THE GREAT RECESSION and DEVELOPING COUNTRIES

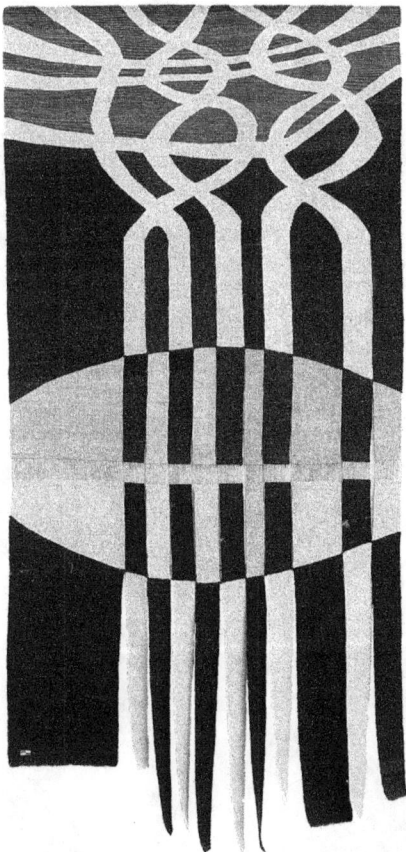

THE GREAT RECESSION and DEVELOPING COUNTRIES

ECONOMIC IMPACT AND GROWTH PROSPECTS

MUSTAPHA K. NABLI, EDITOR

THE WORLD BANK

© 2011 The International Bank for Reconstruction and Development/The World Bank

1818 H Street NW
Washington DC 20433
Telephone: 202-473-1000
Internet: www.worldbank.org

1 2 3 4 13 12 11 10

This volume is a product of the staff of the International Bank for Reconstruction and Development / The World Bank. The findings, interpretations, and conclusions expressed in this volume do not necessarily reflect the views of the Executive Directors of The World Bank or the governments they represent.

The World Bank does not guarantee the accuracy of the data included in this work. The boundaries, colors, denominations, and other information shown on any map in this work do not imply any judgement on the part of The World Bank concerning the legal status of any territory or the endorsement or acceptance of such boundaries.

Rights and Permissions
The material in this publication is copyrighted. Copying and/or transmitting portions or all of this work without permission may be a violation of applicable law. The International Bank for Reconstruction and Development / The World Bank encourages dissemination of its work and will normally grant permission to reproduce portions of the work promptly.

For permission to photocopy or reprint any part of this work, please send a request with complete information to the Copyright Clearance Center Inc., 222 Rosewood Drive, Danvers, MA 01923, USA; telephone: 978-750-8400; fax: 978-750-4470; Internet: www. copyright.com.

All other queries on rights and licenses, including subsidiary rights, should be addressed to the Office of the Publisher, The World Bank, 1818 H Street NW, Washington, DC 20433, USA; fax: 202-522-2422; e-mail: pubrights@worldbank.org.

ISBN: 978-0-8213-8513-5
eISBN: 978-0-8213-8514-2
DOI: 10.1596/978-0-8213-8513-5

Library of Congress Cataloging-in-Publication Data
The Great Recession and the developing countries : economic impact and growth prospects.
     p. cm.
Includes bibliographical references and index.
  ISBN 978-0-8213-8513-5 — ISBN 978-0-8213-8514-2 (electronic)
  1. Financial crises—Developing countries—Case studies. 2. Global Financial Crisis, 2008–2009. 3. Economic forecasting—Developing countries—Case studies. 4. Developing countries—Economic conditions—21st century. 5. Economic development—Developing countries—Case studies. I. World Bank.
  HB3722.G746 2010
  330.9172'4—dc22

                                                                            2010045444

Cover design: W. Drew Fasick, The Fasick Group, Inc.
Cover art: Belkis Balpinar, *World Weave* (tapestry), Turkey.

Contents

v

Boxes

Figures

Tables

Preface

In the more than two years since the eruption of the financial crisis in advanced countries and its spread to become a global economic crisis, attention has been almost singularly focused on short-term developments, tactics for ending the financial chaos and economic collapse and initiating a recovery, and efforts to address the immediate economic and social disruptions caused by the crisis. Much less attention has been paid to the medium- and long-term implications of the crisis for growth, poverty reduction, and—more broadly—development in low- and middle-income countries. To fill this gap, the World Bank's Poverty Reduction and Economic Management Network (PREM) and its Development Economics (DEC) Vice Presidency jointly launched a project to explore how the ongoing crisis, the policy responses to it, and the postcrisis global economy would shape the medium-term growth prospects of developing countries. A selection of 10 countries was studied in order to (a) understand the factors that affected the extent of the economic impact—both in the short and medium term—resulting from the global crisis and (b) help identify policy measures that could support a more inclusive and sustainable growth path—a subject that is of great interest to the World Bank and the development community at large. The goal was not to forecast or predict growth and economic developments in the countries studied, but rather to look at how the medium- to long-term prospects for growth in developing countries might be affected by the way the crisis and the recovery play out and by postcrisis global conditions.

For the country studies, a single illustrative global scenario for the medium term has been used to explore the impact of global economic conditions on growth in developing countries. It would have been useful to explore the impact of alternative scenarios; however, doing so was beyond the scope of this project. In addition, the crisis is ongoing and the recovery is tentative. The conclusions reached within this volume must therefore be understood within the context of these limitations and uncertainties. Nonetheless, we believe that these studies bring a rich set of data and analyses about the Great Recession and its impact on developing countries that will be useful for both the academic and development communities.

This volume is a product of a project undertaken under the leadership and guidance of Otaviano Canuto, Vice President for PREM, and Justin Yifu Lin, Senior Vice President and Chief Economist at the World Bank (DEC); and with the active support of Carlos Alberto Braga, Shahrokh Fardoust, Nadir Mohammed, and Sudarshan Gooptu. A number of colleagues from country teams at the World Bank provided support for the production of the country papers: Jozef Draaisma on Mexico, Miria Pigato on India, and Quang Hong Doan and Martin Rama on Vietnam. Andrew Burns, Mansour Dailami, and Dilip Ratha provided data and advice about the global scenario. Their help and support are gratefully acknowledged. We benefited from useful suggestions and comments made by participants during two seminars held in Washington, DC, December 17–18, 2009, and July 19–20, 2010, during which the papers were reviewed and discussed. The comments from these sessions were taken into consideration in preparing the final papers included in this volume. The July seminar sessions were chaired by Carlos Alberto Braga, Shahrokh Fardoust, Indermit Gill, Marcelo Giugale, Vikram Nehru, and Zia Mohammed Qureshi; the comments from these sessions have been included in this volume as discussant papers. Throughout the project, Rita Akweley Lartey provided excellent administrative support and Utku Kumru provided able and effective research assistance. In addition, Stephen McGroarty, Cindy Fisher, and Nora Ridolfi from the Office of the Publisher provided superb editorial and production support.

Contributors

Editor

Mustapha K. Nabli is Senior Adviser, Development Economics, World Bank.

Chapter Authors

Nguyen Ngoc Anh is Chief Economist, Development and Policies Research Center, Vietnam.

Erhanfadli M. Azrai is Assistant Vice President, Khazanah Research and Investment Strategy, Malaysia.

Fernando de Holanda Barbosa Filho is Professor, Fundação Getulio Vargas, Brazil.

Fernando Blanco is Senior Economist, Africa Poverty Reduction and Economic Management Department, World Bank.

Otaviano Canuto is Vice President and Head of the Poverty Reduction and Economic Management Network, World Bank.

Nguyen Dinh Chuc is Senior Researcher, Development and Policies Research Center, Vietnam.

Dipak Dasgupta is Lead Economist, South Asia Economic Policy and Poverty Sector, World Bank.

Gerardo Esquivel is Professor of Economics, El Colegio de México, Mexico.

Abhijit Sen Gupta is Associate Professor, Jawaharlal Nehru University, India.

Ardo Hansson is Lead Economist, East Asia and Pacific Poverty Reduction and Economic Management Department, World Bank.

Maciej Krzak is Coordinator of the Macroeconomic Team, Center for Social and Economic Research, Poland.

Luis Kuijs is Senior Economist, East Asia and Pacific Poverty Reduction and Economic Management Department, World Bank.

Eric Le Borgne is Senior Economist, East Asia and Pacific Poverty Reduction and Economic Management Department, World Bank.

Justin Yifu Lin is Chief Economist and Senior Vice President, Development Economics, World Bank.

Alvaro Manoel is Senior Economist, Economic Policy and Debt Department, World Bank.

Deepak Mishra is Lead Economist, East Asia and Pacific Poverty Reduction and Economic Management Department, World Bank.

Sheryll Namingit is Analyst, East Asia and Pacific Poverty Reduction and Economic Management Department, World Bank.

Nguyen Duc Nhat is Executive Director, Development and Policies Research Center, Vietnam.

Samuel Pessôa is Professor, Fundação Getulio Vargas, Brazil.

Kaspar Richter is Senior Economist, Europe and Central Asia Poverty Reduction and Economic Management Department, World Bank.

Nguyen Thang is Director, Center for Analysis and Forecasting, Vietnamese Academy of Social Sciences, Vietnam.

Mark Roland Thomas is Lead Economist, Macroeconomics Unit, Europe and Central Asia Poverty Reduction and Economic Management Department, World Bank.

Gallina A. Vincelette is Senior Economist, Economic Policy and Debt Department, World Bank.

Cihan Yalçin is Senior Economist, Macroeconomics Unit, Europe and Central Asia Poverty Reduction and Economic Management Department, World Bank.

Albert G. Zeufack is Director, Khazanah Research and Investment Strategy, Malaysia.

Discussant Paper Authors

Milan Brahmbhatt is Senior Adviser, Poverty Reduction and Economic Management Network, World Bank.

Ishac Diwan is Country Director, Western Africa Region, World Bank.

Shahrokh Fardoust is Director, Development Economics Operations and Strategy, World Bank.

Edgardo Favaro is Lead Economist, Economic Policy and Debt Department, World Bank.

Indermit Gill is Chief Economist, Europe and Central Asia Office of the Chief Economist, World Bank.

Sudarshan Gooptu is Sector Manager, Economic Policy and Debt Department, World Bank.

Brian Pinto is Senior Adviser, Poverty Reduction and Economic Management Network, World Bank.

Martin Rama is Lead Economist, South Asia Office of the Chief Economist, World Bank.

David Rosenblatt is Economic Adviser, Office of the Senior Vice President, Development Economics, and Chief Economist, World Bank.

Luis Servén is Senior Adviser, Development Economics Research Group, World Bank.

Manu Sharma is Junior Professional Associate, Poverty Reduction and Economic Management Network, World Bank.

Shahid Yusuf is Consultant, World Bank.

Abbreviations

ADB	Asian Development Bank
ADLI	agricultural development–led industrialization (of Ethiopia)
ASEAN	Association of Southeast Asian Nations
BCB	Central Bank of Brazil
BNDES	Federal Economic and Social Development Bank (of Brazil)
BNM	Bank Negara Malaysia
BPC	Permanent Benefit for Elderly People (of Brazil)
BPO	business process outsourcing
bps	basis points
BSE	Bombay Stock Exchange
BSE Sensex	Bombay Stock Exchange Sensitivity Index
BSP	Bangko Sentral ng Pilipinas
BSRA	Banking Regulation and Supervision Agency (of Turkey)
BTr	Bureau of the Treasury (of the Philippines)
CA	current account
CB-BOL	Central Bank Board of Liquidators (of the Philippines)
CBRT	Central Bank of the Republic of Turkey
CCT	conditional cash transfer
CDS	credit default swap
CENVAT	central value added tax
CF	Christiano-Fitzgerald (filter)
CONEVAL	Consejo Nacional de Evaluación de la Política de Desarrollo Social (of Mexico)
CONgr	consumption growth

CNI	Confederação National de Indústrias (of Brazil)
CPI	consumer price index
CRR	cash reserve ratio
CSO	Central Statistical Organization (of India)
DBM	Department of Budget and Management (of the Philippines)
DDP	Development Data Platform (of the World Bank)
DOF	Department of Finance (of the Philippines)
DOS	Department of Statistics (of Malaysia)
E&E	electrical and electronics
EC	European Commission
ECBs	external commercial borrowings
EM	emerging market
EMBI	Emerging Markets Bond Index
ERP	Economic Resiliency Plan (ERP)
eop	end of period
EPU	Economic Reports and Economic Planning Unit (of Malaysia)
EU	European Union
FDI	foreign direct investment
FGV	Getulio Vargas Foundation
FII	foreign institutional investment
FRL	Fiscal Responsibility Law (of Brazil)
FSA	Financial Supervision Authority (of Poland)
FY	fiscal year
GDP	gross domestic product
GEP	*Global Economic Prospects* (of the World Bank)
GFCF	gross fixed capital formation
GFS	Government Finance Statistics (of the IMF)
GoE	Government of Ethiopia
GSO	General Statistics Office (of Vietnam)
GST	goods and services tax
GVA	gross value added
HP	Hodrick-Prescott (filter)
IBGE	Brazilian Institute of Geography and Statistics
IMF	International Monetary Fund

INEGI	Instituto Nacional de Estadística y Geografía e Informática (of Mexico)
INVgr	investment growth
IPEA	Institute of Applied Economics Research
IPI	industrial production index
IPO	Imposto sobre Produtos Industrializados (of Brazil)
IPP	Investment Priorities Plan (of the Philippines)
IT	information technology
KLIBOR	Kuala Lumpur interbank offered rate
KRIS	Khazanah Research and Investment Strategy (of Malaysia)
LCU	local currency unit
LGU	local government unit
LOAS	Organic Law of Social Protection (of Brazil)
LT	long term
M1	money supply
M2	M1 plus quasi-money
mma	monthly moving average
MOF	Ministry of Finance (of Malaysia)
MoFED	Ministry of Finance and Economic Development (of Ethiopia)
MOOE	maintenance and other operating expenses
MPI	Ministry of Planning and Investment (of Vietnam)
MSMEs	micro, small, and medium enterprises
NAFTA	North America Free Trade Agreement
NBP	National Bank of Poland
NBS	National Bureau of Statistics (of China)
NEAC	National Economic Advisory Council (of Malaysia)
NEER	nominal effective exchange rate
NEM	New Economic Model (of Malaysia)
NFS	nonfactor services
NICs	newly industrialized countries
NPL	nonperforming loan
NSCB	National Statistical Coordination Board (of the Philippines)
NSO	National Statistics Office (of the Philippines)
ODA	official development assistance
OECD	Organisation for Economic Co-operation and Development

OEF	Oxford Economic Forecasts
PDIC	Philippines Deposit Insurance Corporation
PISA	Programme for International Student Assessment
PPG-ED	public and publicly guaranteed external debt
PPI	private participation in infrastructure
PPP	purchasing power parity
PSBR	public sector borrowing requirement
R&D	research and development
RBI	Reserve Bank of India
REER	real effective exchange rate
s.a.	seasonally adjusted
SMEs	small and medium enterprises
SOE	state-owned enterprise
STN	National Treasury Secretariat (of Brazil)
SVAR	structural vector autoregression
T&C	transport and communication
TFP	total factor productivity
TRP	Tariff Reform Program (of the Philippines)
VASS	Vietnam Academy of Social Sciences
VAT	value added tax
WDI	World Development Indicators Database (of the World Bank)
WEO	*World Economic Outlook* (of the IMF)
WTO	World Trade Organization
yoy	year-on-year

Introduction

Otaviano Canuto and Justin Yifu Lin

While globalization has been a powerful engine of economic growth over the past three decades, it has also posed new problems and challenges, especially for international economic policy coordination. In the past decade, the large and rapid increases in trade, remittances, and international financial flows across borders have been a strong incentive for economic growth, not only in East and South Asia but also in Latin America and Sub-Saharan Africa. And rapid and sustained economic growth in several low- and middle-income economies has been steadily altering the economic weights of different regions in the world economy.

Since the early 1980s, several international crises have revealed new risks associated with large international capital flows, economic booms (Reinhart and Rogoff 2010a), *sudden stops* (Calvo, Izquierdo, and Mejia (2004), and economic busts. The debt crisis in Latin America in the 1980s, the Mexico balance of payments crisis of 1994, the East Asia crisis of 1997, and the Russian Federation crisis of 1998 all underscore the impact of capital flows. Short-term capital *inflows* have supported

Otaviano Canuto is Vice President and Head of the Poverty Reduction and Economic Management Network, World Bank, and Justin Yifu Lin is Chief Economist and Senior Vice President, Development Economics, World Bank.

investment and accelerated economic growth, but they have also posed problems for exchange rate and aggregate demand management at the country level. Sharp short-term *outflows*, in contrast, pose challenges for economic stability at the global-economy level.

Nowhere have the challenges been more visible than in the United States and in other high-income economies after the collapse of the subprime mortgage market and its spread to other financial markets and countries. The crisis has been unprecedented in its origins and unique in its intensity. It originated in a high-income economy and spread rapidly to the rest of the world through financial and trade channels. The crisis led to a 6.5 percent fall in the median GDP growth rate of the Group of Seven (G7) countries between 2007 and 2009, and it has had protracted effects in several low- and middle-income economies in the rest of the world.

The intensity of the crisis has also highlighted the imbalance between the depth and breadth of the problems and the inability of traditional international coordination mechanisms to contain and resolve them. Ad hoc mechanisms created to avoid disruption of the global payments system—led by the U.S. Federal Reserve, the European Central Bank, and the central banks of China, Japan, and several other countries— were effective in averting a collapse of the international payment system and a deeper global economic recession. But the experience has left many treasury and central bank officials around the world concerned that the new risks have yet to be constrained.

The 10 case studies in this volume illustrate the wide range of effects of, and responses to, the global crisis in low- and middle-income economies. While the case studies do not constitute a statistically representative sample of the globe, they illustrate a broad range of experiences in the wake of the crisis and give insights into both the benefits and challenges of globalization. The use of a common methodology in preparing the cases unquestionably facilitates cross-country comparisons and helps identify areas where more study is needed to increase our understanding of the current problems of, and prospects for, developing countries.

The Crisis and Ensuing Recession

As noted earlier, the subprime mortgage crisis broke out in the United States and was transmitted rapidly to other financial markets in the United

States and other advanced countries. It triggered a rapid deleveraging of financial and nonfinancial firms and households, which sharply reduced economic activity during the last quarter of 2007 and the first half of 2008.

The transmission of the crisis worldwide occurred through both financial and trade channels. The financial channel was important not only among advanced economies but also in some middle-income countries that suffered an abrupt reversal of international capital inflows. The reversal was induced, in part, by a rushed liquidation of emerging-market financial positions by private financial funds desperately trying to meet their clients' liquidity demands. These portfolio shifts triggered a plunge in the stock markets of several emerging markets (figure 1.1) and led to sharp depreciations of the exchange rates of several emerging

Figure 1.1. Stock Market Index

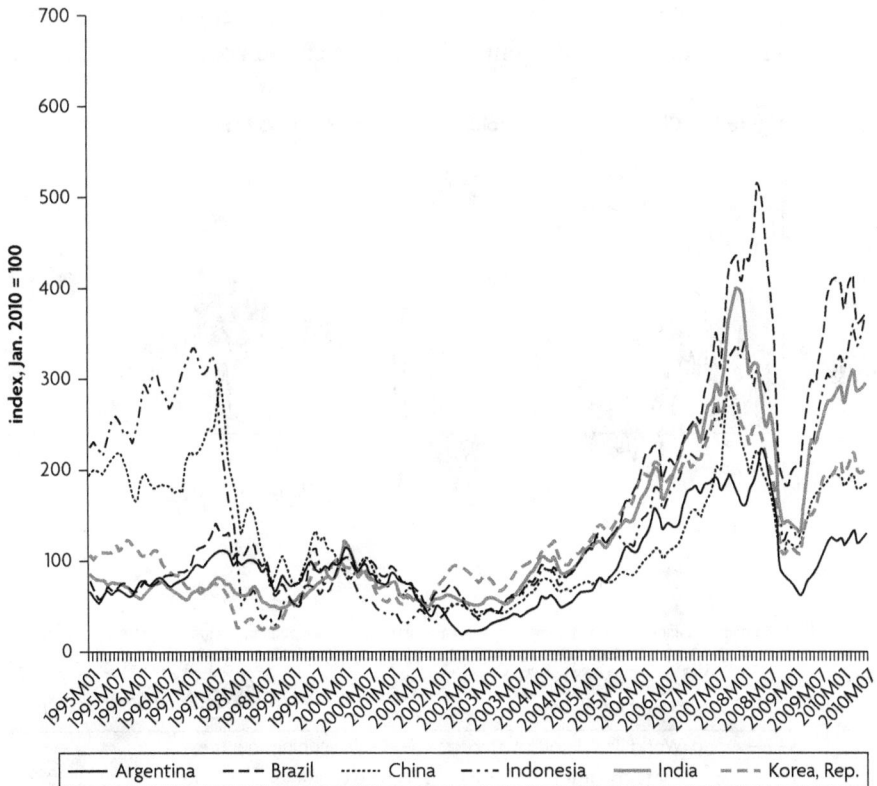

Source: World Bank 2010.
Note: The index is computed using prices quoted in U.S. dollars.

economies (including Brazil and Mexico) in 2008. Coordinated action by central banks was critical for preserving the functioning of the international payments system and smoothing the adjustment. For example, in 2007 and 2008, the U.S. Federal Reserve established a system of reciprocal currency agreements in coordination with other central banks to address the global disruption in dollar funding markets.

A sharp fall in international trade flows affected all countries in the world. According to recent estimates (World Bank 2010), global trade volumes fell by 11.6 percent in 2009 relative to 2008 (figure 1.2). In general, countries that were more dependent on external markets were initially more affected through the trade channel but were also able to rebound more quickly.

The impact of the trade shock on the economies of low- and middle-income countries varied depending on whether the country was mainly an exporter of commodities (minerals, oil, and agricultural products) or an exporter of labor-intensive manufactured goods (as in East Asia

Figure 1.2. Change in Export Volumes over the Previous 12 Months

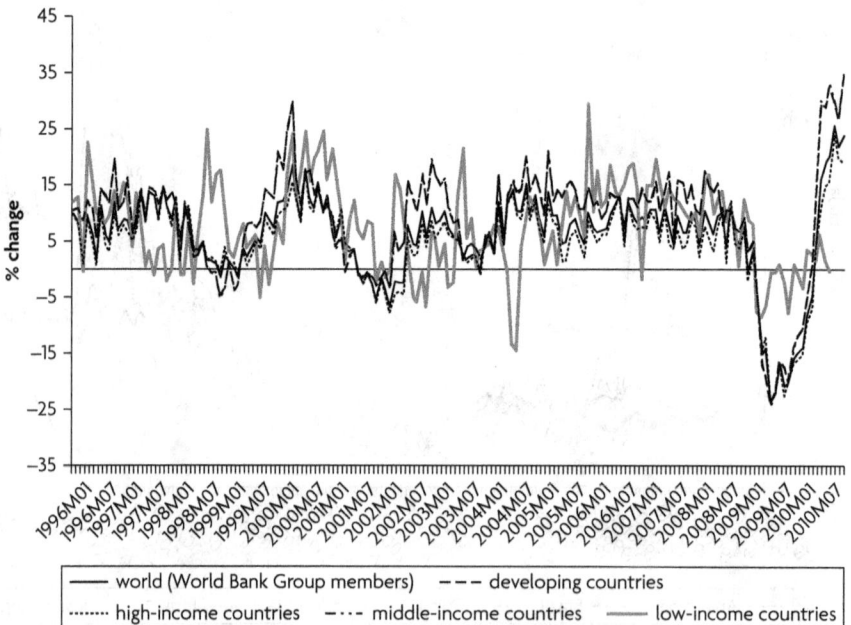

Source: World Bank 2010.

and Mexico). In the first case, the negative shock did not precipitate an immediate fall in economic activity; in the second case, layoffs and a rapid decline in output quickly followed the fall in external demand.

Output responses to the adverse external shocks posed by the global crisis have been quite heterogeneous (table 1.1). The high-income countries, owing probably to their tightly interconnected financial markets, were hit the hardest, with an average fall in the rate of GDP growth of 7.7 percentage points. Middle-income economies followed, posting an average growth rate decline of 6.9 percentage points. And low-income countries suffered the least, experiencing a 1.5-percentage-point fall in GDP growth. Europe and Central Asia and Latin America and the Caribbean posted the largest declines in growth (11.8 and 6.4 percentage points, respectively), followed by East Asia and Pacific.[1] But the dispersion in performance (measured as the standard deviation of the rate of growth of GDP divided by the mean) among middle- and especially low-income countries was much higher than among high-income countries.

The financial and economic crisis struck deeper in countries that had large current account deficits as of 2007.[2] Countries with current

Table 1.1. Change in Real Growth Rate between 2007 and 2009

	By income level					
Statistic	All countries	G7	High-income countries	Developing countries	Middle-income countries	Low-income countries
Median	−5.17	−6.52	−6.92	−3.92	−6.16	−1.55
Mean	−5.94	−6.18	−7.73	−5.30	−6.91	−1.49
Std. dev.	5.88	1.41	3.96	6.32	6.43	4.04
Obs.	183	7	48	135	95	40

	Developing countries by region					
Statistic	East Asia and Pacific	Europe and Central Asia	Latin America and the Caribbean	Middle East and North Africa	South Asia	Sub-Saharan Africa
Median	−3.86	−9.63	−6.49	−0.62	−3.49	−1.95
Mean	−5.20	−11.81	−6.41	−1.49	−3.19	−2.59
Std. dev.	4.15	7.97	3.31	3.23	6.69	5.41
Obs.	18	24	28	12	8	45

Source: Real GDP data are from the World Economic Outlook Database (April 2010), International Monetary Fund.
Note: Income and regional classification follow the World Bank 2010 classification. Change in growth rate is the difference between the real GDP growth in 2009 and real GDP growth in 2007 (in percentage points). Obs. = observations.

account gaps in 2007 that managed to lower their deficits in 2009 performed relatively poorly compared to the rest of the countries (table 1.2, top section); a two-tailed means test indicates that the difference is statistically significant at 1 percent.

In some cases, owing to the sharp reversal in capital flows, the change in the current account balance between 2007 and 2009 amounted to more than 30 percentage points of GDP. (The bottom section of table 1.2 shows countries that experienced the largest swings in their current accounts between 2007 and 2009, from deficit to surplus.) Accompanying the shift in the current account, output growth declined abruptly, with Estonia, Latvia, and Lithuania posting declines in real growth of at least 20 percentage points.

Uncertainties Surrounding the Recovery

World output is projected to grow by 4.6 percent in 2010 after falling by 0.6 percent in 2009 (IMF 2010a). Similarly, though more dramatically,

Table 1.2. Current Account and Growth Performance

	Change in real growth between 2007 and 2009	
	Countries with a CA-to-GDP ratio < 0 in 2007 and ratio in 2007 < ratio in 2009	Rest of the countries
Median	−6.78	−4.45
Mean	−7.47	−4.95
Std. dev.	6.08	5.56
Obs.	72	111
	Means test: t-statistic = 2.89	

Countries that experienced a large swing in the CA balance, from deficit in 2007 to surplus in 2009

Country	Change in real growth between 2007 and 2009	CA-to-GDP ratio in 2007	CA-to-GDP ratio in 2009	Difference between ratios in 2007 and in 2009
Latvia	−27.99	−22.33	9.44	31.77
Estonia	−21.29	−17.81	4.60	22.41
Iceland	−12.44	−16.29	3.79	20.08
Lithuania	−24.80	−14.56	3.82	18.38
Hungary	−7.30	−6.81	0.41	7.21

Source: World Economic Outlook Database (April 2010), International Monetary Fund.
Note: CA = current account.

world trade volume is forecast to rise by 11.3 percent in 2010 after declining by 9 percent in 2009. The projected growth rate of emerging-market economies (6.8 percent) is strong, especially in Asia (9.2 percent), but it is weak among advanced economies (2.6 percent) and especially in the euro area (1.0 percent).

Slower economic growth in most advanced countries is the result of ongoing deleveraging of financial and nonfinancial firms and households, and of new concerns about the level and pace of increase in the public-debt-to-GDP ratios in several advanced economies.

The global crisis has uncovered the vulnerabilities of the international financial system. In the United States, the banking system has stabilized but credit flows have not recovered. And recent developments in Europe concerning the sustainability of the sovereign debt of several countries led to financial turmoil in the spring of 2010 and to a sharp increase in the sovereign government bond spreads of several countries (see IMF 2010a, figure 3). To date, the challenge has been met successfully by the coordinated responses of countries in the region and international financial institutions, but the euro crisis is an indicator of emerging global financial and economic challenges to the capacity for coordinated action by the international community.

The government finances of several advanced economies have clearly worsened. The main reason is the fall in tax revenue caused by the decline of output or the slowdown of economic growth. Fiscal deficits and debt-to-GDP ratios have soared to worrisome levels, and in some cases, sovereign debt concerns have reached perilously risky levels (Reinhart and Rogoff 2010b). The weak state of several economies clearly limits the capacity of treasuries to drastically reduce fiscal deficits without jeopardizing economic recovery. But large fiscal deficits over the medium term do not encourage new investment and economic growth. The challenge of restoring public finances to equilibrium will not be met by short-term deficit reduction measures alone; a successful lowering of fiscal deficits, and of debt-to-GDP ratios, also requires reforms aimed at unleashing private sector investment and economic growth over the medium term (Calvo 2010).

While the recovery in emerging-market economies is strong, the low-interest-rate policy pursued by the main central banks in the world also has implications for capital flows to, and the sustainability of economic growth in, these economies. Low international interest rates encourage capital inflows in pursuit of higher yields in emerging economies and pose such complications as real exchange rate appreciation, rapid growth of credit to the private sector, and, often, a sharp rise in asset prices (IMF 2010b).

Medium-Term Prospects

Globalization has opened up opportunities to narrow the per capita income gap between low- and middle-income countries and advanced economies. Some countries have successfully exploited these opportunities while others have not. Members of the first group have sustained high rates of investment and productivity improvement over decades; members of the second group have not. Although no one set of policies and institutions can guarantee that a country will fall in the first or second group, the ability to exploit opportunities does not develop randomly. The countries that succeed are those that are able to identify and assess their problems and to formulate successful strategies for solving them—and that correct policy mistakes when they become evident.

The assessment of the impact of the global crisis of 2007–09 and the case studies in this volume offer some general lessons for most emerging economies. These lessons are based on the wide range of experiences following the crisis—on the fact that the fall in GDP has been much higher in some countries than in others, and that the recession has been longer and the recovery weaker in some countries than in others. Among the many factors that have contributed to these differences in performance, one stands out: countries that had low external vulnerability at the onset of the crisis suffered, on average, smaller declines in output than the rest. Although measuring vulnerability is a sophisticated undertaking (IMF 2010b), straightforward indicators—such as the current account balance and domestic credit growth—provide a solid starting point. The case studies in this volume clearly illustrate the importance of these indicators.

This volume identifies three main lessons or themes that can be gleaned from the experience of the 10 countries studied:

The importance of *national savings* in reducing external vulnerability cannot be overstated. A country's current account balance is identical to the difference between national savings and investment. An increase in the current account balance may be the result of an increase in savings, a fall in investment, or both. External savings may, and must, be used to accelerate development, but the users are advised to base their decisions on a simple economic calculus: use external financing only if it finances investment with a rate of return higher than the cost of the funds.

The second lesson is that *sound reforms are critical* for countries to benefit from financial and economic globalization. Even if growth is sluggish in advanced countries, emerging-market economies can benefit from access to other markets and technology. But access is not granted automatically; it must be gained by reforming domestic markets and institutions so as to encourage new investment and the absorption of new technology.

Finally, the case studies highlight the *major changes in the economic roles of different regions and countries in the world economy* (table 1.3). During the past decade, economic power has shifted gradually from high-income countries to emerging markets. By 2008, the G7 countries represented less than 60 percent of global output. An even more pronounced change emerges if we use constant purchasing power parity (PPP) dollars instead: G7 countries' share of global GDP was about 50 percent in 1990, but by 2008 their share had fallen to roughly 40 percent.

Underlying this change in share is the fact that developing countries have been growing on average at a faster pace than high-income countries in the past decade. The difference widened over the period, averaging 3.7 percentage points. Every region of the developing world grew faster than the high-income countries. Focusing on the Group of Twenty (G20) developing countries—which represent 80 percent of global GDP in constant U.S. dollars, and 75 percent of global GDP in constant PPP international dollars for 1990–2008—and disaggregating the contribution of developing and developed countries to global growth, a striking picture emerges: in 1990, G20 developing countries produced less than 11 percent of global GDP; by 2008, their share had reached almost 17 percent.

Clearly, while the bulk of the world's GDP continues to be produced in G7 countries, the global economic power balance is changing rapidly.

Table 1.3. The Distribution of Global Economic Activity

	Share in world GDP									
	GDP in constant 2000 U.S. dollars					**GDP in constant 2005 PPP international dollars**				
Year	**G7**	**G20 dev.**	**G20 high**	**G20**	**World**	**G7**	**G20 dev.**	**G20 high**	**G20**	**World**
1990	67.91	10.76	70.94	81.70	100.00	50.54	20.64	53.98	74.61	100.00
1995	66.72	11.60	70.12	81.72	100.00	49.98	21.36	53.86	75.22	100.00
2000	65.43	12.47	68.94	81.41	100.00	48.68	22.69	52.63	75.33	100.00
2005	62.64	14.41	66.36	80.77	100.00	44.86	25.81	48.88	74.69	100.00
2008	59.94	16.42	63.73	80.15	100.00	41.61	28.69	45.58	74.27	100.00

	GDP growth									
	GDP in constant 2000 U.S. dollars					**GDP in constant 2005 PPP international dollars**				
Period	**G7**	**G20 dev.**	**G20 high**	**G20**	**World**	**G7**	**G20 dev.**	**G20 high**	**G20**	**World**
1990–94	2.09	3.44	2.21	2.38	2.34	2.06	2.38	2.26	2.29	2.09
1995–99	2.70	4.39	2.77	3.00	3.10	2.83	4.42	2.90	3.33	3.34
2000–04	2.08	5.45	2.20	2.72	2.86	2.11	5.96	2.29	3.43	3.57
2005–08	1.82	7.70	1.93	2.99	3.25	1.84	7.96	2.01	4.11	4.30

	Contribution to world GDP growth									
	GDP in constant 2000 U.S. dollars					**GDP in constant 2005 PPP international dollars**				
Period	**G7**	**G20 dev.**	**G20 high**	**G20**	**World**	**G7**	**G20 dev.**	**G20 high**	**G20**	**World**
1990–94	1.41	0.38	1.57	1.95	2.34	1.04	0.50	1.22	1.71	2.09
1995–99	1.80	0.52	1.93	2.45	3.10	1.40	0.96	1.55	2.51	3.34
2000–04	1.35	0.70	1.51	2.21	2.86	1.01	1.39	1.19	2.58	3.57
2005–08	1.14	1.13	1.28	2.41	3.25	0.82	2.09	0.98	3.07	4.30

Source: World Development Indicators (2010), World Bank.
Note: dev. = developing countries, high = high-income countries, World = world aggregate reported by World Bank, World Development Indicators database.

Notes

1. See table 1.1, bottom section.
2. Changes in the current account roughly approximate changes in international capital flows.

References

Calvo, Guillermo A. 2010. "To Spend or Not to Spend: Is That the Question?" *VOX*, August 4.

Calvo, Guillermo A., Alejandro Izquierdo, and Luis-Fernando Mejia. 2004. "On the Empirics of Sudden Stops: The Relevance of Balance-Sheet Effects." Working Paper 10520, National Bureau of Economic Research, Cambridge, MA.

IMF (International Monetary Fund). 2010a. "World Economic Outlook: Update." IMF, Washington, DC.

———. 2010b. "How Did Emerging Markets Cope in the Crisis?" http://www.imf. org/external/np/pp/eng/2010/061510.pdf.

Reinhart, Carmen M., and Kenneth S. Rogoff. 2010a. "The Aftermath of Financial Crises." *American Economic Review* 99 (May): 466–72.

———. 2010b. "Growth in a Time of Debt." *American Economic Review* 100 (2): 573–78.

World Bank. 2010. *Global Economic Prospects 2010: Crisis, Finance, and Growth.* Washington, DC: World Bank.

Growth after the Global Recession in Developing Countries

Mustapha K. Nabli

The global financial and economic crisis that engulfed the world since September 2008 will shape the growth and development prospects of developing countries for the foreseeable future. Over the last two years,

Mustapha K. Nabli is Senior Adviser, Development Economics, World Bank. This chapter is based on input and contributions by the authors of the 10 country studies, included as chapters in this book: Nguyen Ngoc Anh, Nguyen Duc Nhat, Nguyen Dinh Chuc, and Nguyen Thang (Vietnam; ch. 12); Erhanfadli A. Azrai and Albert G. Zeufack (Malaysia, ch. 7); Fernando Blanco, Fernando de Holanda Barbosa Filho, and Samuel Pessoa (Brazil, ch. 3); Dipak Dasgupta and Abhijit Sen Gupta (India, ch. 6); Gerardo Esquivel (Mexico, ch. 8); Maciej Krzak and Kaspar Richter (Poland, ch. 10); Eric Le Borgne and Sheryll Namingit (Philippines, ch. 9); Deepak Mishra (Ethiopia, ch. 5); Gallina A. Vincelette, Alvaro Manoel, Ardo Hansson, and Luis Kuijs (China, ch. 4); and Cihan Yalçin and Mark Roland Thomas (Turkey, ch. 11). These contributions are gratefully acknowledged. This work has also benefited from the contribution of Nadir Mohammed, co-leader of the project. Nadeem Ul Haque (consultant) made significant contributions to the paper and Luis Servén made very helpful and insightful comments. The paper benefited also from discussions of all papers included in this book during a seminar held at the World Bank in Washington, DC, July 19–20, 2010. Utku Kumru provided effective and able research assistance.

policy makers have focused on current short-term developments, on how to stop the financial chaos and economic collapse and initiate a recovery, and on how to deal with the immediate economic and social disruptions caused by the crisis. Much less attention has been paid to the medium- and long-term implications of the crisis for growth, poverty reduction, and, more broadly, the development of the low- and middle-income developing countries. The project that gave rise to this volume was designed to fill this gap through a number of country studies.

The goal of the studies was not to forecast or predict growth and economic developments in the countries studied, but rather to look at how the medium- to long-term prospects of growth in developing countries may be affected by the way the crisis and the recovery play out and by the postcrisis global conditions. Understanding these factors in a few countries can help identify policy measures that may help support a more inclusive and sustainable growth path—a subject that is of great interest to the World Bank and the development community at large.

The project was intended to explore these issues through 10 country case studies. The countries include: (low-income) Ethiopia and Vietnam; (low- to middle-income) China, India, and the Philippines; and (upper-middle-income) Brazil, Malaysia, Mexico, Poland, and Turkey. Selected countries are more integrated with high-income countries through trade in manufactures and financial flows, and they are neither commodity dependent nor major oil producers. While this sample of 10 countries is not statistically representative of the group of all developing countries, it includes countries from the full range of income levels and a variety of regional experiences of transmission of the impact of the crisis.

The country studies start by reviewing the growth experience during the precrisis boom period to draw lessons and implications for the medium term. During this period, global conditions, especially in the financial sector, had a large impact on growth in developing countries. Understanding how these global factors impacted developing countries will help understand and assess how future changes may impact growth as well. They proceed to analyze the immediate impact of the global crisis on the developing countries, their policy responses, and their recovery. This will also help draw some conclusions and implications about developments during the crisis that may have an impact in the medium term. Finally, the studies make projections of medium-term growth based on an illustrative global scenario and assess how these prospects may be affected by the crisis. In this work the focus was on average GDP growth, and the studies explore issues of growth volatility and the implications of uncertainty about the possible alternative paths of recovery from the crisis. In many countries, growth volatility before the crisis was high, and it would be of interest to explore whether such volatility would be increased or reduced after the crisis, but these issues were beyond the scope of the study.

The Precrisis Boom: Lessons and Implications for Medium-Term Growth

The review of experience before the global crisis is intended to promote understanding of how global economic conditions affected growth in developing countries before the crisis and draw useful lessons about the implications of changed global conditions after the crisis. Our results and analysis are based on two sources. First is a cross-country analysis of the experience of a sample of about 54 developing countries, for which we have consistent data on the relevant variables. The second source is a set of 10 country case studies, included in this volume, that trace the economies before, during, and after the crisis.

Economic Growth

The period immediately prior to the outbreak of the subprime crisis of 2008–09 (roughly 2003–07) was one of rapid global growth and large capital flows from the advanced to the emerging countries. We call this the "boom" period. During the "preboom" period (1997–2002), two crises affected almost all countries—the East Asia crisis of 1997–98 and the technology crisis of 2001.

For the larger sample of 54 developing countries, the acceleration of actual GDP growth from the preboom to the boom period was 2.0–3.3 percentage points, depending on whether one uses a simple average, the median, or a weighted average (table 2.1).[1] The faster-than-average acceleration in India and China, and their large weight, result in an increase of the weighted average GDP growth from 4 percent during 1997–2002 to 7.2 percent during 2003–07. The exclusion of the three East Asian countries (Indonesia, Malaysia, and Thailand), which were hardest hit by the 1997–98 East Asia crisis, does not change the picture but makes the growth acceleration

Table 2.1. GDP Growth during the Precrisis "Boom" Period

Countries	GDP growth (%)				Potential GDP growth (%) (HP filtered)			
	1997–2002	2003–07	2006–07	Change (2003–07/1997–02)	1997–2002	2003–07	2006–07	Change (2003–07/1997–02)
Sample 54 developing countries								
Simple average	3.5	5.5	6.3	2.1	3.8	5.0	5.2	1.2
Median	3.6	5.7	6.3	2.2	3.8	5.1	5.3	1.3
Weighted average	4.0	7.2	7.9	3.3	4.4	6.5	6.6	2.1
Weighted average (excluding EA-3 countries)	4.2	7.4	8.1	3.2	4.6	6.6	6.7	2.0
Weighted average (EA-3 countries)	1.3	5.6	5.6	4.3	2.4	5.3	5.3	2.9
Sample 10 country case studies								
Simple average	**4.2**	**6.8**	**7.4**	**2.6**	**4.7**	**6.1**	**6.3**	**1.5**
Median	**3.6**	**6.4**	**6.4**	**2.9**	**4.4**	**5.6**	**5.9**	**1.2**
Weighted average	**5.0**	**7.7**	**8.5**	**2.7**	**5.3**	**7.0**	**7.0**	**1.7**
Brazil	2.0	3.8	4.6	1.8	2.4	3.4	3.8	1.0
China	8.4	11.0	12.3	2.6	8.7	10.4	9.8	1.6
Ethiopia	3.4	8.9	11.0	5.5	4.4	8.2	8.9	3.7
India	5.1	8.9	9.4	3.8	5.8	8.0	8.9	2.2
Malaysia	3.3	6.0	6.1	2.7	4.4	5.5	5.5	1.1
Mexico	3.8	3.3	4.0	–0.5	3.4	2.9	3.2	–0.5
Philippines	3.3	5.8	6.3	2.4	3.8	5.3	5.3	1.5
Poland	3.9	5.1	6.4	1.2	4.3	4.4	4.7	0.1
Turkey	2.2	6.9	5.8	4.7	2.8	5.7	6.3	2.9
Vietnam	6.6	8.1	8.4	1.5	6.7	7.7	7.4	1.0

Source: World Bank Development Data Platform (DDP); author's calculations.
Note: EA-3 refers to Indonesia, Malaysia, and Thailand; HP = Hodrick-Prescott.

appear somewhat weaker on average. For the smaller group of 10 countries, the weighted actual GDP growth average increased from 5 percent to 7.7 percent, while the median increased from 3.6 percent to 6.4 percent.

When using a measure of potential GDP growth, estimated using an HP (Hodrick-Prescott) filter,[2] the growth acceleration for the 10 countries was about 1.7 percentage points, or about half the actual GDP growth acceleration. All countries experienced growth accelerations, with the notable exception of Mexico. The acceleration in potential output growth in Poland was insignificant.

For the 54 countries, actual GDP growth was about 0.5 percentage point higher than potential growth during 2003–07.[3] In the case of the 10 countries studied, all countries were experiencing actual GDP growth greater than potential by a margin of between 0.4 percentage point (Brazil, Mexico, and Vietnam) and 1.2 percentage points (Turkey). But toward the end of the boom period, 2006–07, the margin between actual and potential becomes about double that for the 2003–07 period average for most countries, ranging from 0.6 percentage point (Malaysia) to 2.5 percentage points (China). An exception is Turkey, which experienced a large drop in actual output below potential.

The comparison of individual country GDP growth over the two periods—1997–2002 and 2003–07—shows many cases of persistent growth: high growth rates continued to be strong (Mozambique) between periods and even accelerated (China and Vietnam), while large negative growth rates persisted (Zimbabwe). But growth rates show no persistence on average and exhibit mean reversion.[4] This feature can be explained by exogenous shocks, owing to terms of trade, global economic conditions, or idiosyncratic domestic cyclical factors and shocks.[5] One such situation is crisis followed by recovery, as in three East Asian countries (Indonesia, Malaysia, and Thailand) recovering from the severe crisis of 1997–98. Conversely, there are cases of domestic business cycles where the economy was operating at or above its potential growth rate, hitting capacity constraints and slowing growth. This was the case in Turkey, where a peak 9 percent GDP growth rate during 2004–05 was decelerating by 2006–07. In India, growth was slowing by 2007 after it reached highs of 9.5–10.0 percent during 2005–06 (figure 2.1). Ethiopia and Vietnam were also enjoying high growth rates prior to the crisis and showed signs of economic overheating and a likely downward adjustment in growth.

Figure 2.1. Excess of Actual GDP Growth over Potential GDP Growth

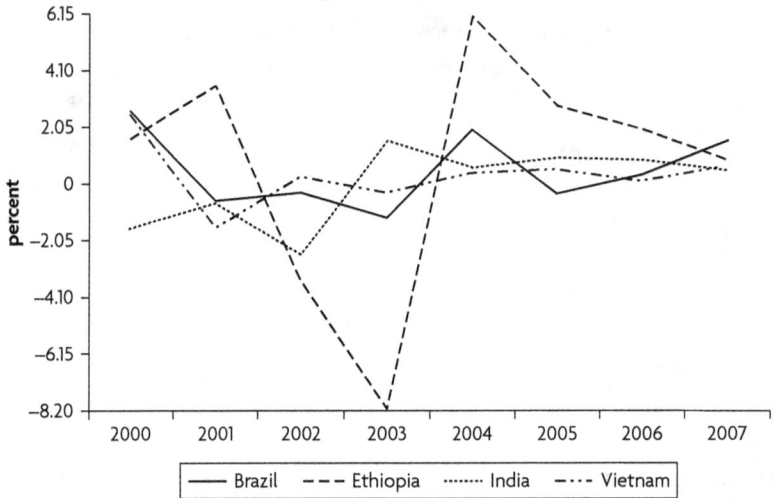

Source: World Bank DDP; author's calculations.

Growth Decompositions. Standard decompositions of actual GDP growth by final demand components show a generalized increase in the contribution of investment demand to GDP growth—from an average of 20–25 percent during 1997–02 to 35–45 percent during 2003–07.[6] But there is a great variety of experiences among the 10 countries studied: an increase from a negative to a large positive contribution of investment growth for Brazil, Malaysia, and Turkey; a persistently low contribution in both periods for the Philippines (5–8 percent); a stable contribution for Mexico (34 percent); and a large decline in the case of Ethiopia. On the other hand, no general pattern is evident in the contributions of domestic consumption and net exports to growth, with a great variety of country experiences. But China is notable, as it shows both a dramatic fall in the contribution of domestic demand (from 58 percent to 13 percent) and rise in net exports (from 5 percent to 39 percent). The case of the Philippines is similar but less extreme. At the other end of the spectrum are Ethiopia and Mexico, which saw high negative contributions of net exports in both periods, and Turkey, which saw negative contributions only during the boom.

We now turn to the role of favorable global economic conditions in terms of large flows of capital and lower cost of capital, higher commodity prices, more trade, and larger remittances and how they contributed to this growth performance. The lessons we can draw from this experience will be helpful for assessing the implications for developing countries of changed global conditions after the crisis.

Financial Channel. For a variety of reasons, global conditions in financial markets eased considerably for developing countries during 2003–07.[7] In nominal terms, yields on 10-year U.S. government bonds fell from an average of 5.5 percent during 1997–2002 to 4.4 percent during 2003–07, and from 5.1 percent to 4.0 percent in the euro area. In real terms, yields declined from 3.2 percent to 1.5–1.8 percent when consumer price index (CPI) inflation is used, but by less if core inflation is used (a decline from 3.1 percent to 2.4 percent on U.S. bonds).

At the same time, financial innovations expanded rapidly and regulatory oversight loosened in advanced country centers. The "shadow banking system" expanded rapidly with the use of securitization and derivatives products. Data from the Bank for International Settlements show international credit expanding at 21 percent per year during 2002–07, twice the rate of growth of global GDP and twice the growth rate in the previous decade.

How did changes in global financial conditions contribute to the acceleration of economic growth in developing countries during 2003–07? The answer to this question is not straightforward for at least three reasons.

First, developing countries implemented a wide range of reforms over the previous decade, especially in the wake of the East Asia crisis. This included liberalization and better regulation of banking sectors and stock markets, and increased openness to foreign capital. Some of these reforms were prompted by previous crises or learning from the experiences of other countries. But some were prompted by the more benign global financial environment itself. Therefore, it is difficult to disentangle the domestic from the external factors in what was observed in terms of increased financial intermediation and cheaper and better access to capital.

Second, there is obviously an interaction between global financial conditions and economic and financial policies and developments in developing countries. For instance, the high saving rates in many developing countries, particularly China, and their macroeconomic policies affect global savings and macro imbalances. These interactions are complex, but we will assume that the main changes in global financial conditions were driven by factors external to developing countries.

Third, during the precrisis period, the huge increase in net capital inflows to developing countries coincided with a large increase in net capital outflows. For many countries, current account surpluses and international reserves increased substantially. This would suggest that the impact of the more benign global financial conditions cannot be found by looking only at the flows of capital to developing countries. The explanation must be much more complex.

Lower Cost of Foreign Capital, Increased Access, and a Surge in Inflows

Average spreads on emerging-market bonds dropped sharply—from about 800 basis points (bps) in 2001 to about 200 bps in early 2007, and further to 168 bps by mid-2007. The domestic reforms and better economic management in developing countries must have contributed to this decline. But the bulk of the decline in risk premiums and borrowing costs for developing countries must be attributed to the similar decreases seen in interest rates and risk premiums in high-income countries.

Net capital inflows (private and official) to developing countries surged from US$223 billion (4 percent of GDP) in 2001 to US$1.1 trillion (9 percent of GDP) in 2007 (World Bank 2010a). Net foreign direct investment (FDI) inflows as a share of developing countries' GDP increased from 2.5 percent in 2001 to 3.9 percent in 2007, while the share of external bond markets and foreign bank lending reached 4 percent of GDP in 2007. The surge in capital inflows took place in all world regions, with the largest gains in relative terms (as a percentage of GDP) in Europe, Central Asia, and South Asia. China, India, the Russian Federation, and Brazil accounted for more than 50 percent of capital inflows, on average, during 2001–07.

But did this surge in net capital inflows translate into increased domestic investment and growth in developing countries?

It is important to note that developing countries' saving rates surged between 2000 and 2007. In view of the phenomenal increases in saving in China (by 18 points of GDP) and India (almost 14 points), the average increase for developing countries was equivalent to about 10–11 points of GDP. But even the median increase was about 4 percentage points of GDP. This implied for many countries a large positive increase in current account balances. In fact, developing countries posted an aggregate current account surplus of US$406 billion in 2007, versus just US$68 billion in 2002. The larger volume of net capital inflows and larger current account surpluses also meant large net capital outflows and increases in reserves. (Total net capital flows—net inflows plus net outflows[8]—is the relevant variable to use in considering the impact on investment and growth.)

World Bank (2010a) finds that a 1-percentage-point increase in capital inflows is associated with a 0.45 percentage-point increase in investment using cross-country regressions. Net capital inflows explain 30 percent of intercountry differences in investment rates (11.5 points between the top and bottom quartiles). And using a panel regression, the study finds that about one-third (1.9 percentage points) of the average increase (of 5.4 percentage points) in investment rates between 2000 and 2007 is accounted for by the reduction in the global cost of capital, 11 percent (0.6 points) by improved domestic financial intermediation, and 25 percent (1.4 points) by improved terms of trade.

The positive correlation between net capital inflows and investment should result in a negative correlation between the current account balance (or total net capital outflows) and economic growth. However, a strand of empirical evidence also finds a positive association between current account balances (surpluses) and economic growth in developing countries (Prasad, Rajan, and Subramanian 2007). This evidence suggests that higher growth rates are associated with higher capital account surpluses (or lower deficits), that is, with higher saving rates while investment rates lag. This would mean that investment in developing countries is not constrained by the lack of domestic resources and is not correlated with total net capital inflows. The weaker growth in investment is explained by weaker financial development or real exchange appreciation in the presence of large capital inflows, which reduces the profitability of investments in tradables.[9]

These conflicting findings can be reconciled if one recalls, from the previous discussion, the many channels through which global financial conditions may affect the domestic economy. Net capital inflows are only one such channel and their impact may depend on the domestic investment climate. The composition of capital inflows may be more important than the total inflows for the quality of investment and growth. Global interest rates and better access to credit may influence domestic financial intermediation and domestic interest rates without significant capital inflows.

Domestic Interest Rates and Banking Intermediation

The easier global financial conditions have also been transmitted to developing economies through their impact on domestic banking intermediation. In combination with domestic reforms, lower inflation, lower international interest rates, lower spreads, and access to foreign capital have helped reduce domestic interest rates and the cost of capital in developing countries and have helped deepen domestic banking intermediation.

Banking intermediation (as measured by claims of deposit money, banks, and other financial intermediaries on the private sector) expanded from 35 percent of GDP in 2000 to 41 percent in 2007.[10] In many cases, this was reinforced through greater participation of foreign banks in domestic financial systems after financial liberalizations in emerging countries. The expansion was most notable in the region of Europe and Central Asia, and in South Asia. World Bank (2010a) finds from a panel regression for the period 2001–07 that a 1 point decline in the global price of risk is associated with an increase of 7.5 percentage points (of GDP) in financial intermediation and a 3.5-percentage-point (of GDP) increase in capital inflows for the average developing country. The growth in banking intermediation in most cases occurred while domestic interest rates were declining, which supported strong domestic demand growth.

But the expansion of banking intermediation was uneven across countries. Many countries experienced a large expansion between 2000 and 2007 (larger than 10 percentage points of GDP), such as Brazil, India, Poland, Turkey, and Vietnam. Others saw a large decline in financial intermediation to the private sector, as in Ethiopia, where government policy favored credit to state-owned enterprises for funding infrastructure projects, and in Malaysia and the Philippines, where private investment was sluggish and declining despite high saving rates.

Lower interest rates, expansion of domestic credit, and greater access to foreign capital increase the demand for investment by private agents.

Composition of Capital Inflows and Financial Engineering

The same level of capital inflows may have a different effect on investment and growth, depending on its composition. Almost all of the 10 country studies highlight the role of larger inflows of FDI in increasing total factor productivity (TFP) growth, including through better access to technology.

The lower cost of capital, moderated risk perceptions, and greater access to international financial markets—together with easing restrictions on capital flows in many developing countries—facilitated access to more complex financial engineering and products that stimulated domestic investment, especially in such markets as infrastructure. This was especially the case in India, but other countries must also have benefited from these services.

The large increase in portfolio capital inflows (from near zero in 2001 to US$160 billion in 2007) contributed considerably to the rise in the market capitalization of developing-country stock markets—which rose on average from 38 percent of GDP in 2000 to 89 percent in 2007.[11] This boom in stock markets was a global phenomenon. The most dynamic countries experienced the largest gains—76 percentage points in India and 94 points in China. Large increases were also experienced by other emerging markets like Brazil and Poland. In Turkey, stock market capitalization doubled from 2002, following the stock market crash of the 2001 crisis, even though the ratio in 2007 returned to the same level as in 2000. The countries that are least dynamic, in terms of investment and economic growth, experienced the smallest gains—Malaysia (recovering from the East Asia crisis), Mexico, and the Philippines.

The rise in equity prices of corporations leads to increases in Tobin's q and also stimulates domestic investment.[12] In the case of India, the study finds a strong impact of stock market capitalization on domestic investment. This effect was likely present and significant in other countries.

Assessing the Impact on Domestic Investment and GDP Growth

While it is difficult to determine the impact of the various financial channels discussed above on investment during the precrisis boom period, for the large sample of 54 countries, the data show that investment rates as a share of GDP increased by an average of 5.3 percentage points during 2000–07, and even more (5.5 points) if we exclude the

three East Asian countries.[13] But these (weighted) averages conceal a lot
of variability and are heavily influenced by three large countries—China,
India, and Vietnam (Asia-3 in figure 2.2)—where the increase was
7–11 percentage points. This increase is much greater relative to what
was observed in East Asia (EA-4: Indonesia, the Republic of Korea,
Malaysia, and Thailand) during 1990–96 (before the 1997–98 crisis)
(figure 2.2). The increase for the other seven developing countries, which
are part of our 10-country sample, is much more moderate. In Malaysia
and the Philippines, the investment rate declined by 4–6 percentage
points of GDP.

The 10 case studies suggest that countries were in different situations
in terms of the extent of their dependence on external finance or the
degree of constraint they faced in financing domestic investment. We find
a group of countries with high saving rates (greater than 25 percent of
GDP by the mid-2000s) and (significantly) positive or increasing current
account balances: China, India, Malaysia, Mexico, and the Philippines.
With a very high and increasing saving rate, Vietnam can be included in

Figure 2.2. Gross Fixed Capital Formation during Precrisis Periods

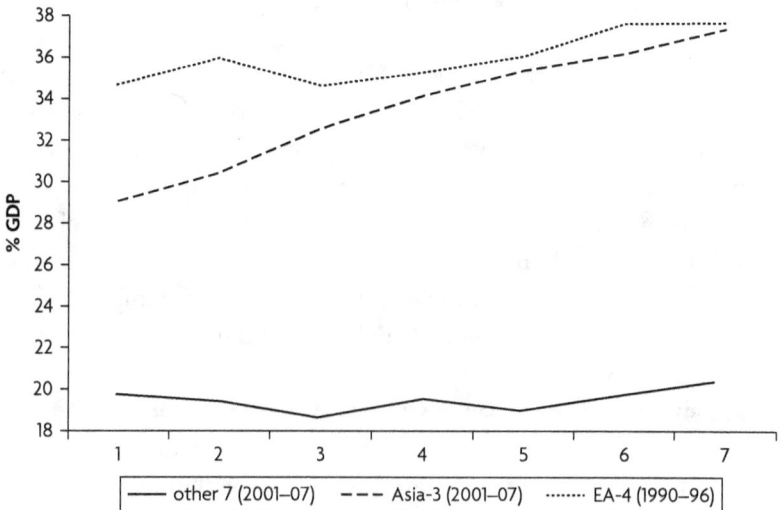

Source: World Bank DDP.
Note: Asia-3 = China, India, and Vietnam; EA-4 = Indonesia, the Republic of Korea, Malaysia, and Thailand;
   Other 7 = Brazil, Ethiopia, Malaysia, Mexico, the Philippines, Poland, and Turkey.

this group despite its declining current account balance. For these countries, the volume of capital flows would have a limited impact on domestic capital accumulation. A second group includes Brazil and possibly Poland, which have low saving rates but are either not external-finance constrained or weakly constrained in view of their even lower investment rates and improving current account balance. A third group can be considered as external-finance constrained in view of their low saving rates, a large (negative) current account balance (Ethiopia), or a deteriorating external balance (Turkey). The volume of capital flows would be a significant determinant of domestic investment for this last group of external-finance constrained countries.

For the more dynamic economies, the impact of a more benign global financial environment is more likely to be found in the composition of capital flows. Larger portfolio flows may stimulate private investment through higher domestic equity prices and Tobin's q, as in the case of India. Larger FDI flows—as in the case of Brazil, India, and Vietnam—would affect the quality of investment and productivity growth. Increased borrowing by the corporate sector may reflect more efficient investment, with access to better financial engineering (as appears to be the case in India).

Trade Channel. The precrisis boom saw a surge of exports from developing countries. This surge was particularly impressive when measured by the ratio of total exports of goods and services to GDP, which increased for a sample of 52 countries during 2000–07 by a weighted average of almost 12 percentage points, and a simple average of 5 points. The increase for the ratio of manufacturing exports to GDP was also significant but more subdued, typically 40 percent that of total exports. For countries such as India, services were a key contributor to increased trade shares.

The empirical literature typically finds a significant effect of trade shares on the level of GDP growth or GDP per capita (Harrison and Rodríguez-Clare 2010). This may be due to "spillover effects" through technological and marketing externalities from production for exporting activities. The impact of exports on growth may also be through "tradables as special," as they allow moving into higher-productivity activities. However, such gains do not require actual exporting, but rather the expansion in the production of tradables. In this case, the effect is captured through the increase in the share of industry in GDP and not the share of exports in GDP (Rodrik 2009).

The deeper integration with the global economy that had been ongoing for the previous two decades must have contributed to the improved growth performance of developing countries during the precrisis boom period. This is particularly true for China and Vietnam, and possibly Poland and Turkey, whose improved competitiveness and productivity may have created a positive feedback loop with increased exports.

Increased growth in demand for exports and of trade shares is a possible channel of impact from global economic conditions on developing countries' growth. But the high rate of export growth of developing countries was not driven by increased import demand growth from rich countries. Indeed, the rate of growth of total imports and of manufactures imports by Organisation for Economic Co-operation and Development (OECD) countries during 2003–07 was the same as (if not lower than) it was during the previous period. However, the rate of increase of OECD imports from developing countries was almost double that of total imports, resulting in a continued increase in the share of developing countries in total imports, as well as in manufacturing imports, of OECD countries from about 18 percent during 1997–2002 to 24 percent during 2003–07. However, this increased market share is largely accounted for by imports from China, and somewhat by Poland, Turkey, and Vietnam. Excluding China, the share of imports of manufactures from developing countries grew only from 11.3 percent during 1997–2002 to 12.1 percent of total OECD imports during 2003–07. Part of the increased share of China, however, probably reflects parts and components produced in other developing countries but transformed further in China before being exported to OECD countries. This also explains part of the surge in South-South trade.[14]

South-South trade was a major driver of the overall expansion of exports by developing countries. The share of developing countries in world import demand increased from about 20 percent in 2000 to 31 percent in 2008 (Canuto, Haddad, and Hanson 2010). Using a gravity model[15] a decomposition of trade growth during 2000–08 shows that higher economic growth rates in low- and middle-income countries explain 51 percent of export growth in the Middle East and North Africa, 42 percent in Europe and

Central Asia, 21 percent in Sub-Saharan Africa, and 18 percent in Latin America and the Caribbean, compared with just 12 percent in East Asia and the Pacific and less than 10 percent in South Asia.

The countries in our sample reflect the average overall experience, but with large variations across countries. Three countries experienced particularly large increases in their trade ratios: China, Poland, and Vietnam. In terms of exports of manufactures as a percentage of GDP, the increase was much smaller in general, but was still quite large for China, Poland, Turkey, and Vietnam. Brazil, Ethiopia, and India recorded small gains in manufactures. Malaysia, Mexico, and the Philippines saw sharp declines in their exports of manufactures.

This analysis shows that high-income countries did not increase their demand for exports of manufactures relative to previous periods. Thus, improved global trade growth was not an important contributor to the improved growth of developing countries during the boom period. Rather, it was improved competitiveness that supported higher growth of exports to high-income countries by a very few developing countries: China, Poland, and Vietnam, and, to a lesser extent, Turkey. These same countries also expanded their trade with non-OECD countries. Another set of developing countries increased their trade of manufactures with other developing countries but to a much smaller extent.

Commodity Prices. The strong global growth during the boom period led to the most marked surge in commodity prices in the past century. The boom covered a wide range of commodity prices and lasted much longer than previous ones. The U.S. dollar price of commodities increased by 109 percent from 2003 to the height of the cycle in mid-2008, or 130 percent since 1999 (World Bank 2009). Nonenergy commodity prices doubled in real terms between 2003 and 2008, while real energy prices increased by 170 percent. For oils and metals, the boom followed an extended period of low or falling prices that created conditions for a low supply response. The boom in agricultural prices reflected rising costs attributable to higher energy costs and rising demand for biofuels.

The relationship between commodity dependence and long-term growth remains subject to considerable debate, with much evidence pointing to a negative relationship. However, for commodity-dependent countries, surges in commodity prices have often been associated with higher growth in the short to medium term. This was the case during the precrisis boom, when the large terms-of-trade improvements for many commodity exporters fueled a growth boom as well, especially in the major oil-exporting countries.

The countries on which we focus in this book are not major commodity exporters, and the role of commodity prices was thus expected to be limited. In our sample of 10 countries, only a few experienced some increase in their goods terms of trade during 2003–07 of more than 1 percent per year: Brazil, Malaysia, and Mexico.

Remittances. Remittance flows to developing countries surged during the 2000s, increasing from US$113 billion in 2002 to more than US$289 billion in 2007, a growth rate of more than 20 percent per year. The simple average ratio of remittances to GDP of developing countries increased from 3.7 percent in 2000 to 5.5 percent in 2007. A few of the countries in our sample did experience a major surge of remittances after 2001 (the Philippines and Vietnam), while others (India, Ethiopia, Mexico, and Poland) experienced a significant increase.

The size and increase in remittances had major effects in many countries. At the microeconomic level, they contributed to lowering poverty and improved living conditions for migrant families. At the macroeconomic level, they helped improve current account balances. In the Philippines, remittances were a main driver of the growth acceleration, as they fueled a surge of private consumption. In Ethiopia, remittances contributed to both higher savings and higher private consumption.

Lessons, Main Messages, and Implications for Postcrisis Growth

The main message from this review of the precrisis period is that countries had a variety of experiences that reflected their specific combinations of domestic and external conditions. These factors included the strength and dynamism of the domestic economy as well as previous and ongoing structural reforms. But external factors were also important and included the impact of global financial conditions, trade in manufactures, and commodity exports.

Keeping this range of experiences in mind, we draw a number of useful lessons for assessing the medium-term impact of the crisis:

- The period 2003–07 saw an acceleration of actual GDP growth in developing countries by 2 to 3.3 percentage points, relative to 1997–2002. But using a measure of potential output, the growth acceleration was only about 1.5 percentage points, about half the actual GDP growth acceleration.
- The exceptionally high actual GDP growth rate of developing countries during the precrisis boom period, especially during 2006–07, cannot be the right benchmark for measuring the impact of the crisis on the growth rate of potential GDP in the medium term. Growth of potential GDP during 2003–07, the more relevant benchmark, was about 0.6 points lower than actual growth, as many countries were on high and unsustainable growth paths during the boom period.
- The impact of global economic conditions on growth during the precrisis boom years was differentiated across developing countries. It depended on domestic economic conditions and external financing opportunities or constraints facing the country. However, in general the financial markets channel was the most important factor, while trade and growth in overall demand from OECD countries was the least important. Larger remittances and improved terms of trade played a significant role in a few countries.
- For countries with low savings, capital flows boosted their growth potential. Even in high-savings countries, the easier global financial conditions still affected growth through various channels: the lower cost of borrowing, which enhanced domestic financial intermediation and led to higher domestic investment; larger portfolio flows, which contributed to higher equity prices, spurring more domestic investment; and better access to foreign capital such as FDI or corporate access to better financial products, which improved the efficiency of domestic investment.
- There was no increase in global trade growth during the boom period, which could have helped improve economic performance in most developing countries. During the past two decades, however, developing countries did increase their trade shares, which helped boost their growth. This was particularly true for China and Vietnam during the boom period; they enhanced their competitiveness and market share, which contributed to their high productivity growth. In the case of China, net exports were a major contributor to GDP growth.

- Increased remittances (Ethiopia, the Philippines, Poland and Vietnam) or improved terms of trade (Brazil, Malaysia, and Mexico) allowed a few countries to improve their current accounts or relieve their external finance constraint. But many remained vulnerable to terms-of-trade shocks and risked becoming finance constrained.

The Crisis, Impact, and Policy Response

While the U.S. subprime crisis, which broke out in August 2007, shook the global economy, it was not expected to lead to what is now widely regarded as the deepest global recession since the Great Depression. At that time, advanced-country economic activity started to slow, and by the middle of 2008 these countries began to experience a mild recession. Emerging and developing economies, however, continued to grow at fairly robust rates, though slower by earlier standards, up until the third quarter of 2008. Early efforts by policy makers sought to deal with the market liquidity and credit concerns arising from worries about the valuation of bad assets and their implications for the solvency of many large financial institutions.

In September 2008, the simmering crisis erupted with the default of a major U.S. investment bank (Lehman Brothers) and the rescue of the largest U.S. insurance company (American International Group). These events were followed by the U.S. government's adoption of a large bailout package in the form of the Troubled Asset Relief Program. It emerged then that toxic assets related to the subprime crisis may have infected not only U.S. banks, but also banks elsewhere in the world. Rescue packages for troubled banks were launched in many countries, while central banks loosened monetary policy to deal with severe liquidity shortages.

Risk premiums jumped everywhere as perceptions of counterparty and solvency risk of the most well-established financial firms came into question. Disorderly deleveraging began to take place: liquid assets were sold at a heavy discount, credit lines to leveraged financial intermediaries were slashed, bond spreads widened sharply everywhere, flows of trade finance and working capital were severely disrupted, banks tightened lending standards further, and equity prices fell steeply.

The financial crisis was unique in that it emerged in the United States and then spread to the rest of the world. The crisis affected the global economy through a range of channels.

The *financial channel* affected many countries in two ways. The first concern was with the health of the financial system and, in particular, the banking system. Almost everywhere, concerns mounted about the counterparty risk and exposure to toxic assets that domestic banks might have. The possibilities of systemic banking problems or bank collapses could not be ruled out. In addition, the breakdown of securitization and the ensuing rise in risk perceptions were leading to a deleveraging process that was drying up liquidity in global markets. The resulting credit crunch hurt even the most highly rated private borrowers—both individual and sovereign. The result was a sharp decline in liquidity in much of the world.

Another financial effect was the drying up of capital flows. As the crisis deepened, uncertainties increased, which led to rising risk premiums, widening spreads, and a flight to quality. The result was a sharp contraction of capital flows to emerging markets, especially in the fourth quarter of 2008.

The *trade channel* hit in the wake of the sharp fall in demand linked to declines in household wealth associated with steep declines in such asset prices as equities and housing. This translated into a sharp drop in demand for exports from emerging markets which were relying on this engine for their growth. In addition the drying up of trade credit increased uncertainties and hindered trade transactions.

These stresses affected real activity in all countries. Industrial production and merchandise trade plummeted in the fourth quarter of 2008 and continued to fall rapidly in early 2009 in both advanced and emerging economies. Demand for investment and consumer goods thus decreased substantially owing to credit disruptions, declining wealth, and rising anxiety. The result was an increase in idle capacity, which rose sharply in almost all countries during this period.

Global GDP is estimated to have contracted by an alarming 6.25 percent (annualized) in the fourth quarter of 2008 (a swing from 4 percent growth the previous year) and to have fallen almost as fast in the first quarter of 2009. The advanced economies experienced an unprecedented 7.5 percent decline in the fourth quarter of 2008. Output in emerging economies contracted by 4 percent in the fourth quarter, mainly through the financial and trade channels.

As global activity slowed, inflation pressures subsided. Commodity prices also plunged from midyear highs in 2008 because of the severe slowdown in the global economy. As a result, 12-month headline inflation in the advanced economies fell below 1 percent in February 2009. Inflation also moderated substantially in the emerging economies. Meanwhile falling profit margins and output declines put pressure on wages and employment. This pressure was partly alleviated by falling exchange rates.

Countercyclical policy was adopted in many countries, according to their circumstances, size of shock, and fiscal space. After the Lehman Brothers collapse, most advanced-country authorities resolved to let no large financial institutions fail. Governments provided support in the form of new capital, guarantees, and special programs for dealing with troubled assets. At the same time, with inflation concerns abated, central banks used a range of measures to ease liquidity and credit market conditions. Interest rates were cut to unprecedented lows—0.5 percent or less in some countries (Canada, Japan, the United Kingdom, and the United States).

Fiscal policy was also used extensively to stimulate demand. Beyond letting automatic stabilizers work, large discretionary stimulus packages were introduced in most advanced economies—notably Germany, Japan, Korea, the United Kingdom, and the United States—and fiscal deficits in the major advanced economies expanded substantially in 2008. As economies continued to slide in the first half of 2009, fiscal stimulus packages were sharply increased in almost all countries.

Immediate Impact of Crisis and Importance of Channels of Impact

The crisis hit most developing countries through the three channels of demand, credit, and financial inflows. Many countries also experienced a negative terms-of-trade shock as commodity prices declined, reflecting weakening demand.

The most visible shock to emerging economies manifested itself through the *exports channel*. The impact of the collapse on trade was straightforward and dependent on the extent of a country's integration into the global trade system, especially in the case of manufactures. While some of these countries were already beginning to show signs of encountering capacity constraints and a possible cyclical correction, the shock that hit them was unexpectedly severe. Much of the impact of the crisis was felt in the last quarter of 2008 and the first quarter of 2009.

Countries saw double-digit declines in exports, with much of the impact felt in the manufacturing sector.

In the Philippines, exports fell by 22 percent in 2009 and imports fell 24 percent with the collapse in global demand for electronics and semiconductors, which accounted for about 60 percent of the country's exports. Brazil, which had seen exports expand by an annual average of 14 percent between 2002–03 and 2007–08, posted double-digit declines in the months following September 2008. In India, manufactured goods exports, which grew by 27.7 percent in 2007–08, declined by 18.8 percent between October 2008 and March 2009. China's export engine was also hit hard, with export growth falling by 25 percent, on an annual basis, in the first six months of 2009. Much of this decline was in manufactured exports. In Turkey, exports contracted by 27 percent annually after the crisis, compared with a 23 percent growth before. Malaysia registered a decline in exports of manufactures of about 30 percent, on an annualized basis, in January 2009. Mexico saw its export growth contract by 26 percent in the first half of 2009. In Vietnam, over the first 10 months of 2009, exports declined by 13.8 percent relative to 2008; for the year as a whole, export growth was –8.9 percent. Even in Ethiopia the growth rate of exports collapsed from 25 percent annually during 2004–08 to –1 percent in 2009.

The *credit channel* hit emerging economies hard. The freeze in credit and money markets in the advanced countries was transmitted to credit markets in other countries very quickly. Uncertainty about exposure to toxic assets heightened counterparty risk everywhere. As a result, credit demand slowed, affecting money markets everywhere. External credit for exporters and small banks vanished. External rollover rates and average maturities fell substantially, while borrowing costs surged. The closing of external credit lines led large corporations to substitute domestic credit for external credit, crowding out smaller firms that rely on domestic credit.

Interestingly, most of the 10 countries in our sample appear to have developed reasonably healthy and well-regulated banking systems. In the wake of the crises of the 1990s (in East Asia, Russia, and Latin America), most countries had built a reasonably conservative regulatory framework that met Basel capital requirements for banks and entailed adequate reserve provisioning. For example, in 2008, Brazil required a capital adequacy ratio of about 11 percent (much higher than Basel II's 8 percent) while banks were holding 17 percent. Improved regulation resulted in little toxic asset exposure on the part of the banks in most of the countries in our study. In Turkey, the banking sector's improved performance and stability was due to the restructuring following the crisis of 2001, effective supervision, and a better regulatory framework. In both reasonably well-regulated banking systems helped mitigate the negative impact of the crisis.

Until September 2008, emerging-market financial systems were relatively sheltered from the global contagion, and economic growth in these countries also remained strong. But the seizure of financial markets in advanced countries following the Lehman Brothers collapse finally triggered liquidity and credit difficulties in developing countries, the stoppage of capital inflows, the soaring of bond spreads, sharp falls in equity prices, and pressures on exchange rates.

The large capital inflows that had stimulated countries in the boom period had already begun to level off when the subprime crisis erupted in 2007. But it was in September 2008 that the real decline in capital flows hit the emerging economies. The initial impact was mainly on portfolio flows. In India, inflows fell from an average of US$45 billion per year during 2003–08 to US$16 billion in 2009. Malaysia lost US$118 billion in the last quarter of 2008. Debt flows, which were much smaller than equity inflows, also slowed, not just because of supply considerations but also because of demand considerations as firms retrenched. FDI flows, however, were more stable as fresh flows slowed but existing commitments were maintained.

The slowdown in (and reversal of) inflows did not last long. Equity markets rebounded quickly as capital flows resumed by the second quarter of 2009. By the end of the third quarter of 2009, the emerging-market index had risen by 52 percent. At the same time, by the second quarter of 2009, creditor banks in advanced economies stopped reducing their exposure to emerging countries. In tandem, most currencies strengthened although they remained below precrisis levels.

During the boom, commodity and fuel producers had experienced terms-of-trade gains, which the crisis eroded fairly quickly; prices of commodities and fuel were corrected sharply in the last quarter of 2008 and the first half of 2009. Despite the steep fall in commodity prices, the terms of trade for commodity producers and the nonfuel-exporting group did not suffer much because the prices of fuel and manufactures also declined sharply with the shrinkage in global demand. On balance, the terms-of-trade shock was small.

Some countries (Ethiopia, India, Mexico, the Philippines, Poland, and Vietnam) benefited from large *remittance inflows* in the precrisis years. During the crisis, remittances did not drop by much, since labor was locked into big projects in such areas as the Middle East. In many cases, remittances in domestic-currency terms actually increased as exchange rates adjusted because of the crisis. Remittances played a countercyclical role and provided funds and liquidity to the economies and the banking systems, and prevented sharp deteriorations in current account balances and reserves.

Policy Response

Learning from previous crises, policy makers in many countries used the global boom period, quite wisely, to develop a reasonably sound macroeconomic policy that reduced debt levels and boosted reserves. Many countries also developed reasonable financial regulatory frameworks and adopted relatively flexible exchange rate arrangements. The preboom period was one of reform for most economies, where measures were adopted to support the budget, open up the trade regime, and adopt better systems of monetary management. In many cases, it was also helpful that the capital account had not been fully opened out.

Exchange rates were not as big an issue as in past crises, in that there were no currency attacks or defenses, nor were there disorderly adjustments or substantial reserve losses. This is because countries no longer instituted hard pegs. All the countries in our sample (except Ethiopia) had a managed exchange rate policy;[16] all pursued a managed float that allowed for quick adjustment. Except for China, all of the countries in our sample let exchange rates adjust rapidly downward in line with evolving market conditions (figure 2.3). Even Ethiopia let its currency depreciate by more than 20 percent since early 2009, and 40 percent over the past two years. As a result, reserves were largely protected, and they were used mainly to counter disorderly market conditions and to augment private credit, including sustaining trade finance.

Figure 2.3. Exchange Rates Adjusted Rapidly

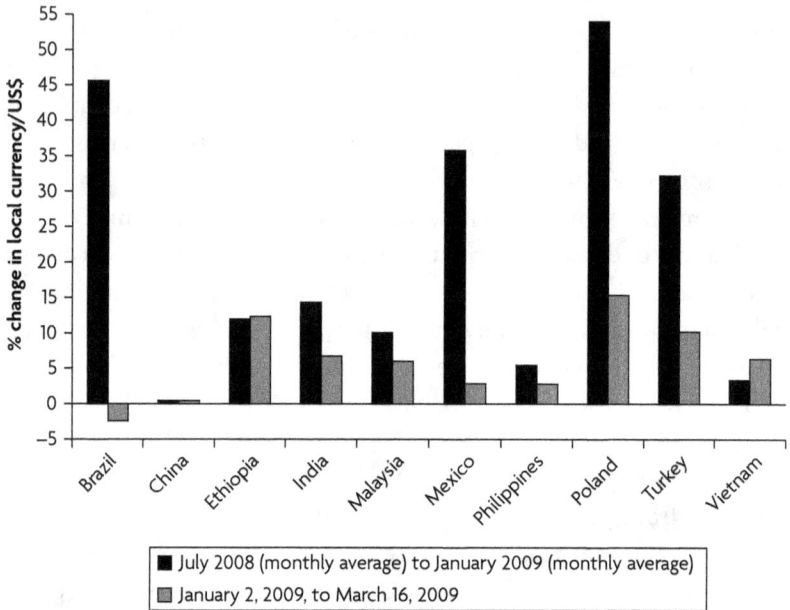

Source: IMF International Financial Statistics; www.exchangerate.com.

The depreciation did not last long, as most of it occurred at the beginning of the crisis, in the last half of 2008 (figure 2.3). In early 2009, most of the countries in our study experienced a smaller depreciation. With the beginning of the turnaround in the third quarter of 2009, exchange rates—especially in Brazil, China, India, Poland, and Turkey—began appreciating. The rapid depreciation at the beginning of the crisis facilitated quick external adjustment and attracted remittances and other inflows while also supporting competitiveness. Because many of the countries had pursued reasonable macroeconomic policies and had well-capitalized banking systems, serious currency mismatches did not emerge, nor did this depreciation lead to any major balance sheet problems. More flexible exchange rate arrangements backed by sound macroeconomic policy and a healthy financial sector may in fact have contributed to the relatively quick adjustment in many countries. In addition, the large capital outflows that took place in the early months of the crisis did not result in large reserve losses, as countries were not actively defending their currencies.

The developing countries in our sample responded to the crisis with countercyclical fiscal and monetary policy, which varied in terms of their nature and strength, taking into account their specific constraints (tables 2.2 and 2.3). They reacted very quickly in dealing with the credit difficulties that were felt right after the Lehman Brothers collapse. Central banks hastened to add liquidity and to lower interest rates and took measures to make liquidity flow through the system (table 2.2).

Table 2.2. Policy Response to the Crisis: Monetary Policy

Country	Monetary easing percent of GDP	Interest rates reduced	Liquidity provision	Reserve requirements reduced
Brazil		13.75% to 8.75%	Yes, 3% of GDP provided by public banks	Yes
China	M2 increased growth of 11%	Cut by 216 bps		From 17.5% to 14–15%
Ethiopia	Tighter monetary policy			Increased before crisis
India	9% of GDP	Repo lowered by 475 bps	Refinance easing, prudential norms relaxed, increase purchase of government debt	CRR reduced by 400 bps
Malaysia		150 bps from 3.5% to 2%		From 3.5% to 1%
Mexico	Yes	375 bps from 8.25% to 4.5%	Yes	
Philippines		From 6% to a 17-year low of 4%	Rediscount window increased, rules relaxed for mark to market	Lowered by 2%
Poland		250 bps to 3.5%	Yes, including credit guarantee by state-owned bank	Lowered 0.5% to 3%
Turkey		Oct. 2008 and Nov. 2009 from 16.75% to 6.5%	Multiple measures to increase liquidity	From 11 percent to 9 percent
Vietnam	No	Base rate from 14% to 7%; subsidy of 4% for working capital and short-term loans	No	No

Source: Country studies in this volume.
Note: bps = basis points; CRR = cash reserve ratio.

Table 2.3. Policy Response to the Crisis: Fiscal Stimulus

Country	Fiscal measures	Other public sector measures
Brazil	Reversible countercyclical stimulus (including automatic stabilizers): 1% of GDP in 2009	Increased credit by public financial sector institutions
	Total change in primary balance between 2009 H1 and 2008 H1 was −3.1% of GDP	
China	Total discretionary multiyear stimulus: 12.5% of GDP. Small part in the budget	2/3 of stimulus is bank lending
	No measure of automatic stabilizers	
Ethiopia	Tighter fiscal policy	Tighter lending to public enterprises
India	3 stimulus packages amounting to 3.5% of GDP. No measure of automatic stabilizers	
Malaysia	Discretionary fiscal measures: 0.7% and then 0.9% of GDP No measure of automatic stabilizers	
Mexico	1 to 1.5% of GDP discretionary measures in 2009	
Philippines	Announced discretionary measures: 4.1% of GDP	
	Overall change in fiscal balance between 2008 and 2009: 2.6% of GDP, includes both discretionary (about 1% of GDP) measures and automatic stabilizers	
Poland	2% of GDP of discretionary measures	
	Increase in deficit in 2009 by 3.6% of GDP, of which half caused by fall in revenues	
Turkey	1.2% of GDP mostly dues to automatic stabilizers	
Vietnam	10% of GDP multiyear discretionary measures	

Source: Country studies in this volume.
Note: H1 = the first half of the year.

Reserve requirements were reduced in almost every country, reflecting their own liquidity needs and inflation considerations. In addition, the use of discount windows was encouraged. In some cases—Brazil, China—public sector banks were used to support the credit needs of the smaller banks. In Vietnam the government extended large subsidies on bank loans to enterprises. Central banks sharply increased direct injections of liquidity as needed in some cases to support the fiscal injection.

Without central bank intervention, the distressed liquidity situation would have led to a collapse of output given the squeeze on working capital and exports. According to the India study, for example, the credit squeeze without central bank intervention (other things being equal) would have led to a fall in GDP growth of an estimated 1.5 percent.

All the economies in our study also used fiscal policy to stimulate demand in the face of collapsing global demand. The stimulus came in many forms, ranging from increases in spending (especially on infrastructure and benefits) to guarantees to the private sector, subsidies, and tax cuts. Countries that used the boom years to develop prudent macro policies (such as Brazil, China, and India) were able to adopt larger stimulus packages. A further stimulus also came in the form of credit extended by state-owned banks and enterprises on behalf of the government in Brazil and China. Our country studies provide measures of the fiscal stimulus (table 2.3). These measures are not strictly comparable, as some include automatic stabilizers while others do not, and some are annual while others are multiyear. But the extent of active fiscal policy varied considerably and depended to a large extent on the fiscal space available to governments. China and Vietnam had the strongest fiscal packages, while Malaysia, Mexico, and Turkey had the weakest.

For some countries the additional expenditures went mostly to infrastructure investment. In the case of China the total multiyear package of 12.5 percent of GDP was only partly through the central government budget (1.18 trillion renminbi out of a total of 4.0 trillion), but the total amount went to various infrastructure projects: transport (38 percent), earthquake reconstruction (25 percent), public housing (10 percent), rural infrastructure (9 percent), technology innovation (9 percent), energy and environment (5 percent), and health and education (4 percent). Like China, Vietnam announced a very large multiyear stimulus package of about 8.5 percent of GDP, of which 6.8 percent of GDP was in expenditures. These expenditures were aimed mostly at infrastructure (77 percent), interest subsidies on working capital loans (15 percent), and other social spending (8 percent).

For other countries the bulk of the additional spending went to current expenditures. In the case of Brazil, 1.8 percent of GDP (out of a total of 1.9 percent between first half of 2008 and first half of 2009) went to increases in civil service wages (+0.7 percent), and in the national minimum wage and social security benefits (+0.8 percent of GDP). The increase in investment expenditures was much more limited at 0.1 percent of GDP. Other measures, which were off-budget, involved increased credit by public sector banks. In the Philippines total budget expenditures increased by 1.4 percent of GDP between 2008 and 2009, with

0.9 percent going to current expenditures (salaries and transfers to local government) and 0.6 percent of GDP to capital outlays. Another part (1.5 percent of GDP) of the stimulus package was off-budget expenditures. The expenditures part of the fiscal stimulus for India (2.9 percent of GDP out of a total of 3.6 percent of GDP increase in the fiscal deficit between 2007–08 and 2008–09) went largely to current expenditures: fertilizer and food subsidies (1.02 percent of GDP), civil service pay (0.47 percent), and farm loan waiver (0.27 percent).

Impact of the Crisis

What impact did the crisis have on emerging markets? In our case studies, most countries saw a sharp decline in growth in the last quarter of 2008, following the Lehman Brothers collapse that triggered the crisis. Growth was reduced in 2008 for all countries compared to the average for 2003–07, except for Brazil and Ethiopia, which did benefit from the commodity boom (figure 2.4).

Figure 2.4. The Impact of the Crisis on GDP Growth

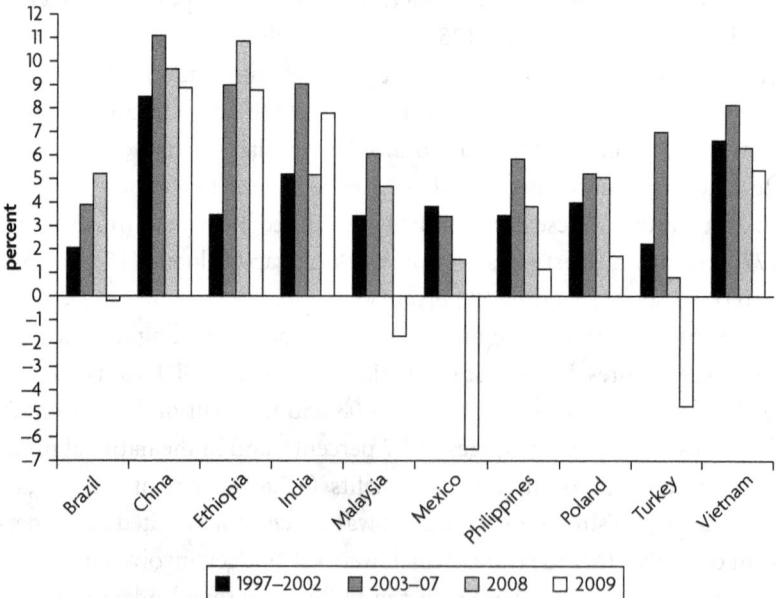

Legend: ■ 1997–2002   ■ 2003–07   ▨ 2008   □ 2009

Source: World Bank DDP; IMF *World Economic Outlook 2010.*

To measure the severity of the crisis's impact, we estimate the output gap as the relative difference in 2009 between actual output and potential output. Specifically, we calculate the absolute output gap as actual output in 2009 minus potential output (calculated as if output increased since 2007 by the precrisis potential growth rate estimated in table 2.5) as a ratio of potential output. To determine the loss to each country relative to its own particular growth potential, we calculate a "relative output gap" as the ratio of the absolute output gap to the precrisis potential output growth rate (figure 2.5).

The countries most severely hurt were Malaysia, Mexico, and Turkey. Prior to the crisis, actual GDP growth in these countries averaged about 5.4 percent and it plunged to −4.3 percent in 2009. The absolute output gap in 2009 was −10.6 percent on average, and as a percent of precrisis potential GDP growth, it was higher than 100 percent (relative output gap) for all countries of this group. For the moderately affected group—Brazil, India, the Philippines, Poland and Vietnam—the output

Figure 2.5. Absolute and Relative Output Gaps, 2009

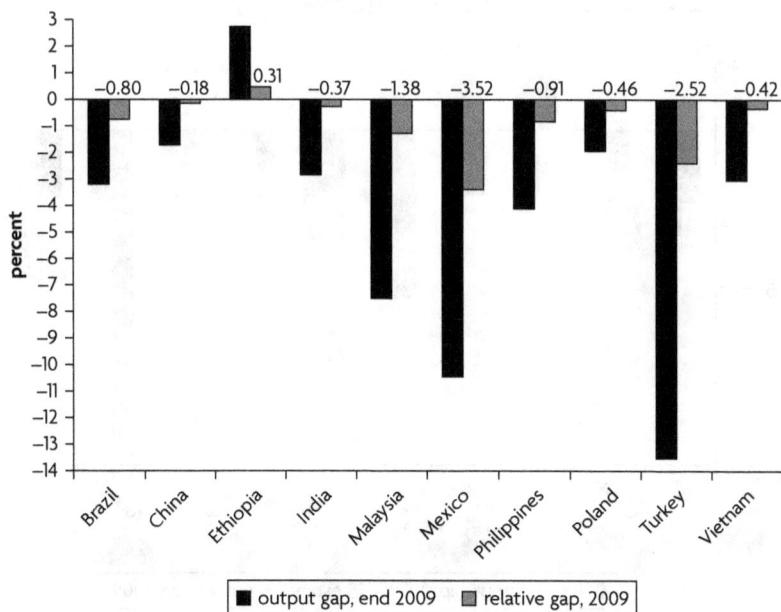

Source: Author's calculations.

gap was about –3 percent on average, about 35–90 percent of the precrisis potential growth rate. China was the least negatively affected, with an output gap of –1.8 percent —only about 18 percent of its precrisis potential growth rate (figure 2.5). Only in Ethiopia did actual output continue to exceed potential output in 2009.

A few recent studies have analyzed the determinants of the severity of impact of the recent crisis, but results vary considerably. In the annex to this chapter, we summarize such findings and analyze these determinants for our sample of 54 developing countries using the output gap in 2009 as a measure of the severity of impact. Our results are similar to those of other authors; the most statistically significant variables, on a consistent basis, are manufactures exports (as a percentage of GDP), leverage, credit growth, current account balance, international reserves, and the ratio of short-term debt to GDP.

But in all cases, regression results show that only 20–40 percent of the cross-country variation is explained. Most of the variation remains unexplained. Figure 2.6 shows the actual versus predicted output gap from a

Figure 2.6. Actual vs. Estimated Output Gap, 2009

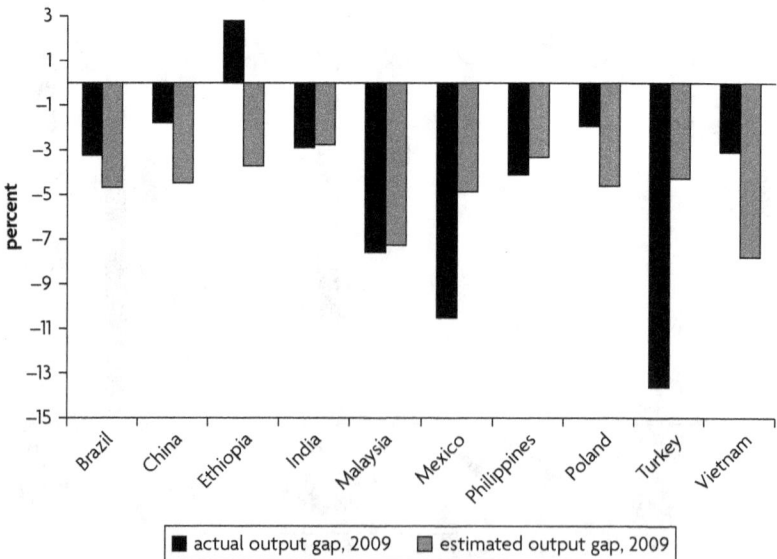

Source: Author's calculations.

typical regression equation.[17] It is striking that the impact of the crisis turns out to be much more severe than what the best regression equation would predict for Mexico, the Philippines, and Turkey. On the other hand, it is better than expected for Brazil, China, Poland, and Vietnam. In the case of Ethiopia, the actual output gap is positive while it would be expected to be significantly negative. Given the limited explanatory power of the econometric analysis, the country studies provide a richer analysis of the factors explaining the differentiated impact across countries.

Undiversified Exports. Countries that had substantial exports of manufactured goods but were not diversified in their product base were hurt most severely. In Mexico and Turkey, growth was sharply negative in 2009 (−6.5 percent for Mexico and −4.7 percent for Turkey). Although Mexico entered the global crisis with greatly strengthened public and private sector balance sheets and healthy banking sectors, the external shock has been substantial, reflecting strong real and financial linkages with the U.S. economy (figure 2.7). With more than three-quarters of exports directed to the United States and strong integration of

Figure 2.7. GDP for Mexico and the United States

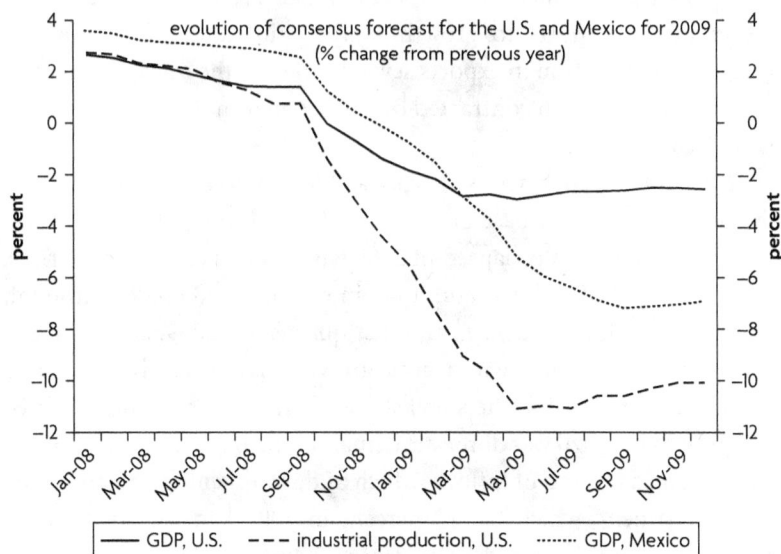

Source: IMF 2010b (figure 2).

production structures among the countries in the North American Free Trade Agreement, the collapse in U.S. industrial production was quickly transmitted to Mexico. Production and trade flows in the automotive industry across North America dropped 40 percent, and the decline in manufacturing activity was also synchronized. In Mexico, services activity also fell sharply—particularly in trade, tourism, and transportation—reflecting the likely presence of strong cross-sectoral spillovers from manufacturing that worsened the collapse in output. Disruptions associated with the H1N1 flu outbreak in the second quarter are estimated to have subtracted an extra 0.5 percent from annual growth.

Turkey was also hit particularly hard through the trade channel. A large part of the contraction in industrial output can be assigned to declines in exports of motor vehicles, basic metal, machinery and equipment, and electronics, which led to a 16 percent decline in industrial production.

Malaysia and the Philippines had built large export-based manufacturing sectors and were hard hit as external demand fell. Because of remittances and limited exposure to high-end manufacturing, the Philippines' growth rate did not contract as sharply as Malaysia's. The Malaysian economy experienced a negative growth rate (−1.7 percent), owing to a sharp reduction in export demand that lowered the contribution of net exports to growth in the third and fourth quarters of 2008. The reduction in exports severely affected the Malaysian manufacturing sector, which contracted by about 6 percent in the first quarter of 2009 (figure 2.8).

Brazil did not contract as sharply as Mexico because it had a more diversified production base and was not as well integrated into world trade. Output growth collapsed in 2009 with a fall in commodity prices, a sharp reversal of inflows, and a fall in demand and credit. Although exports fell by 15.8 percent in the first quarters of 2009, and by about 20 percent for the year, the impact on growth was limited given the large size of the economy and the small share of exports. The main driver of slow growth in Brazil was domestic demand, which fell due to a stoppage of credit and a reversal of inflows. Much of this weakening demand came from investment, which fell 22 percent in 2009. On the supply side, industrial output decreased 12 percent in 2009 as capital accumulation, productivity, and capacity utilization all took a dive.

Figure 2.8. Malaysia: Contributions to Growth by Sector

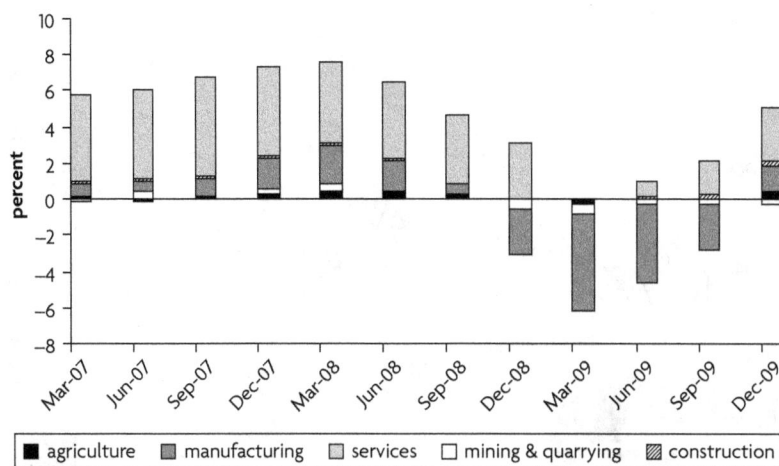

Source: Chapter 7 of this volume.

Domestic Financial Vulnerabilities. The severity of the crisis's impact on developing countries was the result of another major development: domestic financial-sector vulnerabilities attributable to a higher level of leverage and faster credit growth before the crisis.

The case of Turkey illustrates this effect. Turkey suffered from a sharp fall in capital inflows. FDI, which had reached 3.8 percent of GDP in 2006, plunged to about 1 percent in 2009, while private investment contracted by 28 percent in the first three quarters of 2009 (on an annual basis). Net errors and omissions on the balance of payments showed inflows of more than US$14 billion in the first half of 2009, reflecting the repatriation of foreign exchange assets. A stronger banking sector in Turkey after the reforms undertaken from 2001 helped limit the negative financial contagion. However, rapid credit growth prior to the crisis led to almost a doubling of the loan-to-deposit ratio from about 45 percent in 2002 to 80 percent in 2008. When the crisis hit, domestic credit tightened sharply, especially for smaller firms, leading to the shutdown of businesses and increased unemployment (figure 2.9).

The experience of many of the countries studied in this project, however, is not fully consistent with the explanation of excessive domestic financial vulnerabilities. For instance, three countries seriously hurt by the

Figure 2.9. Bank Credit in Turkey

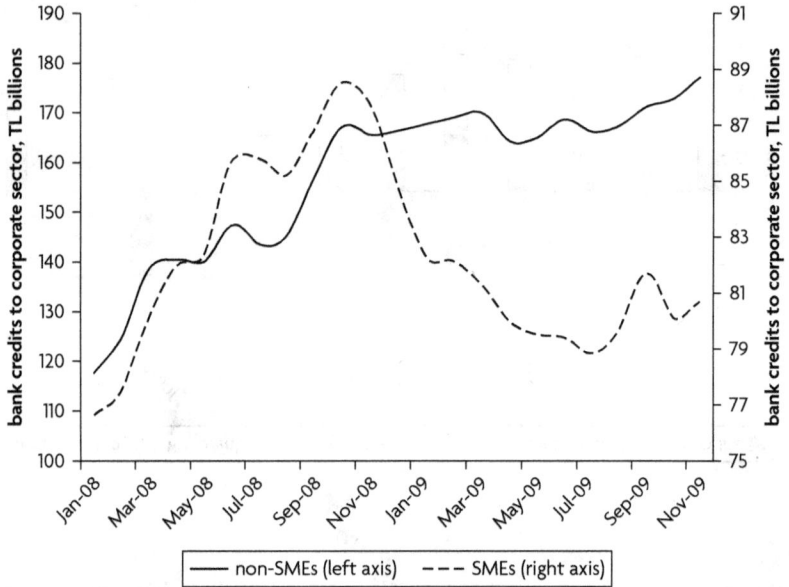

Source: Chapter 11 of this volume.
Note: SMEs = small and medium enterprises.

crisis did not have such vulnerabilities. In the wake of the East Asia crisis, Malaysia and the Philippines recorded slower credit growth and sharply declining loan-to-GDP ratios. Mexico experienced weak domestic credit growth, and its banking sector was relatively sound. But all three countries were seriously hit by the crisis. On the other hand, countries such as Brazil, India, and Vietnam, which did experience rapid domestic growth and higher leverage ratios, were much less severely affected by the crisis.

Current Account Deficits and the Role of International Reserves. In cross-country statistical analyses, the precrisis current account deficit is often found to be a significant determinant of the severity of impact of the crisis. But in our 10 country case studies the existence of large current account deficits played only a very limited role. Only a few of the countries in this study were experiencing significant current account deficits that made them vulnerable to external shocks: Ethiopia, Turkey, and Vietnam. And among these, only Turkey was severely affected by the crisis. Other countries had either current account surpluses or small deficits.

Surprisingly, the 10 country studies did not highlight the role of international reserves in explaining the severity of the impact, even though many showed that the availability of large international reserves allowed the authorities to supply foreign exchange to the private sector in the face of large falloffs in capital flows or to prevent larger domestic currency depreciations. However, econometric evidence points to the importance of reserves in explaining the resilience of emerging economies to crisis. China, India, Malaysia, and Vietnam had international reserves (net of short-term debt) ranging from 20 percent to 40 percent of GDP. Even in Brazil and the Philippines, reserve ratios exceeded 10 percent of GDP. These countries did accumulate large reserves to enable them to self-insure against external shocks through strong countercyclical policy, which limited the loss of confidence and prevented a run on the currency. Mexico, Poland, and Turkey had much lower levels of (net) reserves, which may have prevented them from undertaking more proactive policies. In the case of Turkey, the large current account deficit and a history of recurrent financial crisis, with a low level of reserves, led to a rapid loss of confidence by firms and households, who retrenched, leading to a massive collapse in domestic demand that exacerbated the fall in external demand.

Policy Response and the Role of Nonfinancial Domestic Conditions. The case studies show that the severity of the impact of the crisis was due partly to the countries' vulnerabilities and the extent of their integration with the global economy (which holds more broadly for developing countries). But the severity was also mitigated by the various policy measures taken in unison by advanced countries and followed up by many emerging economies. All of the countries in our case studies responded quickly and some quite strongly to the crisis. Of course, countries that had the fiscal space and large international reserves to allow a strong stimulus and that entered the crisis with strong momentum were able to implement stronger policy responses. These countries were able to soften the adverse impact of the crisis more than the countries that entered the crisis with less room for maneuver (Ostry and others 2010).

The domestic real sector and policy conditions do matter also for a fuller understanding of the variability across countries of the impact of the crisis. These include a range of variables, from the flexibility of markets, to the quality of the business environment and outlook of the business community, and the credibility of government policy.

China, India, and Vietnam were experiencing a positive or improved economic outlook, new or strengthened confidence, and dynamic private sectors. These economies were operating near their potential before the crisis hit. In India and Vietnam, a cyclical correction was under way at the time of the crisis. The crisis did have an immediate impact that shook this confidence, but these countries quickly recovered and retook the initiative. This was also reflected in the nature, extent, and quality of policy response, all of which need to be better understood.[18] China and India were able to take advantage of their large domestic markets and their relatively larger fiscal space and large international reserves to adopt major stimulus packages, thereby mitigating the effects of the crisis. In both of these countries, growth declined but remained high in 2009 (8.8 percent in China and 7.7 percent in India). Vietnam was also able to sustain a growth rate exceeding 6 percent in 2008 and 5.3 percent in 2009, albeit this was a downturn from 8.5 percent in 2007. Growth came from retained momentum of consumption and investment and from a strong agricultural performance, despite a slowdown in construction, services, and the contribution of net exports. These countries were also well positioned, from a competitiveness point of view. Before the crisis, they were enjoying an increasing share of exports in GDP (more than 10 percentage points between 2000 and 2007) and an increased share in imports of OECD countries. They tended to benefit from the global turnaround that began in the second half of 2009.

While experiencing slower growth than the previous group of countries, Brazil and Poland were also experiencing strong momentum before the crisis. Their macroeconomic conditions allowed them to take strong policy action. The severity of the impact of the crisis was much smaller than would have been predicted based on the cross-country regression.

In contrast, the economies of Malaysia, Mexico, and the Philippines were experiencing slow growth, domestic investment was sluggish, and competitiveness weak. Their policy response tended to be weaker and the impact of the crisis much more severe. In the case of Turkey, macroeconomic vulnerabilities and a recurrent history of crises did not allow for a strong policy response, and the impact of the crisis was the most severe.

Ethiopia's experience illustrates also the specific nature of the domestic conditions and the policy response. Based on the econometric analysis in the annex, one would have predicted a mildly negative impact of the crisis on growth. In fact, contrary to what one would have expected for a country with limited trade and financial integration, Ethiopia was seriously affected as export and FDI growth halted and as remittances flows slowed. Given that Ethiopia had serious macroeconomic problems and unsustainable growth, a major growth slowdown was possible. But Ethiopian growth was resilient, slowing from 10.8 percent in 2008 to just 8.7 percent in 2009; this figure was higher than potential GDP growth of 8.4 percent and resulted in a positive output gap. The crisis thus turned out to be an opportunity for Ethiopia to adopt some adjustment measures. The most important of these were fiscal tightening, the elimination of subsidies, and much-needed exchange rate correction to eliminate overvaluation. Donors responded with additional aid, which then stimulated the economy.

Medium-Term Implications of Domestic Developments during the Crisis

The crisis, its direct impact on the domestic economy, and the policy responses may affect medium-term growth through a number of domestic channels.

First, while fiscal policy responses in our sample countries have been agile and in many cases strong, in some cases this can raise concerns about sustainability in coming years. In all countries, the timing and the impact of the withdrawal will be a key issue in the medium term. Our country studies show that most countries (Brazil, India, Malaysia, Mexico, the Philippines, Poland, and Turkey) will need to undertake some type of fiscal consolidation and address varying degrees of fiscal sustainability issues in the coming years. Some, such as Brazil, Malaysia, or Turkey, came into the crisis with less fiscal space than the other counties and will thus probably have to be more aggressive in dealing with the situation. India will also have more limited fiscal space because of its crisis policy response, but it has considerable scope in dealing with fiscal problems because its medium-term growth prospects continue to be good.

Second, we did not find any case in which the global financial crisis precipitated a banking or financial system crisis in the countries studied.[19] In all cases financial systems were quite sound and experienced little direct impact from the crisis. Nonetheless, loan portfolios of banks may need to be watched in the coming period for two reasons. First, during the boom, consumer credit expanded in almost all countries (except Ethiopia). The impact of the crisis could undermine the quality of these loans. Second, policy responses included large increases in liquidity by central banks and, in some cases, the adoption of aggressive credit policies. For example, in Brazil, China, and Vietnam, government policy directed banks and state-owned enterprises to boost lending to infrastructure projects and to maintain some industries that were not performing. Some of this lending may affect the quality of banks' portfolios.

Third, higher unemployment during the crisis may discourage workers from seeking jobs, especially if it translates into prolonged spells of unemployment. This could, in turn, erode marketable skills and destroy human capital. But based on our sample of countries, such concerns do not seem to be highly relevant and are unlikely to have played an important role in the current crisis. The Turkey case study reported a sizable increase in unemployment during the crisis, but a major cause was an increase in labor force participation as workers, especially women, were seeking work opportunities in the face of falling incomes.

Fourth, the crisis may lead to slower accumulation of human capital in developing countries due to lower social spending on health and education. Evidence on this impact is scanty, but the limited data available for a number of countries show that the effect of the crisis on public and private spending on health and education has varied considerably. In general, governments and households tend to protect education over health. Low-income countries are more likely to cut spending on health and education, while middle-income countries tend to increase spending on health and education even when the share in total expenditures is reduced. Many countries have expanded safety nets and protected social spending during the crisis (Lewis and Verhoeven 2010). Thus, this channel of impact seems limited in the case of our sample countries, although further evidence is required.

Finally, the use of fiscal stimulus spending to invest in infrastructure or skills may relieve binding constraints to growth in a country. The large stimulus packages in China and Vietnam were mostly directed toward investment and may have played such a role, but the studies do not show any evidence in this respect.

Main Findings and Messages

- The net effect of the crisis, taking into account policy responses, has varied considerably when measured by the end-2009 output gap. Except for Ethiopia, the output gap was negative. One group of countries was affected moderately, with an output gap of −1.8 percent to −4.2 percent of GDP (Brazil, China, India, the Philippines, Poland, and Vietnam). The countries most severely affected (Malaysia, Mexico, and Turkey) experienced an output gap ranging from −7.6 percent to −13.6 percent.

- The most important negative shock to hit most countries was the collapse in global demand. Countries whose economies were not diversified (Mexico, the Philippines, and Turkey) and dependent on a narrow range of exports of manufactures suffered greater output losses than others.

- Countries that had ample "buffers"[20] for absorbing the shocks and giving them space to take policy action tended to perform better and limit the negative impact of the crisis. For instance, ample fiscal space and high levels of reserves and low levels of short-term debt were major assets that afforded countries substantial policy space and scope to adjust to the negative shock, and gave economic agents confidence that policy action would be taken if needed.

- Another kind of buffer is a sound banking and financial sector. Banking or financial sector problems were limited in the developing countries studied. All countries had implemented adequate regulatory mechanisms so that developing banking systems were protected from toxic assets and had adequate capital and provisioning requirements. The financial shock came mostly in the form of the credit shock, as global liquidity dried up. Factors present before the crisis, such as banking sector vulnerabilities, attributable to rapid credit growth and high leverage, explain only some of the impact.

- Countries that were strongly competitive (China, India, and Vietnam), with large increases in their export-to-GDP ratios and their shares in OECD imports before the crisis, suffered the least adverse impact. These countries also reacted with strong policy responses.

- In response to the crisis and its potentially devastating consequences, policy makers used instruments that were readily available to them, which made for a large variety of policy measures used across countries. Countries like Brazil, China, India, and Vietnam used state-owned banks to channel credit to the productive sector. Others used various tax incentives to support domestic demand, and even incentives to households to buy consumer goods. This makes it difficult to undertake comparative analysis of the effectiveness of policies across countries.
- The policy responses in most countries were timely, strong, and sensitive to macroeconomic realities. Brazil, China, India, and Vietnam put in place fairly strong stimulus packages; those of Mexico and Turkey were less ambitious. Central banks fought back with aggressive monetary policy via increased liquidity and low interest rates.
- Unlike in prior crises, the exchange rate was not a major issue, as countries pursued exchange rate policies that allowed for flexibility to protect reserves. Much of the currency depreciation occurred at the onset of the crisis, which facilitated a faster adjustment.
- There is little evidence of negative impact on human capital accumulation and no information about possible positive effects of increased investments in infrastructure during the crisis on potential growth in the medium term. However, these issues require further analysis.

Medium-Term Growth Prospects

We have discussed how the immediate and (very) short-term losses in output from the financial crisis were substantial, and even severe, for many countries. In the short term and during the recovery phase, growth rates will depend on specific country dynamics, which may imply an actual output growth rate that is below or above potential output growth.

On the other hand, the impact of the current crisis on economic growth will dissipate over the long run, and the standard determinants of growth in both advanced and developing countries will again be the countries' stock of knowledge and technology, the potential for catching up, and the institutions and policies they adopt. It is also clear that future crises and other major shocks are likely to occur and affect economic conditions and outcomes.

But the issue of the impact of the global financial and economic crisis in the medium term is much less clear. Over the next five to seven years, the adverse impact of the crisis on the output gap may persist for some time or be reversed, while the impact on the growth rate is ambiguous.

For countries experiencing a financial or banking crisis, there is much evidence about the medium-term implications. The IMF's *World Economic Outlook 2009* (chapter 4) reviews this evidence. While there is substantial variation across experiences, the *World Economic Outlook* (WEO) finds that output trends remain depressed following banking crises; generally, moreover, output does not rebound over the medium term (seven years after the onset of the crisis) to precrisis levels, but rather remains lower by an average of 10 percent. In about a quarter of the cases, however, output rebounds to precrisis trend levels and even exceeds them. On the other hand, medium-term growth rates tend to return to precrisis levels for most countries. The depressed level of output results in equal parts from reductions in the employment rate, the capital-output ratio, and TFP.

The recent global crisis has been centered in the United States and Europe, and except for a few countries in Eastern Europe or for Dubai, almost no developing or emerging country has suffered a financial crisis since the recent global crisis broke out. This means that the analysis of medium-term implications of financial crises in directly affected countries, reviewed in the WEO, cannot be used to draw lessons and implications for developing countries in the current crisis. The impact of the crisis on developing countries has been mostly indirect, through changed economic and financial conditions at the global level, and the implications for the medium term are much less obvious and more difficult to determine.

The historical experience points to a variety of possible impacts. The Great Depression also originated in the West and had a dramatic and long-term impact on developing countries: output of these countries remained 21 percent lower than precrisis trend levels after seven years. In contrast, the 1990s crisis in Japan, Scandinavia, and Europe had a short-lived and limited impact on developing countries. And its impact on medium-term GDP growth rates varied considerably as well (IMF 2009, box 4.1).

Methodological Framework

Based on our review of the experience of 10 sample countries during the crisis, we concluded in the previous section that the crisis and policy responses did not generate situations of serious internal sustainability or needs for serious macroeconomic adjustment. Thus, after full recovery from the crisis, the possible persistent impact of the crisis on medium-term growth of developing countries would be due almost fully to changed global economic and financial conditions.

In the absence of a well accepted and formal methodology to assess such impacts, we use the 10 country cases to understand the range of experiences and to draw some general lessons and conclusions. We use a hypothetical scenario where the global economy is assumed to fully recover by 2011, and we consider the period 2011–15 as postcrisis. To obtain a measure of the impact of the crisis on medium-term growth, we compare a country's postcrisis (2011–15) potential GDP growth to a counterfactual—that is, the growth path that would have obtained without the crisis. The postcrisis potential GDP growth for each country is the "projected" GDP growth for the period 2011–15, discussed further below. The counterfactual for potential GDP growth, absent the crisis, is the growth rate a given country would have experienced if global economic conditions prevailing before the crisis continued. We assume that a good measure of this growth rate is the estimated potential economic growth rate during 2003–07, obtained by combining two estimates of potential growth as shown in table 2.5 later in this chapter. One estimate is based on the HP filter shown in table 2.1, adjusted to account for some countries' peculiarities. For instance, Brazil's upward continuous shift in growth potential after 2003 is not captured by the HP filter. A similar small upward adjustment was made for Mexico as well. Conversely, the estimate for the Philippines was adjusted downwards in view of the exceptional role played by remittances to stimulate domestic demand and increase capacity utilization during the precrisis period. A similar but smaller adjustment was made for Vietnam. Table 2.5 also shows an alternative estimate of potential GDP growth by the country studies' authors, which sometimes differ from the statistical estimates. We take a simple average of the two estimates as a benchmark or counterfactual of potential growth in the medium term after the crisis.

This approach compares GDP growth rates, which are obtained using two different methods. The postcrisis potential GDP growth is obtained through projections of components of GDP while the measure of potential growth absent the crisis is obtained using a HP filter, which is a statistical method. While this comparison may have some limitations, it is the best we could apply in this project.

Global Economic Conditions, Global Scenario, and Channels of Impact

While long-term forecasts—especially in the wake of a crisis such as the current one—are subject to considerable uncertainty, we use a plausible global scenario to explore and understand the possible impacts. The projections for the main global economic variables in the scenario (table 2.4) are obtained from a number of sources. This illustrative global economic scenario is for the period until 2014–16 and constitutes

Table 2.4. Global Scenario

	1997–2002	2003–07	2008	2009	2010	2011–13	2014–16
GDP growth (%)							
High-income countries	2.6	2.6	0.4	−3.3	1.8	2.3	2.1
Developing countries	3.9	7.1	5.6	1.2	5.2	6.1	5.5
Trade growth (%)							
High-income imports	6.4	6.6	0.7	−15.7	3.5	5.8	4.5
Developing imports	6.2	13.3	7.8	−11.3	6.9	8.6	7.9
High-income exports	5.7	6.6	2.1	−15.4	3.4	5.7	4.6
Developing exports	7.3	12.0	5.3	−11.7	6.4	8.2	7.6
Cost of borrowing							
US LT nominal interest rate (%)	5.5	4.4	3.7	3.3	4.0	5.5	5.0
US LT real interest (%)	3.2	1.5	−0.1	3.6	1.7	2.8	2.7
US LT real interest rate using core inflation (%)	3.1	2.4	1.4	1.6			
EM spreads (bps)	809 (2001)	202 (2007)	415	460	291	258	258
Remittances		**2005–07**					
US$ billions		241	338	317	324	357	461
Growth (%)		20.7	16.7	−6.2	2.2	6.2	8.9

Source: See text.
Note: EM = emerging market; US LT = U.S. long term; blank cells = data not available.

the basis on which our country growth projections are made. The scenario was constructed as of February 2010; it may not necessarily represent the most likely global prospects at the time of publication.

Global Financial Conditions. The most important consequence of the crisis is likely to be the continued tightening of financial market regulations in high-income countries and stricter enforcement of existing regulations. These include tax levies on the banking sector, higher capital requirements, more constraints on leverage and liquidity ratios, more requirements for off-balance-sheet transactions and nonbank subsidiaries, and more scrutiny for nonbank financial institutions that pose systemic risks. Regulation and supervision can be expected to take greater account of interdependencies among financial institutions and macroeconomic risks.[21]

The tighter financial regulations in advanced countries may have beneficial effects on developing countries such as a less volatile macroeconomic environment and more transparency, which reduces risk concerns for all asset classes. The stricter controls and tougher disclosure rules of some market segments in advanced countries may make some developing countries' debt relatively more attractive. Higher capital requirements in high-income countries may increase the relative attractiveness of establishing subsidiaries in developing countries.

Nevertheless, on balance, tighter regulations in high-income countries will likely reduce access to, and the availability and cost of, international finance for developing countries.

Impact on Equity Inflows. Tighter financial conditions are likely to reduce the supply of foreign equity finance to developing-country firms, but the actual effect will vary, depending on the type of equity. FDI flows may decline moderately from the high levels of 3.9 percent of developing-country GDP observed during the precrisis period to 2.8–3.0 percent. On the other hand, portfolio flows may be much more severely reduced.

Impact on Private-Source Debt Flows and Borrowing Costs. The tighter constraints on risk taking and the weaker appetite for risk will reduce the ability of developing-country firms and governments to borrow from banks and issue bonds. The tighter constraints will also dampen interest in project finance, increase its cost, and limit the ability of corporations to use global markets as extensively as they did before the crisis.

Some factors may mitigate these constraints. For instance, the heavy debt burdens in many high-income countries may lead to relatively better risk perceptions for some emerging markets and improve their access to debt markets. At the same time, a more stable financial environment and more transparency may favor the more creditworthy developing countries. The overall effect, however, is likely to be a reduced supply of finance and higher costs for developing countries.

Interest rates in high-income countries are likely to rise from their current low levels with monetary tightening as the recovery takes hold, and as government debt increases sharply. Based on the assumptions in our global scenario starting 2011, the 10-year government yields (United States and Europe) would increase relative to precrisis boom levels by 50–100 bps in nominal terms and by 100–120 bps in real terms.

At present, all risky assets, including emerging market assets, are benefiting from the dollar-funded carry trade, which itself is being partly facilitated by the current relaxed stance of U.S. monetary policy (Dailami 2010). Over the medium term, it seems unlikely that sovereign emerging market debt spreads will narrow again to the level of 150–200 bps seen in 2006 and early 2007. The new equilibrium in the postcrisis era will feature higher market volatility, higher liquidity premiums, and possibly more conservative investment psychology than in the precrisis period. We expect spreads to stabilize at around 250 bps. This implies a further tightening from current levels of 45–75 bps over the next year or so, and 50–100 bps higher than in the precrisis boom.

Impact on Domestic Financial Intermediation. The tighter global financial conditions in the wake of the crisis are likely to affect domestic financial intermediation. Domestic interest rates are likely to increase to reflect the higher costs of international borrowing and tighter monetary policies in developing countries themselves. But the very fast rate of deepening of financial intermediation may also slow relative to the pace of the precrisis period.

Global GDP Growth and Trade. For GDP and trade, we use the baseline forecasts from World Bank (2010a), *Global Economic Prospects 2010*

(GEP), which project that growth in high-income countries will climb to 1.8 percent and growth in developing countries to 5.2 percent in 2010 and to 2.3 percent and 5.8 percent, respectively, in 2011. This follows growth of –3.3 percent for high-income countries and 1.2 percent for developing countries in 2009. The longer-term GEP forecasts are supply side (potential output forecasts) and do not include forecasts of the expenditure-component forecasts beyond 2011. This deficiency is resolved by combining the GEP supply forecasts with the growth and expenditure forecasts of Oxford Economic Forecasts (OEF).[22] More specifically, real GDP growth forecasts beyond 2011 reflect the OEF business cycle forecast, but adjusted to oscillate around the potential GDP as calculated and used in the GEP 2010 publication. Forecasts for import and export volume growth are similarly derived from the OEF forecasts, but adjusted for differences in the overall growth profile using the implied export/GDP and import/GDP elasticities in the OEF forecast.

For the period after 2011, growth is forecast to rise temporarily above trend/potential growth for a few years, as growth recovers to fill the extraordinarily large output gaps. GDP growth in high-income coun-tries is expected to average 2.3 percent during 2011–13 and decline to 2.1 percent afterward, which is about 0.5 percentage point lower than during the precrisis boom.

Growth in imports in high-income countries is expected to slow to 5.8 percent during 2011–13 and to 4.5 percent during 2014–16, which is 0.8–2.0 percentage point lower than during the precrisis period. We should note that, in the context of this analysis, we do not take into consideration the feedback effect of changes in developing-country growth on advanced-country growth. For instance, the projections do not take into account that lower growth in China may in turn lead to lower GDP and trade growth in advanced countries.

Commodity Prices. When the global crisis struck, commodity prices declined sharply from their highs in 2008. But recovery in commodity prices began in March 2009, reflecting that of global economic activity. For the medium term, real commodity prices are expected to remain stable (see World Bank 2010a and b). Energy prices are likely to stabilize at about double the level prevailing in the early 2000s—higher than the low level reached in early 2009 but much lower than the peaks of 2008. Metal prices are expected to continue rising over the next two years, but to moderate and eventually decline afterward, to stabilize at twice the level of the early 2000s. Food prices will moderate as well and stabilize, beginning this year, at levels lower than the 2008 peak but much higher than the lows of the 1990s.

Remittances. Remittance flows are broadly affected by three factors: the total number of migrants and incomes of migrants in destination countries, and (to some extent) incomes in the source country (see Ratha and Shaw 2007). Using a bilateral remittance matrix and estimates of the income elasticity of remittances for each source country during 2001–08, the remittance outflows from each remittance-source country for 2010–18 are estimated using the GDP growth projections in this scenario. The annual growth rate of global remittance flows to developing countries is expected to recover from its very low levels during the crisis to reach an average 6–9 percent over the medium term, but this will be significantly lower than the 20 percent growth of the precrisis boom period.

Postcrisis Growth Prospects

The country studies use a common framework to generate medium-term economic growth projections. Using their intimate and specific country knowledge, data, and available research, most authors produced supply- and demand-side growth projections for 2011–15 while taking the most current projections for 2010 as given.

Using a demand-side approach, the authors projected each component of aggregate demand in order to obtain a GDP growth path. In some cases, they did this using a formal macroeconomic model but in most cases their approach was more pragmatic. At the same time, the authors developed a set of supply-side projections for capital accumulation (consistent with those of investment on the demand side), employment or labor force growth, and TFP growth. The two approaches used together provide a validity and consistency check and also allow us to understand cyclical dynamics. Typically, actual and potential GDP converge by 2011–12.

Table 2.5 presents a summary of country growth projections for the period 2011–15.[23] The postcrisis projections are to be compared to the

Table 2.5. Medium-Term GDP Growth Prospects after the Crisis
(percent)

Country	Actual average GDP growth 2003–07 (1)	Alternative estimates of potential GDP growth just prior to the crisis			Medium-term potential growth after crisis (2011–15) (5)	Output gap 2015 (6)
		HP filter adjusted (2)	Authors estimate (3)	Average col. (2) and (3) (4)		
Simple average	**6.8**	**6.1**	**6.3**	**6.1**	**5.7**	**−6.3**
Weighted average	**8.0**	**7.4**	**7.1**	**7.3**	**6.3**	**−8.2**
Brazil	3.8	3.8	4.5	4.2	4.3	0.1
China	11.0	10.4	10.0	10.2	8.0	−11.8
Ethiopia	8.9	8.2	8.5	8.4	7.8	−0.1
India	8.9	8.0	8.0	8.0	8.5	−0.6
Malaysia	6.0	5.5	5.5	5.5	5.1	−9.4
Mexico	3.3	3.0	3.0	3.0	3.0	−10.0
Philippines	5.8	4.6	4.6	4.6	4.2	−6.2
Poland	5.1	4.4	—	4.4	3.6	−7.3
Turkey	6.9	5.7	5.1	5.4	4.3	−17.7
Vietnam	8.1	7.4	7.5	7.5	8.1	0.5

Source: Column 1, World Bank DDP; column 3, country studies; columns 2 and 4–6, author's calculations.
Note: The weighted averages are computed using 2007 GDP values for all columns. Obtained figures may be somewhat different from those in table 2.1. — = not available.

counterfactual potential growth rate. The growth projections for the 10 countries show that GDP growth would be lower than precrisis potential growth by, on average, 0.4 percentage point (using a simple average) to 1.0 percentage point (using a weighted average, again reflecting the weight of China). But GDP growth after the crisis would be more than 1.1 percentage points lower than actual growth during 2003–07, and even 1.6 percentage points lower using a weighted average.

The individual country projections show a large variety of experiences.

A first group of developing countries—Brazil, India, Mexico, and Vietnam—would see no negative impact of the crisis on their potential growth. However, the reasons vary considerably among the four countries. The output gap practically disappears for Brazil, India, and Vietnam, but remains at about −10 percent for Mexico by 2015.

Brazil has a large domestic market and low dependence on external demand, as well as favorable macroeconomic conditions, which enabled the government to pursue an effective countercyclical policy. The country is expected to see a very strong recovery in 2010, with GDP growth climbing to 7.0 percent; but growth is likely to slow to 4.3 percent over the medium term, roughly approximating the precrisis potential growth rate.

Brazil's low dependence on export markets and the product and geographical diversification of its exports imply that slow global demand will have a limited impact. The investment-to-GDP ratio is expected to increase from 17 percent during the crisis to 20 percent toward the end of the period. With low (and stable) saving rates, the current account balance will likely deteriorate. Brazil is expected to finance this deficit without problem, mostly through increased FDI flows. Low indebtedness should make access to foreign capital easy, and growth should not be finance constrained. But the continuation of lax fiscal policy and tighter monetary policy would constrain investment and growth.

With TFP growth slightly below the precrisis level, and assuming no major structural policy changes, GDP growth is mainly determined by capital accumulation. This scenario does not take into account the effects of the recently discovered oil reserves, which should have major positive implications for Brazil.

India was enjoying strong growth acceleration before the crisis; its potential growth increased from 5.5–6.0 percent during 1997–2002 to 8.0 percent during 2003–07.[24] Despite the cyclical slowdown, growth momentum remained strong. India was hit hard by the crisis, mainly through the external demand channel, and reduced credit and capital flows. But growth resumed in the third quarter of 2009 as capital inflows picked up and the strong policy measures adopted began to stimulate demand. In FY2009–FY2010, the economy slowed to an average growth rate of 6.4 percent. However, in the medium term, 2011–15, growth is expected to average about 8.5 percent—above the 8 percent potential output growth estimated before the crisis.

The large size of the Indian economy and the dominance of domestic factors make it less sensitive to changes in global economic conditions. While the slowdown in global growth and tighter global financial conditions may reduce the growth of exports and the volume of capital flows to levels lower than before the crisis, they are expected to remain robust enough to be consistent with the potential growth rate. Based on a recovery of global trade of 6–7 percent a year, and with India maintaining its low-cost advantage in manufacturing and in knowledge-based manufacturing and services, it is expected to see exports rise by at least 10 percent per year in real terms. Since import growth will be similar, net exports would not change very much. Services exports will remain strong. With the high savings rate—which is likely to remain high, at about 37 percent of GDP in the coming period—investment is unlikely to be constrained by any reduced availability of external finance. Indeed, some argue that India may become a more attractive destination for foreign capital, as its relative riskiness would improve with the worsening of fiscal positions in many rich countries. Even so, the less benign financial environment may limit the gains India enjoyed from using more efficient international financial intermediaries.

India's projected high growth rate is likely to be supported by a pickup in investment to an annual growth rate of about 12 percent during 2011–14, albeit still below the peak of 17 percent in 2006–07. The strong corporate balance sheets and positive prospects for the stock market should restore investment to a robust growth. The current low interest rate scenario is helping investment. However, the monetary policy goal of keeping rates low to maintain a real deposit rate of about 2–3 percent appears uncertain with the recent pickup in inflation. Already, the issue now is whether or not to curb excessive capital inflows.

On the supply side, labor productivity and TFP growth will both continue to improve as recovery sets in and investment enables robust capital accumulation and technological advancement. While somewhat slower than during the boom period, they remain consistent with the lower (than actual) potential growth path.

Vietnam, like India, is expected to return to a robust growth path of 8.1 percent per year in the medium term—growth that is higher than the relatively high potential GDP growth experienced before the crisis. The output gap would disappear by 2015. Vietnam was able to limit the immediate negative impact of the crisis, despite some macroeconomic weaknesses precrisis. It has been experiencing a strong recovery in 2010, with an expected GDP growth of 8.2 percent. The dynamism and diversification of Vietnam's exports should continue after the crisis, underpinning a strong performance.

Mexico is likely to experience a potential growth rate of 3 percent after 2011, a performance that is similar to the one during the precrisis period. The output gap for Mexico would remain large at about −10 percent by 2015, with little recovery compared to 2009. Mexico did not benefit from the precrisis boom, as it did not experience any growth acceleration due to the favorable global environment. Its growth remained low, and the economy showed little dynamism. It was hit very hard by the crisis, mostly through the trade channel. The large output gap in the aftermath of the crisis allows scope for a higher growth rate over the medium term without the threat of capacity constraints. But a number of constraints tracing back to the precrisis period are likely to limit potential growth. Mexico will continue to be constrained by a lack of diversification of exports and dependence on the U.S. recovery. On the fiscal side, it needs to undertake a painful fiscal adjustment to fill the gap that resulted from the precrisis spending boom financed by oil revenue. The financial sector is expected to be a drag on growth in the medium term, owing to the excessive credit growth to the private sector (mainly consumption credit). The worsening of portfolio quality implies less scope for credit expansion. And the constraints of the financial sector have been worsened by the growing pressures, during the crisis, on the balance sheets of some banks, which are owned by global banks, and on some nonbank financial intermediaries (see IMF 2010b).

The countries of the second group are likely to experience significant loss in GDP growth relative to precrisis conditions: Turkey (−1.1 percentage points), Poland (−0.8 point), Ethiopia (−0.6 point), the Philippines (−0.4 point), and Malaysia (−0.4 point).

Turkey suffered a large immediate negative impact from the crisis that will continue into the medium term. Potential GDP growth is estimated to decline from the precrisis rate of more than 5.4 percent to 4.3 percent in the medium term (2011–15). The output gap is expected to reach −17.7 percent of GDP by 2015, a record compared with the other countries. The output gap is expected to reach −17.7 percent of GDP by 2015, a record compared with the other countries. Turkey's strong growth precrisis was driven largely by the improved policy environment following the country's 2001 economic crisis. Access to foreign capital improved and trade substantially increased, especially with the European Union. Turkey also adopted a strategy based on manufactured exports, which expanded rapidly over the boom years.[25] Potential output growth improved by almost 3 percentage points during the precrisis boom. In the current scenario, however, the worsening of global conditions is likely to reduce access to foreign capital and slow export growth. This will be reflected in a slowdown in both capital accumulation and TFP growth during 2011–15.

While investment weakened from 21.8 percent in 2008 to about 16.5 percent in 2009, it is expected to recover to 18.8 percent in 2012 and 22 percent in 2015. The rise in investment will be constrained by low domestic savings and harder access to foreign capital. Capital inflows are expected to grow by about 4 percent per year until 2015, lower than the 6.8 percent in 2003–07. An important cause of weakening investment has been the contraction in capacity utilization in manufacturing— from 78 percent in 2007 to 65 percent in 2009, which represents nearly 18 percent of its potential. It will therefore take some time for investment in Turkey to return to precrisis levels.

Exports will recover relatively quickly owing to a rising share of exports going to neighboring countries and favorable expectations about export orders. Nevertheless, the contribution of net exports to GDP growth is estimated to be negative—nearly 0.4 percentage point on average during 2011–15—because of the relatively faster growth of imports. The import growth, in turn, is based on the expectation that domestic demand will stay strong while terms of trade deteriorate as a result of higher commodity prices (mainly energy).

Poland, unlike the rest of Europe, and even its own neighbors, is experiencing a rapid recovery with GDP growth projected to reach 3.9 percent in 2011 before easing to 3.5 percent by 2013. The output gap will reach –7.3 percent by 2015. The average medium-term GDP growth rate of 3.6 percent is lower than the potential growth estimate of 4.4 percent before the crisis due to a variety of factors. Slower growth in the European Union (EU) and of global trade would tend to lower GDP growth in Poland, given its need to rebalance its sources of growth toward exports and the tradables sector. A declining supply of labor growth will also reduce the potential growth rate of Poland. However, the expected large increase in EU funds for investment in infrastructure and human capital will limit or reverse the possible negative impact of external financial conditions and provide a strong stimulus for economic growth. Poland will continue to be an attractive destination for FDI and other capital flows.

Ethiopia's medium-term potential growth rate is likely to be 7.8 percent, 0.55 percentage point lower than the precrisis estimate. Given that Ethiopia continued to grow in the aftermath of the crisis at higher than potential GDP growth, the output gap would practically disappear by 2015. This is mainly the result of domestic economic factors, but it also reflects expected changes in global economic conditions.

Ethiopia was experiencing a surge in economic growth from 2004, led largely by peace, political stability, and policy initiatives to invest in infrastructure and diversify exports. Its potential GDP growth rate, during the precrisis boom, is estimated to have reached 8.35 percent per year as it became an attractive destination for FDI and workers' remittances, and as exports surged. But the economy was overheating prior to the recent global crisis, with domestic absorption increasing by 15 percent or more and actual GDP growing by 11–12 percent. This situation was not sustainable, and growth was expected to slow as macroeconomic policy was adjusted. As it turns out, the crisis hit Ethiopia much harder than expected. Export growth collapsed, remittance flows and FDI slowed, and aggregate demand growth declined substantially. But thanks to Ethiopia's relatively limited integration into the world economy, sustained aid flows, and active policies—including a large currency depreciation—GDP growth declined somewhat but remained strong. The slower rates of growth of remittances and of FDI are likely to affect private consumption and investment growth and to contribute to a slowdown in potential growth.

The Philippines is expected to see GDP growth of 4.2 percent postcrisis, versus precrisis potential growth of 4.6 percent. The output gap would be −6.2 percent by 2015. On the supply side, the decline in potential growth reflects both slower capital accumulation and productivity growth. Investment demand is likely to be weaker because of the higher cost of capital and continued weak investment climate. The manufacturing export sector is expected to face weaker global demand for electronics and semiconductors, while business process outsourcing should stay strong. Overall, the contribution of net exports to growth will be near zero. In addition, fiscal space constraints imply lower public consumption growth. All of these factors are likely to translate into a weaker labor market and lower private consumption growth.

Malaysia, after suffering a large negative crisis impact in 2009, has experienced a strong rebound in 2010, owing to supportive policies and the rebound in Asia. The precarious fiscal situation precrisis (and two fiscal stimulus packages), however, will require the government to curtail its expenditures in the medium term. Private consumption is expected to grow more slowly as a result of the household sector's high leverage. While Malaysia is likely to benefit from strong growth in commodities trade, noncommodity export growth will remain weak as the country works to upgrade its manufacturing capacity and diversify away from labor-intensive industries. Potential GDP growth in the medium term would reach 5.1 percent which is lower than the precrisis potential growth rate of 5.5 percent, and the output gap will be large at −9.4 percent by 2015.

Finally, growth projections for China show the largest fall in potential growth—by a full 2 percentage points, from 10 percent during the precrisis period to 8.0–8.5 percent during 2011–15, and even to 7.7 percent by 2015.

China's composition of growth is set to change substantially, with a rebalancing in favor of domestic demand due to slower global demand and slower growth in market share. The contribution of net exports to GDP growth is expected to decline from about 2.6 percentage points to zero because of saturation effects in several sectors and limited demand growth. Consumption demand should remain strong while investment growth slows. While China faces no constraints on external finance, the tighter global financial conditions would imply a higher cost of capital and a lower capital-output ratio.

On the supply side, the growth slowdown, relative to the precrisis potential, can be expected to come from various growth sources— mainly a slower rate of capital accumulation and employment growth (−0.8 percentage point). Although China may face weaker TFP growth, the fundamental competiveness of its manufacturing is strong—even with some currency appreciation and wage increases, competitiveness should be maintained. Major investment in infrastructure during the crisis may relieve binding constraints to growth.

Although the reduction in China's potential growth seems to be significant, much of this "adjustment" is not due only to the recent financial crisis. In particular, the lower employment growth is the result of demographic changes, while part of the very high growth in the precrisis period (2006–08) was fueled by very high levels of investment, which were unsustainable.

The Chinese authorities' policy response to the crisis has created possible vulnerabilities. The massive growth in bank lending for infrastructure projects and the buildup of excess capacity in many industries may weaken the quality of bank portfolios. The credit expansion has also fueled a heated real estate market, characterized by rapid rises in property prices. These will require monetary tightening or restraint, which could affect investment demand. Overall, though, these vulnerabilities appear manageable.

Diverse Experiences and Lack of Simple Rules to Predict the Impacts of the Crisis

A key lesson emerging from the studies is that there are no simple rules, no set of variables that allow one to fully predict the severity of the crisis's impact on countries. A large component of the degree of impact seems to be quite specific and the result of a complex interaction among domestic economic conditions, the momentum of growth, and the nature and size of the channels of impact. This message is quite similar to what was observed during the precrisis boom years where the impact of more favorable global conditions on countries depended to a large extent on domestic economic conditions, and where it was difficult to disentangle the domestic and international factors.

Of course, some countries—such as Eastern European countries not covered in the project—that had large current account deficits, problems with banking system balance sheets, and inadequate regulation, did suffer greatly. The review of the country cases in this study showed also that the presence of some vulnerabilities was likely to result in a more severe impact of the crisis. These vulnerabilities included excessive concentration of exports, fast credit growth, high leverage, and large current account deficits. At the same time, countries that had buffers such as a high level of reserves, ample fiscal space, and a well-regulated banking system managed to limit the severity of the impact of the crisis. However, in a number of cases it was not easy to determine ex ante which countries would be most severely hit just by looking at their macroeconomic initial conditions or the extent of their dependence on trade. In addition, one could not predict which countries would be most affected in the medium term based on how severely they were affected right after the crisis.

The cases of China and India illustrate the point. Abstracting from the cyclical factors and short-term macroeconomic adjustments that may have been needed, these countries have strong fundamentals in terms of macroeconomic balances and structural reforms. They would have continued to experience strong economic growth in the medium run, albeit slower than during the precrisis boom period. Their potential growth was on an upward trend, and investment rates were high and booming. India and China had high saving rates and an expanding current account surplus. They were experiencing large capital inflows in the boom period. The main effect of these inflows, and the easing of global financial conditions, was reflected not in higher investment, but rather in the composition of these flows and their impact on the efficiency of investment. The lower cost of borrowing was also reflected in a deepening of domestic financial intermediation, and large portfolio flows contributed to the boom in domestic equity markets. Both countries were improving their trade market shares and were highly competitive (India mostly in the services sector). Both had a strong policy response and recovered rapidly. But China was heavily dependent on manufacturing exports; while it expanded market shares, its competitiveness was coming under pressure. The expected weaker global environment is thus likely to complicate the adjustment, and the prospects are for China to grow at a lower rate than before the crisis. In contrast, India has been less dependent on manufacturing, and its trade shares remain at the early stages of expansion. It still has scope to increase competitiveness and see strong export growth, as well as strong flows of FDI. Its attractiveness to foreign capital is expected to improve. India is expected to experience even higher growth after the crisis.

The cases of Mexico and Brazil illustrate the point in a different way. Mexico stands out among the sample countries as recording the slowest growth (3.3 percent during 2003–07) and no acceleration during the global boom. Indeed, during the boom, its investment rate declined[26] and its competitiveness weakened. As a less dynamic economy, it did not experience larger capital inflows or gains in equity markets during the boom. It suffered a serious loss during the crisis, and growth is likely to continue to be slow in the medium term. Brazil, however, was experiencing improved growth prospects attributable to structural reforms and better macroeconomic management. Its potential growth was on an upward trend, even though it remained relatively weak. It continued to have some structural problems, such as low savings, low competitiveness, and a heavy dependence on commodity exports. The large capital inflows during the precrisis period were not important as an aggregate source of finance for Brazil, but in the form of FDI were a source of dynamism for investment. Overall, both Mexico and Brazil are expected to experience the same or a slight decline in potential growth in the medium term compared with the precrisis period. In both cases, attaining higher growth rates in the coming period would require further structural reforms to boost competitiveness.

Main Findings and Messages

- The impact of the crisis on the medium-term prospects (2011–15) of developing countries is likely to be moderate, with the average GDP growth rate about 0.4–1.0 percentage points lower during than potential growth before the crisis. This impact is much lower than what would have been obtained by comparing the projected postcrisis potential GDP growth rate to the actual growth rate before the crisis. The impact is highly variable among countries. Some countries are expected to see almost no impact, while many others will experience a significant negative impact.
- By 2015, the output gap is likely to average about −6 to −8 percent of GDP for the 10 countries. It is expected to vary considerably across countries; for example, it could be −18 percent of GDP for Turkey but almost disappears for Brazil, Ethiopia, India, and Vietnam.
- In exploring the prospects for medium-term growth, the country studies have shown that it is hard to separate the effects of domestic factors from global economic conditions. For example, the strongly optimistic scenario for India and Vietnam and the moderately optimistic scenario for Brazil reflect, to a large extent, a broadly positive outlook related mainly to domestic factors and the momentum of the economy. By comparison, the strong negative impact for China reflects the adjustments that the economy would need to take in any case.

One general principle seems to be held firmly: countries that enjoy strong fundamentals—not only macroeconomic balances, but also structural—seem best able to minimize the impact of the crisis. Strong growth momentum, high savings, a healthy financial sector, more diversified exports, a good margin for fiscal space, large reserves, and an ability to take policy-appropriate action are all features associated with experiencing a less severe impact. Conversely, countries with structural problems that weaken their competitiveness are most vulnerable to external shocks. This is illustrated in the cases of Mexico, Malaysia, the Philippines, and Turkey.

Policy Issues and Implications

The 10 country case studies in this project are not sufficient to allow statistical inference and provide strong conclusions applicable more generally. Nonetheless, they are rich enough to permit a number of conclusions and to suggest some policy implications.

Learning, the Global Crisis, and Its Management

One general observation emerging from the country studies is the capacity many emerging-market countries have developed for dealing with crises. Various country studies cite the lessons that have accumulated and that have helped countries deal with highly volatile, dangerous, and unpredictable situations. Almost all countries have been proactive and flexible, taking timely policy measures that have helped minimize the immediate cost of the crisis, guided by their specific economic circumstances.

Policy Issues and Domestic Reforms

The previous discussions suggest a number of directions for policies that relate to the prevention of crises, the immediate response to crises, and the medium-term impact. The analyses and findings of this volume relate mainly to middle-income countries, and these lessons are of primary relevance to those countries. Nonetheless, the lessons largely apply to low-income countries as well.

Preventing and Mitigating the Impact of Crises. One of the major lessons of the crisis and how it impacted developing countries is that the creation of buffers before crises plays a key role in explaining the resilience of economies. Some of these buffers, such as a high level of net reserves, may be a costly self-insurance, but the benefits if a crisis materializes may be enormous. However, what may be efficient at the individual country level may be inefficient and even impossible globally. More efficient global solutions are required that provide countries with the policy buffers and insurance they need in case they are subject to such major shocks.

Other buffers may be just part of prudent policies, such as maintaining a low level of public debt and fiscal discipline, a low current account deficit, or a sound financial system. These buffers provide policy makers with enough policy space to take action when needed. They may even preclude the need for action, as the mere existence of the buffers enhances confidence and may make policy action unnecessary.

Another policy issue that requires further analysis and scrutiny is that of trade-offs between short-term benefits from policy action and potential longer-term costs. In some cases governments used the crisis as an opportunity to increase public sector salaries, which helps stimulate aggregate demand in the short run and mitigate the impact of the crisis. But when such increases in salaries, and even increases in public employment, are permanent, this makes the budget more rigid and reduces room for fiscal policy in the future. Another example is the use of public sector banks to channel credit to state-owned enterprises or the private sector in order to compensate for the retrenchment of private credit institutions during a crisis. This can be effective in the short run and stimulate investment, but it may run counter to the requirements in the longer run of the more efficient market-based allocation of credit. In addition, the credit allocations may turn out to be inefficient and end up as contingent liabilities of the government budget.

Governments had to face such trade-offs because they had to use the policy instruments that were most readily available and that could be implemented without much delay. It is preferable if policy makers could build ex ante a set of policy instruments that could be deployed almost automatically in case of crisis. These "automatic adjusters" would work like automatic stabilizers but would be triggered by policy makers.

Uncertainties about the Recovery and Policy. The global recession is not over. The recovery is uncertain and scenarios of a protracted recovery or even a double-dip recession are still possible. The country case studies in this volume did not explore such scenarios and the implications of such uncertainties. A related issue is the possible increase in volatility in the aftermath of the crisis as evidenced by the recent financial turmoil in Europe. The course of fiscal policy in high-income countries and the implications for trade and capital flows to developing countries will be sources of volatility, as well as the effects of the recent surges in capital flows to emerging markets and the risks they create of pressures in asset markets.

While they may have to deal with such increased uncertainties and volatility, developing countries will have more limited scope for policy action compared with the situation that prevailed in 2008–09. For instance, in the area of fiscal policy, many countries will have a weaker "buffer" to deal with another global demand shock. The country studies show that while there were no cases of serious fiscal sustainability issues resulting from the immediate impact of the crisis or the policy responses, most countries will need to undertake some type of fiscal consolidation and address varying degrees of fiscal sustainability issues in the coming years. The ability of these countries to use countercyclical fiscal policy is limited. Similarly, for many countries, such as China or Brazil, that used policy-induced increases in lending by public sector banks, the use of this instrument will be more limited given the level of exposure and risks.

Policy Issues for the Medium Term. Country studies provide many examples of domestic reforms that could be undertaken by governments and that would easily compensate for any negative impact of the global crisis in the medium term.

For a few countries, authors present alternative scenarios to the base case to illustrate the potential gains from reforms. In *Brazil*, an alternative scenario based on a strong domestic reform agenda—including tax and labor reform, social security reform, and tighter monetary policy—would generate growth of 6 percent, or a gain of 1.5 percentage points relative to the base case. With higher savings, lower government consumption, and looser monetary policy, investment would grow much faster, reaching 24 percent of GDP. Under a reform scenario, GDP growth in *the Philippines* could reach 6 percent. Reforms would include fiscal consolidation and tax reform, which would support increased investment in infrastructure and social spending. Exports of commodities, which are constrained by infrastructure, would expand considerably. Together with reforms in the investment climate, this would spur investment and attract more FDI. In *Malaysia*, a reform scenario would boost growth during the postcrisis period from 5.1 percent to 5.8 percent or even 6 percent under implementation of a New Economic Model that emphasizes a reorientation of public expenditures toward public investment, reduction in subsidies, an improved business environment, and a stronger private sector. In the case of India, the authors do not produce a full scenario but mention the potential for an accelerated growth path of 9–10 percent compared with the base case of 8.5 percent.

For the other countries, the authors of the country papers did not prepare alternative scenarios but argued for policy reforms that improve performance. These typically involve structural reforms to boost competitiveness, domestic resource mobilization for investment, and—in the case of larger countries such as China and India—a rebalancing of growth toward domestic markets.

In addition, for most countries, there is a need for fiscal consolidation. As we pointed out above, authors of country studies, with the exception of China and Vietnam, argued that governments need to take action through higher taxes or tighter spending to maintain or achieve fiscal sustainability.

The second major area of domestic reforms concerns education, labor markets, and skills, which are high on the agenda for Brazil, India, Mexico, Poland, Turkey, and Vietnam. In China's case, labor market issues are viewed from the perspective of an improved framework for domestic migration to facilitate the growth of the services sector and urbanization. The third area of reform relates to improved infrastructure services through larger investment or more efficient public services. This is highlighted as important or at least mentioned in the cases of Brazil, India, Mexico, Ethiopia, the Philippines, and Vietnam. In the case of Poland, the large EU funds would be used to overcome infrastructure bottlenecks. The fourth area of reforms is that of the business environment, which is high on the agenda for the Philippines and Malaysia, and reform of the state-owned-enterprise sector in Vietnam.

Two additional policy concerns are not widely recognized or mentioned but appear as important ones for some countries. The first one is about innovation, industrial upgrading, technological catch-up, and structural transformation. The issues of innovation and technological catch-up are high on the agenda for China, Malaysia, and Poland. Issues of structural transformation are raised in the case of China in the context of rebalancing toward services, and in the case of India in the context of the need for an agricultural sector revolution. In Ethiopia, the related issue of the reform of industrial policy is a major policy concern. The second concern is about the financial sector. In the case of China, reform of the financial sector is high on the agenda in order to improve the allocation of credit toward services and smaller, privately owned firms. These reforms are all the more important in view of recent massive growth in bank lending, especially lending for infrastructure projects and to the regional governments. The risks of overinvestment and misallocation of investment, and of asset prices bubbles from rapid credit growth, require careful management and supervision of the banking sector. Similar issues exist in Brazil, with required further credit market liberalization, reduction of public banks' subsidized credit, and increased private sector participation. During the crisis, the government used public sector banks to rapidly expand domestic credit in response to the crisis. The resulting risks, as well as the additional fiscal costs due to large volumes of subsidized credit, need to be addressed and the soundness of the banking system preserved. Large subsidies to bank lending are also a major issue in Vietnam.

South-South Trade

During the precrisis boom, South-South trade played an important role in boosting performance in many developing countries. While trade volume growth of the OECD countries was steady, South-South trade increased strongly, mirroring the surging economic growth in developing countries.

This trend is set to continue and become even stronger after the crisis. Economic growth in the advanced countries is likely to remain muted, and trade growth with OECD countries will be slower. As discussed above, China's trade with the OECD and its gains in trade shares can be expected to grow much less than before the crisis. Some of the South-South trade that is linked to Chinese exports to the OECD countries will be affected. But as the developing countries experience a powerful recovery and strong growth in the medium term, South-South trade will become the most dynamic component of global trade. As developing countries see their growth dampened by the slower growth in, and trade with, advanced countries, they can be expected to seek out markets in Southern partners, for both trade and investment.

South-South FDI should also thrive with trade. This should help countries continue increasing their integration with, and benefits from, the global trade system. This includes commodity-exporting countries, which can be expected to deepen their ties with emerging economies and become major trading partners.

Helping External Finance Constrained Countries
Invest in Infrastructure

Many developing countries did not appear to be constrained by a lack of external finance as they increased their investment during the precrisis "boom." Their situation seems unlikely to change after the crisis. These countries' high saving rates are greater or increasing faster, than their investment rates. But even in such countries, access to international financial markets with better financial products and engineering can support higher (or higher-quality) investment, as in infrastructure. The tighter global financial conditions expected after the crisis may limit the development prospects of these countries.

Some countries were constrained by a lack of external finance during the boom period, and they are likely to remain so in the future. Other countries were not so constrained during the precrisis boom period, but could become so in the future if they experience significant negative terms-of-trade shocks. For these countries, access to external finance could be important for their growth prospects.

Global policy makers should focus their attention on how to improve the access of developing countries to external finance if market conditions tighten. In this context, international financial institutions can play a role. The returns to such improved access could also be important for the global economy, if it helps stimulate global demand and increase growth in the advanced countries with high excess production capacity.

Annex: Explaining the Output Gap

A number of recent studies have attempted to explain the severity of the impact of the crisis on GDP growth. Blanchard, Faruqee, and Das (2010) explain the difference between actual growth from the fourth quarter of 2008 to the first quarter of 2009 and average growth during 1995–2007 for 33 emerging-market countries. They find that countries with higher debt-to-GDP ratios performed worse than the rest, controlling for other factors. The study also finds evidence for the negative impact of trade exposure (exports as a share of GDP weighted with partner growth); however, the effect is not always significant.

A similar study by the World Bank (2010c) focuses on the decline in actual growth rates between 2007 and 2009 for 103 countries. The study finds that the countries with high trade openness were more vulnerable to crisis. In terms of the financial vulnerabilities, the evidence suggests that countries with high precrisis credit growth and highly leveraged economies faced sharper declines in growth. Finally, the study also finds that countries with higher precrisis inflation and lower fiscal space for countercyclical policies suffered greater collapses in growth. However, given that many countries were already experiencing slower growth before the crisis, the degree to which this collapse is attributable to the aforementioned macroeconomic variables in these studies is questionable. To overcome this problem, Berkmen and others (2009) focus on revisions of projections for GDP growth in 2009 instead of actual growth rates for two sets of countries (40 emerging countries and 126 developing countries, using two different sources of growth forecast revisions), comparing forecasts before and after the intensification of the crisis in September 2008. For the emerging countries, they find that growth revisions were most sensitive to financial vulnerabilities measured by credit growth and leverage. For the broader set of developing countries, the trade channel and monetary policy (exchange rate flexibility) played a significant role as well. Countries that rely heavily on advanced manufacturing exports and that have fixed-exchange-rate regimes were more severely affected by the global crisis. They find little or no evidence for the impact of the fiscal position and other policy/institutional variables on growth revisions.

For this project, we undertake a study similar to that of Berkmen and others (2009). Our set of countries includes 54 developing (low- and middle-income) countries, none of which rely heavily on commodity exports. Our analysis overcomes the problem of measurement of the severity of impact by using the output gap, measured as the difference between actual and potential GDP growth in 2009, which ranges from −14 percent to 9 percent. We include the typical variables used in this type of analysis—trade variables, financial variables, and different combinations of fiscal/monetary variables—in our regressions. The results from a few selected regressions are included in table 2A.1.

The most statistically significant variables, on a consistent basis, are manufactures exports (as a percent of GDP), leverage, and the short-term debt-to-GDP ratio. Although overall trade exposure appears to matter for postcrisis economic growth, its effect is insignificant. On the other hand, heavy reliance on manufactures exports seems to have undermined the growth prospects of the developing countries in our sample. Similarly, those countries that had financial vulnerabilities before the crisis—such as higher leverage ratios and faster domestic credit growth—have performed worse. The current account balance (as a percent of GDP) is also significant in several regressions; however, the explanatory power is not strong in some cases. We find that international

Table 2A.1. Regression Results: The Impact of the Global Financial Crisis
(dependent variable: actual output gap, 2009)

	1	2	3
Trade channel			
Manufacturing Exports (% GDP)	−0.092** (0.039)	−0.137*** (0.040)	−0.141*** (0.051)
Financial channel			
Leverage	−0.038** (0.014)	−0.040*** (0.014)	
Cumulative credit growth	−0.013 (0.007)		
Short-term debt-to-GDP ratio			−0.291*** (0.094)
Total reserves-to-GDP ratio			0.122** (0.061)
Foreign assets and liabilities (% GDP)		0.011 (0.007)	
Current account surplus (% GDP)		0.200*** (0.071)	
Observations	49	40	51
R-squared	0.32	0.45	0.33

Source: Author's calculations.
Note: Standard errors are reported in parentheses.
*** $p < 0.01$, ** $p < 0.05$, * $p < 0.1$

reserves have a significant effect on the output gap at the 5 percent confidence level, with larger resources mitigating the negative impact of the crisis. Short-term debt is significant at the 1 percent confidence level and affects growth negatively. A 1-percentage-point increase in short-term debt (as a percent of GDP) leads to a reduction in the output gap of 0.29 percentage point. We do not find strong evidence for the role of fiscal and monetary policies for growth. Countries that were targeting inflation seem to have performed better than those that were not; however, this result does not seem strong or robust.

Notes

1. The figures in the tables may sometimes differ from those in the individual country studies because of the use of different time periods.
2. The Hodrick-Prescott (HP) filter is a statistical method that produces a smoothed series of data points based on an original series that is much more volatile. The method minimizes the sum of the (squared) distance between the smoothed (HP-filtered) and the original series and of the (squared) difference in the changes in the values of the smoothed series. In this case, the HP filter was applied to the log of GDP per laborer for the period 1990–2007.
3. Actual growth was typically lower during the previous period than potential by a similar amount.
4. Mean reversion suggests that when one considers a time series of GDP growth rates, annual observations tend, on average, to revert to the mean of the series. The mean reversion of growth rates was pointed out by Easterly and others (1993).
5. That cyclical factors play an important role is evidenced by the fact that the negative relationship between the change in average growth rate and the level of the growth rate during the previous period is much stronger when actual GDP growth is used rather than potential GDP growth. The coefficient of a simple regression is -0.72 in the case of actual GDP growth and only -0.32 for potential GDP growth, and the statistical significance is much stronger as well.
6. This applies for both the average for the large sample of 54 countries and the limited sample of 10 countries studied.
7. The information cited in this section relies heavily on World Bank (2010a).
8. The current account balance is a good measure of total net capital inflows (i.e., net capital inflows plus net capital outflows), subject to changes in international reserves.
9. The data relating to the precrisis period for our sample of 54 countries are consistent with this view. The change in current account balances (the balance between domestic saving and investment) is either uncorrelated or even

positively correlated with changes in GDP growth between the periods 1997–2002 and 2003–07.

10. Weighted averages are used for the sample of 54 countries.

11. The sample includes 36 countries for which data are available.

12. Tobin's q is usually measured as the ratio of the value of a corporation's current stock market capitalization to its book value.

13. Investment rates are calculated based on gross fixed capital formation and GDP measured in current prices. The picture is broadly similar using constant price data.

14. The same picture emerges if one looks at data on exports from developing countries. For instance, the growth rate of exports of manufactured goods in real terms to OECD countries changed little between 1997–2002 and 2003–07. It even declined for a large number of countries. However, the growth rate of exports to non-OECD countries almost doubled between the two periods.

15. In a gravity type model, bilateral trade flows are explained by the characteristics of the bilateral relationship such as distance between trading partners, the weight of each one of the economies, the prevailing trade restrictions, and so on.

16. Countries except China managed the peg quite flexibly.

17. We use regression 1 from the annex table to obtain this figure.

18. See IMF (2010a) for a recent analysis of the determinants of policy response.

19. Of course, the exception was the effect in a number of Central and Eastern European countries, but not in Poland, which is one of our country studies.

20. Using the term suggested by Luis Servén in his comments on this chapter (which are included in this volume).

21. A more detailed analysis of financial conditions after the crisis is developed in World Bank (2010a), chapter 3.

22. Please refer to http://www.oef.com for more detail regarding their forecasts, methodology, and models.

23. When authors present demand- and supply side projections that are different, we have used in these calculations those which correspond to the supply-side projections, which better reflect the potential GDP growth.

24. For India, we are using data for GDP at market prices, which can be quite different for some years from GDP at factor cost.

25. The share of mid- and high-technology products increased from 5 percent in 1980 to 14 percent in 1990 and 43 percent in 2005. Turkey is now the sixth largest producer of automobiles in Europe.

26. Based on the gross fixed capital formation measure. In contrast, gross capital formation increased significantly during the period 2001–08.

References

Berkmen, P., G. Gelos, R. Rennhack, and J. P. Walsh. 2009. "The Global Financial Crisis: Explaining Cross-Country Differences in the Output Impact." Working Paper WP/09/280, International Monetary Fund, Washington, DC.

Blanchard, O. J., H. Faruqee, and M. Das. 2010. "The Initial Impact of the Crisis on Emerging Market Countries." Manuscript, International Monetary Fund, Washington, DC.

Canuto, O., Mona Haddad, and Gordon Hanson. 2010. "Export-Led Growth v2.0." Economic Premise Note 3, World Bank, Washington, DC.

Dailami, M. 2010. "Finding a Route to New Funding." *Credit* (January).

Easterly, W., M. Kremer, L. Pritchett, and L. H. Summers. 1993. "Good Policy or Good Luck? Country Growth Performance and Temporary Shocks." *Journal of Monetary Economics* 32: 459–483.

Harrison, A., and A. Rodríguez-Clare. 2010. "Trade, Foreign Investment and Industrial Policy," in Dani Rodrik and Mark Rosensweig (eds), *Handbook of Development Economics*. New York: North-Holland.

International Monetary Fund. 2009. *World Economic Outlook.* Washington, DC: IMF.

IMF (International Monetary Fund). 2010a. "How Did Emerging Markets Cope in the Crisis." Strategy, Policy and Review Department, Washington DC.

International Monetary Fund. 2010b. "Mexico: 2010 Article IV Consultation." IMF staff report, Washington DC.

Lewis, M., and M. Verhoeven. 2010. "Financial Crises and Social Spending: The Impact of the 2008–2009 Crisis." World Bank, Washington, DC.

Ostry, J., A. R. Ghosh, K. Habermeier, M. Chamon, M. S. Qureshi, and D. B. S. Reinhardt. 2010. "Capital Inflows: The Role of Controls." Position Note, SPN/10/04, International Monetary Fund, Washington, DC.

Prasad, E. S., R. Rajan, and A. Subramanian. 2007. "Foreign Capital and Economic Growth." *Brookings Papers on Economic Activity* 38(2007-1):153–230.

Ratha, D., and W. Shaw. 2007. "South-South Migration and Remittances." Working Paper 102, World Bank, Washington, DC.

Rodrik, D. 2009. "Growth after the Crisis." Harvard Kennedy School, Cambridge, MA, May 1.

World Bank. 2009. *Global Economic Prospects 2009: Commodities at the Crossroads.* Washington DC: World Bank.

———. 2010a. *Global Economic Prospects 2010: Crisis, Finance, and Growth.* Washington, DC: World Bank.

———. 2010b. "Global Commodity Markets: Review and Price Forecast: A Companion to Global Economic Prospects 2010." World Bank, Washington, DC.

———. 2010c. "From Global Collapse to Recovery: Economic Adjustments and Growth Prospects in LAC." Office of the LAC Regional Chief Economist, World Bank, Washington, DC.

Discussant Paper

Comment on "Synthesis: Growth after the Global Recession in Developing Countries"

Luis Servén

This crisis is very different from the recurrent emerging-market crashes of the 1990s. Those crises were almost invariably self-inflicted by policy mistakes. In this episode, however, developing countries have been "innocent bystanders," hit by a tidal wave from the North. In this sense, the crisis is a stark reminder of the dual effects of international integration: it opens new growth opportunities for developing countries but also makes them vulnerable to new risks stemming from global shocks. Moreover, the crisis has underscored that such shocks can arise not only from world financial markets, but also from goods markets, as shown by the collapse of global trade. In other words, "sudden stops" can affect international goods flows just as they affect international financial flows.

In the aftermath of the crisis, the academic and policy communities have embarked on a number of stock-taking exercises to derive relevant policy lessons—which, given the nature of the crisis, are likely to have

Luis Servén is Senior Adviser, Development Economics Research Group, World Bank.

important consequences for countries' future aggregate risk management strategies. Against this background, the current study has two distinguishing features. First, it takes a medium- to long-term perspective, in contrast with most other assessments, which focus on the short-run impact of the turmoil. The underlying presumption is that the crisis may have brought about some lasting changes in the environment that developing countries will face for years to come. Second, it is based on case studies of selected developing countries. Methodologically, this allows a much richer analysis than do the routine cross-country empirics, but it also poses a well-known trade-off in terms of the comparability of the country analyses and the generality of their findings.

Before the Crisis

The paper stresses that developing-country growth had exceeded its trend ("potential growth" in the text) in the years immediately preceding the crisis. Closer inspection reveals that this phenomenon was much more marked for middle-income countries than for low-income ones.[1] Nevertheless, the paper is right that precrisis growth performance cannot be taken as a guide to medium- and long-term prospects postcrisis.

In addition to rapid growth, the paper documents how the run-up to the crisis was preceded by escalating commodity prices, surging capital flows, compressed sovereign spreads, and other classic features of booms. However, as the paper also hints, there was considerable diversity across developing countries along important dimensions, such as their current account performance or the composition of capital inflows. This diversity was certainly reflected in countries' diverse fortunes after the crisis. Perhaps a more systematic documentation of precrisis similarities and differences across the sample countries along key dimensions of performance would help drive home the point.

One critical dimension of cross-country heterogeneity was the buildup of what I will term "buffers" (or cushions) in the upswing.[2] Following the turmoil of the Asia and Russian Federation crises, many (but certainly not all) developing countries undertook efforts to fortify their fiscal positions, by reducing deficits and containing public indebtedness, and to strengthen their monetary policy institutions and lower inflation—for a number of emerging markets, through the adoption of inflation targets by newly independent central banks. Most emerging markets, particularly in East Asia, embarked on a policy of large-scale foreign exchange reserve accumulation to guard against the possibility of "sudden stops" (Jeanne and Ranciere 2009) and, in many cases, also in pursuit of a neo-mercantilist policy of exchange rate undervaluation in support of export-oriented growth (Korinek and Servén 2010). Indeed, by the end of 2008, the combined reserve holdings of emerging markets were three times those of industrial countries (Servén and Nguyen 2010).

In addition, many developing countries took steps to limit their vulnerability to shocks by containing currency and maturity mismatches. Emerging markets made efforts to substitute domestic for foreign currency borrowing. There was also a generalized shift in the composition of their net external liabilities away from debt instruments and toward equity-related liabilities. This resulted in a form of international financial integration that was less vulnerable to liquidity crunches and rollover risk. Lastly, enhanced regulation and supervision of banking systems raised deposit-to-loan ratios in many countries, thereby helping shelter banking systems from disturbances in wholesale financial markets. However, these macroprudential trends were considerably weaker in much of emerging Europe and Central Asia; and on the eve of the crisis in 2007, several countries in the region displayed a high proportion of foreign currency liabilities, negative net debt positions vis-à-vis the rest of the world, and low deposit-to-loan ratios in their banking systems.

The Impact of the Crisis

The global crisis had heterogeneous short-run effects across developing countries. Indeed, as the paper stresses, its country-specific impact was not governed by exact rules. But this, of course, does not mean that the impact was random. On the contrary, some general principles help predict the different country impacts with reasonable accuracy; they are closely related to the diversity in the creation of buffers just described, and this relationship offers valuable policy insights regarding the management of macroeconomic risks.

The crisis has entailed a global liquidity crunch and a world trade collapse. Simplifying to the extreme, the effects of these two shocks on different countries can be seen as the result of two main factors: country exposures and policy responses. We address them in turn.

Exposure to the real shock—the trade collapse—was primarily a matter of a country's degree of trade openness. Other things being equal, more open countries were hit harder. It is important to keep in mind, however, that this factor works in reverse in the recovery; that is, countries more open to trade also benefit more quickly from the postcrisis rebound in world trade. Indeed, this was the case in a number of East Asian countries. The paper highlights one important dimension of trade exposure, namely, the role of trade in manufactures, over and above trade openness more broadly: for a given degree of trade openness, countries whose export baskets were more heavily tilted toward manufactures were hit harder by the trade collapse. This finding should be taken with caution because the case studies purposely exclude commodity-exporting countries. Nevertheless, it seems consistent with the view that demand for manufactures, particularly consumer durables, is likely more sensitive to the cycle (and to liquidity conditions) than demand for other types of goods.

The paper also argues that undiversified export baskets tend to make countries more vulnerable to the trade shock. It is not clear, however, how diversification across export goods would have played out in the face of a common shock affecting, to a first approximation, the demand for all goods. Nor is it obvious whether the relevant dimension of diversification is across export goods, as claimed in the paper, or across customers. The latter could explain, for example, the strong negative effect of the crisis on Mexico's exports, which would have been driven by the above-average short-run contraction of aggregate demand in the United States—by far Mexico's biggest trading partner.

In turn, exposure to the liquidity shock is determined by countries' financing needs. These reflect, on the one hand, their current account gaps, which require new financing, and on the other hand their (net) short-term debt plus the rollover needs of debt of longer maturities. Short-term financing of banks from wholesale markets was an important element here, as shown by Raddatz (2010)—banking systems more exposed to such markets suffered comparatively more when wholesale financing dried up across the world. In several of these dimensions, emerging Europe and Central Asia lagged behind, as already noted, which helps in understanding why the crisis had a bigger short-term impact there than in other developing regions.

What about policy responses? There has already been considerable discussion in the policy community about the large role that countercyclical fiscal and monetary policies have played across the world, and specifically in emerging markets, in mitigating the impact of the crisis. Many observers have likewise underscored the valuable contribution of flexible exchange rate regimes in easing the adjustment of relative prices and thus containing the contractionary adjustment of output and employment. The paper offers some additional detail on these policy responses in the sample countries.

From a cross-country perspective, a rapidly growing number of empirical studies[3] confirm that the heterogeneity in the impact of the crisis can be traced to suitable measures of these exposures and policy responses—such as trade openness, current account deficits, debt-related financial openness, fiscal procyclicality, initial inflation, and measures of banking system fragility (such as the loan-to-deposit ratio and the [over-]expansion of credit prior to the crisis). Of course, these studies leave unexplained much of the cross-country variation in outcomes, a gap that case studies such as those summarized in this paper can help bridge.

The key issue, however, is that the room for policy responses arises from the creation of buffers in the upswing. Building a stronger fiscal position in good times allows an expansion of the deficit in bad times. Containing inflation in the upswing helps establish the credibility that permits a monetary easing in the downswing. Financial de-dollarization provides room for real depreciation without wreaking havoc on firms' and banks' balance sheets. This central role of buffers may not be fully apparent in regressions that combine measures of buffers with policy responses because such exercises fail to stress how the latter critically depend on the former.

In this regard, recent analyses suggest that precrisis international reserve holdings (preferably measured net of short-term foreign liabilities) are the best predictor of the incidence of the crisis in a variety of dimensions (Frankel and Saravelos 2010). In light of the logic above, this is hardly surprising. A bigger stock of international reserves helps by both reducing exposure to external liquidity shocks and creating scope for the deployment of expansionary macroeconomic policies. Curiously, however, the case studies fail to highlight the role of reserves, perhaps again because they do not trace the deployment of countercyclical policies to the maneuverability afforded by external liquid assets. Indeed, at the height of the crisis, some emerging markets appeared to take the key role of reserves to the extreme, as shown by their seeming reluctance to use their external liquid assets for fear of upsetting market confidence. This hints at a "fear of losing reserves," which represents a 180-degree turn from the "fear of floating" of the 1990s (Aizenmann and Sun 2009).

And after the Crisis?

Assessing the effects of the crisis on the medium- and long-term growth prospects of developing countries is a task fraught with uncertainty. Any such assessments should be taken with a grain of salt, but extra caution is advisable in this case, as world markets—especially financial markets—have yet to settle in the wake of the turmoil.

The paper sets out to accomplish this task by ostensibly comparing "potential" growth in the sample countries before and after the crash. In reality, what it does is somewhat different. It compares trend growth prior to the crisis (constructed using a Hodrick-Prescott filter) with a sort of model-based forecast of growth after the crisis, built from assumptions about the global real and financial environment.

This exercise yields "before versus after" changes in growth rates that appear relatively modest on average but exhibit considerable variation across the sample countries. Still, it is not entirely clear how these figures should be interpreted. They do not capture, strictly speaking, the "impact of the crisis," in the sense of holding all other factors constant. Indeed, as the paper recognizes, some of the changes in growth performance would have happened even in the absence of the global shock (this is explicitly noted, for example, in connection with the projected slowdown of China's growth). Moreover, the projected changes are positive in some cases and therefore ill suited for attribution to the global crash.

Conceptually, one can take a step back and ask what has changed after the crisis to alter the growth prospects of developing countries. Many possible elements come to mind, but two stand out: the growth prospects of rich countries and the trends in global financial markets.

Despite the seeming appeal of the "multipolarity" view of the postcrisis world, the fact is that industrial countries still dominate global demand trends. As recently as 2005, they accounted for 75 percent of world GDP (in dollar terms). Hence, their postcrisis growth performance is one of the crucial unknowns. And much of the uncertainty surrounding rich-country growth prospects reflects the uncertain timing of the withdrawal of the big fiscal stimulus that they deployed in response to the crisis. The pace of the withdrawal seems to be speeding up, particularly in Western Europe. Absent a vigorous private sector reaction, the result could be a longer-lasting global demand slump—perhaps more so than envisaged in the paper.

In turn, world financial markets will have to adjust to changed conditions after the crisis, at least in two major dimensions. The first one is the ongoing tightening of financial regulation across the world, which is widely expected to involve tougher capital and liquidity restrictions for financial intermediaries. In principle, this should result in an increase in the cost and/or scarcity of financing, which could be particularly harmful to developing countries with large external financing needs. It is true that it might also help achieve a more stable international financial environment with less volatile flows, which in turn might improve long-term growth. But this beneficial effect is unlikely to materialize in the near term.

The other dimension concerns the greatly increased debt burden of rich countries in the aftermath of the crisis, which is likely to put heavy pressure on global financial markets for years to come, potentially crowding out borrowers from developing countries. Again, there may be a silver lining in the form of improved risk ratings of emerging markets relative to those of rich countries, owing to the much more favorable debt prospects of the former. But on the whole, the most likely scenario is one of tighter financial conditions worldwide.

Obviously, these are highly tentative forecasts, and there is much uncertainty about how the postcrisis global scenario will really shape the affairs of developing countries. One way to highlight this uncertainty, and to assess the magnitude of its growth implications, would be to compare the likely performance of developing countries under alternative global scenarios. This approach is similar to the one taken in some of the country studies to illustrate the impact of domestic reform scenarios.

Indeed, what can developing countries do in the new global environment? Other things being equal, limited growth by rich countries and tight financing across the world should imply diminished growth for developing economies. But other things need not remain equal, and there is scope for developing countries to take actions that improve their medium- and long-term growth prospects under these changed world conditions.

The biggest payoff is likely to result from domestic reforms to enhance productivity growth. In most developing countries there is still a lot to gain from unleashing the forces of competition and innovation and by streamlining burdensome regulations that constrain the efficient allocation of resources. Human capital and infrastructure shortages remain severe constraints to growth in many countries as well, and public policies to address them could yield big growth dividends. The need for these types of reforms has long been acknowledged, but they become all the more pressing under less favorable global conditions.

A rebalancing of growth in surplus emerging markets—reducing their dependence on rich-country aggregate demand in favor of domestic absorption—could also help speed their growth. However, as already explained, the crisis has, if anything, increased countries' incentives to hoard large volumes of foreign reserves, and the easiest way to achieve this is by restraining domestic demand—exactly the opposite of the rebalancing strategy. Hence the prospects for a significant rebalancing in emerging markets are far from clear.

Lastly, numerous observers have expressed hope that expanding South-South trade could counteract weakening import demand from the North and thereby sustain global demand. But it is not obvious that South-South trade can continue to flourish without vigorous growth in the North. The reason is that much of that trade likely reflects the increasing fragmentation of the global production chain—purchases and sales between developing countries of components and intermediates that are ultimately linked to exports of final goods to rich countries. Hence, the suspicion is that a large share of South–South trade is indirectly driven by demand from the North. The magnitude of that share is a topic that deserves deeper analysis.

Notes

1. According to the Penn World Tables, the median growth rate of middle-income countries exceeded 5 percent every year during 2004–07, after hovering between 3 percent and 4 percent during 1998–2003. In contrast, median growth in low-income countries during 2004–07 was only slightly higher than in the preceding decade.
2. In the case of Latin America, this is documented by World Bank (2010).
3. See, for example, Blanchard, Faruqee, and Das (2010), Calderón and Didier (2010), Corbo and Schmidt-Hebbel (2010), or Frankel and Saravelos (2010).

References

Aizenmann, J., and Y. Sun. 2009. "The Financial Crisis and Sizable International Reserves Depletion: From 'Fear of Floating' to the 'Fear of Losing International Reserves'?" Working Paper 15308, National Bureau of Economic Research, Cambridge, MA.

Blanchard, O., H. Faruqee, and M. Das. 2010. "The Initial Impact of the Crisis on Emerging Market Countries." Unpublished, International Monetary Fund, Washington, DC.

Calderón, C., and T. Didier. 2010. "The Great Collapse of 2009." Unpublished, World Bank, Washington, DC.

Corbo, V., and K. Schmidt-Hebbel. 2010. "The International Crisis and Latin America: Growth Effects and Development Strategies." Unpublished, World Bank, Washington, DC.

Frankel, J., and G. Saravelos. 2010. "Are Leading Indicators of Financial Crises Useful for Assessing Country Vulnerability? Evidence from the 2008–09 Global Crisis." Working Paper 16047, National Bureau of Economic Research, Cambridge, MA.

Jeanne, O., and R. Ranciere. 2009. "The Optimal Level of Reserves for Emerging Market Countries: Formulas and Applications." Unpublished, revised version of IMF Working Paper 06/98, International Monetary Fund, Washington, DC.

Korinek, A., and L. Servén. 2010. "Undervaluation through Foreign Reserve Accumulation: Static Losses, Dynamic Gains." Policy Research Working Paper 5250, World Bank, Washington, DC.

Raddatz, C. 2010. "When the Rivers Run Dry: Liquidity and the Use of Wholesale Funds in the Transmission of the U.S. Subprime Crisis." Policy Research Working Paper 5203, World Bank, Washington, DC.

Servén, L., and H. Nguyen. 2010. "Global Imbalances before and after the Global Crisis." Policy Research Working Paper 5354, World Bank, Washington, DC.

World Bank. 2010. "From Global Collapse to Recovery: Economic Adjustment and Growth Prospects in Latin America and the Caribbean." Paper presented at the 2010 IMF–World Bank Spring Meetings, Washington, DC.

Resilience in the Face of the Global Crisis

Fernando Blanco, Fernando de Holanda
Barbosa Filho, and Samuel Pessôa

Brazil is emerging from the global financial crisis in a strong position. The country's resilience during the recent financial turmoil and its strong, rapid recovery have generated renewed optimism about Brazil's ability to weather adverse shocks and bolstered confidence in its overall economic growth potential.

Brazil's adoption of far-reaching structural reforms and price stabilization initiatives in the 1990s, followed by the consistent pursuit of sound macroeconomic policies in the 2000s, have strengthened the country's resistance to external shocks and improved its medium-term growth prospects.

A favorable external environment has contributed to these achievements, but sound policy decisions have been central. Brazil took advantage of the pre–global crisis boom period (2002–08) to sharply reduce its fiscal and external vulnerabilities. This consolidation ultimately served as a kind of insurance, safeguarding the economy against the negative fiscal and external shocks triggered by the crisis. Furthermore, the Brazilian

Fernando Blanco is Senior Economist, Africa Poverty Reduction and Economic Management Department, World Bank; Fernando de Holanda Barbosa Filho is Professor, and Samuel Pessôa is Professor, Fundação Getulio Vargas, Brazil.

government's successful promotion of macroeconomic stability and structural reforms have enhanced its growth potential, as evidenced by the strong productivity gains in the precrisis period.

Nevertheless, despite its considerable advances in structural stability and macroeconomic management, the global crisis has hit Brazil hard. The immediate and most important impact was on financial markets, reflected in both external and domestic credit curtailment and a sharp depreciation of the Brazilian currency, the real. On the real side, the drop in exports linked to falling commodity prices, the contraction of global demand for manufactures, and the sharp decline in investment led to a GDP contraction of 3.6 percent in the fourth quarter of 2008, and 1 percent in the first quarter of 2009.

Yet the solid macroeconomic fundamentals established in the precrisis period, combined with effective countercyclical policies, enabled Brazil to mount a swift and strong recovery, which was already evident in the second quarter of 2009. Sovereign spreads have rebounded quickly, and the exchange rate and domestic capital markets have since returned to levels prevailing in the preboom period. Furthermore, Brazil's robust economic fundamentals have allowed the government to adopt emergency measures to alleviate the liquidity crunch and implement countercyclical policy responses to shore up domestic demand. Brazil's large domestic market and correspondingly low dependence on external demand, along with the essential soundness of the domestic financial system, have further contributed to the rapid resumption of economic activity since the second quarter of 2009.

Notwithstanding its impressive resilience, Brazil's economy still faces several challenges to its ability to sustain rapid growth. The most important of these are the country's low saving and investment rates. Meanwhile, high tax rates and a distortive taxation system, cumbersome social security regulations, and a lack of further reforms to improve the investment climate significantly inhibit saving and investment by households and firms.

In this chapter, we assess the reasons for Brazil's strong performance during and immediately after the global crisis and analyze how the anticrisis policy responses and the postcrisis global economy may shape the country's medium-term growth. We will first describe the economic history of Brazil and its relationship to the worldwide economy in the period leading up to the global crisis and then assess the immediate impact

of the crisis and the government's policy response. We conclude by exploring Brazil's medium-term growth prospects in the wake of the global crisis.

Pre–Global Crisis: From Price Stabilization to Strong Macroeconomic Foundations

Throughout the 1990s, Brazil implemented a series of far-reaching structural reforms, including successful price stabilization policies, and developed a consistent macroeconomic policy framework designed to establish
a more stable, resilient, and dynamic economy. Over time these structural
reforms, combined with the consistent pursuit of sound and appropriate
macroeconomic policies and supported by a generally favorable external
environment, played a central role in solidifying the country's macroeconomic foundations and bolstering its economic growth potential.

The economic reforms, price stabilization, and the adoption of a consistent macroeconomic framework can be divided between two periods
covering four government administrations (figure 3.1). The first period,

Figure 3.1. Growth and Brazil's Sovereign Risk, 1994–2009

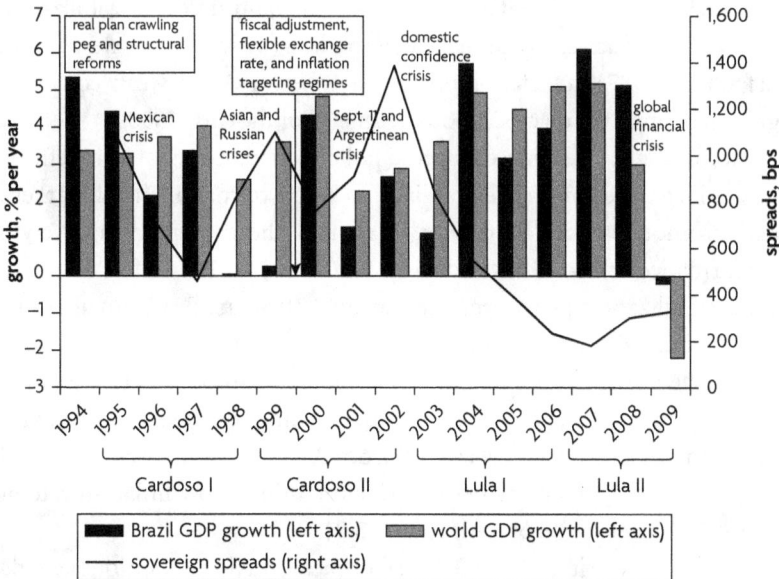

Source: IBGE (Brazilian Institute of Geography and Statistics); World Bank; JP Morgan.
Note: bps = basis points.

from 1994 to 2002, corresponds to the two terms of President Fernando Henrique Cardoso. It was marked by successful price stabilization, a massive structural reform program,[1] extreme volatility resulting from the country's fiscal and external vulnerabilities and a series of external shocks, the adoption of a more consistent economic policy in 1999, and the credibility crisis related to the transition to a new presidential administration in 2002. The second period, running from 2003 to 2008, covered the two mandates of President Luiz Inácio Lula da Silva (the second of which will end in 2010). This period was characterized by the further entrenchment of the macroeconomic policy framework established in 1999 and by the easing of fiscal and external vulnerabilities, which enabled Brazil to achieve investment-grade status in 2008. Economic growth performance improved substantially during this time (the average growth rate was 4.2 percent).

We will next look at how the external environment affected Brazil's economic situation and how global conditions interacted with domestic economic policies during the two precrisis periods (1994–2002 and 2003–08).

The Precrisis, Preboom Period, 1994–2002

The Brazilian economy emerged from the 1980s in a difficult macroeconomic situation. Persistent high inflation, several unsuccessful stabilization plans, a lack of access to external credit markets (owing to the external debt default of 1987), a deteriorating fiscal trajectory, and weak economic growth defined the macroeconomic scenario of the early 1990s.

Accordingly, Brazilian economic policies were dominated by efforts to stabilize the economy, reestablish access to external financial markets, and promote structural reforms to remedy the disappointing growth performance of the 1980s and early 1990s. In July 1994, after six failed price stabilization plans over the previous 10 years, Brazil finally initiated a successful price stabilization effort embedded in the Real Plan. Established during the first term of President Cardoso, and based on a crawling peg exchange rate as nominal anchor, the Real Plan brought inflation under control, lowering it from 2,500 percent per year in 1994 to less than 10 percent in 1995 and maintaining a low inflation rate of about 5 percent to the present (figure 3.2).

In parallel, during 1995–98, Brazil implemented an ambitious agenda of structural reforms. These encompassed trade openness; liberalization of the capital account; administrative, civil service, and social security

Figure 3.2. Growth, Inflation, Stabilization Plans, and Debt Crises, 1980–95

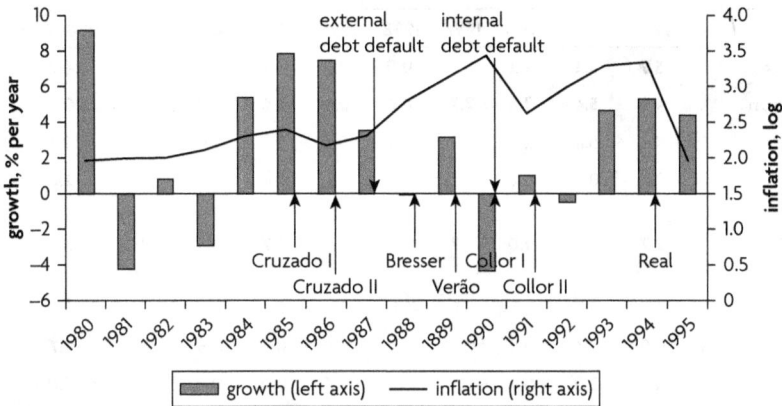

Source: IBGE.

reforms; privatization; the overhaul of regulatory frameworks for privatized services; reform of both the private and state banking systems; and the elimination of price controls.

These reforms led to a modest improvement in growth: from 1994 to 2002, average annual GDP growth increased to 2.7 percent—up from 2.1 percent in the previous decade—driven by rising domestic demand. With the strong increase in real income generated by the abrupt fall in inflation and the more stable economic environment, consumption—mainly private consumption—surged. It became the main driver of growth during this period, rising 20 percent (with private consumption growing 17.6 percent), and accounted for 85 percent of total growth. Following a rapid rise in the aftermath of price stabilization, investment made a modest contribution to growth, representing the remaining 15 percent (table 3.1, figure 3.3).

The net contribution of the external sector to Brazil's GDP growth was negligible, owing to a strong increase in imports coupled with modest export growth that resulted from the new fixed-exchange-rate regime. The external environment was nevertheless essential to the stabilization effort, as a larger supply of imports (and the appreciated exchange rate) helped keep prices under control. Imports tripled between 1994 and 1997, shifting a positive trade balance of US$20 billion into a deficit of similar magnitude by 1997. External conditions also allowed Brazil to finance its large trade and current account deficits via foreign direct

Table 3.1. Decomposition of GDP Growth, 1994–2002
(percent)

	1994	1995	1996	1997	1998	1999	2000	2001	2002	1994–2002
GDP growth	**5.9**	**4.2**	**2.2**	**3.4**	**0.0**	**0.3**	**4.3**	**1.3**	**2.7**	**24.2**
Consumption	**4.6**	**5.4**	**1.6**	**2.2**	**0.2**	**0.6**	**2.6**	**1.0**	**2.2**	**20.2**
Private	4.5	5.1	2.1	1.9	−0.4	0.2	2.5	0.4	1.1	**17.6**
Government	0.1	0.2	−0.4	0.3	0.6	0.3	0.0	0.5	0.9	**2.8**
Capital formation	**2.7**	**1.8**	**1.0**	**1.7**	**-0.5**	**-2.1**	**1.7**	**−0.5**	**−2.0**	**3.8**
Fixed capital formation	2.7	1.5	0.3	1.5	−0.1	−1.4	0.8	0.1	−0.9	**4.5**
Increase in stocks	0.0	0.3	0.8	0.2	−0.4	−0.7	0.9	−0.5	−1.1	**-0.7**
External sector	**−1.4**	**−3.0**	**−0.5**	**−0.5**	**0.3**	**1.7**	**0.0**	**0.8**	**2.5**	**0.0**
Exports	0.4	−0.2	0.0	0.7	0.3	0.4	1.2	1.0	0.9	**4.8**
Imports	−1.9	−2.8	−0.5	−1.2	0.0	1.3	−1.2	−0.2	1.6	**-4.8**

Source: IBGE; IPEA (Institute of Applied Economics Research).

Figure 3.3. Contribution to Growth by Demand Component, 1994–2002

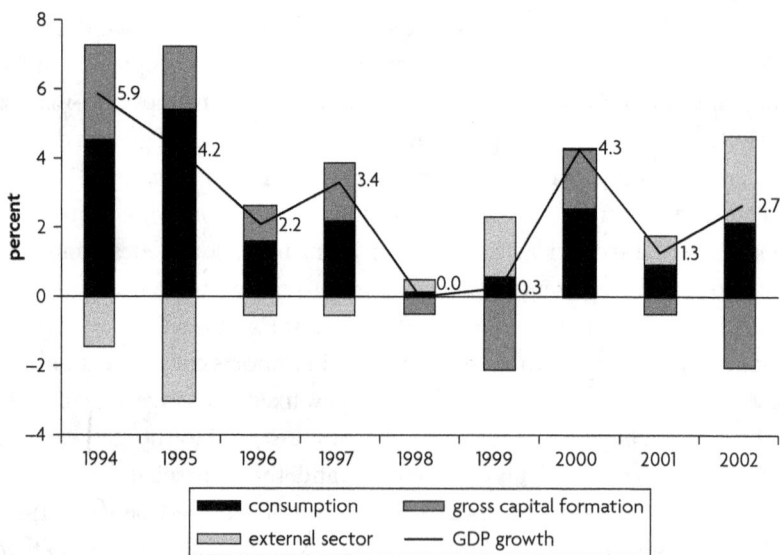

Source: IBGE; IPEA.

Table 3.2. Exports, Imports, and Terms of Trade, 1994–2002
(US$ millions)

	1994	1995	1996	1997	1998	1999	2000	2001	2002
Export value of goods and services	46,702	49,544	52,785	59,870	59,037	55,205	64,584	67,545	69,913
% GDP	8.5	6.4	6.3	6.9	7.0	9.4	10.0	12.2	13.9
Merchandise exports	42,674	45,988	47,240	52,623	50,736	47,551	54,187	56,121	57,337
Of which: Manufactures exports	24,959	25,565	26,411	29,192	29,380	27,331	32,559	32,959	33,069
Services exports	—	4,929	5,038	6,876	7,897	7,194	9,498	9322	9551
Import value of goods and services	26,142	58,750	67,065	77,269	75,722	63,382	72,444	72,654	61,749
% GDP	7.3	7.6	8.0	8.9	9.0	10.8	11.2	13.1	12.2
Merchandise imports	21,040	49,972	53,346	59,747	57,714	49,210	55,783	55,572	47,241
Of which: Manufactures imports	—	—	36,076	42,660	42,620	36,582	39,851	40,922	34,008
Services imports	—	12,412	13,719	17,522	18,008	14,171	16,660	17,081	14,509
Terms of trade (index)	92.9	103.2	102.8	109.1	107.4	93.2	96.2	96.0	94.7
Remittances	59	60	197	253	282	310	237	270	293
% GDP	0.01	0.01	0.02	0.03	0.03	0.05	0.04	0.05	0.06

Source: IBGE; IPEA.
Note: — = not available.

investment (FDI) and portfolio investment inflows (table 3.2; see also table 3.4, which provides FDI data).

At the sector level, GDP growth patterns were closely correlated with the evolution of the industrial sector. Brazil's initial GDP growth acceleration was driven by robust but temporary industrial growth during 1994–96. Likewise, economic deceleration in 1996 was associated with a stagnation of industrial activity. Agriculture maintained a positive growth rate during 1994–99, while services grew steadily during the same period, increasing its relative share in GDP (figure 3.4).

After a decade of continuous decline, total factor productivity (TFP) grew strongly but briefly, as a result of the short-run effects of price stabilization and of economic reforms—particularly the promotion of trade openness and increased FDI, which facilitated a large increase in capital goods imports and technology transfer. From 1994 to 1999, TFP contributed 0.2 percentage points to growth, representing 10 percent of

Figure 3.4. Growth and Share of GDP by Sector, 1994–2002

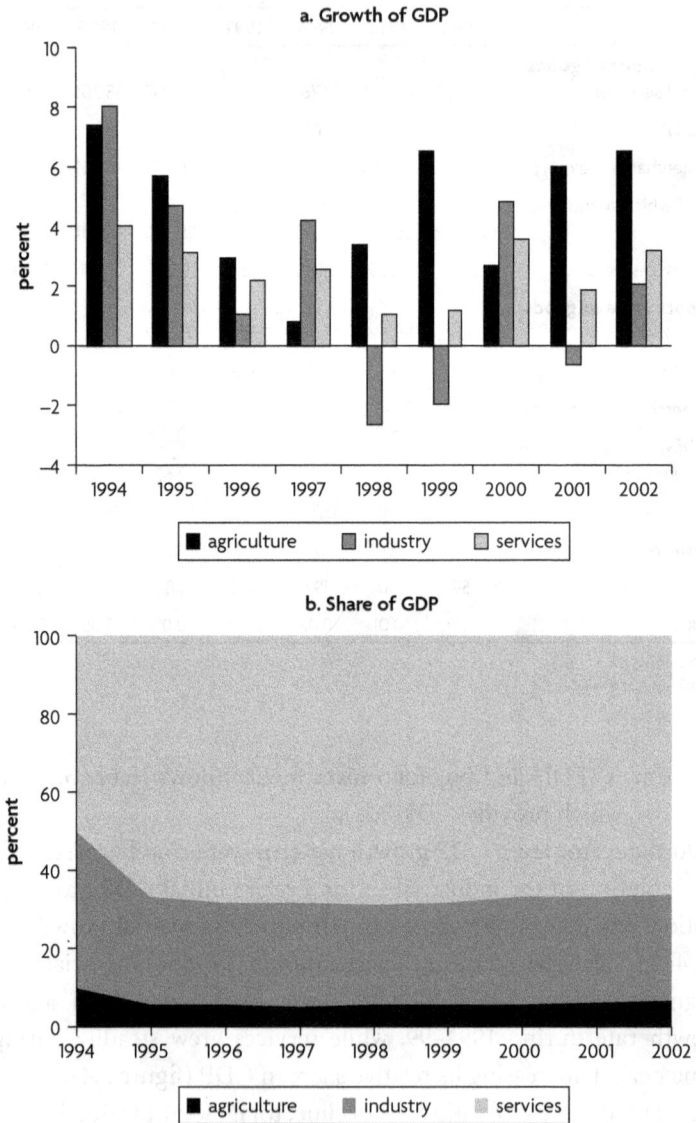

a. Growth of GDP

b. Share of GDP

Source: IBGE.

total growth. Physical capital and labor contributed 1.2 and 0.6 percentage points, representing 50 percent and 23 percent of total growth, respectively. Human capital's contribution was 0.4 percentage points, representing 17 percent of total growth. From 1999 to 2001, several negative shocks, the rigidity of the crawling exchange rate, and the increasing vulnerability of the economy reversed the positive contribution of productivity to growth. As a result, TFP fell continuously from 1999 to 2002, having a negative contribution of −1 percentage point to growth (−38 percent of total growth) during the period. During the same period, labor, physical capital, and human capital accumulation all contributed positively to GDP growth (table 3.3).[2]

The effects of economic stabilization and increased growth on poverty reduction were immediate and substantial, demonstrating how previous inflation had mainly hurt the poor: in 1993, one year before price stabilization, the proportion of people below the poverty line was 42 percent, whereas in 1995, one year after price stabilization, this proportion had dropped to less than 34 percent. Improvements in employment indicators, especially in formal employment and labor income, were also key contributors to the declining poverty rate (see figure 3.9 later in the chapter).

Until 1998, however, fiscal reform lagged reforms in other areas. Indeed, increasing fiscal fragility was the main reason for the high volatility and economic stagnation of the latter part of the 1990s. Fiscal disequilibrium in Brazil has a long history and deep roots. From around 1950 through the 1970s, the expansion of the public sector was driven by an explicit

Table 3.3. Growth Decomposition, 1994–2008

	Output (Y)	Total factor productivity (TFP)		Human Capital[a] (H)		Physical capital[b] (K)		Labor[c] (L)	
	Growth rate	Contribution to growth level	Contribution to growth percentage	Contribution to growth level	Contribution to growth percentage	Contribution to growth level	Contribution to growth percentage	Contribution to growth level	Contribution to growth percentage
1994–99	2.5	0.2	10.0	1.2	50.0	0.4	17.0	0.6	23.0
1999–2002	2.7	−1.0	−38.3	1.1	40.2	1.1	41.3	1.5	56.8
2002–08	4.0	1.1	28.9	0.9	22.4	0.6	14.5	1.4	34.2

Source: Barbosa Filho and Pessôa 2009.
a. Human capital is measured by the rate of participation, and labor income was calculated as a function of education and experience.
b. Physical capital is measured by the existing capital stock adjusted by capacity utilization.
c. Labor is measured by actual employment (number of hours worked).

development strategy that relied on strong state intervention in the economy. During this period, Brazil recorded one of the highest growth rates in the world. But the expansionary fiscal policy that underpinned this growth strategy proved unsustainable. The growing fiscal imbalance and the resultant macroeconomic instability slowed economic growth in the 1980s, and the country found itself mired in rapidly accumulating public debt accompanied by rising inflation.

Low growth, high inflation, and increasing fiscal disequilibria characterized the macroeconomic context in which the country initiated its redemocratization process in 1985. The increasing demand for social services that resulted from increased political openness heightened the pressure on the fiscal accounts.[3] The 1988 Constitution generated its own expenditure pressures due to the expansion of state social responsibilities; a fiscal federalism tax structure and intergovernmental transfer system; universal access to health care, education, and social security; and an expansion of the compensation structure for public sector employees, which included employment tenure, several bonuses that raised total salaries, and a very generous pension system. The effects of the 1988 Constitution on fiscal sustainability would have been immediately evident, but inflation masked the fiscal disequilibria that continued to widen during the late 1980s and early 1990s.

With the end of the inflationary period, the country's fiscal deterioration became visible. Previously, inflation served not only as a source of revenue, but also as a useful mechanism for deflating government expenditures in real terms. This loss of maneuvering space in which to adjust expenditures, combined with the lack of decisive fiscal reforms and the high interest rates mandated by the anti-inflationary policy, resulted in expanding government deficits and a large increase in the public debt. The subnational governments experienced a similar situation. In 1997, the federal government assumed the debts of 25 of the 27 states that were unable to meet their debt service obligations. Indeed, during the 1980s and 1990s, the fiscal behavior and indebtedness of state and municipal governments in Brazil became an important source of macroeconomic instability (World Bank 2009).[4]

The government's primary balance shifted from a surplus equivalent to 5.6 percent of GDP in 1994 to –1 percent in 1998, while overall balances deteriorated from –5 percent of GDP in 1994 to –8 percent in

1998. Net public debt grew from 32 percent of GDP in 1994 to 40 percent in 1998. The unfavorable debt dynamics of the period reflected the decline in primary balances, the high interest rates needed to stabilize the economy along with the large share of debt indexed to it, and the strong accumulation of contingent liabilities.

The cleaning up of private banking institutions' balance sheets and the capitalization of public banks also generated fiscal costs. Several private banks faced balance sheet deterioration linked to the rapid transition to a low-inflation scenario. The Brazilian Central Bank (Banco Central do Brasil, BCB) was forced to bail out two large private financial institutions and to initiate a banking system restructuring and strengthening program. On the public side, the aggressive use of federal financial institutions to stimulate economic activity through subsidized credits in the 1970s led to the accumulation of contingent liabilities that threatened the solvency of the public sector in the new price stabilization context. The costs of capitalizing public banks to clean their balance sheets amounted to 6 percent of GDP. Finally, the balance sheets of banks owned by state governments were also cleaned by the federal government.

While the fiscal costs were considerable, the cleaning up of private and public banks allowed the government to impose a successful program to restructure the banking system. The program has been one of the reasons behind the strength of the Brazilian financial system since 1997. The BCB adopted a very conservative regulatory framework and a tight supervisory apparatus, enforcing high capitalization ratios and adequate capital provisions. In addition, high reserve requirements to manage liquidity also favored a prudent credit expansion. Additional instruments—such as the Deposit Insurance Fund (Fundo Garantidor de Créditos) and the Brazilian Payment System (Sistema Brasileiro de Pagamentos)—were created to guarantee creditors' rights and ensure the quick identification of systemic risks. The justification for the establishment of a deposit insurance system was the urgent need to strengthen the banking system's safety network, both to minimize the economic and social costs of a possible bank run and to prepare for the potential threat that a banking crisis would pose to the gains achieved during the previous period of economic stability. The experience and the costs of cleaning up financial institutions also favored significant efforts and investments in oversight activities by the BCB (box 3.1; World Bank 2001, 2002).

Box 3.1. Financial Sector Reforms, 1995–2008[a]

Financial sector reforms in Brazil occurred in three stages:

- In the first stage (1995–97), in response to a wave of bank failures, mergers, and acquisitions (3 out of the 10 largest banks were liquidated) precipitated by the new price stabilization policies, financial reforms were aimed at addressing the insolvency of private and public banks.
- In the second stage (1997–2002), policy actions were aimed at enhancing the regulatory and oversight frameworks.
- In the third stage (2003–08), efforts were concentrated on expanding access to credit and increasing financial intermediation.

This sequencing closely reflects the government's focus on specific policy objectives; the improvements in financial regulation and oversight continued in the third stage, and the initial measures on the expansion of credit access were taken in the second stage.

1995–96: Private Bank Restructuring Program (PROER): This program included the government's payment of deposits to failed banks; the capitalization of some private banks was contingent upon broad restructuring measures designed to enhance their financial soundness and integrity.

1995: Deposit Insurance Fund (FGC): The FGC is a depositors' insurance fund similar to the U.S. Federal Deposit Insurance Corporation (FDIC), an autonomous institution created to protect small account holders and prevent systemic banking risks. The establishment of the FGC was accompanied by legislation intended to avoid bank failures and to hasten their resolution.

1997–99: Restructuring and Privatization Program for State-Government-Owned Banks (PROES): This program was designed to reduced credit expansion to financial institutions owned by the states, to avoid the use of public banks to finance state government deficits, and to increase the participation of the private sector so as to foster more competition and facilitate the exit of insolvent institutions that were not complying with minimum prudential norms.

1998–2002: This period saw the harmonization of financial accounting, auditing, and reporting standards with internationally recommended best practices by International Accounting Standards Board (IASB), the International Federation of Accountants (IFAC), and the Bank for International Settlements (BIS) for the provisions of losses, the consolidation of financial statements for financial institutions, and disclosure practices.

2000–02: The federal government's ongoing reform of public banks: Further reform efforts succeeded in improving the efficiency and transparency of the three largest federal banks, Banco do Brasil, Caixa Econômica Federal, and Banco Nacional de Desenvolvimento Econômico e Soical (National Treasury to the Federal Economic and Social Development Bank, BNDES), expanding the oversight power of the central bank and separating their balances from government accounts.

2001: Introduction of the Bank Credit Bond (Cédula de Crédito Bancário): The Bank Credit Bond is a bank credit—an asset-backed security where the underlying asset represents a bank claim. This instrument increased the safety of financial institutions' credit transactions.

2001–02: The Brazilian Payments and Settlement Systems (SBP): This program was aimed at reducing systemic risks, limiting the central bank's exposure to losses in the settlement system, and transferring the remaining risk to private sector participants in the payments system under new rules and oversight. Under this system, interbank fund transfers could now be permanently settled on a real-time basis.

2001: Initial opening of the Credit Risks Center: The Credit Risks Center is an online database at the BCB designed to enhance debtor screening.

2002: Establishment of new laws governing Brazil's Securities Commission (CVM): These measures enhanced the enforcement capacity and independence of this commission to oversee mutual funds and pension funds.

2002: The introduction of Credit Investment Funds (FDIC): These funds can hold securities based on any credit receivable, including mortgages.

2004: Signing of the Bankruptcy Law: This law increased flexibility for liquidation and the restructuring of firms in bankruptcy, enhanced private creditors rights, and simplified asset sales processes.

2004: New regulations allowing the use of payroll bills, social security benefits, and social protection transfers as collateral for consumer credit. This measure was designed to increase access to credit by low-income consumers and to reduce credit risks spreads.

2004: The Brazilian Payment System and Risk Center database became fully operational.

2005: Reform of Housing Credit Legislation: These reforms allowed the use of properties as collateral, increasing the participation of the private sector in housing financing.

2004–07: The adoption of Basel II: Capital requirement ratio minimum levels (PRE) as fixed in order to improve the regulatory structure of the capital maintained by financial institutions.

2005–07: Expansion of Credit Securitization: New instruments established for housing, agriculture, and agribusiness.

2008: The adoption of more stringent regulations than those recommended by Basel II: New regulations are put in place for interest rate and exchange rate exposures, and the minimum level for PRE is set at 11 percent (the Basel II minimum level is 8 percent).

2008, October: The FGC guarantee to small banks that faced liquidity problems in the aftermath of the global financial crisis was increased.

a. For a more detailed description of financial sector reforms, see World Bank (2001) and World Bank (2002).

Fiscal deterioration, coupled with the crawling-peg exchange rate regime amid increasing trade openness and capital account liberalization, resulted in a substantial deterioration of external accounts and increased external indebtedness. Meanwhile, the strong increase in private consumption reduced domestic saving. Declining domestic saving and increased capital accumulation led to a rapid deterioration of external balances. Already in 1995, the trade balance had shifted to a deficit of US$10 billion for the first time since 1982. The current account deficit expanded sharply from US$1.8 billion (or 0.3 percent of GDP) in 1994 to US$30 billion (or 4 percent of GDP) in 1997–98. External debt surged from US$148 billion (25 percent of GDP) in 1994 to US$242 billion or (33 percent of GDP) in 1998. The strong capital account portfolio investment inflows, resulting from high domestic interest rates and FDI related to privatization, financed the expanded current account deficit. Portfolio investments soared to US$51 billion in 1994 (from US$12 billion in 1993 and remained at about US$20 billion through 1998. FDI surged to US$29 billion in 1997–98 from about US$2 billion in 1994.

Fiscal and external disequilibria made Brazil extremely vulnerable to contagion effects. In 1995, the Mexican crisis obligated the Brazilian government to increase interest rates to defend the exchange rate and interrupted the strong economic acceleration initiated with the successful price stabilization. The Asian and Russian crises in 1997 and 1998 also strongly affected the Brazilian economy. Speculative attacks against the real demanded firm monetary tightening, with widespread effects on economic activity and public debt dynamics. Additionally, the government used exchange rate–indexed bonds to avoid exchange rate depreciation pressures; the strategy appeared to be effective in the short run, but ultimately introduced additional risk into the composition of public debt.

Deteriorating macroeconomic conditions led to economic stagnation in 1998, dragging down the average growth rate during 1995–98 to 2.4 percent, a rate only slightly higher than that experienced in the 1980s (considered the "lost decade"). Furthermore, a marked decrease in the capital accumulation rate, lower productivity, a weak labor market, and rising poverty interrupted the positive trends initiated with the launch of the Real Plan in 1994. In addition to low growth and high interest rates, the government's failure to address the deteriorating fiscal accounts rendered public and external debts increasingly unsustainable.

After the Brazilian authorities' unsuccessful efforts to defend the currency following the Russian crisis—which included raising the headline interest rate to 30 percent, signing an additional Stand-By Arrangement with the International Monetary Fund (IMF) for US$43 billion, and international reserve losses of US$30 billion—the government in January 1999 had to abandon the crawling-peg exchange rate regime. This led to a rapid depreciation of the exchange rate and disruption of domestic financial markets. To avoid further depreciation, the government was forced to raise interest rates to 45 percent from 30 percent in December 1998. Given the large share of public bonds indexed to the exchange and interest rates, public debt jumped to 47 percent of GDP. Economic activity plummeted, with industrial production and capital accumulation falling sharply. Last but not least, inflation increased substantially because of the exchange rate depreciation, placing at risk the most important achievement of the Real Plan—price stability.

In this context, the government adopted a new economic policy framework built on strong fiscal discipline, inflation targeting, and flexible exchange rate regime. The previous policy of fiscal laxity was replaced by a tight fiscal policy aimed at reducing indebtedness and restoring fiscal sustainability. To restore its credibility, the government announced a primary fiscal target of 3.3 percent (versus a deficit of 1 percent in 1998).

To consolidate its new tighter fiscal stance, the government strengthened controls on subnational fiscal performance by enacting the Fiscal Responsibility Law (FRL) in May 2000. The FRL explicitly prohibited debt-refinancing operations between different levels of government—moderating the moral hazard problem in intergovernmental fiscal relations associated with sequential bailouts—and set limits on personnel costs, borrowing, and indebtedness. The approval of the FRL allowed Brazil to exert institutional control over subnational fiscal policy and also send a signal to the market of the institutional strengthening of fiscal discipline. Monetary policy adopted an inflation-targeting regime. Finally, a flexible exchange rate regime replaced the crawling peg that had supported price stabilization under the Real Plan.

The effects of the shift to this more consistent macroeconomic policy framework showed up surprisingly quickly (table 3.4). Despite the substantial exchange rate depreciation, the inflation-targeting regime managed to keep inflation under control. The increase in national debt

Table 3.4. Brazil's Macroeconomic Indicators, 1994–2002

Indicator	1994	1995	1996	1997	1998	1999	2000	2001	2002
National accounts									
GDP (US$ billions)	546	769	840	871	844	587	645	554	504
Population (millions)	159.3	161.6	164.2	166.6	169.2	171.7	174.2	176.7	179.1
Population growth (%)	1.5	1.5	1.5	1.5	1.4	1.4	1.4	1.4	1.4
GDP per capita (US$)	3,430	4,756	5,115	5,228	4,998	3,418	3,701	3,133	2,815
Real GDP growth (%)	5.3	4.4	2.2	3.4	0.0	0.3	4.3	1.3	2.7
Supply side									
Agriculture growth (%)	7.4	5.7	3.0	0.8	3.4	6.5	2.7	6.1	6.6
Industry growth (%)	8.1	4.7	1.1	4.2	−2.6	−1.9	4.8	−0.6	2.1
Services growth (%)	4.0	3.2	2.2	2.6	1.1	1.2	3.6	1.9	3.2
Demand side									
Consumption growth (%)	5.9	7.0	2.0	2.6	0.2	0.7	3.0	1.2	2.6
Investment growth (%)	13.0	8.1	5.7	9.7	−2.7	−12.2	10.3	−2.6	−5.2
Investment (% GDP)	20.7	18.3	16.9	17.4	17.0	15.7	16.8	17.0	16.4
Public sector	3.6	2.3	2.0	1.7	2.4	1.4	1.8	2.0	3.7

(continued)

Table 3.4. *(continued)*

Indicator	1994	1995	1996	1997	1998	1999	2000	2001	2002
Private sector	17.1	16.0	14.9	15.7	14.6	14.3	15.0	15.0	12.7
Gross national savings (% GDP)	20.4	15.9	14.1	13.9	13.0	12.4	13.0	12.8	14.7
External sector									
Trade balance (US$ billions)	10.5	−3.5	−5.6	−6.8	−6.6	−1.2	−0.7	2.7	13.1
Current account balance (US$ billions)	−1.8	−18.4	−23.5	−30.5	−33.4	−25.3	−24.2	−23.2	−7.6
Current account balance (% GDP)	−0.3	−2.4	−2.8	−3.5	−4.0	−4.3	−3.8	−4.2	−1.5
Foreign direct investment (US$ billions)	2.1	4.4	10.8	19.0	28.9	28.6	32.7	22.5	16.6
International reserves (US$ billions)	39.8	51.8	60.1	52.2	44.6	36.3	33.0	35.9	37.8
External debt (US$ billions)	148	159	180	200	242	241	236	226	228
External debt to exports (%)	341	342	377	377	473	503	429	388	377
Interest payments to exports (%)	18.7	22.9	26.7	27.5	30.0	36.5	31.0	30.0	23.6
Nominal exchange rate (end of period)	0.84	0.97	1.04	1.12	1.21	1.79	1.95	2.32	3.53
Real effective exchange rate (2,000 = 1)	97.3	110.5	112.2	118.0	120.8	140.2	100.0	84.2	82.2
Public sector									
Primary balance (% GDP)	5.6	0.3	−0.1	−1.0	0.0	3.2	3.5	3.4	3.5
Overall balance (% GDP)	−24.7	−6.5	−5.3	−5.5	−7.0	−5.2	−3.4	−3.3	−4.4
Net public sector debt (% GDP)	43.8	29.5	31.9	32.8	39.4	48.5	47.7	52.3	50.5
Prices and economic activity									
Consumer inflation (%)	2,287	71.9	18.2	7.7	4.1	4.9	7.5	6.9	12.5
Headline interest rate (avg. %)	3,490	54.5	27.4	22.8	24.3	24.7	17.6	17.5	19.2
Unemployment (%)	5.5	5.0	5.8	6.1	8.3	8.2	7.9	6.8	11.7
Industrial capital utilization (%)	79.8	83.2	81.6	83.5	81.7	80.5	82.8	81.7	79.4

Source: BCB (Central Bank of Brazil); IBGE; IPEA.

was halted, and the growth rate accelerated in 2000 to 4.3 percent after two years of stagnation. On the demand side, capital accumulation and the external sector led the recovery, while on the supply side, industry was the driving force.

The Pre–Global Crisis Boom Period, 2002–08

The adverse shocks of 2001–02 demonstrated that, despite Brazil's reform efforts, serious fiscal and external vulnerabilities remained.[5] These shocks reduced access to international capital, leading to the resumption of exchange rate depreciation and to higher inflation. Consistent with the inflation-targeting regime, and in an effort to avoid further depreciation, the government had to interrupt the previous declining trend of domestic interest rates and sign a new IMF Stand-By Arrangement for US$15 billion. As a result, Brazil's economic growth rate fell to 1.3 percent in 2001 and 2.7 percent in 2002, bringing the average growth rate for the period 1998–2002 to just 2 percent, the same level experienced in the 1980s. Exchange rate depreciation, high interest rates, a dangerous public debt composition, and low growth renewed doubts about the sustainability of Brazil's public and external debt.

The deterioration of Brazil's economic situation coincided with the presidential elections in 2002. A significant political shift was expected as the leftist candidate, Lula da Silva, emerged as the favorite in the electoral campaigns. Markets were concerned about the continuity of the sound but nascent and politically vulnerable economic policies adopted since 1999, as well as about the current administration's ability to curb increasing public debt despite strong fiscal reform efforts. These uncertainties triggered a credibility crisis that rocked the domestic financial markets. Between March and September 2002, the exchange rate depreciated by 60 percent, sovereign spreads reached 2,400 basis points (bps), the stock market index fell 30 percent, interest rates increased from 16.3 percent to 21 percent, and public debt reached a full 58 percent of GDP. In August, a third IMF Stand-By Arrangement, in the amount of US$30 billion, was endorsed by presidential candidate Lula, who publicly committed to maintaining the economic policy framework established in 1999 and to honoring the agreements made with the IMF.

Concerns that the discontinuity of the prevailing macroeconomic framework could lead to a debt default precipitated a strong and convincing economic policy credibility response during President Lula's first term (2003–06). Upon taking office, the new administration tightened fiscal and monetary policies. Primary surplus targets were increased to 4.5 percent of GDP from the previous target of 3.3 percent, which had been in place since 1999, and interest rates were lifted to 26.5 percent to dampen inflationary pressures related to the real depreciation. The government also adopted a debt management strategy focused on aggressively reducing the volume of U.S. dollar–indexed debt and began to gradually increase the proportion of fixed-interest-rate debt. The authorities also lengthened debt maturities to lessen vulnerabilities associated with exchange and interest rate fluctuations and rollover risks. With these measures, the government reduced the fiscal dominance on monetary and exchange rate policies. Taking advantage of strong political support in the early stages of its term, the new administration received congressional approval for a second round of social security reforms. Further reforms included the approval of a bankruptcy law and improvements in the domestic credit markets, especially concerning the housing and consumer lending sectors, which sharply increased available credit.

The strong commitment to prudential macroeconomic policies was decisive in achieving a substantial improvement in market sentiment. This improvement was reflected in reduced sovereign spreads and steady improvement of credit ratings, which culminated in Brazil's winning investment-grade rating in 2008 by the three major international credit rating agencies.

Further strengthening of the macroeconomic management framework during 2003–08, along with the favorable external scenario, enhanced Brazil's fiscal and external solvency positions. Strong government balances led the public debt-to-GDP ratio to fall to 38 percent in 2008 (from 57 percent at the end of 2002). The strong fiscal adjustment allowed not only the reduction of debt levels but also the altering of its composition through an effective implementation of a debt management strategy designed to reduce exposure to exchange and interest rate shocks. As a result, the share of debt linked to the exchange rate fell from 35 percent in 2002 to negative territory (the government is a creditor in this instrument) in 2005, and it remained negative until 2008. Debt indexed to the interest rate fell from 42 percent in December 2002 to 31 percent in 2008, while the share of fixed bonds increased from 2 percent in 2002 to 27 percent in

2008. Average bond duration increased from 11 months to 27 months between 2002 and 2008. As the change in debt composition posed increased financing costs (bonds denominated in real and fixed-rate bonds being more expensive), this debt strategy released monetary policy from fiscal dominance. It has served as a type of insurance against macroeconomic shocks, which frequently combine exchange rate and interest rate shocks and increased rollover risks.

Brazil's inflation-targeting regime has been very successful in anchoring inflation expectations. Operationally independent, the BCB has been able to control inflation and progressively reduce interest rates. Inflation fell to about 4.5 percent in 2007–08 from 12.5 percent in 2002, and BCB targets have been regularly met since 2003. The strong commitment to inflation targeting reduced inflation expectations. Consistent with lower inflation and inflation expectations, the BCB cut the headline interest rate from a peak of 26.5 percent in 2003 to 13.75 percent at the end of 2008.

Brazil's external sector showing benefited from the new exchange rate flexibility and the global economic boom and contributed decisively to improving external sustainability indicators. Bolstered by higher commodity prices, exports grew steadily from US$60 billion in 2002 to US$198 billion in 2008 (table 3.5). Associated with the diversification of exports destination (regional trade and South-South trade) manufactured exports also experienced a very impressive growth. The Brazilian trade surplus widened from US$13 billion in 2002 to more than US$40 billion in 2005–07 and fell to US$25 billion in 2008 due to the economic activity acceleration.

Commodity prices played an important role in improving Brazil's external sector performance. Nevertheless, it is useful to assess its net contribution to the trade balance, not just its impact on exports. While Brazil is an important commodity exporter, it is also a large commodity importer. The net trade commodity index (a weighted average of the prices of commodities exported and imported by Brazil) did not exhibit the strong increase observed in the commodity price export index (figure 3.5). This is confirmed by the modest rise of about 13 percent in Brazil's terms of trade in 2003–08.

A second consideration is that while Brazilian commodity exports increased, manufacturing exports surged as well. Furthermore, while higher commodity prices explain the increased share of commodities in

Table 3.5. Exports, Imports, and Terms of Trade, 2002–08
(US$ millions)

	2002	2003	2004	2005	2006	2007	2008
Export value of goods and services	69,913	83,531	109,059	134,403	157,283	184,603	228,393
% GDP	13.9	15.1	16.4	15.2	14.4	13.8	14.2
Merchandise exports	57,337	69,263	96,678	118,529	137,807	160,649	197,942
Of which: Manufactures exports	33,069	39,764	53,137	65,353	75,018	83,943	92,683
Services exports	9551	10,447	12,584	16,047	19,476	23,954	30,451
Import value of goods and services	61,749	63,668	80,097	97,956	120,467	157,795	220,247
% GDP	12.2	11.5	12.1	11.1	11.1	11.8	13.7
Merchandise imports	47,241	48,290	62,836	73,600	91,351	120,622	173,107
Of which: Manufactures imports	34,008	34,099	43,585	51,090	61,343	81,085	115,843
Services imports	14,509	15,378	17,261	24,356	29,116	37,173	47,140
Terms of trade (index)	94.7	93.4	94.2	95.0	100.0	102.1	105.7
Remittances	293	269	354	325	397	497	730
% GDP	0.06	0.05	0.05	0.04	0.04	0.04	0.05

Source: IBGE; IPEA.

Figure 3.5. Commodity Prices for Exports and Net Trade, 2002–09

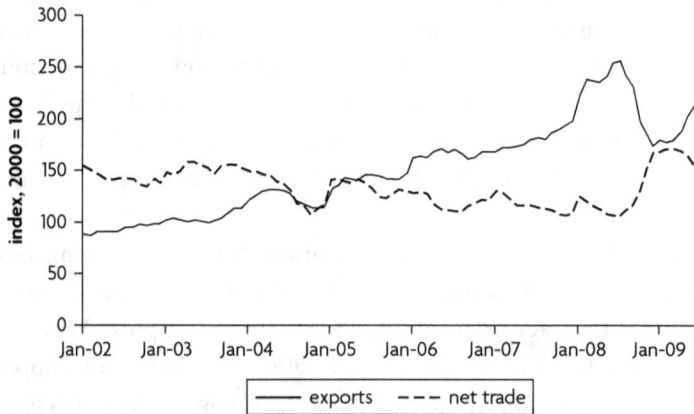

Source: BCB.

Brazilian export values, the volume of manufactured exports expanded more than that of commodity exports—demonstrating that Brazilian exports are well diversified in terms of products. From 2002 to 2008, the volume of manufactured exports grew by 41 percent while the volume of commodity exports grew by 36 percent. In addition, Brazil has diversified its export destinations in recent years. The commodity price boom thus appears to have had an indirect positive impact on Brazilian exports, as countries importing Brazilian manufactures (especially regional trade partners) posted substantial terms-of-trade gains that allowed them to boost their demand for Brazilian products. Between 2002 and 2008, exports volume to Mercado Común del Sur (Mercosur) countries grew by 150 percent, to the Asia-Pacific region by 52 percent, and to the European Union by 30 percent, while exports to the United States (the most important destination) fell by 18 percent, promoting a major diversification. High trade diversification in terms of products and destinations has provided the Brazilian economy with additional insurance against future macroeconomic shocks.

Brazil's sizable trade surpluses resulted in a decisive improvement in its current account balance. After more than a decade of deficits, Brazil enjoyed consecutive current account surpluses from 2003 to 2007. In 2008, however, with strong investment growth and high profit and dividend remittances related to the acceleration of economic activity, the current account shifted to a deficit of 1.8 percent of GDP.

The robust external performance and increased capital flows led to the accumulation of large international reserves, which surged from US$37 billion in 2002 to US$206 billion in December 2008. The growing strength of Brazil's external position allowed the country to easily repay its entire outstanding obligations to the IMF in December 2005. The government anticipated the end of Stand-By Arrangements with the IMF in 2002 and with the Paris Club of official creditors in 2006, as well as the retirement of its Brady Bonds[6] in 2006. Total external debt fell to US$200 billion (from US$210 billion in 2002), with public debt dropping to US$67 billion (from US$110 billion in 2002). As a result, the Brazilian public sector's external net debt in 2008 was negative, and Brazil's external debt sustainability indicators have improved considerably. As noted earlier, declining public and external debt resulted in Brazil's attaining investment-grade status in 2008.

Strong export growth reduced Brazil's interest-payments-to-exports ratio from 24 percent in 2002 to 7.1 percent in 2008. Similarly, the debt-to-export ratio decreased dramatically—from 377 percent in 2002 to 135 percent in 2008. The accumulation of reserves and reduced external public debt represented the Brazilian government's use of macroeconomic and fiscal policy as a means of purchasing a type of "insurance" against future shocks during the worldwide economic boom.

An additional positive development was the change in the composition of the country's net external liabilities. Substituting for indebtedness, portfolio investment in fixed income had been the most important source of capital account inflows until 1998. From 1998 to 2006, FDI replaced portfolio investment as the primary source of capital inflows. Portfolio investment reasserted its importance in 2007–08, but investment in equities was now its most important component. Spurred by the increasing importance of FDI and portfolio investment in equities, changes in net external liabilities introduced a pro-cyclical orientation to the current account, as dividends and profit flows are more sensitive to the business cycle than debt interest payments. This change in the composition of net external liabilities represented a further type of insurance against adverse shocks to the domestic economy: because these net liabilities generate outflows that are pro-cyclical, they fall during crisis periods, thereby reducing the pressure on the current account (figure 3.6).

Figure 3.6. Net External Liabilities, 2001–09

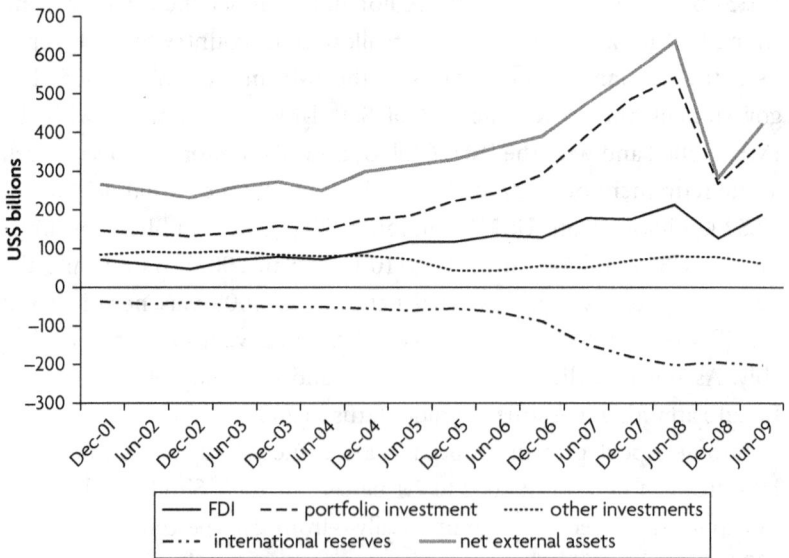

Source: BCB.

Brazil's GDP growth strengthened substantially in the mid-2000s. After growth slowed in the wake of the strong contractionary fiscal and monetary policies adopted in 2003, the economy grew at an average annual rate of 4.8 percent during 2004–08, well above the average rate of 2.6 percent during 1994–02. This growth cycle was driven mainly by domestic demand (table 3.6, figure 3.7). Expanding domestic consumption led the recovery in 2004 and sustained an average GDP growth rate of more than 5 percent until 2008. Final consumption represented 75 percent of this growth, with private consumption accounting for 60 percent of accumulated GDP growth. The improvement in Brazil's macroeconomic fundamentals stimulated investment, which averaged 14 percent growth between 2006 and 2008. As a result, investment also increased its contribution to growth (to 23 percent). The external sector contributed the remaining 2 percent to accumulated GDP growth during 2002–08.[7]

The strong performance of the external sector had been fundamental in the earlier recovery period of 1999–2003. In 1999, and again in 2001–03, the growth of net exports compensated for the fall in domestic demand. The exchange rate depreciations of 1999, 2001, and 2003, along with the positive external environment, fostered the growth of export demand, averting a more severe economic slowdown. Therefore, contractionary periods are characterized by a robust external sector that serves as a buffer against the business cycle. Economic expansions, by

Table 3.6. Decomposition of GDP Growth, 2002–09
(percent)

	2002	2003	2004	2005	2006	2007	2008	2009	2002–08
GDP growth	2.7	1.1	5.7	3.2	4.0	6.1	5.1	−0.2	27.8
Consumption	2.2	−0.2	3.2	3.1	3.6	4.7	4.5	3.2	21.1
Private	1.1	−0.4	2.3	2.6	3.1	3.7	4.1	2.4	16.6
Government	0.9	0.2	0.8	0.4	0.5	1.0	0.3	0.7	4.3
Capital formation	−2.0	−0.3	1.9	−0.4	1.7	2.8	2.8	−3.5	6.4
Fixed capital formation	−0.9	−0.8	1.4	0.6	1.6	2.3	2.3	−1.9	6.5
Increase in stocks	−1.1	0.5	0.5	−1.0	0.1	0.5	0.5	−1.6	−0.1
External sector	2.5	1.7	0.7	0.5	−1.4	−1.4	−2.2	0.1	0.4
Exports	1.6	0.2	−1.6	−1.1	−2.1	−2.3	−2.1	1.6	−7.4
Imports	0.9	1.5	2.3	1.5	0.8	0.9	−0.1	−1.4	7.8

Source: IBGE; IPEA.

Figure 3.7. Contribution to Growth by Demand Component, 2002–09

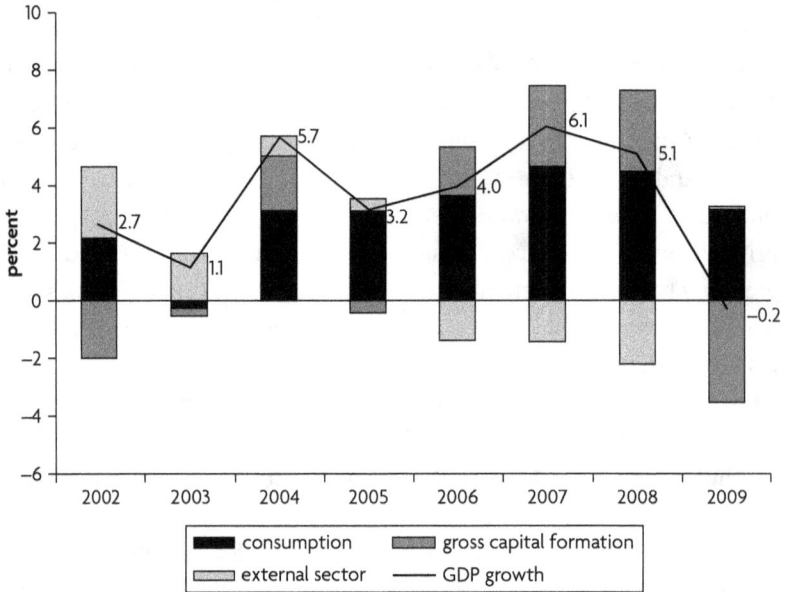

Source: IBGE; IPEA.

contrast, are fueled by increased domestic demand. This increase leads in turn to increased imports, switching the net contribution of the external sector from positive to negative. In addition, the exchange rate appreciation in 2003–08 also contributed to the rise in imports, further reducing the net contribution of the external sector to GDP growth.

In this context, the role of global financial conditions during the boom years was more important for reducing macroeconomic vulnerabilities, as it allowed the shift in the country's debt asset-liability structure, rather than supporting a growth acceleration based on the increase of external savings and increasing current account deficits. Actually, external savings were negative, as the country was able to generate continuous current account surpluses. Nonetheless, as noted above, benign global financial conditions allowed Brazilian banks and firms broader access to capital markets, reducing their financing costs and promoting the expansion of credit. In addition, large capital flows allowed a valorization of domestic assets, which indirectly had a positive effect on investment.

At the sectoral level, the 2004 recovery was again led by industry (figure 3.8). The increase in commodity prices resulted in growth rates in the agriculture sector exceeding 5 percent since 2006. Fostered by strong domestic demand and rising consumption, the contribution of

Figure 3.8. Growth and Share of GDP by Sector, 2002–08

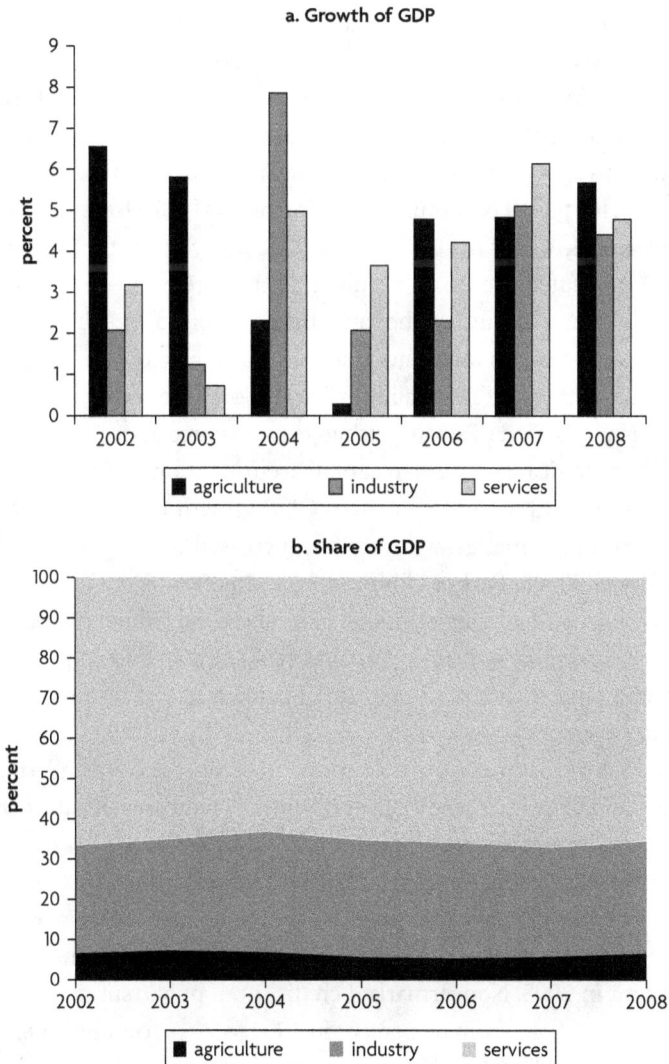

a. Growth of GDP

b. Share of GDP

Source: IBGE.

the services sector to GDP stayed consistently positive. The strong performance of all three sectors left sectoral GDP composition unchanged during the period.

Another benefit of the acceleration of economic growth in the pre-global crisis period was the substantial and consistent growth of factor productivity. From 2002 to 2008, the contribution of TFP to growth averaged 1.1 percentage points and accounted for 29 percent of growth. Physical capital and human capital continued to contribute positively to GDP growth (0.9 and 0.6 percentage points) and accounted for 22 percent and 15 percent of growth, respectively. Labor contributed 1.4 percentage points or 34 percent of GDP growth.

Productivity growth has benefited from the structural reforms of the 1990s and the global economic expansion of 2003–08. However, the negative external shocks of the late 1990s and the first years of the 2000s appear to have prevented the positive effects of these reforms on productivity from fully materializing. At the same time, a more competitive economy has increased Brazil's ability to take advantage of global expansions, as evidenced by the increase in all Brazilian exports (not only commodities) even during a period of strong exchange rate appreciation.[8]

Higher physical and human capital accumulation and increased productivity brought a higher potential GDP growth rate. Studies indicate that Brazil's potential growth rate has increased to 4.5 percent (OEDC 2009; Bonelli 2005; Barbosa Filho and Pessôa 2009).

Another recent development that may have contributed to productivity growth has been the impressive expansion of credit in the economy. Credit has been growing at annual rates of 15 percent in real terms since 2003, fostered by such reforms as the bankruptcy law, enhanced access to credit for many low-income groups (due to more liberal collateral rules for housing and consumer credit), the creation of credit securitization instruments, and improved access to external credit markets by Brazilian firms and banks. As a result, the credit-to-GDP ratio soared from 26 percent in 2002 to 40 percent in 2008. In addition, the private sector and foreign financial institutions' share of total credit grew from 55 percent in 2002 to 65 percent in 2008. Nonearmarked credit (non–public subsidized credit) also raised its share, from 60 percent in 2002 to 72 percent in 2008.

While the credit expansion increased delinquency and nonperforming loan (NPL) rates in the months leading up to the crisis, the Brazilian banking system has remained solid. Profitability, solvency, and asset quality indicators have all been strong. As a whole, the ratio of capital to risk-weighted assets was 17 percent before the crisis, in August 2008, well above the minimum 11 percent required by Brazilian law and by Basel II. Recent changes in regulations fostered this increase in capital adequacy ratios.

Social Protection. On the social side, higher growth—as reflected in rising labor income and employment—and the introduction of enhanced social policies helped reduce poverty and income inequality. The poverty rate fell from 33 percent in 2003 to 22 percent in 2008, paced by increases in labor income, a sharp fall in unemployment, and well-targeted conditional cash transfer programs. From 2003 to 2008, labor income increased by 20 percent in real terms, while the unemployment rate fell from 12 percent in 2003 to 8 percent in 2008. In total, more than 30 million people freed themselves from poverty between 2002 and 2008. Income inequality also fell, with the Gini index dropping from 0.58 in 2003 to 0.56 in 2008 as a result of a reduction in educational disparities, substantial increases in the national minimum wage, and the expansion of cash transfer programs. The country's major conditional cash transfer program, Programa Bolsa Familia, contributed substantially to reducing poverty in the past decade (figure 3.9), especially extreme poverty. The incidence of extreme poverty would be an estimated 9 percent without Bolsa Familia transfers, instead of the observed 7.5 percent; this represents a reduction in extreme poverty of almost 15 percent.

The Brazilian government's establishment and expansion of a broad social protection network has further bolstered domestic demand. The incorporation of a large part of the population into the social protection network has not only expanded the domestic market, but also hedged against the effects of economic activity and employment fluctuations on income, as the cash transfers received by the beneficiaries are not sensitive to macroeconomic cycles.

Challenges to Long-Term Growth. Despite these remarkable improvements, the Brazilian economy before the global crisis still faced challenges in guaranteeing sustainable growth in the long run. The first of

Figure 3.9. Poverty Rates and Conditional Cash Transfers, 1992–2008

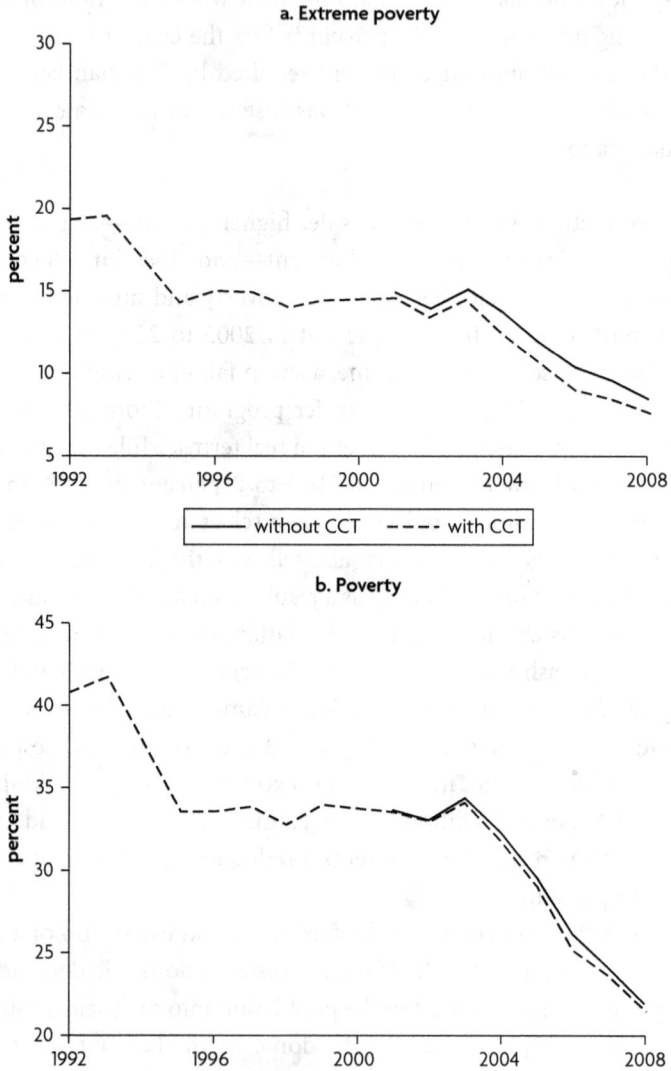

a. Extreme poverty

without CCT   ---- with CCT

b. Poverty

Source: IBGE; authors' calculations.
Note: CCT = conditional cash transfer.

these was the low domestic saving and investment rates. Recent increases notwithstanding, domestic saving and capital formation have been fluctuating between 15 and 20 percent of GDP, levels that may pose an obstacle to more robust and sustained growth (table 3.7). Low domestic

Table 3.7. Brazil's Macroeconomic Indicators, 2002–08

Indicator	2002	2003	2004	2005	2006	2007	2008
National accounts							
GDP (US$ billions)	504	552	664	882	1,089	1,333	1,613
Population (millions)	179.1	181.5	183.8	186.1	188.2	190.1	192.0
Population growth (%)	1.4	1.3	1.3	1.2	1.1	1.1	1.0
GDP per capita (US$)	2,815	3,043	3,610	4,741	5,788	7,013	8,399
Real GDP growth (%)	2.7	1.1	5.7	3.2	4.0	6.1	5.1
Supply side							
Agriculture growth (%)	6.6	5.8	2.3	0.3	4.8	4.8	5.7
Industry growth (%)	2.1	1.3	7.9	2.1	2.3	5.2	4.4
Services growth (%)	3.2	0.8	5.0	3.7	4.2	6.1	4.8
Demand side							
Consumption growth (%)	2.6	−0.3	3.9	3.9	4.5	5.9	5.4
Investment growth (%)	−5.2	−4.6	9.1	3.6	9.8	13.5	13.8
Investment (% GDP)	16.4	15.3	16.1	15.9	16.4	17.5	19.0
Public sector	3.7	2.6	3.2	3.3	3.3	3.3	3.3
Private sector	12.7	12.7	12.9	12.6	13.1	14.2	15.7
Gross national savings (% GDP)	14.7	16.0	18.5	17.3	17.6	17.5	16.9
External sector							
Trade balance (US$ billions)	13.1	24.8	33.7	44.7	46.1	40.3	24.8
Current account balance (US$ billions)	−7.6	4.2	11.7	14.0	13.6	1.6	−28.2
Current account balance (% GDP)	−1.5	0.7	1.8	1.6	1.3	0.1	−1.8
Foreign direct investment (US$ billions)	16.6	10.1	18.1	15.1	18.8	34.5	45.1
International reserves (US$ billions)	37.8	49.3	52.9	53.8	85.8	180.3	206.8
External debt (US$ billions)	228	235	220	188	199	240	267
External debt to exports (%)	377	322	228	159	145	149	135
Interest payments to exports (%)	23.6	19.4	14.8	12.2	10.8	9.5	7.1
Nominal exchange rate (end of period)	3.53	2.89	2.65	2.34	2.14	1.77	2.3
Real effective exchange rate (2000 = 100)	82.2	77.4	81.8	100.3	112.9	123.3	130.8
Public Sector							
Primary balance (% GDP)	3.5	3.9	4.2	4.4	3.9	3.9	4.1
Overall balance (% GDP)	−4.4	−5.1	−2.8	−3.4	−3.5	−2.7	−1.9
Net public sector debt (% GDP)	50.5	52.3	47.0	46.5	44.7	42.0	36.0
Prices and economic activity							
Consumer inflation (%)	12.5	9.3	7.6	5.7	3.3	4.1	5.9
Headline interest rate (avg. %)	19.2	23.8	16.4	19.1	15.3	12.0	12.5
Unemployment (%)	11.7	12.3	11.5	9.8	10.0	9.3	7.9
Industrial capital utilization (%)	79.4	80.5	83.3	84.5	83.3	85.1	85.2

Source: BCB; IBGE; IPEA.

savings implies that increased investments need to be financed by external savings (de Melo and Mogliani 2009).

Of course, low domestic savings are related to the government's low saving capacity. Despite the strong fiscal reform effort of the past decade, fiscal adjustment has been accomplished by curtailing public investment and increasing taxes. In particular, given Brazil's fiscal adjustment requirements, the growth of current expenditures—especially social-security payments and public sector salaries—significantly narrowed the fiscal space for investment. Government investment fell to less than 2 percent of GDP during the adjustment phase of 2003–04, rising to just 3 percent in 2007, a low level by historical and international standards. In addition, the fiscal adjustment was based on an extraordinary tax collection effort. The tax burden grew to exceed 36 percent of GDP in 2008 (up from 25 percent in 1994). Low public investment and high government consumption and taxation continue to limit Brazil's growth potential (Blanco and Herrera 2007).

Furthermore, the modest contribution of human capital to growth suggests the need for better educational attainment and health outcomes. Despite the recent increase in these indicators, human capital growth in the past 16 years has been very low, at just 0.1 percent a year. While the country has achieved universal primary education, and while labor force schooling has increased, the acceleration of human capital accumulation will require public sector reforms to improve the quality of educational services.

Finally, the resumption of the structural reform agenda would substantially increase Brazil's growth potential. On the external front, despite the increased importance of trade to the country's economy, Brazilian markets remain relatively closed, not only because of the size of the domestic economy relative to the external sector, but also because of lingering tariff protection. Low dependence on foreign economies and international markets could prove to be an advantage in the event of future worldwide economic crises, but in general low openness implies that macroeconomic adjustment could require further changes in the exchange rate and shifts in factor allocation and economic activity. On the domestic side, labor and financial market reforms to enhance labor flexibility and the country's competitiveness would further alleviate the negative shocks the country has been forced to weather in the current global crisis.

The Global Financial Crisis and the Brazilian Economy

The impact of the global financial crisis on Brazil's economy has been immediate and extensive. Financial indicators fell sharply; access to credit was interrupted; capital flowed out and export demand collapsed, leading to a significant real depreciation; industrial production plummeted; and employment and labor income fell. But the country's solid macroeconomic fundamentals and a rapid and vigorous government response have contributed to a remarkably quick and robust recovery. Enhanced fiscal and external solvency led to the rapid return of capital flows, and financial indicators swiftly rebounded to the levels prevailing in the late 1990s and early 2000s. The government's credit, monetary, and fiscal stimulus package spurred the resumption of economic activity and the recovery of employment and labor income. Nonetheless, the global crisis interrupted the period of economic expansion that Brazil had enjoyed since 2003, and GDP growth in 2009 was slightly negative (a rate of −0.2 percent).

We will now describe the impacts of the global financial crisis on the Brazilian economy, the economic mechanisms by which those effects were realized, the government's policy response, and the rapid recovery after the crisis. We then discuss the factors that led to the recovery and, in particular, the considerable role of the sound macroeconomic policies adopted in the previous decade.

Impact Channels and Initial Effects

The immediate effects of the global financial crisis included contagion in financial markets, capital outflows, a lack of access to external credit, and a fall in commodity prices that put pressure on the exchange rate and further curtailed both external and domestic credit. From September 2008 through March 2009, the São Paulo Stock Market Index (Ibovespa) fell 25 percent, sovereign spreads increased 77 percent, and the Brazilian real depreciated by 40 percent (figure 3.10).

Credit Channel. The contraction of external credit markets was particularly damaging. External credit for exporters and small banks vanished. External rollover rates and average maturities fell sharply, while borrowing costs increased. The closing of external credit lines forced large corporations to turn to domestic credit markets, crowding out smaller

Figure 3.10. Sovereign Spreads, Exchange Rate, Stock Market Index, Commodity Prices, Exports, and External Balances

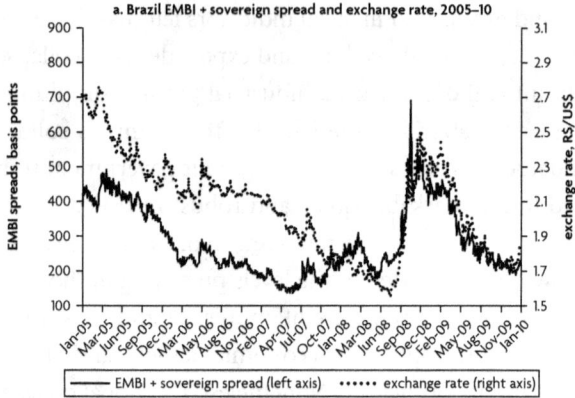

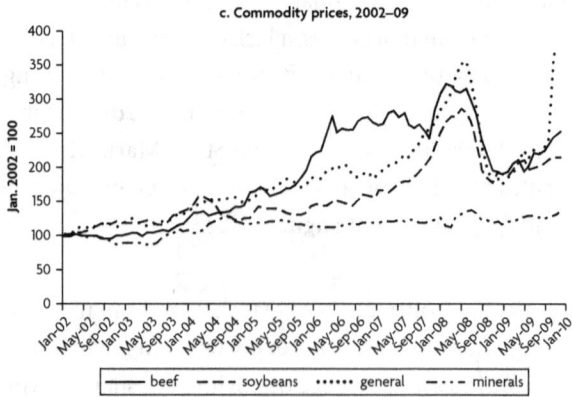

a. Brazil EMBI + sovereign spread and exchange rate, 2005–10

— EMBI + sovereign spread (left axis)   ⋯⋯ exchange rate (right axis)

b. Ibovespa stock market index, 2005–10

c. Commodity prices, 2002–09

—— beef   – – – soybeans   ⋯⋯ general   – · – minerals

d. Monthly trade balance, exports, and imports, 2002–09

US$ millions

23,000

18,000

13,000

8,000

3,000

−2,000

Dec-01 Apr-02 Aug-02 Dec-02 Apr-03 Aug-03 Dec-03 Apr-04 Aug-04 Dec-04 Apr-05 Aug-05 Dec-05 Apr-06 Aug-06 Dec-06 Apr-07 Aug-07 Dec-07 Apr-08 Aug-08 Dec-08 Apr-09 Aug-09 Dec-09

——— exports   – – – imports   ·········· trade balance

e. Current account and foreign direct investment, 2002–10

% GDP

5

3

1

−1

−3

−5

Sep-02 Jan-03 May-03 Sep-03 Jan-04 May-04 Sep-04 Jan-05 May-05 Sep-05 Jan-06 May-06 Sep-06 Jan-07 May-07 Sep-07 Jan-08 May-08 Sep-08 Jan-09 May-09 Sep-09 Jan-10

——— current account   – – – foreign direct investment

f. Exports and commodity prices, 2002–10

exports, US$ millions

23,000

18,000

13,000

8,000

3,000

−2,000

commodity prices, 2002 = 100

400

350

300

250

200

150

100

50

0

Jan-02 May-02 Jan-03 May-03 Jan-04 May-04 Jan-05 May-05 Jan-06 May-06 Jan-07 May-07 Jan-08 May-08 Jan-09 May-09 Jan-10

——— exports, US$ millions (left axis)   – – – commodity prices (right axis)

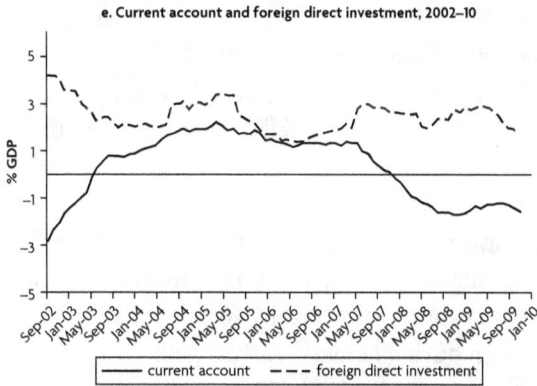

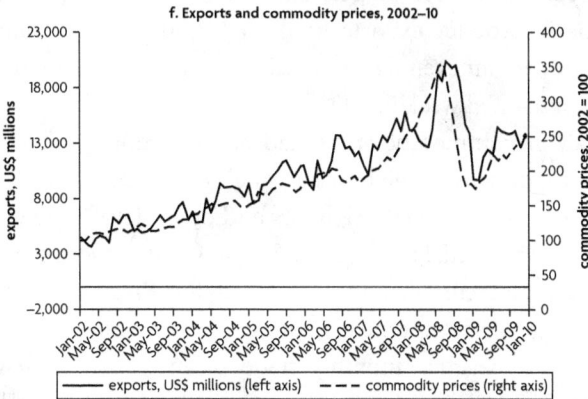

Source: BCB; IPEA.
Note: EMBI = Emerging Markets Bond Index.

firms that had previously relied on domestic credit. In addition, the sudden and dramatic exchange rate depreciation led to large losses for Brazilian corporations that used exchange-based derivatives contracts. Small financial institutions were particularly hurt by the credit crunch, as they depended on wholesale funds and foreign credit lines. The increase in NPLs put additional pressure on the cash position of these institutions and triggered a run on small banks. Nevertheless, because the larger banks enjoyed considerable liquidity and reliable access to additional funding, the effects of the confidence crisis on small institutions did not spread to the whole financial system.

Domestic credit, which had been growing at monthly rates of 2–3 percent since 2005, slowed to just 0.2 percent in January and 0.1 percent in February 2009. Consumer credit was the most affected, having been hit early in the last quarter of 2008; the effects spread to corporate credit at the beginning of 2009, which fell 0.8 percent in January.

Exports Channel. The slump in global economic activity reduced both commodity prices (by more than 30 percent) and export demand for Brazilian manufactures. The drop in commodity prices and global demand caused exports to decline by 40 percent, from a monthly average of US$20 billion during January–August 2008 to less than US$12 billion during September 2008–March 2009. The falling commodity prices caused basic product exports to drop by 30 percent. Manufactures exports suffered an even deeper decline (33 percent), and, unlike basic products, remained weak in 2009.

The fall in commodity prices had an additional indirect effect on Brazilian exports. As noted earlier, the main importers of Brazilian manufactures—its regional neighbors and other developing countries—also suffered substantial terms-of-trade losses that reduced their purchasing capacity and curtailed their demand for Brazilian manufactures. In January 2009, the combined fall of export commodities and manufactures led to a negative monthly trade balance for the first time in seven years. However, the domestic economic deceleration simultaneously reduced imports from a monthly average of US$18 billion basis to one of US$10 billion, and monthly trade balances quickly returned to the positive levels that prevailed before the crisis, though at a drastically reduced volume. Spurred by the fall in the trade balance, the deterioration of the current account balance, already evident at the start of 2008, accelerated. But the contraction of economic activity narrowed the current account deficit.

Capital Flow Channel. Another impact of the crisis was the shifting direction of capital flows. While FDI flows were not reduced substantially, portfolio investment outflows were massive. Indeed, FDI and portfolio investments responded very differently to the crisis, establishing trends that continued into the recovery period, which began in March 2009. From September to December 2008, FDI flows reached US$20 billion and then peaked at US$45 billion for all of 2008. In 2009, however, FDI flows were substantially lower, at US$26 billion—43 percent less than in 2008.

Portfolio investments, on the other hand, shifted direction in September 2008. From September 2008 to March 2009, portfolio investment outflows totaled US$23 billion. Nevertheless, portfolio inflows recovered strongly after March 2009 and totaled US$46 billion for the full year 2009. These sizable capital inflows contributed to the appreciation of the Brazilian real since March 2009 (figures 3.10 and 3.11).

Figure 3.11. Capital Inflows, 2002–09

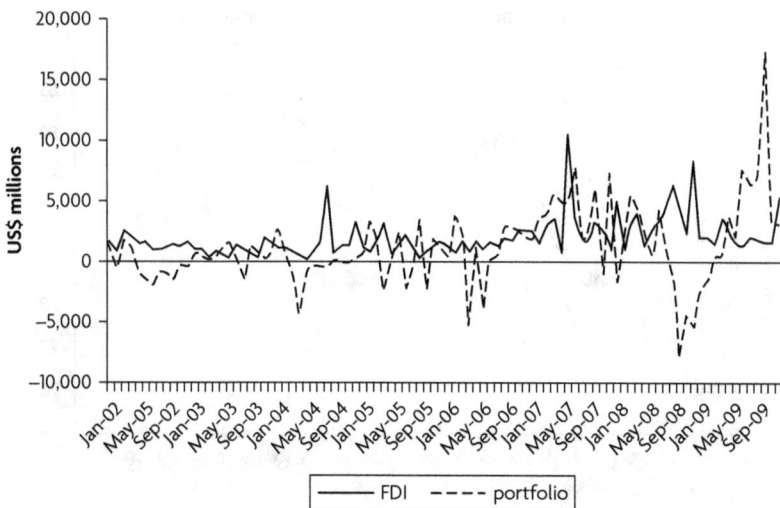

Source: BCB.

The Real Economy Channel. The effects of the crisis on Brazil's real economy were also sharp and immediate. After 12 consecutive quarters of expansion, GDP contracted in the fourth quarter (Q4) of 2008 by 3.4 percent (quarter on quarter) and in Q1 2009 by 1.0 percent (figure 3.12). This decline was driven by the shrinking credit supply, which interrupted the

Figure 3.12. GDP Growth, Industrial Production, Unemployment, and Inflation

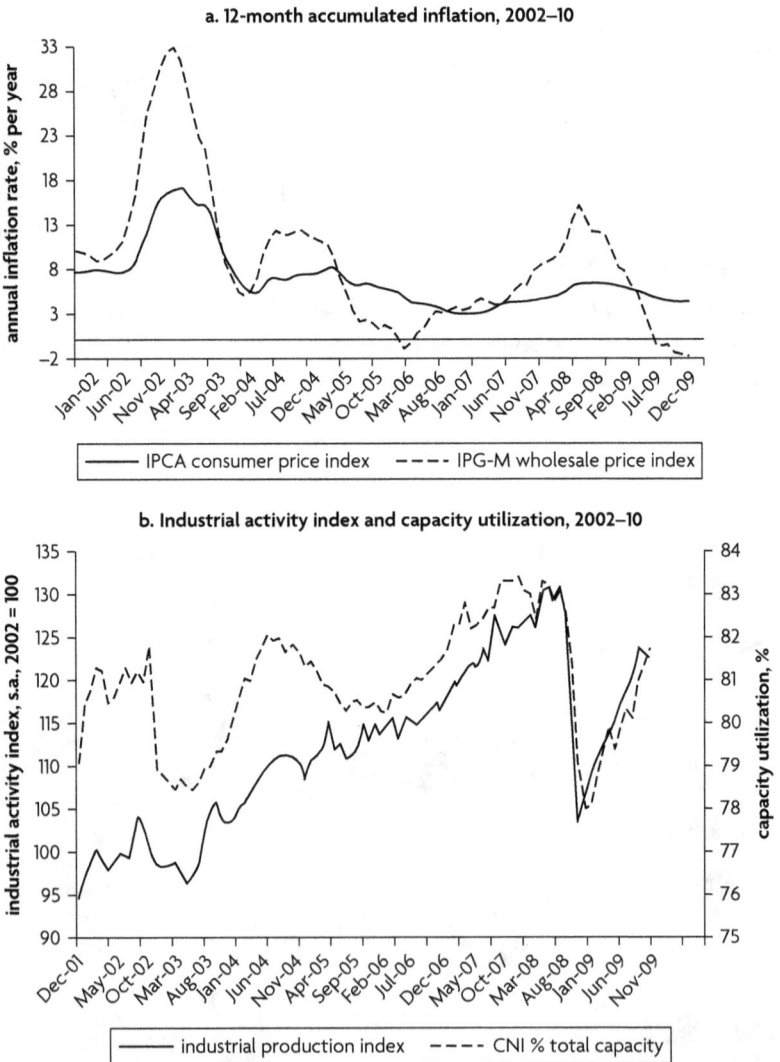

a. 12-month accumulated inflation, 2002–10

b. Industrial activity index and capacity utilization, 2002–10

c. Unemployment rate, 2002–10

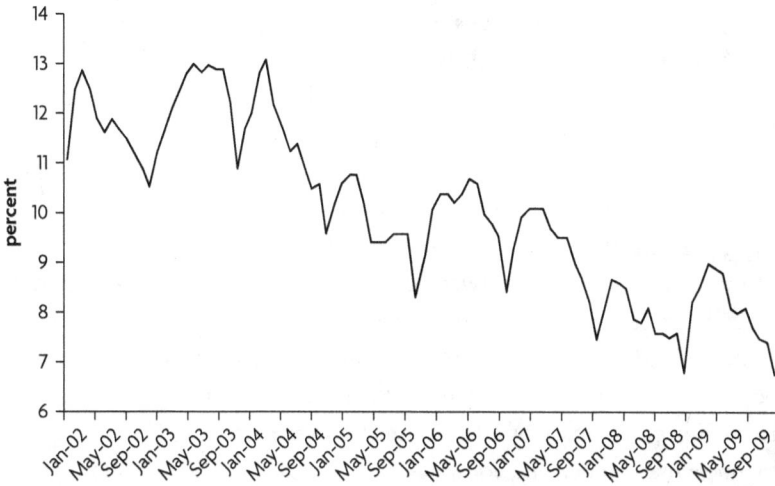

d. Contribution to GDP growth by demand components, 2004–10

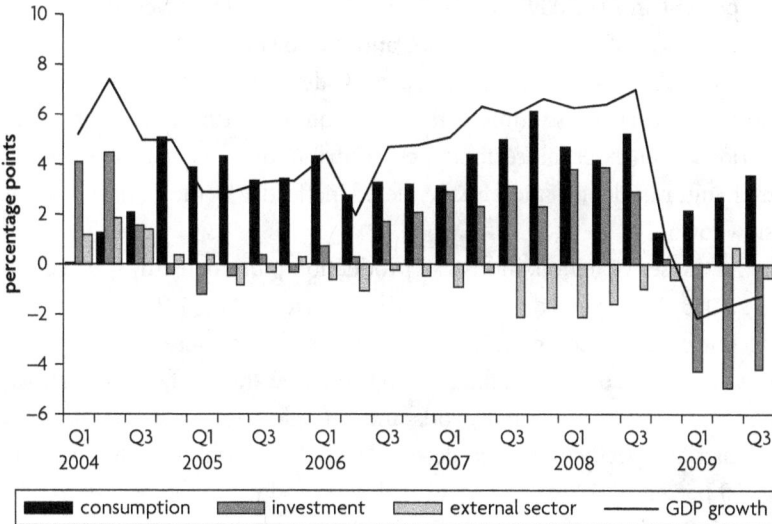

consumption   investment   external sector   GDP growth

Source: IBGE; IPEA; FGV (Getulio Vargas Foundation).
Note: CNI = Confederação Nacional de Indústrias; s.a. = seasonally adjusted.

rising trends in investment and durable goods consumption of the pre-crisis period. The high inventories at the end of 2008 (and their exhaustion after the crisis) added further downward pressure, while the disruption in the credit markets caused a sharp drop in investment, which, in turn, has been the main cause of slowing GDP growth. Investment demand was the most affected, dropping by 9.1 percent in Q4 2008 and 12.3 percent in Q1 2009, for a total drop of 22 percent in the two quarters following the crisis. Household consumption fell by 1.4 percent in Q4 2008 but recovered immediately in Q1 2009, when it grew by 0.6 percent. Government consumption grew by 0.3 percent and 0.8 percent in the same quarters, contributing positively to GDP growth. Exports fell by 4.1 percent in Q4 2008 and 15.8 percent in Q1 2009, for a total of 20 percent. In terms of categories, manufactured exports suffered the deepest slump, with a fall of more than 30 percent between 2008 and 2009. With the quick recovery of commodity prices, exports of basic products fell only 5 percent. In terms of destination, trade with Mercosur was the most affected (falling by 36 percent). Exports to the United States fell by 30 percent and exports to the European Union by 20 percent. However, trade with China increased by more than 50 percent, compensating partially for the losses in regional and developed markets. Imports also fell by 7 percent in Q4 2008 and 12 percent in Q1 2009, for a total of 18 percent. But given the reduced participation of the external sector and the collapse of domestic demand, the contribution of weakening external demand to the downturn was limited. Nevertheless, unlike the situation in previous contractionary periods, the external sector's net contribution was negative because exchange rate depreciation was rendered ineffective by the global economic slowdown.

At the sectoral level, industrial production plummeted by 8 percent in Q4 2008 and dropped an additional 3.2 percent in Q1 2009, for a total decline of 12 percent in the first two quarters after the onset of the financial crisis. Associated with the fall in credit shortage and the fall in investment demand, output of capital goods and durable goods suffered the most. Industrial capacity utilization declined from 87 percent in September 2008 to 78 percent in March 2009. Agricultural production fell by 2 percent in Q4 2008 and by 1.4 percent in Q1 2009, for a total decline of 3.5 percent. Services fell by 0.5 percent in Q4 2008 but recovered immediately, rising 0.6 percent in Q1 2009. Market-based GDP growth forecasts were revised downward from a positive 5 percent before September 2008 to a negative 1.5 percent in March 2009.

The labor market was already feeling the effects of the downturn by the end of 2008. After years of sustained employment growth, unemployment rates spiked, especially in January, when urban unemployment experienced its largest increase ever—to 8.2 percent from 6.8 percent in December. About 650,000 formal sector workers lost their jobs in December 2008, mostly in export-oriented states like São Paulo. The bulk of the initial job losses were caused by a sudden freeze in hiring in the formal sector. While the impact was felt mainly in formal export and industrial jobs, other sectors were also hit. This initial pattern reflected the decline in export demand for manufactures and basic goods. Formal retail sector employment, which was increasing in November 2008 (with 77,000 new jobs added), began falling in January 2009 and continued falling, indicating that impacts on domestic employment demand had extended beyond export-oriented firms. The widening scope of the crisis was also evident in the informal sector. Informal workers suffered smaller initial job losses, but declines in informal employment were sustained throughout April and May, especially because of the reduced number of self-employed and household workers.

After falling temporarily in September 2008, real wages in metropolitan areas continued to increase until the end of 2008 and resumed their normal decreasing seasonal trend in the first months of 2009 (figure 3.13). Accordingly, the proportion of people living below the poverty line (those with an income of less than half the minimum wage of about US$230) displayed the same pattern, falling until December 2008 and then rising again until March 2009.[9]

Given the decline in output and capacity utilization, TFP dropped 2.9 percent in the Q3 2008 and accounted for 85 percent of the total output fall. The reduction of capacity utilization accounted for 35 percent of this drop, while capital and labor accumulations were each responsible for −10 percent (figure 3.14).

The Government's Policy Response

The credibility built up over the previous decade allowed the government to swiftly adopt strong anticrisis measures. The government's response consisted of steps to alleviate the liquidity squeeze and the adoption of countercyclical monetary and fiscal policies and measures to expand the supply of credit made available by public sector financial institutions.

The government's first reaction was to alleviate the liquidity squeeze affecting Brazilian corporations, exporters, and small financial institutions. The central bank took several steps to inject liquidity into

Figure 3.13. Wages and Poverty in Metropolitan Areas, 2002–09

Source: IBGE; authors' calculations.

Figure 3.14. GDP Growth Decomposition, 2003–10

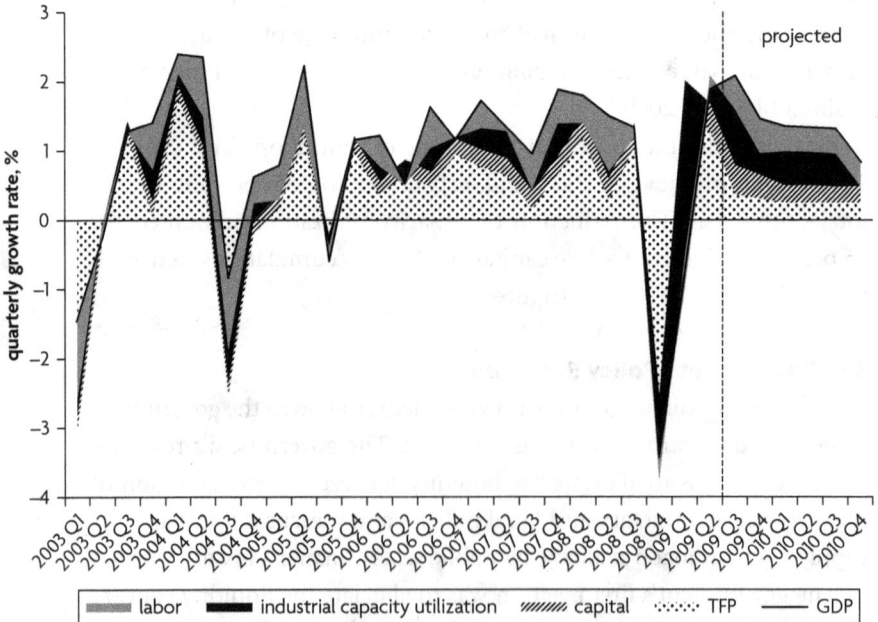

Source: IBGE; authors' calculations.

domestic markets and provide foreign exchange to Brazilian corporations with obligations abroad. To alleviate private sector problems in raising resources in domestic and foreign markets and to avoid steeper exchange rate depreciation, the government:

- made several reductions in reserve requirements,
- gave direct support to small financial institutions experiencing liquidity constraints,
- gave incentives to large financial institutions to buy smaller ones with liquidity problems,
- held repo-credit line auctions in U.S. dollars for exporters, and
- sold international reserves to give an injection to the spot exchange rate market.

To avoid further contagion of the financial system stemming from the difficult liquidity conditions faced by small banks, Brazil's Deposit Insurance Fund's deposit threshold was increased. Incentives for large banks to use the reduction in reserve requirements to transfer resources to small banks also injected liquidity to smaller financial institutions, eliminating any possibility of a systemic crisis in the domestic financial sector. In addition, public banks massively increased their lending to industry and agriculture in order to compensate for the contraction of the private credit supply. The government's swift response successfully normalized credit market conditions almost immediately. Domestic credit and access to foreign credit have since returned to their precrisis levels.

The BCB's strong reputation for controlling inflation allowed it to initiate an aggressive reduction in interest rates. The moderating inflation coupled with the economic slowdown opened space for the easing of monetary policy. Consistent with the fall in inflation and inflation expectations, the central bank cut the policy interest rate by 500 bps, from 13.75 percent in September 2008 to 8.75 percent in July 2009 (a historical low) and maintained its throughout 2009.

The government complemented these measures by adopting a countercyclical fiscal stance, but there is some controversy about the actual size and countercyclicality of the fiscal stimulus. A large portion of the increase in government expenses in 2009 was the result not of the new expansionary fiscal policy, but of decisions made before the emergence of the global crisis, including increases in public sector wages and social security benefits. Indeed, before the crisis the Brazilian government had been accelerating its current spending through increases in operating costs, public employees' wages, and social protection transfers. By the time the crisis broke out, the government had already expanded its recurrent spending. This limited the fiscal space for discretionary increases, and the countercyclical fiscal stimulus consisted primarily of tax breaks and the acceleration of preplanned capital investment.

The combination of falling revenues linked to the economic slowdown, increases in current expenditures, tax breaks, the effect of automatic stabilizers, and increases in capital spending reduced the public sector's consolidated primary surplus to 2.4 percent of GDP in January–June 2009 from 5.9 percent in the year-earlier period. As a result, net public debt expanded from 39 percent of GDP in December 2008 to 44 percent in July 2009.

While the discretionary portion of the fiscal stimulus aimed at cushioning the effects of the financial crisis has been relatively small, the fall in government revenues and the increase in current spending resulting from previous government decisions and automatic stabilizers' effects have been substantial and are the main reasons for the deterioration of government fiscal balances during the first semester of 2009 (table 3.8). The federal primary surplus fell to 1.3 percent in January–June 2009, down from 4.4 percent in the same period in 2008—a drop of 3.1 percent of GDP, or 71 percent from its previous level.[10]

The causes of the narrowing of the federal primary surplus include the effect of the economic slowdown on tax revenues, the cost of the countercyclical fiscal stimulus package, and the increase in nonreversible current expenditures. Federal revenues declined by 1.2 percent of GDP, accounting for 39 percent of the decline in the primary surplus. About 25 percent of the narrowing in the primary surplus, or −0.8 percent of GDP, can be attributed to the economic slowdown itself.

During January–June 2009, current expenditures as a share of GDP grew by 1.8 percentage points relative to January–June 2008, accounting for 57 percent of the federal government's primary surplus reduction (table 3.8). Increases in civil service wages amounted to 0.7 percentage point, or 22 percent of the decline in the primary fiscal balance. Increases in the national minimum wage, with concomitant effects on social security and other social protection benefits (such as the Permanent Benefit

Table 3.8. Decomposition of Federal Government Primary Balance Reduction, 2008–09

	2008, Jan–Jun (% GDP)	2009, Jan–Jun (% GDP)	Change (% GDP)	Percent change	Contribution to the primary balance reduction (%)
Total revenue	24.7	23.5	-1.2	-4.9	38.9
Treasury	19.6	18.0	–1.6	–8.3	51.4
Taxes	9.4	8.7	–0.7	–7.6	22.8
Of which: Income tax	5.3	5.0	–0.3	–6.2	10.5
Federal VAT–IPI	1.0	0.7	–0.3	–32.9	10.5
Other revenues	10.3	9.4	–0.9	–8.7	28.6
Social security contributions	5.3	5.7	0.4	7.2	–12.1
Expenditures	**20.3**	**22.2**	**1.9**	**9.4**	**61.1**
Current expenditures	19.6	21.4	1.8	9.1	57.3
Personnel	4.3	5.0	0.7	16.3	22.4
Social security benefits	6.6	7.1	0.5	8.3	17.4
Intergovernmental transfers	4.5	4.4	–0.1	–1.8	–2.6
Operating costs	2.9	3.4	0.5	18.0	16.5
Unemployment insurance	0.5	0.7	0.2	35.8	6.2
Social protection (BPC, LOAS)	0.6	0.7	0.1	13.5	2.4
Subsidies	0.2	0.0	–0.2	–100.0	–5.8
Investment expenditures	0.7	0.8	0.1	17.2	3.9
Primary balance	**(4.4)**	**(1.3)**	**(3.1)**	**70.9**	**100**

Source: STN=National Treasury Secretariat; authors' calculations.
Note: VAT = value added tax; IPI = Imposto sobre Produtos Industrializados.

for Elderly People [BPC] and the benefits from the Organic Law of Social Protection [LOAS]), amounted to 0.8 percentage point, representing about 25 percent of the decline in the primary surplus. Given the importance of government consumption and the broad coverage of the social security and social protection networks, this expansion of wages and benefits prevented a further drop in private consumption demand.

As noted above, the contribution of reversible, countercyclical fiscal stimulus has been limited. Including automatic stabilizers (lower income tax receipts and increased unemployment insurance payouts), discretionary tax cuts (temporary cuts to the tax on industrial products [Imposto sobre Produtos Industriais] and taxes on financial operations [Impostos sobre Operações Financeiras] to foster economic activity and increase available credit), and the acceleration of government investment expenses, the countercyclical stimulus amounted to 1 percent of GDP, and accounted for only 30 percent of the decrease in the primary surplus.

The main component of the government's stimulus program was the credit supplied by public financial institutions. This credit expansion was financed by two loans amounting to R$180 billion (US$100 billion)—about 6 percent of GDP—in 2009 and 2010 from the National Treasury to the Federal Economic and Social Development Bank (Banco Nacional de Desenvolvimento Econômico e Social, BNDES) to allow the latter to expand its subsidized credit supply to the industrial sector. To finance BNDES activities, the Treasury issued bonds that increased its gross debt by 6 percent of GDP. As the Treasury lending to BNDES is registered as an asset in the government's book while it issues government bonds (liability) to lend to the BNDES, the effect on government net debt is neutral. Nonetheless, it has an implicit fiscal cost as the spread between the rate paid by government bonds and the rate charged by the government to the BNDES, the Long-Term Interest Rate (Taxa de Juros de Longo Prazo), which in turn is the rate used by the BNDES for its loans to the industrial sector (added by an operational spread). This cost increases with the spread and the amount of BNDES credit. In fact, the spread multiplied by the amount of BNDES lending is a subsidy from the government to the private sector.[11]

In addition, as part of its anticrisis package, the government created a new housing program for low-income households financed by the Federal Severance Bank (Caixa Econômica Federal). The government also made credit lines available through the Bank of Brazil (Banco do Brasil) to support agricultural exporters affected by the credit squeeze.[12]

The expansion of public banks' available credit was rapid and strong and led to a large increase in the total credit-to-GDP ratio, from 36 percent in August 2008 to 45 percent in December 2009. Credit from public financial institutions grew from 11 to 19 percent of GDP in the same period, while credit from private and foreign institutions grew from 25 percent of GDP to 26 percent. As a result, the public banks' share in total outstanding credit grew to 42 percent in December 2009 from

34 percent in September 2008. While the expansionary stimulus provided by public banks appears to have been effective in restoring the overall credit supply, the long-term effects of this strategy on the balance sheets of public financial institutions may prove to be important, and contingent liabilities may emerge in the future. Another potential long-term effect is the reversal of the previous trend of increasing participation by private banks and nonsubsidized credit in domestic credit markets observed in the past few years.

Reaping the Benefits of Consistent, Prudent Policies

Brazil has been able to avoid a deeper economic downturn and to quickly work its way through the global crisis because of its strong macroeconomic foundations (built and reinforced over the previous decade), a solid financial sector, and swift government policy responses. Since the second quarter of 2009, financial, external, and economic activity has recovered robustly. Improvements in the global economic environment have also contributed substantially. In 2009, the Ibovespa stock market index grew by 77 percent, sovereign spreads returned to their precrisis levels of about 250 bps, and the Brazilian real appreciated by 25 percent from its low in December 2008, also returning to its precrisis level. Capital inflows resumed their precrisis trend and closed out 2009 with an impressive net inflow of US$46 billion. The country's international reserves reached US$239 billion in December 2009, well above their precrisis high of US$205 billion in August 2008.

The easing of monetary policy, the expansion of the credit supply by public banks, tax breaks for durable goods consumption, the increase in government consumption, and the recovery of commodity prices have enabled a rapid and strong economic recovery. In Q2 2009, GDP grew by 1.1 percent and consolidated its gains in Q3 2009 with a growth rate of 1.3 percent. Capped by a GDP growth rate of 2 percent in Q4 2009, the Brazilian economy ended the year with only a slight overall decline of 0.2 percent (table 3.9). First- and second-quarter GDP growth figures in 2010 and market forecasts for 2010 suggest a strong GDP expansion of about 7 percent.

The solvency of the financial system has been a further stabilizing factor. By the end of 2008, the liquidity squeeze had relaxed and the credit supply resumed its increasing trend. The financial sector did not

Table 3.9. Summary Impact of the Crisis

	1997–2002	2003–07	Change from 1997–2002 to 2003–07	Highest two-year average value before crisis	Expected potential value just prior to the crisis	2008	2009	Total loss during 2008–09 compared to potential (% GDP)
GDP growth (%)	2.0	4.2	2.2	5.6	4.5	5.1	−0.2	5.0
TFP growth (%)	−1.1	1.4	2.5	2.4	2.0	2.4	−2.2	4.2
Exports growth (%)	8.7	7.7	−1.0	12.0	5.0	−0.6	−10.3	25.0
Exports (% GDP)	8.6	13.0	4.4	14.0	15.0	13.8	11.2	6.0
Investment (% GDP)	17.2	16.9	−0.3	19.1	20.0	20.0	16.7	4.0
Capacity utilization (%)	80.5	84.0	3.5	85.0	87.0	85.2	79.5	7.5
Capital inflows (% GDP)	3.1	1.4	−1.7	4.0	4.0	1.7	4.2	−0.2
Fiscal deficit (% GDP)	4.8	3.1	−1.7	2.1	1.5	1.9	3.5	2.0

Source: IBGE; BCB; authors' calculations.

experience an asset crisis similar to that observed in many developed (and some emerging) economies. In addition, the market value of Brazilian banks did not fall either during or after the crisis.[13] The prudent regulatory framework and tight oversight mechanisms had ensured high reserve ratios by Brazilian banks in the precrisis period, reinforcing their stability during the crisis. Furthermore, given their good financial condition, Brazilian banks were able to increase their reserves during the crisis. In addition, the profitability of domestic banks did not decline during the crisis—yet another crucial difference from the experience of more developed economies. Finally, because of the conservative regulatory regime, the capitalization ratio of Brazilian banks has remained at about 17 percent, well above the minimum level recommended by Basel II (8 percent) and required by Brazilian legislation (11 percent). On the whole, the banking sector has weathered the global crisis extremely well, strengthening the resilience of the Brazilian economy as a whole (Cirne de Toledo 2009).

Meanwhile, domestic demand has driven the recovery of GDP growth. Consumption was the main component of economic activity in the first part of 2009, while capital formation rebounded strongly in the second part. Fueled by the fiscal stimulus measures, government consumption grew by 4.5 percent in Q1 2009 (relative to the year-earlier quarter) and remained steady in the following quarters, then fell slightly to 3.7 percent for 2009 as a whole. Following a 1.8 percent drop in Q4 2008, household consumption bounced back in 2009, growing by 2.4 percent, maintaining a 1.5–2.0 percent growth rate in Q2–Q4 2009, and reaching an annual growth rate of 4.1 percent for the year.

After an 11 percent slump in Q4 2008 and Q1 2009, capital formation grew by 2 percent in Q3 2009 and recovered vigorously in Q3–Q4 2009, with growth rates of 6.7 percent and of 6.6 percent, respectively. But the accumulated decline in capital formation in 2009 reached 17 percent, which shows that investment has been the demand component most affected by the global crisis.

After a combined fall of 21 percent in Q4 2008 and Q1 2009, exports grew 7 percent in Q2 2009. But they stagnated thereafter due to the weaker economic recovery of Brazil's key trading partners and the appreciation of the exchange rate, beginning in March 2009. The net result was 10 percent decline in 2009. The flexible exchange rate's buffering function was unable to shore up exports given the worldwide economic slowdown. Imports also experienced a modest 4 percent recovery in Q2 2009 and rose a further 1.8 percent in Q3 2009 after plummeting 25 percent in the previous semester. As a result, imports fell 11 percent in 2009.

At the sectoral level, after falling steeply after the crisis, industry also recovered steadily and posted a 1.5 percent growth rate in Q2 2009 followed by 3 percent in Q3 and 4 percent in Q4, substantially mitigating an overall drop of 5.5 percent in 2009. Agriculture lagged the other sectors, falling continuously until Q3 2009, stabilizing in Q4, and closing the year with a total decline of 5 percent. Services posted a positive growth rate ranging between 1.5 percent and 3 percent in 2009 and recorded a growth rate of 2.6 percent for the year.

The overall decline of 0.2 percent of GDP in 2009 was smaller than expected in the wake of the crisis. The government's effective policy response, and especially its efforts to reestablish credit and reduce interest rates along with tax breaks for vehicles and durable goods, seems to have avoided a deeper slump. While it is difficult to estimate the impact of the global crisis in the absence of the government's policy response (the counterfactual), the evolution of market expectations regarding GDP growth in 2009 reveal how market participants perceived the impact of the crisis before the government's response had been announced. Prior to the crisis, GDP was expected to grow by about 4 percent (figure 3.15). At the beginning of 2009 these expectations were sharply lowered and a GDP decline of about 1.5 percent was expected. The recovery of economic activity since the second quarter led to a gradual revision of market expectations, and by the end of the year GDP growth rate expectations were near zero. The improvement in market expectations can be partly attributed to the government's policy response and to general confidence in the continuity of its sound economic policies.

A further positive development has been the solid performance of the labor market. By the end of 2009 the unemployment rate had hit a historic low, and job creation returned to the level in the first part of 2008. Wages and poverty in metropolitan areas also improved during the year. The quick recovery of job creation, the decline in unemployment, and the rise of labor income—together with the expansion of the credit supply—has bolstered domestic consumption demand. High levels of domestic demand in turn helped shield the Brazilian economy during the financial crisis.

Figure 3.15. Market Expectations for 2009 GDP Growth

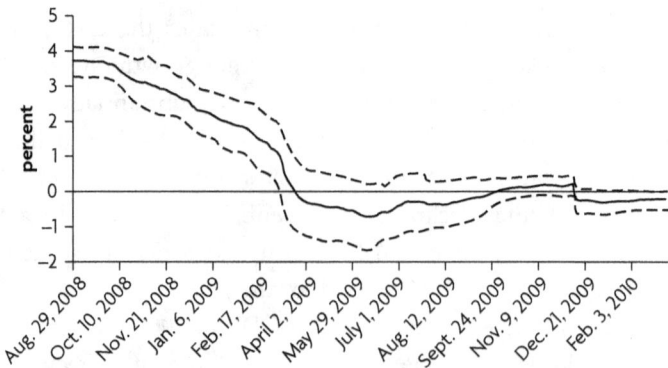

Source: BCB.

Projections for productivity, capital, and labor accumulation, as well as capacity utilization, all indicate a strong recovery in potential GDP growth in 2010. Currently, this recovery is being driven by increased capital utilization followed by the resumption of TFP growth. Increases in capital accumulation and employment began in the third quarter of 2009, and by the end of 2010 potential GDP growth is expected to reach an annual rate of about 4.5 percent, the same level before the global crisis.

Medium-Term Growth Prospects

With the more intense effects of the global crisis continuing to diminish and normalcy returning, expectations about Brazil's medium-term growth prospects are highly positive. The strong performance of the Brazilian economy during the crisis has eliminated any remaining skepticism about the stability of Brazil's macroeconomic foundations or its ability to cope with severe adverse external shocks. The country's strong resilience, coupled with its rapid and sustained economic recovery, has generated renewed optimism about Brazil's growth potential.

In a sense, the global crisis has provided Brazil's economy an opportunity to pass a severe stress test and to demonstrate that its robust economic performance in 2003–08 could not be attributed only to favorable external conditions. Brazil's encouraging performance during this stress test has placed it in a better position than it was in before the crisis. The recovery of FDI and portfolio investment flows since March 2009 has demonstrated the country's heightened attractiveness to international investors. And the evolution of exchange rates, sovereign spreads, domestic stock markets, and other financial indicators all illustrate the strength and durability of the economy.

In addition, the swift recovery of GDP and the remarkable effectiveness of the Brazilian government's response to the crisis have highlighted the growing importance of domestic demand as a driving force for economic growth and clearly demonstrated the country's ability to sustain growth based on its huge domestic market despite adverse external conditions.

Having looked at the country's precrisis macroeconomic conditions, the immediate impact of the global crisis, the policy response, and the initial recovery, we will next evaluate the medium-term prospects for the Brazilian economy and describe how the new global economic context will affect the country's macroeconomic climate and its economic growth potential.

The projections we will present indicate that the new global scenario characterized by lower economic growth, reduced trade and capital flows, and higher financial costs will have a moderate impact on Brazil's macroeconomic stability. Nevertheless, given tighter external credit conditions, the country will need to enhance its ability to generate domestic savings to sustain its medium-term potential GDP growth. In addition, the implementation of pending structural reforms will be important for strengthening factor accumulation and productivity growth.

In sum, the financial crisis and the global economic scenario projected for the coming years have made Brazil's economic growth prospects more linked to the country's ability to increase savings and resume its structural reform agenda than on any external or circumstantial factors.

The logical starting point for assessing the medium-term effects of the global financial crisis on the Brazilian economy is an analysis of the domestic macroeconomic conditions that prevailed at the end of 2009. These conditions can be summarized as

- a strong recovery of domestic GDP growth (with an annual growth rate of about 6 percent in Q3–Q4 2009) driven by domestic consumption and investment demand, increased government deficits resulting from the increased spending, and diminished tax revenue mandated by the fiscal stimulus package;
- a low saving rate perpetuated by higher government and private consumption;
- declining trade and current account balances owing to weakened export demand combined with the swift recovery of import demand;
- the emergence of inflationary pressures that will likely require the tightening of monetary policy, given the increase in capacity utilization (even in a context of investment recovery); and
- strong capital inflows—mainly portfolio flows—attributable to large interest rate differentials that will cause the steady appreciation of the exchange rate, which in turn will reinforce the decline in external balances.

Global conditions affecting the Brazilian economy can be summarized as

- a slow recovery in the more developed economies (with projected growth rates of –2 percent in 2009, 3 percent in 2010, and 3.5 percent in 2011 and 2012);
- the gradual recovery of global trade values and commodity prices;
- the reduction of fiscal stimulus measures and monetary tightening in developed economies expected to begin at the end of 2010, which will increase financing costs in emerging economies;
- large capital portfolio inflows derived from carry trades in the short run, which should recede in the medium term as interest rate differentials diminish; and
- a slow recovery of FDI flows.

The baseline scenario assumes no changes in major monetary or fiscal policies (table 3.10). This scenario indicates a strong recovery of as much as 7 percent in 2010 followed by a growth rate deceleration in 2011. In fact, a slowdown in GDP growth is expected in 2011, owing to the leveling off of domestic private demand growth as a result of the monetary tightening initiated in April 2010. The projection indicates a gradual increase in growth rates to about 4.5 percent in 2013 and beyond (a level lower than in 2007–08, but similar to the average growth rate for 2003–07).

The recovery of 2010 is expected to be led mainly by investment and, to a lesser extent, by private consumption. Between 2010 and 2014, investment growth is expected to stabilize at about 6.5 percent (the average level for the precrisis period); this implies the recovery of the investment-to-GDP ratio from 17 percent in 2009 to about 20 percent by the end of the projection period. Given that the baseline scenario assumes the government will be unable to reduce its consumption immediately because of irreversible increases in recurrent spending mandated by the stimulus package, and the cost of the presidential and gubernatorial election cycles in 2010, the increase in investment will need to be financed by external savings (as domestic savings will continue to fluctuate between 15 and 17 percent of GDP). This scenario thus anticipates a considerable deterioration in the current account balance in 2010 and an average deficit equal to 2.5 percent of GDP in the following years.

Table 3.10. Demand-Side Growth Projections

	2003–07	2008	2009	2010	2011	2012	2013	2014	2012–15
GDP (% per year)	4.2	5.1	−0.2	7.0	4.0	4.2	4.5	4.5	4.3
Gross fixed capital formation (% per year)	6.4	13.6	−17.5	16.0	6.0	6.5	6.5	7.0	6.5
Private consumption (% per year)	3.8	7.0	4.1	6.0	5.0	5.0	4.5	4.5	4.7
Public consumption (% per year)	3.1	1.6	3.7	4.0	3.0	3.0	3.0	3.0	3.0
Export growth	9.3	−0.6	−11.4	3.0	4.0	4.5	5.0	6.0	5.0
Import growth	11.7	18.0	−10.3	10.0	8.0	7.0	7.0	8.0	7.5
Memo:									
Current A/C balance (% GDP)	1.1	−1.8	−1.7	−3.5	−3.0	−2.5	−2.5	−2.5	−2.5
Capital inflows (% GDP)	1.3	1.8	4.2	4.0	2.0	1.5	1.5	1.5	1.5
Change in reserves (% GDP)	2.4	0.0	2.5	0.5	−1.5	−1.0	−1.0	−1.0	−1.0
Fiscal balance (% GDP)	−3.5	−1.9	−3.5	−3.5	−3.0	−3.0	−2.5	−2.5	−2.7
Public debt-to-GDP ratio (%)	44	38	43	43	42	41	40	38	40

Source: IBGE; BCB; authors' calculations.

In the short run, the massive capital inflows in 2009, which are expected to be sustained in 2010, should make external financing needs easy to fulfill. Furthermore, the historically high capital flows observed in 2009 in a context of declining investment indicate the presence of carry trades that could support the formation (real or perceived) of asset bubbles and promote the overappreciation of the exchange rate.

From 2010 on, the expected recovery of FDI should finance the sizable current account gaps that will result from the increasing investment and sluggish domestic savings projected for the period. Even in a context of reduced capital flows (which is not a likely scenario in the short run but will become more likely over the medium term), and given the country's low indebtedness and high foreign exchange reserves, Brazil's external position is projected to remain sustainable. After the fiscal expansion of 2009–10, the growth of public consumption is expected to recede slightly, and government balances and debt should decrease as a result of the recovery of economic activity—which will favor positive debt dynamics. While Brazil's fiscal position is also projected to remain sustainable, the effect of increasing government consumption amid an investment recovery would require additional monetary tightening to keep inflation under control. Consequently, a policy mix consisting of steady fiscal expansion and tight monetary policy would reinforce the deterioration of the trade and current account balances. Higher interest rates will continue to attract large capital inflows and contribute to the appreciation of the exchange rate. Despite the different policy framework (based on a flexible exchange rate and an inflation-targeting regime), this policy mix is similar to the government's policy stance during 1994–98, Brazil's current, much-improved macroeconomic foundations (particularly its low indebtedness and enhanced asset composition) would allow this mix to be sustained during the projection period without the country experiencing the instability it suffered in the 1990s.

The scenario depicted above implies that in the absence of further adverse shocks and policy shifts, Brazil will preserve its strong macroeconomic fundamentals, secure its fiscal and external sustainability, and reach GDP growth rates similar to those in the precrisis period. Nevertheless, given the government's difficulties in reducing consumption in the short term, the low-savings equilibrium will be preserved. Thus, the most likely policy stance will continue to be a tight monetary policy combined with a somewhat lax fiscal policy that constrains private investment and GDP growth potential.

The scenario for the supply side assumes a fall in TFP growth in 2009 followed by an annual TFP growth rate of 1 percent, which is slightly below the average observed between 2003 and 2007, and much lower than that in 2006–08. This conservative projection is based on the assumption of a lack of major structural reforms, continuing limits on access to export markets, and no significant changes in FDI flows (beyond what would be consistent with the expectation of a slow worldwide recovery). As employment is assumed to grow at the same rate as in 2003–08, the country's growth potential will depend primarily on capital stock accumulation. Given the low investment levels assumed in this baseline scenario, after a strong rebound in 2010 potential GDP will return to a modest growth rate of about 4 percent, which is lower than during the precrisis economic boom. Assuming a TFP growth rate of

1.5 percent for 2010–14, the average potential GDP growth rate rises to 5.1 percent for the period.[14]

The supply-side projection indicates that, in a lower TFP growth scenario, the economy would operate at full capacity (table 3.11). This finding reinforces the potential role of monetary tightening to curb inflationary pressures. As described above in the demand-side projections, monetary tightening would favor the appreciation of the exchange rate, reduce the country's competitiveness, and further worsen its external balances.

We project an alternative scenario to illustrate the effect of a policy mix consisting of a tighter fiscal policy and a less contractionary monetary policy. This alternative scenario also assumes the resumption of a structural reform agenda. Fiscal policy in this scenario assumes a gradual reduction of government consumption that creates scope for added government investment. Given the tighter fiscal policy, a lower interest rate is assumed to be needed to curb inflation. In terms of structural reform, we assume a tax and a labor reform effort aimed at reducing the cost of capital and labor together with a social security reform package designed to increase not only government saving but also private saving. In this scenario, as a result of the projected higher government investment (a corollary of lower government consumption) and higher private investment (a corollary of lower interest rates and taxes), the investment rate rises gradually from the current 16 percent to

Table 3.11. Supply-Side Growth Projections
(TFP growth of 1%)

	2003–07	2008	2009	2010	2011	2012	2013	2014	2012–15
GDP (% per year) with TFP growth of 1%	4.0	5.1	−0.2	5.5	4.0	4.1	4.1	4.1	4.1
GDP (% per year) with TFP growth of 1.5%	4.0	5.1	−0.2	6.2	4.6	4.8	4.8	5.0	4.9
Employment (% per year)	2.4	1.9	−0.2	2.4	2.4	2.4	2.4	2.4	2.4
Capital stock (% per year)	1.8	3.1	3.0	2.5	3.4	3.7	3.7	3.7	3.7
TFP growth (% per year)	1.0	2.6	0.7	1.0	1.0	1.0	1.0	1.0	1.0
TFP growth (% per year)	1.1	2.6	0.7	1.5	1.5	1.5	1.5	1.5	1.5

Source: IBGE; authors' calculations.

24 percent in 2013. In turn, lower government consumption and the new social security reforms would increase domestic saving rates from the current 15 percent of GDP to 20–22 percent (the exchange rate will appreciate less with a looser monetary policy). The current account balance would be slightly higher than the one projected in the baseline scenario, averaging a deficit of 2.2 percent of GDP. Finally, these structural reforms would foster productivity growth, which is expected to reach a rate of 1 percent. Under this scenario, while the external and fiscal equilibria are basically similar to the baseline scenarios, the GDP growth rates could reach 6 percent annually.[15]

In summary, the projection exercise suggests that the impact of the global financial crisis on Brazil's medium-term growth prospects will be temporary and modest. Indeed, both scenarios assume the same external conditions described above. Given the size of the domestic economy and the relatively limited openness of Brazilian markets, GDP growth rates will continue to depend primarily on domestic factors rather than external ones. In the event of a slow recovery in the global economy, the country's specific economic policy mix and the resumption of its structural reform agenda will be the most relevant factors in determining its medium-term growth performance. In this sense, the global financial crisis has not changed the nature of Brazil's fiscal and structural challenges, though it has increased their relative importance.

Brazil's Enhanced Economic Resilience, Future Growth, and Challenges

The government's sound policy choices made in the context of the positive external conditions of the pre–global crisis period have served to insure the Brazilian economy against adverse shocks and ultimately enabled the country to successfully weather the financial crisis. The foundations built over the previous decade, as well as the experience of the crisis itself, have come to represent valuable assets, which have greatly enhanced Brazil's short- and medium-term economic growth prospects. In the wake of the crisis, a number of specific advantages have become apparent. These include

• a recent expansionary cycle based on productivity growth and capital accumulation,

- low public and external indebtedness,
- a flexible exchange rate regime,
- an improved government debt profile and net external asset composition,
- a strong and sustainable financial sector,
- substantial and increasing domestic demand, and
- trade diversification.

First, the return of productivity growth and capital accumulation to the levels prevailing during the precrisis economic boom suggests that the current recovery will be sustainable as long as domestic and external macroeconomic conditions remain reasonably stable. Productivity growth and capital accumulation are highly dependent on a stable macroeconomic environment, increased FDI flows, and access to external financing. Given Brazil's strong reputation—a reputation that has only been enhanced by the crisis—these conditions seem to be highly probable, at least in the short run.

Second, pending the resolution of several major fiscal reform issues, low public and external indebtedness may allow Brazil to maintain an active fiscal policy in the coming years. This will enable the country to sustain economic dynamism, even with low global economic growth and finance external deficits stemming from domestic demand expansion, without placing its fiscal and external sustainability at risk. Of course, as saving rates are likely to remain low, external liquidity conditions will affect Brazil's ability to finance domestic expansion through external savings.

Third, the flexible exchange rate has enhanced the country's ability to accommodate shocks, while an improved government debt profile has attenuated the effects of exchange rate adjustments on debt sustainability, thereby freeing monetary and exchange rate policy from fiscal dominance. In addition, the newly enhanced composition of net external liabilities has made them pro-cyclical, thus preventing deterioration of the current account balance during adverse shocks and promoting external debt sustainability.

Fourth, the solid financial system has been a key stabilizing factor, as the effects of the global financial crisis were not transmitted through domestic financial channels. While not immune to the effects of the crisis, the financial sector did not succumb to systemic risks—an experience mirroring that of the economy as a whole. Strong solvency, low leverage, and good asset quality allowed the financial sector to function properly during the crisis. Rollover constraints and liquidity shortages faced by small financial institutions and corporate exposure to foreign exchange liabilities were localized problems that did not affect the solvency of the financial sector.

Fifth, the large domestic market and consequent low level of dependence on external demand enhanced the government's ability to use countercyclical policies to stabilize economic growth. As described above, given the size of the Brazilian economy, the importance of the external sector has been largely restricted to contractionary periods. Before the global financial crisis, adverse shocks had been cushioned by exchange rate depreciation, and economic slowdowns were less severe as a result. However, the worldwide nature of the financial crisis rendered exchange rate adjustments ineffective as global export demand did not respond to price movements. Therefore, countries that were highly dependent on export demand were among the most strongly affected. By contrast, because of the size of the Brazilian domestic market, expansionary periods have been driven by increases in domestic demand and as a result fiscal and monetary impulses in a context of solid macroeconomic fundamentals were efficient in promoting a quick and strong recovery. This advantage is particularly relevant in the expected future context of lower global economic growth.

Finally, trade diversification, along with the country's low dependence on the performance of the external sector, represents yet another asset that reduces country risks by limiting external vulnerability. Brazil is both an exporter and an importer of commodities, as well as semi-manufactured and manufactured products. This diversification makes the country's terms of trade less sensitive to international price movements, increasing its resilience to price shocks. In addition, the destinations of exports and origins of imports are also well diversified, and therefore localized crises have only a minimal impact on overall trade.

In addition, Brazil's advantages have been considerably bolstered by the recent discovery of huge oil reserves, which could make Brazil the world's fifth-largest oil producer in the medium term. If the Brazilian government is able to establish and enforce an integrated policy for managing its oil reserves—one that encompasses the fiscal, monetary, and trade policy elements of prudent, growth-oriented resource management—this massive infusion of natural assets will decisively increase Brazil's growth potential and enhance further the country's attractiveness to foreign investors.

Yet, despite Brazil's positive prospects in the short and medium term, uncertainties remain regarding long-run economic growth. Brazil still faces the challenge of implementing the structural reform agenda of the precrisis period. In addition, the medium-term effects of the crisis and the apparent permanence of certain policies adopted in response to it could impact the country's medium-term growth prospects. Indeed, the way in which the government will dismantle its anticrisis package may have as strong an effect on the country's medium- and long-term growth prospects as the resumption of its structural reform agenda.

The most important pending issue is fiscal reform. While the decline in the primary surplus should not put fiscal solvency at risk in the short run, the irreversible nature of a large part of the stimulus package could reduce the already small space for discretionary countercyclical fiscal policies. With higher levels of mandatory recurrent spending, fiscal policy options for reestablishing the declining trend of indebtedness will continue to be restricted to further increases in taxation and reduced public investment, either of which would hurt growth.

If these complex issues are not addressed, Brazil may have increasing difficulty in achieving positive primary balances through further rises in taxation or investment cuts (as the tax burden is already quite high, while public investment is relatively low). Even with low public and external indebtedness, a scenario of permanently declining government and external balances would not be desirable. The potential inability of the government to reverse the fiscal stimulus could put pressure on long-term interest rates, crowding out private investment or leading to a rapid deterioration of the current account that would further raise external financing costs.

The resumption of key structural reforms designed to increase the competitiveness of the country is another challenge—one that has only become more urgent. Reform areas encompass credit and labor markets, trade policy, and public sector improvements in service delivery and in both physical and human capital accumulation.

While the strict regulation of financial markets and the low leverage of Brazilian financial institutions have prevented a systemic crisis, and the active participation of public banks has mitigated the effects of the worldwide credit squeeze, financing capital accumulation will require credit market liberalization, the review of public banks' subsidized credit, and increased private sector participation. Again, the return of public banks' credit to normal levels will be crucial, not only to ensure the long-term health of the domestic capital market, but also to reduce the fiscal costs associated with interest rate differentials between the government's financing costs and the rates charged by public banks.

Similar observations can be applied to labor market reforms. While the strict regulation of labor markets has helped prevent a sharper rise in unemployment during the crisis, a more flexible labor market and lower labor costs will be necessary to increase the contribution of labor accumulation to growth potential.

The responsible exploration of the country's recently discovered oil reserves is another important challenge for postcrisis economic policy. The ways in which the expected increase in national wealth will alter the current policy framework will determine the extent to which Brazil is able to exploit this discovery to enhance its economic growth. The government will need to launch a competent and sophisticated economic policy response to deal with increased commodity dependence, exchange rate appreciation pressures, more volatile public finances, and possible Dutch disease effects on the competitiveness of nonresource exports.

Public sector reforms aimed at altering the current government expenditure composition would further improve the country's growth potential. There is consistent evidence that the growth effects of Brazil's public spending would increase given greater capital investment in economic infrastructure. The experience of the past several years—with weak investment expenditure execution and problems in adopting a fiscal stimulus based on added investment during the crisis—shows that the economic importance of increased capital spending does not automatically imply that Brazil will immediately benefit from, or even be able to bring about, a larger allocation of budgetary resources to infrastructure. Unless the public sector is able to identify economically viable projects and execute them efficiently, capital spending will not necessarily generate high-return economic assets, and thus will not necessarily contribute to higher sustained growth.

Finally, despite substantial progress in reducing both poverty and income inequality, and in enhancing the effectiveness of social protection instruments during the crisis, long-term economic growth and the reduction of poverty and income inequality will depend mainly on improvements in educational attainment. Reforms aimed at enhancing the effectiveness of educational services will be essential for fostering a sustainable "pro-poor" growth cycle.

While these challenges are substantial, they are far from insurmountable. Over the past decade, the Brazilian government has demonstrated an increasing propensity for circumspect, forward-looking policy decisions backed by consistent enforcement, and the experience of the global financial crisis has revealed the government's capacity to respond quickly and effectively to unforeseeable shocks. These developments are highly encouraging in and of themselves, yet it is the extent to which they reflect the Brazilian government's growing reputation for sound economic policy making that may ultimately have the greatest impact on Brazil's medium-term growth prospects.

Notes

1. Trade liberalization and privatization processes were initiated during the administration of President Fernando Collor (1990–92). However, the administration's failure to stabilize the economy derailed its economic reforms.
2. The reverse contributions of human capital and TFP during this period resulted from the inclusion of human capital in the growth accounting exercise presented in this study and from how the information was used. Most growth decomposition exercises in Brazil have not included human capital, and thus productivity estimates have normally regarded human capital changes as part of TFP. This is why these estimations show a positive and more stable TFP performance for this period. In addition, the measure of human capital used in this study includes not only a quantitative component (participation rates), but also the return on human capital expressed as labor market wages. As wages vary with the economic cycle, so too does this measure of human capital. Given that TFP is estimated as the residual, it displays higher volatility when this measure of human capital is used.
3. Increasing fiscal disequilibria were a main reason for the failure of the two stabilization attempts implemented by the new democratic government in 1986 and 1987.

4. The subnational bailout of 1997 was the third since 1989. The federal government refinanced the states' external debts in 1989, the states' debts with federal financial institutions in 1993, and the states' bond debts in 1997. In 2000, the federal government restructured the debt of 180 municipal governments. Total refinanced subnational debt in 1989–2000 amounted to about 15 percent of GDP. Unlike the previous debt refinancing, in 1997, as part of the agreement the federal government simultaneously negotiated fiscal adjustments and structural reforms with the states as conditions for the debt-rescue package.

5. These negative shocks in 2001–02 included a domestic energy crisis; a slowing world economy; increased risk aversion in markets following the attacks of September 11, 2001; Argentina's debt default; and market concerns ahead of Brazil's presidential elections.

6. U.S. dollar–denominated bonds were issued mostly by Latin American countries in the 1980s and were named after U.S. Treasury Secretary Nicholas Brady.

7. The contribution of the external sector refers to net trade or net exports (exports minus imports) and this was low. Considering the individual contribution of exports to growth, it is possible to conclude that exports had a strong contribution to growth,

8. On the contrary, the exchange rate appreciation may also have helped increase country competitiveness, as it stimulated the increase of capital goods imports and imported components of Brazilian manufactures.

9. This monthly poverty measure is not compatible with the measure presented in figure 3.9. There are two basic differences between them. The first is that the poverty measure in figure 3.9 corresponds to per capita household income (which does not include solely labor income), while the measure used in figure 3.13 defines poverty by labor income alone. The second difference is coverage: the measure used in figure 3.9 covers 27 states and includes both rural and urban areas. The poverty measure in figure 3.13 covers only the 11 largest metropolitan areas, which together represent 60 percent of the Brazilian population. As rural areas are generally poorer than metropolitan areas, the poverty level in figure 3.9 is higher.

10. Subnational governments reduced their primary surplus to 1.1 percent of GDP in January–June 2009, down from 1.4 percent of GDP during the same period of 2008.

11. The average spread from 2007 to 2009 was 4.5 percentage points.

12. As the loan will be financed by the issuance of federal debt, it will increase indebtedness. Capitalization of public banks and lending operations to them are off-budget operations that are not treated as government expenses. Therefore, this expansion is not included in the fiscal stimulus described above. In addition, given the interest rate differentials between government debt and lending rates applied by BNDES, the expansion of the credit supply by public financial institutions generates a sizable fiscal cost.

13. On the contrary, the share of banks' market value in the Ibovespa stock market increased to levels higher than in the precrisis period. By comparison, while in

2007 the three largest American banks had a market value five times superior than the value of the three largest Brazilian banks, in 2009 this ratio fell to 2:1.

14. The supply-side GDP projection assumes that the marginal productivity of capital is constant (which also implies a constant incremental capital-output ratio); therefore, the stock of capital is determined endogenously.

15. Here it is important to mention that a constant marginal productivity of capital (i.e., a constant incremental capital-output ratio) could be considered an optimistic assumption that would lead to a higher GDP growth.

References

Bacha, E. L., and R. Bonelli. 2004. *Accounting for Brazil's Long Term Growth*. Rio de Janeiro: Casa das Garças.

Barbosa Filho, F. H., and S. A. Pessôa. 2009. "Educação, Crescimento e Distribuição de Renda: A Experiência Brasileira em Perspectiva Histórica." In *Educação Básica no Brasil*, ed. Fernando Veloso, Samuel Pessôa, Ricardo Henriques, and Fábio Giambiagi. São Paulo: Elsevier Editora Ltda.

Barbosa Filho, F. H., S. A. Pessoa, and F. Veloso. 2010. "Evolução da Produtividade Total dos Fatores na Economia Brasileira com Ênfase no Capital Humano—1992–2007." *Revista Brasileira de Economia*. Forthcoming.

Blanco, F. A., and S. Herrera. 2007. "The Quality of Fiscal Adjustment and the Long Run Impact of Fiscal Polciy in Brazil." Paper presented at the Banca D'Italia Workshop, Perugia, March 29–31.

Bonelli, R. 2005. "Economic Growth and Productivity Change in Brazil." In *Brazil Investment Climate Assessment*. Washington, DC: World Bank.

Cirne de Toledo, M. G. 2009. "Avaliação da Crise: O Sistema Está Sólido?" In *Risco e Regularaçao: Por que o Brasil Enfrentou Bem a Crise Financeira e Como Ela Afetou a Economia Mundial*, ed. F. Giambiagi and M. Garcia. Rio de Janeiro: Campus-Elsevier.

de Melo, L., and M. Mogliani. 2009. "Current Account Sustainability in Brazil: A Non-Linear Approach." Economic Department Working Paper. OECD, Paris.

De Paiva Abreu, M., and R. L. F. Werneck. 2005. "The Brazilian Economy from Cardoso to Lula and the Interim View." Economics Department, Pontifical Catholic University of Rio de Janeiro, Texto para Discussão 504.

OECD (Organisation for Economic Co-operation and Development). 2009. *OECD Economic Survey of Brazil*. Paris: OECD.

Pessôa, S. A., V. Gomes, and F. Veloso. 2003. "Evolução da Produtividade Total dos Fatores na Economia Brasileira: Uma Análise Comparativa." *Pesquisa e Planejamento Econômico* 33 (3): 389–434.

Werneck, R. L. F. 2009. "Setting up a Modern Macroeconomic Policy Framework in Brazil, 1993–2004." Working Paper 45, Commission on Growth and Development, Washington, DC.

World Bank. 2001. "Brazil: Proposed First Programmatic Financial Sector Adjustment Loan." Program Document, Report P7448-BR, World Bank, Washington, DC.

———. 2002. "Brazil: Proposed Second Programmatic Financial Sector Adjustment Loan." Program Document. Report P24067-BR. World Bank, Washington, DC.

———. 2003. "Brazil: Stability for Growth and Poverty Reduction." Economic and Sector Work Report 25278-BR. World Bank, Washington, DC.

———. 2007. "Brazil: Improving Fiscal Conditions for Growth." Economic and Sector Work Report 35595–BR. World Bank, Washington, DC.

———. 2009. "Brazil: Topics in Fiscal Federalism." Economic and Sector Work Report, World Bank, Washington, DC.

Comment on "Brazil: Resilience in the Face of the Global Crisis"

David Rosenblatt

This is an excellent paper in that it provides an overview of the history of economic policy in recent decades, as well as a thorough and balanced analysis of the domestic policy response to the global crisis. The paper offers exquisite detail on the economy's evolution and the policy-making process before and after the global crisis. The evaluation of the strengths and weaknesses of the crisis response is well prepared. It is thus difficult to disagree with the analysis and main conclusions of the paper.

My comments focus on three areas: (1) the role of exports in recent macroeconomic performance, (2) the interpretation of the estimates of total factor productivity (TFP), and (3) international perspectives with regard to the Brazilian experience.

The Role of Exports

It is a simple accounting fact that the level of net exports is not a major direct contributor to the changes in aggregate demand in Brazil over

David Rosenblatt is Economic Adviser, Office of the Senior Vice President, Development Economics, and Chief Economist, World Bank.

the period. The demand-side growth accounting is undeniably correct. On the other hand, net exports can never be a major and sustained contributor to growth, broadly speaking. By definition, if net exports grow faster than total GDP, then the trade surplus is on an explosive path—even as a share of GDP. When one considers export-led growth, the "action" is generally hidden on the supply side. As the economy opens, the tradables sector expands more rapidly than overall GDP, jobs are subsequently created in the tradables sector, and much of the increase in domestic consumption demand could actually be driven by this process.

Figure D3.1 provides evidence that export-intensive industrial production sectors did in fact grow faster than other industrial sectors prior to the global crisis. Naturally, export-oriented sectors also contracted more rapidly during the crisis. It would be interesting to explore in more detail where jobs were created prior to the crisis (or subsequently

Figure D3.1. Industrial Production (Physical Quantities) by Export Intensity (Annual Averages)

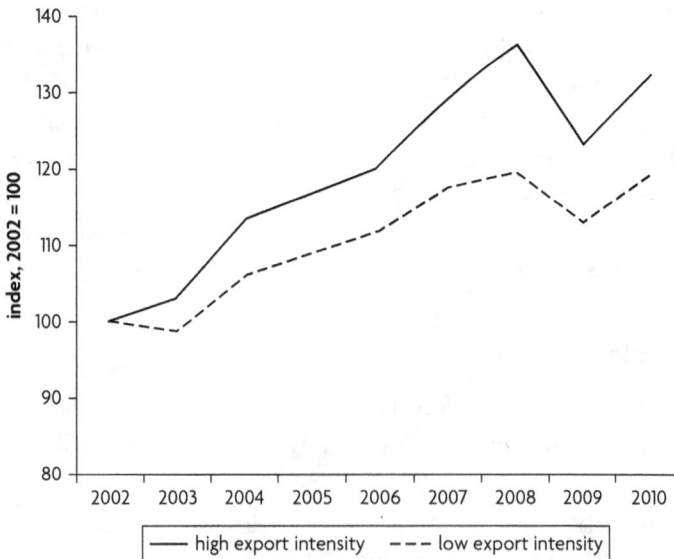

Source: Brazilian Institute of Geography and Statistics (IBGE).

destroyed during the crisis) to understand better the full impact of trade on recent economic developments in Brazil.

Interpretation of the Estimates of TFP

In growth decompositions, as a residual, anything unaccounted for becomes part of measured TFP. In the case of Brazil, this may have particular significance given the important role of natural resource–intensive sectors in recent economic growth. It could also be important in projecting future TFP growth given the potential for a substantial increase in oil production based on recent discoveries. In terms of recent history, figure D3.2 provides an example of the expansion of land use, which must have made some quantifiable contribution to agricultural sector growth.

International Perspectives

Brazilian fiscal and monetary policies leading up to the crisis were clearly of tremendous help in preparing the economy and in dampening the effects of the global crisis. It is important to note, however, that the effect of a lower degree of exposure to trade (as a share of GDP)—often cited as a kind of advantage during the crisis—may be overstated. As noted above, much of the trade impact may be hidden on the supply side, requiring further analysis. Also, using international perspective, figure D3.3 shows that other, more open economies (e.g., China and the newly industrialized countries [NICs] in Asia) showed a fairly similar performance during the global crisis.

Another perspective is longer-term performance relative to relevant comparators. Figure D3.3 also shows that over the medium-term projection period, Brazilian growth would lead to very gradual convergence with advanced economies (discounting population growth differentials); however, the growth rates are only on a par with some more advanced Asian NICs, and the convergence process would be extremely gradual.

Also, using a longer-term historical comparison, figure D3.4 shows that Brazil has not necessarily outperformed the other large economy of Latin America: Mexico. Clearly, since the last recession (2000–02),

Figure D3.2. Area Planted

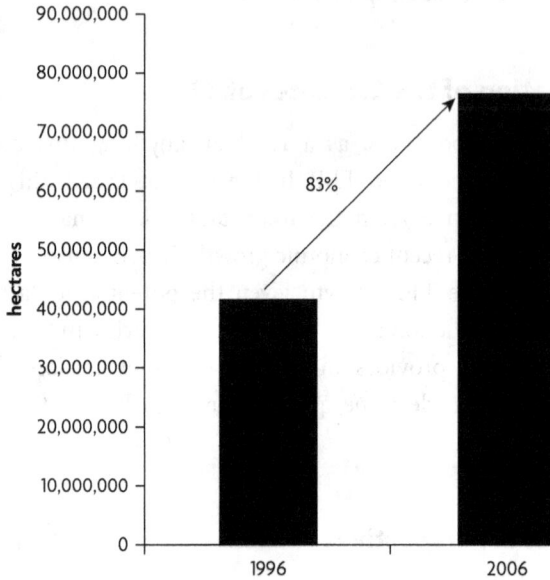

hectares (y-axis): 0 to 90,000,000

1996 · 2006 · 83%

Source: IBGE.

Brazil's economy outperformed Mexico. But this episode followed a relatively poor performance for the 1990s—even compared with Mexico, thanks to the "V-shaped" recovery from the Tequila Crisis and the initial gains from the creation of the North American Free Trade Agreement (NAFTA). Moreover, there is some irony to Mexico's success in "upgrading" to almost all manufactures in exports and not developing a more diversified basket, with more traditional natural resource–intensive exports. During the precrisis commodity boom, Mexico did not experience the same terms-of-trade gains that Brazil experienced. In addition, there is some irony in the geographic "advantage" of Mexico's location next to the U.S. market: the "easy" export gains to the NAFTA market subsequently left Mexico's export base exposed to the epicenter of the global economic crisis. Mexico is the topic of another chapter; however, these points may be of interest

Figure D3.3. Real GDP Growth: Brazil and Selected Country Groups

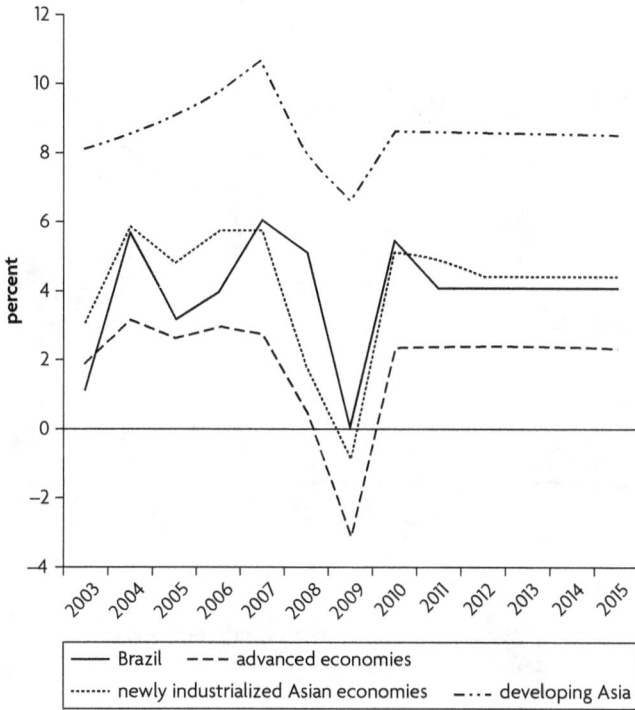

Source: IMF World Economic Outlook Database.

in understanding the degree of Brazilian "exceptionalism" in recent economic performance.

Final Comments

In brief, the Brazil paper constitutes an excellent contribution to this volume. The final section provides a thorough and thoughtful discussion of the specific countercyclical measures taken by the Brazilian government during, and prior to, the global crisis. As noted above, one might desire more detail on the sources of growth on the supply side and on the role of exports. One might also benefit from more caveats on the improved growth of TFP during 2005–08. Both of these adaptations might inspire a bit more caution about the medium-term growth projections.

Figure D3.4. Real GDP per Capita

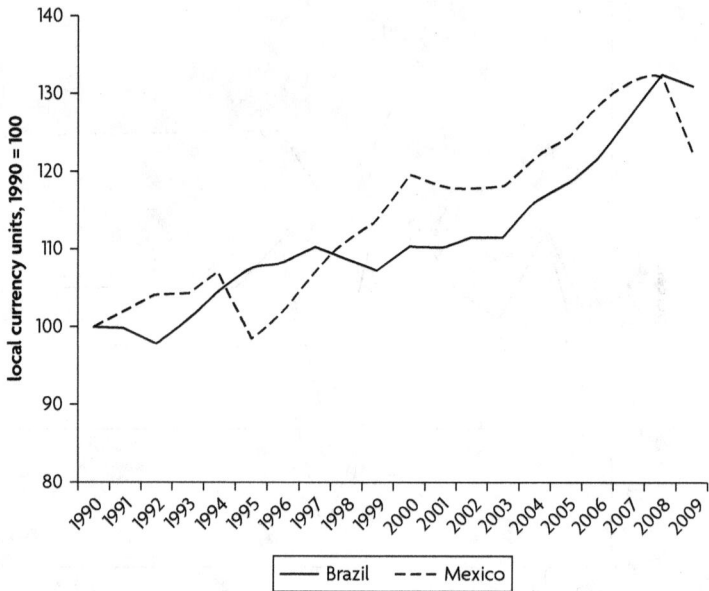

Source: World Bank, World Development Indicators Database; author's estimates.

China | 4

Global Crisis Avoided, Robust Economic Growth Sustained

Gallina A. Vincelette, Alvaro Manoel,
Ardo Hansson, and Luis Kuijs

This chapter explores how the ongoing economic crisis, the policy responses to it, and the postcrisis global economy will affect China's medium-term prospects for growth, poverty reduction, and development.

The chapter begins with a review of China's precrisis growth experience, summarizing China's growth, poverty reduction, and human development achievements over the 30-year period of reform and globalization. It then discusses the pace, composition, sources, and financing of China's growth during 1995–2007 and the impact of key external and domestic factors. We identify several challenges emanating from China's precrisis policies and assess the impact of the global crisis

Gallina A. Vincelette is Senior Economist, and Alvaro Manoel is Senior Economist, Economic Policy and Debt Department, World Bank; Ardo Hansson is Lead Economist, and Louis Kuijs is Senior Economist, East Asia and Pacific Poverty Reduction and Economic Management Department, World Bank. The authors would like to thank Carlos A. Primo Braga, Milan Brahmbhatt, Nadeem Ul Haque, Ivailo Izvorski, Naoko Kojo, Lili Liu, Nadir A. Mohammed, Mustapha K. Nabli, Vikram Nehru, Tatiana Rosito, and Shahid Yusuf, and participants of the two World Bank Workshops on Crisis and Medium-Term Prospects for Growth (Washington, DC, December 17–18, 2009, and July 19–20, 2010) for useful discussions and comments on earlier drafts of this paper.

on China's economy in 2009, as well as its likely impact in 2010. We then examine the government's policy response, focusing on fiscal and monetary stimulus measures. We conclude with a look at China's medium-term growth prospects and the main policies needed to move it to a robust and sustainable growth path.

Precrisis, Preboom, and the Global Boom

Since 1978, China's government has consistently undertaken economic reforms and opened up the economy to the outside world, fueling impressive economic growth. China's gross domestic product (GDP) has grown by an average annual rate of nearly 10 percent in real terms since 1978, compared with 4 percent for all developing countries. Although China's per capita GDP is still modest (about US$3,300 in 2008), it had become the world's third largest economy by 2007 (measured in current exchange rates). China's share of world trade in 2008 was 10 percent, compared with the U.S. share of 12 percent and the European share of 16 percent. And in 2009, China edged out Germany to become the world's largest exporter.

China's strong growth has sharply reduced the share of the population in poverty. Using China's official poverty standard, the poverty rate in rural China fell from 18.5 percent in 1981 to 2.8 percent in 2004, and the number of rural poor fell from 152 million to 26 million. Measured by the World Bank poverty standard, China's poverty reduction has been even more striking. The fraction of the population below the poverty line declined from 65 percent to 10 percent in this period, and the absolute number of poor fell dramatically—from 652 million to 135 million, or by over half a billion people. Measured by the new international poverty standard of US$1.25 per person per day, poverty levels are higher, but the decline since 1981 has been no less impressive—from 85 percent in 1981 to 27 percent in 2004. Preliminary analysis of trends during 2004–07 suggests further progress in poverty reduction, with poverty measured by the World Bank standard likely to have fallen further to 4 percent from about 10 percent.[1]

China has also made great strides in improving human development indicators. It has already achieved most of the Millennium Development Goals, or is well on the way to achieving them. As a result, China is now at a very different stage of development than it was at the dawn of the economic reforms at the start of the 1980s. It has become a booming lower-middle-income country strongly integrated into the global economy.

Economic Performance before the Crisis

During the precrisis period, China posted impressive growth rates. Average annual growth between 1995 and 2007 was 9.7 percent. The economy experienced a slight dip after the Asian financial crisis of 1998, but rebounded quickly in the following years (figure 4.1).

China's strong economic performance in this period was influenced by both external and domestic factors:

- *During 1995–2001, growth in global output and export demand was robust and stable.* As financial markets developed, developing countries' access to financing became easier, although flows were still moderate and spreads fluctuated. Primary commodity prices were generally low. During this period, China, like its neighboring economies, was hurt by the Asian crisis. While it was not at the epicenter of the crisis, it did not remain unscathed, and its growth decelerated until 1999.
- *The global picture began to change around 2002.* Although growth in advanced countries slowed beginning in 2001 and throughout the boom period, growth accelerated in developing countries, including China, with trend growth appearing to decouple from that of developed countries. Regionally, the impact of the Asian crisis had long subsided, partly because of improved policies and technology,

Figure 4.1. China GDP Growth Rate, 1995–2007

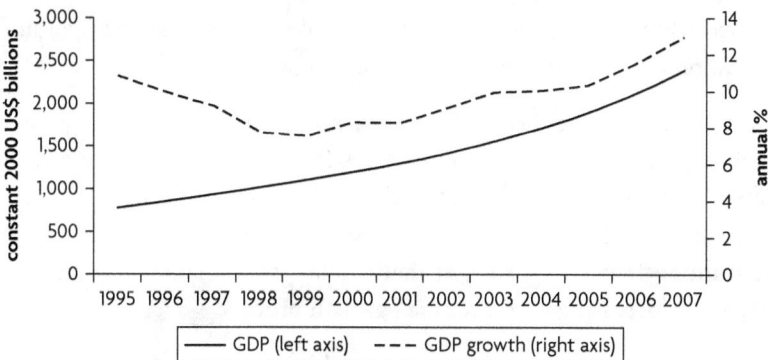

Source: World Bank.

but also because of a more favorable global economic environment. With ample global savings and financial innovation, risk premiums fell to unprecedented lows.

- *International trade and capital flows accelerated.* Trade flows grew very rapidly, with expanding global demand facilitating export-led growth. During much of this period, China's exports grew at more than 20 percent a year, in real terms. As the global economy boomed, commodity prices increased sharply. Together with high export demand and easy financing, this contributed to an investment boom in the developing world. Capital flows to developing countries (mostly to the private sector) were around five times their average levels before 2002. China, however, bucked this trend by becoming an even larger net exporter of capital, with current account surpluses averaging 6.1 percent of GDP during this period. Stock markets boomed globally—and especially in developing countries.

- *China's growth was also fueled by the fruits of reforms and public investments that made labor and capital more productive.* Key reforms— including those implemented in response to the Asian crisis— consisted of China's accession to the World Trade Organization and the reforms it catalyzed; the restructuring and privatization of state-owned enterprises (SOEs); the privatization of social housing; policy adjustments that facilitated a sustained flow of "surplus" labor from rural areas to urban areas, engendering the process of urbanization; and improved macroeconomic management. Major investments were made in areas such as roads, ports, and airports. A significant share of China's post–Asian crisis investment served to remove critical bottlenecks to growth, generating high rates of return and laying the foundation for the next wave of development.

Growth in China has been increasingly capital intensive, with high (and rising) savings and investment rates. A look beyond aggregate growth rates reveals several key characteristics of China's recent growth pattern.[2] Analyses of the sources of China's economic growth using a growth accounting framework suggest that capital accumulation has played a large and increasing role in China's growth process:

- Investment in factories, buildings, and infrastructure increased from 35 percent of GDP in 2000 to about 43 percent in 2007. This was accompanied by a corresponding increase in gross national saving from 37 percent of GDP to about 54 percent.

- The contribution of capital accumulation to labor productivity growth increased from 2.9 out of 6.4 percent a year in 1978–94 to 5.5 out of 8.6 percent in 1994–2009 (box 4.1).

Box 4.1. Growth Accounting for China

Physical capital accumulation in China has been sizable and growing. Several studies have used growth accounting to analyze the sources behind China's rapid growth of the past 25 years. These studies find that, respectable productivity growth notwithstanding, the contribution of physical capital accumulation has been of major significance, reflecting the increasing investment-to-GDP ratio. Capital accumulation's contribution to GDP growth was much larger in 1994–2007 than it was in 1978–94, reflecting the rapid investment growth in the past decade. Kuijs and Wang (2006) conducted a growth accounting exercise for 1978–2004 using consensus assumptions on the key parameters. They found that the contribution of capital accumulation to GDP growth was considerably larger in 1994–2007 than in 1978–94, reflecting the rapid investment growth in the past decade, while TFP growth declined relative to the first period.

What explains labor productivity growth? A useful way of looking at these trends is to decompose labor productivity growth into TFP growth and the contribution of capital accumulation (higher K/L). The contribution of capital accumulation to labor productivity growth increased from 2.9 out of 6.4 percent a year in 1978–94 to 5.5 out of 8.6 percent in 1994–2009 (table B4.1.1). This is very high, and explains more than two-thirds of the difference in labor productivity growth between China and other countries and regions. Under most assumptions that were examined, TFP growth is estimated to have declined over time. With overall employment growth slowing, the contribution of labor growth has been modest, especially over the last decade.

Table B4.1.1. Sources and Aspects of Growth, 1978–2015
(average annual increase, %)

	1978–94	1994–2009	2009–15
GDP growth	9.9	9.6	8.3
Employment growth	3.3	1.0	0.2
Labor productivity growth	6.4	8.6	8.1
From TFP growth	3.0	2.7	2.2
From higher H/L	0.5	0.3	0.5
From higher K/L ratio	2.9	5.5[a]	5.2
Memorandum items (%)			
Investment/GDP ratio (period avg.)	30.1	39.8	47.7

Source: NBS (National Bureau of Statistics); World Bank staff estimates.
Note: Methodology as in Kuijs and Wang (2006), but with human capital. TFP = total factor productivity; H/L = human capital – labor ratio; K/L = physical capital – labor ratio.
a. The contribution from higher K/L is much higher in 2000–09 than in 1994–99.

- Contrary to popular belief, China's total factor productivity (TFP) growth has been higher relative to most other countries, but most of the difference in GDP growth performance between China and other countries has been due to increasing levels of capital accumulation.

The bulk of China's investment has been financed domestically. Foreign direct investment (FDI) played an important role in China's development, particularly in transferring technology and linking China to global markets. However, at 3–4 percent of GDP, FDI has not been the main source of financing for China's growth. Furthermore, FDI as a share of GDP was actually lower during 2002–07, when China's growth rate accelerated further. FDI as a share of GDP fell from 4.2 percent in 1995–2001 to 3.0 percent in 2002–07. Instead, domestic savings has been the key source of financing in China. Thus, even as the investment-to-GDP ratio increased by 8 percentage points from 2000 to 2007, savings far outpaced investment. As a result, China's external current account surplus rose from 1.7 percent of GDP in 2000 to almost 11 percent of GDP in 2007.

Household savings are relatively high in China; but this has not been the main force driving the impressive increase in domestic savings in the past 10 years. Households in China save more than those in the Organisation for Economic Co-operation and Development countries, partly because of the lack of social safety nets. However, with household income accounting for some 60 percent of GDP, and with households typically saving 25–30 percent of their income, China is not out of line with its Asian comparators. Household savings declined somewhat as a share of GDP in 1995–2001 and rose somewhat after 2001 (figure 4.2).

Much of the increase in China's domestic saving came from the enterprise sector and the government.[3] Since the late 1990s, rising enterprise savings have helped increase economywide saving under China's capital-intensive, industry-led growth model,[4] which has boosted productivity in industry. With surplus labor in agriculture still sizable, wages lagged productivity, especially at the lower end of the wage scale, even as skilled workers saw wages rise more rapidly. As a result, enterprise profits and savings increased as a share of total income.

As for the government, its revenues have grown sharply because so much of it derives from taxes on corporate and industrial activity. Government revenues from land sales have also increased over time.

Figure 4.2. Saving and Investment in China

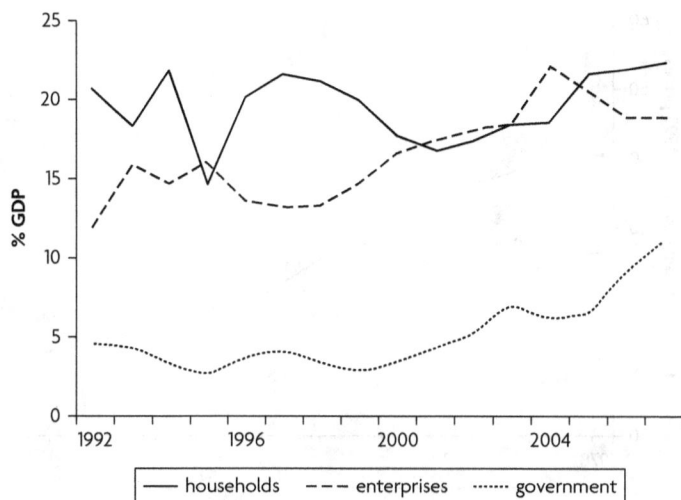

Source: CEIC China Database; World Bank staff estimates.
Note: Flow-of-funds data.

Thanks to China's traditionally conservative fiscal policy, government expenditure has been less than revenue. In particular, the government's current spending has lagged because Beijing has traditionally set aside a large share of revenues to finance investment.

Much of China's GDP growth since the early 1990s has come from the explosive growth in industrial production. Industrial value added has increased by an annual average rate of 12.3 percent during 1990–2007, and the share of industry in GDP (in current prices) rose from 41 percent to almost 49 percent—among the highest for any country since the 1960s. In fact, the increase would have been larger but for declining relative prices in industry. In constant 1995 prices, the share of industry in GDP rose from 37 percent in 1990 to 54 percent in 2007 (figure 4.3). During 2003–07, the industrial sector contributed 60 percent of total GDP growth; just 5 percent was from agriculture and 35 percent was from the services sector.

On the whole, more than 80 percent of the growth in industry during 1993–2005 was due to higher labor productivity (figure 4.4) rather than more employment. This is attributable mainly to the large-scale investment effort and increased capital-to-labor ratio. Of course, the low

Figure 4.3. Industry Has Driven Growth

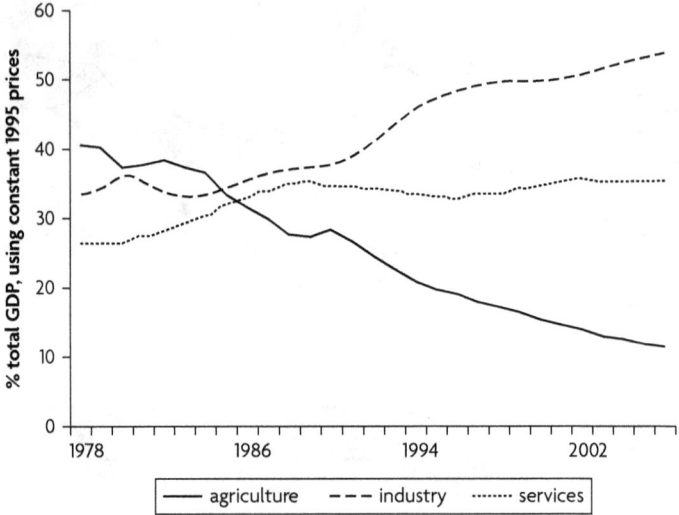

Source: NBS; authors' estimates.

Figure 4.4. Labor Productivity in Industry Has Soared

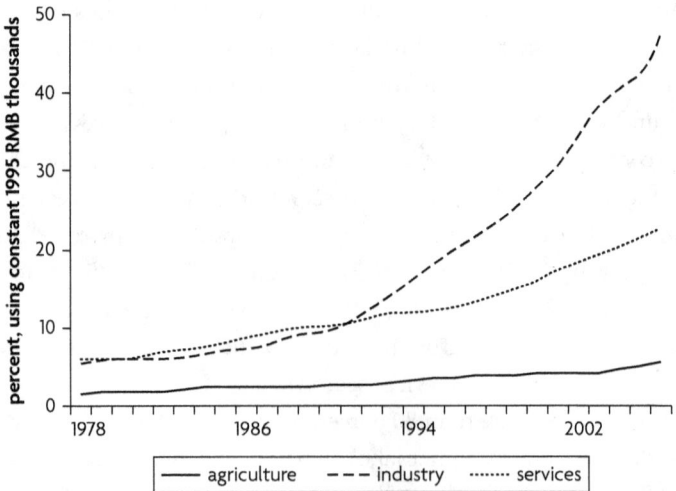

Source: NBS; authors' calculation.

growth of industrial employment in this period masks important net movements of labor out of SOEs into private sector firms.

As in other successfully industrializing countries, Chinese government investment has been a key component of industry growth. Public investment, as reported by flow-of-funds data, averaged 6 percent of GDP during 1995–2007, including capital transfers. Rising levels of public investment were supported by strong growth in tax collections and other revenues (for example, land transfers by local governments) and by limits on current spending. As a substantial amount of investment is financed through special-purpose municipal investment companies, total public investment was even higher.

China's traditional capital-intensive, industry-led growth pattern is amplified by its policies. The government has favored industry and investment over the services sector and domestic consumption in several ways:

- *Policies have encouraged saving and investment.* Government spending has been geared to investment in physical infrastructure instead of current spending on health and education. Apart from its obvious direct effect, this has increased precautionary saving by households. In addition, investment has been encouraged by several features of the tax system, by the exemption of SOEs from paying dividends, and by the channeling of capital transfers and loans to SOEs and SOE-type entities.
- *Investment in industry has been encouraged through the financial system.* Commercial bank lending rates have been kept low for those with access to financial markets. Access has been easier for large industrial firms, which has promoted capital-intensive industrial development. The People's Bank of China reports that small and medium enterprises)—which are far more prevalent in services than in industry—account for more than half of GDP, but receive less than 10 percent of total bank loans.
- *Industrialization has also been promoted by keeping the prices of key inputs low.* Besides capital, these inputs include energy, electricity, utilities (including water), land, and low pricing of environmental impacts.
- *Promoting industrial development has meant that services-sector development was not given priority.*[5] Recognizing this, China's State Council in March 2007 called for opening up several services sectors—including telecommunications, railways, and civil aviation—to private and

foreign investors and for improving the legal framework to stimulate the services sector.

• *The containment of migration into urban areas has shaped the capital-intensive nature of growth.* The speed and nature of migration has been affected by the Hukou system of residency permits, regulations discriminating against migrant workers, the nonportability of labor and social benefits, and land tenure policies. As a result, much of the migration has taken place in the form of a growing "floating," rather than permanent, population.

While these policies have contributed to China's export-led growth model, exchange rate policy has also been instrumental. In particular, the reluctance to let the exchange rate appreciate in line with the rapid productivity gains in manufacturing—which have outpaced those for most of China's trading partners—has stimulated the production of tradable goods and services. Nominal and real effective exchange rates for the renminbi (the Chinese currency, whose unit is the yuan) are now broadly at their 2000 level (figure 4.5). But the exchange rate policy in China is evolving: on June 19, 2010, the government decided to return to a managed floating-exchange-rate regime that allows for movements in

Figure 4.5. China's (Effective) Exchange Rate Trends

Source: CEIC China Database; World Bank staff estimates.
Note: NEER = nominal effective exchange rate; REER = real effective exchange rate.

the exchange rate based on market supply and demand and with a reference to a basket of currencies.

The capital-intensive, industry-led growth model, accompanied by an undervalued currency, has served China well in many respects. The high savings and investment, combined with respectable rates of technological progress, have led to rapid growth of China's production capacity. In recent years, potential GDP growth—or the capacity to produce—has been rising in line with actual GDP growth to more than 10 percent a year (figure 4.6). This means that the economy can grow rapidly without running into the kinds of constraints often faced by emerging-market countries, such as high inflation, large current account deficits, and bottlenecks in the real economy. Thus, the policies cited above have been key elements of a pro-growth policy package that also includes good macroeconomic management, trade liberalization, a favorable setting for FDI, good infrastructure, and pro-growth local governments.

Nonetheless, China's capital-intensive, industry-led growth model has also raised several risks:

- *This growth pattern has created fewer urban jobs than would a more labor-intensive model and has increased urban-rural inequality.* Industry creates

Figure 4.6. Actual and Potential GDP Have Grown Steadily in Recent Years

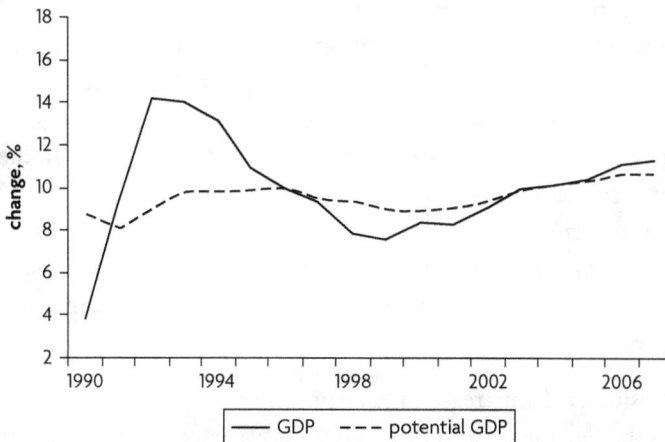

Source: NBS; World Bank staff estimates.
Note: Potential GDP is estimated using a growth accounting framework with Cobb-Douglas production function.

fewer urban jobs than does the services sector, and during 1993–2007, more than 80 percent of the growth in industry came from higher labor productivity instead of from new employment. Indeed, industrial employment grew by just 2.3 percent per year during 1993–2007, compared with annual value added growth of 11.7 percent. Since the mid-1990s, this has limited the movement of people out of agriculture and the rural areas, where productivity and income are much lower (productivity in agriculture is about one-sixth that of the rest of the economy). While the share of total employment in agriculture fell rapidly during 1978–95, the share did not fall much from the mid-1990s until around 2003. The reduction seems to have accelerated since then, and the share fell to less than 41 percent in 2007. Nonetheless, this is high relative to other countries at a similar stage of development. The divergence of productivity, however, has underscored rural-urban income inequalities. It is an important reason for the widening in the rural-urban income gap from 2.2 in 1990 to 3.3 in 2007, as well as in the increase in overall income inequality as measured by the Gini coefficient.

- *Much of China's growth has stemmed from the increased production of manufactured goods, with a tendency to expand current account surpluses.* Under the investment-heavy pattern of growth, and with surplus labor in agriculture keeping wage growth low relative to the rapid productivity gains, production in China has tended to outstrip domestic demand. From the perspective of China's external balance, the strong growth of manufacturing output means continued strong export growth; however, import growth has been more subdued, partly because of increasing import substitution. As a result, the current account surplus is widening steadily.

- *Industry-led growth (including construction) has made particularly intensive use of energy, primary commodities, and other resources, with a damaging effect on the environment.* China's overall reliance on these inputs is high due to the size of its industrial sector.

The flipside of the increase in enterprise income and buoyant tax revenues is the decline, as a share of GDP, in wage and household incomes (figure 4.7). This decline has been the main cause of the falling share of consumption in GDP since the late 1990s. A decline in households'

Figure 4.7. The Wage Share Has Declined

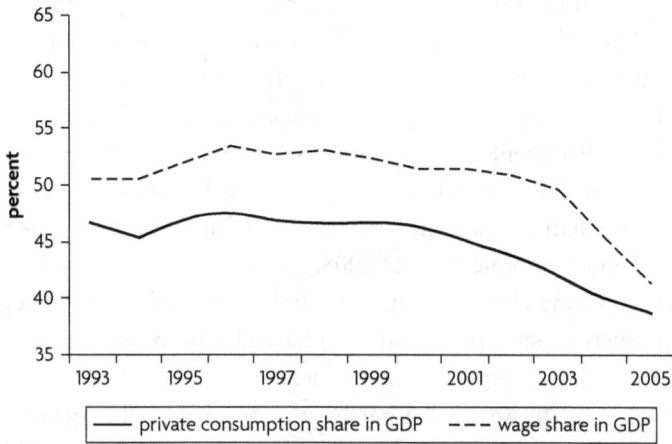

Source: National Resource of Statistics. Wage share data are from *Statistical Yearbook.*

investment income, driven by declining interest rates, has amplified the reduction in the share of household income in GDP.[6]

Precrisis Policies and Postcrisis Challenges

- How attributable were the rate and pattern of Chinese growth during the precrisis boom (2002–07) to improved longer-term growth potential, and how attributable were they to cyclical factors?
- How—and to what extent—did the precrisis global boom affect China's potential growth rate?
- Did China's precrisis policies increase or mitigate its vulnerability to external shocks and global reversals?

China's growth rate during 1995–2007 is mainly a reflection of a high and relatively stable underlying growth potential, and to a lesser extent cyclical factors. China's potential GDP growth rate has increased since the late 1990s, after moderating earlier (figure 4.6, box 4.1). On average, actual growth during 1995–2007 was in line with potential growth, being slightly above potential growth in 1995 and 2007, while falling nearly 2 percent below it during the Asian crisis.

The increase in estimated potential growth during the current decade was due primarily to a rise in the investment rate from 37 percent in

1995–2001 to 42 percent in 2002–07. These high and rising investment rates reflected the policies discussed earlier, as well as a strong outlook for (and actual performance of) China's exports and capacity bottlenecks in some sectors. These high investment rates and the continued robust underlying TFP growth were also supported by a favorable external environment and a solid record of reform and macroeconomic management. Tentative estimates suggest that the economy was operating at more than full capacity in 2006–07, before it was hit by the global financial and economic crisis of 2008.

Despite China's high and stable underlying growth potential, cyclical factors (such as net exports and FDI) have also been important. In particular, the 2.6 percentage point increase in the contribution of net exports to growth was fueled partly by strong external demand. While access to external financing was negligible in aggregate terms, FDI has been important for supporting growth through structural changes and increased productivity. More than half of China's exports are produced (at least partly) by foreign firms, and FDI has had positive spillover effects on other firms (Xu and Sheng 2010).

While internal migration has been a critical part of China's growth story, external migration has not been important. Recorded private transfers averaged only 0.7 percent of GDP per year during 1995–2007.

China's precrisis policies helped protect the economy against external shocks and global reversals. These policies also put China in a strong position to respond to the crisis with substantial monetary and fiscal easing. The main monetary and fiscal policies included the following:

- *Prudent fiscal policies*, which left China with generally low budget deficits and reported public debt below 20 percent of GDP as it entered the crisis
- *Fairly prudent monetary policy*, with tightened controls on bank lending during periods of perceived overheating (a preemptive "deleveraging," which left banks with relatively low loan-to-deposit ratios)[7]
- *A cautious approach to financial sector liberalization* and opening up of the capital account

Partly because of these policies, China substantially increased its foreign reserves and kept external debt at a low level. China accumulated nearly

US$2 trillion of foreign reserves, equivalent to more than 20 months of imports, and its external debt was only about 10 percent of GDP.[8]

The evolution of China's macroeconomy during the precrisis period and the role of its economic policies reflected the authorities' degree of policy maneuverability. First, the average annual growth rate during 1995–2007 was impressive (9.7 percent), suffering only a slight dip after the Asian crisis (figure 4.1). Second, growth has been increasingly capital intensive, and much of it has been financed domestically—largely by the enterprise sector and the government (box 4.1 and figure 4.2). And third, the economy has seen periods of overheating, when GDP outpaced potential GDP growth, creating a positive output gap. This happened before the Asian crisis and again (in a less pronounced way) during the precrisis period (figure 4.6), when the economy was beginning to overheat again.

Precrisis policies, however, also left the country exposed to external shocks. To the extent that both structural and exchange rate policies supported rapidly rising exports and trade surpluses, they left China more vulnerable to any sudden decline in export demand. The managed nature of the exchange rate regime also reduced the independence of monetary policy to respond to domestic needs. Moreover, the developments in the equities and private housing markets have introduced new potential transmission channels for external shocks. These markets did exhibit volatility in recent years, especially in the equity market. However, the equity market is less important to the real economy than it is in many other countries, and was thus not the primary channel through which the recent crisis affected the Chinese economy.

Global Crisis: Impact and Policy Response

The financial crisis that originated in the developed world intensified in September 2008 in the United States and began to spread globally. Since Lehman Brothers' bankruptcy, many other systemically relevant financial institutions (such as Freddie Mac, Fannie Mae, AIG, Merrill Lynch, and CitiGroup) have faced serious financing difficulties.

In spreading beyond the United States and beyond the financial sector into the international money and capital markets, the previously heavy capital inflows to emerging-market economies quickly and abruptly reversed. These developments did not leave China unaffected.

Channels of Transmission in China

Limited exposure to toxic assets in the developed world and a fairly closed capital account shielded China from the initial financial turmoil of 2008. Furthermore, China's strong fiscal position, highly regulated domestic and recently recapitalized banking sector, large foreign reserves, and low short-term debt helped the country mitigate the external shock.

Despite its favorable initial macroeconomic position, China began to feel the effects of the crisis in November 2008. The impact has been mainly through the trade channel, and not so much through private capital flows and the financial sector.

Trade channel. The real sector has been the main channel through which the global crisis has affected China. In the last quarter of 2008, China's exports declined dramatically. Since the onset of the crisis, exports shifted from 20 percent annual growth to an annualized contraction of more than 25 percent in early 2009. The sharp fall in exports cut growth in the fourth quarter of 2008 to its lowest rate in more than a decade.

A large part of the export contraction was the result of reduced exports of machinery, transport equipment, and manufactured goods (figure 4.8). Negative growth in China's major trading partners—namely, Europe and the United States, where demand plunged—is the main reason for the steep drop in Chinese exports. Export growth continued to remain subdued throughout 2009, with exports to all markets contracting. This strong decline had additional effects on the real economy, including on investment in the manufacturing sector and in the labor market.

The outlook is for exports to remain restrained given the subdued global economy. As the global economy gradually starts to recover, China's export growth is expected to improve. However, a sharp rebound is unlikely.

Import growth, on the other hand, has risen substantially, as the stimulus package has increased China's appetite for investment goods and raw materials. Indeed, real imports rebounded to levels higher than before the crisis. The growth in import volumes has shifted to positive territory for all types of products except electronics and light manufactures, which are affected by still-subdued processing trade. Owing to these strong imports, China's trade surplus is narrowing substantially. And, in combination

Figure 4.8. Export Growth (Year-on-Year) by Commodity Group

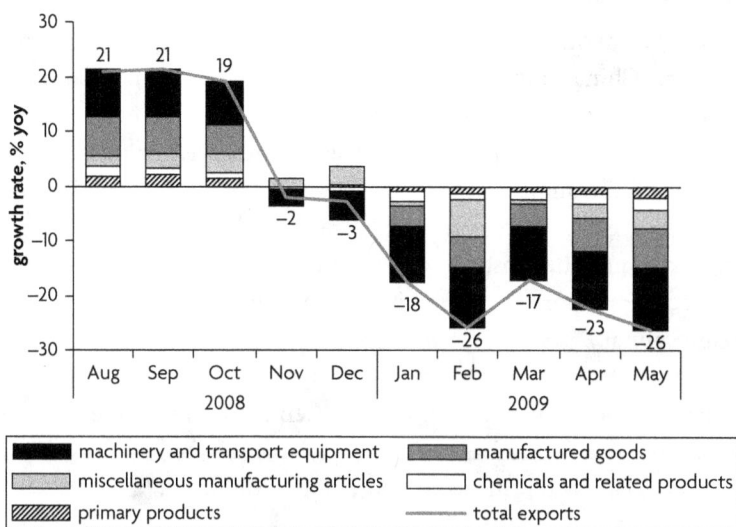

Source: World Bank; China Monthly Update (April, May, June, July 2009).
Note: yoy = year-on-year.

with the unlikelihood of a sharp export rebound, China's trade surplus may shrink further in the near term before it recovers.

Private capital flows. For many countries, another major source of vulnerability in the face of the global crisis is the massive contraction of private capital flows worldwide. Net private capital flows to emerging economies in 2009 are less than half of the US$392 billion of 2008, and far below the record US$890 billion in 2007 (see IIF 2009).

While China as a net capital exporter is less affected by such developments, virtually all categories of capital flows to China were hurt after September 2008. Nonresidents continued to sell equities; they also shifted to selling debt securities and selectively withdrawing deposits held with domestic banks. Inflows of FDI slowed sharply as companies began delaying new commitments and new construction. Lending by foreign banks also slowed.

More recently, capital flows to China have begun to recover, and official foreign exchange reserve accumulation has regained strength. After an abrupt decline in foreign investment in the fourth quarter of

2008 and first quarter of 2009, gross FDI inflows revived in the second quarter of 2009. Despite the shrinking current account surplus, which narrowed by about a third in the first half of 2009 (relative to the previous year), China's official foreign exchange reserve accumulation has regained momentum because of valuation gains and net inflows of financial capital (figure 4.9). The headline reserves figure reached a record US$2.3 trillion as of September 30, 2009.

China is likely to continue to attract capital inflows in the near term. Good growth prospects and strong asset market performance are expected to support the attractiveness of China as a destination for foreign capital.

Financial channel. In contrast to other emerging-market economies, China's financial sector has not been seriously affected by the crisis. Its banks were largely untouched because of the following:

- The banking reforms undertaken in early 2000, when the state asset trust cleaned up the nonperforming loans of the banking sector and left the banking system solvent

Figure 4.9. Foreign Exchange Reserve Accumulation

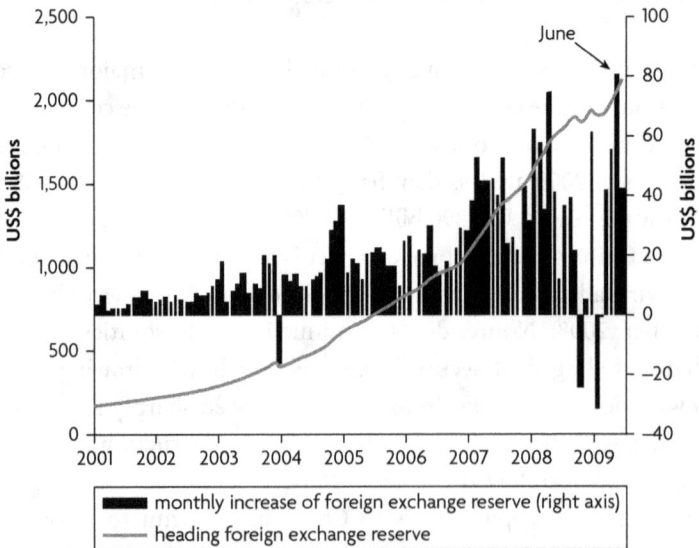

Source: CEIC China Database; World Bank staff estimates.

- The financial system's limited exposure to the toxic assets of the developed world
- The country's minimal reliance on foreign capital for financing economic growth in recent years

While the Chinese government generally does not report in detail on the holdings of financial entities, some commercial banks have disclosed their low levels of exposure to subprime U.S. mortgages relative to their total investments. For example, the Bank of China (one of China's largest state-owned commercial banks and the largest foreign exchange lender) is among the banks with the greatest exposure to U.S. asset-backed securities. Still, its reported exposure to U.S. mortgage-related securities fell from some 3.5 percent of its overall investment securities portfolio in March 2008 to only 1.4 percent in October 2008.

Instead of relying on foreign savings to finance economic activity, China's banks have deleveraged in recent years. With a considerable saving-investment surplus, China has been able to generate and intermediate financing domestically. Unlike many other emerging markets, the country has remained self-sufficient and was able to continue to lend to domestic agents soon after the crisis broke out. A sharp expansion in domestic bank lending is expected to keep fueling growth in the short term.

Policy Responses and the Strong Fiscal Stimulus

In contrast to other crises, policy makers around the world have responded speedily and forcefully to limit the effects of the rapidly deteriorating financial conditions of late 2008. Like many other countries, China launched expansionary monetary and fiscal policies to offset the fast slowing in economic activity worldwide, cushioning the drag from declining world demand and falling private investment.

Loose monetary policy. China radically changed its monetary policy stance in the last quarter of 2008 following a collapse in export markets, a freezing of upstream industrial activity, and declining housing prices. From a tight monetary policy incorporating inflation expectations, the authorities switched to looser monetary policies aimed at boosting credit expansion and supporting economic activity.[9] The central bank began injecting substantial liquidity into the banking system, starting in the last quarter of 2008 (table 4.1).

The aggressive easing of monetary policy supported an extraordinary expansion in bank lending. The year-on-year increase in bank lending climbed from 18.8 percent in the last quarter of 2008 to 29.8 percent in the first quarter of 2009—and to 34.3 in the second quarter. New lending amounted to about 30 percent of GDP in 2009 (figure 4.10).

To ease bank lending in late 2008, the central bank lifted credit quotas and cut interest rates five times (by a total of 216 basis points) during September–December. In large part, the injection came about because

Table 4.1. Monetary Indicators, 2008–09
(% change from previous year period)

	2008				2009	
	Q1	Q2	Q3	Q4	Q1	Q2
M1	18.0	14.0	9.2	9.0	17.0	24.8
M2	16.2	17.3	15.2	17.8	25.4	28.4
Bank loans	14.8	14.1	14.5	18.8	29.8	34.4

Source: CEIC China Database; World Bank staff estimates.
Note: M1 = money supply; M2 = M1 plus quasi-money.

Figure 4.10. New Banking Lending

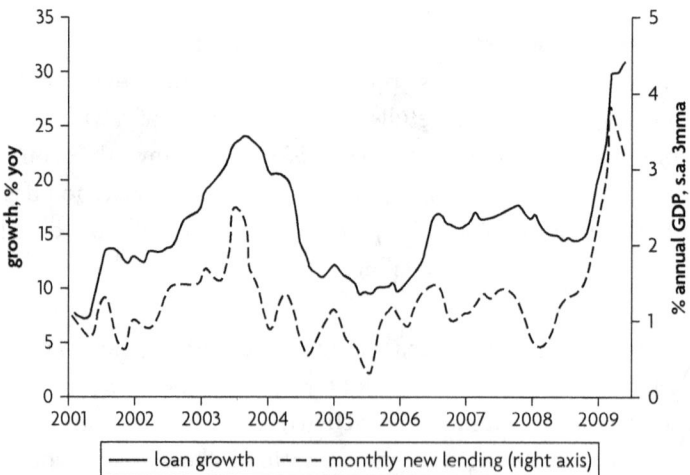

Sources: CEIC China Database; World Bank staff estimates.
Note: mma = monthly moving average, s.a. = seasonally adjusted.

of lower required reserve ratios, which went from 17.5 percent to 14–15 percent. Most banks have sizable capital bases and, so far, low nonperforming loans. Loan-loss reserves have also been increased. Bank profits are, however, being squeezed by falling loan rates and higher provisioning costs, and many need to raise capital after the lending surge.

China's effective exchange rate continues to hover around its U.S. dollar peg. Since the end of 2008, the renminbi has been repegged to the dollar. However, a large and increasing part of China's trade is with countries other than the United States. Thus, as a result of the dollar's movement relative to other currencies, changes in China's trade-weighted exchange rate have differed significantly from movements against the dollar. China's nominal effective exchange rate (NEER) appreciated 12.3 percent between July 2005 and early March 2010, after depreciating in 2000–05, and is now roughly at the level prevailing in 2000 (figure 4.5). This is also true for the consumer price index–based real effective exchange rate (REER). Moreover, large movements in the U.S. dollar versus other currencies have meant that since the repegging against the dollar at the end of 2008, the renminbi has moved up and down recently against the currencies of most of its trading partners. With respect to China's largest trade partner's currency, the EU's euro, the renminbi has appreciated since November 2009.

Fiscal expansion. China's fiscal policy response to the crisis has been bold and effective. In November 2008, the government announced a two-year fiscal stimulus package amounting to Y 4 trillion (US$590 billion). The expansionary fiscal policy aimed to dampen the impact of falling exports and weaker private domestic demand (box 4.2).

Substantial fiscal space combined with strong external confidence allowed the authorities to adopt such a large fiscal package. China had huge fiscal space (unlike most other emerging countries) thanks to its high level of domestic savings, strong external confidence, and low interest rates and spreads. Furthermore, a long track record of fiscal discipline has reduced public debt, allowing China to increase spending and lower taxes without triggering fiscal sustainability concerns. This is true even though total public debt is higher than the headline number of 20 percent of GDP, including the debts incurred by investment platforms associated with local governments.

In addition to the magnitude of the fiscal stimulus, the government front-loaded investment spending and deployed it rapidly. Starting in the

Box 4.2. China's Fiscal Stimulus Package

In November 2008, the government announced a bold two-year fiscal stimulus package amounting to Y 4 trillion (about US$590 billion, or 12.5 percent of 2009 GDP). The central government accelerated the approval process for new projects. The package also envisaged a significant share of the investments being implemented by local governments. The budget allocation under the stimulus package is summarized in table B4.2.1.

Table B4.2.1. Budget allocation under the government of China stimulus package

	Budget, yuan billions	% of total
Total stimulus package, 2008 Q4 to 2010 Q4	4,000	100
Central government new investments	1,180	30
Strategic investment		
Public housing	400	10
Rural infrastructure (electricity, water, and roads)	370	9
Transport and big infrastructure projects (railway, road, airport, irrigations and electricity grid)	1,500	38
Health and education (including building schools and hospitals/clinics)	150	4
Energy and environment (including water and sanitation, sewage, and restoration)	210	5
Technological innovation	370	9
Postearthquake reconstruction	1,000	25

Source: National Reform and Development Commission website, http://en.nrdc.gov.cn.

The Y 4 trillion fiscal stimulus package includes the following components:

- Infrastructure (including rural), transport, and energy investment projects account for 52 percent of the total; this share rises to 77 percent if postearthquake reconstruction spending is added.
- Central government's new investment amounts to Y 1.18 trillion (US$173 billion); Y 104 billion (US$15 billion) was spent in 2008, Y 487.5 billion (US$71 billion) is budgeted for 2009, and Y 588.5 billion (US$86 billion) will be spent in 2010.
- Investments in fixed assets, such as machinery and equipment, were also further encouraged through reforms to the value added tax (VAT), which the government estimated would reduce the corporate tax burden by Y 120 billion (US$18 billion) in 2009.

The impact of the consumption-oriented fiscal measures is more modest. Despite the overwhelming focus on investment, some consumption and social welfare programs are being developed:

- The government has sharply increased financial support for low-income groups and subsidies for the rural sector, including a program that provides a 13 percent subsidy on home appliances (color TVs, refrigerators, washing machines, cell phones).
- In June 2009, the State Council approved a pilot scheme to launch a trial of rural pensions. The amount allocated by the federal government starts out small (about Y 3 billion), but the government plans to extend the program to all rural areas and supplement it with local government budgets; it also includes a self-funded component.
- Earlier in 2009, the government announced a health care reform plan to make health care more accessible and affordable. Spending commitments under this plan are sizable, including wider coverage for medical insurance.

last quarter of 2008, the quickly deployed public investment included major infrastructure projects and rebuilding efforts after the Sichuan earthquake.[10]

Additional measures supported domestic demand more generally. These included lower taxes, subsidies, and pension increases. Other fiscal policies targeting specific industries were also introduced. Strategic plans have been designed to support individual industries—retooling factories, improving energy efficiency, encouraging innovation and research and development spending, and consolidating those industries with excess capacity.

China's fiscal stance has changed dramatically with the stimulus that has boosted aggregate demand. The country's robust growth in 2009 was linked to a massive investment-led stimulus (5.9 percent of GDP) centered on infrastructure, combined with increases in transfers, consumer subsidies, and tax cuts. Only a small portion of the fiscal stimulus was reflected in the budget; the deficit rose moderately from 0.4 percent of GDP in 2008 to 2.8 percent in 2009. Bank lending contributed most of the fiscal stimulus (almost two-thirds) and the lending surge was fairly broad-based: infrastructure made up half of total medium- and long-term lending in 2009, but medium- and long-term lending to manufacturing, real estate (including mortgages), and other sectors also more than doubled (figure 4.11).

Figure 4.11. New Medium- to Long-Term Banking Lending, 2006–09

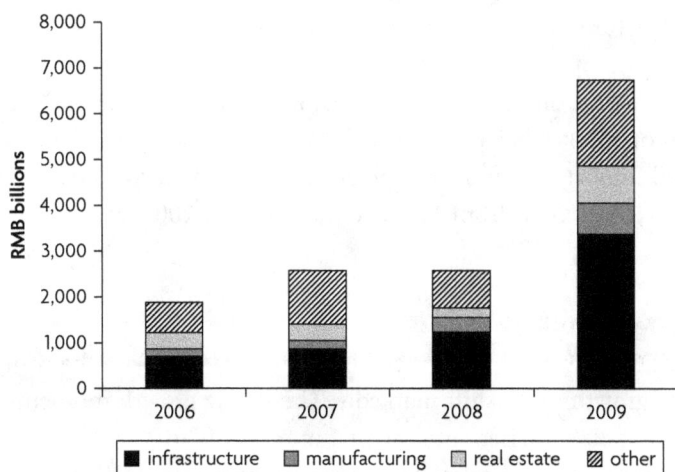

Source: The People's Bank of China; World Bank staff estimates.

Overall, China has shown a large capacity for countercyclical fiscal spending, especially on government investment projects (notably, infrastructure) that have helped put the economy back on a growth path. Besides the positive, short-term Keynesian impact on aggregate demand, which was felt in late 2008 and in 2009, infrastructure investments also tend to be good for medium- and long-term growth, as they relieve constraints by boosting productive capacity and GDP potential.

Although the impact of consumption-oriented fiscal measures was more modest, household consumption growth has remained steady. After weakening in early 2009, labor market conditions have improved and employment and wage growth have held up well through early 2010. Income and consumption have also been further supported by falling consumer prices during much of 2009, which boosted purchasing power; higher government transfers; lower consumption taxes for small cars; and subsidies for rural consumption of electronic appliances.

China's Short- and Medium-Term Prospects

China's large fiscal and monetary stimulus has supported an economic recovery, despite the sharp fall in exports associated with the global recession. The stimulus was the main cause of China's real GDP growth of 8.7 percent in 2009. Although most of the stimulus has shown up in infrastructure-oriented, government-sponsored investment, some has been consumption-oriented; and domestic demand growth has been broad-based. Consumption has remained robust, in large part because the labor market has held up well. The strong domestic demand has buoyed import volumes, and the current account surplus narrowed to 6.1 percent of GDP from 11 percent of GDP in 2007, even with sharp declines in import prices.

Short-Term Outlook

Real GDP growth is likely to remain strong this year, with the composition of growth set to shift markedly. The strong growth momentum at the end of 2009 carried into the first months of 2010, with particularly strong exports, retail sales, and industrial production. We project real GDP growth of 9.5 percent for 2010 as a whole. Exports are set to grow robustly as global demand recovers. Although imports should outpace exports somewhat, net external trade should add modestly to real GDP growth. Real investment growth, however, may be only about half the rate it was last year. In a heated housing market, real estate investment should grow well. On the other hand, government-led investment—the key driver of growth in 2009—is bound to decelerate considerably. In 2011, we expect overall GDP growth to remain strong, with a broadly similar composition as this year's.

With this scenario, the trade surplus (in U.S. dollar terms) may narrow in 2010 because of a projected decline in the terms of trade. The current-account surplus may expand somewhat this year and the next, owing mainly to higher income earned on China's foreign reserve holdings.

While inflation has turned positive, it is likely to remain modest in 2010. Consumer prices picked up in the second half of 2009, led by higher food prices. Nonetheless, inflation will likely average a modest 3.5–4 percent in 2010 as global price pressures remain subdued, China-specific factors behind food price increases abate, and the authorities act decisively to curb core inflation pressures.

The heated real estate market, however, will keep property prices rising rapidly. Prices in the large cities in February 2010 averaged more than 30 percent above those of the previous year, and further increases are in sight. This has prompted policy measures to expand supply and curb speculation, although the government is cautious in its policy response and does not want to reduce real estate activity.

China will need to take a less accommodative macroeconomic policy stance in 2010 to contain the emerging risks. The world economy is still subdued, with output below potential in many countries. China's growth, however, has been strong and, unlike most other countries, its overall output is near potential. The absence of a significant output gap means that China needs to assume a macroeconomic stance different from that of most other economies. Even though inflation risks remain modest because of the weak global environment, the macro stance should be considerably tighter in 2010 than in 2009; this will be necessary to manage inflation expectations and contain the risks of a property bubble and strained local government finances.

In general, the key economic issues in China are quite different from what they are in most other countries:

- *The 2010 budget presented to the National People's Congress rightly implies a broadly neutral fiscal stance.* The 2010 fiscal deficit is now targeted to remain largely unchanged from 2009. However, world economic prospects are still uncertain, and flexibility in implementation is important. This points to the need for contingency plans and, equally important, room for automatic stabilizers to work.

- *Monetary policy needs to be tighter than last year, and the case for exchange rate flexibility and increased monetary independence from the United States (and the dollar) is getting stronger.* A higher renminbi exchange rate can help reduce inflation pressures and rebalance the economy. The case for a larger role for interest rates in monetary policy is strong. Also, if policy makers remain concerned about interest rate–sensitive capital flows, more exchange rate flexibility would help.

- *Given that most of the stimulus package took the form of increased bank lending, concerns have arisen about the effect this will have on the quality of bank portfolios.* A potential risk is that overall economic growth in China could markedly slow in 2010 (and beyond), cutting into the profits of private and state entities, which would in turn create problems in repaying outstanding bank loans. This risk appears minimal, however, and building on the momentum shown in the first months of 2010, economic growth is likely to remain strong in 2010 (9.5 percent). Another mitigating factor is the expected deceleration of government-led investment, the driver of credit growth in 2009. Furthermore, the authorities have outlined a less expansionary monetary policy stance for 2010: overall credit growth is targeted at about 18 percent (versus 30 percent in 2009), monthly credit quotas should keep lending growth in check, and the reserve-requirement ratio has been raised twice to withdraw liquidity.

- *Ensuring financial stability includes mitigating the risk of a property price bubble and ensuring the sustainability of local government finances.* With regard to the property market, stability calls for an appropriate macro stance and improving the functioning of markets. Concerns about the affordability of housing for lower-income people are best addressed by a long-term government support framework. The authorities have rightly increased vigilance over lending by local government investment platforms. Given China's solid macroeconomic position, local financial problems are unlikely to cause systemic stress;

however, the flow of new lending to the various platforms needs to be contained, and local government revenues need to be less dependent on land transaction revenues.

In the medium term, China's recovery can be sustained only with a successful rebalancing of its economy. This calls for more emphasis on consumption and services and less on investment and industry. As China's leaders (including Premier Wen Jiabao) have noted, the global crisis makes rebalancing China's economy all the more urgent. This is because global demand and export growth are expected to be weak, even in the medium term—reducing GDP growth, all else being equal.[11] In addition, China's rebalancing will be helpful in addressing the global imbalances, whose resolution requires that countries like China pursue policies to lower their surpluses.

Following on earlier initiatives, the government took steps in 2009 to rebalance and boost domestic demand. For example, it expanded the role of the government in financing health, education, and social safety nets; improved access to finance and small and medium enterprise development; and contained resource use and environmental damage. These are useful steps, but more policy measures are needed to rebalance growth, given the strong underlying momentum of the traditional pattern. More must be done in all these areas.

More generally, in the years ahead, China will need to undertake two types of structural reform to ensure a successful economic rebalancing and sustained growth:

- *Policy reforms to help channel resources to sectors that should grow in the new environment, instead of to sectors that have traditionally been favored and done well.* Financial sector reform can improve the allocation of capital (and access to finance) for the private sector, service-oriented and smaller firms, and households. Also, the expansion of the dividend payment policy for SOEs can improve the allocation of SOE profits. Adjustment of prices and taxation of resources and strengthening of the renminbi exchange rate can shift production from industry to services. A stronger real exchange rate would support consumption by reducing the prices of tradable goods domestically and increasing labor income at home. It would also give incentives for greater investment in domestically oriented sectors by increasing their relative competitiveness. Thus, despite the problems that it may cause for exporters, further real appreciation of the renminbi is desirable, given China's policy priorities. In addition, opening up several service sectors to the private sector and removing unnecessary regulation and restrictions could boost growth and employment.

- *Policy reforms to support more thriving domestic markets; to encourage successful, permanent urbanization; and to achieve a more vigorous, services sector–oriented domestic economy.* China needs more migrants to settle permanently in the cities. Urban dwellers consume more than rural people and spend much more on services. In addition to opening up services sectors, other key policies to promote successful, permanent migration are further liberalization of the Hukou (household registration) system; land reform; and reform of the intergovernmental fiscal system (to give municipalities the resources and incentives to provide basic public services to migrants). Significant increases in household debt are also feasible. In 2007, the household debt-to-GDP ratio was below 20 percent in China, compared with 100 percent in other Asian countries, and 110 percent in the United States and United Kingdom (see Lardy 2009). With regard to international economic relations, China must (as its leaders have stressed) avoid protectionism, as exports are critical to the recovery of the world economy.

Medium-Term Outlook

Successful implementation of the reforms cited above cannot be taken for granted. Nonetheless, China's medium- and long-term economic prospects look good, as they continue to be supported by broadly appropriate economic policies and institutions and a capable government.

Our medium-term projections on the expenditure components of GDP are based on the following assumptions:

- *Private consumption grows broadly in line with real household income.* As to its determinants, our medium-term outlook for the urban labor market suggests continued robust wage and employment growth. Moreover, further fiscal support to household disposable income is expected in the coming years, with continued—and substantial—increases in government spending on health, education, and social security (even though the overall fiscal stance is expected to remain broadly neutral).

- *The rebalancing of the pattern of growth planned by the government is likely to lead to a somewhat declining share of investment to GDP in the medium term.* However, boosted by the 18 percent investment surge in 2009, the starting level is high, and expectations for investment remain strong. Investment is thus likely to continue growing robustly in the coming years.

- *Exports depend on the strength of world imports.* China's exports have continued to gain market share, and we expect Chinese exports to continue gaining market share in the coming six years—but at a slower pace, owing to saturation effects. In addition, overall market growth is likely to be more subdued than in the past 10 years. In all, in this scenario real export growth is expected to taper off to about 6.5 percent by 2015.

- *Sustaining past patterns, processing import volumes[12] will grow broadly in line with processing export volumes, and nonprocessing imports (used in the domestic economy) will grow broadly in line with domestic demand.* In all, we expect imports to outpace exports somewhat in the medium term, reflecting substantial growth differentials between China and the rest of the world, and some rebalancing. Given this assumption, China's trade surplus in our scenario is smaller compared to the precrisis levels.

Based on these assumptions and projections, GDP growth in China would taper off from 9.5 percent in 2010 to 7.5 percent in 2015. Table 4.2 presents the main variables of the medium-term scenario.

At the same time, we also expect China's potential output growth to slow during 2010–15. The investment projections mentioned above imply a mild decline in the ratio of investment to GDP. On this basis, increases in the capital-to-output ratio are expected to moderate but remain substantial, thus representing a significant contributor to productivity and GDP growth. Demographic projections imply a further moderate decline in the growth of the working population and overall employment. TFP growth is assumed to slow somewhat, as the scope for reaping economies of scale in manufacturing may diminish, leading to a more subdued global trade outlook. But TFP growth should remain

Table 4.2. China: Medium-Term Scenario, 2010–15
(% change, unless otherwise indicated)

	2000	2001	2002	2003	2004	2005	2006	2007	2008	2009	2010f	2011f	2012f	2013f	2014f	2015f
The real economy																
Real GDP	8.4	8.3	9.1	10.0	10.1	10.4	11.6	13.0	9.6	8.8	9.5	8.7	8.0	7.9	7.8	7.6
Domestic demand[a]	7.5	8.5	8.6	10.2	9.7	8.1	9.7	10.8	9.4	13.9	9.7	8.7	8.4	8.2	8.1	8.0
Consumption[a]	8.9	6.6	6.6	5.9	6.8	7.3	8.4	10.2	8.8	9.9	9.6	9.3	9.2	9.1	9.0	8.9
Gross capital formation[a]	5.2	12.0	12.1	16.9	13.6	9.0	11.1	11.4	10.2	18.3	9.7	8.0	7.5	7.3	7.1	6.9
Contribution to GDP growth (pp)																
Domestic demand[a]	7.4	8.3	8.4	9.9	9.5	7.9	9.4	10.4	8.8	12.8	9.1	8.3	8.0	7.9	7.8	7.7
Net exports[a]	0.0	0.0	0.7	0.1	0.6	2.5	2.2	2.6	0.8	-4.0	0.4	0.4	0.0	0.0	-0.1	-0.1
Contribution net exports (pp)[b]	—	—	—	—	—	—	3.8	3.5	1.8	-4.8	0.4	0.4	0.0	0.0	-0.1	-0.1
Exports (goods and services)[b]	30.6	9.6	29.4	26.8	28.4	24.3	24.0	20.0	8.6	-10.4	14.7	9.4	7.0	6.8	6.7	6.5
Imports (goods and services)[b]	24.5	10.8	27.4	24.9	22.7	11.4	16.1	14.2	5.1	4.3	16.4	9.2	8.3	8.2	8.1	8.0
Potential GDP growth	8.7	9.0	9.1	9.7	10.0	10.2	10.5	10.4	10.1	10.0	9.3	8.8	8.5	8.2	7.9	7.7
Output gap (pp)	-1.1	-1.8	-1.8	-1.6	-1.5	-1.3	-0.2	2.3	1.8	0.6	0.8	0.7	0.3	0.0	-0.2	-0.3
CPI increases (period average) (%)	0.4	0.7	-0.8	1.2	3.9	1.8	1.5	4.8	5.9	-0.7	3.7	2.8	2.8	2.8	2.8	2.8
GDP deflator	2.1	2.1	0.6	2.6	6.9	3.8	3.6	7.4	11.4	-2.1	2.8	2.6	2.3	2.0	2.0	2.0
External terms of trade	—	—	—	—	—	—	-0.8	-0.9	-4.3	8.6	-2.9	-0.1	1.1	0.7	0.7	0.7

Fiscal accounts (% GDP)

Budget balance[c]	-2.5	-2.3	-2.6	-2.2	-1.3	-1.2	-0.8	0.6	-0.4	-2.8	-2.8	-2.8	-2.8	-2.8	-2.8	-2.8
Revenues	13.5	14.9	15.7	16.0	16.5	17.3	18.3	19.9	19.5	20.6	19.6	19.8	20.0	20.2	20.4	20.6
Expenditures	16.0	17.2	18.3	18.1	17.8	18.5	19.1	19.3	19.9	23.4	22.4	22.6	22.8	23.0	23.2	23.4

External account (US$ billions)

Current account balance (US$ bn)	21	17	35	46	69	161	250	372	426	297	322	359	391	415	438	458
As share of GDP (%)	1.7	1.3	2.4	2.8	3.6	7.2	9.4	11.0	9.4	6.1	5.8	5.6	5.4	5.0	4.7	4.3
Foreign exchange reserves (US$ bn)	—	—	403	610	819	1,066	1,529	1,946	2,400	2,767	3,148	3,550	3,970	4,411	4,870	

Other

Broad money growth (M2), eop (%)	14.0	14.4	16.8	19.6	14.6	17.6	16.9	16.7	17.8	27.0	17.0	—	—	—	—	

Source: NBS; The People's Bank of China; Ministry of Finance; World Bank staff estimates.

Note: The data are not adjusted for accumulation of arrears in tax rebates to exporters during 2000–02, and the repayment of these arrears in 2004 and 2005. Such an adjustment would increase the deficit in 2000–02 and lower it in 2004–05. f = forecast; — = not available.

a. World Bank estimations using data on contribution to growth (Table 2–20 in China Statistical Yearbook 2009, National Bureau of Statistics of China).

b. World Bank staff estimates based on trade data for goods from the Custom Administration, adjusted for estimated difference in price development for services trade.

c. For 2009 and 2010 this is the commitment data presented to the National People's Congress.

respectable as improvements in education continue to support human capital. In all, potential GDP growth would continue to approximate actual GDP growth, declining from about 10 percent in recent years to 7.7 percent in 2015.

Innovation, technological catch-up, and increased TFP will be critical factors in China's economic growth in the medium term. Concerns about job creation in the enlarged and more technologically advanced services sector will have to be addressed in the new industrial policy.

As noted earlier, China has seen a much milder recession than most other countries and a much smaller output gap; we project a continuing small output gap in the medium term. Actual overall output should also remain relatively close to potential output, continuing the track record since the late 1990s. Inflation is likely to remain moderate in the medium term, largely because of the subdued global inflation pressures expected in the coming years. In general, with growth and macro stability likely to remain in place, policy attention should shift to the structural reforms necessary to rebalance the economy and sustain productivity growth.

A number of factors, however, pose risks to these benign medium-term scenarios. Externally, the world economy is slowly getting back on track but it will take a long time to normalize all financial and trade transactions. Since the second quarter of 2009, the world economy has shown notable signs of stabilization. Industrial production in industrial and emerging economies has recovered, the intermediation function of the financial system has increased, and trade has slowly picked up. However, achieving a comprehensive and broad-based recovery will be a slow, difficult, and complicated process, as Premier Wen Jiabao has indicated: "It would require long-term, concerted efforts by every country in the world."

Domestically, while China's financial sector has shown its resilience to the global turmoil, risks to credit quality exist. These stem from the recent massive growth in bank lending, especially lending for infrastructure projects, and the buildup of excess capacity in some tradable industries. Despite the signs of economic recovery, incentives for overinvestment are present. Therefore, policy makers should keep a watchful eye on the rapid credit growth and should strictly supervise banks.

Another domestic risk involves local government finance. As indicated in box 4.2, local government investment helped prop up growth in

2009. However, a significant portion of this investment (bank loans jumped to Y 7.4 trillion at the end of 2009 from Y 1.7 trillion at the end of 2007) was financed through the borrowings of urban development and investment companies used by local government (Wolfe 2010). If some of the projects financed by these loans prove unable to generate enough revenue, either the state-owned banking sector or central and local governments will have to take on the costs.

While progress has been made in increasing the market's role in determining the exchange rate of the renminbi, China's failure to make the exchange rate regime more flexible could increase the risks of macro vulnerability. A more flexible exchange rate policy would make monetary policy more independent, allowing it to mitigate the impact of external and domestic shocks (IMF 2009). This motivation has become more important as China's cyclical conditions have diverged from those in the United States, which is the current anchor for monetary and exchange rate policy.

Finally, the Chinese authorities will have difficulty pursuing structural reforms in the face of resistance from those benefiting from current policies. For example, it may prove difficult to open up several services sectors to private sector participation or to reform the intergovernmental fiscal system to diminish fiscal inequality.

In sum, successful economic rebalancing could help China sustain medium- and long-term economic growth. Its success, however, depends mainly on the pace and sequence of domestic policies aimed at deriving more growth from consumption and less from investment and exports. Bringing about this change will have global implications. If it is achieved, and if it is combined with the successful rebalancing efforts of other countries, it will help reduce global current account imbalances and lead to a healthier pattern of global growth. For China, however, the more successful the rebalancing effort, the more sustainable will be its future growth path.

Summary and Concluding Remarks

Since the late 1970s, China has experienced impressive GDP growth, averaging 8.9 percent per year during 1995–2001. GDP growth accelerated even further during 2002–07, to an annual average of 11 percent.

China's powerful investment-heavy, industry-led pattern of growth was fueled by the recovery from the Asian crisis, a strong reform agenda, and an active public investment program. Amid a favorable global environment characterized by expanding global demand, Chinese exports surged by about 20 percent annually during 2002–07. While China attracted a large amount of FDI during this period—equal to 3–4 percent of GDP—current account surpluses stayed large, averaging more than 6 percent of GDP. Domestic savings have been the key source of investment financing in China. Were it not for the global crisis, China's potential annual growth rate would have been about 10 percent.

When the crisis hit, China had strong macroeconomic fundamentals with large current account surpluses, low public and external debt, and substantial foreign exchange reserves. Moreover, China's limited exposure to toxic assets in the developed world and its relatively closed capital account shielded it from the initial financial turmoil of 2008. But beginning in November 2008, China's real economy began to feel the effects of the crisis, especially through the trade channel. Export growth plummeted in early 2009, contracting by 25 percent year on year. To counter the effects of the rapidly deteriorating economic conditions of late 2008, the Chinese authorities took strong and quick action: a huge fiscal stimulus package equivalent to 12.5 percent of 2008 GDP and a substantial loosening of monetary policy. The measures limited the impact of the crisis, and economic growth reached 8.8 percent in 2009.

Looking beyond the global crisis, the growth slowdown in advanced countries, and especially slower export demand, can be expected to have a significant impact on China's medium-term potential growth. All else being equal, we estimate that a 10-percentage-point drop in the growth of exports will result in a 2-percentage-point reduction in GDP growth over the medium term—down to about 8 percent annually.

While signs of stronger domestic demand were already evident in 2009, it remains unclear how much the recovery can be sustained in the absence of government stimulus. The government's ability to adopt a more active and sustained policy of rebalancing its economic structure away from dependence on exports and investment to domestic consumption, accompanied by other structural reforms, will be critical. Only such a rebalancing will mitigate the impact of the crisis and put China on a renewed long-term growth path.

Notes

1. Concerns about the distributional impacts of the growth process have led to a debate. For a recent review, see Chaudhuri and Ravallion (2007).
2. This section draws on Kuijs (2005) and Kuijs and Wang (2006).
3. See Kuijs (2005) and (2009) for details.
4. The exact breakdown of the increase in China's domestic savings in recent years is not yet fully clear, with the headline national accounts data in the flow of funds difficult to line up with data from the household survey, the industrial survey, and fiscal information. Large discrepancies have also appeared in the flow-of-funds data themselves, suggesting that the asset data imply higher enterprise saving and lower household and government saving in recent years than the headline flow-of-funds data shown in figure 4.2.
5. A 2003 World Bank report concluded that "service sector development suffers from restrictions and regulation and a lingering bias against private ownership." The OECD (2005) saw similar room for improvement by removing entry and other barriers to the development of services industries.
6. This implication is from Aziz and Cui (2007).
7. The ratio of loans to GDP decreased from a peak of 130 percent in early 2004 to 92 percent in mid-2008.
8. At the end of 2007, gross external reserves were reportedly almost 700 percent of short-term external debt by remaining maturity.
9. Until the fourth quarter of 2008, the central bank had been pursuing a tight monetary policy to prevent a spiral of inflation expectations. These inflationary pressures were arising from food and commodity price increases and rising asset prices, and the tight monetary policy aimed to stop overheating in high-growth sectors. Controls on new lending and credit ceilings (partially voluntary) were put in place.
10. The quick response of government spending partially reflected the fact that a large share of the program had already been drafted for reconstruction after the earthquake in May 2008.
11. Guo and N'Diaye (2009) show that maintaining the current export-oriented growth over the medium to long term would require significant gains in market share through lower prices across a range of industries. This achievement, without consideration of the lower global demand following the current crisis, would necessitate higher productivity subsidies and lower profits. Evidence suggests it will be difficult to accommodate such price reductions. Furthermore, experiences from Asian countries also suggest that there are limits to the global share a country can attain.
12. Processing trade refers to importing all or part of the raw and auxiliary materials, parts and components, accessories, and packaging materials from abroad in bond, and reexporting the finished products after processing or assembly by enterprises in China.

References

Aziz, Jahangir, and Li Cui. 2007. "Explaining China's Low Consumption: The Neglected Role of Household Income." IMF Working Paper 07/181, International Monetary Fund, Washington, DC.

Chaudhuri, Shubham, and Martin Ravallion. 2007. "Partially Awakened Giants: Uneven Growth in China and India." In *Dancing with Giants: China, India and the Global Economy*, ed. L. Alan Winters and Shahid Yusuf, 175–210. Washington, DC: World Bank, and Singapore: Institute for Policy Studies.

Guo, Kai, and Papa N'Diaye. 2009. "Is China's Export-Oriented Growth Sustainable?" IMF Working Paper 09/172, International Monetary Fund, Washington, DC.

IIF (Institute of International Finance). 2009. *Capital Flows to Emerging Market Economies*. Washington, DC: IIF.

IMF (International Monetary Fund). 2009. *World Economic Outlook October 2009: Sustaining the Recovery*. Washington, DC: IMF.

Kuijs, Louis. 2005. "Investment and Savings in China." Policy Research Working Paper 3633, World Bank, Washington, DC.

———. 2009. "Policies Drive Chinese Saving." *China Economic Quarterly* (4th quarter).

Kuijs, Louis, and Tao Wang. 2006. "China's Pattern of Growth: Moving to Sustainability and Reducing Inequality." *China & World Economy* 14 (1): 1–14.

Lardy, Nicholas R. 2009. "China: Leading the Global Economic Recovery." Paper presented at the Global Economic Outlook Meeting, Washington, DC, September 17.

OECD (Organisation for Economic Co-operation and Development). 2005. *Economic Surveys: China*. Volume 2005 (September 13).

Wolfe, Adam. 2010. *Beware! Here Be UDICs: Demystifying China's Local Government Debts*. New York: Roubini Global Economics.

World Bank. 2003. "Country Economic Memorandum." Washington, DC.

Xu, Xinpeng, and Yu Sheng. 2010. "Productivity Spillovers from Foreign Direct Investment: Evidence from Firm-Level Data in China." Paper submitted to the Hong Kong Institute for Monetary Research for a research conference on China's economy, January 11–12.

Comment on "China: Global Crisis Avoided, Robust Economic Growth Sustained"

Shahid Yusuf

The paper provides a concise overview of recent macroeconomic developments in China, forecasts for the medium term, and policy suggestions on rebalancing the Chinese economy. By and large, China emerges from this with flying colors:

- Rapid growth has been sustained over the past decade with relatively stable prices.
- The fast growth has cut poverty to 4 percent.
- Over half of China's growth has been derived from domestically financed capital investment and much of the rest from gains in total factor productivity (TFP), which are the highest in the world.
- Thanks to conservative fiscal policy, public indebtedness is low and the government has plenty of fiscal space.
- China's competitiveness has made it the world's largest exporter, and its external-account surpluses have resulted in a vast accumulation of foreign exchange reserves that safeguard the economy from the

---

Shahid Yusuf is Consultant, World Bank.

sudden stops of capital and the speculative flight of capital that traumatized the East Asian region during the 1997–98 crisis.

With the help of a massive (US$590 billion) two-year fiscal and financial stimulus equivalent to 12.9 percent of GDP in 2008, China weathered the global downturn of 2008–09 and, amazingly, posted a growth rate of 8.8 percent when most other economies contracted or at best grew by 3–4 percent.

While the advanced economies are anticipating anemic growth over the medium term, China, according to the projections in the paper, could grow by 9.5 percent in 2010 and average GDP growth of about 8 percent a year through 2015, with current account surpluses averaging a little less than 5 percent of GDP.

How can one be critical of such a performance? No country is perfect, however, and concerns remain. Echoing the call for rebalancing heard in China and in policy-making circles worldwide, the paper recommends that China revalue its currency so as to reduce its trade surplus and encourage domestic consumption by households, particularly of services. Household consumption could also be stimulated through ongoing measures to expand the social safety net and improve access to education and health services, as these would reduce the propensity to accumulate precautionary savings.

This is the "new conventional wisdom" on the shortcomings of China's performance and medium-term policy agenda. There is certainly some truth to it, although the paper could usefully go beyond the frequently reiterated nostrums and take a more critical approach. It could discuss the need for a coordinated approach to adjustment—with China's main trading partners pursuing aggressive demand management and competitiveness-enhancing policies alongside China's own— and probe in more detail the implications of China's rebalancing for future potential growth and employment. In this context, a number of questions and scenarios could have been explored by the paper, which are discussed below.

With the markets for some of China's export mainstays showing signs of saturation and with the U.S. and EU markets growing more slowly, could a significant weakening of demand further narrow China's trade surplus? If so, by how much does China's real effective exchange rate

(REER) need to appreciate to achieve the desired adjustment, and exactly what degree of adjustment of China's external balance is being sought (by China, by the United States, and by the East Asian economies)? There is a large literature on China's exchange rate that has wrestled with these questions; it would be helpful for the reader if the paper sorted through the evidence (beyond noting the appreciation that has occurred) and the competing claims and arrived at a well-reasoned position—both on the degree of appreciation and on what it could be expected to achieve, with some assumptions regarding China's expected inflation rate and the actions of its main trading partners.

The paper does not make clear that significant adjustment is likely even with a moderate appreciation of the REER. Household consumption has been growing at a robust 8 percent in real terms. The paper assumes that it will grow somewhat faster, but by 2015 domestic savings will still be 49 percent of GDP. There is a reference to robust growth of investment, but with the stimulus being wound down and investment in real estate, manufacturing, and infrastructure likely to ease, investment could return to the precrisis level of about 42 percent by 2011–12, which would also be consistent with GDP growth rates of 8 percent. This would result in current account surpluses of 8 percent, or even more. Where is the rebalancing?

If investment does remain robust and is maintained at approximately 45–46 percent of GDP, what kinds of activities will absorb this capital? Is there overcapacity in many manufacturing industries or not? If rebalancing induces more investment to flow into services, which services activities are poised for rapid expansion? Are these tradable or nontradable services? And could these become a source of exports in the future (as the Chinese are fast learners, and China's deficit on the services account could shift into a surplus)?

China's focus on growth derives in large part from the need to generate jobs—in particular, well-paid jobs. The manufacturing sector has amply fulfilled that role and, by registering high rates of productivity growth, is accommodating fairly steep increases in wages. Can a slowing of economic growth to below 8 percent and an increase in the share of services in GDP continue to generate the number of well-paid jobs (as distinct from the "McJobs" that only contribute to widening inequality) China needs to absorb the anticipated increments in the urban labor force (natural and through migration)? Moreover, if growth dips to the

7–8 percent range—or even less—would investment remain in the range of 42–45 percent of GDP (or decline into the 30–40 percent range, which happened in other East Asian countries after the 1997–98 crisis), and how would this investment be distributed intersectorally to produce such low-growth outcomes?

Suppose that instead of rebalancing by raising consumption and, as a result, reducing the growth of investment, exports, and GDP, China continues to pursue rapid growth with investment and research and development spending as the principal drivers. What, then, could be the potential growth rate over the next five years? To arrive at this number we need to know China's capital/labor (K/L) ratios relative to those of the United States and Japan in the principal two-digit industries, productivity differentials between Chinese industries and U.S. industries, the scope for technological catch-up in the key industries, and the potential for stimulating growth through innovation. My guess is that there is ample scope for raising K/L ratios in China closer to an advanced-country optimum (in manufacturing and services) and that wide productivity and, to a lesser extent, technology gaps remain. By narrowing these and through innovation (as the authors briefly note), China could sustain annual TFP growth close to 4 percent for several more years with the help of high investment rates. With investment rates of 42–45 percent and continuing productivity and technology catch-up in both manufacturing and services, China's growth potential is likely to be in the range of 10–11 percent, rather than 8–9 percent.

The paper could have assessed China's adjustment options in a global context and focused on its growth potential, with a high-growth scenario as a point of reference. If, as indicated, rebalancing through 2015 increases the share of consumption by a couple of percentage points, reduces growth by as much as 3 percentage points by diminishing the marginal product of capital (and raising the incremental capital-output ratio); and reduces the current account surplus by just 1.2 percent of GDP in five years, this would be a lose-lose scenario for China. The economy would sacrifice a lot of growth and catching up, and the increasing global share of exports and large current account imbalances would not placate China's critics in the deficit countries.

By digging deeper into the issue of rebalancing, the analysis could provide many more policy-relevant insights on the issues of growth, the changing sectoral (and intrasectoral) composition of GDP, and household savings that (given population aging, the shortage of caregivers for the aged, rising medical expenses, and uncertainties regarding the adequacy of safety nets and the government's ability to deliver on promised services one or two decades into the future) might not be excessive. Household savings may in fact be excessively low in many of the advanced economies that are treated as comparators.

Ethiopia 5

Sustaining Rapid Growth amidst Global Economic Crisis

Deepak Mishra

When the global crisis first hit, there were two predominant opposing views among analysts in Ethiopia on how it would affect the country. One view was that because of its relative insulation from the global economy, the impact would be weak or nonexistent. The other view was that Ethiopia had in fact become more closely integrated with the global economy over time and would be substantially affected—given that prices had begun converging with world levels, exports had risen sharply, foreign direct investment (FDI) had increased, and the economy had become more dependent on external savings. As things turned out, the global crisis has had a substantial effect on Ethiopia's external sector, but overall, real gross domestic product (GDP) growth has held up quite well. Why and how did this happen?

We begin by examining the direct and indirect impact of the global crisis on the Ethiopian economy. We consider the direct impact by comparing the change in the levels of exports, private transfers (including remittances),

---

Deepak Mishra is Lead Economist, East Asia and Pacific Poverty Reduction and Economic Management Department, World Bank. The author thanks the following people for their useful comments and assistance: Isaac Diwan, Nadeem ul Haque, Chandana Kularatne, Mirafe Marcos, Mustapha K. Nabli, Mefin Girma Bezawagaw, and Utku Kumru.

and private capital flows after the crisis with their potential levels in the absence of a crisis. We then explore the indirect effect by assessing the impact of the crisis on aggregate demand and supply and, thus, on the overall growth rate of the economy. Finally, we consider Ethiopia's prospects for recovery from the crisis and its medium-term growth outlook.

Differing Views on the Impact of the Global Crisis

As noted above, there were two prevailing—and opposing—views on the impact of the global crisis on Ethiopia when it broke out. Those arguing that the impact would be zero or minimal pointed to the government's conscious (and, in their view, prudent) policy of not liberalizing the economy, especially the financial sector. Ethiopia has no foreign banks, no stock market, and no corporate bond market, and the private sector is not allowed to engage in external borrowing, except for a small amount of trade and suppliers' credit. Even the government does little external borrowing apart from official sources. Foreign investors are not permitted to invest in many sectors, such as transport, communication, banking, insurance, construction, and power. As a result, the levels of foreign investment and exports are modest relative to the size of the economy, in comparison other developing countries (figure 5.1a).[1] The channels of transmission through which the global crisis could be transmitted to Ethiopia were therefore either weak or nonexistent.[2]

Those arguing that the economy would be greatly affected by the crisis held that Ethiopia was not the paragon of autarky it was in the past, as its goods market had rapidly integrated with the rest of the world and its economic growth had become increasingly dependent on external savings. Some recent studies have shown that domestic prices in Ethiopia, which were below international levels for many years (after accounting for duties, freight, insurance, and other charges), have begun gradually converging with global prices—indicating Ethiopia's steady integration with the rest of the world. Thus, while merchandise imports made up only 13 percent of GDP in the mid-1990s, the share had risen to 30 percent by the middle of the first decade of the 2000s. Similarly, private capital flows (which is mostly FDI) in Ethiopia was nonexistent at the end of fiscal year 1994 (FY94)[3] but exceeded US$800 million in FY08[4] (figure 5.1b). Private transfers were less than US$270 million in

Figure 5.1. How Integrated Is Ethiopia with the Global Economy? (Cross-Country vs. Time Series)

a. Exports and foreign investment in selected developing countries

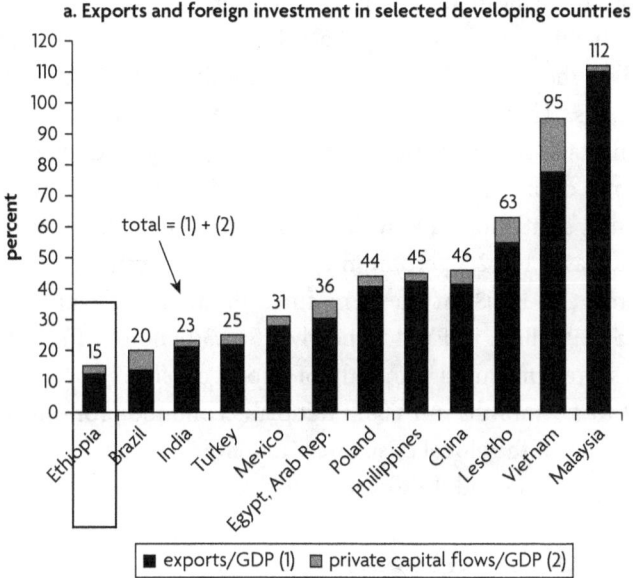

b. Ethiopia's increased reliance on foreign private savings over time

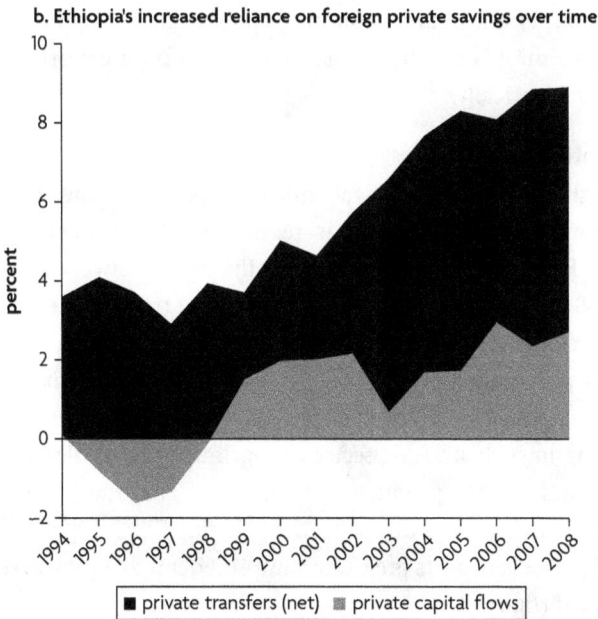

Source: World Bank Live Database 2009; National Bank of Ethiopia; Ministry of Finance and Economic Development (MoFED), Government of Ethiopia (GoE); International Monetary Fund (IMF).

FY94, but rose tenfold, to nearly US$2.4 billion, by FY08. As a result, Ethiopia had become increasingly exposed to external shocks and could not afford to be indifferent to the problems in the world economy.

Assessing the impact of the global crisis on Ethiopia, however, is complicated by the country's own macroeconomic problems predating the global crisis. These problems took the form of high inflation and a severe shortage of foreign exchange, beginning in the mid-2000s. Despite the absence of droughts, which tend to affect its agricultural production, the country's inflation rate, which was in the single digits in previous years, increased to 12.3 percent in FY06, to 15.8 percent in FY07, and to 25.3 percent in FY08. At the same time, the trade imbalance widened from US$1.9 billion in FY04 to nearly US$5.3 billion in FY08. International reserves, measured in months of import cover, fell from 3.7 months in FY04 to 1.9 months in FY08. Ethiopia's economic problems in FY09 (the first year of the global crisis) were therefore a by-product of both its domestic problems and the external shocks.

Assessing the Direct Impact

The global financial and economic crisis coincided with a sharp slowdown in Ethiopia's international trade, with both exports and imports falling dramatically.

International Trade

Although exports are a relatively small component of the Ethiopian economy, they have grown rapidly in recent years. Until the early 2000s, the value of Ethiopia's exports and imports fluctuated between US$500 million and US$1.5 billion, showing a modestly rising trend. For example, during FY97–FY03 (the "preboom" period), exports grew at an annual average rate of 4 percent and imports at 7 percent. The government adopted a new industrial policy in FY02 that provided attractive incentives for firms operating in such strategic sectors as agribusiness, textiles and garments, leather and leather products, and flowers. This fueled an increase in exports, as well as their diversification. During FY04–FY08, (the "precrisis boom" period), exports grew at an unprecedented annual average rate of 25 percent (figure 5.2).

The precrisis boom period was also one of the most favorable periods for economic growth in Ethiopia's history. It was marked by peace,[5]

Figure 5.2. Ethiopia's Merchandise Trade Slowed Considerably after the Global Crisis

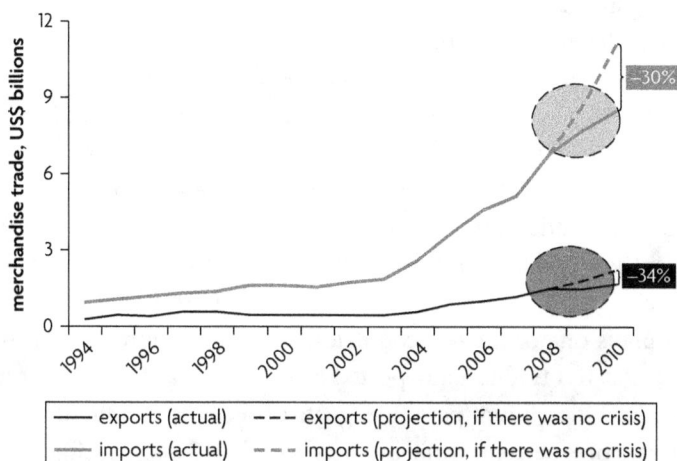

Period	Growth rate of	
	Exports (%)	Imports (%)
1991–96 (transition)	16	3
1997–2003 (preboom)	4	7
2004–08 (precrisis boom)	25	30
2009 (first year of crisis)	–1	13
2010 (second year of crisis)	14	12

Source: National Bank of Ethiopia; MoFED, GoE; IMF.

political stability,[6] good weather, sizable debt relief, and a global war on terror that raised Ethiopia's geopolitical profile and attracted additional aid. These factors, along with an infrastructure boom led by public enterprise and financed with easy money, triggered an economic boom that made Ethiopia one of the fastest-growing countries in Africa—posting five consecutive years of double-digit growth. This helped trigger an unprecedented level of growth in imports; starting from a modest 7 percent annual growth in the preboom period, imports expanded 30 percent annually during the precrisis boom period (figure 5.2).

In 2009, the first year of the crisis, export growth fell to –1 percent and import growth to 13 percent. The corresponding numbers for 2010 are projected as 14 percent for exports (a strong positive shift) and 12 percent for imports (a slight worsening) (figure 5.2). These figures are much below the potential levels that would have prevailed in the absence of the global financial crisis. Indeed, by the end of FY10, Ethiopia will have exported 34 percent less goods relative to what it could have exported had there been no crisis. The corresponding number for imports is 30 percent.

Ethiopia is one of the few countries that export more services than goods, and it has traditionally posted a positive balance on its services account. In the preboom period, exports of services grew at an annual average rate of 9 percent, while imports grew by 12 percent (figure 5.3). Like merchandise trade, services trade accelerated in the precrisis boom period, with exports and imports growing at an annual average rate of 20 percent and 25 percent, respectively. Had these growth rates been maintained for another two years, in FY10 Ethiopia would have posted a deficit on its services account for the first time.

Trade in the service sector has been affected by the global economic crisis, although the effects have taken a year longer to manifest here than in other sectors. In FY09, services exports jumped 21 percent while imports grew 3 percent, widening the surplus in the services account. This led some to conclude—prematurely—that trade in services would remain unaffected by the global economic crisis and that the crisis might even be good for Ethiopia's external balance. Unfortunately, in FY10 services exports fell by 4 percent and imports by 6 percent, dashing any such hopes. The decline is much steeper if the results are compared with the potential growth rates in the absence of the global financial crisis. At the end of FY10, Ethiopia's exports of services will be 22 percent lower relative to a no-crisis scenario; the corresponding figure for imports is even larger, at 61 percent (figure 5.3).

Private Transfers and FDI

Private transfers constitute the single largest source of foreign exchange earnings for Ethiopia—higher than international trade, external aid, or private transfers. With more than 3 million Ethiopians living around the

Figure 5.3. Trade in Services Also Slows after the Crisis, Albeit with a Lag

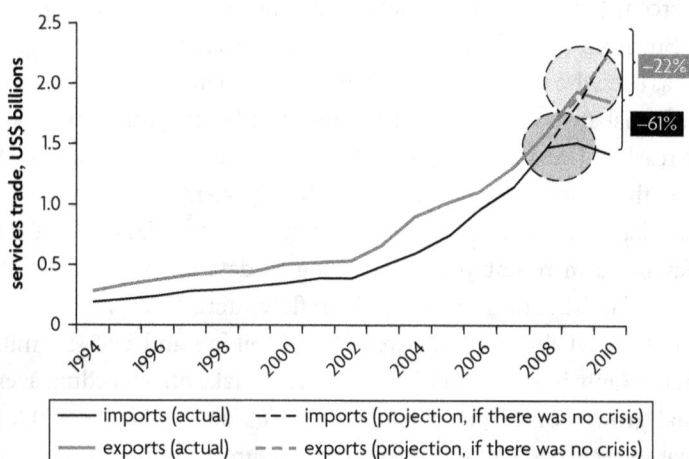

	Growth rate of	
Period	Exports (%)	Imports (%)
1991–96 (transition)	7	4
1997–2003 (preboom)	9	12
2004–08 (precrisis boom)	20	25
2009 (first year of crisis)	21	3
2010 (second year of crisis)	–4	–6

Source: National Bank of Ethiopia; MoFED, GoE; IMF.

world—mostly in the United States, the Middle East, and South Africa—and many of them skilled professionals with higher earnings, remittances to Ethiopia have grown rapidly in recent years. Private transfers also include funds channeled through nongovernmental organizations for developmental activities. Total transfers thus generated nearly US$2.4 billion of hard currency for the country in FY08.

While remittances at the global level declined by nearly 6 percent during FY09, they rose in Ethiopia by 13 percent to US$2.7 billion. Although

private transfers in FY10 are expected to decline marginally (about
0.4 percent), they seem to be holding up quite well, from a global perspective. But from a time series perspective, the deceleration in the growth
rate has been drastic. Specifically, had the growth in private transfers continued unabated at the level of the precrisis boom period, they would
have reached US$4.2 billion in FY10, compared to an estimated US$2.7
billion; this represents a decline of nearly 55 percent (figure 5.4).

FDI has been the fastest-growing component of Ethiopia's balance
of payments in recent years. According to data of the National Bank
of Ethiopia, the country had no FDI inflows until FY97. Between FY97
and FY05, FDI fluctuated between US$7 million and US$150 million
annually. Only in FY06 did FDI really start to take off, recording average
annual growth of 45 percent between FY05 and FY08. In FY09, FDI
increased by 8 percent and is expected to jump another 20 percent in
FY10. While FDI flows into Ethiopia have held up quite well from a
global perspective, their growth rate has slowed. Indeed, had FDI maintained its precrisis boom period growth rate, it would have reached
nearly US$1.8 billion by FY10. The actual value, however, is more likely
to be about US$1.1 billion, a decline of almost 70 percent from the
no-crisis scenario (figure 5.4).

Figure 5.4. Flow of Private Transfers and FDI Are Also Affected by the Global Crisis

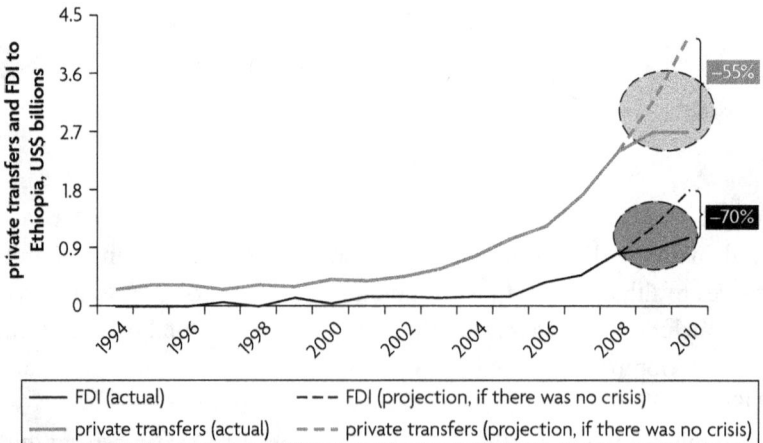

Source: National Bank of Ethiopia; MoFED, GoE; IMF.

Our assessment so far indicates that Ethiopia's external sector has been severely affected by the global economic crisis. Although in absolute terms the decline in the growth of exports, imports, private transfers, and FDI appears small relative to what more open economies have experienced, it is nevertheless significant relative to the precrisis boom period levels in Ethiopia. These findings also support the view that Ethiopia's economy has become increasingly more integrated with the rest of the world and more dependent on foreign capital to finance its growth.

Assessing the Indirect Impact

Given the serious impact of the crisis on the external sector, one would expect Ethiopia's economic growth rate to have decelerated sharply in the wake of the crisis. After all, trade constitutes nearly 35 percent of Ethiopia's GDP, and foreign private savings and private transfers account for more than half of total investment. One would therefore assume that the fall in these variables would be reflected in a weaker overall growth rate.

Surprisingly, however, Ethiopia's economic growth seems to have been largely unaffected by the crisis. In the preboom period, because of the war with Eritrea and drought in FY02 and FY03, real GDP grew at the slow rate of about 4.5 percent annually. The precrisis boom period saw a dramatic acceleration of growth to an annual average rate of 11 percent. Government estimates show that Ethiopia's economy grew 8.7 percent in FY09, and we estimate that it is likely to grow by 8.2 percent in FY10.[7] Extrapolating GDP using the growth rate of the precrisis boom period, we find only a marginal difference between projected and actual GDP— actual growth being 5 percent lower than the projected rate for real GDP, and only 3 percent lower for nominal GDP (figure 5.5). To better understand why the decline in GDP is considerably lower than the decline in external sector variables, we need to take a closer look at the components of GDP.

Impact on Aggregate Demand and Its Composition

Private consumption has historically been the main driver of aggregate demand in Ethiopia (figure 5.6). The share of private consumption (denoted as C) in aggregate demand has generally been about 80–85 percent, and the

Figure 5.5. Ethiopia's GDP Continues Growing Strongly amid the Global Crisis

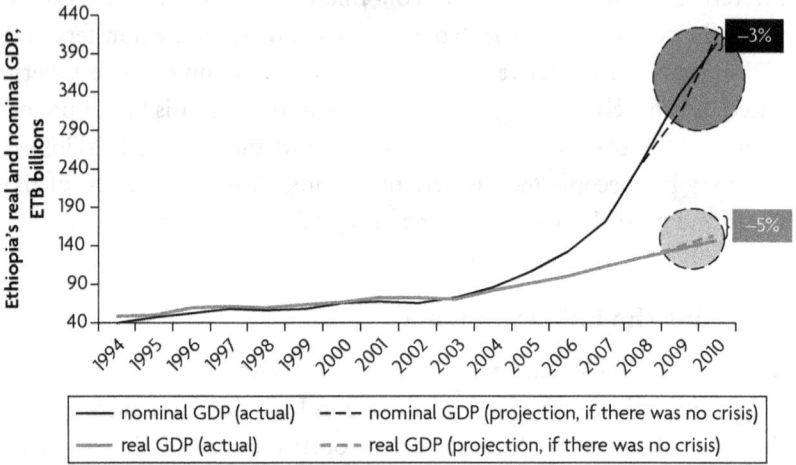

Source: World Bank Live Database 2009; National Bank of Ethiopia; MoFED, GoE; IMF.
Note: ETB = Ethiopian birr.

Figure 5.6. Ethiopia's Rapid Growth in Aggregate Demand Not Curbed by the Global Crisis

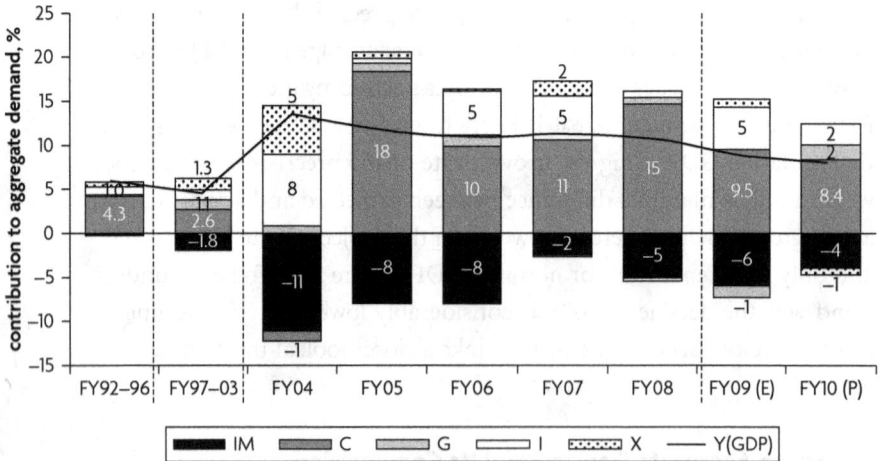

Source: World Bank Live Database (2009); National Bank of Ethiopia; MoFED, GoE; IMF.
Note: The sum of the contributions of *C, I, G* and (*X – IM*) do not add up to the real GDP growth rate because of large error terms for certain years. *C* = private consumption; *I* = investment; *G* = government consumption; *X* = exports; *IM* = imports; *X – IM* = net exports; E = estimate; P = projection.

share of investment (denoted as *I*) has hovered in the 20 percent range. A large part of *C* and *I* are met by imports, whose share has fluctuated by about 35–40 percent of aggregate demand in recent years.

Following the onset of the global crisis, aggregate demand continued to grow at a healthy pace of 8.7 percent. Yet Ethiopia's economy was slowing even before the onset of the crisis. The growth rates in the precrisis boom period were 13.6 percent (FY04), 11.8 percent (FY05), 10.8 percent (FY06), 11.5 percent (FY07), and 10.8 percent (FY08). Therefore, the estimated growth rates of 8.7 percent in FY09 and 8.2 percent in FY10 do not represent a huge deceleration in output growth. However, the composition of aggregate demand has changed considerably. The contribution of private consumption to aggregate demand growth has gradually fallen from an average of 12 percent in the precrisis boom period to 9.5 percent and 8.4 percent in FY09 and FY10, respectively. This decline is mirrored by a gradual decline in the contribution of imports, especially in FY10.

The preceding discussion raises a number of questions. What explains the large contribution of private consumption in the precrisis boom period, and how was it financed? Second, what led to such a sharp drop in the contribution of private consumption and investment in the crisis year? How did Ethiopia manage to keep its growth rate so high despite a near-collapse in the growth of private consumption and investment following the crisis? We turn to these questions next.

Impact on Aggregate Supply and Its Composition

Ethiopia has witnessed a gradual sectoral transformation of its economy. The share of agriculture in aggregate GDP has declined from nearly 60 percent in FY94 to 45 percent in FY08. Its contribution to growth rate has declined even faster—from 7 percent in FY04 to a projected 2 percent in FY10 (figure 5.7). The decline in the importance of agriculture has been matched by a gradual increase in the shares of both industry and services. The services sector seems to have become the driving force of growth in recent years.[8]

The global crisis appears to have had little effect on the trend growth rate across the real sectors (figure 5.7). As noted earlier, Ethiopia's economy was slowing even before the onset of the crisis, and the postcrisis growth rates fall roughly along this trend line. In the first year of the

Figure 5.7. Sectoral Contribution to Ethiopia's Growth Rate

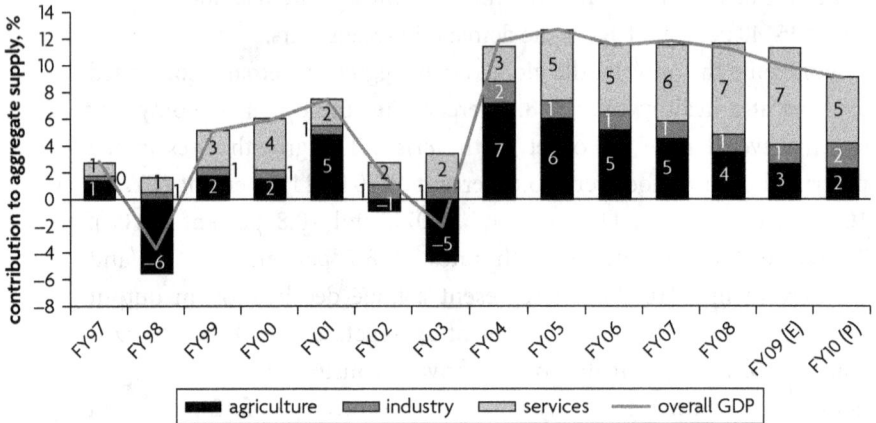

Source: World Bank Live Database 2009; National Bank of Ethiopia; MoFED, GoE; IMF.
Note: E = estimate; P = projection.

crisis, the supply side showed practically no change except for a small decline in the contribution of agriculture. Agriculture growth is largely a function of weather and is unrelated to global events. In the second year of the crisis, the manufacturing sector appears to have gained strength, boosted by the devaluation of the birr.

Explaining the Rapid Growth of the Precrisis Boom Period

The robust growth in private consumption and public investment in the precrisis boom period was financed largely by a rapid expansion of domestic credit and foreign savings. According to an IMF staff report (2008), broad money growth has remained high, driven mainly by credit expansion to the public sector—particularly to public enterprises.[9] Since FY05, domestic credit to public enterprises has grown at an annual average rate of 65 percent (figure 5.8a). This surge in credit has been used primarily to build and upgrade the much-needed infrastructure network of the country, including roads, hydropower dams, and the telecom system. At the same time, a booming economy encouraged the Ethiopian diaspora to send a lot more money home; private transfers

Figure 5.8. Easy Money and Increased Remittances Partly Finance Ethiopia's Economic Boom

a. Growth rate of selected monetary indicators

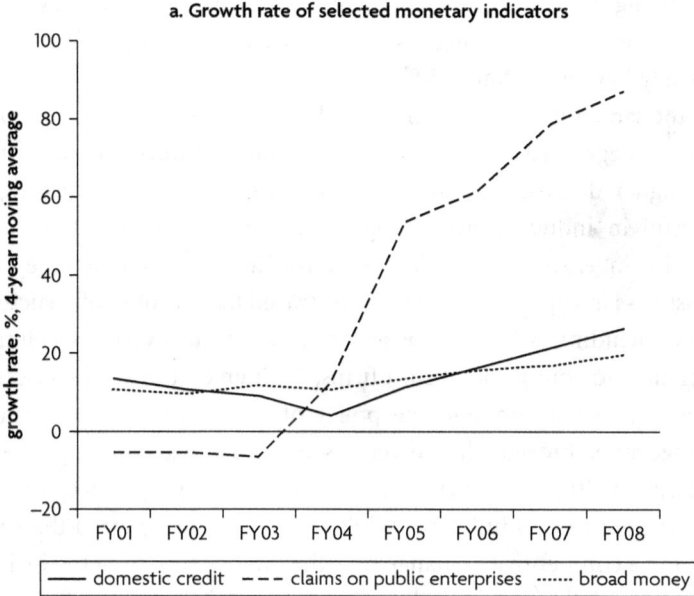

domestic credit   — — — claims on public enterprises   ······· broad money

b. Robust growth in private consumption has been financed by these factors

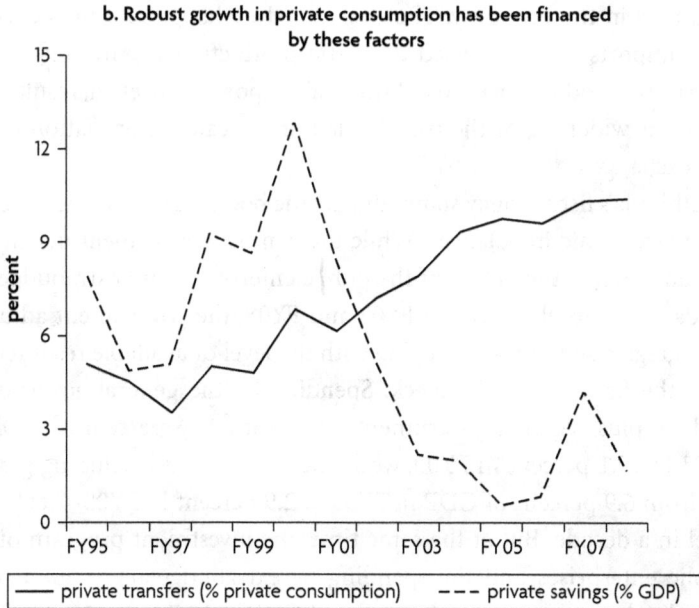

private transfers (% private consumption)   — — — private savings (% GDP)

Source: World Bank Live Database 2009; National Bank of Ethiopia; MoFED, GoE; IMF.

thus accounted for nearly 9 percent of private consumption during the precrisis boom period. Also, the highly negative real interest rate in the banking sector engendered a culture of borrowing and excessive consumption. Private savings as a share of GDP fell precipitously from its already low levels (figure 5.8b).

At the same time, an overvalued exchange rate meant that the robust growth in aggregate demand came from increased imports rather than from higher domestic production. While the government was highly successful in inducing strong aggregate demand growth, it was less successful in ensuring a healthy response from the supply side. The sluggishness in aggregate supply can be traced to a number of structural factors, including weak private sector capacity, an investment climate less friendly to young and upstart firms, the high cost of such services as transport and telecom, and the policy of maintaining an overvalued exchange rate. Indeed, the currency's real exchange rate appreciated by nearly 35–40 percent between FY03 and FY08, largely because of a persistent increase in inflation. While the authorities realized the value of having a competitive exchange rate, they were hamstrung by the high and rising inflation rate and did not want to stoke further inflationary pressures in the economy. The overvalued exchange rate thus encouraged imports and depressed domestic production (figure 5.9). So, as global commodity prices rose, Ethiopia's import bill swelled, resulting in a further widening of the trade deficit and greater appreciation of the real exchange rate.

Ethiopia's fiscal policy stance during the boom years also increased its macroeconomic imbalances. While the general government deficit was low and falling, the deficit of the public enterprises and extrabudgetary funds grew rapidly. Between FY03 and FY08, the government adjusted its aggregate spending in keeping with the level of available resources to keep the fiscal deficit in check. Spending by the general government (federal plus regional governments) fell from 23.6 percent of GDP in FY03 to 19.1 percent in FY09, while the fiscal deficit (including grants) fell from 6.9 percent of GDP in FY03 to 2.9 percent in FY08—its lowest level in a decade. But at the same time, the investment program of the public enterprises and the spending by extrabudgetary funds is estimated to have risen from 5.9 percent of GDP to 10.7 percent—the latter figure estimated to be more than the combined capital budget of the

Figure 5.9. Overvalued Exchange Rate Encourages Imports over Domestic Production

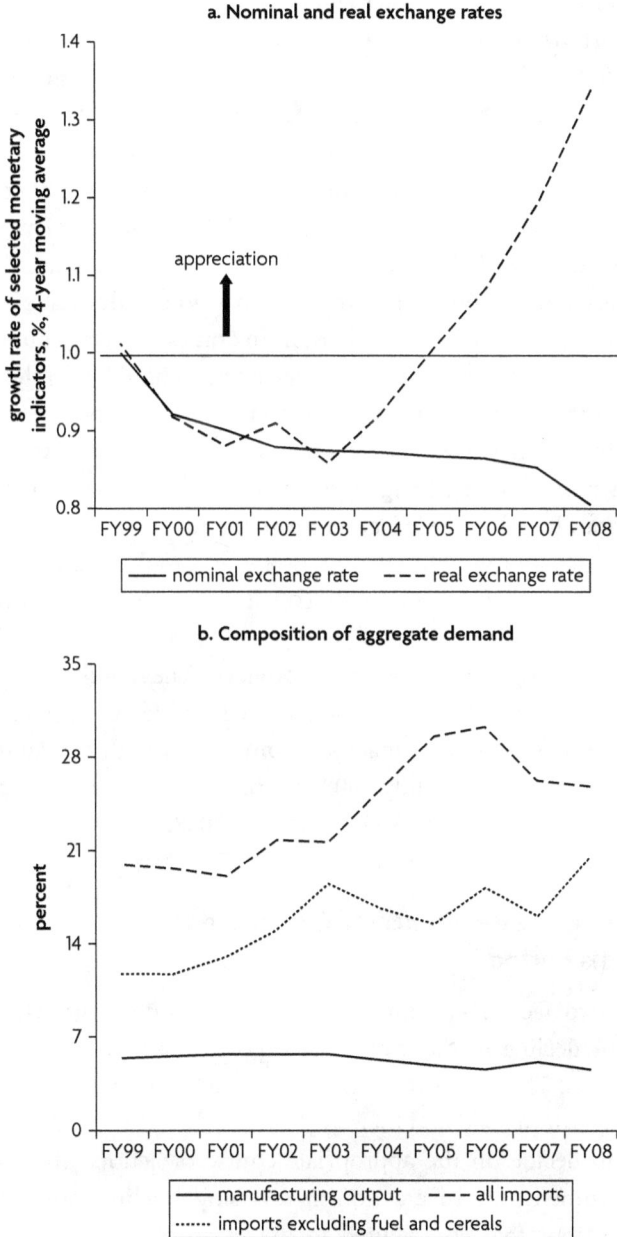

a. Nominal and real exchange rates

appreciation

nominal exchange rate   — — — real exchange rate

b. Composition of aggregate demand

manufacturing output   — — — all imports
.... imports excluding fuel and cereals

Source: World Bank Live Database 2009; National Bank of Ethiopia; MoFED, GoE; IMF.

federal and 11 regional governments. According to the IMF (2008), borrowing by public enterprises played a significant role in loosening the fiscal stance and contributing to higher inflation.

In short, while structural policies pursued by the Ethiopian authorities limited the impact of the crisis, macroeconomic policies worsened the impact. The government's long-standing policy of not liberalizing its financial sector helped limit the spread of financial contagion. But at the same time, the authorities' accommodating monetary stance increased the economy's vulnerability to global shocks.[10] The government strategy to invest heavily in infrastructure and social services as a way to jump-start growth did lead to robust expansion in domestic demand. However, since this was financed not from domestic savings but through rapid growth of reserve money, it created excess liquidity in the system. While the general government pursued a prudent fiscal policy, the public enterprises were reckless in their investment programs. At the same time, an overvalued exchange rate encouraged imports over domestic production. Together, these factors created a growing imbalance between domestic demand growth and the domestic supply response and laid the groundwork for a rising trade deficit. As global commodity prices increased steeply in 2007–08, foreign inflation was imported into Ethiopia, pushing its inflation to a record level. The rapidly rising import bill quickly drained Ethiopia's foreign exchange reserves, plunging the country into its worst-ever macroeconomic crisis, with annual inflation peaking at 64 percent in July 2008 and international reserves falling to just four weeks of import cover by October 2008.

Explaining the Resilience of Growth in the Postcrisis Period

At least two factors explain Ethiopia's robust output growth despite the major decline in the growth of exports, remittances, and private capital flows. The first is the timely response by donors in significantly increasing external aid and thereby providing breathing space for policy makers to decide on the appropriate course of action. The second is the government's decisive action in reversing or eliminating many of the distortions that contributed to the macroeconomic vulnerability in the first place.

Large Infusion of External Aid

Despite its low per capita income and high level of poverty, Ethiopia is not one of the largest recipients of external aid in Africa. Aid to Ethiopia has been subject to sharp fluctuations in the past, declining during its war with Eritrea (FY98–FY99) and again in FY06 owing to postelection violence. In per capita terms, aid to Ethiopia is less than US$30, well below the Sub-Saharan African average. However, external aid to Ethiopia has surged in recent years, largely in the form of long-term loans and from such nontraditional sources as the governments of China and India.

The onset of the global crisis coincided with a sharp increase in external aid to Ethiopia. Faced with the twin crises of high inflation and a severe shortage of foreign exchange, the government had begun asking donors to boost their aid well before the global crisis erupted. By the time the donors responded, the impact of the crisis had become more visible; the additional aid in FY09 thus could not have come at a better time. The higher level of aid was maintained in FY10, especially after Ethiopia agreed to an IMF-supported adjustment program, which provided an additional US$400 million in aid in FY10. Consequently, the level of total external aid in FY10 was 21 percent higher than it would have been had the donors maintained their precrisis aid growth rates (figure 5.10).

The Government's Policy Response

The government took a number of measures to address the domestic economic imbalances and mitigate the impact of the exogenous shocks. Since the country's aggregate demand was running ahead of its efforts to expand the economy's aggregate supply capacity, the authorities had to, in the short run, take steps to curb excess demand. Pursuing tight fiscal and monetary policies in the midst of a global crisis may seem counterintuitive, but it was justified, since Ethiopia's fundamental problem was a domestic imbalance that had been made worse by the external shocks.

Some of the key reforms undertaken so far include the following:

- *Depreciating the local currency.* The Ethiopian birr has been allowed to depreciate in a step-wise fashion by nearly 40 percent against major currencies since January 2009. After a series of depreciations, the

Figure 5.10. Ethiopia Sees Sharp Rise in External Aid Postcrisis

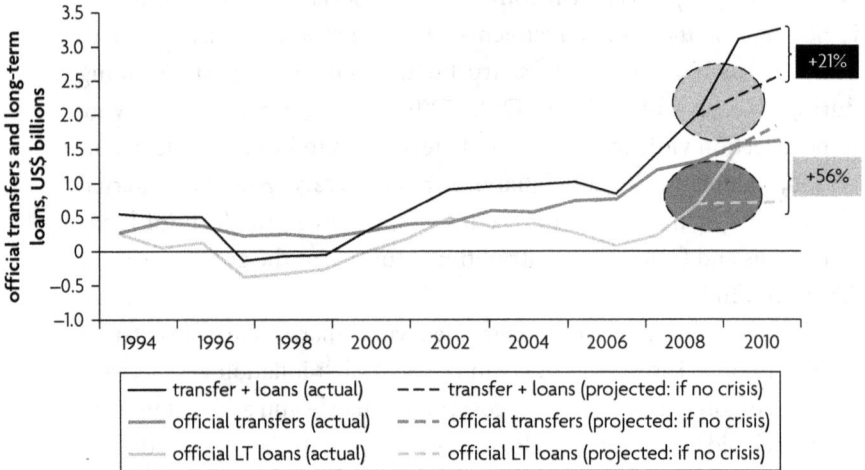

Source: World Bank Live Database 2009; National Bank of Ethiopia, Ministry of Finance, GoE; and IMF.
Note: LT = long-term.

premium in the parallel foreign-exchange market has fallen to less
than 5 percent.

- *Eliminating domestic fuel subsidies.* The government eliminated the
  fuel subsidy in October 2008 by adjusting regulated domestic prices
  to the import parity level: prices of gasoline, diesel, fuel oil, and kerosene were raised 6 percent, 39 percent, 32 percent, and 50 percent,
  respectively.[11] The authorities also dismantled the old pricing system,
  replacing it with a new one in which domestic fuel prices are reviewed
  and adjusted on a monthly basis.

- *Tightening fiscal policy and ceasing domestic borrowing.* The federal
  government cut domestic borrowing to zero in FY09 by limiting
  spending and enhancing revenue mobilization through administrative measures. The central government fiscal deficit was reduced from
  2.9 percent of GDP in 2007–08 to 1.1 percent in 2008–09.

- *Reducing the domestic borrowing of public enterprises.* Public enterprise
  borrowing was reduced to 2 percent of GDP in 2008–09, as compared
  with 4.4 percent in 2007–08, by limiting these enterprises' investment
  activities and by repaying the debt of the Oil Stabilization Fund. The

government also established an interagency committee to monitor the activities of key public enterprises and public institutions.

- *Tightening monetary policy.* The National Bank of Ethiopia kept broad money growth below 20 percent in 2008–09, versus about 23 percent in 2007–08. Building on earlier increases in reserve requirements (in July 2007 and April 2008) that helped trim banks' excess reserves, the NBE closely monitored and controlled reserve money creation arising from its net lending to the government.

- *Curbing inflation expectations.* To dampen inflation expectations and soften the impact of inflation on the most vulnerable populations, the government imported 520,000 metric tons of food grains (about 3.5 percent of domestic production) using its own resources and sold part of it to the urban poor at a subsidized price. It also temporarily abolished the value added tax, turnover tax, and surtaxes on some food items, and increased the cash-for-work wage rate (and the cash transfer rate for labor-poor households) in its rural Productive Safety Net Program from 6 Ethiopian Birr to 8 Birr a day.

Of all the policy measures, the one with the largest impact on medium-term growth is likely to be the decision to correct the overvaluation of the real exchange rate. As Ethiopia's structural transformation takes shape and FDI inflows increase, a competitive exchange rate should spur domestic production. Already evident in FY10 is a modest switch in the aggregate expenditure from tradables to nontradables (figure 5.6). The contribution of imports to aggregate demand growth has declined from an average of 8 percent in the precrisis boom period to 4 percent in FY10. However, the corresponding numbers for aggregate domestic demand $(C + I + G)$ are 16 percent and 13 percent, respectively—indicating that at least 1 percent of aggregate demand has switched from imports to domestic production.[12]

Ethiopia's ability to sustain rapid growth, however, will largely depend on the breadth and depth of its structural reform. Real GDP growth, though extremely high, has been on a declining trend since before the current global crisis. In our view, this is largely because the structural reforms initiated in the early 2000s have just about run their course. The country can reap considerable benefits by gradually correcting some of its domestic distortions (box 5.1).

Box 5.1. Structural Reforms That Could Spur Growth

Ethiopia's economy is characterized by many domestic distortions, which it needs to address while gradually opening its economy to international competition.

Needed structural reforms include the following:

Improving the investment climate. The government needs to implement a second-generation industrial policy that is flexible in its approach and encourages the discovery of new industries apart from strategic priority sectors—both for exports and for the domestic market. This includes creating an incentive regime that enables "pioneer firms" (firms introducing new products/services and/or firms engaged in major technological upgrading) to negotiate a more tailored incentives package.

Establishing a public-private sector dialogue forum, which can be an effective mechanism for strengthening dialogue and feedback between the public and private sectors and a key input into business-related policy formulation. Also, approval of the revised Trade Practices Proclamation Act will help address unfair competition in all sectors and segments of the economy.

Modernizing the financial sector. Ethiopia will benefit by adopting a long-term national architecture for a modernized national payment system, developing a long-term business strategy for the Credit Information Center, and creating a Central Depository System and Transaction Disclosure/Records System (back end of the stock market) to help increase transparency in the financial transactions in the growing over-the-counter stock market.

Developing a competitive telecom sector. The country needs a competitive telecom sector; this can be achieved by allowing private sector entry into all segments of the telecom market and by constituting a strong and independent regulatory body to oversee the liberalized environment.

Improving the land market. Ethiopia needs to establish an efficient land and real estate market by creating a transparent and effective system of land development and administration.

Recovery and Medium-Term Growth Prospects

Ethiopia's medium-term outlook depends on the availability of foreign savings to support economic expansion. Throughout the precrisis boom period, the economy suffered a pervasive shortage of foreign exchange. Indeed, the lack of sufficient foreign exchange—which reflects structural distortions in the economy—is the binding constraint on Ethiopia's growth prospects.

Any projection of growth for Ethiopia must therefore begin with a realistic assessment of its balance of payments position. We project each component of the balance of payments separately: merchandise exports and imports, private transfers, exports and imports of nonfactor services, private capital flows, and external aid. We project each of these variables using a number of domestic and global parameters. We readjust these flows to ensure that there is no funding gap, that is, that the balance of payments remains sustainable over the forecast period (which means that international reserves are enough to cover more than two months of imports). We project that as the impact of devaluation slowly takes hold, the contribution of net exports to GDP growth will gradually turn positive, from −5.3 percent as of FY10 to 0 percent by FY12 (table 5.1).

Table 5.1. Ethiopia: Medium-Term Scenario, 2010–13

	FY06	FY07	2008	2009	2010f	2011f	2012f	2013f
Real GDP growth at market price (%)	10.8	11.5	10.8	8.7	8.2	8.0	7.6	7.6
Domestic demand growth (%)	13.8	12.9	13.2	10.6	9.9	8.0	5.4	6.0
Consumption	11.9	11.0	16.5	8.4	10.4	9.1	5.0	6.4
Gross capital formation	21.3	19.5	2.1	18.7	8.1	4.2	6.8	4.7
Contribution to GDP								
Domestic demand	16.2	15.5	16.1	13.1	13.0	9.8	7.5	7.6
Net exports	−7.9	−0.9	−5.5	−5.2	−5.3	−1.6	0.0	−0.8
Statistical errors	2.6	−3.2	0.2	0.8	0.5	−0.2	0.1	0.7
Contribution net exports								
Exports of G & NFS	0.1	1.5	−0.4	0.8	−0.8	1.8	1.9	2.2
Import of G & NFS	−8.0	−2.4	−5.1	−6.0	−4.5	−3.4	−1.9	−3.0
Potential GDP growth	8.5	8.5	8.5	8.5	8.5	8.5	8.5	8.5
Output gap	2.3	3.0	2.3	0.2	−0.3	−0.5	−0.9	−0.9
CPI increase (period average) (%)	11.6	17.2	30.5	24.4	5.6	8.4	6.6	6.1
GDP deflator	11.6	17.2	30.5	24.4	5.5	9.1	7.5	7.0
External terms of trade	3.5	−1.3	1.9	7.8	12.2	−2.1	0.1	0.8
External accounts (US$ billion)								
Current account balance	−1.4	−0.9	−1.5	−1.6	−2.4	−2.9	−2.6	−2.4
As share of GDP (%)	−9.1	−4.5	−5.6	−5.1	−7.9	−9.3	−7.5	−6.7
Foreign exchange reserves (US$ bn)	1.2	1.3	0.9	1.5	1.9	2.2	2.4	2.6

Source: World Bank; International Monetary Fund; staff estimates.
Note: f = forecast; G = goods; NFS = nonfactor services; CPI = consumer price index.

We project the remaining components of aggregate demand individually. Government consumption (G) is estimated from the authorities' medium-term fiscal framework. We calculate investment (I) based on future investment projections of key state enterprises and the framework (which together account for 75 percent of total investment in the country), and we assume that private investment will be a certain proportion of FDI. Private consumption (C) is the residual in the aggregate demand equation.

The results of this exercise and the key underlying assumptions (table 5.1) show that the Ethiopian economy was growing well above its potential growth rate during the precrisis boom years; we estimate the potential growth rate by averaging the difference between the cyclical component of the output growth and the actual output growth during FY01–FY08. The potential growth rate is thereby estimated at 8.5 percent.[13] During the crisis years, the actual growth rate fell below potential output growth, and we expect it to gradually converge to its potential in the outer years. As our projection shows, we do not expect the Ethiopian economy to continue growing above its potential output growth rate, since the favorable global conditions of the precrisis boom period are unlikely to be replicated in the near term.

The actual growth rate is likely to be below the potential growth rate in the foreseeable future for many reasons. Ethiopia's actual output growth rate will remain below its potential growth rate of 8.5 percent in the medium term (figure 5.11), largely because the structural reforms required to permanently raise Ethiopia's aggregate supply function either are not in place or will take considerable time to take effect (box 5.1). Moreover, the favorable weather of the past six years is unlikely to continue indefinitely. The country will, however, continue to benefit from increased foreign investment from China, India, and a few other emerging markets, and will begin to reap the benefit of recent years' increased investment in hydropower. However, the impact of these variables on potential output growth will take some time to manifest.

Concluding Remarks

Ethiopia's economy has been experiencing macroeconomic difficulties for some time now, initially because of domestic factors and later as a result of external shocks. With the objective of modernizing its economy

Figure 5.11. Ethiopia's Medium-Term Growth Prospects under Two Scenarios

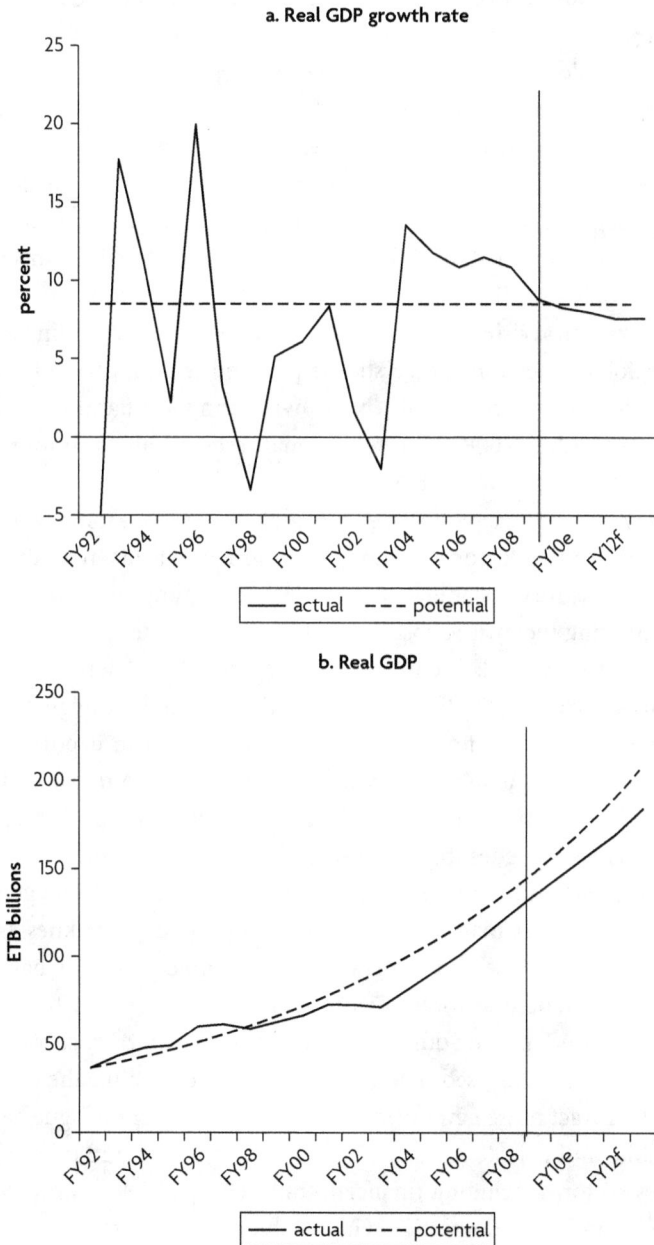

a. Real GDP growth rate

b. Real GDP

Source: World Bank; IMF.
Note: e = estimated; f = forecast.

and transforming its society, the government adopted a strategy in the early 2000s of investing heavily in infrastructure and social services. This strategy was carried out largely by public enterprises financed by a rapid expansion of domestic credit. The strategy was highly successful in stimulating aggregate demand, but aggregate supply has been less responsive owing to weakness in private investment. This has created a growing imbalance between domestic demand growth and the domestic supply response, and has laid the groundwork for rising inflation and widening trade deficits. While mired in its own domestic macroeconomic problems, Ethiopia was hit with a series of unprecedented external shocks—first rising commodity prices and later plummeting exports and a global recession. These shocks plunged the country into one of its worst-ever macroeconomic crisis, with annual inflation peaking at 64 percent in July 2008 and international reserves falling to four weeks of import cover by October 2008.

But Ethiopia has withstood the global crisis reasonably well so far, thanks to two factors. First, the government has taken a number of decisive measures to stabilize the economy, including such bold reforms as eliminating fuel price subsidies and allowing the birr to depreciate by more than one-third. Second, donor partners have stepped up their assistance during FY09–FY10, offsetting the decline in foreign exchange earnings associated with slower or negative growth in exports, remittances, and FDI. As a result growth has not suffered much and poor households have been given considerable protection since a large part of donors' assistance goes to protect spending in social sectors.

Nevertheless, Ethiopia may not be able to take full advantage of the global recovery, as many of the economy's structural weaknesses have remained unaddressed. Ethiopia's macroeconomic problems have both cyclical and structural roots. To its credit, the government has taken a number of measures to address the cyclical factors, but structural distortions remain unaddressed. These include the need to refine the industrial policy to attract more new businesses, promote a better dialogue between the public and private sectors, create a more efficient and cost-effective services sector—including financial, transport, and telecommunication services—and raise domestic savings. Ethiopia is unlikely to experience rapid and sustained growth as long as these structural distortions remain a millstone around the economy's neck. We therefore estimate that the average real GDP growth rate in the medium term will be about 7.5 percent, below its potential growth of 8.5 percent.

Notes

1. The 12 countries included in figure 5.1 were initially part of this study. Since then case studies for two countries have been dropped from the project. Data for all countries except Ethiopia are from the World Bank's Live Database. All data for Ethiopia are from national sources.

2. The following remark by Ethiopia's Prime Minister captures the sentiment widely shared by policy makers there about the impact of the global crisis: "It is projected that the global crisis will continue to prevail for the next two or three years[;] on our side there is a hope that our economy will continue to grow at the same pace" (http://allafrica.com/stories/200903060610.html).

3. A study by Leoning, Durevall, and Ayalew (2009) finds that international price movements explain a large portion of Ethiopia's inflation during 2000–08. The IMF (2009) argues that Ethiopia's recent inflation was the result of a one-time increase in the price level to one comparable with global levels.

4. Ethiopia's fiscal year runs from July 1 to June 30. Throughout this chapter, for convenience, fiscal year 1993–94 is referred to as FY94, and similarly for other years.

5. The border war with Eritrea ended in a decisive victory for Ethiopia. International public opinion also turned critical of Eritrea and supportive of Ethiopia.

6. Following a split in the rank and file of the Tigray People's Liberation Front (TPLF) in 2001, the faction led by the current prime minister emerged as a politically stronger and more cohesive force than before. While national elections in 2005 were marked by violence and loss of international goodwill toward the government internally, the incumbent party, the Ethiopian Peoples' Revolutionary Democratic Front (EPRDF), emerged more powerful and better organized.

7. Our real GDP growth rate numbers are the same as the government's numbers until FY09, but we differ in future projections.

8. The source of this large, robust increase in services sector GDP in recent years is not well understood. There has been a persistent discrepancy between the government's own projections of services sector output and those of the IMF and the World Bank. A recent IMF mission found that many of the parameters used in estimating services sector GDP are outdated and are not consistent with data from other sources.

9. The problem was made worse in 2007, when the central bank temporarily resumed providing direct advances to the government in response to commercial banks' request to rediscount treasury bills.

10. Also see World Bank 2008.

11. Fuel subsidies are not necessarily a pro-poor measure. Laderchi and Raj Kumar (2008) suggested that subsidies for petroleum products, including kerosene, are captured disproportionately by the rich. The lowest-income quintile receives less than 10 percent of total subsidies, while the top quintile receives about 44 percent.

12. In a surprise move, Ethiopia depreciated its currency further by 16 percent in August 2010. This step is believed to spur domestic production and increase the level and diversity of its export basket.

13. A potential output growth rate of 8.5 percent may appear too high, but during the past 10 years Ethiopia's economy has grown at an annual average rate of 8.1 percent. During this period it has fought a war with its neighbor (Eritrea), invaded Somalia (2006–08), had a severe drought (2002–03), was on the brink of a balance of payments crisis, experienced extremely high inflation (peaking at 64 percent), and experienced some unprecedented violence following one of its national elections (in 2005). It is hard to imagine a worse scenario than this, and yet the growth rate has been a robust 8.1 percent.

References

IMF (International Monetary Fund). 2008. "The Federal Democratic Republic of Ethiopia: 2008 Article IV Consultation—Staff Report." IMF Country Report 08/264, IMF, Washington, DC. http://imf.org/external/pubs/cat/longres .cfm?sk=22226.0.

———. 2009. "The Federal Democratic Republic of Ethiopia: Request for a 14-Month Arrangement under the Exogenous Shock Facility-Staff Report." Country Report 09/296, IMF, Washington, DC. http://www.imf.org/external/ country/ETH/index.htm.

Laderchi, R. Caterina, and Andrew Sunil Rajkumar. 2008. "Benefit Incidence Analysis of Petroleum Subsidies in Ethiopia." Policy Note, World Bank, Washington, DC.

Leoning, L. Joseph, Dick Durevall, and Yohannes Ayalew. 2009. "Inflation Dynamics and Food Prices in an Agricultural Economy: The Case of Ethiopia." Policy Research Working Paper 4969, World Bank, Washington, DC.

World Bank. 2008. "Finding Lasting Solutions to Ethiopia's Macroeconomic Problems: Some Options." Policy Note, World Bank, Washington, DC.

Discussant Paper

Comment on "Ethiopia: Sustaining Rapid Growth amidst Global Economic Crisis"

Ishac Diwan

This is a very nice article—concise, with clear, rich arguments and well-designed graphs that speak a thousand words.

The punch line is delivered early: Ethiopia is no longer the paragon of autarky that we have gotten used to hearing about. It has been greatly affected by the recent global crisis, both because several of its channels of interaction with the global economy have become powerful over time, and because Ethiopia has faced the crisis with large macroeconomic imbalances. Growth has continued but it remains below potential. The chapter's main arguments are as follows.

- Precrisis, the economy was overheating, driven by high public investment. Inflation reached 25 percent in 2008 (it peaked at 64 percent in July 2008) and the balance of payments deficit stood at US$5 billion that year.
- The collapse in the growth of foreign direct investment (FDI) and of private transfers, which were financing the growing precrisis

Ishac Diwan is Country Director, Western Africa Region, World Bank.

external-payments deficit, led to a devaluation-induced adjustment (especially a reduction in imports).

- It is posited that the crisis hit exports (which suffered a 25 percent decline), FDI, and remittances (which fell in 2010 by 55 percent and 70 percent, respectively, relative to their precrisis trends), but that GDP was only 5 percent lower (cumulative), owing to fast adjustment (devaluation essentially) and the accompanying increase in official development assistance.
- GDP remains below potential because of structural weaknesses.

So the story is essentially about foreign exchange as the main constraint to growth. The precrisis rapid increase in FDI and remittances afforded some slack for a few years and larger imports allowed higher growth (infrastructure and housing, facilitated by easy credit). But the economy had to adjust suddenly when the global crisis reduced credit and imports, although this was partially cushioned by an increase in official development assistance and resumed expansion of exports.

This simple one-gap model view of the Ethiopian economy is essentially right. However, I suggest that several structural complexities be considered in parallel, as these have implications for both the causes and the consequences of the shock. These are mainly related to (a) the role and dynamics of agriculture in the economy, (b) the need to build infrastructure for long-term growth, and (c) the need to create urban jobs. I will illustrate this point with three remarks on specific aspects of the adjustment and growth processes in Ethiopia: the behavior of exports, the causes of the precrisis overheating, and prospects for medium-term growth.

What Drives Exports?

It is tempting to attribute much of the behavior of exports to exchange rate movements and external demand, as the author does. In this view, exports collapsed postcrisis because global demand collapsed, and they have since started to grow again because the large devaluation improved Ethiopia's competitiveness.

Precrisis exports grew fast (more than 25 percent a year). This growth must have been led by agricultural products. Generally, such exports are not very sensitive to exchange rates as their prices tend to adjust quickly to international prices. So why did they fall postcrisis (at a rate of −1 percent) and then recover rapidly (to a rate of more than 13 percent)? It is conceivable that the demand for roses would fall in a time of global crisis, but much of the agricultural exports is thought to be food products going to China and India.

I speculate, and this needs to be researched, that there are two main reasons for this dynamic (with the global crisis and exchange rate movements being lesser factors). First, agriculture expansion may have been slowing precrisis, because of factors inherent to the sector (such as an increasing scarcity of land), possibly indicating the end of the decade-long smallholder expansion. If this is true, it would have important implications for the future. Second, the local demand for food may have played an important role in the dynamics of exports. Precrisis consumption of agricultural output first fell, with a shift to food exports and a catch-up with international prices (as recognized in the paper). By the time of the crisis, domestic consumption had begun to catch up, owing to higher urban incomes (most of them construction boom related), which can explain the slack in exports by 2009. But then the crisis hurt incomes and there was a shift back to exports (which rose to 13 percent in 2010).

Why Did the Economy Overheat Precrisis?

This is an important issue in the Ethiopian context, as high growth is perceived to be a national priority. In particular, it is important to try to disentangle internal from external balance constraints. As the paper explains, the main constraint to growth is the availability of foreign exchange. Increased levels of FDI and remittances before the crisis allowed a one-shot gain but did not resolve the structural weaknesses attributable to low (but rising) exports. Lack of foreign exchange leads to inflationary pressures. But was the economy also overheating precrisis because of the slow supply response by nontradables? The good news is that inflation seems to have been dominated by increased food prices. This is puzzling, given that food production was rising sharply over the period. The author explains this, convincingly, by attributing it to the rise in domestic prices to international levels, as part of the process of opening up the economy to exports. It seems that several factors exacerbated the food price increases. Precrisis, farmers increased their production and incomes, but the low level of development of financial markets initially fostered food storage as a means of saving, which pushed food prices even higher; food price increases were also worsened by the international hike in food prices (and with July being the height of the dry season). Since inflation was most likely driven by food prices, it is possible that Ethiopia has gotten better at alleviating the domestic supply response constraints and could thus be able to sustain high growth rates as long as foreign exchange is available. There are several examples of supply constraints that have become more flexible with time (e.g., from energy, skills, cement, and credit coming under control). The ability to manage local scarcities better along a high-growth path (as long as sufficient foreign exchange is available) remains an important issue for the future.

Structural Issues and Reforms for Future Growth

The paper argues that better policies are needed to generate future growth. Yes, but which policies? The areas outlined in the paper are not connected convincingly to the characterization of the structure of the economy. The Ethiopian authorities, I have no doubt, will accuse the Bank of being ideological in its choice if the link between structures and policy recommendations is not tight. While the recommended improvement in the investment climate may seem to be a no-brainer, why should the liberalization of the banking sector, telecommunications, and land sectors be priorities? Are these measures in particular perceived to be effective constraints to growth in Ethiopia at this juncture of its development to merit that the government invests its meager management and political capitals in these areas?

A growth diagnostic is not provided, but it is clear from the paper that while growth did not collapse postcrisis, it was already slowing down before the crisis. The crisis itself did not affect the main source of growth—agriculture. The main questions in Ethiopia from a growth perspective should therefore be: can agriculture remain a key growth engine in the future?

Is ADLI (the Ethiopian model of agricultural development–led industrialization) still an effective strategy? Are small farmer–led exports tapering off already? Has the rural hoarding problem been resolved? The government view is that making ADLI work well requires that efforts be continued to find ways to recycle the rural rent faster and more effectively by opening up rural markets for consumer and investment products (ideally, produced locally), expanding saving instruments in rural areas (to reduce the incentives to store grain), and making the land market more effective as a store of wealth.

A new policy issue is whether new FDI in agriculture, which the government has been encouraging, can supplement smallholder farming as a dynamic source of growth. Progress on this front requires that the difficult issues related to movement of labor (restricted by ethnic conflicts in the low lands of the country), access to water, and access to land be resolved in favorable ways.

ADLI focuses on agriculture. It foresees second-round effects in urban areas as the demand by richer farmers of consumer products, produced in urban areas, picks up. This channel has, however, remained elusive, for various reasons. So how can Ethiopia create urban jobs in the short term? Has there already been a structural break with export-focused industries taking off? I think not. The urban housing boom—built on remittances, credit, and cheap imports—has dominated the recent past but is not sustainable. What other activities can create urban jobs? How to encourage manufacturing? Does a model built around export processing zone and labor-intensive manufactures address the main binding constraints of the sector?

Finally, it is important to note that the prospect of large exports of hydropower to Ethiopia's neighbors is an important development from a foreign exchange constraint perspective. More exports would allow more scope for infrastructure finance and would generate domestic-demand-induced growth.

It seems to me that analysis along these lines would be needed to be in a position to offer more valuable advice to Ethiopia on how to improve its growth performance.

Rapid Recovery and Stronger Growth after the Crisis

Dipak Dasgupta and Abhijit Sen Gupta

After every economic crisis in its postindependence history—and there have been at least five—India's economic growth became stronger, suggesting a capacity to learn and modify its policy approaches, with the help of strong institutions. The boom period 2002–07 (corresponding to fiscal years [FY] 2003–08)[1] was a major episode for India, when rising private investment financed by domestic savings led to a rapid growth acceleration. India also greatly benefited from expanding foreign trade and capital flows during this period—not because they added to aggregate demand or the supply of additional savings, which they did in some

Dipak Dasgupta is Lead Economist, South Asia Economic Policy and Poverty Sector, World Bank, and Abhijit Sen Gupta is Associate Professor, Jawaharlal Nehru University, India. Contributions from Mohan Nagarajan, Ulrich Bartsch, Farah Zahir, Luis Servén, Monika Sharma, and other colleagues who worked on the *India Crisis Report* and associated papers (draft of 2009) are gratefully acknowledged. Several parts of this article use sections from that draft report, especially chapter 2 (coauthor Mohan Nagarajan). Comments on an earlier version of this paper by Mustapha Nabli and others are acknowledged. None of these individuals are responsible for the views expressed in this article.

measure, but rather because they induced productivity gains, greater competition, and efficiency in product and factor markets.

Nonetheless, when the crisis hit, India was already experiencing a sizable cyclical slowdown, caused by domestic overheating and other supply side constraints. These have exacerbated the downturn. India's policy response has been swift and sizable and has counteracted much of the downturn. By March 2009, India was already recovering, and in the most recent quarter (quarter 4, FY10), growth has accelerated to as much as 8.6 percent.

Turning to prospects, we conclude that India's fundamentals remain strong and should allow recovery with sustained medium-term annual growth of about 8.5 percent. This would be much faster than the earlier cyclical downturn (1996–2001), but below the peak rate in the precrisis boom period (2002–07). The expected fast growth owes to India's strong private investment, ample savings, a young population, fast rates of productivity growth, and policy making that responds to and learns from past experiences. Nevertheless, we expect that slower world growth and domestic supply constraints will lower India's growth from precrisis boom levels. But India will benefit from maintaining strong openness, whether or not the global economy recovers swiftly or sputters; and capital flows may well be driven countercyclically to India, as growth prospects slow in the rest of the world and brighten in India. The engine of global trade should also continue to work in India's favor, even with a slow recovery in global growth.

The Context for India's Growth Performance

Crises often bring change, and precrisis growth rates are rarely a good predictor of postcrisis growth, as demonstrated by the wide range of country experiences (Dasgupta 2000; Kraay 1998).[2] Countries that have solid policy settings—prudent and flexible macroeconomic policies, open economies, sound institutions, and political stability—seem to recover fastest. India seems to fit this pattern, which helps in understanding the global crisis and its possibly limited medium-term effects.

Growth

In contrast to most other countries, where the pattern has been that "one decade's growth star usually falls to earth the next" (World Bank 2006), India so far seems to have defied the trend. At least five major economic crises or cycles, whether of domestic or external origin, have driven long-term change in India's economic policies and performance (figure 6.1). In each such episode, India's political leadership and economic institutions altered their policies based on lessons learned from experience and from seeing what seems to have worked elsewhere (e.g., the former Soviet Union, the United States, and China). As a result, growth has strengthened after each crisis episode. The 1991 balance of payments crisis and the subsequent response was an important—if not the most important—historical event for India, whereby it opened its economy widely, dismantled trade barriers, and deregulated the domestic economy. The latest global economic crisis has also been a watershed event, with significant negative effects on India (although less than earlier feared). Some medium-term institutional policy changes in response to this latest episode will improve India's economic performance.

Figure 6.1. India: Episodes of Long-Term Growth

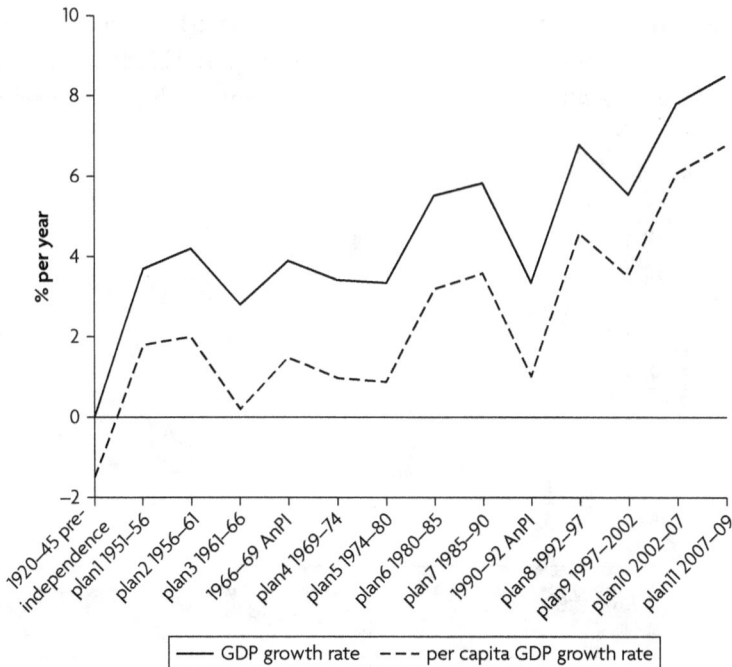

Source: Reserve Bank of India, Handbook of Statistics.
Note: AnPl = annual plan.

Poverty

Stronger economic growth in India has also substantially reduced the incidence of long-term poverty (figure 6.2). By 2005, the poverty rate had dropped to less than a third of households. However, poverty measurement has lagged growth measures. Due to the absence of data since 2005, we cannot estimate the likely impact of growth on poverty in the most recent period or the effects of the current global crisis. Most observers point to rising inequality and disparities, the result of a lower elasticity of poverty reduction in the recent period. But the effects of the current crisis are likely to have been relatively limited, since many of the poor are still heavily concentrated in rural areas, with relatively few direct linkages to the global economy.

Per Capita Income

The faster economic growth and slowing rate of population increase have led to a sharp rise in per capita income in India, especially since 2000. Immediately before the current crisis, India's annual growth rate exceeded 8 percent, with annual per capita growth escalating to more than 6 percent by the early 2000s—historically unprecedented levels. This dramatic acceleration of growth (along with some appreciation of the exchange rate)

Figure 6.2. India: Poverty Trends

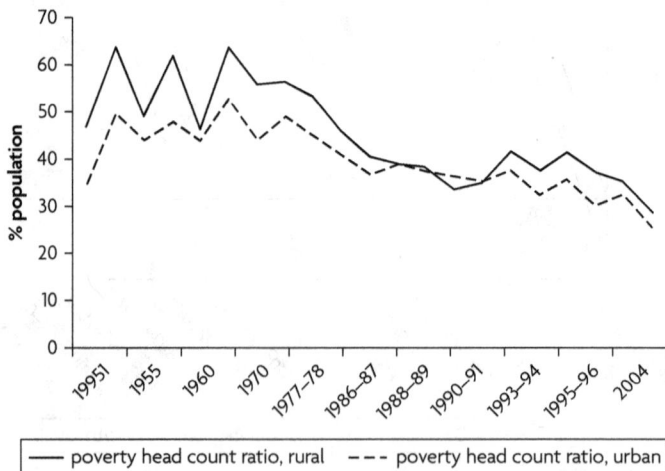

Source: Planning Commission.

Figure 6.3. India: Trends in Per Capita Income

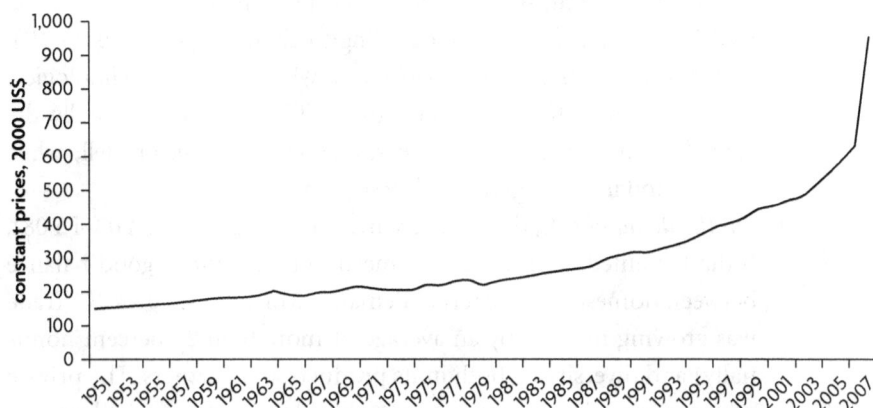

Source: World Bank, World Development Indicators Database.

nurtured the first visible signs of middle-class prosperity, with per capita incomes accelerating to about US$1,000 (figure 6.3), the threshold of middle-income status. India has also joined the ranks of the leading emerging markets and the largest economies in the world (ranked 10th, compared to 50th in 1980). India, along with China and other fast-growing economies, started attracting heavy inflows of foreign direct investment (FDI) and portfolio capital. Its foreign exchange reserves also swelled, and exports and outward orientation rose dramatically paced by fast-growing services and manufacturing. The economy, thus, appeared to have reached a new growth potential. Inequalities persisted, however, and the gap in per capita income between the poorest and richest states widened from about 1:3 in the 1960s to about 1:5 in the early 2000s.

Recent Structural, Cyclical, and Policy Drivers of Precrisis Growth

- *On the supply side,* during the precrisis period (FY03–FY08), India appeared to benefit from a young population and an ongoing demographic transition (low dependency rates), which potentially boosted annual growth by 1–2 percent; large and increasing domestic savings (36 percent of GDP in FY08), which financed much of the high and accelerating investment rates and rising capital stock; heavy remittances from abroad that boosted national savings and covered the greater part of the trade deficit; sharply rising education attainment; accelerating trade integration (with trade doubling to about 40 percent of GDP); and growing FDI and portfolio flows, which boosted technological "catch-up" and total factor productivity (TFP) growth. Sectorally, the contribution of agriculture (the slowest-growing sector) fell, while services and industry grew the fastest (figure 6.4).

- *On the demand side,* during the same precrisis period (FY03–FY08), India benefited from a large domestic market and a good balance between domestic and external demand, which fueled growth. Trade was growing rapidly (by an average of more than 25 percent nominally) and diversifying both in its products and partners. The private sector remained the largest engine of domestic investment and growth, and several enterprises became global players. The private sector accounted for about 80 percent of the sharply rising investment rate (about 37 percent of GDP in FY08) (figures 6.5 and 6.6). The well-developed financial sector grew rapidly. Credit growth averaged well

Figure 6.4. Sectoral Shares of GDP

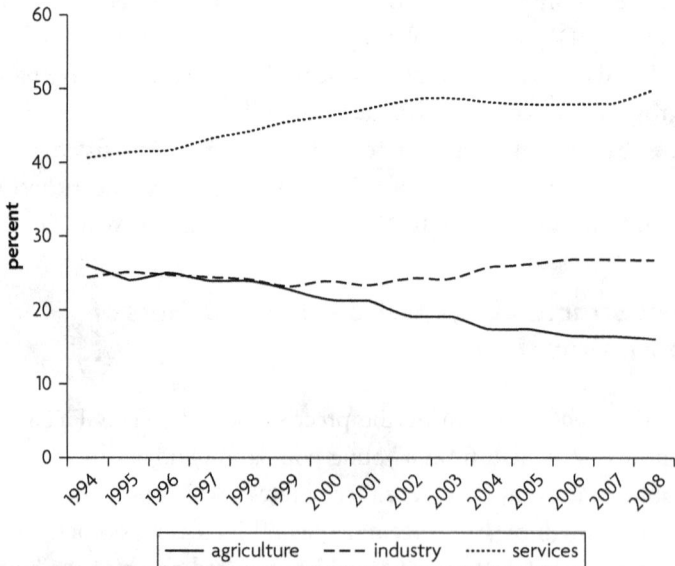

Source: World Bank, World Development Indicators Database.

Figure 6.5. India: Rising Investment Rates and GDP Growth

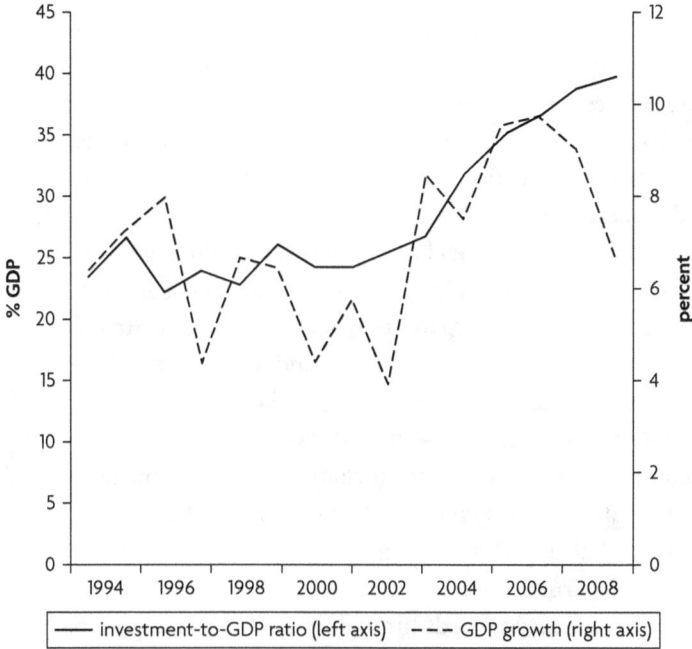

Source: World Bank, World Development Indicators Database.

Figure 6.6. India: Contributions to GDP Growth

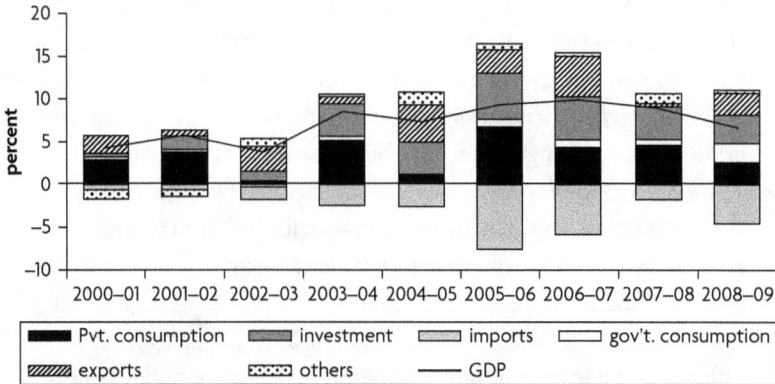

Source: Reserve Bank of India, *Handbook of Statistics.*

over 20 percent a year (more than 15 percent in real terms) and credit deposit rates increased sharply. In addition, India had a thriving stock market (capitalization of over 100 percent of GDP) with a significant foreign investor presence (15 percent of the market).

- *Tax policies* were progressively overhauled during the period, with the goal of simplifying the system and broadening the tax base, redirecting taxes from production and trade to incomes and consumption, and reducing tax rates to ensure compliance. The tax changes were a huge success. Key elements included a new value added tax system in 2005 (replacing cascading sales taxes, as well as falling import and excise taxes), an electronic taxpayer information base (boosting income taxes and corporate taxes), and simplified and lowered tax rates and exemptions (income taxes, corporate taxes, and capital gains). The result was sharply rising (faster than expected) tax-to-GDP ratios.

- *Public spending and pricing* (including subsidy) policies were aimed at alleviating growing income distribution problems (widening rural-urban, skilled-unskilled, regional-state, and caste-tribe-household disparities), rural poverty and human capital (public education), and some infrastructure needs through investment in urban roads, power, and energy. The effectiveness and efficiency of spending was a big concern. The larger public enterprise sector still accounted for a sizable share of the economy, although the share had fallen drastically over the past six decades. Because political backlash precluded any serious attempt at privatization, efforts focused instead on divestiture (through stock markets) and greater autonomy, performance benchmarking, and competition. Despite large gains in taxes, India posted persistent and large fiscal deficits (averaging over 7 percent of GDP, with debt-to-GDP ratios reaching 80 percent), but these deficits were easily financed.

- The *macroeconomic policy mix* was characterized by: a generally prudent and cautious approach, with low tolerance for inflation or growth instability; heavier reliance on monetary policies for aggregate demand management, because fiscal policy was harder to operate; managed exchange rates (but with growing flexibility), partly in response to greater capital inflows; and a long-standing reputation for effective policy conduct by the Reserve Bank of India (RBI) as well as other institutional checks and balances (including a well-functioning Securities and Exchange Board and a constitutionally independent Finance Commission).

- *Easing capital controls.* Capital controls, both on domestic outflows and inflows, were eased gradually and in a calibrated fashion over time. This easing has coincided with large and growing volumes of foreign capital inflows.

Precrisis Growth Policies and Performance

India's recent growth policies and performance can be divided into three distinct periods (table 6.1). The first is the slow-growth period, during FY98–FY02, when India's annual growth fell to an average of about 5.5 percent from 6.8 percent previously (i.e., the period of initial recovery from the 1991 balance of payments crisis and subsequent reforms). The second period is FY03–FY08, the golden period of faster precrisis growth just before the 2008 global financial events. And the third phase is FY09–FY10, when India and other countries were hit by global financial shocks.

Table 6.1. India: Key Macroeconomic Indicators, FY98–FY10
(period averages, unless otherwise indicated)

	FY98–FY02	FY03–FY08	Est. FY09–FY10
1. GDP (US$ billions)	**442.2**	**784.5**	**1183.2**
Per capita (current US$)	438.4	706.2	1010.0
Population growth (% per year)	2.0	1.8	1.7
GDP growth (% per year, at factor cost)	**5.5**	**8.0**	**7.1**
Per capita GDP growth (% per year)	**3.5**	**6.2**	**5.4**
Agriculture growth	2.1	2.9	0.9
Industry growth	4.3	9.0	6.6
Services growth	7.9	9.6	9.1
Consumption growth (% per year)	5.1	5.7	6.0
Gross fixed capital formation growth (% per year)	5.3	17.1	7.2
Bombay Stock Exchange index (change in percent, end of period, US$)	−20.3	607.9	−20.1
2. Shares of GDP (% GDP)			
Consumption	79.7	70.7	65.8
Investment	24.8	31.0	37.1
Gross domestic savings	23.5	32.6	36.5
Net exports	−4.4	−1.6	−2.8

(continued)

Table 6.1. (continued)

	FY98–FY02	FY03–FY08	Est. FY09–FY10
3. Current account balance (% GDP)	–0.6	–0.1	–1.8
Net invisibles receipts	2.6	4.9	7.1
Merchandise exports	8.9	12.2	14.1
Merchandise imports	12.1	17.1	22.9
Export growth (% per year)	8.3	26.8	4.1
Real effective exchange rate (index 2000 = 100)	98.1	101.4	103.2
Trade/GDP (% GDP)	21	30	37
4. Net capital inflows (US$ billions, annual average)	7.6	44.5	15.6
As percent of GDP (%)	2.3	4.3	1.8
5. Fiscal balance (% GDP)	–9.0	–7.2	–9.8
Debt/GDP (% GDP)	67.5	79.6	78.3
6. Money supply growth (% per year)	16.6	17.8	17.0
Credit growth (% per year)	16.2	25.9	16.3
Inflation (% per year)			
CPI	6.3	4.8	7.0
WPI	4.9	5.0	5.8
7. Reserves (US$ billions, end of period)	51	299	290
Months imports (period average)	8.1	13.3	12.3
Percent of GDP (end of period)	11	26	24
8. Global high-income GDP growth (% per year)	**3.1**	**2.6**	**–1.6**
9. Global trade growth (% per year)	**6.4**	**7.7**	**–3.0**

Source: Economic Survey, Government of India; Reserve Bank of India; World Development Indicators Database; International Monetary Fund (IMF) International Financial Statistics and World Economic Outlook.
Note: CPI = consumer price inflation; WPI = wholesale price inflation.

The First Low-Growth Phase. During FY98–FY02, global GDP growth was, in fact, quite strong; but India suffered from two external events: the East Asian crisis and its aftermath (as large exchange rate changes in East Asia put India at a competitive disadvantage), and the impact of nuclear sanctions (i.e., reduced access to markets). India's growth slowdown also originated from internal shocks. Agriculture suffered two droughts, first in FY98 and again in FY01. Industrial growth averaged just 4 percent a year, as domestic demand slowed sharply. Services growth was higher, at around 8 percent, but was hit by a slowing of exports in FY01 (owing to the U.S. technology sector crisis in 2000). Nominal dollar export growth averaged only about 6 percent per year. Imports also did not revive, and the trade-to-GDP ratio was essentially flat (as large exchange rate devaluations in East Asian countries took away market shares). The East Asian crisis and global capital market fears also reduced the Bombay Stock Exchange (BSE) index sharply; it fell by 20 percent over the period. With asset values falling and a general demand slowdown, domestically and in key export sectors, the real crunch hit on the investment side. Investment rates, which were previously climbing in response to the earlier reforms, collapsed from about 27 percent of GDP in FY98 to 22 percent by FY02.

Policy responses such as raising policy interest rates in response to the East Asian crisis did not help. The fiscal situation approached crisis levels, partly because of the domestic slowdown and revenue shortfalls, but also because of a surge in civil service salaries and added fiscal spending. As a result, the government had very little fiscal space to adopt countercyclical fiscal policy to restore growth. Higher financing requirements pushed up interest rates further. Fortunately, thanks to higher salaries and government consumption during the period, total annual consumption growth held up well at 5.1 percent. Without this, the growth slowdown in India would have been even worse. The extended downturn in the late 1990s and early 2000s was reflected in weak growth, despite a relatively benign global economic growth climate.

The Second High-Growth Phase. During FY03–FY08, India's growth accelerated dramatically, matching rates in East Asia and China. Indian growth surged (along with that of many other developing countries) at a time when world economic growth, especially in industrial countries, was not particularly robust. In fact, as a result of the events of September 11, 2001, and as a result of earlier shocks, economic growth slowed substantially in industrial countries. However, this growth slowdown in industrial countries and the resulting low interest rates may have sparked faster growth in large, reforming emerging markets such as India, as they began to attract greater investment.

What is notable therefore is that during this phase, growth rates in India began to accelerate and to diverge from global growth, especially in industrial countries. Indeed, the relationship between GDP growth in

India and in the rest of the world weakened considerably after 2001 (figure 6.7). Bhanumurthy and Kumawat (2009) confirm that the elasticity of India's growth relative to that in industrial countries or world GDP fell to about 0.4 during FY03–FY08, even with the Indian economy's much higher levels of trade and capital flow integration. Other studies also confirm a relatively low elasticity—not unexpected given that India's trade share of GDP is still only about 40 percent—although an open economy still benefits from the long-term productivity growth that comes from trade and competition.

Figure 6.7. India Decoupling? India and U.S. GDP Growth Rates

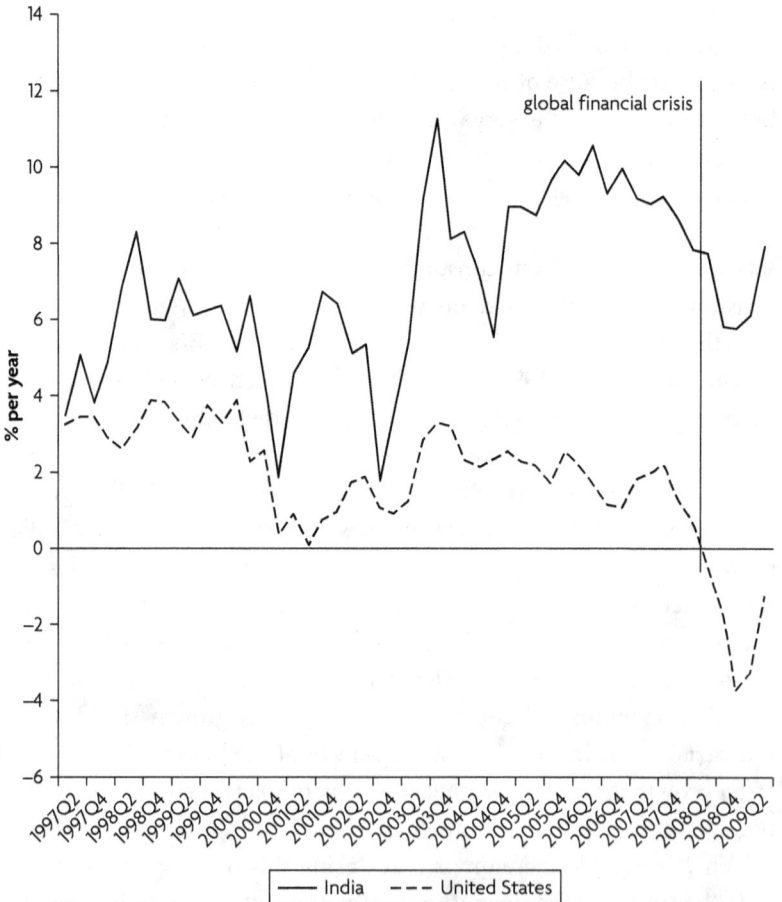

Source: IMF International Financial Statistics.

So, given slower world growth, what factors drove India's faster growth, and what were the links to global markets? Our earlier data (table 6.1) and analysis suggest five important factors.

The first, of course, was the *massive surge in private domestic investment*, which grew at an annual average rate of 17.1 percent during FY03–FY08, three times faster in than the previous period (and compared with historical averages) (figure 6.8). This investment boom was unprecedented in India's modern economic history and drove India's rapid growth in this period. It also lifted India's investment rates up near those in East Asia. The investment rate rose from about 22 percent in FY03 to about 37 percent by the end of FY08.

The second was the *sharp rise in private savings*, which fully financed the surge in private investment. The result was a shrinking current account deficit. The main reason for higher saving rates, however, was not increased private household savings, but rather higher corporate savings (profits and retained earnings) and public savings (associated with narrowing fiscal deficits linked to cyclical growth improvements and better tax collection).

The third was a *massive surge in private capital inflows*—FDI, external commercial borrowings (ECBs) by Indian corporations, portfolio capital inflows, and minimal short-term inflows. As a result, annual average capital

Figure 6.8. India: Investment Cycles as the Prime Driver of Faster Growth

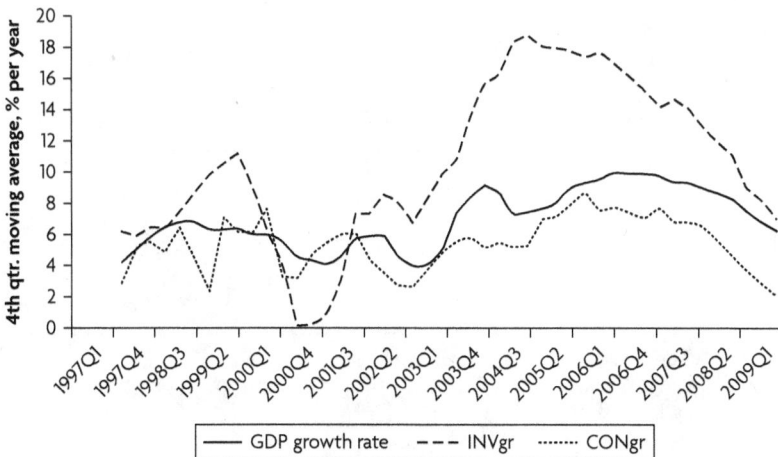

Source: Reserve Bank of India, *Handbook of Statistics*.
Note: INVgr = investment growth; CONgr = consumption growth.

inflows rose to over US$44 billion a year (although the peak, US$124 billion, actually occurred later in the period, in FY08). These levels far exceeded the 4 percent of GDP. The surge in capital inflows was reflected in a large rise in the stock market valuations of Indian companies, which increased about fivefold during these six years. The equity boom also allowed Indian corporations to borrow externally to more easily finance the investment boom without ratcheting up debt-to-equity ratios. ECBs played a key role.

Fourth was the *accumulation of foreign exchange reserves*. Foreign reserves by the end of the period reached about one-quarter of GDP (figure 6.9). The counterpart of this accumulation was a clear policy goal of maintaining real exchange rates, which the central bank, the RBI, largely achieved (except for a significant appreciation at the end of the period). In addition, the RBI attempted to sterilize the impact of capital inflows and reserves growth. Apart from the fiscal costs of increasing sterilization, it accommodated part of the surge in capital inflows by expanding the domestic money supply. As a result, domestic credit growth reached an annual growth rate of about 26 percent by the end of the period. Inflation remained moderate at the end of FY08, thanks to falling global prices, elimination of trade barriers on imports, and lower

Figure 6.9. India: Gross Capital Inflows and Foreign Reserves Addition

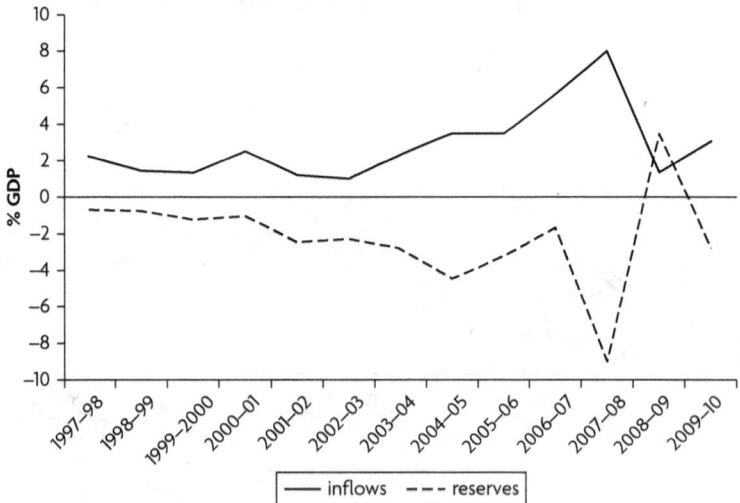

Source: Reserve Bank of India, *Handbook of Statistics*.
Note: Addition to foreign reserves is treated per convention as negative, and vice versa.

prices of tradables, as well as adequate rainfall, bumper harvests, and low food prices throughout the period. Agricultural production also boomed.

Fifth was the *surge in trade* and in the economy's openness to trade (figure 6.10). In this respect, India was helped by favorable global conditions. Global trade during FY03–FY08 expanded by nearly 8 percent per year, even with the reduced industrial country growth. The U.S. economy's heavy consumption drove world trade growth while its expanding current account deficits were being financed by the growing reserves and external savings of China, India, and others. Merchandise export growth was about 25 percent per year, and net services exports also expanded sharply (reflecting surging workers' remittances—in addition to the surge in outsourced business process services). India's imports also surged and the trade-to-GDP ratio virtually doubled, increasing the impact of global know-how and competition.

In sum, as Prime Minister Manmohan Singh remarked, the FY03–FY08 phase was an unusually benign one for Indian economic growth. World trade boomed and capital inflows to developing countries surged, with low interest costs and spreads. At the same time, foreign investors were looking to invest long-term—and in risk-sharing forms. Indian companies were

Figure 6.10. India's Trade Growth

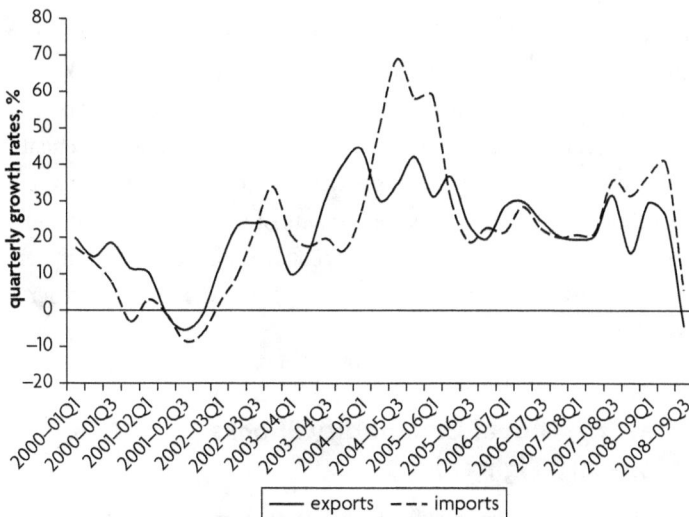

Source: Reserve Bank of India, *Handbook of Statistics.*

also able to borrow abroad at low cost, even as their escalating valuations and strong performance made them attractive long-term bets for overseas investors. The overall effect was a rise in India's potential growth rate, earlier pegged at about 5–6 percent a year, to about 8–9 percent. Nevertheless, while capital inflows and global demand (rising exports) helped fuel India's economy during the faster boom period, domestic demand clearly played a much bigger role (figure 6.6 and annex table 6A.2). The higher domestic demand was mainly the result of higher investment, as domestic consumption growth barely changed, staying at about 5 percent, the same as the previous period. Net exports also added very little.

Finally, not only was investment rising faster, but TFP also grew more rapidly. Average annual TFP growth was about 3.4 percent, versus only about 1 percent during 1996–2001 (see table 6.9 later in this chapter). The slowdown in TFP growth during 1996–2001 was undoubtedly partly cyclical, reducing TFP growth during that phase by about 1 percent per year; Collins (2007) and our estimates suggest that the TFP growth during 1990–2003 was about 2 percent per year. Conversely, during the subsequent fast-growth period, procyclical TFP growth was higher, by about 0.5 percent per year, with cyclically adjusted TFP growth potentially rising to near 3 percent per year. Increased openness, trade, investment in new plants and machinery, and structural change in faster-growing sectors all contributed to these gains.

The third phase of the recent evolution of the Indian economy is represented by the impact of the global economic crisis during FY09–FY10. What is important to note is that there were three other factors that preceded the direct financial impacts of the global crisis: (a) overheating of the economy, as quarterly GDP growth began to exceed the capacity of the domestic economy; (b) severe impacts of the rise in global commodity prices; and (c) a slowdown in the cyclical engine of domestic demand, which especially affected investment. These are discussed further in the next section.

Overheating, Global Commodity Shocks, and Monetary Tightening

Having discussed the reasons for India's high growth rates during the precrisis period, we now turn to the reasons for the sharp drop in annual growth in FY09 to a low of 6.7 percent, which recovered marginally to 7.4 percent in FY10. The reasons include structural, cyclical, and domestic policy developments, as well as the external environment.

The growth slowdown was also attributable to the serious global commodity price shocks that hit India in late 2007. These shocks weakened domestic demand, resulted in net terms-of-trade losses of about 4.5 percent of GDP, and fueled domestic inflation, which peaked at 12.6 percent. The RBI further tightened monetary policy to dampen inflation expectations, raising the cost of borrowing. Global capital also began flowing out and stock market valuations began a rapid decline.

A key contributor to the growth slowdown was the fact that India was already in a cyclical downturn in FY09, owing mainly to the cyclical slowing of domestic investment (box 6.1). The downturn in the investment cycle was in turn the result of rising labor costs, infrastructure constraints, limited skills among workers, falling profitability, slowing sales, and an appreciating exchange rate—all indicators of wider economic "overheating." The investment cycle downturn would have undermined GDP growth even more had it not been for the good weather, unexpectedly strong agriculture production, and expansionary fiscal policy and public spending.

India's most recent growth cycle began in 2001, peaked in FY07, and started decelerating in FY08 (figure 6.11). Annual GDP growth accelerated to a record of almost 10 percent over several quarters during FY05–FY07. But following that, quarterly GDP growth started to slow.

India's monthly index of industrial production (IIP), a leading economic barometer, provides corroborating evidence. The IIP growth rate peaked in January 2007, and then dropped even more sharply than the GDP slowdown.

Binding Constraints to Expansion

Investment cycles in India (as elsewhere) were initially characterized by a rise in corporate profitability, growing cash inflows, good access to credit, and rising expectations of future growth. Matching this was a rise in stock market valuations of companies and their ability to finance the surge in investment. The turning point came with the emergence of binding constraints to expansion and profitability. Expansion in production capacity could not be sustained by market demand or skill shortages that raised wage rates. Infrastructure bottlenecks began to

Figure 6.11. India's Cyclical Growth Slowdown Prior to Financial Crisis

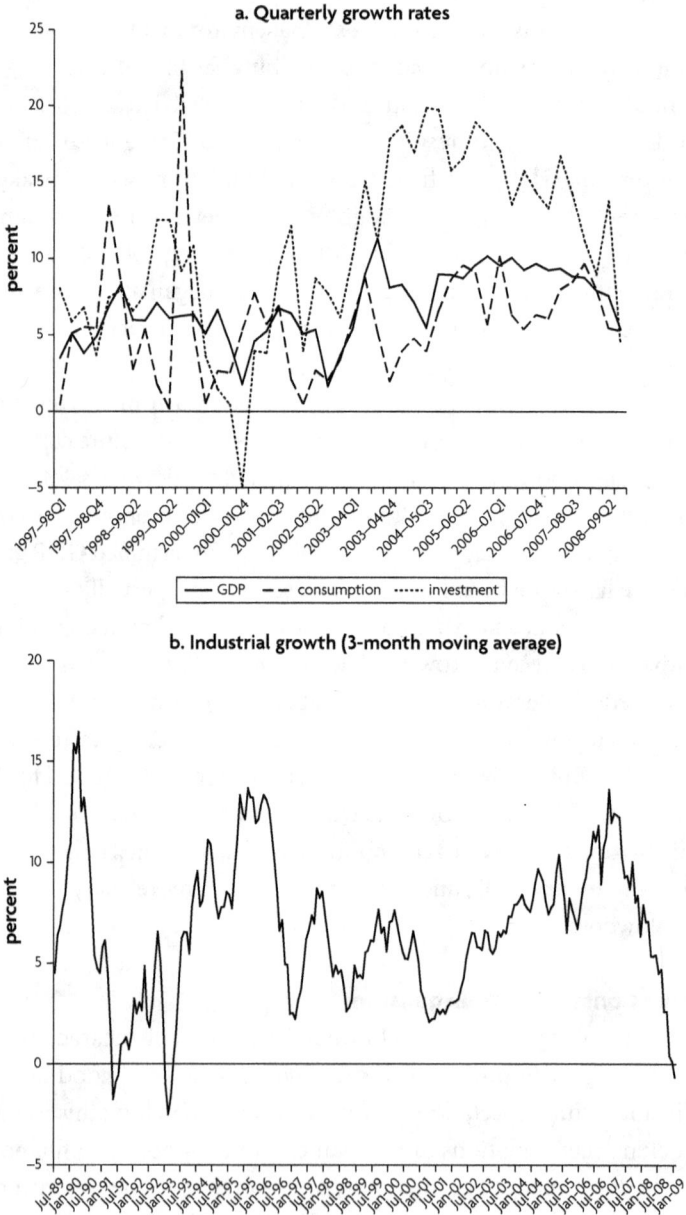

a. Quarterly growth rates

b. Industrial growth (3-month moving average)

Source: Reserve Bank of India, *Handbook of Statistics*; Central Statistical Organization (CSO).

Box 6.1. Was High Growth Sustainable?

In trying to analyze whether the economy was in fact overheating in 2007–08, it is crucial to compare actual with potential output. In the recent growth acceleration, high investment rates increased capacity in the Indian economy, so potential output was expanding as well as actual output. However, the growth of actual output was faster than the growth of potential output, and a positive output gap developed. Capacity constraints and bottlenecks then caused inflation, curtailed investment, and eventually forced output back in line with capacity.

Figure B6.1.1. Output Growth and Output Gap

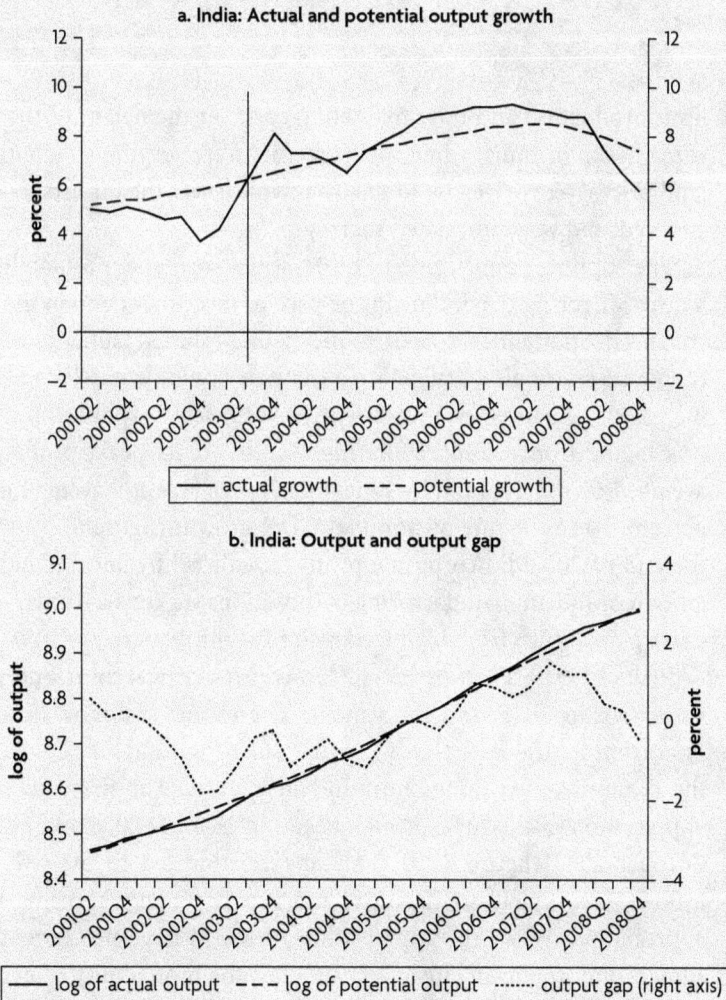

a. India: Actual and potential output growth

b. India: Output and output gap

Source: Reserve Bank of India, *Handbook of Statistics;* authors' estimates.

(continued)

limit production and raise marketing costs. At the height of the investment boom in India, when major sectors were surging simultaneously, land prices were driven up to unsustainable levels, the infrastructure was strained, and wages escalated sharply.

The "tipping point" came in FY08, when corporate profitability took a dive. Mirroring the decline in the pace of investment and in the industrial production index, corporate profitability started falling sharply. The corporate sector also chalked up a massive rise in debt, which had been increased to finance new investment. Nevertheless, corporate profitability was falling from exceptionally high levels. At its peak, profit growth averaged 60 percent, and by June–July 2007 it was still averaging 30–40 percent, twice the rate of nominal GDP growth (figure 6.12). Only by the end of 2007 did corporate profit growth fall by another half. Sales growth of Indian manufacturing corporations suggests a similar picture: a sharp downturn from high levels after the third quarter of FY07.

Reduced export competitiveness was also a critical contributor to the slowdown in GDP and investment. The export sector was especially important for the fastest-growing manufacturing and services sectors of the economy. Two things hurt Indian exports. The first was a sharp appreciation of the rupee, which began in October 2006 and peaked in October 2007 (figure 6.13). This appreciation led to massive capital inflows, incomplete sterilization, and a policy stance favoring further appreciation. While the appreciation provided large net gains to consumers and importers, it sharply reduced the profitability of exporters. This, in turn, led to a severe slowdown in export growth and a reduction in export shares in key markets for such major growth sectors as textiles

Figure 6.12. Indian Corporate Performance Prior to the Crisis

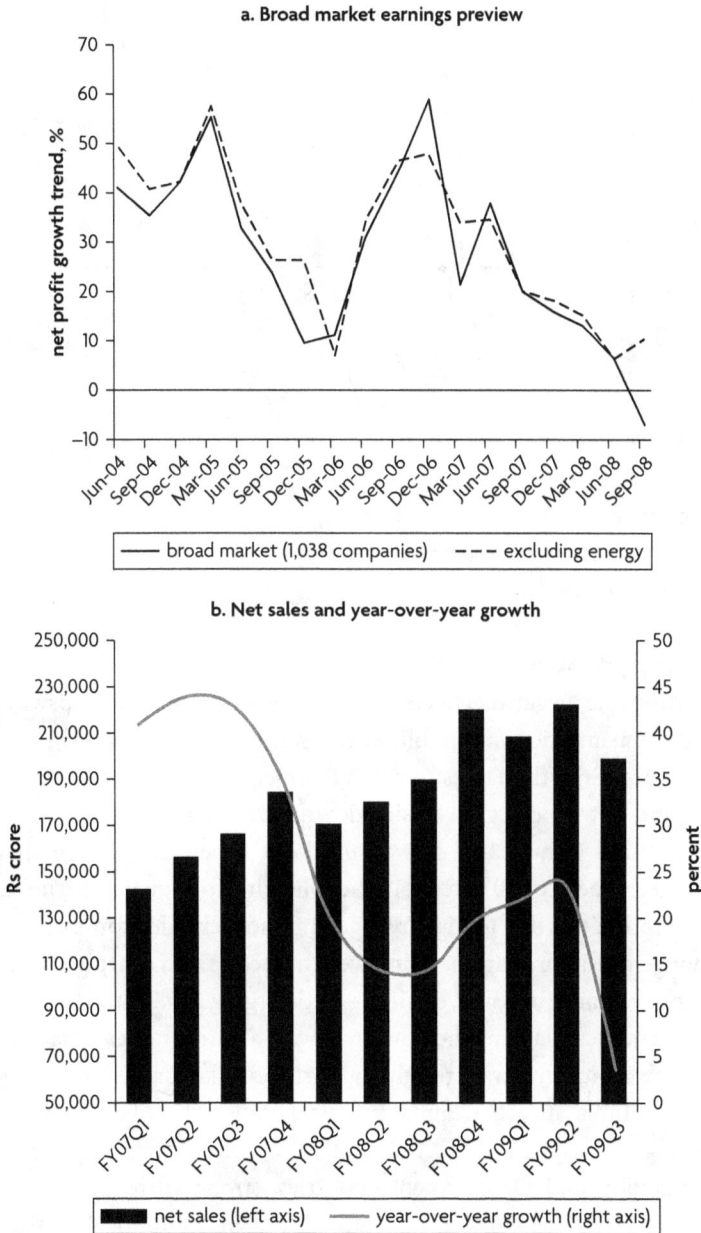

a. Broad market earnings preview

broad market (1,038 companies) --- excluding energy

b. Net sales and year-over-year growth

net sales (left axis) year-over-year growth (right axis)

Source: Capitaline and IMaCS analysis.

Figure 6.13. Effective Exchange Rates Prior to the Crisis

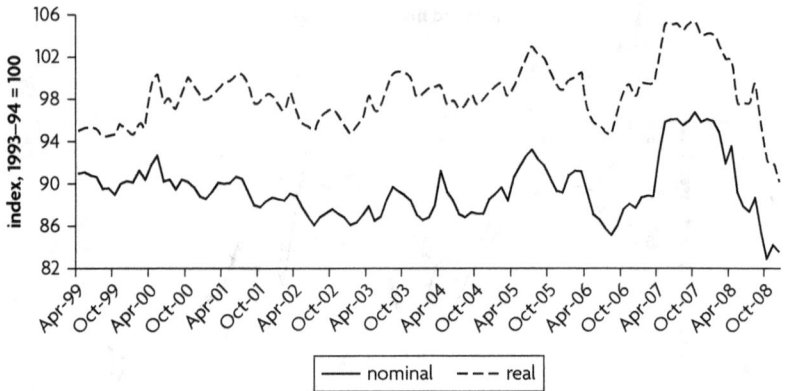

Source: Reserve Bank of India, *Handbook of Statistics.*

and garments. Another factor hurting exports was infrastructure constraints, which were especially limiting during the period of rapid domestic growth.

Offsetting Positive Factors

Offsetting the negative effects of the slowdown were an upswing in private consumption and public spending, and an unexpected boom in agriculture. Growth in consumption dampened the effects of the investment and net export growth slowdowns. By the last quarter of FY07, consumption growth had slowed to about 5 percent; it then sharply climbed to a peak of 10 percent in the following four quarters. The rising consumption was due to higher wages and household incomes, aided by exchange rate appreciation, rising wealth effects from sharply escalating asset prices (land, housing, equities), and surging government spending.

Also counterbalancing the slowdown were a number of external factors, including capital inflows, strongly supportive stock markets, and a lagging euphoria. India attracted capital inflows because of its fast growth rate, widening interest rate differential with the Organisation for Economic Co-operation and Development countries, strong currency, and easier conditions for foreign investment. Strong foreign institutional investment (FII) inflows increased stock market valuations fourfold, with the BSE index rising from 5,000 in April 2004 to more than 20,000 in January

2008. At its peak, FII accounted for 19 percent of stock market capital-ization, comparable to the level for the Republic of Korea—and larger relative to many other emerging markets. Indian companies benefited from stronger FDI inflows and ECBs. Cumulative FDI inflows amounted to US$51 billion during FY05–FY08, nearly five times the flows in the pre-vious four years. The stock of outstanding ECBs more than doubled from US$27 billion in March 2006 to over US$62 billion in March 2008.

Did Poor Policy Cause the Precrisis Growth Slowdown?

While public spending supported faster growth during the precrisis downturn, the inability to address infrastructure, skills shortages, and other bottlenecks may have contributed to the slowdown. Another key question was whether a tight monetary policy also contributed to the cyclical downturn. Surprisingly, we find that monetary policy was remark-ably accommodative and had little effect on the investment and growth slowdown. Key policy rates were on a downtrend in the early part of the decade, interspersed with periods of relatively stable rates in between, as the RBI tried to stimulate growth after the slump of the late 1990s to early 2001. The RBI reduced both repo and reverse repo rates by almost 1,000 basis points (bps) between 2000 and 2004, while the cash reserve ratio (CRR) dropped by 400 bps. Inflation was more volatile, declining initially and then increasing from May 2002. From 2004 onward, the RBI modestly widened the band between the repo and reverse repo rates to allow a more flexible band of choices of monetary policy; it also moder-ately increased nominal policy rates as inflation began to rise. Between April 2004 and March 2007, the RBI increased policy rates and the CRR by 150 to 200 bps. This widened the band between the repo and reverse repo from 100 to 150 bps in early 2007. Between April 2007 and June 2008, policy rates were unchanged, even as inflation rose dramatically. Instead, the CRR increased by just 225 bps (from 6 percent to 8.25 percent). None of this can be interpreted as sharp monetary tightening, given that infla-tion went from 6.6 percent in March 2007 to 11.8 percent (an increase of more than 500 bps) by June 2008.

Management of Commodity Shocks, Inflation, and Fiscal Deficits

Between October 2007 and late March 2008, wholesale price inflation more than doubled—from 3.1 percent to 7.4 percent—and then peaked at 12.6 percent at the end of August 2008. The main cause of the uptick in inflation was a firming of global prices of food grains, cement, steel, edible oil, and crude oil. The global oil price soared from US$71 a barrel in June 2007 to about US$136 in June 2008 (table 6.2).

In addition to the rise in commodity prices and inflation, three additional shocks hit the Indian economy:

- A large deterioration in external terms of trade (equivalent to about 4.5 percent of GDP), which expanded the current account deficit by about the same magnitude.

Table 6.2. India: Key Policy Rates and Inflation

Date (month/ day/ year)	Reverse repo rate (%)	Repo rate (%)	CRR (%)	WPI (%)	Date (month/ date/ year)	Reverse repo rate (%)	Repo rate (%)	CRR (%)	WPI (%)
3/31/04	4.50	6.00	4.50	4.60	11/10/07	6.00	7.75	7.50	3.20
9/18/04	4.50	6.00	4.75	7.90	4/26/08	6.00	7.75	7.75	8.30
10/2/04	4.50	6.00	5.00	7.10	5/10/08	6.00	7.75	8.00	8.60
10/27/04	4.75	6.00	5.00	7.40	5/24/08	6.00	7.75	8.25	8.90
4/29/05	5.00	6.00	5.00	6.00	6/12/08	6.00	8.00	8.25	11.70
10/26/05	5.25	6.25	5.00	4.50	6/25/08	6.00	8.50	8.25	11.90
1/24/06	5.50	6.50	5.00	4.20	7/5/08	6.00	8.50	8.50	12.20
6/9/06	5.75	6.75	5.00	4.90	7/19/08	6.00	8.50	8.75	12.50
7/25/06	6.00	7.00	5.00	4.70	7/30/08	6.00	9.00	8.75	12.50
10/31/06	6.00	7.25	5.00	5.40	8/30/08	6.00	9.00	9.00	12.40
12/23/06	6.00	7.25	5.25	5.80	10/11/08	6.00	9.00	6.50	11.30
1/6/07	6.00	7.25	5.50	6.40	10/20/08	6.00	8.00	6.50	10.80
1/31/07	6.00	7.50	5.50	6.70	10/25/08	6.00	8.00	6.00	10.70
2/17/07	6.00	7.50	5.75	6.00	11/3/08	6.00	7.50	6.00	8.70
3/3/07	6.00	7.50	6.00	6.50	11/8/08	6.00	7.50	5.50	8.70
3/31/07	6.00	7.75	6.00	5.90	12/8/08	5.00	6.50	5.50	6.80
4/14/07	6.00	7.75	6.25	6.30	1/5/09	4.00	5.50	5.50	5.20
4/28/07	6.00	7.75	6.50	6.00	1/17/09	4.00	5.50	5.00	0.00
8/4/07	6.00	7.75	7.00	4.40					

Source: Reserve Bank of India.
Note: WPI = wholesale price inflation.

- A growing quasi-fiscal deficit arising from sharply rising off-budget energy subsidies (as oil price rises were not fully passed through).
- An expanding on-budget deficit—the result of massive farm loan waivers, increased spending on social sectors, and large increases in civil service salaries in the FY09 budget.

All of these liabilities appeared likely to worsen the central government's fiscal deficit, including off-budget liabilities, from about 4.5 percent of GDP in FY08 to more than 6.1 percent. The general government deficit looked set to expand to more than 9 percent of GDP from 7 percent in FY08.

Capital Flow Reversals. About the same time, India began to face a reversal of FII inflows. Portfolio inflows turned negative, and during April–June 2008, net outflow totaled US$5.8 billion. With higher oil imports, the current account gap required additional financing. But the large stock of foreign reserves (US$315 billion) and continued FDI and remittance inflows provided an adequate cushion to prevent a run on the rupee. With accelerating FII outflows, the BSE fell rapidly from a high of nearly 21,000 to a 10-month low of about 14,000.

Monetary Conditions. While policy rates were left unchanged throughout FY08, the CRR was raised four times (from 6 percent to 7.5 percent) in a mild attempt to cool the growth in credit and the money supply, which was essentially accommodating inflation. The impact on gross bank credit and nonfood credit growth was more pronounced. Both gross bank credit and nonfood credit growth decreased from 28 percent in FY07 to 22 percent in FY08. Broad money (M3), however, increased by 21 percent in FY08, almost the same as in the previous year, and further to 22 percent by May 2008, owing to the partial sterilization of foreign inflows.

Macroeconomic policy makers thus faced three main dilemmas:

- With the spike in domestic inflation generalizing, what could be done to manage the trade-offs posed by attempts to tighten monetary policy (to reach inflation targets) while dealing with a slowing economy?
- With the sharp prospective widening of the twin deficits, and the political constraints to fiscal policy, what instruments were available to moderate a potential boom-bust cycle?

- With FII flows reversing, what policy stance was needed with respect to reserves and the exchange rate?

Eventually, the government took a series of carefully calibrated steps to achieve a soft landing, with the announced GDP growth target of 7.0–7.5 percent and inflation moderating to single-digit levels. First, in April 2008, the RBI announced a policy to continue monetary tightening, hiking the CRR in two steps by 50 bps (and raising the CRR once again in May 2008) and policy interest rates by 25 bps in June 2008. Second, the government accommodated the foreign capital outflows with a combination of reserve drawdown and moderate exchange rate depreciation. Third, the central government raised retail energy prices by 10–17 percent (on top of a small 3–4 percent adjustment in February 2008) and implemented other measures to limit the off-budget liabilities attributable to public sector oil companies. Finally, the authorities adjusted some trade and price policies (export bans and restraints, lower import tariffs, and higher export taxes) to soften the impact of imported inflation.

The Effects of the Global Financial Crisis, FY09–FY10

The global financial crisis erupted at this time of slowing growth momentum in India. Like other emerging markets, India was affected by the crisis—through the channels of trade, credit, and capital flows—and the impact was more severe than initially anticipated. The impact was strong because India, in the previous two decades, had increasingly integrated itself with the world economy through trade and investment financing links in the fastest-growing parts of the economy. These included the new manufacturing sector, traditional export-oriented sector, and fast-growing services exports—as well as corporate borrowers accessing external financing and investing globally, and a high volume of financing from the rest of the world that substituted for more expensive and less flexible domestic bank financing. Thus, the direct effects of the crisis were substantial. But the most important channel for transmitting the global shock was indirect: the loss of domestic consumer and investor confidence, the shrinking of domestic financial credit markets (despite their limited exposure to offshore financial markets), and the negative wealth effects of stock market losses.

Trade

The most visible manifestation of the shock was the plunge in exports. Merchandise exports had previously increased at an average rate of 25 percent, tripling between FY03 and FY08 to US$159 billion. Services exports grew more than fourfold to US$87 billion in FY08. But after September 2008, merchandise exports fell dramatically, as in other countries. The sharp exports slowdown reduced GDP growth by about 1 percentage point.[3]

Manufactured goods exports, which grew at a nominal rate of 27.7 percent in FY08 relative to FY07, shrunk by 18.8 percent during October 2008–March 2009. Some of the worst-affected sectors were gems and jewelry, textiles, leather and leather products, cotton and man-made yarn, tea, marine products, and handicrafts. As most of these sectors are labor intensive, job losses were significant.

Services exports also slowed, although not as severely. Export of "miscellaneous services," including software, financial, business, and communication, had been increasing at an average rate of 37 percent during FY04 to FY08, driven by a booming global economy. In contrast, during April–December 2008, the annual growth of these services exports slumped to less than half, or 18 percent.

Credit Channel

The credit channel took a strong hit. After September 2008, interbank call money rates spiked to more than 20 percent, even with much of the banking sector in the public domain. This was due largely to heightened risk aversion resulting from reports that some of Indian private banks had exposure to toxic assets. The RBI stepped in quickly and announced a host of measures, including cuts in key policy rates, increasing the attractiveness of nonresident Indian deposits, and added liquidity support through the liquidity assistance financing window.

Prior to September 2008, the RBI's main concern was containing inflation, and monetary policy was geared to achieving that goal. However, once the crisis affected India and financial conditions tightened, the RBI rapidly changed gears and focused on supporting growth and maintaining financial stability. It reduced the repo rate and the CRR by 400 bps and the reverse repo rate by 250 bps.

Public sector banks increased their lending even as private and foreign banks were withdrawing. Corporate demand for credit shifted to domestic banks as overseas financing dried up. Exacerbating the problem was a sharp drop in flow of nonbank resources to the commercial sector. While funds from domestic sources declined by 31 percent, funds from foreign sources experienced a drop of 34 percent (table 6.3).

Credit growth rate strongly decelerated in the wake of the crisis (figure 6.14). Nonfood credit (more than 97 percent of total credit) witnessed a dramatic slowdown from October 2008, despite banks lowering interest rates. Bank credit growth fell from a peak of 30 percent to about 17 percent in March 2009, due to a dim outlook for the economy and an uncertain funding environment. Sectors hit hard by the global meltdown—like small and medium enterprises (SMEs), textiles, and real estate—found it hard to access credit. Despite the RBI lowering policy rates and provisioning norms and reducing risk weights on exposures, lending rates have not fallen by a corresponding amount. The slowdown in domestic credit could potentially cut some 1.5 percentage points off expected growth in the Indian economy.

The final negative impact of the shock was the outflow of foreign capital and sharply rising costs of external funding. Their higher costs

Table 6.3. Flow of Nonbank Resources to the Commercial Sector
(Rs billions)

	2007–08	2008–09
Domestic Resources	**2,745.63**	**1,914.70**
Public issues by nonfinancial entities	344.13	135.59
Gross private placements by nonfinancial entities	323.06	391.13
Net issuance of commercial papers	313.51	200.04
Net credit by housing finance companies	86.93	164.38
Gross accommodation by Indian financial institutions	−11.74	72.46
Nonbanking Financial Companies	203.04	−30.12
Foreign sources	**1,486.70**	**981.22**
External commercial borrowings/foreign currency convertible bonds	630.08	275.88
American depository receipts/global depository receipts	249.72	46.87
Short-term credit from abroad	415.65	122.52
Foreign direct investment to India	191.25	535.95
Total nonbank credit	**4,233.23**	**2,895.92**

Source: Reserve Bank of India's Macroeconomic and Monetary Developments, January 2009.

Figure 6.14. Credit Growth Weakens

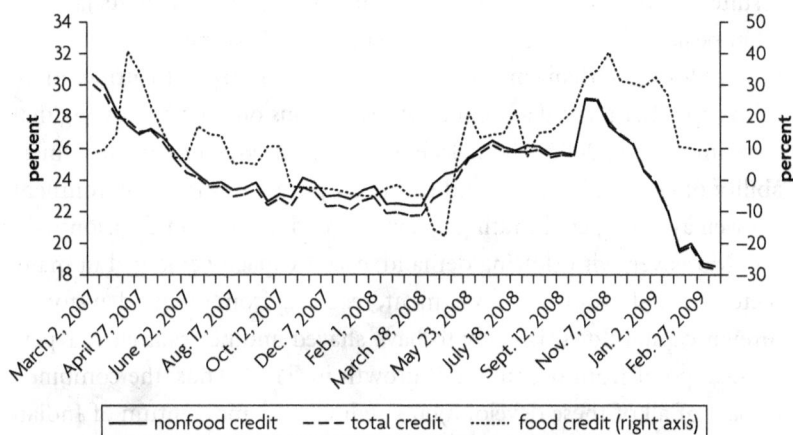

Source: Reserve Bank of India, *Handbook of Statistics.*

Table 6.4. External Financing for Emerging Asia
(US$ billions)

	2006	2007	2008	2009 forecast
External financing, net				
Private flows, net	258.9	314.8	96.2	64.9
Equity investment, net	122.6	112.9	57.9	85.7
Direct investment, net	87.2	148.6	112.7	79.3
Portfolio investment, net	35.5	−35.7	−54.7	6.5
Private creditors, net	136.3	201.9	38.2	−20.8
Commercial banks, net	90.5	155.7	29.8	−25.3
Nonbanks, net	45.8	46.2	8.4	4.5
Official flows, net	−3.3	10.7	16.1	−1.1
International financial institutions	−6.8	0.6	2.2	3.2
Bilateral creditors	3.5	10.1	13.8	−4.3
Resident lending/other, net	−207.7	−158.0	−125.5	−90.0
Reserves (− = increase)	−337.5	−587.8	−373.1	−448.3

Source: IIF 2009.

showed up in rising spreads and increased perceptions of credit risk and
(risk aversion behavior) in global financial markets. Indian corporations, like others, suffered a sudden large drop in external financing
(table 6.4). Outflows of FII, which began in early 2008, sharply accelerated after September 2008, with a net outflow of US$7.6 billion between

then and March 2009. Most of the outflow was in the equity market, and resulted in the BSE falling by more than 50 percent between its January 2008 peak and March 2009. ECBs, which had become a key source of finance for the Indian corporate sector, also fell sharply. To attract more ECBs, the RBI relaxed a number of restrictions on such borrowing that were imposed in 2007. These declines, along with the increasing vulnerability of corporate profits and of the corporate business environment (as well as falling credit ratings), complicated investment decisionmaking. Moreover, with slowing demand, excess capacity emerged in many sectors. The slowdown in investment, resulting from the sudden stop in foreign capital flows, is likely to have shaved another estimated 1 percentage point from overall GDP growth in FY10. Thus, the combined impact of all of these developments reduced the momentum of Indian growth in FY10, slowing it from the 6.5–7.0 percent expected earlier to a now possible 3.0–3.5 percent.

Much of this slowdown is due to the global weakening of private capital flows to emerging countries. While all components of net private capital inflows have slowed, the largest drop is in net bank lending, forecast to shift from a net inflow of US$30 billion in 2008 to a net outflow of US$25 billion in 2009 (IIF 2009). In contrast, FDI flows remained relatively buoyant as cumulative inflows of FDI in April 2008–January 2009 rose to US$24 billion, compared to US$15 billion in the same period a year earlier.

Financial Markets

Financial markets tightened after the collapse of Lehman Brothers, with the call money rate rising to 20 percent (figure 6.15). While some domestic factors—such as advance payment of taxes and withdrawal of bank deposits for festival shopping—tightened liquidity conditions, the rise was largely attributable to the liquidity squeeze associated with the sudden stop in foreign capital flows and the freezing up of the interbank market. The uncertainty about various Indian banks' exposure to toxic assets resulted in banks being unwilling to lend to one another, even though most banks were in the public sector. Credit default swap spreads for Indian banks rose sharply in October–November 2008 as the risk perception of the stakeholders of these banks rose substantially.

A sharp drop in nonbank financing for the corporate sector worsened the downturn. While the flow of funds from domestic sources fell

Figure 6.15. Effects of the Crisis on India's Financial Markets

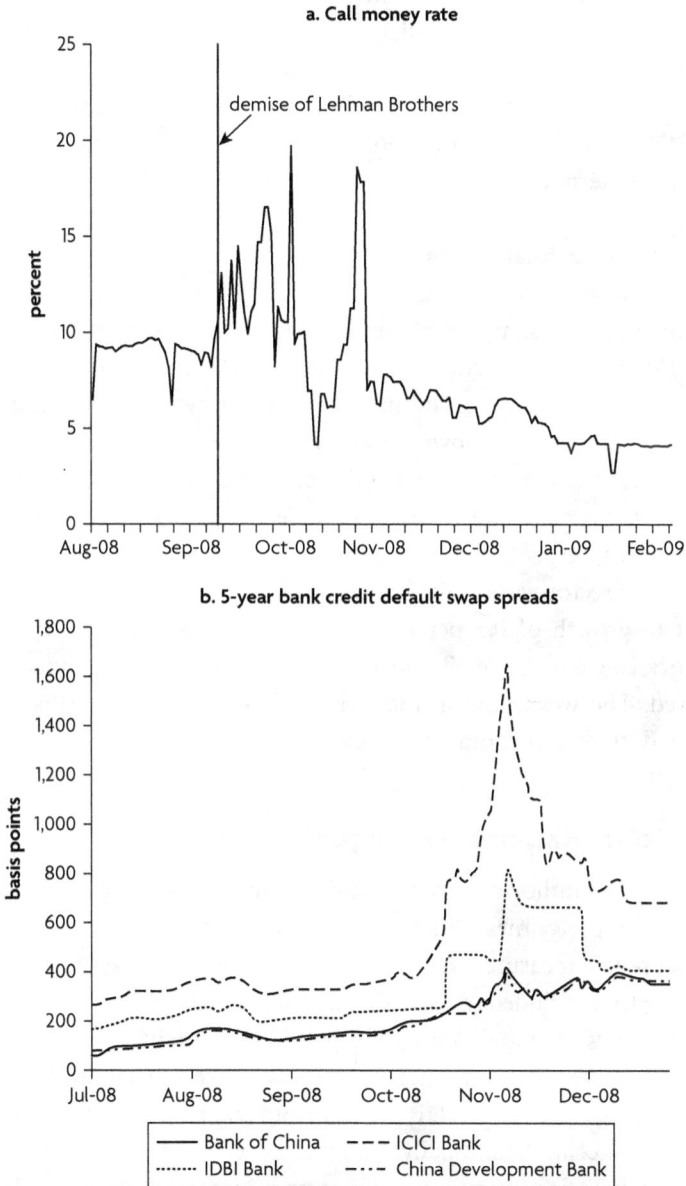

a. Call money rate

b. 5-year bank credit default swap spreads

Legend: Bank of China — — — ICICI Bank ········ IDBI Bank — ·· — China Development Bank

Source: Reserve Bank of India, *Handbook of Statistics*; Global Economic Monitor.

30 percent, foreign funding declined 34 percent. Among the former, fundraising through public issues, the issuance of commercial paper, and accommodation by Indian financial institutions fell substantially relative to previous years. The strong decline in foreign funds was mitigated by a near tripling of FDI inflows, as other financing sources (such as ECBs, Global Depository Receipts, American Depository Receipts, and short-term credit) fell by 60 percent or more.

Impact on the Real Sector

Given the domestic effects of the crisis as manifested in domestic confidence losses, financial market losses, and wealth effect losses, the global financial crisis has had a profound impact on India's real economy (figure 6.16). The industrial sector, which was already witnessing a growth slowdown, saw further deceleration. During October 2008–March 2009, the capital and basic goods sectors grew on average by only 6.4 percent and 1.9 percent, respectively, versus 10.2 percent and 3.8 percent, respectively, during April–September 2008. The intermediate goods sector was hit the hardest and shrunk by 4.8 percent, in contrast to growth of 0.5 percent in the earlier period. Within the core sectors, coal and crude oil were affected most, and cement and steel also slowed. The weakening in the industrial sector was associated with a sharp decline in corporate investment.

The Policy Response and Impact

The Indian authorities reacted quickly and proactively to the global crisis with policy measures that have considerably mitigated its impact. Initial policy measures were focused mainly on monetary and banking sectors; they included massive liquidity injections, re-attracting or slowing outflows of global capital, and providing guarantees and finance to troubled sectors. These monetary policies are likely to have added at least 2 percentage points to GDP growth from the baseline expectations of 3.5–4.0 percent. Additionally, the government announced and implemented three fiscal stimulus packages since December 2008, and they are likely to have added at least 1 percentage point to GDP growth. Some of the massive discretionary measures undertaken prior to the onset of the crisis—such as the hike in public sector employee salaries, the extension

Figure 6.16. Real Sector Impact of the Global Crisis

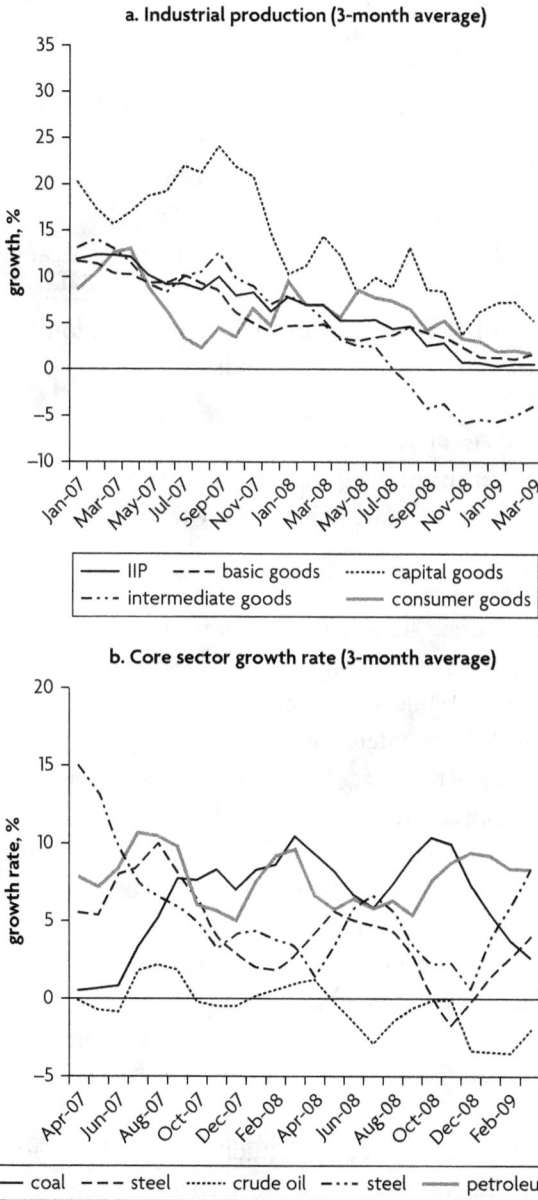

a. Industrial production (3-month average)

Legend: IIP — basic goods --- capital goods .... intermediate goods -•-• consumer goods

b. Core sector growth rate (3-month average)

Legend: coal — steel --- crude oil .... steel -•-• petroleum refinery

Source: CSO.
Note: IIP = index of industrial production.

of the National Rural Employment Guarantee Act countrywide, and higher minimum support prices for farmers—also helped boost aggregate demand. Thus, the policy measures taken together offset at least about 3.0–3.5 percentage points decline in the GDP growth rate, with overall GDP growth now estimated at 7.4 percent in FY10. This is a remarkable turnaround—and far better than earlier expected, especially given the recent drought affecting Indian agriculture. Moreover, the global policy responses to the financial crisis and its effects may have even had some unintended benefits for India. This is because of the dramatic reduction in global central banks' policy interest rates to near zero and the easing of global commodity prices and inflation, both of which allowed much lower interest rates in India.

Monetary and Fiscal Stimulus

The Indian government adopted a series of strong monetary and fiscal measures to arrest the downswing in growth in the wake of the global crisis.

Monetary Measures. To meet the immediate shortage of foreign exchange in the face of declining capital flows, the RBI tapped its foreign exchange reserves. While this accentuated the liquidity constraints in the economy, the RBI countered it by introducing a series of measures (table 6.5). The CRR and statutory liquidity ratio were reduced by 400 and 100 bps, respectively. The government introduced a number of refinance windows, including the Small Industries Development Bank of India and the Export-Import Bank of India, which provided liquidity to small industries and exporters. The government also relaxed prudential norms with respect to provisioning and risk weights. It also enhanced foreign exchange liquidity by increasing the interest rate ceiling on nonresident deposits, easing restrictions on ECBs, and short-term credits, among other things. Moreover, the central bank ceased issuing bonds under the Market Stabilization Scheme, which were used extensively in FY08 to absorb excess liquidity by sterilizing foreign capital flows. Instead, the RBI resorted to buying back these securities. Such key policy rates as the repo and reverse repo rates were reduced by 425 and 275 bps, respectively, to stabilize money market interest rates, which had spiraled after the Lehman Brothers collapse. To facilitate government

Table 6.5. Monetary Policy Measures

Measure/Facility	Amount (Rs billions)	Share in GDP (%)
Monetary policy operations	3,266.16	6.14
1. Cash reserve ratio reduction	1,600.00	3.01
2. Open market operations	688.35	1.29
3. MSS unwinding/desequestering	977.81	1.84
Extension of liquidity facilities	1,650.12	3.10
1. Term repo facility	600.00	1.13
2. Increase in export credit refinance	255.12	0.48
3. Special refinance facility for scheduled commercial banks	385.00	0.72
4. Refinance facility for Small Industries Development Bank of India/National Housing Bank/Export Import Bank	160.00	0.30
5. Liquidity facility for nonbanking financial companies through special purchase vehicles	250.00	0.47
Total	4,916.28	9.24
Memo		
Statutory liquidity ratio reduction	400.00	0.75

Source: Mohan 2009.

borrowing, the RBI also agreed to purchase government securities through open market operations. These measures sought to offset the contraction in RBI's balance sheet—attributable to a decline in foreign assets—by expanding domestic assets. The various measures had the potential for releasing liquidity equal to more than 9 percent of GDP.

Fiscal Measures. The government sought to bolster aggregate demand through a series of fiscal stimulus measures consisting of tax cuts and additional spending (table 6.6). Quantifying spending measures is relatively easy compared to tax cuts, as tax cuts in turn depend on the growth rate of the economy. In addition, under the two supplementary demands for grants, the government has sought additional resources involving a net cash outlay to boost aggregate demand. These reflected a number of measures announced in FY09, but for which funds were not provided, like the farm loan waiver and implementation of the sixth pay commission. Surging commodity prices led to a sharp rise in the subsidy bill, as the government did not allow the entire price rise to be passed on to

Table 6.6. Fiscal Stimulus Measures

Measure/Facility	Amount (Rs billions)	Share in GDP (%)
Precrisis stimulus	**958.30**	**1.95**
1. Fertilizer subsidy	449.00	0.83
2. Sixth pay commission	254.30	0.47
3. National Rural Employment Generation Scheme	105.00	0.19
4. Farm debt waiver	150.00	0.27
5. Food subsidy	106.00	0.19
Fiscal stimulus I (December 2008)	**314.50**	**0.58**
1. Additional plan spending	200.00	0.37
2. 4% reduction in CENVAT	100.00	0.18
3. Export incentives and refund of terminal excise duty/central sales tax	14.50	0.03
Fiscal stimulus II (January 2009)	**300.00**	**0.57**
1. Additional market borrowing for states	300.00	0.57
Fiscal stimulus III (February 2009)	**291.00**	**0.51**
1. Service tax reduction	140.00	0.25
2. Excise duty reduction	85.00	0.15
3. Customs duty reduction	66.00	0.11
Total	**1,863.80**	**3.60**

Source: Author's calculations.
Note: CENVAT = central value added tax.

consumers. The various measures outlined in the stimulus packages included a reduction in service tax and excise duties; additional plan expenditure by the central government, as well as allowing state governments to borrow more; and support for exports, textiles, infrastructure, and SMEs. As a result of these steps, the FY09 fiscal deficit of the central government surged from a budgeted 2.5 percent of GDP to an estimated 6.1 percent.

Rapid Recovery from Global Crisis

Since March 2009, the Indian economy has made a rapid recovery. Several early leading indicators were already pointing to such a recovery by the middle of the year, including Nomura's Composite Leading Index, the ABN Amro Purchasing Manager's Index, and UBS's Leading Economic Indicator. The recovery hypothesis was also supported by impressive early showings of sectors like steel, cement, auto, and port traffic. Cement shipments grew 10 percent in March 2009, while container traffic expanded by 9.8 percent after declining 26 percent in February 2009. The World Steel Association had expected India to be the only large economy to witness a spike in steel consumption (of 1.7 percent) in 2009. The expansion in India's telecommunications subscriber base also held up, and wireless subscriber growth was expected to be about 30 percent in 2009. Anecdotal evidence also pointed to growth starting among SMEs, which were earlier constrained by the liquidity crunch and fall in exports. Core sectors—including crude oil, petroleum refining, coal, electricity, and steel—recorded encouraging growth of 2.9 percent in March 2009, relative to the previous year, and above the average of 2.7 percent for FY09 as a whole.

By the end of 2009, these early indicators of rapid recovery were borne out, confirming that the Indian economy had made a faster-than-expected recovery. Quarterly GDP growth picked up to almost 8 percent by the second quarter of FY10, and strengthened further to 8.6 percent in the last quarter of FY10, boosting overall economic growth in F10 to as much as 7.4 percent. Much of the growth was boosted by a massive surge in industrial production—especially manufacturing, which grew by a torrid 18 percent (figure 6.17a). Services also grew rapidly, as did trade. Exports increased for three months, fueled by the global recovery, while import growth surged with the accelerating domestic recovery. In less than two quarters, Indian economic growth was very quickly rebounding to precrisis levels of 8 percent. Indeed, India's recovery was as strong as China's bounce-back.

Accompanying this rebound, however, was a rising inflation rate. Wholesale price inflation (WPI) converged with consumer price inflation and food prices were rising along with core inflation (figure 6.17b). Clearly, India was starting to hit up against some supply side (rather than demand-side) bottlenecks to growth, especially with fast-recovering private consumption and investment demand. Beginning in late 2009 and early 2010, the RBI began tightening the capital account on ECB norms that it had earlier relaxed; the RBI also started raising the CRR and policy interest rates in small steps from their previously very low

Figure 6.17. Industrial Production Surges to Precrisis Levels, as Does Inflation

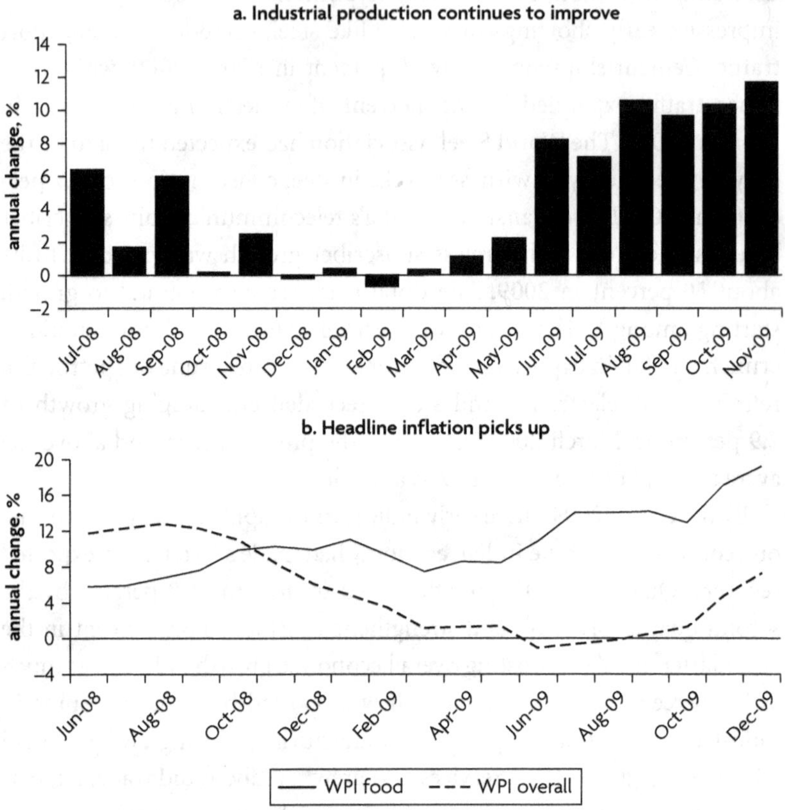

a. Industrial production continues to improve

b. Headline inflation picks up

——— WPI food   – – – WPI overall

Source: CEIC Data Ltd.
Note: WPI = wholesale price inflation.

levels, signaling its gradual exit from the exceptional monetary stimulus measures.

Also supporting this recovery was improved financial flows from abroad and a recovery in domestic confidence (figure 6.18) The Indian equity market, which had slumped from a peak of 20,000 in January 2008 to 8,000 in March 2009, recovered substantially to cross 14,000 in late May; the market has since improved by another 20 percent, with levels hovering close to precrisis ones. Part of the explanation was the postelection results rally in May (which led to a rise of over 2,000 points in one day) because of the stability that the results ensured. The rally was also

Figure 6.18. Capital Flows Return and Stock Markets Improve

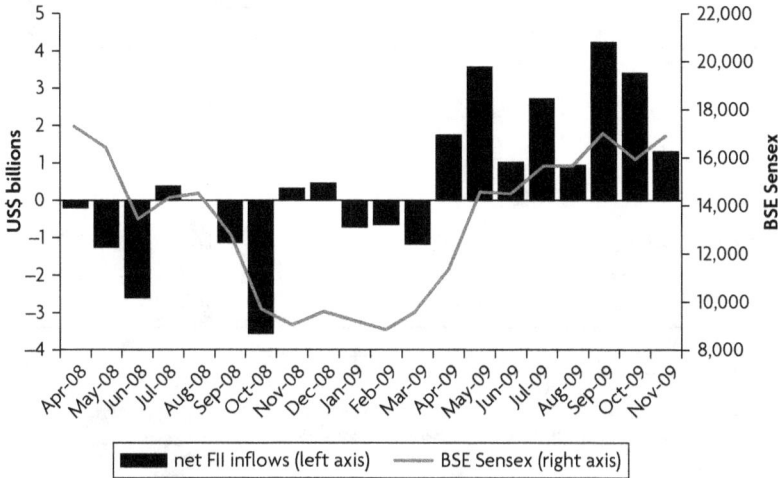

Source: Reserve Bank of India; IMF International Financial Statistics.
Note: FII = foreign institutional investor; BSE Sensex = Bombay Stock Exchange Sensitivity Index.

helped by a strong recovery in FII net inflows, which turned positive after staying in negative territory for most of October 2008–March 2009 Along with the return of FII and the weakening of the dollar, the rupee has also appreciated significantly, and foreign reserves have started to grow.

Medium-Term Growth Prospects

What are India's medium-term growth prospects? Can the country restore growth to its precrisis levels, or will growth be markedly slower as a result of slower global growth? Will medium-term growth be led by high rates of domestic investment and savings? What role will global factors play, and how should Indian macroeconomic policies seek to make conditions more supportive of sustained and faster growth?

We start first with a possible baseline scenario of medium-term prospects.[4] We project that medium-term sustainable growth will be about 8.5 percent (table 6.7). This is greater than the preboom precrisis period average of 5.5 percent; it is due to the impact of reforms and the new dynamism already apparent during this period, but offset by policy and international conditions. However, our forecast of 8.5 percent sustainable

Table 6.7. India: Actual and Projected Growth in the Medium Term

	Actual FY06–FY08	Estimated FY09–FY10	Projected FY11–FY15
Private consumption (% per year)	9.0	3.5	6.0
Public consumption (% per year)	7.2	15.1	−0.5
Investment (% per year)	15.0	7.8	12.0
GDP (% per year, at market prices)	9.5	6.4	8.5
Memo			
Nominal export growth	25.5	4.1	12.0
Nominal import growth	23.7	17.8	10.0
Current A/C balance (% GDP)	−1.2	−1.6	−1.5

Source: Reserve Bank of India, *Handbook of Statistics*; authors' calculations.
Note: A/C = account.

Table 6.8. Forecast Annual Growth Rates: Base Case
(% per year)

	FY09	FY10	FY11	FY12	FY13	FY14	FY15
GDP at factor cost	6.7	7.4	8	8.5	9	8.5	8.3
GDP at market prices	5.1	7.7	8.1	8.3	8.8	8.7	8.5

Source: CSO; authors' estimate.

growth will be significantly lower than the peak growth of nearly 10 percent that India achieved during the boom precrisis years—a rate that was not sustainable with the overheating evident earlier.

While our medium-term growth figure of 8.5 percent is an average for the entire period FY11–FY15, we envisage a cycle that starts with slower growth from current levels and then picks up to higher levels before moderating. (See table 6.8 for the proximate annual forecasts underlying the average period forecast.) Obviously, shocks—whether of domestic or external origin—will affect the projected growth path. The predicted average period growth is consistent with supply-side forecasts.

The Domestic Investment Cycle

A great deal of India's medium-term growth prospects hinge on a recovery of investment. This requires overcoming

- the down-cycle that started autonomously because of supply-side pressures (overheating, exchange rate appreciation, skills shortages, and infrastructure shortages);

- the global commodity shocks that led to lower aggregate demand because of tighter monetary policy measures; and
- stresses of the 2008 global economic crisis, which led to problems in trade and financing (slower credit growth, falling FII, and falling stock prices).

Looking at the broader picture, financing is much less an aggregate macroeconomic constraint, since large domestic savings are easily available—primarily from household and corporate savings. The biggest immediate driver of investment appears to be confidence in domestic and foreign markets.

We see good reasons to expect that annual investment growth rates, which fell from a peak of about 17 percent in FY06 to a low of about 4 percent in FY09, should recover rapidly to a sustainable level of about 12 percent annually in the medium term. Household domestic savings continue to be high (reflecting demographics), and corporate profitability has been buoyant even with the downturn because of scale and efficiency improvements. The stock markets, in turn, have recovered to their near-historic highs and are above FY08 levels (although still below their peaks), largely because of the inherent strengths of corporate balance sheets and growth prospects.

Monetary policy will aid the recovery, since real interest rates have been lowered sharply globally, and Indian interest rates will follow that parity condition with lower country risks. A sustainable real deposit rate in India of about 2–3 percent will be consistent with buoyant investment (and consumption) demand. Some policy shocks are always possible, and are likely to be more on the upside (lower real interest rates) than on the downside (sudden monetary policy tightening to deal with inflation), given slower global growth and low interest rates abroad. The role of foreign portfolio preferences is also likely to remain strongly positive with the prospect of faster growth in India relative to the rest of the world.

Investment prospects also depend heavily on rising aggregate growth and demand. With immediate growth prospects ahead of about 8–9 percent for real GDP, profitability will be reasonably high (as is currently evident). On the supply side, wages have moderated, and two years' worth of cumulative skills supply should prevent immediate skill shortages. We also expect that infrastructure bottlenecks will be eased,

owing to the slowdown and the completion of several investment projects in key sectors (power, roads, telecommunications, and ports). In
other words, faster growth is also possible because the economy has
operated well below potential output over some 24 months. Thus, there
is little reason to expect severe skill or infrastructure constraints to
growth. Conversely, infrastructure financing and prospects will receive
considerable policy attention, especially access to preferential financing
and demand from public sources. The government's new budget for
FY11 preserves a sharp rise in infrastructure spending.

As to financing from global sources, FDI inflows remain very strong,
and FII inflows can be expected to recover to medium-term trends (as
both are currently doing). Indian corporations are also relatively conservative. Despite capital expenditures largely funded by debt in the past two
years with a significant share of ECBs, the leverage ratio of the Indian
corporate sector is still low relative to international levels. The aggregate
debt-to-equity ratio peaked at 0.84 in FY02, but thereafter declined to
0.62 in FY06 before increasing marginally to 0.64 in FY08. While the
debt-to-equity ratio of BSE-500 companies has increased marginally
from a low of 0.56 in FY05 to 0.60 in FY08, the debt-to-equity ratio of
BSE Small Cap companies has declined steadily from FY02.

The sharp drop in ECBs, along with FII outflows and limited issuance
of fresh equity, will hamper corporate investment immediately ahead.
However, foreign capital inflows have begun to recover. Since March,
ECB financing for Indian corporations has picked up sharply, and in the
medium term, Indian corporations can expect to receive more—not
less—financing, both as a result of easing of policy and greater supply
from abroad (countercyclical to global trends). Already, Indian policy
makers are discussing whether to curb excessive capital inflows.

Nevertheless, the projected infrastructure investment target of
US$500 billion during 2007–12 will be difficult to achieve. The target
was based on increasing the share of infrastructure investment in India
to 8 percent of GDP. Of these, about 30 percent (US$150 billion) is
expected to be through private participation. In the past three years, private sector participation in infrastructure has increased for a variety of
reasons such as improved macroeconomic fundamentals, increased ability to pay for infrastructure services, progress toward full cost recovery
with the use of efficient subsidies, gradually improving access to both

foreign and domestic capital, gradually improving access to long-term financing, fiscal incentives (such as tax rebates), and increasing clarity in policy and regulatory frameworks. At the end of FY09, outstanding investments in the infrastructure sector were valued at about US$706 billion.[5] The most recent data suggest that private participation in infrastructure (PPI) has held up very well in India: about 40 percent of total developing country investment in PPI projects in the first three quarters of 2009 was accounted for by India—with US$25 billion invested in 33 projects and the average project size increasing to US$638 million in 2009. Thanks to the growing depth and liquidity of domestic financial markets, the growth of these infrastructure projects was largely financed domestically. The top four lead arrangers in the entire Asia Pacific region were Indian banks.

Domestic Consumption Growth

Domestic consumption growth is much less volatile and is endogenous to growth. With steady GDP expansion, a young population, and life-cycle consumption behavior, there is little reason to expect any sharp departures from past medium-term trends. While private consumption growth fell sharply in FY09 (to about 2.5 percent), it was due largely to the sharp falloff in growth, higher inflation, and possible changes in asset prices and wealth effects—much of which has been reversed in the past few months of 2010. Barring agricultural shocks (which are not anticipated), therefore, there is little downside to baseline assumptions of 5.5–6.0 percent annual consumption growth.

Global Trade and Exports. Global real trade growth is expected to recover to at least 6–7 percent per year and to far exceed world GDP growth. If—as expected—India maintains its low-cost advantages (especially in manufacturing and in knowledge-based manufacturing and services), and if exchange rates are kept competitive, exports should rise by at least 10 percent per year in real terms, or about 12–15 percent in nominal terms, and potentially more. Import growth should also be similar and should follow GDP growth; such a level of import growth should be easily financed by exports, remittances, and services earnings. Thus, we do not expect net exports to change very much or to contribute much to growth changes. Instead, rising trade ratios will have their main impact through raising productivity. Annual TFP growth of at least 2 percent per year (as historically) is therefore a reasonable assumption.

Global Growth Slowdown. As noted earlier, slowing global growth—other than through its effects on global trade—should barely affect India's medium-term growth prospects. Barring a sudden shock or another deep recession, India is relatively immune in the medium term. A global medium-term growth slowdown of 1 percentage point in advanced countries (say, from 3 percent to 2 percent per year) would reduce India's annual GDP growth from, for example, 8.5 percent to about 8 percent—hardly notable within the variance of India's own growth path. Alternative estimates of the elasticity of India's GDP growth to world GDP growth are sometimes even lower, ranging from 0.15–0.2, with 0.4 as the upper-bound elasticity.

Capital flows, in contrast, should be countercyclical (relative to global growth) and favor India, relative to prospects in advanced countries. This is partly because of a widening of investors' appetite for portfolio diversification, since faster growth and long-term returns are consistently higher in India than in advanced countries. In the short term, India should actually gain from slow growth and demand for financing and savings in the advanced countries, as relatively faster GDP growth and earnings in India attracts more of such long-term capital. Still, the overall pool of financial savings may contract relative to the pre-2008 crisis episode, and India may well receive significantly less aggregate flows of foreign capital intermediation. While this would not be central for financing, it would be an issue for financial intermediation efficiency. Therefore, the right policy choice is to enhance the functioning and efficiency of domestic capital markets in the medium term.

It also bears remembering that the past episode of investment buoyancy was relatively unaffected by the surge in global capital flows, because at the margin, it was absorbed in the accumulation of reserves. The biggest gains were the financial deepening and efficiency effects, which India will continue to benefit from even if total flows are reduced.

Policy Effects. We expect that India has the potential to gain a lot from this crisis in terms of policy and institutional learning. We see financial sector policies being strengthened, capital markets being deepened, monetary policy shocks being reduced, and prudent capital account opening. The only major downside will be the effects of fiscal deterioration after this crisis. This effect will be to delay the ability of public investment to bounce back, possibly causing (at the margin) a relative slowdown in the supply of public goods (such as education and infrastructure), and also potentially raising domestic interest rates. If the effect of this shock is a not-so-transient raising of medium-term government bond yields—and, hence, market interest rates by, say, 100 bps at the margin—it could slow GDP growth by up to about 0.5 percentage points in the medium term. However, this can be offset by fiscal management improvements, and India may well undertake these. The recent Thirteenth Finance Commission has proposed reducing fiscal deficits quickly to about 5.5 percent of GDP by FY15, and a target debt-to-GDP ratio of about 67 percent (from the current 80 percent or so) in the medium term. The government has accepted these targets, and the FY11 budget is based on that proposal and path of fiscal adjustment. Much of the fiscal adjustment should occur as a result of faster growth and cuts in spending, as well as significant privatization—all of which are feasible.

The other major policy improvement will be India's development of domestic capital markets and deepening their intermediation—which has already started. Intermediaries such as private equity funds, mutual funds, bond funds, insurance funds, private pension funds, and other financial intermediaries are all substantially boosting their onshore presence in India. These are endogenous responses to India's growing capital structure and financing needs and, with policy enhancements on the regulatory side, should steadily boost the domestic financing of investment.

A Supply-Side View

The supply-side picture also confirms medium-term annual growth projections of about 8.0–8.5 percent. India's steady improvement in historical growth in output per worker primarily reflects faster capital-per-worker growth (table 6.9)—rising especially fast in the most recent periods—and steady human capital gains, as India completes its nearly universal primary education and extends gains to secondary and tertiary levels. The growth of output per worker has, in turn, been aided by rising TFP growth and the benefits from openness and technological catch-up.

Data in table 6.9 are broadly comparable with other estimates, such as OECD (2007) and Collins (2007), in the sense that both also expect

Table 6.9. Supply-Side Factors behind India's Growth Prospects
(growth rate %)

	1960–70	1970–80	1980–90	1990–2003	1996–2001	2002–07	Est. 2008–09	Proj. 2010–20
GDP (at factor cost)	3.7	3.1	5.5	5.8	5.4	8.0	7.0	8.5
GDP per worker	1.8	0.7	3.5	4.0	3.5	6.1	5.3	6.5
Capital per worker	1.3	0.7	1.1	1.5	2.0	2.3	1.9	2.5
Human capital/ worker	0.2	0.3	0.4	0.5	0.5	0.6	0.4	0.5
TFP	0.7	−0.2	2.1	2.0	0.9	3.1	2.7	3.0
Labor force	1.9	2.4	2.0	1.8	1.9	1.9	1.7	2.0
Memo								
Population	2.3	2.2	2.2	2.1	1.8	1.8	1.7	1.7

Source: World Bank, World Development Indicators Database; OECD; authors' estimates.
Note: Data are in calendar years.

that after eliminating the effects of cyclical factors and agricultural output variations, an increasingly larger contribution to growth originates from capital formation, while TFP growth continues to improve steadily. The cyclical effects are obvious when comparing the two subperiods 1996–2001 and 2002–07. But even with the crisis downturn, the estimated slow-down effects in 2008–09 (calendar years) are much less pronounced than in 1996–2001(calendar years). Thus, reforms and developments, especially additions to capital stock since 2001, have raised the economy's potential output growth well above that prevailing during 1996–2001.

Overall, therefore, India's medium-term growth prospects remain robust at about 8.5 percent per year, fueled by gains on the supply side (young population, high savings/investment, catch-up, and TFP gains from rising trade), while private investment remains the aggregate supply and demand-side engine driving medium-term growth.

Upside Potential and Downside Risks

While our baseline forecasts suggest 8.5 percent noninflationary medium-term growth, there is scope for accelerated growth of about

9 percent per year, and potentially even faster. Indeed, the government has set a target of such a rate of growth. This is predicated on a stronger supply response in agriculture, as well as higher investment rates and modestly higher factor productivity. If sustained, these would allow India to attain growth rates of 10 percent and higher toward the end of this decade. The potential output gap that opened up during the crisis also allows scope for this upside potential, although the gap is not very large. On the downside, three main factors may lead to slower growth: rising real interest rates, an appreciation of the rupee, and continued slow growth in the rest of the world. Rising real domestic interest rates would most likely result if fiscal adjustment is slower than envisaged and increased borrowing forces rates higher. External shocks could also complicate the picture, especially if global growth is much slower than assumed. Other global shocks could include higher commodity price inflation, especially for petroleum and food, and sudden reversals of capital flows because of shocks in global financial markets. India's external remittances are large, now nearly 4 percent of GDP, and are relatively steady and diversified (with overseas workers going to the Persian Gulf and a wide array of advanced countries). And even in this crisis, remittances have exhibited little volatility; indeed, receipts have risen in much of the period under review. Domestic shocks that could undermine fast growth include the possibility of rising core inflation (and, hence, tighter monetary policies and higher interest rates), which would force demand-side moderation as well as agricultural supply shocks. On the supply side, other risks include rising skill shortages and growing infrastructure deficits (e.g., power, water, transport).

Inflation is an immediate concern; core inflation has risen to about 7–8 percent, up from the precrisis levels of 4–6 percent. Much of it appears to be related to the rising food inflation, which should abate as better weather returns and expected supply responses materialize. Fiscal vulnerability is also high because of the consolidated general government's heavy debt (debt-to-GDP ratio of about 80 percent) and large deficits after this crisis. If both are unexpectedly persistent and rising, medium-term growth could fall by about 1.0–1.5 percentage points below the forecast level, down to 7.0–7.5 percent annually. Externally, if commodity prices were to worsen sharply, the effects would be of similar magnitude.

Concluding Remarks: Policy and Institutional Underpinnings of India's Faster Growth and Prospects for the Future

From a comparative standpoint, one of the enduring puzzles of India's recent growth spurt (FY03–FY08) before this crisis, and the one that is now emerging, is the role that policy and institutional reforms play in driving and sustaining such growth accelerations. This chapter has alluded to one key strength of India's institutional setting: its well-established policy-making setting and its ability to learn from its own history and that of others. However, the question persists: was India's recent growth acceleration of FY03–FY08 due merely to "good luck" or to accelerated reform? And if such reforms are fundamental, what are the key challenges ahead if India is to sustain its recovery from this crisis? While these were not the main questions directly framed to the authors by the organizers of this book, later peer reviews have suggested that we at least provide some possible pointers to readers and researchers. We therefore address this topic in conclusion with three or four broader observations that might be helpful.

The first is that there is as yet no settled answer, either generally or in India's particular case, as to why growth accelerations occur and what sustains them. A body of work is still evolving, after the earlier work, for example, by Hausmann, Pritchett, and Rodrik (2004), which noted both the existence and the importance of such growth accelerations and their relative rarity. In India's case, the argument still rages as to whether the growth acceleration started in the 1970s, in the 1980s, or in the 1990s. As we have argued, what is much more interesting in India's case is that growth crises have been periodic, and the ability of policy makers to produce growth accelerations after such pauses is far more interesting than when they have happened. We argue, furthermore, that is it is not any single body of Washington-style consensus economic reforms that produce better results, but the ability of policy makers to address the most critical constraints to growth at any one point of time—be it food and agriculture, services, labor markets, or infrastructure—combined with the confidence and ability of its larger public and private sector settings to respond to such reforms.

The second is that there is very little doubt that India's growth spurt in the FY03–FY08 period was a major event because of its strength (doubling per capita growth from the previous 3 percent to about 6–7 percent currently) in relation both to its own history and to that of comparators such as China and East Asia. But here, too, the mystery of India's previous growth spurt episodes persists in two very important respects: (1) there was no single political economy or policy reform that decidedly spurred such an acceleration, and (2) the growth that took place, on the other hand, was not simply "good luck" but was attributable to the impacts of an accretion of macroeconomic and structural policy improvements across a wide range of fronts that this chapter has addressed—from the improvement of tax policies, to the liberalization of FDI policies, the steady opening of the economy, the growth of infrastructure, the development of skills, and managing the complex political economy in favor of faster growth with equity. This process has been given various names by other authors, ranging from "a gradualist and evolutionary transition model" (Ahluwalia 1994), to a shift to a "pro-market attitudinal" orientation (Rodrik and Subramaniam 2004) and the more radical "end of license raj reforms" (Srinivasan 2005).

Perhaps the most important aspects of the reform process in India are as noted in a contemporaneous lecture by a leading reform counsel (Rangarajan 2006, 3): "India's economic reforms are unique in two important respects—not because of the content of the reforms but because of the context in which we are pursuing them. First, we are implementing them in a democratic context....second, in a decentralized context. This has...meant restraint, even compromise, deliberate decision-making and slow progress...making haste slowly....(and adding) to the credibility and robustness of our reform."

We have preferred to call it more simply an endogenous process of reform, insofar as such reforms essentially take place in the most binding areas endogenously as pressure groups and lobbyists of the private sector coalesce, as internal bureaucratic policy makers address increasingly costly constraints or attempts to take advantage of new opportunities, and as political actors trade off the costs and benefits of policy alternatives. The steady accretion of such improvements, and the ability to take decisive steps when needed, especially in crises, are the two hallmarks of success. The period FY03–FY08 simply benefited from an acceleration of such a process with improved opportunities and openness to the rest of the world, nothing more, compared to a much more difficult previous five years when growth stalled after the 1991 reforms.

The third observation is that such growth accelerations have eventually and ultimately depended on (1) the creation of conditions for rising private investment, and hence expansion of private opportunities; (2) the reduction of entry barriers and the enhancement of competitiveness and openness; and (3) the adequacy of financing, driven by enhanced profitability and financial innovation with strong financial institutions. Given India's per capita income and structural opportunities, the scope for such growth has been and will remain enormous—be it in the form of the telecommunications boom, the construction boom, the manufacturing boom, or the infrastructure boom that is ongoing and will continue. Sound macroeconomic policies are essential, especially for policies supporting high savings and domestic investment capabilities (which India, as a large country with a young population, similar to the case of China, is capable of sustaining). But also essential is the internal capacity to develop and implement the reforms needed to open up such areas in the increasingly expanding circle of opportunities discussed earlier in this chapter.

Looking ahead, the acquisition of new skills sets in the labor force, labor regulations, manufacturing capacity, services opportunities, a second agricultural revolution, urbanization, water, power, and energy are all key "reform" constraints and opportunities that will likely be dealt with "endogenously." India has been doing this and will likely also follow the successful lessons and examples of other fast-growing economies in Asia and elsewhere, rather than a standard "template" of prescriptive reforms. Exactly of which of these "reforms" are crucial and when they are likely to be undertaken cannot be presupposed—aside from what is known widely (e.g., infrastructure gaps, skills gaps, urbanization gaps, labor regulations). It is possible that India, like other countries, may slip into less certain institutional waters with some unanticipated domestic or external challenge. But at the moment its institutional capacity for endogenous innovation and improvement ("reforms," in other words) appears reasonably promising for fueling rapid and sustained growth.

Finally, one of the more difficult challenges ahead in this broader setting is whether India, like other countries, will manage now to find the right mix of growth-enhancing policies and institutions versus inequality-reducing policies. There is a rising tension between the two, especially as far as public policies and spending are concerned. While this article is overtly focused on growth, it is inclusive growth that is the most pressing public policy challenge. How India's institutions respond to this challenge will be of great significance in the coming years.

Annex

Table 6A.1. India: Basic Macroeconomic Indicators

	FY95	FY96	FY97	FY98	FY99	FY00	FY01	FY02	FY03	FY04	FY05	FY06	FY07	FY08	FY09
GDP (US$ billions)	323.5	356.3	388.3	410.9	416.3	450.5	460.2	477.9	507.2	599.5	700.9	810.2	914.9	1,176.9	1,159.2
GDP per capita (current US$)	363.2	391.5	418.5	434.4	431.8	458.3	453.4	464.4	484.9	564.5	649.6	739.2	821.3	1,040.6	1,009.7
Population growth (% per year)	2.3	2.0	2.0	1.9	1.9	2.0	3.3	1.4	1.7	1.5	1.6	1.6	1.6	1.5	1.5
GDP growth (% per year, at factor cost)	6.4	7.3	8.0	4.3	6.7	6.4	4.4	5.8	3.8	8.5	7.5	9.5	9.7	9.2	6.7
GDP growth by sector (% per year)	6.4	7.3	8.0	4.3	6.7	6.4	4.4	5.8	3.8	8.5	7.5	9.5	9.7	9.0	6.7
Agriculture	4.7	−0.7	9.9	−2.6	6.3	2.7	−0.3	6.3	−7.2	10.0	−0.1	5.3	3.7	4.7	1.6
Industry	9.3	11.6	6.7	3.7	4.1	4.6	6.4	2.7	7.1	7.4	10.3	8.1	13.6	9.3	3.1
Services	5.9	10.1	7.6	8.8	8.3	9.5	5.7	7.2	7.5	8.5	9.1	11.3	10.2	10.4	9.3
GDP growth by demand component (% per year)															
Private consumption	4.9	6.1	7.8	3.0	6.5	6.1	3.4	6.0	2.9	5.9	5.2	9.0	8.2	9.8	6.8

(continued)

Table 6A1. (continued)

	FY95	FY96	FY97	FY98	FY99	FY00	FY01	FY02	FY03	FY04	FY05	FY06	FY07	FY08	FY09
Gross fixed capital formation (% per year)	—	—	—	6.0	7.4	11.2	-0.0	7.4	6.8	13.6	18.9	15.3	14.4	15.2	4.0
Share of GDP (% GDP)															
Private consumption	65.9	64.6	65.7	64.3	64.5	64.4	64.0	64.5	63.3	61.8	58.7	57.6	55.9	55.0	54.7
Gross fixed capital formation	22.1	24.4	23.1	23.0	22.8	23.4	22.7	23.6	23.8	24.9	28.4	31.0	32.5	34.0	34.8
Gross domestic savings	21.9	24.4	24.4	22.7	23.8	22.3	24.8	23.7	23.5	26.4	29.8	31.8	34.2	35.7	37.7
External sector															
Trade balance (US$ billions)[a]	-8.4	-11.6	-14.1	-14.2	-11.1	-13.8	-10.8	-8.3	-7.0	-3.6	-18.3	-28.7	-32.3	-54.1	-69.6
Current A/C balance (US$ billions)	-3.8	-5.9	-4.6	-5.5	-4.0	-4.7	-2.7	3.4	6.3	14.1	-2.5	-9.9	-9.6	-17.0	-29.8
Foreign direct investment (US$ billions), net	1.0	2.1	2.8	3.6	2.5	2.2	3.3	4.7	3.2	2.4	3.7	3.0	7.7	15.4	17.5

Foreign reserves (US$ billions)	25.2	21.7	26.4	29.4	32.5	38.0	42.3	54.1	75.4	111.6	140.1	150.9	198.7	309.3	251.0
In months of imports	8.4	6.0	6.5	6.9	8.2	8.2	8.8	11.5	14.0	16.7	14.1	11.5	12.5	14.4	10.2
External debt (US$ billions)	99.0	93.7	93.5	93.5	96.9	98.3	101.3	98.8	104.9	111.6	133.0	138.1	171.3	224.6	229.9
External debt to exports (%)	300.1	236.4	224.6	207.3	204.0	184.5	164.2	159.8	140.8	119.9	103.5	84.8	84.5	87.6	83.2
Interest to exports (%)	13.4	12.7	10.8	10.6	10.0	9.4	8.4	7.2	7.0	5.0	4.7	2.4	3.1	3.6	3.3
Nominal exchange rate (end of period)	31.5	34.4	35.9	39.5	42.4	43.6	46.6	48.8	47.5	43.4	43.8	44.6	43.6	40.0	51.0
REER (index 1993–94 = 100)	104.3	98.2	96.8	100.8	93.0	96.0	100.1	100.9	98.2	99.6	100.1	102.4	98.5	104.8	94.4
Public sector[b]															
Primary balance (% of GDP)	1.9	1.6	1.2	2.1	3.7	3.8	3.6	3.7	3.1	2.1	1.3	1.2	1.0	0.9	2.6
Overall balance (% of GDP)	8.2	7.6	6.5	6.4	7.3	9.3	9.6	9.6	10.1	9.7	9.1	7.6	5.5	6.0	8.6

(continued)

Table 6A.1. (continued)

	FY95	FY96	FY97	FY98	FY99	FY00	FY01	FY02	FY03	FY04	FY05	FY06	FY07	FY08	FY09
Net public debt (% of GDP)	75.6	71.7	68.0	69.8	70.1	72.6	76.2	81.2	85.6	86.9	85.8	83.3	80.2	78.0	78.6
Economic activity															
Unemployment (%)	—	4	—	—	—	—	—	4	—	—	—	5	—	—	—
Industrial capital utilization (%)	—	—	—	—	—	—	—	—	—	—	—	—	—	—	—

Source: CSO; Reserve Bank of India; World Bank, WDI 2009.
Note: REER = real effective exchange rate; — = not available.
a. Goods and services.
b. General government, including central and states.

Table 6A.2. India: Decomposition of GDP Growth
(percent)

	FY95	FY96	FY97	FY98	FY99	FY00	FY01	FY02	FY03	FY04	FY05	FY06	FY07	FY08	FY09
Total GDP growth rate (%, at factor cost)	6.4	7.3	8.0	4.3	6.7	6.4	4.4	5.8	3.8	8.5	7.5	9.5	9.7	9.2	6.7
Total GDP expenditures															
Final consumption	76.7	75.5	76.4	75.7	76.8	77.4	76.6	76.9	75.1	73.1	69.4	68.0	66.1	65.1	66.3
Private consumption	65.9	64.6	65.7	64.3	64.5	64.4	64.0	64.5	63.3	61.8	58.7	57.6	55.9	55.0	54.7
Government consumption	10.8	10.9	10.7	11.4	12.3	12.9	12.6	12.4	11.9	11.3	10.7	10.5	10.2	10.1	11.6
Investment	23.5	26.6	22.1	23.9	22.6	26.1	24.2	24.2	25.2	26.8	31.6	34.8	36.4	38.7	39.7
Gross fixed capital formation	22.1	24.4	23.1	23.0	22.8	23.4	22.7	23.6	23.8	24.9	28.4	31.0	32.5	34.0	34.8
Increase in stocks	1.4	2.2	-1.0	0.9	-0.1	1.9	0.7	-0.1	0.9	0.9	1.9	2.6	2.6	3.6	3.5
Net exports	-0.3	-1.2	-1.2	-1.3	-1.7	2.0	-0.9	-0.9	-1.0	-1.3	-1.8	-2.8	-3.0	-3.6	-5.4
Export	10.0	11.0	10.5	10.8	11.2	11.7	13.2	12.8	14.5	14.8	18.1	19.9	22.2	21.2	22.7
Import	10.3	12.2	11.7	12.1	12.8	13.6	14.2	13.6	15.5	16.1	19.9	22.7	25.2	24.7	28.0
Errors	0.1	-0.9	2.7	1.7	2.2	-1.5	0.1	-0.2	0.6	1.4	0.8	0.0	0.6	-0.3	-0.7

Source: CSO; Reserve Bank of India; World Bank, WDI 2009.

Table 6A.3. India: Domestic and International Financial Intermediation

	FY95	FY96	FY97	FY98	FY99	FY00	FY01	FY02	FY03	FY04	FY05	FY06	FY07	FY08	FY09
Money supply															
Annual growth (%)	22.4	13.6	16.2	18.0	19.4	14.6	16.8	14.1	14.7	16.7	12.3	21.2	21.5	21.2	19.0
Policy interest rate (reverse repo rate)	—	—	—	—	—	—	—	7.0	6.0	5.0	4.75	5.5	6.0	6.0	3.5
Foreign banks															
Share of assets owned (%)	7.3	8.0	8.3	8.2	8.1	7.5	7.9	7.3	6.9	6.9	6.5	7.2	7.9	8.4	8.5
Credit market															
Total credit growth (% per year)	26.6	20.2	13.2	14.5	13.0	15.4	14.4	12.5	28.4	17.5	37.3	40.5	28.2	28.7	17.5
Total credit (% GDP)	18.2	18.6	18.2	18.9	18.6	19.2	20.4	21.2	25.3	26.4	31.8	39.2	43.6	49.1	51.2
Credit to the private sector growth (% per year)	23.1	17.7	9.2	15.1	14.5	18.3	15.8	11.8	18.3	13.0	26.0	32.2	25.8	20.9	24.6
Credit to the private sector (% GDP)	56.8	57.2	56.6	56.7	56.2	57.1	57.0	56.3	57.1	57.8	62.9	68.8	71.9	74.0	71.7
Headline lending interest rate	15.0	16.5	14.5	14.0	12.0	12.0	11.5	11.5	10.8	11.1	10.6	10.5	12.3	12.5	12.0
Capital markets															
Price index (base year 2000)	3,261.0	3,366.6	3,360.9	3,892.8	3,740.0	5,001.3	3,604.4	3,469.4	3,048.7	5,590.6	6,492.8	11,280.0	13,072.1	15,644.4	9,708.5
Market capitalization (% GDP)	42.9	44.2	33.7	36.7	31.1	46.8	27.2	26.9	23.3	43.6	53.9	84.3	85.9	108.8	58.0
Inflation (% per year)															
Consumer price index	7.6	10.0	9.4	7.0	13.1	3.4	3.7	4.3	4.1	3.7	4.0	4.2	6.4	6.2	9.1
Wholesale price index	12.6	8.0	4.6	4.4	5.9	3.3	7.2	3.6	3.4	5.5	6.5	4.5	5.3	4.8	8.3
Total capital inflows (% GDP), net															
Foreign direct investment, net	0.3	0.6	0.7	0.9	0.6	0.5	0.7	1.0	0.6	0.4	0.5	0.4	0.8	1.3	1.5
Portfolio, net	1.2	0.8	0.9	0.4	0.0	0.7	0.6	0.4	0.2	1.9	1.3	1.5	0.8	2.5	-1.2

Source: CSO; Reserve Bank of India; World Bank, WDI 2009.
Note: — = not available.

Table 6A.4. India: External Trade

	FY95	FY96	FY97	FY98	FY99	FY00	FY01	FY02	FY03	FY04	FY05	FY06	FY07	FY08	FY09
Total exports of goods and services (% GDP)	10.2	11.1	10.7	11.0	11.4	11.8	13.4	12.9	14.7	15.5	18.3	20.1	22.2	21.8	23.8
Merchandise exports	8.3	9.1	8.8	8.7	8.2	8.3	9.9	9.4	10.6	11.1	12.2	13.0	14.1	14.1	15.1
Manufactures exports	6.3	6.7	6.3	6.5	6.2	6.6	7.5	7.0	7.9	8.1	8.7	9.0	9.3	8.7	—
Services exports	1.90	2.06	1.92	2.29	3.17	3.49	3.54	3.59	4.09	4.48	6.17	7.12	8.06	7.65	8.73
Total imports of goods and services (% GDP)	12.8	14.4	14.3	14.4	14.1	14.9	15.8	14.7	16.1	16.1	20.9	23.6	25.7	26.4	29.8
Merchandise imports	11.1	12.3	12.6	12.5	11.4	12.3	12.6	11.8	12.7	13.3	17.0	19.4	20.8	21.9	25.4
Manufactures imports	2.4	2.9	2.6	2.4	2.4	2.0	1.9	2.1	2.7	3.0	3.6	4.6	5.1	5.0	—
Services imports	1.7	2.1	1.7	2.0	2.6	2.6	3.2	2.9	3.4	2.8	4.0	4.3	4.8	4.5	4.4
Remittances (% GDP)	2.3	2.2	2.9	2.6	2.2	2.5	2.6	3.0	3.1	3.3	2.7	2.8	3.0	3.3	3.6
Terms of trade (index, base 1978–79 = 100)[a]	139.5	134	124.3	145.6	161.4	152.9	122.2	123.6	111	126.8	123.8	164.1	175.9	212.1	—

Source: CSO; Reserve Bank of India; World Bank, WDI 2009.

Note: — = not available.

a. Gross terms of trade implies volume index of imports expressed as a percentage of volume index of exports.

Table 6A.5. Impact of the Crisis: Summary

	FY98 to FY03	FY04 to FY08	Change from FY98–FY03 to FY04–FY08	Highest 2-year average before crisis	Expected potential value just prior to the crisis	FY09	FY10
GDP growth (%, at factor cost)	5.2	8.9	3.7	9.6	8.0	6.7	7.4
TFP growth (%)	0.9	3.4	2.5	3.5	3.0	2.7	3.0
Export growth (%)	8.3	25.4	17.1	25.8	20.0	13.8	-3.6
Export (% GDP)	10.4	28.1	17.7	32.0	20.0	13.3	-5.1
Gross fixed capital formation (% GDP)	22.9	29.8	6.9	32.5	34.0	32.9	32.8
Capital inflows (% GDP) (eop)	2.1	4.6	2.5	6.8	4.5	0.5	4.1
Fiscal deficit (% GDP)	9.0	7.1	-1.9	10.6	5.5	8.7	9.8

Source: Reserve Bank of India, *Handbook of Statistics*; authors' estimates.

Note: eop = end of period.

Table 6A.6. Demand-Side Growth Projections

	Actual FY06–FY08	Estimated FY09–FY10	Projected FY11–FY15
Private consumption (% per year)	9.0	5.1	6.0
Public consumption (% per year)	7.2	13.6	−0.5
Investment (% per year)	15.0	5.6	12.0
GDP (% per year, at market prices)	9.5	6.4	8.5
Memo			
Export growth	20.0	−2.5	12.0
Import growth	16.0	−3.0	10.0
Current A/C balance (% GDP)	−1.2	−1.6	−1.5
Capital inflows (% GDP)	6.4	1.8	4.0
Change in reserves (% GDP)	6.5	−1.5	4.0
Fiscal balance (% GDP)	−6.0	−10.0	−6.5
Public debt/GDP (% GDP)	78.0	81.0	70.0

Source: Reserve Bank of India, Handbook of Statistics; authors' estimates.
Note: Annual data not available.

Notes

1. Fiscal years in India run from April to March, and the convention (as followed in this article) is that the ending year is denoted as the relevant fiscal year; for example, the fiscal year covering April 2009–March 2010 is denoted as FY10. All data reported in this paper refer to fiscal years unless otherwise noted.
2. See also World Bank (2006, chapter 1).
3. The impact appears smaller than usually presumed, because it operates through net exports rather than gross exports. That is the correct measure, even if the gross exports impact also provides a useful alternative measure. This is because the exports and imports are not necessarily in the same sectors and are complicated by oil sector exports and imports, which are both large and affected by large independent swings in prices.
4. The forecasts in this article are based in part on judgments and in part on simulation results from a small macro-model for the Indian economy, which is in line with others in the forecasting and policy analysis system tradition. It is a highly aggregated two-country model with four endogenous variables for India and three for a composite "rest of the world." The model parameters (coefficients in the equations) are based on Bayesian estimation techniques using quarterly data for the period 1991–2008. The smallness of the model allows for a straightforward interpretation of results, in contrast to many richer, more complicated dynamic stochastic general equilibrium models that often become "black boxes."

However, because of its aggregate nature, it should be understood more as a coherent framework for thinking about macroeconomic policy questions rather than as a dependable forecasting instrument. Annual forecasts other than GDP are not reported.

5. From the Centre for Monitoring Indian Economy; conversion factor: US$1 = Rs 49.00 (does not include urban development).

References

Aguiar, M., and G. Gopinath. 2007. "Emerging Market Business Cycles: The Cycle Is the Trend." *Journal of Political Economy* 115 (1): 69–102.

Ahluwalia, Montek S. 1994. *India's Economic Reforms*. Oxford: Merton College.

Akin, Cigdem, and M. Ayhan Kose. 2007. "Changing Nature of North-South Linkages: Stylized Facts and Explanations." Working Paper 07/280, International Monetary Fund, Washington, DC.

Banga R., and S. Bathla. 2008. "Impact of Trade on Employment, Wages and Labor Productivity in Unorganized Manufacturing in India." Paper presented at the conference "How the Poor Are Affected by Trade," New Delhi, October 14–16.

Bhanumurthy, N. R., and Lokendra Kumawat. 2009. "External Shocks and the Indian Economy: Analyzing through a Small, Structural Quarterly Macroeconometric Model." MPRA Working Paper 19776, University Library of Munich, Munich.

Borchert, Ingo, and Aditya Mattoo. 2009. "The Resilience of Services Trade." Policy Research Working Paper 4917, World Bank, Washington, DC.

Chand, R. 2008. "Prospects of Achieving a 4 Percent Growth Rate in Agriculture during the Eleventh Plan." *NAAS News* 8 (July–September): 3.

Collins, Susan. 2007. "Economic Growth in South Asia: A Growth Accounting Perspective." In *South Asia Growth and Regional Integration*, ed. Sadiq Ahmed and Ejaz Ghani. Delhi: Macmillan and World Bank.

Dadush, Uri, and Dipak Dasgupta. 2000. "The Benefits and Risks of Capital Account Openness." In *Capital Flows without Crisis? Reconciling Capital Mobility and Economic Stability*, ed. Dipak Dasgupta, Marc Uzan, and Dominic Wilson. London: Routledge.

Dasgupta, Dipak. 2000. "A Bump in the Long Road? Revisiting Growth Prospects in East Asia Beyond the 1997 Crisis." In *Papers and Proceedings*, APEC Economic Committee Symposium, Tokyo.

Dasgupta, Dipak, et al. 2007. "Monsoons and Its Impact on Agriculture and GDP Growth in India." *Echoes Magazine* 7.

Economist. 2008. "The Decoupling Debate." March 6.

Hausmann, Ricardo, Lant Pritchett and Dani Rodrik, 2004. "Growth Accelerations." NBER Working Paper W10566, National Bureau of Economic Research, Cambridge, MA.

IIF (Institute of International Finance) 2009. "Capital Flows to Emerging Economies." *Institute of International Finance* (January 29).

India, Ministry of Labour and Employment, Labour Bureau. 2009a. *Report on Effect of Economic Slowdown on Employment in India (October–December 2008)*. Chandigarh.

Jadhav, Narendra. 2003. "Capital Account Liberalization: The Indian Experience." APD Seminar Paper, New Delhi.

Kraay, Art. 1998. "The Aftermath of Crises." Background paper for *Global Economic Prospects Report 1998/99*. World Bank, Washington, DC.

McKinsey & Company. 2009. "Building India, Financing and Investing in Infrastructure." McKinsey & Company India Office, Mumbai and Gurgaon.

———. 2009b. "Report on Effect of Economic Slowdown on Employment in India (January 2009)." Appendix. Chandigarh.

Mohan, Rakesh. 2009. "Global Financial Crisis: Causes, Impact, Policy Responses and Lessons." RBI Bulletin (May): 879–904.

OECD (Organisation for Economic Co-operation and Development). 2007. *India: OECD Economic Survey*. New Delhi: Academic Foundation.

Panagariya, Arvind 2002. "India's Economic Reforms, What Has Been Accomplished? What Remains to Be Done?" ERD Policy Brief 2, Asian Development Bank, Manila.

Patnaik, Ila, and Ajay Shah. 2009. "Why India Choked When Lehman Broke." In *India Policy Forum 2008–09*, ed. Suman Bery, Barry Bosworth, and Arvind Panagariya. New Delhi: NCAER and Brookings Institution Press.

Prasad, Eswar. 2008. "Some New Perspectives on India's Approach to Capital Account Liberalisation." Paper prepared for presentation at the Brookings-NCAER India Policy Forum, New Delhi, July 15–16.

Rakshit, Mihir. 2009. "India amidst the Global Crisis." *Economic and Political Weekly* 44 (13): 94–106.

Rangarajan, C. 2006. "Economic Growth and Issues of Governance," The Seventh D.P. Kohli Memorial Lecture, delivered by the Chairman, Economic Advisory Council to the Prime Minister of India, New Delhi, June 1. http://eac.gov.in/aboutus/ch_speech.htm.

Ratha, Dilip, and Sanket Mohapatra. 2009. "Revised Outlook for Remittance Flows 2009–2011: Remittances Expected to Fall by 5 to 8 Percent in 2009." Migration and Development Brief 9, World Bank, Washington, DC.

Reddy, Y. V. 2000. "Operationalising Capital Account Liberalisation: Indian Experience." *Reserve Bank of India Bulletin* (October).

Rodrik, D. 1998. *Institutions, Integration and Geography: In Search of the Deep Determinants of Economic Growth*. Boston: Harvard University.

Rodrik, Dani, and Arvind Subramaniam, 2004. "From 'Hindu' Growth to Productivity Surge: The Mystery of the Indian Growth Transition," IMF Working Paper, International Monetary Fund, Washington, DC.

Sen, Amartya. 1989. "Indian Development: Lessons and Non-Lessons." *Daedalus* 118 (4).

Servén, Luis, et al. 2009. "Corporate Investment in India in the 2000s." Unpublished document, World Bank, Washington, DC.

Sinha, Anushree. 2009. "Impact of Global Slowdown on Employment and Income in India: A CGE Model Analysis." Forthcoming World Bank Working Paper, National Council of Applied Economic Research and World Bank.

Srinivasan, T. N. 2005. "Comments on 'From Hindu Growth to Productivity Surge: The Mystery of the Indian Growth Transition.'" *IMF Staff Papers* 52 (2): 229–33.

Srinivasan, T. N., and Suresh Tendulkar. 2003. *Reintegrating India with the World Economy*. Washington, DC: Institute for International Economics.

Subbarao, Duvvuri. 2009a. "India—Managing the Impact of the Global Financial Crisis." Speech delivered at the Confederation of Indian Industry's National Conference and Annual Session 2009, New Delhi, March 26.

———. 2009b. "Impact of the Global Financial Crisis on India: Collateral Damage and Response." Speech delivered at the symposium "The Global Economic Crisis and Challenges for the Asian Economy in a Changing World," Institute for International Monetary Affairs, Tokyo, February 18.

Unni, J. 2006. "Employment Trends and Earnings in the Informal Sector." In *India: Meeting the Employment Challenge*. Conference papers from "Conference on Labour and Empoyment Issues," Institute for Human Development and World Bank, New Delhi, July 27–29.

World Bank. 2006. *Inclusive Growth and Service Delivery: Building on India's Success*. Washington, DC: World Bank.

———. 2008. "India's Employment Challenge: Creating Jobs, Helping Workers." World Bank, Washington, DC.

———. 2009a. *How Should Labor Market Policy Respond to the Financial Crisis?* Washington, DC: World Bank.

———. 2009b. "India Crisis Report." Unpublished draft. World Bank, Washington, DC.

Comment on "India: Rapid Recovery and Stronger Growth after the Crisis"

Martin Rama

This is an ambitious paper that seeks to answer three major questions at once:

- What explains India's growth acceleration prior to the global crisis?
- How did the crisis affect India's short-term performance?
- Will India's medium-term growth prospects be affected by the crisis?

The chapter is well written and contains a wealth of information and analysis, which certainly makes for interesting (and pleasant) reading. Most likely, the answers provided to these three questions are right. However, the links among the three issues are not always straightforward, and a skeptical reader may not be convinced by the answers, despite their plausibility.

Main Comments

Was the acceleration of growth due to good policies or to good luck?
One of the main drivers of India's rapid growth was the increase in the

Martin Rama is Lead Economist, South Asia Office of the Chief Economist, World Bank.

investment rate, closely related to the increase in the saving rate. An increase in the saving rate is the "second dividend" one would expect from a rapid demographic transition, and it has played to the advantage of many countries in Asia before benefiting India. Admittedly, saving rates have increased for the corporate sector more than for the household sector, but the distinction is sensitive to profit-retention policies by enterprises, and in a country where few of them are public, those policies are an accounting choice more than anything else. The paper refers only in passing to the "first dividend" from the demographic transition, namely, the increase in employment rates (or in the share of "working capitas per capita"). And while it provides the basic elements of a growth decomposition, it makes no reference to the contribution of structural change (i.e., productivity gains from labor moving out of agriculture). Also, the significance of terms-of-trade effects, reaching at times 4.5 percent of GDP, is frequently mentioned. Therefore, it would seem that forces beyond the control of the authorities, such as demographics and international price fluctuations, could be responsible for much of the variation in GDP growth rates. Admittedly, the paper reports strong fluctuations in total factor productivity growth. But not much is said about the reasons underlying those fluctuations. In sum, in order to claim that "arguably the most important part" of India's growth acceleration prior to the crisis was the policy response to the 1991 balance of payments crisis," the paper should first show that "good luck" does not account for the bulk of the acceleration in growth rates.

What were the key reforms behind the acceleration of growth? The paper argues that after the 1991 balance of payments crisis, "India opened its economy sharply." However, no information is provided on which measures were adopted, so that for a reader unfamiliar with India's case, it is difficult to tell through which channels greater openness led to India's well-known successes (in increasing its exports of goods and services). For sure, the trade-to-GDP ratio increased, but nothing is said on the level of tariff and nontariff barriers, so that it is difficult to link de facto openness to trade liberalization. As for the opening of the capital account, the paper makes it clear that inflows were mostly sterilized, so as to avoid real-exchange-rate appreciation. If capital inflows simply resulted in larger international reserves, capital account liberalization could impact growth only through its effect on the efficiency of capital markets. And there is evidence on the surge of stock market capitalization and the like, but little information is provided on the policy reforms behind those improved indicators. The paper is more convincing in arguing that important progress was made on tax policy. But it also depicts a situation in which the efficiency of public spending is dubious, privatization has made little progress, large fiscal deficits are persistent, and fiscal policy is hard to operate. So, fiscal policy is another unlikely candidate for explaining India's growth acceleration. For a skeptical reader, all this reinforces the point made earlier, that the acceleration of growth may be more the result of good luck than of good policy.

Why does decoupling from global trends matter? Quite a lot of space is devoted to arguing that India's growth slowdown had started prior to the global crisis. And the evidence presented is convincing. However, it is less clear that this decoupling of the business cycle is helpful in understanding either India's recovery in the aftermath of the crisis or what its growth prospects are in the medium term.

How relevant was the policy response to the global crisis? There is no doubt that the Indian economy has bounced back strongly and that India is one of the star performers in the aftermath of the global crisis. It is less obvious that this stronger-than-expected recovery is due mainly to the stimulus policies adopted by the government. With increasing openness to capital flows and a deliberate effort to avoid swings in the real exchange rate, monetary policy is essentially endogenous. Credit policy affects the composition of the monetary base (the faster the credit growth, the lower the level of international reserves) but not money supply. In several places, the paper shows that the growth of broad monetary aggregates such as M3 experienced very little variation in recent years, despite the swings in monetary policy. Admittedly, the expansionary monetary stance adopted by the government as a response to the global crisis might have been instrumental in preventing a collapse in the growth of M3. From this perspective, in the absence of such response the crisis would have been more severe. But the additional liquidity injected (equivalent to 9 percent of GDP) was mostly offset by the 7 percent of GDP lost in international reserves. The net outcome was an almost unchanged growth rate for broad monetary aggregates, and therefore it is difficult to attribute the strong recovery to easy money. A similar case can be made for fiscal policy. The paper reports an impressive array of stimulus measures, adding up to 3.6 percent of GDP. And yet, the primary deficit increased by just half that amount. Again, echoing the point made on the reasons for the strong performance before the global crisis, attributing economic performance to specific policies is challenging. There is no doubt that Indian authorities succeeded in quickly restoring confidence, which was fundamental. But stimulus policies might have played a more important role through their impact on investor confidence than through their boosting of domestic demand.

Which policy levers does the government of India have at this point?
Accepting that the acceleration of growth in the wake of the 1991 balance of payments crisis was due to the strong policy response by the government, the question is: what will be the policy response to the 2008–09 global crisis? It is clear that the margin for maneuvering in relation to macroeconomic policy is limited (see the previous point). Monetary policy is arguably endogenous and fiscal policy is severely constrained. In the absence of more fiscal space, addressing the bottlenecks in infrastructure and skills will be difficult. The paper credibly claims that these bottlenecks will not be binding for the next couple of years. But sooner or later, they will. There are several references to financial deepening as the next policy frontier. However, the analysis does not imply, at any point, that capital market inefficiencies are among the main obstacles to rapid growth in India. Needless to say, financial deepening can do no harm. But much the same as for trade liberalization in the precrisis period, a skeptical reader could wonder whether financial liberalization will really boost growth in the postcrisis period. Moreover, there are a few other policy areas that are not mentioned at all. The paper makes clear that progress on privatization has been limited, and some would argue that overstaffing is one of the main reasons for this. But while the author emphasizes the need to increase capital market efficiency, there is no reference to labor market policies. More generally, labor and skills are conspicuously absent from the discussion, even when

it is dealing with growth decomposition. While describing the baseline scenario, the authors claim that "the medium-term sustainable growth will be about 8.5 percent. This is greater than the preboom precrisis period average of 5.5 percent ... due to the impact of reforms." But it remains unclear which reforms the authors refer to.

Postcrisis Growth Prospects Depend on Restoring Fiscal Discipline and Private Investor Confidence

Erhanfadli M. Azrai and Albert G. Zeufack

Malaysia, the third most open economy in the world, was one of the hardest hit by the 2008 global financial crisis. The initial impact was a demand shock manifest mainly in the form of a dramatic fall in exports of electrical and electronic products. The crisis did not affect the financial sector, largely because of sustained reforms implemented since the 1997–98 financial crisis. Although there was virtually no exposure to toxic assets, the downturn had a significant impact on industrial production, output, and capital markets.

The 2008 crisis may lower Malaysia's average growth rate in the medium term, partly because the economy did not fully benefit from the global trade boom led by China and India, and also because it entered

Erhanfadli M. Azrai is Assistant Vice President, and Albert G. Zeufack is Director, Khazanah Research and Investment Strategy, Malaysia. The authors thank Mustapha K. Nabli and Nadeem ul Haque for guidance throughout the project; Shahrokh Fardoust for insightful comments and suggestions; and Utku Kumru, Ahmad R. Nungsari, and participants at the World Bank "The Crisis and Aftermath" workshops in December 2009 and July 2010 for useful comments. All errors and omissions are the authors. Views expressed in this chapter do not represent the opinions of the World Bank or Khazanah Research and Investment Strategy and should be solely attributed to the authors.

the crisis with limited fiscal space, which in turn limited its fiscal stimulus options. Nonetheless, a sustained implementation of the country's New Economic Model (NEM) could return it to its pre-2008 growth trajectory. Ultimately, Malaysia's medium-term growth prospects will hinge on the recovery of its private investment and productivity improvements.

We begin by looking at Malaysia's pre-2008 growth experience and its relationship to the global economy. We then assess the immediate impact of the crisis and the Malaysian government's policy response and consider the country's medium-term prospects.

Malaysian Precrisis Growth

Malaysia's openness to the global economy is reflected in the fact that the value of its trade is equivalent to 200 percent of its GDP and that 45 percent of its exports are electrical and electronics (E&E) components and products whose main markets are the United States and Europe. This external orientation and broad openness to trade, however, increases the country's vulnerability to external shocks. Indeed, Malaysia's economic growth has been greatly undermined by virtually all of the global crises of the past 35 years (figure 7.1).

The 1974 oil crisis hurt the Malaysia economy as the country was not yet a net oil exporter. In 1986, the collapse in commodity prices severely hurt the country's main exports, including rubber and tin. After the 1986 crisis, Malaysia diversified its manufactured exports to a range of products by attracting a substantial inflow of foreign direct investment (FDI). At the same time, Malaysia launched several large infrastructure projects such as the North-South Expressway to improve connectivity between major cities.

Malaysia has been vulnerable to various external shocks. But it was the 1997–98 Asian financial crisis, which started in Thailand and spread throughout the region, which had the most dramatic impact on Malaysian economic growth. The government took several drastic measures to contain the crisis, including depreciating the currency, fixing the exchange rate at 3.8 ringgit (RM) to the U.S. dollar, and imposing capital controls while rejecting a program of structural adjustment supported by the International Monetary Fund (IMF). The government also restructured and recapitalized banks. However, in 2001, the bursting of

Figure 7.1. Real GDP Growth, 1970–2009

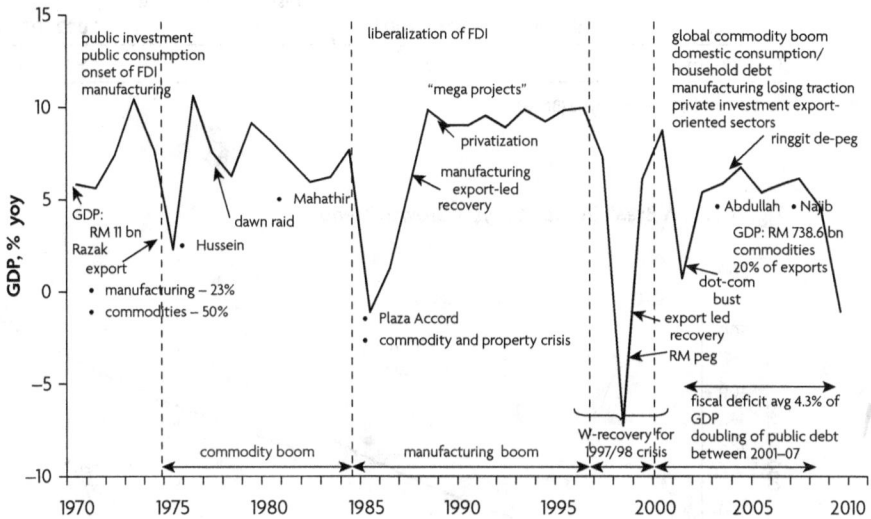

Source: Various Ministry of Finance (MOF) Economic Reports and Economic Planning Unit (EPU) Malaysia Five-Year Development Plans; Khazanah Research and Investment Strategy, Malaysia (KRIS).

the U.S. dot-com bubble hurt Malaysia in the form of reduced demand for its electronic products.

Malaysia's Growth Path Has Shifted downward since the Asian Crisis

Malaysia, the former growth superstar has lost its luster since the 1997 crisis, and its growth trajectory has shifted downward. Despite the rapid global economic expansion during 2003–07, Malaysia's real GDP grew at a slower rate, and it could not attain the growth level that prevailed before the Asian crisis (see annex 7B). While countries such as China, India, and Vietnam invested massively between 2003 and 2007, increased their exports to the rest of the world, and implemented policies that better positioned them to respond to the 2008 crisis, Malaysia's policy actions were timid and its economic performance modest. Malaysia's real GDP growth between 1987 and 1997 averaged 8.9 percent annually. The annual average real GDP growth rate between 2002 and 2007 was merely 5.9 percent (table 7.1), well below the country's potential. Nungsari and Zeufack (2009) argue that Malaysia appeared to be stuck in the "middle-income trap."[1]

Table 7.1. Malaysia's Real GDP Growth

	1994–2001	1997–2002	Highest growth before Asian crisis	2002–07
GDP (% yoy)	5.6	3.5	10.0	5.9

Source: Bank Negara Malaysia (BNM).

Figure 7.2. A Break in the Malaysia Growth Trend

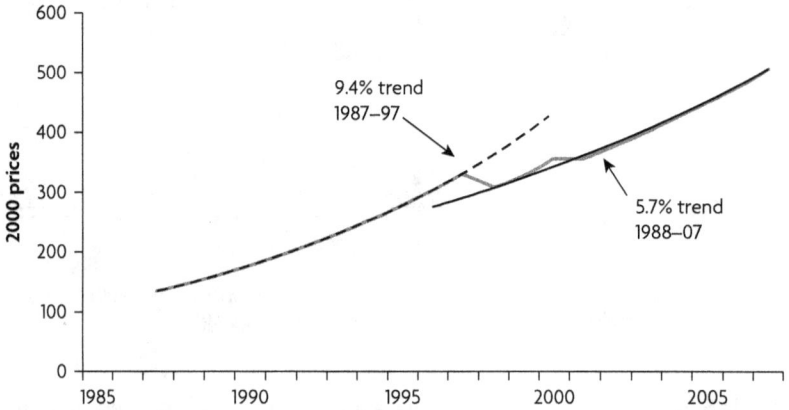

Source: World Bank 2008.

This relatively weak performance took place despite very favorable external conditions. Indeed, from 2001 onward, following the dot-com bubble burst, the cost of financing was at historically low levels and inflation was relatively benign at the global level. World trade grew rapidly, and global investment growth (in real terms) averaged 5.8 percent. Levels of real GDP growth for the large emerging economies, China and India, were 10.7 percent and 8.1 percent, respectively.

A study by the World Bank (2008) suggests that large transitory shocks impose substantial and permanent costs when they occur in high-growth economies. This may explain why Malaysia's growth trend shifted considerably downward after the East Asian financial crisis at the end of the 1990s (see figure 7.2). Interestingly, of all the East Asian countries hit by the 1997 crisis, Malaysia was still the farthest from its precrisis growth trajectory in 2009.

Sources of Growth. Using a growth-accounting framework, World Bank (2008) sheds more light on the impact of the Asian crisis by analyzing the sources of growth a decline in labor force participation and a reduced rate of population growth appear to have contributed to the slowdown. More important, labor productivity was halved, from an average of 5.5 in 1987–97 to 2.9 between 1998 and 2007. A decomposition of the changes in labor productivity shown in table 7.2 reveals that almost all the fall can be attributed to a slower accumulation of capital per worker from 3.4 percent per year in 1987–97 to only 1 percent during 1998–2007. The contribution of improvement in educational attainment remained flat and gains in total factor productivity (TFP) averaged 1.7 percent per year in 1987–97 and 1.6 percent per year in 1998–2007. The TFP's gain of only 0.9 percent per year for the full two decades highlights the large loss during the crisis period.

Growth Engine Lost in 1997 Has Never Been Replaced. Malaysia experienced a boom in private investment between 1988 and 1996; its annual growth rate during the boom averaged about 23 percent. Private investment accounted for the bulk of gross fixed capital formation, while public investment remained almost constant as a percentage of GDP. After the financial crisis, private investment dropped to half its value, the largest contraction in private investment in four decades.

As shown in figure 7.3, the investment rate fell from more than 40 percent of GDP in 1995–97 to only about 20 percent in recent years, which is below the rate needed to support 6–7 percent GDP growth. Capital accumulation, the engine driving Malaysian growth before the

Table 7.2. Sources of Growth, Total Economy, 1987–2007
(percent)

Total Economy	1987–2007	1987–97	1998–2007
Output per worker	3.7	5.5	2.9
Contribution of			
Capital	2.5	3.4	1.0
Education	0.3	0.3	0.3
Land	0	0	−0.1
Factor productivity	0.9	1.7	1.6

Source: EPU; World Bank 2008.
Note: The calculations for 1987–2007 include 1998 (the peak of the Asian crisis) whereas 1998 is not included in the calculations for 1998–2007.

Figure 7.3. A Collapse in Investment amid High Savings

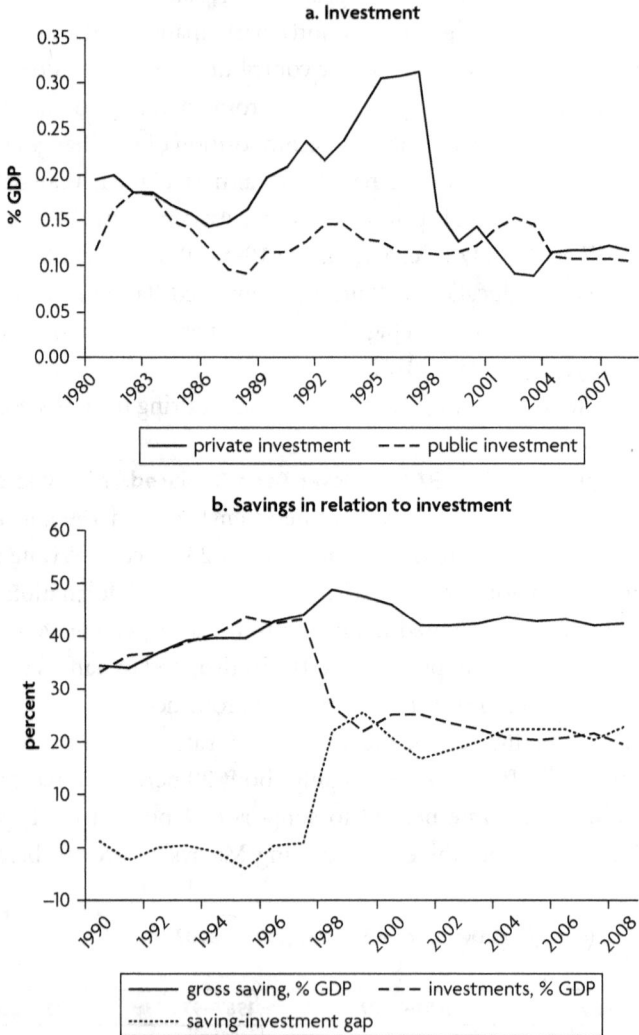

a. Investment

private investment   - - - public investment

b. Savings in relation to investment

——— gross saving, % GDP   - - - investments, % GDP
·········· saving-investment gap

Source: BNM Monthly Statistical Bulletin (www.bnm.gov.my).

Asian crisis and the key to understanding the East Asian "miracle" clearly ran out of fuel. The current low rate of capital accumulation emerges as the major supply-side constraint on growth.

Most troubling is the fact that investment collapsed despite high saving rates in Malaysia. The saving rate, which climbed slowly from about

34 percent in 1990 to 48 percent in 1998, dropped to 41.8 percent in 2001. Since 2001, the saving rate has remained at about 40 percent. The saving-investment balance therefore remains high given the larger drop in investment.

It may be that capital accumulation has reached the decreasing returns phase, in which case, it is unlikely to ever return to its precrisis level. But there could be some more structural barriers to investment. There are unfortunately very few studies on why private investment has not recovered in Malaysia, see Tuah and Zeufack (2009) for a survey. Guimaraes and Unteroberdoerster (2006) suggest that besides macroeconomic conditions, a shift in investors' perceptions, which may have been triggered by the crisis itself or by prolonged overinvestment, appears to have contributed to the sharp decline in private investment in recent years. A study by Ang (2008) using data from 1960–2005 suggests that a drop in aggregate output, higher real user cost of capital and macroeconomic uncertainty have negatively impacted private investment. Tuah and Zeufack (2009) highlight the complementarity between public investment in infrastructure and private investment and the role of political and policy uncertainties. In a region where most countries compete for the same pool of FDI, the differential in corporate income tax with neighboring countries might have led some firms to settle in Singapore for example, lowering FDI flows to Malaysia.[2]

An alternative explanation of Malaysia's poor investment performance is the political economy of the pre–2008 crisis period. The political transition between Prime Ministers Tun Mahathir and Tun Badawi in 2004 led to increased political and policy uncertainty. In order to differentiate himself from his powerful and charismatic predecessor, Badawi froze several infrastructure projects, alienating the private sector and creating a rift with Mahathir. As a result, the country entered a political and policy uncertainty phase that led to the resignation of Badawi in 2009. Also, it is possible that the reinforcement of affirmative action policies favoring the Bumiputera[3] under the Badawi Administration led the domestic investment community, most of whom is ethnic Chinese, to adopt a wait and see attitude or seek investment opportunities abroad.

Contributions to GDP Growth. Since the 1997 crisis, private consumption has replaced investment as the main growth driver, with its contribution to growth surging to 93 percent in 2008—from only 32 percent in 2002

Figure 7.4. Contribution to GDP Growth

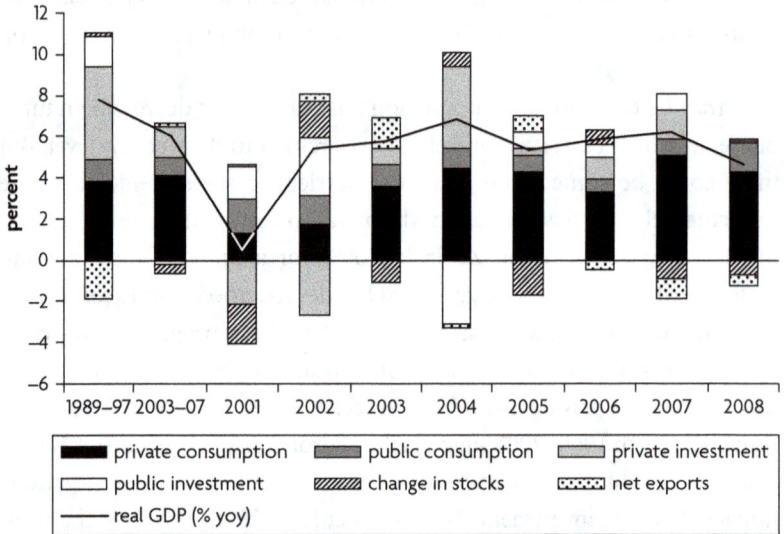

Source: BNM Monthly Statistical Bulletin (www.bnm.gov.my).

(figure 7.4). This shift in growth drivers contributed to lower growth, as private consumption is a less powerful engine than investment was in the pre–Asian crisis era (see annex 7B).

From a sectoral perspective, services contributed as much as 85 percent to real GDP growth in 2008, versus 55.3 percent in 2002. However, the services sector, given its current structure, is unlikely to drive growth at the rates necessary to achieve high income levels by 2020. Malaysia's services sector remains one of the most restricted in the world and is still largely domestically oriented, operated, and owned.

Commodities still constitute a large share of GDP (figure 7.5). The share of agriculture as a percentage of GDP has grown in recent years, mainly because of the increase in value added for major agricultural commodities—such as rubber and crude palm oil—together with the boom in prices and volume. In 2006–07, high energy prices have made palm oil–based biofuel commercially viable, further driving the demand for—and price of—palm oil upward. Primary commodities played a critical role in the Malaysian economy in the pre-2008 crisis period. Indeed, commodities were the main driver of Malaysian exports since

Figure 7.5. Agricultural Contribution to GDP

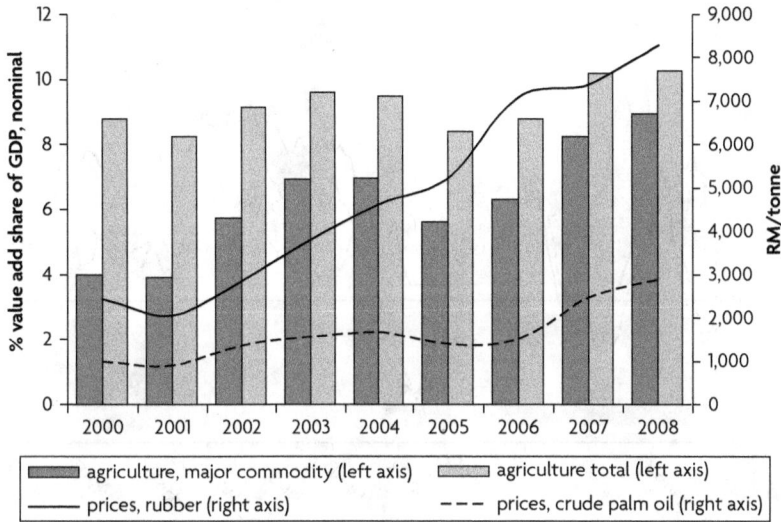

Source: Department of Statistics (DOS; www.statistics.gov.my).

2003. As of 2008, about 90 percent of the agricultural sector's contribution to GDP came from commodities.

Malaysia Did Not Fully Benefit from the Global Trade Boom

In contrast to most economies in Asia, Malaysia did not fully benefit from the global boom in trade led by China and India between 2002 and 2007. Malaysia's trade to North Asia did grow; however, the growth came from commodities—and more from prices than volumes. For manufacturing, capacity utilization was lower than in the preboom period, and export volumes did not increase significantly (figure 7.6). Just like Mexico, Malaysia has remained overreliant on the U.S. market for its manufacturing products, especially from the E&E sector. Compared with other countries' export growth, Malaysia seems to lag behind (figure 7.6).

East Asian countries took advantage of the relatively good global economic conditions during 2002–07 to strengthen their economic and financial fundamentals and raise their market shares (table 7.3). They improved their fiscal and external debt positions, built up their foreign

Figure 7.6. Exports Growth

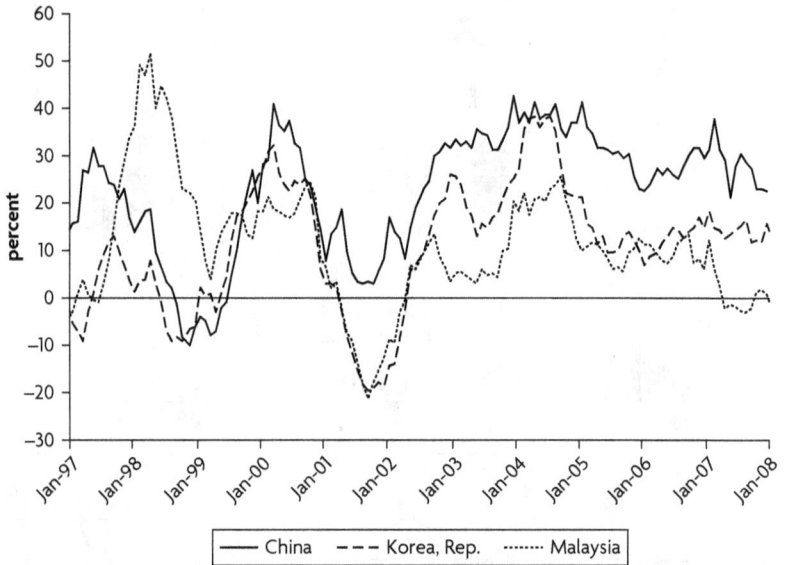

Source: CEIC (www.ceicdata.com).

Table 7.3. Growth in the Volume of World Merchandise Trade by Selected Region and Economy, 2000–08
(annual percentage change)

Exports				Imports		
2000–08	2007	2008		2000–08	2007	2008
5	**6**	**1.5**	**World**	**5**	**6**	**1.5**
2.5	5	1.5	North America	3	2	−2.5
3.5	6.5	6	United States	3	1	−3.5
3.5	4	0	Europe	3	4	−1.5
3.5	3.5	−0.5	EU (27)	3	3.5	−1.5
10	11.5	5.5	Asia	8	8	4.5
20.5	19.5	8.5	China	16	14	4
−4	−20.5	−11	Hong Kong SAR, China	3	7	−2
12.5	13	7.5	India	13.5	16	14
6	9.5	2	Japan	2.5	1.5	−2
8	8.5	4.5	Six East Asian traders[a]	5.5	5	4
5	4	−4.6	Malaysia	6	5	−6.8

Source: World Trade Organization (WTO).

a Hong Kong SAR, China; Republic of Korea; Malaysia; Singapore; Taiwan, China; and Thailand.

exchange reserves, and reformed their banking sectors. As a result, they were better positioned to avoid the worst effects of the crisis. Asian exports grew by an average of 8 percent per year during 2000–08, while Malaysia's real exports grew by just 5 percent.

Before the crisis, the capacity utilization rate of Malaysia's export-oriented industries was about 75–80 percent, peaking at 88 percent in 2003 (figure 7.7). Similarly, growth of noncommodity exports—chemicals, manufactured goods, and machinery and transportation goods—also declined from a 2004 peak. The import growth of intermediate goods has shown a similar trend. Also, Malaysia's terms of trade were on a slight downward trend from around March 1999 through March 2008.

Exchange Rate and Monetary Policy

During the Asian financial crisis, as conditions in the domestic and regional economies worsened, the Malaysian government took the bold step of prohibiting the internationalization of the ringgit and adopting a

Figure 7.7. Capacity Utilization

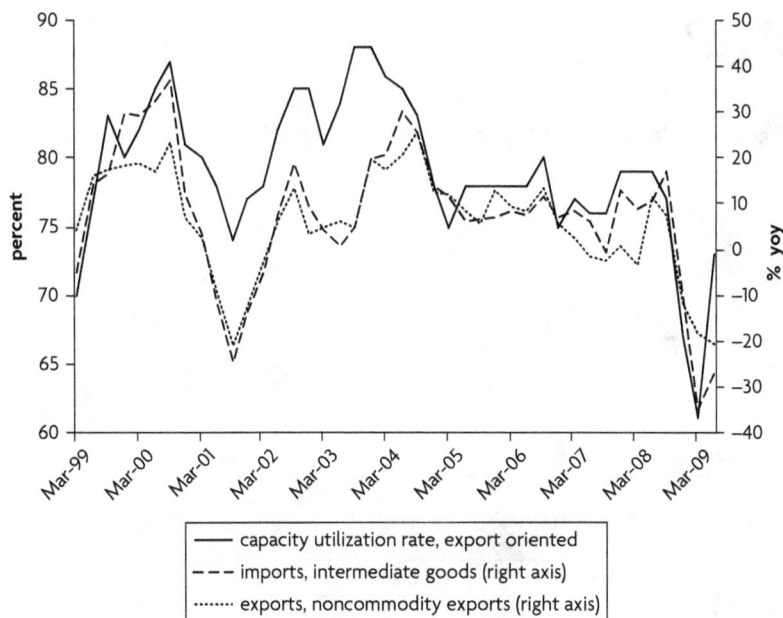

Source: DOS.

fixed-exchange-rate regime. The ringgit was pegged to the U.S. dollar in September 1998 to insulate the economy from external uncertainties and further disruptions. The fixed-rate regime was probably retained too long; it was finally removed in July 2005. During the fixed-rate period, the ringgit's real effective exchange rate depreciated, thus boosting exports. But after the end of the peg, the ringgit appreciated steadily against the currencies of Malaysia's trading partners, dampening external demand for Malaysian products (figure 7.8). Most firms then kept afloat by hiring more foreign unskilled labor. Probably because of the overall political and policy uncertainty characterizing the years of Malaysian Prime Minister Badawi, the ringgit appreciation did not lead to an increase in capital inflows. Both equity and FDI inflows remained subdued during the precrisis period.

The Banking Sector

The current global crisis did not hit Malaysia's financial sector because of the sustained reforms it implemented since the 1997–98 Asian financial crisis. Malaysia had limited direct exposure to the toxic assets that damaged American and European banks in 2008. The country's banks suffered no systemic failures, as sufficient capital and low levels of nonperforming loans (NPLs) put them on a stronger footing in dealing with the crisis.

Figure 7.8. Manufacturing Exports Growth and Real Effective Exchange Rate

Source: DOS; IMF.
Note: REER = real effective exchange rate.

Table 7.4. Financial Sector Indicators

Banking system	1996	1997–98	2008
Number of institutions	89	80–86	54
Average total assets per institution (RM billion)	7.1	9.6	40.4
Risk-weighted capital ratio (%)	10.6	10.5	12.7
Core capital ratio (%)	9.0	8.9	10.6
Return on assets (%)	2.0	−0.9	1.5
Return on equity (%)	27.5	−12.3	18.5
Net NPL ratio (%)	3.0	13.2	2.2
Gross NPL ratio (%)	3.9	18.7	4.8

Source: BNM.

After the Asian crisis, Bank Negara Malaysia (BNM) embarked on a strategy to consolidate a highly fragmented domestic banking system (table 7.4). The system consisted of 71 institutions before the crisis, but the number was cut to 30 domestic banking institutions organized in 10 domestic banking groups by 2002. Recognizing that the financial sector in Malaysia had to be strengthened further, BNM launched a Financial Sector Master Plan in 2001. The plan set a medium- and long-term agenda of strengthening the financial sector. It emphasized putting in place capacity-building initiatives covering the banking sector, insurance sector, and Islamic banking sector, as well as the development of financial institutions, alternative modes of financing, and the Labuan International Offshore Financial Centre.

By the end of 2007, the consolidation of the banking sector and reforms in risk management practices were showing positive results. With a stronger balance sheet, Malaysian financial institutions are now resting on a firmer foundation allowing them to venture into new businesses and countries, and are better equipped to withstand shocks. The risk-weighted capital ratio of the banking sector stood at 12.7 percent and the net NPL ratio at 2.2 percent at the end of 2008.

Fiscal Space

Entering the global crisis, Malaysia had limited fiscal space, and this narrowed its options for fiscal stimulus. The government has run continuous deficits from 1998 to 2008 (figure 7.9), and the debt level has more

Figure 7.9. Fiscal Position of the Malaysian Government

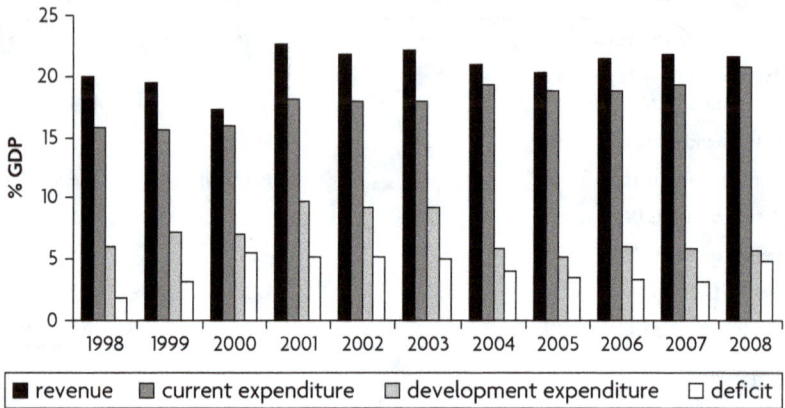

Source: BNM; MOF (www.treasury.gov.my).

than doubled since 2002—from US$33.9 billion at the end of 2002 to around US$85.5 billion by the end of 2008.[4] Even though Malaysia's debt-to-GDP ratio did not grow disproportionately, the high debt level left the government with little scope for added leveraging. The rising government debt has a crowding-out effect and carries the risk of further downgrade in sovereign ratings, which raise the cost of funding for the private sector.

The Malaysian government's revenue structure poses a long-term and structural public finance challenge. The tax base is narrow and the country is increasingly dependent on oil-based revenues. Although petroleum accounts for about 20 percent of exports, it constitutes 40–45 percent of government fiscal income, derived from taxes, dividends, and royalties. Direct tax revenue from the petroleum industry has grown steadily—from about 11 percent of total revenue in 1994 to 30 percent in 2008. Under nontax revenue, petroleum royalties and dividends from PETRONAS[5] contributed about 78 percent in 2008, compared with 33 percent in 1994. As a consequence, price volatility of crude oil greatly affects the government's budget planning. At the current production rate, Malaysia will be able to produce oil for up to 18 years only and natural gas for 35 years, which raises concerns about long-term fiscal sustainability.

On the spending side, operating expenditure (relative to development spending) has been trending upward. Fiscal injections to prop up consumption were maintained since the 1999 crisis. Government operating expenditure increased consistently from around 15 percent in 2000 to around 20 percent in 2008. In contrast, development expenditures that were close to 10 percent of GDP in 2003 were halved by 2008. Public debt grew from around 35 percent of GDP in 2000 to 45 percent in 2004 and Malaysia had debt-to-GDP ratio of 41 percent in 2008, one of the highest debt-to-GDP ratios in the South-East Asia region (figure 7.10). A combination of procyclical fiscal policy, the missed opportunity to review and rationalize public expenditures to improve their efficiency, and the lack of new sources of revenues between 2002 and 2007 therefore explain why Malaysia had a limited fiscal space entering the 2008 crisis.

The Immediate Impact of the Global Crisis

As noted earlier, the main impact of the 2008 crisis on Malaysia was on trade; the financial impact was quite limited. The first impact was a demand shock, felt mainly as a sharp fall in exports of electrical and

Figure 7.10. Public Debt and Budget Balance as Percentage of GDP

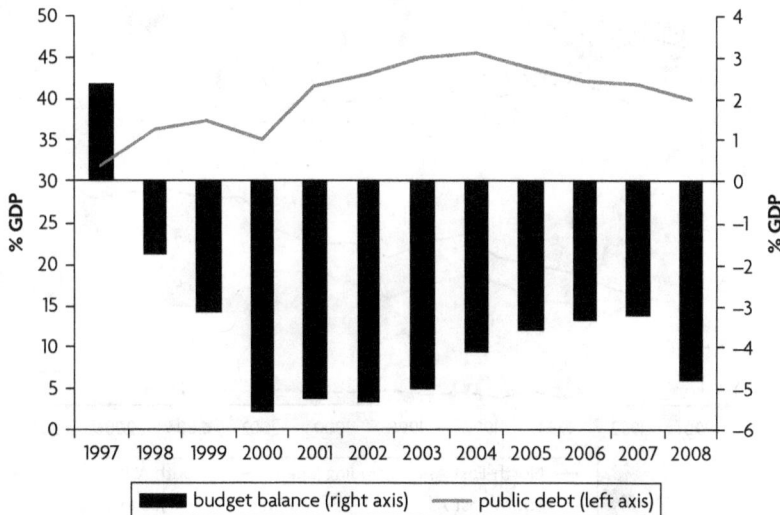

Source: MOF.

electronic products. Malaysia's over-reliance on the U.S. market for E&E
products, which constitute the bulk of Malaysian exports, was the main
channel of the shock's transmission. Twenty percent of Malaysian
exports go to the United States; indeed, the percentage could well be
higher, as indirect exports through third countries are not properly
accounted for (figure 7.11).

As manufactured goods account for about 78 percent of total exports,
and E&E exports account for the bulk of exports, any shift in U.S. domestic demand strongly affects Malaysia's export performance (figure 7.12).
This over-reliance on the U.S. market led to a sizable drop in industrial
production and output.

Because Malaysia's export sector is integrated into regional production and trading networks, the amount of goods exported—both
directly and indirectly—to the West fell substantially. Indeed, some of
Malaysia's exports to China are intermediate inputs to products that
eventually find their way to the West. In terms of products, the large
decline in the E&E sector, a subset of the machinery and transport
equipment sector, led the way.

Figure 7.11. Export Destinations for Malaysia's Manufactured Products

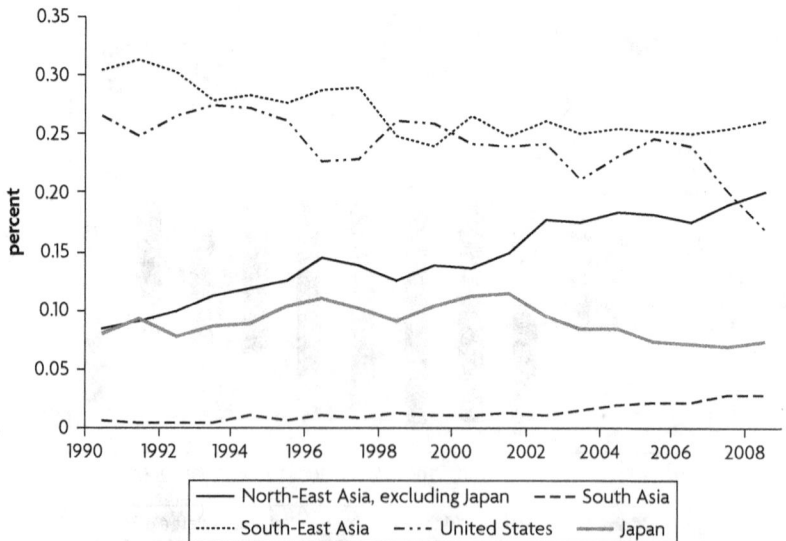

Source: CEIC.

Figure 7.12. Contribution to Exports Growth by Destination

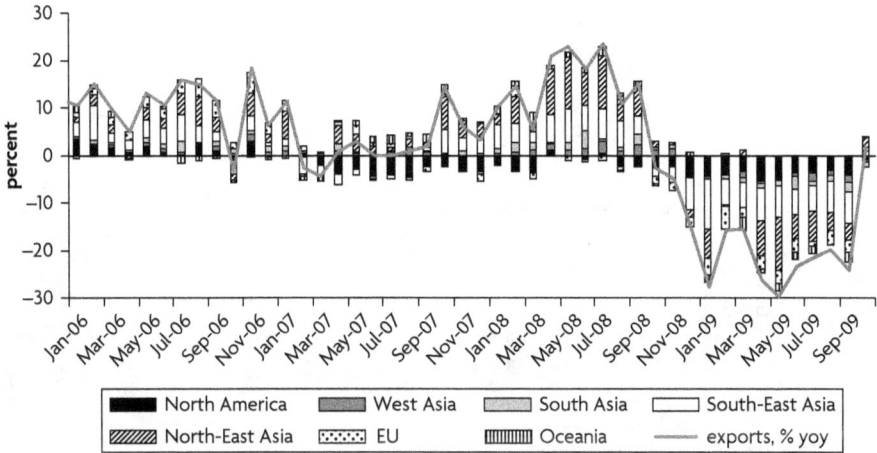

Source: KRIS; DOS.

Analysis of exports value index suggest that manufacturing exports have been contracting in volume since 2007 and the global crisis has only made the situation worse. In terms of destinations, the drop in exports was led mainly by the decline in exports to North Asia and North America. Commodity prices have also fallen sharply after the financial crisis, the result of lower demand for commodities in the West and expansions of supply in response to the higher prices from 2004 to 2008. Also, the export volume index for commodities shows a negative growth in the months after the global crisis with no recovery since.

Capital Outflows

The crisis has also resulted in outflows of foreign portfolio capital. The country's overall balance of payments showed a large surplus for several years, but the tide turned suddenly because of large net outflows in the financial account due to significant portfolio divestment by foreign investors—particularly in the second half of 2008 (figure 7.13). The 2008 financial account showed a net outflow of US$35.4 billion.

Malaysia's overall balance of payments posted a surplus of US$7.8 billion in the second quarter of 2008 but shifted to a deficit of US$9.4 billion in the third quarter, with and the shortfall widening to US$18.5

Figure 7.13. Net Funds Inflow

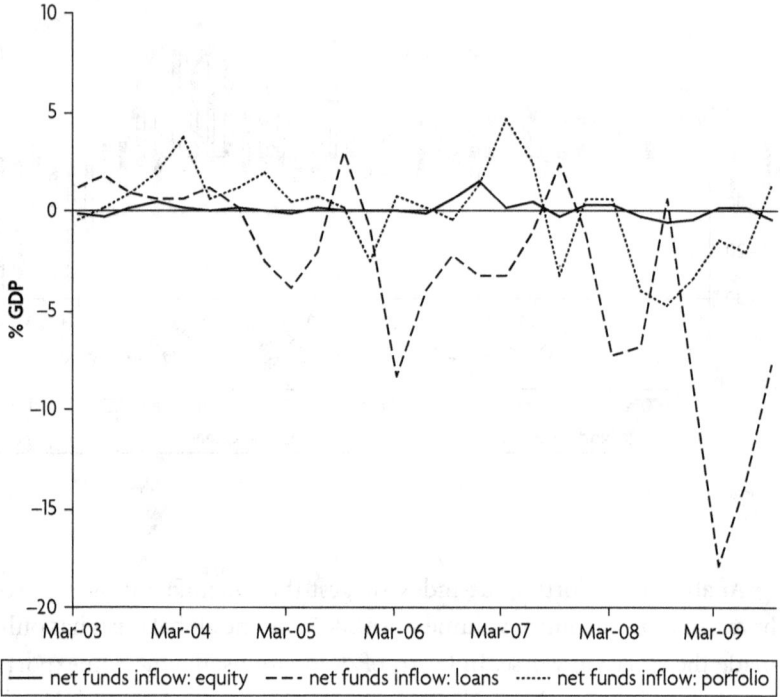

Source: CEIC; BNM.

billion in the fourth quarter. For the full year of 2008, Malaysia saw an overall net outflow of US$5.4 billion. The change in Malaysia's balance-of-payments trend has also been reflected in the country's falling foreign reserves (Figure 7.14). Reserves had climbed steadily to a peak of US$122.8 [RM 410.8] billion in June 2008, then fell to US$113.3 [RM 379] billion in September, and further to US$94.7 [RM 316.8] billion in December.

The outflow may have been the result of the withdrawal of foreign equity funds from Asia. This could reflect a greater aversion to risk as the bond market in emerging markets saw an increase in yields, or it could be a sign of a crisis-triggered capital outflow to lower cost countries, since Malaysia can no longer support low–value added industries.

Figure 7.14. International Reserves and MYR/US$ Exchange Rate

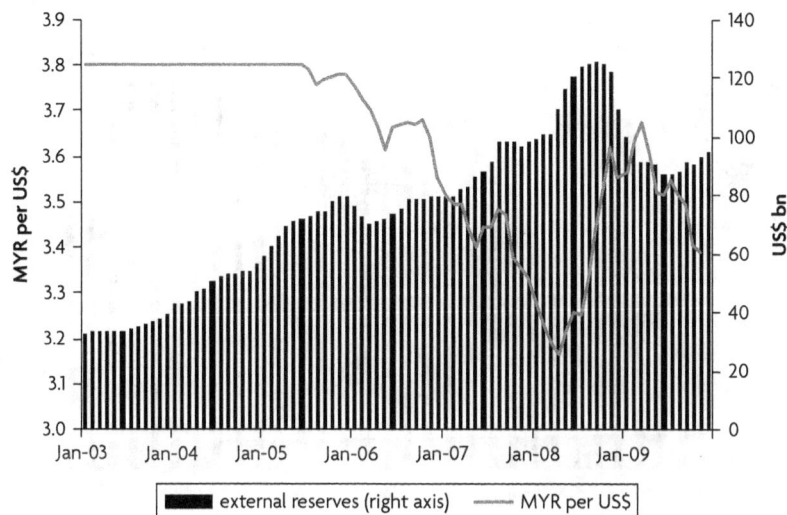

Source: CEIC; BNM.

Employment

Malaysia's output losses have been large, and portfolio investment has fallen sharply; however, the excess capacity generated by the demand shock did not have much impact on unemployment, as foreign unskilled workers served as a buffer (see annex 7B). The adjustment in the labor market took the form of a shedding of foreign labor. The Malaysian economy has been operating at full capacity since the 1990s. The expansion of manufacturing and plantations was therefore possible only with the influx of foreign labor from Indonesia, southern Thailand, Sri Lanka, and the Philippines. Interestingly, the unemployment rate did not change significantly during the crisis (figure 7.15). The prohibitive retrenchment costs required by Malaysian labor law may have forced firms to adopt more creative solutions to managing the downturn than just firing staff.

The Banking Sector

Malaysia's banking sector as a whole held up well in the face of the global financial crisis. The reforms instituted in the years after the Asian financial crisis had clearly strengthened the sector. The crisis affected only the higher-end residential property sector, credit cards, and purchases of

Figure 7.15. Labor Force and Unemployment

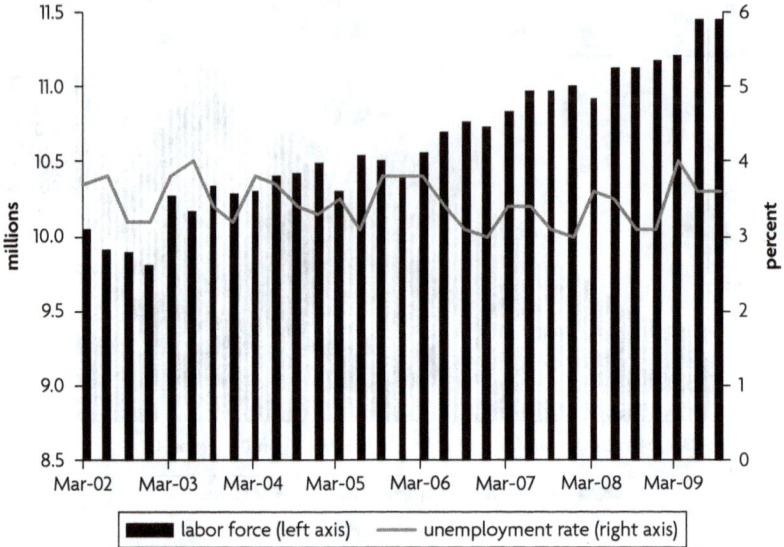

Source: DOS.

fixed assets—excluding land and buildings. The banking system recorded an increase in the amount of NPLs in these categories in the last quarter of 2008. As a whole, the banking sector was not a transmission channel for the crisis.

The Impact on Output

As a result of the crisis, net exports contributed negatively to overall output in the third and fourth quarters of 2008 (figure 7.16). Then, in the first quarter of 2009, inventories declined massively, dragging down real GDP growth. The growth of private consumption slowed as a result of the uncertain external environment. Malaysian manufacturing sector was the worst hit after the global crisis. The sector started contracting in the fourth quarter of 2008 as shown in figure 7.16.

In the Midterm Review of the Ninth Malaysia Plan (2006–10), the government expected real GDP to grow 6.0 percent from 2008 to 2010. Using 6.0 percent as the potential real GDP growth and 2007 as the base year, the output gap in 2009 could have been as high as –8.2 percent of potential GDP (tables 7.5 and 7.6).

Figure 7.16. The Loss of Output and the Slowdown in Growth

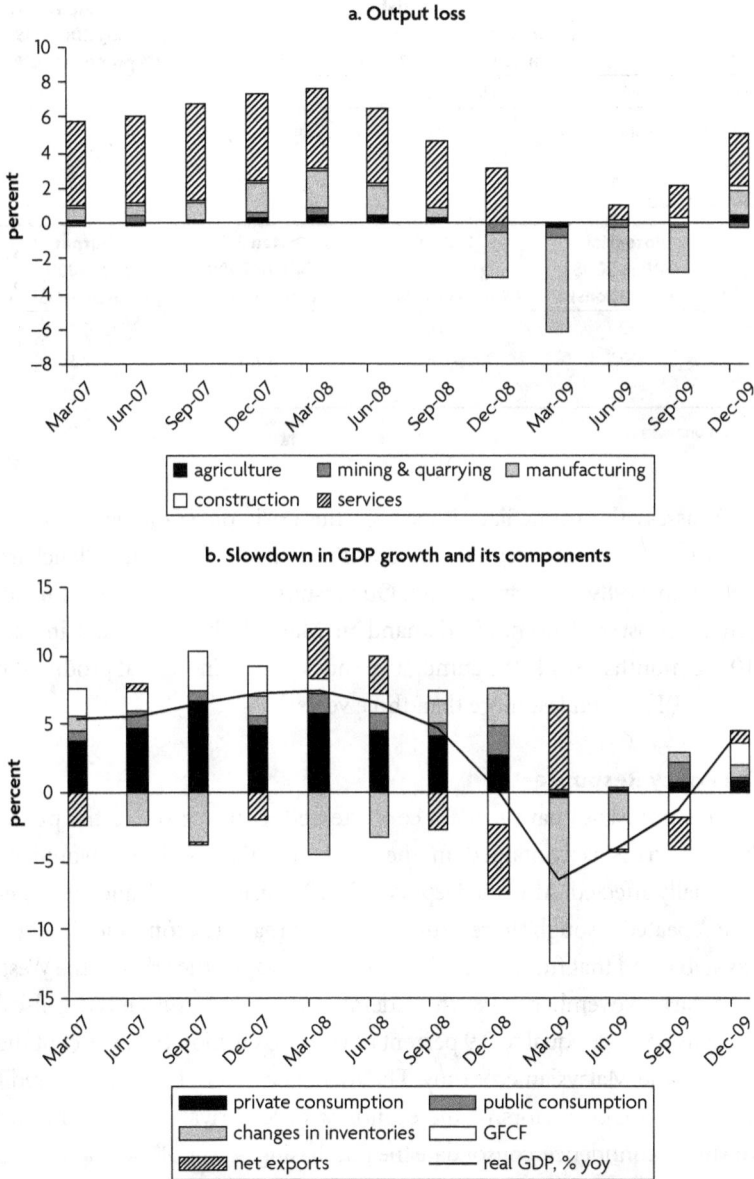

a. Output loss

- agriculture   ■ mining & quarrying   □ manufacturing
- □ construction   ▨ services

b. Slowdown in GDP growth and its components

- ■ private consumption   ■ public consumption
- □ changes in inventories   □ GFCF
- ▨ net exports   —— real GDP, % yoy

Source: DOS; KRIS.
Note: GFCF = gross fixed capital formation.

Table 7.5. The Cost of the Crisis Is High, Measured in Output Gap

	Expected potential medium-term growth just prior to the crisis (2008)	2008	2009	Total output loss during 2008–09 (% potential GDP)
Real GDP (% yoy)	5.5 to 6.0	4.6	–1.4	–7.3 to –8.1

Source: Ministry of Finance 2010.

Table 7.6. Output Gap

Potential GDP growth (2008–09)	Potential GDP in 2008 (RM billions)	Output gap (2008) (% potential GDP)	Potential GDP in 2009 (RM billions)	Output gap (2009) (% potential GDP)
5.0	532.7	–0.3	556.7	–6.4
5.5	532.7	–0.8	562.0	–7.3
6.0	535.2	–1.3	567.3	–8.2

Source: KRIS calculation.

To assess the immediate impact of the crisis on Malaysia, we use a structural vector autoregression (SVAR) analysis, following Blanchard and Quah (1989) (see annex 7A). Our results suggest that a fiscal injection to boost real domestic demand in Malaysia has a limited impact (10–12 months), while the cumulative shock on the industrial production index (IPI) would last more than three years.

The Policy Response

Various ministries have made a concerted effort to convey to the public that the crisis is contained in the West and that Malaysia would be minimally affected. Also, the Deputy Prime Minister and Finance Minister have repeatedly sought to reassure the public that the economic situation was stable and that fundamentals were strong despite the crisis in the West.

In early November 2008, the federal government announced a fiscal stimulus package equal to 0.9 percent of GDP to cushion the impact of the crisis on the Malaysian economy. The main goals were to maintain credit flow to all major sectors of the economy, boost private investment and consumer confidence, consolidate the purchasing power of the population, and mitigate unemployment. To heighten the impact of the stimulus package, the government gave priority to projects with high multiplier effects and low import content. In addition, the government accelerated the registration process for aid recipients and the recruitment of contract-based civil servants in critical positions. The government's reduction of contributions to the Employees Provident Fund from 11 percent to 8 percent has also helped increase consumers' disposable income.

The fiscal stimulus also sought to pump-prime the construction sector. Among the measures adopted was the construction of more low- and medium-cost houses under various programs. Other notable efforts include the resumption of abandoned housing projects along with upgrading, maintaining, and building the new public transportation network, schools, and hospitals in major cities. The government has allocated US$84.8 [RM 300] million to the development corridors authorities[6] to provide training and employment opportunities.

The government also set up a US$169.7 [RM 600] million assistance guarantee scheme to provide financing to small and medium enterprises (SMEs). Since SMEs constitute 99 percent of all businesses in Malaysia, this has proven to be a vital measure in ensuring the continuity of their operations, since banks were initially reluctant to lend.

The worsening recession in 2009 rendered the first fiscal stimulus inconsequential and necessitated a second stimulus. In March 2009, the government unveiled the second stimulus, amounting to 9 percent of GDP. The second stimulus proved to be more comprehensive. Some 25 percent of the stimulus consisted of fiscal injection: about 42 percent in guarantee funds, some 17 percent in equity investments, about 12 percent in private finance initiative and off-budget projects, and 5 percent in tax incentives. The "mini budget" also highlighted four main goals:

- Reducing unemployment
- Easing the burden on the people
- Helping the private sector cope with the crisis
- Building capacity for the future

Although these goals were similar to those of the first stimulus plan, their financial composition reflected a change in priority. The government has given more emphasis to promoting private investment and building long-term productive capacity.

In March 2009, the government reduced the price of gas supplied to the energy sector by 25 percent; as a result, prices fell by 32 percent for the industrial sector and other end users to help businesses weather the crisis. With the lower gas price, average electricity prices for households have fallen by 2.5 percent. Industrial users would pay 5 percent less on average, while commercial users would get a 2.7 percent reduction. Even though it looked massive, only 25 percent of the second fiscal stimulus took the form of direct fiscal injection. The rest was in the form of financial guarantees, equity investments, and private finance initiatives. But the financial guarantees fund the Malaysian government, enabling it to ensure the continued flow of credit to businesses.

In February 2009, Fitch Ratings lowered Malaysia's local-currency rating to negative (from stable). Fitch blamed the downgrade on Malaysia's high fiscal deficit, public debt, and the expectation that the country's fiscal position would worsen in 2009–10. Then in June 2009, Fitch cut Malaysia's long-term local-currency rating further to single-A from single-A-plus on concerns about the growing budget deficit. The rating cut was soon reflected in a wider yield spread between 1-year and 10-year Malaysian government securities as uncertainty increased. This has affected the corporate bond yield, effectively raising interest rates for corporate borrowers.

Within three months, the central bank reduced the interest rate from 3.5 percent in December to 2.0 percent in March to help stimulate economic activity. BNM also injected liquidity into the market by reducing the statutory reserve requirement to 1 percent in February 2009 from 3.5 percent in December 2008 (figure 7.17).

Figure 7.17. KLIBOR and Fed Fund Rate

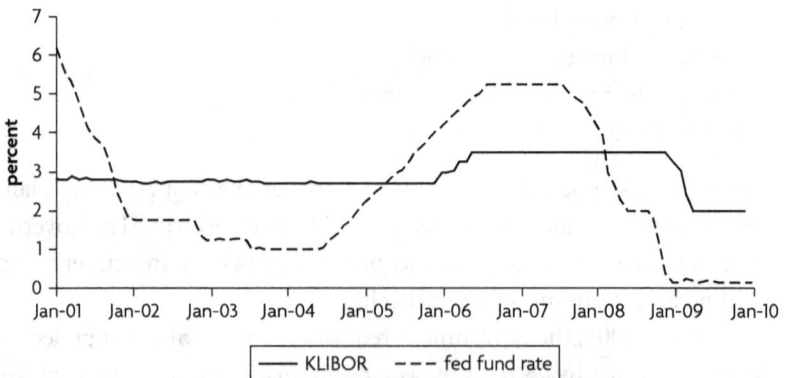

Source: BNM.
Note: KLIBOR = Kuala Lumpur interbank offered rate.

Figure 7.18. Loan Growth and Loan Deposit Ratio

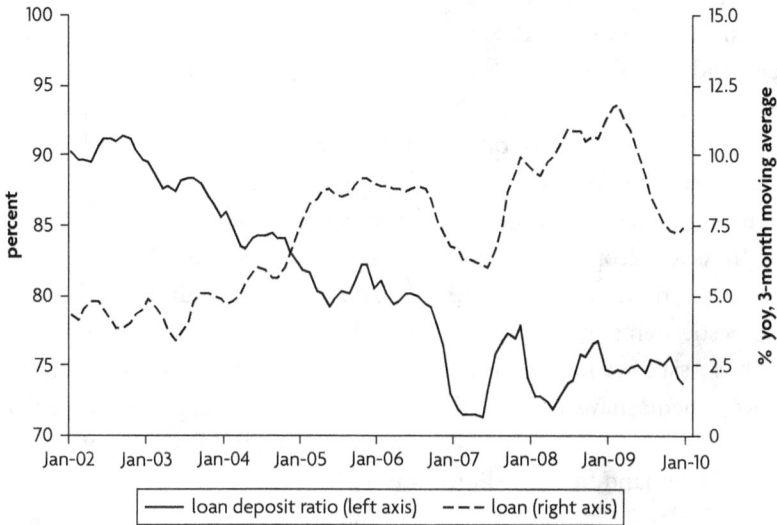

Source: BNM.

In response to the lower interest rate, commercial banks have reduced their base lending rate to 5.5 percent. Even with the reduced interest rates, loan growth slowed to about 7 percent in January 2010, reflecting soft consumer and business confidence (figure 7.18).

Malaysia's Medium-Term Growth Prospects

At the global level, the banking sector seems to have stabilized after a round of bailouts by central banks and governments. The market is therefore experiencing improved liquidity and reduced lending spreads, two measures of a successful credit-easing policy. The possible return of confidence may be causing a rebound in the equity market. Moreover, the "flight to quality" phenomenon is reversing as capital flows back into emerging markets. But even though it seems that the capital market is slowly returning to normal, banks are still in the process of deleveraging.

The global macro picture in the real sector is less certain, as the global crisis has affected the real economy in several ways. First, as capital flowed into safer assets (such as U.S. Treasuries), less capital was available for corporate borrowing, leading to higher lending rates. These higher rates, in turn, reduced output as firms delayed investments while households saved more and delayed consumption. Also, a drop in overall domestic demand in the developed countries triggered massive unemployment. Second, as highly leveraged households faced higher interest rates and lower asset prices—prerequisites of debt overhang—they spent less. The contraction in demand by both firms and consumers in the developed countries reduced their demand for imports, especially from Asia.

In Asia, a drop in U.S. and the Euro zone demand for Asian products has affected the industrial output of export-oriented industries, although domestic demand has somewhat cushioned the blow. Central banks across Asia have lowered interest rates to stimulate output growth, and governments have embarked on countercyclical fiscal stimuli. But it remains unclear whether Asian domestic demand can fully offset the drop in demand from the Euro zone and America.

In Malaysia, as in the rest of Asia, the crisis seems to have been short-lived. A recovery of the industrial production index (IPI) seems to have started in March 2009 (figure 7.19). While the government has

Figure 7.19. U.S. New Orders and Malaysia's Industrial Production Growth

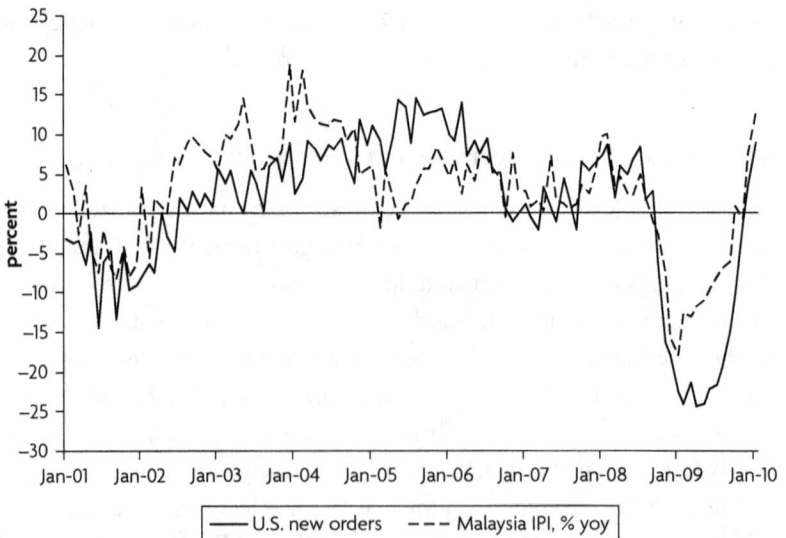

Source: CEIC; DOS.

attributed the recovery to its stimulus package, simulations from the SVAR analysis should lead to added prudence. The supply shock may take more than 12 months to fully dissipate, see annex 7A. Sustained recovery will depend on the government's policies in the next couple of years.

Impact of Reforms and Trends in Key Macro Variables

On the fiscal front, in the medium term, the government will have no choice but to cut the deficit in the medium run by further reducing operational expenditures and expanding the tax base. Returning to the path of fiscal consolidation will be critical to improving the country's recently downgraded sovereign rating. Malaysia's Ministry of Finance has announced a 15 percent cut in operating expenditures for the next budget. However, with general elections looming in less than two years, sustaining fiscal discipline will be a daunting task.

We expect that domestic consumption, the main driver of growth since the Asian financial crisis, will continue to hold up, although households are relatively highly leveraged. As of the end of 2009, the household debt-to-GDP ratio averaged 66.5 percent, the highest in Asia after the Republic of Korea. Although the unemployment rate has been kept below 4 percent, an increasing duration of unemployment, especially among fresh college graduates, coupled with high levels of household indebtedness may weaken domestic household consumption growth, making it harder to mitigate the slowdown in external demand.

While the central bank's policy remains accommodative to growth, the external rebalancing between Asia's export-led growth model and the current-account imbalances in the West may dampen trade between Asia and the West. This, in turn, may reduce trade in manufactures between the Asian countries. Being plugged into the regional supply chain, Malaysia may feel the pinch as trade contracts.

We expect that interest rates will increase over the medium term owing to higher risk aversion and tighter regulations. The increased risk aversion and lower capital availability will make capital more expensive. After a huge surge in the crisis period following flight-to-quality assets (such as U.S. government bonds), the strip spreads[7] of Asia and Malaysia have stabilized at a level higher than in the precrisis period (figure 7.20). The higher spread rate of the Emerging Markets Bond Index for both

Figure 7.20. EMBI Global Strip Spread

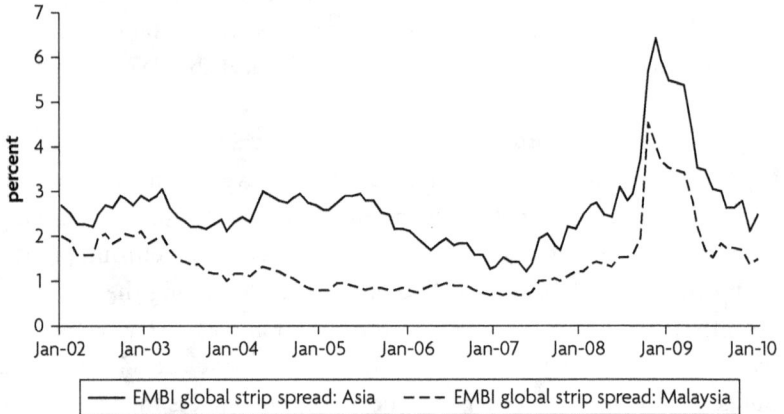

Source: JP Morgan Dataquery.
Note: EMBI = Emerging Markets Bond Index.

Malaysia and the Asia region reflect a higher level of risk aversion for both government and corporate bonds.

The rise in international interest rates can be expected to hit the Malaysian corporate sector hard. Although the sector has pared down its external debt over the past decade, learning the lessons from the Asian financial crisis, the rise in spreads will hurt as both the private sector and the nonfinancial public enterprises have increased their external debt from 2008. The global financial crisis will likely increase the cost of borrowing from external sources, providing an incentive for firms to borrow domestically. This could in turn raise the risk of financial crowding out as 96 percent of government's debt is financed domestically.

Domestic interest rates are expected to remain supportive of growth as the central bank (BNM) promotes maximum sustainable growth with price stability. BNM has seen the crisis as having a serious and long-term effect, hence the reduction of both the overnight policy rate and statutory reserve requirements to stimulate the domestic economy.

Since BNM has never used interest rate policy to influence the exchange rate, the movement in foreign interest rates will have little impact on domestic rates, which will likely remain accommodative (at about 2.75–3.5 percent) during 2012–15. In recent years, the average interest rate hovered around 3–3.5 percent, which could be the "normal" rate for BNM. Meanwhile, if international capital flows back into Malaysia, thus increasing liquidity in the market, BNM will gradually remove the excess liquidity by raising the reserve requirement in the medium term.

We expect that inflation in Malaysia will continue to be benign, but it would experience spikes if the government reviews food and energy subsidies, leading to price adjustments. Although the government continues to maintain a price ceiling on a list of consumer goods—such as fuel, sugar, flour, rice, cooking oil, condensed milk, and bread—it reviews the price ceilings regularly. The government has announced early in 2010, its intention to cut the subsidy on electricity generation by gas to 0 from 70 percent over 15 years. Were this removal or adjustment of the price ceilings to happen, it would create a one-off inflation rate spike.

FDI inflows volumes are likely to slow down as Malaysia focuses more on attracting a different kind of FDI, more knowledge driven and less capital intensive. The downward trend in FDI may be further accentuated unless a large-scale liberalization of Malaysia's protected services sector lures in a new generation of FDI. In February 2010, the government announced the liberalization of 17 services subsectors. This wave of liberalization included ending the requirement for 30 percent Bumiputera participation in the 17 services subsectors.[8] The government has also committed to extending the list of services subsectors to be liberalized, but the list is still awaited.

In order to tap the regional markets, Malaysian companies will continue to invest abroad in areas of competitive advantage. These would include but not be limited to palm oil, oil and gas, financial services, and communications. Such investments would allow companies over the medium term, to grow and become regional and global champions.

The ringgit can be expected to appreciate, loosely following the Chinese renminbi in the medium term. However, it is likely to be driven rather by commodity trade and portfolio capital inflows in the short run. Although the ringgit's short-term prospects are only minimally affected by the renminbi, the Chinese currency's long-term appreciation will affect the ringgit's movements. The ringgit's appreciation, which started after the end of the peg to the U.S. dollar in 2005, is therefore likely to continue.[9] BNM will however be wary of stern appreciation as this could jeopardize Malaysia export competitiveness relative to regional peers.

An improvement in world trade driven by growth in developing Asia will boost commodity trade more than the manufacturing trade in Malaysia. Commodity trade is expected to register strong growth after the crisis since the large developing economies (such as China and India) will likely continue to grow at a rapid pace. This would benefit the commodity sector products, especially palm oil and petroleum. As a major exporter of palm oil products, Malaysia would stand to gain from the fast growth in China and India. Oil production may not have a significant impact because Malaysia's output comes from a mature field; unless new fields are discovered, production will be stable, approximating the current rate.

Malaysia, like many East Asian economies, rode the export-led bandwagon to high growth for decades. Thus, its export-oriented economy is highly vulnerable to global demand, a vulnerability that was clearly evident during the crisis. The manufacturing sector in Malaysia may be forced to upgrade—that is, to "shape up or ship out." There will be no other option but to climb the technology and value ladders as labor costs increase and policies on unskilled labor will very likely tighten up. Since world growth in the West will be slower going forward, manufacturing export growth can be expected to weaken. Profit margins will be squeezed by stronger competition from other emerging countries in labor-intensive industries; and currency appreciation in line with the renminbi will hurt companies operating on thin profit margins. The Malaysian fiscal incentive system will need to be revamped to adapt to this new reality, attracting investment in areas where the main production factor is not capital or equipment, but rather intangible knowledge.

To broaden the tax base and reduce the tax rate, the government has proposed introducing a goods and services tax (GST) as a form of value added tax. However, the actual implementation may be hampered by political considerations. Apart from introducing the GST system, the government should also consider reviewing the subsidy structure to better target recipients. A broadly targeted subsidy system will distort the price signal in the economy and distort incentives to invest. Therefore, both the GST and subsidy targeting should be complemented by a social safety net program that will help cushion the impact of these reforms.

Recognizing the need for reform of the civil service, the government is making efforts to enhance the country's competitiveness by improving the business environment. The government and business community formed the Special Taskforce to Facilitate Business (Pemudah) to improve the business environment and reduce bureaucratic red tape. Six National Key Result Areas—safety, education, infrastructure, corruption, equality, and public transportation—were introduced to improve the delivery of public services. These initiatives, if implemented properly, should yield strong benefits in the medium term.

On the structural front, Malaysia will be hard-pressed to diversify export markets away from the developed world and tap demand in such emerging markets as China, India, and Indonesia. As the share of intraregional trade increases in Asia, commodity trade will be sustained. However, consumption of final goods will also increase to serve about a billion new Asian middle-income consumers. Ultimately, medium-term growth prospects in Malaysia will depend heavily on private investment recovery and productivity improvements.

Medium-Term Projections

To assess the impact of fiscal consolidation, reductions in subsidies, and increases in public investments, we conduct a simulation using the Oxford Economics model with the base case assumptions given in table 7.7.

Fiscal revenue from the petroleum sector is a main source of government income; but, given the declining rate of production, the fiscal position will be strained. During 2003–07, oil production contracted by an average annual 3.0 percent. For the projection, we assume flat production expansion (table 7.8).

The base case results presented in table 7.9 suggest that Malaysia's average GDP growth between 2010 and 2015 will be around 5.1 percent, which is lower than the 5.9 percent recorded between 2002 and 2007. As the global economy recovers between 2010 and 2012, Malaysia will benefit

Table 7.7. Base Case Assumptions
(percent)

	2008	2009	2010	2011	2012	2013	2014	2015
U.S. interest rate	3.7	3.3	4.0	5.1	5.8	5.6	5.0	5.0
Euro zone interest rate	4.3	3.8	4.1	5.0	4.8	4.6	4.6	4.6
U.S. real interest rate	−0.1	3.6	1.7	2.6	2.9	2.8	2.6	2.8
Euro real interest rate	1.0	3.6	2.9	3.3	2.8	2.6	2.6	2.6
U.S. inflation	3.8	−0.3	2.2	2.5	2.9	2.8	2.4	2.2
Euro zone inflation	3.3	0.2	1.2	1.7	1.9	2.0	2.0	2.0
Malaysia bank lending rate	—	5.62	6.65	6.72	6.72	6.72	6.72	6.72
Malaysia policy rate	—	2.12	2.7	2.75	3.0	3.0	3.0	3.0

		Actual					Projected				
Commodity	Unit	1970	1980	1990	2000	2009	2010	2011	2012	2015	2020
Energy											
Coal, Australia	US$/mt	7.8	40.1	39.7	26.3	71.8	80.0	85.0	85.0	75.0	80.0
Crude oil, average	US$/bbl	1.2	36.9	22.9	28.2	61.8	76.0	76.6	76.6	77.8	79.8
Natural gas, European	US$/mmbtu	0.4	4.2	2.8	3.9	8.7	8.3	8.5	8.8	9.5	10.0
Natural gas, U.S.	US$/mmbtu	0.2	1.6	1.7	4.3	3.9	6.0	7.0	7.5	9.0	9.5
LNG, Japanese	US$/mmbtu	—	5.7	3.6	4.7	8.9	8.8	9.0	9.3	10.0	10.5

Source: Oxford Economics (www.oef.com).
Note: mt = metric ton; bbl = barrel; mmbtu = 1 million British thermal units; LNG = liquefied natural gas; — = not available.

from stronger external demand and private consumption because of a supportive monetary stance and the spillover effect of fiscal stimulus. Private consumption will continue to drive the economy, but the appreciating Malaysian ringgit will boost consumption-based imports. Total investments would grow by an annual average 4.3 percent during 2010–15, slightly lower than investment growth in 2002–07.

We project that between 2013 and 2015, Malaysia will experience lower growth, with the government no longer able to prop up the economy and the private sector unable yet to pick up the slack. If the government continues to expand both government consumption and investment by 5.5 percent annually, the fiscal deficit will continue to hover around 7 percent of GDP, which in turn will nudge the government debt-to-GDP ratio upward to 52 percent in 2015.

Table 7.8. Long-Term Scenario

	2003	2004	2005	2006	2007	2003–07	2008	2009	2010p	2011p	2012p	2013p	2014p	2015p
Bank lending rate (%)	6.1	6.0	6.0	6.6	6.7	**6.3**	6.7	5.6	6.0	6.3	6.3	6.3	6.3	6.3
Overnight rate (%)	2.7	2.7	2.7	3.4	3.5	**3.0**	3.5	2.1	2.6	3.0	3.0	3.0	3.0	3.0
Oil production (%)	5.7	2.4	–16.4	–2.8	–4.0	**–3.0**	3.5	13.5	0.0	0.0	0.0	0.0	0.0	0.0
Base case government investment (% yoy)	0.0	–21.3	7.0	6.0	9.6	**0.2**	0.8	12.9	9.3	5.5	5.5	5.5	5.5	5.5
Government consumption (% yoy)	9.4	8.2	5.6	4.9	6.9	**7.0**	10.9	3.8	–2.7	1.5	5.5	5.5	5.5	5.5
With fiscal reforms														
Government investment (% yoy)	0.0	–21.3	7.0	6.0	9.6	**0.2**	0.8	12.9	9.3	5.0	6.0	7.0	7.0	7.0
Government consumption (% yoy)	9.4	8.2	5.6	4.9	6.9	**7.0**	10.9	3.8	–2.7	1.5	2.0	2.0	2.0	2.0

Source: Authors' assumptions.

Note: p = projected.

Table 7.9. Base Case Results
(change %)

	GDP	Private consumption	Government consumption	Investment	Exports	Imports	Consumer price index
1994–2001	5.57	5.11	5.73	3.81	9.81	8.50	2.71
2002–07	5.89	8.03	7.69	4.84	7.67	8.90	2.27
2010–15	5.11	4.55	4.13	4.33	7.96	8.57	2.30
2009	–1.72	0.78	3.70	–5.53	–10.15	–12.45	0.58
2010	5.49	3.85	–2.70	6.99	7.36	9.45	1.66
2011	5.56	4.85	5.50	2.60	8.59	9.01	1.93
2012	6.12	5.99	5.50	6.12	8.56	9.28	2.74
2013	4.89	5.20	5.50	2.26	8.06	8.20	2.71
2014	4.20	3.84	5.50	3.12	7.68	7.99	2.38
2015	4.42	3.55	5.50	4.93	7.48	7.51	2.37

	Current account balance (% GDP)	Fiscal balance (% GDP)	Public debt (% GDP)	Short-term interest rate (%)	Spread	Real interest rate (%)	Exchange rate (RM/US$)
2009	17.22	–8.07	50.77	2.12	1.43	1.54	3.52
2010	15.50	–8.44	43.31	2.60	2.23	0.94	3.36
2011	14.78	–7.63	44.23	3.00	0.79	1.07	3.24
2012	12.84	–7.28	45.20	3.00	–1.17	0.26	3.15
2013	10.61	–7.25	46.65	3.00	–1.58	0.29	3.08
2014	10.06	–7.21	49.06	3.00	–1.55	0.62	3.01
2015	9.30	–7.46	51.99	3.00	–1.54	0.63	2.97

Source: Authors' calculations.

Table 7.10 presents results of a scenario where the government imple-
ments reforms announced in the New Economic Model (NEM; see
box 7.1) and the Malaysia tenth five-year development plan unveiled in
June 2010. If these policy pronouncements are implemented, the government is expected to increase public investments and contain public
consumption by cutting subsidies. Between 2003 and 2007, subsidies
ballooned to about 8 percent of current expenditure, or 1.6 percent of
nominal GDP. Our reform assumptions presented in table 7.8 consider
a gradual reduction in subsidies, given the political sensitivities in a
potential pre-election year. Reducing subsidies in stages between 2011

Table 7.10. Results: Scenario with Reforms
(change %)

	GDP	Private consumption	Government consumption	Investment	Exports	Imports	Consumer price index
1994–2001	5.57	5.11	5.73	3.81	9.81	8.50	2.71
2002–07	5.89	8.03	7.69	4.84	7.67	8.90	2.27
2010–15	5.82	5.11	1.22	8.91	7.93	8.77	2.26
2009	−1.72	0.78	3.70	−5.53	−10.15	−12.45	0.58
2010	5.49	3.85	−2.70	6.99	7.36	9.45	1.66
2011	4.99	4.63	2.00	1.54	8.55	8.72	1.92
2012	6.29	5.65	2.00	10.68	8.68	9.59	2.72
2013	6.52	6.13	2.00	11.94	8.16	8.81	2.79
2014	5.64	5.09	2.00	11.62	7.48	8.41	2.23
2015	6.01	5.29	2.00	10.71	7.34	7.63	2.24

	Current account balance (% GDP)	Fiscal balance (% GDP)	Public debt (% GDP)	Short-term interest rate (%)	Spread	Real interest rate (%)	Exchange rate (RM/US$)
2009	17.22	−8.07	50.77	2.10	1.43	1.54	3.52
2010	15.50	−8.44	42.34	2.60	2.23	0.94	3.36
2011	15.03	−7.26	42.02	3.00	0.78	1.08	3.24
2012	13.00	−6.52	42.64	3.00	−1.18	0.28	3.15
2013	10.20	−6.01	43.67	3.00	−1.59	0.21	3.07
2014	9.06	−5.42	44.68	3.00	−1.57	0.77	3.00
2015	7.91	−5.15	44.47	3.00	−1.56	0.76	2.93

Source: Authors' calculations.

Box 7.1. Malaysia: Old and New Economic Models

The New Economic Model was drafted by the National Economic Advisory Council (NEAC) and published in March 2010 at the request of the Prime Minister of Malaysia. The mandate of the NEAC, an independent body composed of nine international and local experts of the Malaysian economy, is to formulate an economic transformation model for the country. The council is expected to provide a fresh, independent perspective in transforming Malaysia from a middle-income economy to a high-income economy by 2020.

The first report of the NEAC reaffirmed the need for a "big push" to propel Malaysia into an Advanced Nation by 2020. The three-pronged strategy is built around inclusiveness, sustainability and achieving high income status.

(continued)

Box 7.1 (continued)

Implementation of the New Economic Model is expected to generate large benefits to businesses. It would lead to an overall improvement in the environment for Investment through increased market transparency, absence of rent-seeking and quotas and a predominance of the rule of law. Equally important would be a significant reduction in the regulatory burden. Unnecessary licensing would be eliminated, so would be undue delays in approvals. Finally, better human capital provision coupled with increased liberalization of all sectors and transparency of government would create the conditions for higher productivity and restore business confidence.

The table below presents the difference between the old and the New Malaysian Economic Models.

	Old model	New model
1.	Growth through factor accumulation (capital and labor)	Growth through productivity
2.	Dominant state participation	Private sector–led growth
3.	Centralized strategic planning	Localized autonomy in decision making
4.	Balanced regional growth	Cluster-corridor based economic activities
5.	Favor specific industries and firms	Favor technologically capable industries and firms
6.	Export markets dependence (G-3)	Asian and Middle East orientation
7.	Restrictions on foreign skilled workers	Retain and attract skilled professionals

Source: NEAC 2010.

and 2013 would translate into a reduction in current expenditure of 2 percent annually, which in turn would slow the growth of government consumption to 2 percent annually after 2011.

Although the government has committed itself to continue to divest state-owned enterprises, the decline in total public investment resulting from divestiture will be smaller than the increase in public investment in infrastructure. The composition of public investment will change from nonfinancial public enterprises to public infrastructure, but total public investment will continue to rise. We project that public investment will expand at an increasing pace of 5–7 percent annually. Increasing public investment—especially in public infrastructure—will, in turn, revive private investment because of the complementarities between these two variables (Tuah and Zeufack 2009).

The results of these simulations suggest that the recent crisis, although short-lived, might lower Malaysia's average growth in the medium term. But the change in trajectory may not be comparable with how the East Asia crisis derailed Malaysian growth. We expect the annual average GDP growth rate to be 5.1 percent during 2010–15, lower than the 5.9 percent growth rate achieved during 2002–07.

A successful implementation of the NEM (the "reform scenario"), however, could boost average annual GDP growth to 5.8 percent during 2010–15, a rate close to that prevailing before the global crisis. The sources of this stronger growth will be private consumption and renewed private investment, with associated increases in capital goods imports. Malaysia could, however, start reaping the fruits of sustained reform momentum as early as 2012, in which case the average growth rate would exceed 6.0 percent, reaching 6.5 percent in 2013, driven by stronger private investment.

Conclusion

We have explored how the 2008 global financial crisis, the policy responses, and the postcrisis global economy will shape Malaysia's medium-term growth prospects. We found that Malaysia's economic performance during 2002–07 was far from stellar. The country did not fully benefit from the global boom in trade, and was neither at its full potential nor in a good fiscal position when the crisis hit. As a result, Malaysia was one of the worst-hit countries by the crisis. Its total output loss during 2008–09, relative to potential output, was 8.8 percent of GDP. Net capital outflows hit a record US$33.5 [RM 118.5] billion, and reserves contracted by US$30 billion.

Entering the 2008 crisis, Malaysia had limited fiscal space, reducing its options for economic stimulus. The government has run continuous deficits from 1998 to 2008. Government operating expenditure increased consistently from around 15 percent in 2000 to around 20 percent in 2008, while development expenditures fell from 10 to 5 percent of GDP between 2003 and 2008. Public debt grew from around 40 percent of GDP in 2000 to 45 percent in 2004 and was 41 percent in 2008, one of the highest debt-to-GDP ratios in the South-East Asia region.

A combination of pro-cyclical fiscal policy, the missed opportunity to review and rationalize public expenditures to improve their efficiency, and the lack of new sources of revenues between 2002 and 2007 explain why Malaysia had a limited fiscal space when the 2008 crisis hit. The government's response to the crisis was therefore timid, compared to China for example, and gradual. The two stimulus packages announced in early November 2008 and March 2009 totaled 2.9 percent of GDP in direct fiscal injection.

The Malaysian financial sector remained sound during the crisis because of sustained reforms implemented after the 1997–98 Asian crisis and its very limited direct exposure to the toxic assets. Also, the excess capacity generated by the demand shock did not have much impact on unemployment, as the adjustment in the labor market took the form of shedding foreign labor.

Looking forward, while growth prospects for Malaysia in 2010 are positive and the mood in policy-making circles is rather triumphant, our results from an SVAR model suggest more caution. We find that a fiscal injection to boost the real domestic demand has limited impact (10–12 months) in Malaysia, while the cumulative shock on IPI would last more than three years. In addition, the fiscal consolidation process begun in 2003 has been derailed and fiscal sustainability is now a matter of concern. In the medium term, the government will have no choice but to reduce the deficit by further cutting back operational expenditures and expanding the tax base. However, with general elections looming in less than two years, maintaining fiscal discipline will be a challenge.

The cost of borrowing from external sources will very likely increase, providing an incentive for firms to borrow in their domestic markets. In Malaysia, this could raise the risk of financial crowding out as 96 percent of the government's debt is financed domestically. Domestic interest rates will remain supportive of growth, and inflation will continue to be benign. However, inflation will experience spikes if the government reduces subsidies on food and energy, a policy measure currently under consideration. The exchange rate will loosely follow the Chinese renminbi in the medium term but may be driven by commodity trade and portfolio capital inflow in the short term.

Malaysia will be hard-pressed to shift its export markets away from the developed world toward emerging China, India, and Indonesia. Also, the Malaysian manufacturing sector will be forced to upgrade or give up. There will be no other option but to climb up the technology and value ladders as labor costs will continue to increase and policies on foreign unskilled workers will likely become less permissive. The Malaysian fiscal incentive system will need to be revamped to adapt to this new reality, attracting investment in areas where the main production factor is knowledge rather than capital or equipment.

Our projections suggest that average annual GDP growth in Malaysia could be 5.1 percent during 2010–15, lower than the 5.9 percent growth rate realized during 2002–07. However, a successful implementation of the NEM could bring the country back to its pre–2008 crisis growth trajectory. If the reforms announced in the NEM and 10th Malaysia plan are implemented, Malaysia's real GDP could grow by an annual average rate of 5.8 percent between 2010 and 2015. Also, benefits from these reforms could be felt as early as 2012, with growth exceeding 6 percent and reaching 6.5 percent in 2013.

The "great recession" 2008 may have been short-lived in Malaysia, but global economic recovery remains uncertain. Ultimately, the medium-term growth prospects for Malaysia will depend heavily on its government's capacity and ability to implement the announced reforms, leading to private investment recovery and productivity improvements. Actual and potential investors have taken a "wait and see" attitude regarding Malaysia and this is likely to further jeopardize the country's hopes of becoming a high-income economy by 2020.

Annex 7A: Assessing the Immediate Impact of the Crisis—An SVAR Analysis

To assess the immediate impact of the crisis on Malaysia, we use an SVAR, following Blanchard and Quah (1989). Long-run restrictions are identified based on Mundell-Fleming's framework to model the response of industrial output to real supply, real demand, and nominal shocks. We use monthly data for the industrial production index (IPI), the real interest rate (the average lending rate by commercial banks minus the inflation rate), and the nominal effective exchange rate from January 2009 to May 2009.

The variance decomposition analysis (figure 7A.1) shows that changes in the IPI were largely driven by real demand and real supply shocks, with more than 50 percent of the changes attributable to the real supply shock.

Our results suggest that a fiscal injection to boost real domestic demand in Malaysia has a limited impact (10–12 months), while the cumulative shock on the IPI would last more than three years (figures 7A.2 and 7A.3).

The impulse responses indicate that the effect of a real demand shock to the economy will completely disappear in 12 months, as will the nominal monetary shock. However, a real supply shock has a cumulative effect that peaks after 12 months before stabilizing (figure 7A.2). Both real demand and nominal shocks will have a temporary effect on production as shown in figures 7A.3 and 7A.4.

Figure 7A.1. Variance Decomposition

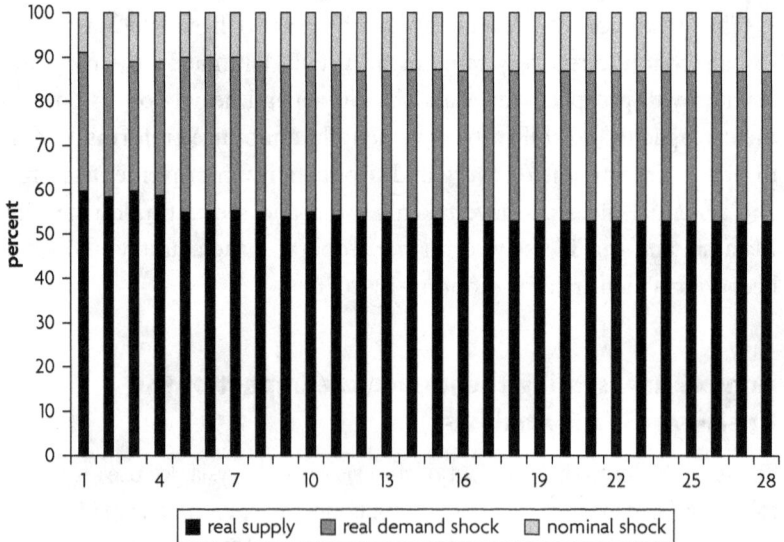

Source: Authors' calculations.

Figure 7A.2. IPI Impulse Response to Supply Shock

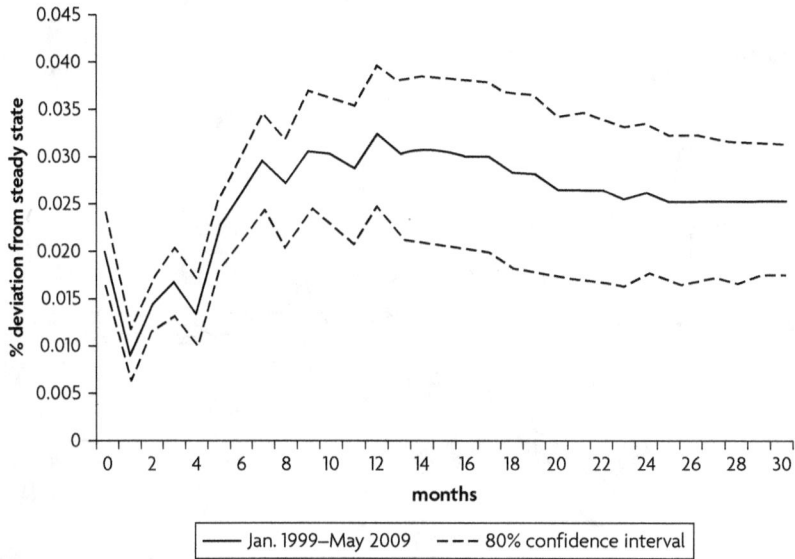

Source: Authors' calculations.

Figure 7A.3. IPI Impulse Response to Real Demand Shock

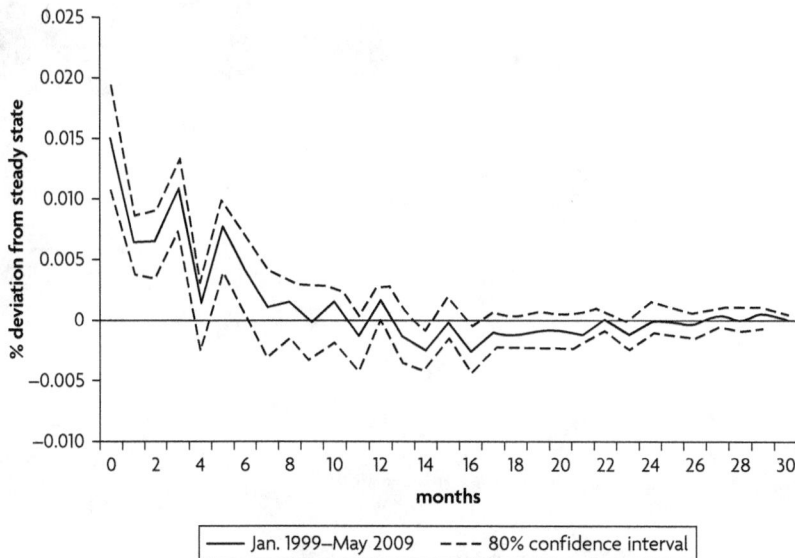

Source: Authors' calculations.

Figure 7A.4. IPI Impulse Response to Nominal Shock

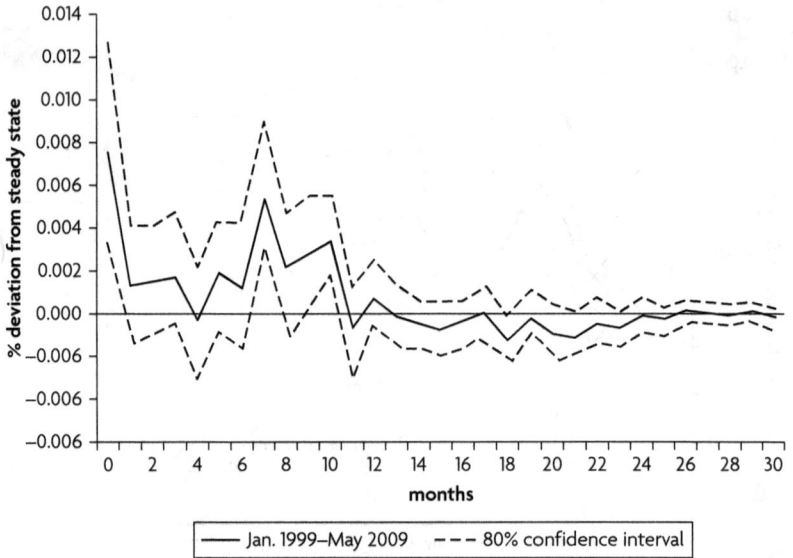

Annex 7B: Malaysia Macroeconomic Indicators

Malaysia	1994	1995	1996	1997	1998	1999	2000	2001	2002	2003	2004	2005	2006	2007	2008	2009
GDP per capita (current US$)	3,703.8	4,293.5	4,763.8	4,622.5	3,255.3	3,485.2	3,991.1	3,864.4	4,111.1	4,399.3	4,876.8	5,279.5	5,878.4	6,850.1	7,991.7	6,759.1
Population growth (% per year)	2.8	2.9	2.3	2.4	2.4	2.4	3.5	2.2	2.2	2.1	2.1	2.2	2.0	2.0	2.1	2.1
GDP growth (% per year)	9.2	9.8	10.0	7.3	−7.4	6.1	8.9	0.5	5.4	5.8	6.8	5.3	5.9	6.2	4.6	−1.7
GDP growth by sector (% per year)																
Agriculture	−1.9	−2.5	4.5	0.7	−2.8	0.5	4.3	−0.2	2.9	6.0	4.7	2.6	5.2	1.4	4.7	0.4
Industry	11.4	11.4	18.2	10.1	−13.4	11.7	20.7	−4.3	4.1	9.2	9.6	5.2	6.7	3.2	1.6	−9.3
Services								4.1	5.8	4.2	6.4	7.3	7.5	9.7	7.3	3.4
GDP growth by demand components (% per year)																
Private consumption	9.4	11.7	6.9	4.3	−10.2	2.9	13.0	3.0	3.9	8.1	9.8	9.1	6.8	10.4	8.5	0.8
Gross fixed capital formation	16.1	22.8	8.2	9.2	−43.0	−6.5	25.7	−2.1	0.6	2.8	3.6	5.0	7.5	9.6	0.8	−5.5
Government consumption	7.9	6.1	0.7	5.7	−8.9	17.1	1.6	15.7	11.9	8.6	7.6	6.5	5.0	6.5	10.9	3.7
Exports	21.9	19.0	9.2	5.5	0.5	13.2	16.1	−6.8	5.4	5.1	16.1	8.3	6.6	4.5	1.3	−10.1
Imports	25.6	23.7	4.9	5.8	−18.8	10.6	24.4	−8.2	6.2	4.5	19.6	8.9	8.1	6.0	1.9	−12.5
Share of GDP (% GDP)																
Private consumption	48.1	47.9	46.0	45.3	41.6	41.6	43.8	46.1	45.0	44.6	44.0	44.8	45.0	45.8	45.2	50.2
Government consumption	12.3	12.4	11.1	10.8	9.8	11.0	10.2	12.0	13.0	13.0	12.6	12.3	11.9	12.2	12.5	14.3

(continued)

Malaysia	1994	1995	1996	1997	1998	1999	2000	2001	2002	2003	2004	2005	2006	2007	2008	2009
Gross fixed capital formation	40.2	43.6	42.5	43.1	26.8	21.9	25.3	25.1	23.5	22.4	21.0	20.5	20.8	21.7	19.6	20.4
Exports	89.2	94.1	91.6	93.3	115.7	121.3	119.8	110.4	108.3	106.9	115.4	117.5	116.5	110.5	103.6	96.9
Imports	90.8	98.0	90.2	92.4	93.7	96.3	100.6	93.0	91.1	87.3	95.0	94.6	93.9	90.2	80.5	75.4
Gross domestic savings	35.1	33.9	37.1	37.0	39.9	38.3	35.9	32.3	31.9	34.9	35.1	34.5	36.7	37.2	36.7	30.8
External sector																
Trade balance (US$ bn)	1.6	-0.1	3.9	3.5	17.5	22.6	20.8	18.4	18.1	25.7	27.6	33.2	36.7	37.3	51.3	38.3
Current account balance (US$ bn)	-4.5	-8.6	-4.5	-5.9	9.5	12.6	8.5	7.3	7.2	13.4	15.1	20.0	26.2	29.2	38.9	32.0
Foreign direct Investment (US$ bn)	4.3	4.2	5.1	5.1	2.2	3.9	3.8	0.6	3.2	2.5	4.6	4.0	6.1	8.5	7.4	4.1
International reserves (US$ bn)	25.5	23.9	27.1	20.9	25.7	30.6	28.4	29.6	33.4	43.9	65.9	69.9	82.2	101.1	91.2	95.5
In months of imports	4.6	3.3	3.6	2.7	4.6	4.8	3.6	4.1	4.4	5.4	6.7	6.4	6.7	7.2	6.1	7.9
External debt (US$ bn)	30.3	34.3	39.7	47.2	42.4	41.9	41.9	45.1	48.3	48.6	52.2	52.0	52.5	53.7	54.6	48.4
External debt to Exports (%)	44.0	39.6	41.5	48.8	49.4	42.3	36.3	42.9	43.4	39.5	34.9	30.9	27.3	24.7	22.4	24.7
Interest payments to Exports (%)	8.9	7.0	8.8	7.3	7.1	4.8	5.6	5.9	7.1	7.8	6.2	5.6	4.0	4.6	3.6	5.1
Nominal exchange Rate (eop)	2.6	2.5	2.5	3.9	3.8	3.8	3.8	3.8	3.8	3.8	3.8	3.8	3.5	3.3	3.5	3.4
Public sector																
Primary balance (% GDP)	5.7	3.8	3.4	4.6	0.7	-0.5	-3.0	-2.5	-2.8	-2.5	-1.8	-1.4	-1.2	-1.2	-3.1	-5.5
Overall balance (% GDP)	2.3	0.8	0.7	2.4	-1.8	-3.2	-5.5	-5.2	-5.3	-5.0	-4.1	-3.6	-3.3	-3.2	-4.8	-7.6
Net Debt (% GDP)	47.6	41.1	35.3	31.9	36.4	37.3	35.2	41.3	43.0	45.1	45.7	43.8	42.2	41.7	41.5	52.0

Economic activity																
Unemployment (%)	2.9	2.8	2.5	2.5	3.2	3.4	3.1	3.7	3.5	3.6	3.6	3.6	3.3	3.2	3.3	3.7
Decomposition of GDP growth (%)																
Total GDP growth rate	9.2	9.8	10.0	7.3	-7.4	6.1	8.9	0.5	5.4	5.8	6.8	5.3	5.9	6.2	4.6	-1.7
Total GDP expenditures	100.0	100.0	100.0	100.0	100.0	100.0	100.0	100.0	100.0	100.0	100.0	100.0	100.0	100.0	100.0	100.0
Final consumption	60.0	64.7	33.8	35.7	76.1	46.6	63.2	563.8	59.7	82.4	79.3	90.5	62.7	88.3	112.3	-47.4
Private consumption	49.2	57.1	32.9	27.1	63.1	19.4	61.2	255.7	33.1	63.1	64.7	75.2	52.1	75.8	83.6	-20.6
Government consumption	10.8	7.6	0.9	8.6	13.0	27.2	2.0	308.2	26.6	19.3	14.6	15.3	10.6	12.5	28.8	-26.9
Investment	68.0	93.5	35.8	53.2	251.7	-28.6	63.6	-100.7	2.7	11.5	11.7	19.6	26.4	32.1	3.6	63.0
Gross fixed capital formation	68.0	93.5	35.8	53.2	251.7	-28.6	63.6	-100.7	2.7	11.5	11.7	19.6	26.4	32.1	3.6	63.0
Net exports	-32.2	-46.8	38.9	-3.1	-241.6	86.9	-44.8	19.5	4.5	24.7	0.6	20.9	0.7	-7.0	-6.7	28.5
Exports	187.7	172.0	86.8	68.7	-6.2	248.3	220.0	-1,579.7	111.1	96.1	253.2	179.6	132.3	84.6	31.3	611.0
Imports	219.9	218.8	47.9	71.7	235.4	161.4	264.8	-1,599.3	106.7	71.3	252.6	158.8	131.6	91.6	37.9	582.5
Contribution to growth (ppt)																
Final consumption	5.5	6.4	3.4	2.6	-5.6	2.9	5.6	2.9	3.2	4.8	5.4	4.8	3.7	5.5	5.2	0.8
Private consumption	4.5	5.6	3.3	2.0	-4.6	1.2	5.4	1.3	1.8	3.7	4.4	4.0	3.0	4.7	3.9	0.4
Government consumption	1.0	0.7	0.1	0.6	-1.0	1.7	0.2	1.6	1.4	1.1	1.0	0.8	0.6	0.8	1.3	0.5
Investment																
Gross fixed capital formation	6.3	9.2	3.6	3.9	-18.5	-1.8	5.6	-0.5	0.1	0.7	0.8	1.0	1.5	2.0	0.2	-1.1
Increase in stocks																
Net exports	-3.0	-4.6	3.9	-0.2	17.8	5.3	-4.0	0.1	0.2	1.4	0.0	1.1	0.0	-0.4	-0.3	-0.5
Exports	17.3	16.9	8.7	5.0	0.5	15.2	19.5	-8.2	6.0	5.6	17.2	9.6	7.7	5.2	1.4	-10.5
Imports	20.3	21.5	4.8	5.3	-17.3	9.9	23.5	-8.3	5.8	4.1	17.1	8.5	7.7	5.7	1.8	-10.0

(continued)

Malaysia	1994	1995	1996	1997	1998	1999	2000	2001	2002	2003	2004	2005	2006	2007	2008	2009
Money supply																
M1 annual growth (%)	16.8	13.2	14.9	11.8	−29.7	28.4	7.7	−1.3	11.8	16.0	11.2	8.7	12.2	18.7	9.0	0.3
M2 annual growth (%)	11.5	18.5	18.5	16.0	0.2	12.1	10.0	9.1	3.9	8.1	11.7	6.3	11.5	10.5	11.3	2.0
Credit market																
Total credit growth (% per year)	13.2	28.5	28.2	27.4	−0.2	−1.7	9.2	4.8	6.5	6.4	3.2	5.8	6.9	6.5	17.2	
Total credit (% GDP)	115.0	124.8	141.7	118.2	167.4	150.1	138.4	146.5	143.6	139.8	127.5	122.6	123.6	118.3	111.2	131.3
Headline lending interest rate			10.1	11.5	9.7	7.8	7.5	6.7	6.5	6.1	6.0	6.1	6.6	6.3	5.9	4.8
Capital market																
Price index (base year 2000)	971.2	995.2	1238.0	594.4	586.1	812.3	679.6	696.1	646.3	793.9	907.4	899.8	1096.2	1445.0	876.8	1272.8
Market capitalization (% GDP)	2.7	2.4	2.8	2.3	1.2	1.5	1.6	1.2	1.3	1.3	1.4	1.3	1.3	1.6	1.2	1.2
Inflation (% per year)																
CPI	2.1	3.2	3.3	2.9	5.3	2.5	1.2	1.2	1.6	1.2	2.2	3.3	3.1	2.4	4.4	1.1
WPI	4.9	5.5	2.3	2.6	10.8	−3.3	3.1	0.5	−0.8	4.6	7.0	6.9	6.7	4.6	8.5	−8.8
Total capital inflows (net) (% GDP)																
FDI (net)	5.8	4.7	5.0	5.1	3.0	4.9	4.0	0.6	3.2	2.2	3.7	2.9	3.9	4.5	3.3	
Portfolio (net)	7.5	2.5	3.7	−10.6	−0.4	0.3	−2.7	−0.6	−1.4	2.6	7.3	−1.5	1.7	3.7	−11.9	−2.5
Interest rate spreads on external debt (% per year)																
Government			0.5	2.0	6.2	1.7	2.4	2.1	2.1	1.0	0.8	0.8	0.7	1.2	3.7	1.4
Corporate								2.9	2.7	1.6	1.1	1.2	0.9	1.8	5.1	1.8

Source: BNM; World Bank; IMF; WTO; authors' calculations.

Note: eop = end of period; ppt = percentage points.

Notes

1. The "Middle Income Country Trap" is a development stage that characterizes countries squeezed between low-wage producers and highly-skilled, fast-moving innovators (Gill and Kharas 2007).
2. Corporate Income Tax in Singapore is 20 percent against 26 percent in Malaysia.
3. The Bumiputera are the native people of the Malay archipelago who constitute the largest ethnic group in Malaysia. Under the New Economic Policy implemented since 1971, they enjoy an affirmative action program that grants them various special economic and social privileges. One of the most contentious privileges is the requirement for 30 percent equity to be owned by the Bumiputera in most new investments.
4. The ringgit was pegged at 3.8 per U.S. dollar from 1999 to 2005 and has appreciated steadily since.
5. PETRONAS is the government-owned oil and gas company.
6. In 2007, as part of its regional development policy, the Malaysian government created five development corridors: the Northern Corridor (Utara), the Southern Corridor (Iskandar), the Eastern Corridor and Sabbah and Sarawak.
7. Strip spreads or calendar strips are simultaneous purchase (or sale) of futures positions in consecutive months.
8. The requirement for 30 percent Bumiputera participation was abolished for the manufacturing sector in the mid-90s to attract more FDI in Malaysia.
9. The Malaysian ringgit surged to a 13-year high at RM 3.13 per U.S. dollar, in reaction to the foreign exchange liberalization measures announced by Bank Negara Malaysia on August 18, 2010. Year to date, the ringgit has appreciated by 9 percent in 2010.

References

Ang, J. B. 2008. "Determinants of Private Investment In Malaysia: What Causes the Post-Crisis Slumps." *Contemporary Economic Policy.*

BNM (Bank Negara Malaysia). Annual Reports Series. BNM, Kuala Lumpur.

———. 2001. The Financial Sector Master Plan. BNM, Kuala Lumpur.

Blanchard, O. J., and D. Quah. 1989. "The Dynamic Effects of Aggregate Demand and Supply Disturbances." *American Economic Review* 79 (4): 655–73.

Gill, I., and H. Kharas. 2007. *An East Asian Renaissance: Ideas for Growth.* Washington, DC: World Bank.

Guimaraes, R. F., and O. Unteroberdoerster. 2006. "What's Driving Private Investment in Malaysia?: Aggregate Trends and Firm-Level Evidence." *IMF Working Paper* 06, 190, IMF, Washington, DC.

Ministry of Finance, Malaysia. 2010. *Economic Report 2008/2009.*

National Economic Advisory Council, Malaysia. 2010. New Economic Model.

Nungsari, A. R., and A. G. Zeufack. 2009. "Escaping the Middle Income Trap." In *Malaysia 2057: Readings on Development.* Ed. N. Radhi and S. Alias. Khazanah Nasional.

Tuah, H., and A. G. Zeufack. 2009. "Determinants of Private Investment in Malaysia: The Role of Public Infrastructure." Working Paper, Khazanah Research and Investment Strategy, Khazanah Nasional Berhad, Kuala Lumpur.

World Bank. 2008. "Measuring the Contribution to GDP and Productivity of the Malaysian Services Sector." World Bank, Washington DC.

Discussant Paper

Comment on "Malaysia: Postcrisis Growth Prospects Depend on Restoring Fiscal Discipline and Private Investor Confidence"

Shahrokh Fardoust

Malaysia has been identified by the Growth Commission as one of only 13 economies in the world that has grown at a rate exceeding 7 percent a year for more than 25 years (Commission on Growth and Development 2008). In fact, for the past 40 years, Malaysia has been enjoying relative prosperity, driven largely by bountiful endowments of natural resources, including oil and timber, as well as by a dynamic manufacturing sector. The proportion of people living in poverty has fallen from more than 50 percent of the population in the 1960s to about 4 percent now. However, in the aftermath of the Asian crisis (1997–98), something fundamental may have changed, with the economy losing some of its dynamism and with growth slowing markedly over the past decade.

More recently, in 2008–09, the Malaysian economy, one of the most open economies in the world, was hit hard by the global crisis. The impact came mainly through the trade channel and, to a lesser extent,

Shahrokh Fardoust is Director, Development Economics Operations and Strategy, World Bank.

through the financial channel, owing to turbulence in the international financial markets. As a result, the economy contracted in 2009 for the first time in more than a decade. Although the economy is beginning to rebound, helped by the global recovery and by expansionary domestic macroeconomic policies, its future course is uncertain, with weakness in export demand and battered investor confidence weighing heavily on its prospects.

A key question confronting policy makers, therefore, is whether there is a set of policy reforms and structural changes that can be implemented in a timely manner to enable the Malaysian economy to regain its former dynamism and competitiveness. Some observers are concerned that the economy may suffer further deceleration in growth and loss of export market share over the medium term as a result of the crisis and in light of global economic conditions that likely will continue to be more difficult compared with the last decade.

Main Comments

The chapter by Azrai and Zuefack provides a fairly detailed analysis of the macroeconomic and financial impact of the global crisis on Malaysia. By presenting a compelling story about how the global crisis affected the economy, the chapter attempts to respond to the above-mentioned questions. The authors' forward-looking analysis explores how the government's policy responses are likely to affect the medium-term growth prospects of the Malaysian economy.

In my view, the discussion makes several timely contributions to the current policy debate on Malaysia. In this context, a key finding concerns the initial conditions of the Malaysian economy: it did not fully recover its dynamism in the post–Asia crisis period, it did not fully benefit from the rapid global economic and trade growth during 2002–07, and it was unable to regain its full potential or productive capacity before the onset of the current global crisis. Most important, the Malaysian authorities may have lacked the sufficient policy space that could have been used as a buffer against the external shock generated by the global crisis. This last point is a key finding of recent studies by the World Bank, the International Monetary Fund, and this volume, on how developing countries have coped with the global economic crisis (World Bank

2010a; IMF 2010). This body of work has shown that countries that improved policy fundamentals in the precrisis period—reducing their vulnerability and strengthening their buffers against external shocks— were able to reap the benefits of these reforms during the crisis.[1]

Thus, the second important point made by the Azrai-Zuefack chapter is that that economic weaknesses and insufficient policy space in the post–Asia crisis period increased Malaysia's vulnerability to subsequent external shocks. In fact, Malaysia was one the hardest-hit developing countries during 2008–09. It suffered a total output loss of more than 8 percent of GDP (output gap as a percentage of potential GDP), as estimated by the authors—compared with, for example, 3–5 percent for Brazil, China, Ethiopia, India, the Philippines, and Poland.

Interestingly, as Azrai and Zuefack argue, Malaysia's vulnerability to external shocks could have been even greater had it not been for the fact that its financial sector remained generally sound because of sustained reforms implemented after the Asia crisis. The authors also claim that, to date, the crisis has had a limited effect on unemployment because of adjustments in the labor market that include the shedding of foreign labor, which constitutes about 20 percent of the labor force. This policy is likely to have long-term implications for the Malaysian economy. However, the authors do not provide an in-depth analysis of the effects of this labor shedding on the future of the labor market. There is evidence that shifts to self-employment have been particularly strong, which may be associated with a rise in informal employment, as would be expected during a downturn. Generally, patterns of employment and wage dynamics during the global crisis have tended to vary across sectors, partly reflecting exposures to external demand (World Bank 2010b).

I have three general comments on the chapter.

First, the authors argue that Malaysia did not benefit from the global post–Asia crisis boom. In fact, GDP growth dropped sharply during this period. Whereas from 1987 to 1997 the economy grew at an average annual rate of about 9 percent, it fell to less than 6 percent during 2003–07. Furthermore, during this same period, Malaysia's investment rate fell from 40 percent of GDP to just 20 percent. These massive shifts represent a major break in performance that must have resulted from a fundamental shock to the system from the Asia crisis, which may have also had important political and social consequences. However, it is not clear from the discussion what specifically caused the sharp downturn. Is Malaysia caught in the "middle-income trap"?[2] And could this "trap" have political and social roots?

This leads to my second general comment, which is that the chapter is largely silent on political and social factors that may have played a key role in reducing private investment and redirecting a portion of FDI to other, more dynamic economies in the region. In fact, despite its fairly comprehensive macroeconomic and financial analysis, the Azrai-Zuefack contribution does not offer much analysis on how political and social developments may have actually constrained Malaysia's policy space in recent years.

My third comment concerns the role of China's economy, both in terms of its interactions with the Malaysian economic recovery and, more specifically, through its increased competition with Malaysian exports to third markets over the medium term. This important link could have been explored in greater depth, as China is Malaysia's largest trade partner in Asia. Although growth in exports is likely to slow over the next 18 months owing to weak global demand, exporting to China is likely to remain strong as China's manufacturing sector moves up the value chain, boosting demand for Malaysia's electronic goods. In fact, the recovery in global external demand, which is of critical importance to Malaysia's economy, is increasingly tied to China's rapid economic growth.

The prospects for Malaysian exports will also depend in part on the evolution of China's exchange rate policy. The Chinese government has set a long-term goal of achieving a more flexible exchange rate regime and a more interest-rate-oriented monetary policy. The current divergent cyclical positions between the United States and China may speed up this process. Potential strengthening and increased flexibility of the Chinese exchange rate versus the U.S. dollar may provide room for other countries in Asia to strengthen their exchange rates and flexibility over time. However, potential strengthening of the real exchange rates in Asia is likely to put additional stress on Malaysian firms, which already face pressure to improve cost efficiency and become more competitive in global markets in order to preserve market share (World Bank 2010b).

Specific Comments

The authors do not indicate what really accounts for the substantial drop in private investment in recent years (from about 30 percent of GDP in the mid-1990s, to 9.5 percent by 2004, and to only 4 percent in 2009). Some recent analyses have shown that this may have been the result of overinvestment (particularly in the construction sector), as well as the relatively limited profitability of earlier investments. The drop in investment may have also been due to the lack of adequate financing for small- and medium enterprises (Guimares and Unteroberdoerster 2006). Moreover, the chapter's estimates for total factor productivity (TFP) growth raise some questions. Azrai and Zeufack show that, while growth in output per worker declined sharply from 5.5 percent a year during 1987–97 to less than 3 percent in 1998–2007, mainly because of a sharp reduction in the contribution of capital, TFP growth remained more or less unchanged at about 1.7 percent a year for 1987–97 and 1.6 percent a year for 1998–2007. It is also not clear how TFP growth was maintained in the face of a sharp decline in private investment. A sudden decline in private investment must have had at least some adverse effects on the pace of technical progress in Malaysia through research and development spending, imports, or foreign direct investment, for example, all of which are major determinants of TFP growth.

The analysis would benefit from a more detailed discussion of the new US$70 billion reform package, the New Economic Model (NEM). An explanation would be helpful of how the NEM will address the main challenges posed by the current crisis, as well as overcome problems that may have led to the middle-income country trap situation. For example, does the model address upgrading Malaysia's technology sector and advancing up the value chain to enhance competitiveness? Based on recent press reports, the reforms under the NEM will focus on privatization, the sale of government land, reassessment of various fiscal subsidies, removal of restrictions on foreign investment in services, and reform of the educational system.

Deep reforms are needed to spur investment and innovation to enhance the economy's dynamism and competitiveness. These include measures to diversify the economy, bring about a level playing field for domestic and foreign investors, encourage domestic demand, and enhance the economy's buffers to increase Malaysia's resilience to external shocks. These reforms are expected to have the desired effects on Malaysia's high savings rate, but relatively low level of private investment.

The current debate in Malaysia on the need to reduce dependence on external markets could lead to inward-looking policies that may further reduce the economy's competitiveness in the global economy and lead to further deceleration of growth over the medium term. Malaysia will need to continue to embrace globalization and accept that a structural shift in the economy may be necessary to produce a more diversified range of goods and services for export. This point is also made by Azrai and Zuefack.

Finally, looking forward, the authors argue that the 2008–09 crisis may lower Malaysia's average growth in the medium term. GDP growth could be about 5 percent a year between 2009 and 2015, compared with about 6 percent between 2002 and 2007. However, the authors also argue that a successful implementation of the NEM program would bring the country back to its pre-2008 crisis growth trajectory. Malaysia could grow substantially faster, however, if the government's reform program is implemented in a timely way—the authors claim that increased momentum could be felt as early as 2012 if sustained reform is enacted quickly. I agree with the authors that, while measures adopted by the authorities may have defused the crisis, it is still critically important to restore private investor confidence. Although growth has rebounded strongly in 2010, private investment and FDI remain depressed. Private investment could be revived only after a bulk of critical reforms are implemented. Furthermore, because of the difficult fiscal situation prior to the crisis, which has been complicated by fiscal stimulus packages, fiscal sustainability may become a matter of concern. Thus, over the medium term, the government may be required to reduce the fiscal deficit by both reducing spending and expanding the tax base, actions that are likely to introduce additional uncertainty to the political economy of the reforms.

Notes

1. More specifically, the initial impact of the crisis appears to have been less pronounced in those countries that had better precrisis policies and had reduced their vulnerabilities to external shocks. A relatively higher level of international

reserve holdings, for example, helped protect countries from the real and financial consequences of the global crisis. Moreover, those countries that entered the crisis with more policy space were better able to react quickly with sizable fiscal and monetary stimulus packages.

2. This refers to countries that grow rapidly for a couple of decades and then stall, or continue growing at a significantly slower pace, a circumstance that has been shown in a number of countries in Latin America, such as Brazil and Mexico.

References

Commission on Growth and Development. 2008. "The Growth Report: Strategies for Sustained Growth and Inclusive Development." Washington, DC.

Guimaraes, Roberto, and Olaf Unteroberdoerster. 2006. "What's Driving Private Investment in Malaysia? Aggregate Trends and Firm-Level Evidence." IMF Working Paper WP/06/190, IMF, Washington, DC.

IMF (International Monetary Fund). 2010. "How Did Emerging Markets Cope in the Crisis?" Washington, DC. http://www.imf.org/external/np/pp/eng/2010/061510.pdf.

World Bank. 2010a. "From Global Collapse to Recovery: Economic Adjustment and Growth Prospects in LAC." Semiannual Report of the Office of the Chief Economist for the Latin America and the Caribbean Region, prepared in collaboration with the Research Department at the World Bank.

———. 2010b. "Economic Monitor: Growth through Innovation," Washington, DC, April.

Large, Immediate Negative Impact and Weak Medium-Term Growth Prospects

Gerardo Esquivel

The crisis that put the global financial system on the brink of total collapse in late 2008 will undoubtedly have a profound impact on the world economy. The crisis was far from being only a financial one; it will also be very costly in terms of output and employment. Indeed, at some point in 2009, and for the first time in several decades, all developed countries were simultaneously in recession (OECD 2009).

The cost of the crisis, however, has not been confined to the developed world or to those countries whose financial sectors had strong links to the U.S. financial system. The process of globalization and economic integration that took place in recent decades has led to the first truly global crisis of the modern age. This crisis will have important implications for many developing countries, not just because of the output contraction of 2009, but also because the postcrisis international economic scenario will be much different from the one anticipated in the precrisis era. For example, the medium-term growth prospects of the world

Gerardo Esquivel is Professor of Economics, El Colegio de México, Mexico. The author thanks Isabel Cueva and Williams Peralta for their excellent research assistance.

economy will likely be considerably different (presumably smaller) from what was expected earlier. For this reason, it is important to understand the interaction between the international economic environment and the performance of local economies, not just during the crisis but also in its aftermath. While several recent studies have focused on the social and economic impacts of the crisis and on the domestic policies deemed necessary to counteract its immediate negative effects and address its predictable sequels, we attempt to go beyond this short-term analysis and explore how the ongoing global crisis, the domestic policy response, and the postcrisis global economy will shape the medium-term growth prospects of the Mexican economy. This case study is particularly relevant, not just because of Mexico's importance in Latin America, but also because Mexico is the Latin American country most affected by the current crisis in terms of output and economic activity. In fact, given the economic contraction in 2009, Mexico was the most adversely affected country in the entire Western Hemisphere.

We begin by describing the precrisis growth experience in Mexico. We review the impact of the crisis on Mexico and its policy responses, as well as present estimates of potential output, output gaps, and total factor productivity (TFP) in Mexico. We then analyze the aftermath of the crisis and discuss Mexico's medium-term growth prospects.

The Preglobal Boom Period (1995–2002)

At the beginning of this period, Mexico was in the midst of an economic and financial crisis that had begun in late 1994, when it became known that Mexico did not have enough foreign exchange reserves to meet its foreign-currency-denominated short-term obligations. The ensuing devaluation of mid-December 1994 and the sharp increase in both interest rates and prices that followed in early 1995 complicated the economic situation even further.

The currency crisis rapidly became a full-blown financial and economic crisis when a large number of people started to default on their credits as a result of the sudden and sharp increase in interest rates. This was particularly problematic because Mexico had recently reprivatized its banking system and banking loans of all types (for consumption, mortgages, and commercial) had soared in the previous five years. Most of these loans had been contracted on a variable interest rate, and debtor's quality had deteriorated substantially throughout the lending boom process. Banking regulation, on the one hand, had been too lax for too long, and many banking institutions had granted credits to clients lacking capacity to pay.

As a direct consequence of the crisis, Mexico had to fix and reorganize its whole financial sector. In the absence of a deposits protection fund, the government bailed out a large segment of the banking sector and had to directly intervene in several financial institutions. In some cases, these institutions were fully revamped and resold to the private sector. There were also several mergers and acquisitions, and the structure of the banking sector changed radically toward a more modern financial sector dominated by large multinational players. In addition, the Mexican government improved supervision mechanisms and established tighter regulations.[1]

As a result of the crisis, poverty in Mexico increased substantially between 1994 and 1996. For example, extreme (food-based) poverty in Mexico rose from 21 percent of the total population in 1994 to 37 percent in 1996. Similar increases were observed in two alternative definitions of poverty, capabilities-based and assets-based, which reached 47 and 70 percent of the total population by 1996, respectively. Starting in that year, poverty in Mexico began a steady decline, but it was not until 2002 that it returned to its precrisis levels.

Exit from the so-called Tequila Crisis was based on an export-led growth model, which was accompanied by a rapid increase in the formation of capital. Exports took off after 1995, when they increased from about 12 percent of GDP to represent close to 25 percent of GDP by 2000. On an index basis, exports increased threefold between 1993 and 2000, whereas internal demand increased only by less than 40 percent in the same period.

During the process of economic recovery, Mexico's GDP grew at an annual rate of 5.5 percent between 1995 and 2000. If we include in the computation the two recessionary years of 2001 and 2002, Mexico's GDP growth rate is reduced to only about 4 percent per year, which, although smaller, is still above the average annual GDP growth rate for the post-1986 period (3 percent per year).

During this period of relatively rapid economic growth, job creation also took place at a relatively fast pace. For example, about one million formal jobs per year were created between 1995 and 2000. This was undoubtedly the period with the fastest rate of formal job creation in Mexico during the past three decades. Obviously, rapid job creation and positive economic growth rates help to explain the reversal in poverty rates that was observed throughout this period.

Mexico was able to exit from its deep crisis as a result of the combination of three different but related factors: first, the U.S. economy was enjoying its strongest and largest expansion of the postwar era, and therefore, demand for Mexican exports was growing at a fast pace; second, the North American Free Trade Agreement (NAFTA) had just been enacted, which in turn also boosted Mexican exports because one of the main implications of the trade agreement was the reduction in tariff barriers for Mexican exports entering U.S. territory;[2] and, third, the sharp devaluation of the Mexican peso in December 1994 made Mexican goods even more attractive for U.S. consumers. The latter allowed Mexican exports to the United States to grow even faster than they would have in the absence of either the devaluation or NAFTA.

In general, Mexico was able to exit quickly from the crisis due to its strong ties with the U.S. economy. These links were already quite strong before NAFTA, and they became even stronger after the enacting of the trade agreement. For example, before NAFTA, close to 80 percent of total Mexican exports went to the U.S. market. By 2000, this share had already increased to 90 percent. The increase in foreign trade between Mexico and the United States also strengthened the synchronization between these two economies, as will be discussed later.

The Precrisis Period

Sometime around 2002, developed countries began a period of rapid economic expansion that triggered a sharp rise in worldwide demand for commodities and manufactured goods. This set the stage for the global boom of 2002–07, as countries with both strong industrial bases and abundant natural resources faced rising external demand. These countries participated in and benefited from this period of economic expansion, which reinforced the initial expansion of the developed countries.

Some of the main beneficiaries of this boom were thus commodity-producing countries. Among them, several Latin American countries faced a particularly positive terms-of-trade shock that provided them with additional resources and allowed them to grow at their fastest rates since the 1970s. For Mexico, however, the precrisis global boom was not as favorable. The post-2002 rapid expansion of the world economy had only a small positive effect on Mexico's terms of trade, contrary to the experience of such countries as Bolivia, Chile, Peru, and the República Boliviariana de Venezuela, whose terms of trade improved substantially during this period. The precrisis global boom had three important implications for the Mexican economy.

First, the economy of the United States, Mexico's main trading partner, grew at a relatively rapid pace during 2002–07 (2.8 percent per year), which greatly helped to sustain the economic growth of Mexico during that period (3.3 percent per year).

Second, the price of oil, one of Mexico's most important export products, surged during the boom—after a prolonged period of relatively low prices—and reached a historic peak by 2008. The price of Mexican oil (which is heavier and cheaper than other types) rose from less than US$22 a barrel in 2002 to almost US$80 by the end of 2007. This boosted the total flow of resources to Mexico by about US$84 billion during 2003–07.

Another effect of the global boom on Mexico's economy during 2002–07 was the huge increase in remittances received by Mexican households from abroad. The inflow of remittances increased from less than US$10 billion in 2002 to more than US$26 billion in 2007. As a result, remittances became one of Mexico's most important sources of foreign exchange, even surpassing the income received from tourism-related activities or through foreign direct investment (FDI).

The rapid increase in the supply of foreign exchange that resulted from the higher oil income and remittances led to strong appreciation pressures on the peso exchange rate in 2004 and beyond. The central bank—Banco de México—responded by increasing its stock of foreign exchange reserves and by sterilizing these operations to avoid monetization pressures. Hence, during 2002–07, reserves increased from US$48 billion to more than US$78 billion—an increase of more than 60 percent. This helped strengthen Mexico's external position; for example, the ratio of short-term external debt to foreign exchange reserves declined from 32 percent in 2002 to less than 10 percent in 2007.

Despite Mexico's slight economic growth acceleration during this period, the country benefited surprisingly little from the precrisis global boom (average GDP growth increased by just 0.1 percentage point, as shown in table 8A.6 in the annex). This can be partly explained by the lack of fundamental or structural changes in the Mexican economy in previous years. Indeed, the Mexican government has made no progress on its structural reform agenda since the late 1990s. This is the result of the combination of two elements: reform fatigue and a divided government.[3] The reform fatigue is associated with the failure, perceived or real, of some of Mexico's most important previous reforms, such as privatization and pension reform. And starting in 1997, the party in power has not been able to simultaneously achieve a majority in Congress, and this has severely complicated policy making in the country. Thus, a political consensus on structural reforms has not been possible, and only a few relatively minor reforms have been approved in recent years.

The arrival of other strong players in the global economy—such as China and India, who compete with Mexico in terms of products (manufactures) and markets (the United States)—has also affected the perception and competitiveness of the Mexican economy. Since China entered the World Trade Organization, it has displaced Mexico as the second most important U.S. trade partner.

More importantly, the lack of dynamism of the Mexican economy is strongly associated with relatively low levels of TFP. Several recent estimates, using a variety of methodologies, have shown that TFP growth in Mexico has been either negative or modest during the past three decades (figure 8.1 and table 8A.3).[4]

By the end of the global boom, due to the policy decisions made during this period, Mexico was in a dual position in terms of confronting what was coming. On the one hand, it had strengthened its external position by reducing its external debt burden, increasing its foreign exchange reserves, and showing improvement in all of its external vulnerability indicators. But, on the other hand, Mexico was in a weakened fiscal situation as a result of having financed its current expenditures with oil revenues, which are characteristically volatile and uncertain.

Figure 8.1. Income per Worker and TFP Annual Growth, 1980–2007

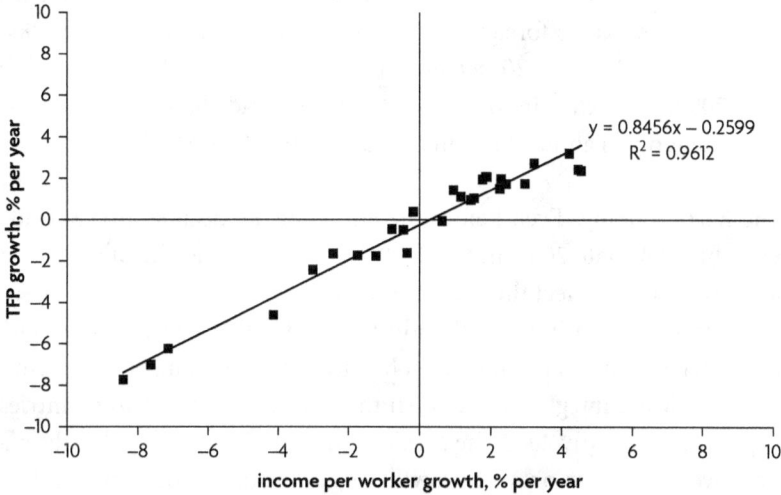

$$y = 0.8456x - 0.2599$$
$$R^2 = 0.9612$$

Source: World Bank data; author's estimates.

The Immediate Impact of the Crisis

The global financial and economic crisis had an immediate and broad-based impact on the Mexican economy. This was transmitted to Mexico in several ways.

Channels of Transmission

The crisis was transmitted to the Mexican economy through the channels of trade, remittances, tourism, FDI, external financing, exchange rate volatility, and oil prices. All of these channels had a negative impact on the Mexican economy and highlight why Mexico was the most affected country in the Western Hemisphere—and one of the most affected in the world—by the global crisis.

Exports. A key transmission channel has been Mexico's trade relationship with the United States—the destination for nearly 80 percent of its exports. Indeed, the collapse in U.S. demand for durable goods led to a sharp contraction in the demand for some of the most important Mexican export products such as automobiles (–24 percent) and electronic appliances (–19 percent). Likewise, the weakening of the U.S. economy triggered a sharp fall in demand for Mexican oil (–39 percent). As a result, Mexico's foreign trade grew at a relatively low rate in 2008 and fell by more than 20 percent in 2009 in nominal dollar terms. By mid-2009, the decline in Mexico's total foreign trade had reached almost 35 percent on an annual basis in nominal terms (figure 8.2).

The Real Economy. Even before the effects of the decline in U.S. trade were fully felt (late 2008 and early 2009), however, the global crisis had already begun to affect the Mexican economy through the real sector. In fact, the slowdown in the U.S. industrial sector that began in late 2007 coincided with a similar slowing in Mexican industry. This was the result of the growing integration between the industries of the two countries (figure 8.3). By early 2008, the Mexican industrial sector was already at a negative rate of year-on-year growth, suggesting that both industries had begun contracting even earlier than had trade.

Figure 8.2. Annual Growth of Foreign Trade (Imports and Exports), 1992–2010

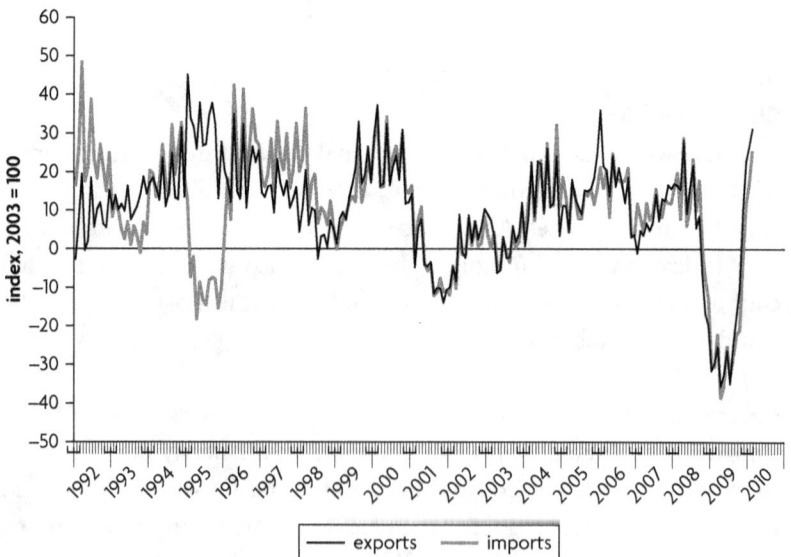

Source: Instituto Nacional de Estadística y Geografía e Informática (INEGI).

Figure 8.3. Mexico and the United States: Industrial Activity Indexes, 1980–2010

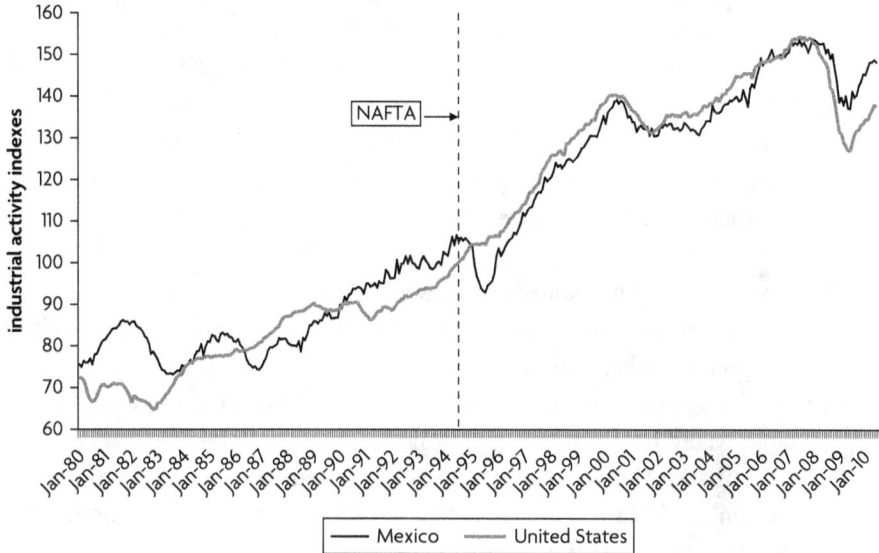

Source: INEGI and Federal Reserve.
Note: Seasonally adjusted data (Mexico 1993 = 100, United States 1994 = 100).

Remittances. Another channel of transmission of the shock were the remittances that Mexicans living abroad (mainly in the United States) sent back to Mexico. Although remittances are, in relative terms, far more important for Central American and Caribbean countries, Mexico had nonetheless become the second-largest recipient of remittances in the world, and remittances accounted for about 2.5 percent of total Mexican GDP in 2007. Since the beginning of the crisis, this flow has steadily diminished, and as of early 2010 it was almost 20 percent lower than two years before.

Several studies have shown the close connection between employment indicators in the United States and the level of remittances to Mexico.[5] This is because many Mexican workers who had originally migrated to the United States to work in agriculture switched jobs to move into the then-booming housing sector, where they could earn higher salaries. But, the contraction in the U.S. economy began precisely in the construction sector, thus immediately reducing the level of remittances to Mexico, which began their decline in August 2007.

Tourism. Tourism flows to Mexico were also affected by the crisis, as personal spending on travel and entertainment is highly responsive to changes in income. The number of tourists visiting Mexico from the United States and from Europe fell substantially in 2009 (a 16.9 percent drop in the first half of 2009). This was aggravated by the H1N1 flu outbreak that hit Mexico in late April and early May 2009, raising fears of a new pandemic, which led to an even sharper reduction in the number of tourists to Mexico in the April–June period (–27.6 percent).

Foreign Direct Investment. FDI and external financing to Mexico have also fallen as a result of the global credit crunch and the pullback in financial markets. In 2009, several investment (mainly infrastructure) projects in Mexico were set aside because of the lack of long-term financing. Many other productive projects were postponed or canceled by multinational firms owing to the lack of liquidity. In all, capital inflows diminished from 2.7 percent of GDP in 2007 to only 2.2 percent in 2009, a 20 percent reduction.

The Exchange Rate. Exchange rate volatility has also increased since the onset of the crisis. In October 2008, right after the collapse of Lehman Brothers, uncertainty around the world increased and a "flight to quality" occurred across all countries—both emerging and developed. This meant that even after massive interventions in the foreign exchange market, the currencies of many emerging-market countries depreciated by 20–30 percent. The average peso exchange rate went up from almost 11 pesos per dollar in early 2008 to about 13.5 pesos in 2009.

Oil Prices. Finally, the collapse of oil prices has had a major impact on the Mexican economy. The price of Mexican oil, which had reached US$120 a barrel, fell to half that price in 2009 (although it later experienced a recovery). This sharp price decline translated into a substantial fall in Mexican oil exports and, even more important, a large drop in government revenues, which depend heavily (about 40 percent) on oil revenues. As a result, the collapse of oil prices, together with a reduction in the level of oil extraction, has dramatically reduced public sector revenues and generated a fiscal gap in public finances of nearly 3 percent of GDP.

All of these sources of shock took a toll on domestic demand, and particularly on private consumption and gross fixed capital formation. Private consumption fell by more than 6 percent in 2009 relative to 2008, and fixed capital formation dropped by 10.1 percent. The total GDP loss during 2008–09, relative to Mexico's potential GDP level, is estimated at close to 11 percentage points. Most of it is explained by a loss in TFP growth equivalent to 8.8 percent of GDP (table 8A.6).

Policy Responses

Although it is true that the magnitude of the crisis surprised almost everyone, the Mexican government clearly underestimated the situation in two crucial aspects: first, the scope of the crisis itself, which was initially perceived as relatively mild and confined mostly to the financial sector; and, second, its impact on the Mexican economy.

The main reason the local authorities expected a limited impact on the Mexican economy was that the country's financial sector was safe and sound as a result of the stricter regulation that was put in place during the restructuring of the financial sector following the 1995 crisis. According to the authorities, the fact that Mexico had been adhering to a strict fiscal discipline in recent years, that domestic inflation was relatively low, and that Mexico's financial institutions were not engaged in the type of operations that had led to the collapse of several U.S. financial institutions, would be sufficient to make the Mexican economy relatively immune to the international crisis.

The problem with this reasoning, however, was that the crisis was far from being only a financial one. It was also a crisis of the real sector of the economy and, as such, it was going to affect other economies through a multiplicity of channels. In the end, the intensity of the impact would depend, among other things, on the degree of economic integration with the U.S. economy. A faulty diagnostic explains the late and timid response of the Mexican authorities in confronting the crisis.

On the fiscal policy front, the Mexican government announced in the spring of 2008 the creation of an infrastructure fund that was intended to have a countercyclical impact. Most of the resources in this fund were not new, however, coming from existing accounts that were dispersed across the different ministries. In addition, the government announced that several existing stabilization funds could be used if necessary to maintain the level of expenditures in the event that revenues proved lower than expected. In late 2008 and early 2009, the Mexican government announced several other measures to mitigate the negative impact of the crisis. The programs originally included fiscal, social, and labor measures to confront the impending crisis. The magnitude of the fiscal impulse was estimated by the International Monetary Fund (IMF) at 1.0–1.5 percent of GDP (IMF 2009b, 2009c). However, given the cut in government spending in the second half of 2009, the fiscal impulse actually implemented was likely even lower than originally estimated.

In any event, cross-country comparisons with the fiscal measures implemented by other countries show that the Mexican response was much lower (CEPAL 2009; OECD 2009). Nevertheless, the government's response at least did not make things worse for the Mexican economy. This is because government consumption increased in 2009 by nearly 2.3 percent in real terms, which helped mitigate the contraction in other demand components.

On the monetary policy front, the Banco de México's response to the crisis was late and timid. In fact, throughout 2008 (and despite the clear signs of further deterioration in economic activity), the central bank's main concern remained the inflationary pressures emanating from the rapid rise in food prices. For this reason, contrary to what others central banks around the world were doing, the Banco de México increased the interest rate in the summer of 2008 on three occasions (figure 8.4). These policy decisions, which increased the interest rate gap between Mexico and the United States, also contributed to a further rise in the amount of foreign portfolio inflows. This outcome again increased the vulnerability of Mexico's exchange rate to a sudden stop or reversal of capital flows, which was precisely what occurred in September–October 2008, after the collapse of Lehman Brothers.

It was not until early 2009, when the recession was already well established in the country and when the target interest rate in the United States was already close to zero, that the Banco de México finally started to reduce its target interest rate (figure 8.4). Even then, it did so in relatively small steps, first by 25 basis points (bps) and only later by 75 bps. All in all, the central bank reduced the interest rate in Mexico from 8.25 percent to 4.5 percent over seven months. But by that time,

Figure 8.4. Target Interest Rates in the United States and Mexico, 2008–09

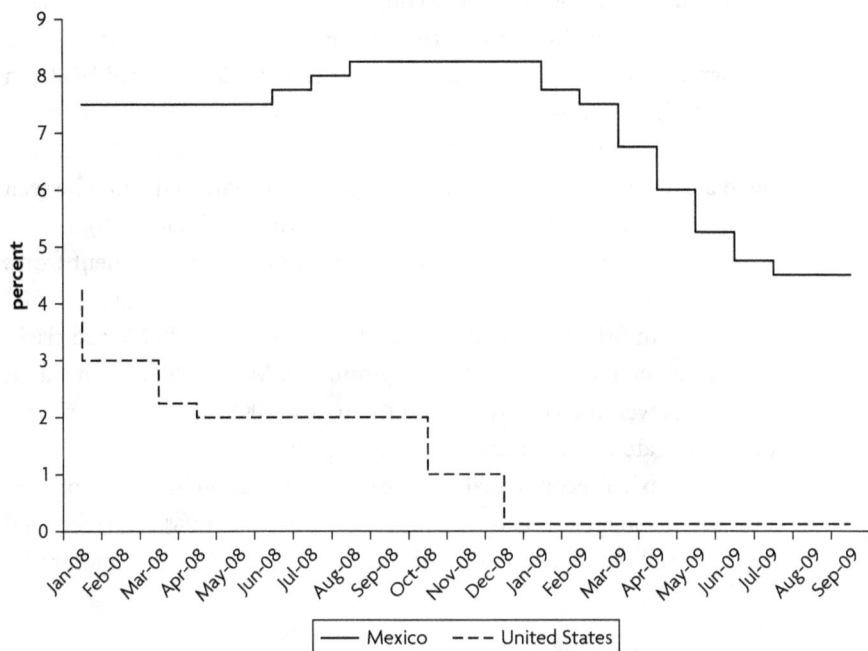

Source: Banco de México; Federal Reserve.

most of the negative effects of the global crisis had already been transmitted to the Mexican economy.

The Mexican authorities reacted more appropriately, however, to other aspects of the crisis. For example, they intervened through the development banks to provide liquidity and to maintain fully functioning credit markets amid the worst phase of the financial crisis (following the collapse of Lehman Brothers). Likewise, the Mexican central bank also reacted in a timely way to avoid a larger (and presumably costlier) depreciation of the domestic currency. In October 2008, the Banco de México implemented a mechanism for a foreign exchange reserves auction, which sold off more than US$10 billion. This prevented a much larger depreciation of the Mexican peso, which, at least from the central bank's perspective, could have generated serious inflationary pressures.

Effects on Output and Employment

As noted earlier, the Mexican economy was one of the most affected in the world by the global crisis; GDP, for example, contracted by 6.5 percent in 2009, the largest annual decline in Mexico since 1932. On a quarterly basis, Mexico's GDP fell by more than 10 percent in the second quarter of 2009, relative to the year-earlier quarter (figure 8.5). Such a contraction was not just the largest since 1981, but could be seen as constituting an economic depression (Barro and Ursúa 2008).

The Mexican economy was also hit hard on the employment front. The open unemployment rate reached 6.3 percent in August 2009 (7 percent in urban areas), its highest level since the 1995 Mexico crisis. Unemployment climbed steadily beginning in May 2008, when it was at its lowest level in recent years, and by August 2009 the monthly unemployment rate was 3 percentage points higher.

With Mexico's economically active population approaching 45 million in 2009, this suggests that the number of unemployed in Mexico increased by 1.35 million over a 15-month period. We get a similar picture by

Figure 8.5. GDP Growth Rate, 1981–2009

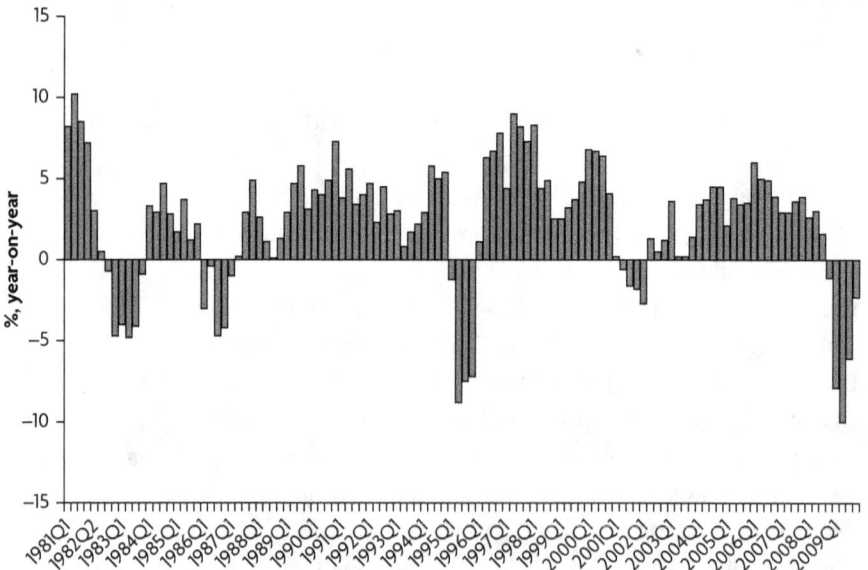

Source: INEGI.

looking at the number of workers registered at the Mexican Institute of Social Security. According to the institute, the number of formal jobs in Mexico fell by 400,000 in 2009. Such a contraction represents a decline of almost 3 percent in the total number of formal job posts. The rest of the unemployed came from the informal sector or from among new entrants into the labor force.

Many other indicators suggest that the labor market in Mexico at the beginning of 2010 was extremely weak. The share of underemployed, for example, was close to 9 percent of the total economically active population, while it usually fluctuates around 6 percent. This also suggests than an additional 1.35 million Mexican workers are now underemployed as a result of the crisis.

In summary, the global crisis has had a very strong negative impact on the Mexican economy. The impact has been large by any standard and is explained by the combination of at least two main factors:

- Mexico's heavy dependence on the U.S. economy, which made it highly vulnerable to U.S. economic conditions on many fronts such as exports, remittances, and tourism
- Mexico's delayed and weak policy response, exemplified by its late reduction in interest rates and weak fiscal stimulus, relative to other countries

Potential Output, the Output Gap, and Total Factor Productivity

We now present estimates of potential output, the output gap, and TFP, measures on which we will base our analysis of the global crisis's effects on Mexico's medium-term economic prospects.

We first estimated Mexico's potential output using quarterly data from 1989 to 2009. A problem with this estimation, however, is that in 2009 Mexico was already facing a severe economic contraction. Given that standard estimates of potential output use backward-looking information, this could complicate the precise identification of potential output, particularly at the end of the sample.[6] For this reason, in addition to the most common approach to the estimation of the potential output (the Hodrick-Prescott filter), we used two alternative methods that correct the estimation at the end of the sample: the St. Amant–Van Norden and the Christiano-Fitzgerald approaches (box 8.1).

Box 8.1 also shows the results for potential GDP using the three approaches. Figure 8.6 shows the output gaps implicit in the application of each of these methodologies. As can be seen, they all produce relatively similar results. The first three shaded areas correspond to the recession periods, as defined in Acevedo (2009), and the last one represents the recent crisis using the same criteria.

Total Factor Productivity

We first provide a summary description of the evolution of output per worker, capital stock per worker, and TFP[7] in Mexico during different subperiods (table 8A.3 and figure 8.7). In general, these results are in line with previous findings reported in, for example, Faal (2005) and García-Verdú (2007)—that is, TFP and output per worker grew rapidly between 1950 and 1981, and then began a steady decline that reached a trough during the crisis of 1995. Since then, these variables, together

Figure 8.6. Output Gaps, 1989–2009

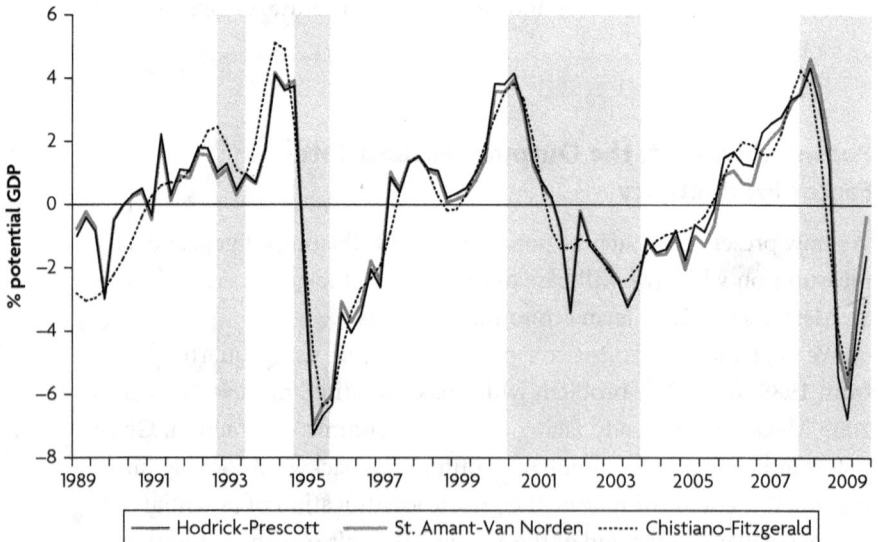

Source: Author's estimates.
Note: Shaded areas indicate recession periods.

Box 8.1. Estimating Potential Output

The level of potential output is commonly defined as the level that could be produced if the economy were at full employment or at the natural rate of unemployment. In practice, potential output is usually estimated using a statistical filter and the output gap is the percentage deviation of observed output relative to its potential level. In particular, the Hodrick-Prescott (1997) filter (HP, hereafter) is commonly used to obtain the output trend at a given point in time, using past and future observations. However, where future observations are scarce, the HP filter will often fail to measure the cyclical component of output. This problem is particularly relevant at the end of the sample, which is usually the most relevant point from a policy making perspective, since it will give an indication of the level of the current output gap. In the literature, at least two alternatives have been offered: the St. Amant–Van Norden (1997) filter and the Christiano-Fitzgerald (2003) filter. These two methods have been reported as being superior to the HP methodology in correcting the end-of-sample problem (see, for example, Anton 2010).

The Hodrick-Prescott (HP) Filter
If y_t denotes the logarithm of real GDP, the HP filter decomposes the time series into a cyclical component y_t^c and a trend y_t^*. Obtaining the HP trend involves minimizing the objective function

$$\sum_{t=1}^{T} (y_t - y_t^*)^2 + \lambda \sum_{t=2}^{T-1} [(y_{t+1}^* - y_t^*) - (y_t^* - y_{t-1}^*)]^2,$$

where the parameter λ defines the smoothness of the trend. That is, the larger the value of λ, the smoother the trend component. It is obvious that if $\lambda = 0$, the trend will simply equal the original series. However, as λ approaches infinity, the trend corresponds to a straight line. For quarterly data, the conventional value for λ is 1,600.

The St. Amant–Van Norden (SAVN) Filter
The SAVN filter is an extension of the HP filter. This method consists of including an additional term to the minimization problem:

$$\sum_{t=1}^{T} (y_t - y_t^*)^2 + \lambda \sum_{t=2}^{T-1} [(y_{t+1}^* - y_t^*) - (y_t^* - y_{t-1}^*)]^2 + \lambda_{ss} \sum_{t=T-j}^{T} (\Delta y^* - u_{ss})$$

The new term penalizes the deviation of the trend growth relative to the long-run output growth rate at the end of the sample. There are two new parameters in the minimization problem: the long-run growth rate of the series u_{ss} (which is a constant determined by the researcher) and the penalty parameter λ_{ss}, which smoothes the trend in the last j observations of the sample.

The Christiano-Fitzgerald (CF) Filter
Christiano and Fitzgerald (2003) proposed a method based on a band-pass filtering for recovering the trend of a time series with periodicity between a lower (p_l) and an upper bound (p_u). This filter requires an infinite amount of data to derive an optimal trend. Hence, the proposed filter is a linear approximation of the optimal filter. To decompose the original series it is assumed that the data are generated by a random walk (this assumption is likely false in many cases), and the following expression is estimated:

$$y_t^* = B_0 y_t + B_1 y_{t+1} + \dots + B_{T-1-t} y_{T-1} + \tilde{B}_{T-t} y_T + \dots B_{t-2} y_2 + \tilde{B}_{t-1} y_1$$

(continued)

Box 8.1 *(continued)*

where coefficients B_t are weights that are variable over time and are functions of the p_l and p_u values.

It is clear that the CF filter is also exposed to the end-of-sample problem, but even so it has been reported that the CF estimation of the output gap performs better than the HP methodology (Anton 2010; Christiano and Fitzgerald 2003).

Results

The results of applying the previously described methodologies to the Mexican case for the period from 1989 to 2009 using quarterly data are shown in the accompanying graph.

Figure B8.1.1. Mexico's GDP: Observed and Potential

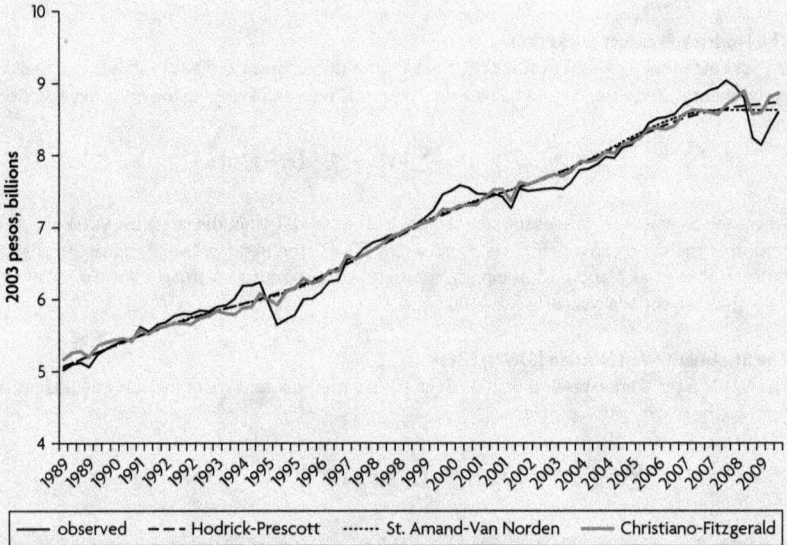

Source: INEGI; author's estimates.

with the capital stock per worker, began to recover, and all simultaneously reached a peak in 2007. In 2009, output per worker and TFP fell again by a similar magnitude as during the crisis of 1995.

Medium-Term Perspectives

We now describe our medium-term perspectives (tables 8A.7 and 8A.8), which assume no important structural reforms in Mexico in the next few

Figure 8.7. Output, Capital, and TFP, 1950–2009

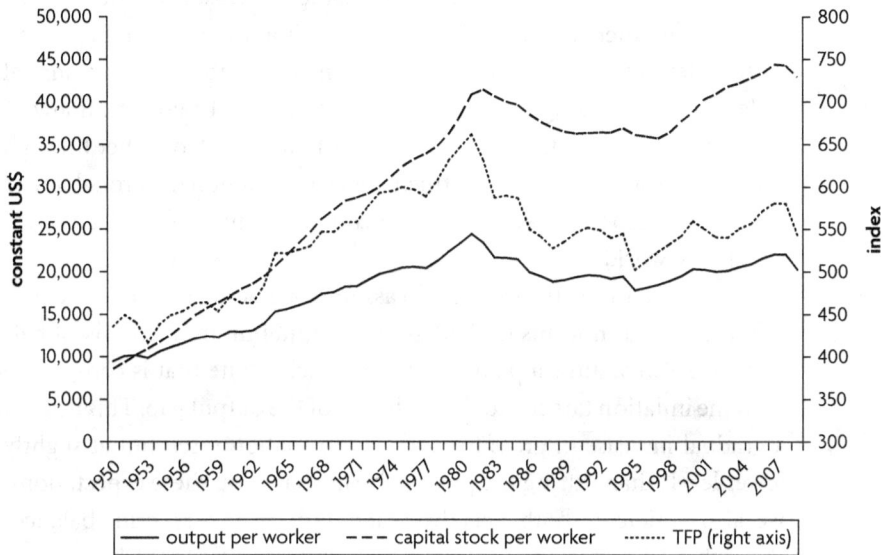

Source: World Bank data; author's estimates.

years or, in the event that some are approved, that they will have effects only over the longer run. We also assume that Mexico's GDP will be demand determined until the current output gap is fully closed and that it will be supply determined thereafter. Note that TFP growth in table 8A.8 is the trend TFP growth and not the one that we expect to observe, which is presumably higher.

The 2010–15 scenario was built using estimates for external trade, commodity prices, remittances, inflation, interest rates, and high-income countries' GDP growth (as provided by World Bank staff). These estimates, however, were in some cases adjusted based on our expectation of the evolution of some domestic variables in order to ensure macroeconomic consistency. For example, our GDP forecast for Mexico is slightly less optimistic in the short run and more optimistic in the medium run relative to the global scenario provided by World Bank staff. In this sense, our forecast for Mexican GDP growth during 2010–12 is slightly lower than the consensus, and also lower than the IMF forecast for two reasons: first, because it considers a stronger effect of the anticipated sluggish growth of the U.S. economy on Mexico; and, second, because it assumes a scenario where the Banco de México either increases the interest rate earlier than other central banks or allows an important real appreciation of the Mexican currency in order to reach (or approximate) its annual inflation target throughout the period (3 percent ± 1 percent). If any of these events occurs, demand will be lower than expected, either through the effects of a decrease in investment and consumption or through lower net exports associated with the loss of competitiveness of Mexican products in the world market.

In general, the 2010–15 scenario assumes a gradual return to the precrisis situation in terms of TFP growth, capital inflows, and fiscal balance. We also assume a path for the real interest rate that is compatible with the inflation target and the evolution of the output gap. This implies a gradual increase in gross fixed capital formation rates, but at slightly lower levels than during the precrisis years. Based on these expectations, we also anticipate both negative trade and current account balances throughout the period. Given the size of these deficits, and given our expectations on the evolution of capital inflows, we also anticipate a steady accumulation of foreign exchange reserves at a rate similar to that of the precrisis period. Finally, we also forecast moderate increases in both public and private consumption. Public consumption is expected to grow at rates lower than GDP to compensate for the deficits associated with the crisis years and to incorporate the expected reduction in oil revenues. Private consumption, on the other hand, is expected to grow at higher rates than GDP.

On the supply side, we anticipate a return to precrisis TFP growth rates, in part fueled by the continued accumulation of human capital (which is not disaggregated in our estimates of table 8A.3, and which may therefore be accounted for as an increase in TFP). Also, note that the expected path for TFP in Mexico during the crisis aftermath is similar to that in the postcrisis of 1994–95. In this sense, we expect Mexico's TFP to return to its 2007 level by 2014.

With all these projections at hand, we developed a forecast for Mexico's GDP from 2010 to 2015. In so doing, we have assumed that GDP will be demand determined while the ouptut gap is negative and will be supply determined afterward. (The expected path of GDP growth is depicted in figure 8.8, and specific year growth forecasts are shown in

Figure 8.8. Mexico's GDP: Observed, Potential, and Forecasts

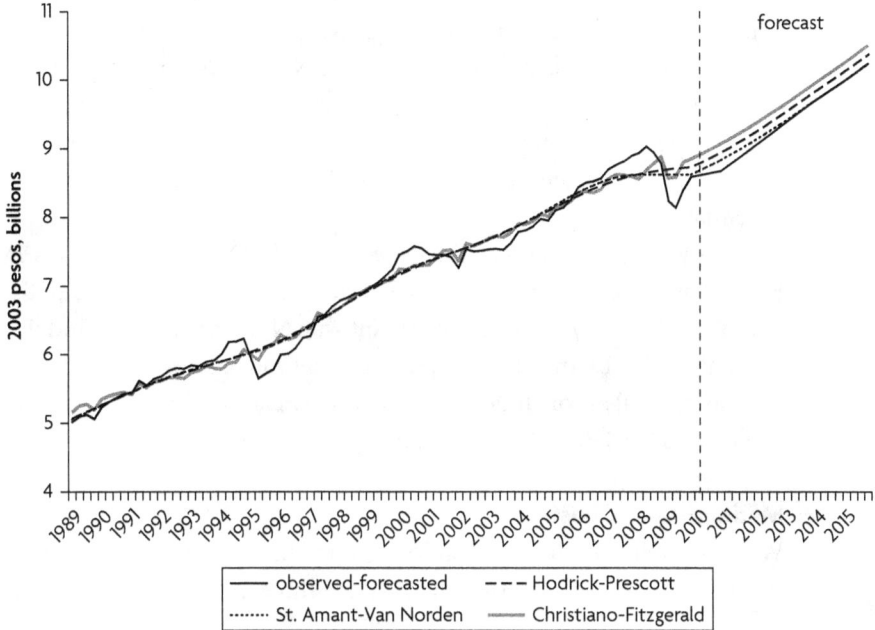

Source: Author's estimates.

table 8A.7.) Figure 8.8 also shows the projected potential GDP lines that are consistent with our supply-side forecasts and using our three alternative estimates of potential output described above.

The most remarkable characteristic of this projection is the downward shift in the evolution of both potential and projected output. This forecast is somehow consistent with the key stylized facts in IMF (2009d), and also with results described in IMF (2010). According to the former, after a crisis GDP does not return to its precrisis trend, although medium-term growth rates do tend to do so eventually. In the case of Mexico, medium-term potential output growth is projected to return to a 3 percent annual rate, which is precisely the growth rate projected to occur once the transition ends. Even though we assume a return to precrisis TFP growth rates, the expected postcrisis medium-term GDP growth rate (3.0 percent from 2014 on) is lower than those observed in the precrisis period (3.3 percent). Interestingly, the projected GDP growth path for Mexico will not reach its potential level in two of our estimates of potential output: the Hodrick-Prescott and the Christiano-Fitzgerald estimates. Mexico's projected GDP reaches its potential level only in the St. Amant–Van Norden estimates, which, as described earlier, correct the estimation at the end of the sample and could therefore be more appropriate in the current context. For this reason, we prefer the St. Amant–Van Norden estimates for Mexico's potential GDP.

Finally, figure 8.9 shows the expected evolution of output gaps in Mexico over the medium term. As described earlier, the output gap disappears only when we use the St. Amant–van Norden estimates, and this will only occur by the end of 2013. Using all the previously mentioned estimates, we also conclude that Mexico's per capita GDP will return to its precrisis level only by late 2013 or early 2014.

Medium-Term Constraints

We expect relatively low GDP growth for the Mexican economy over the medium term, because Mexico will face three major obstacles to its

Figure 8.9. Output Gaps, 1989–2015

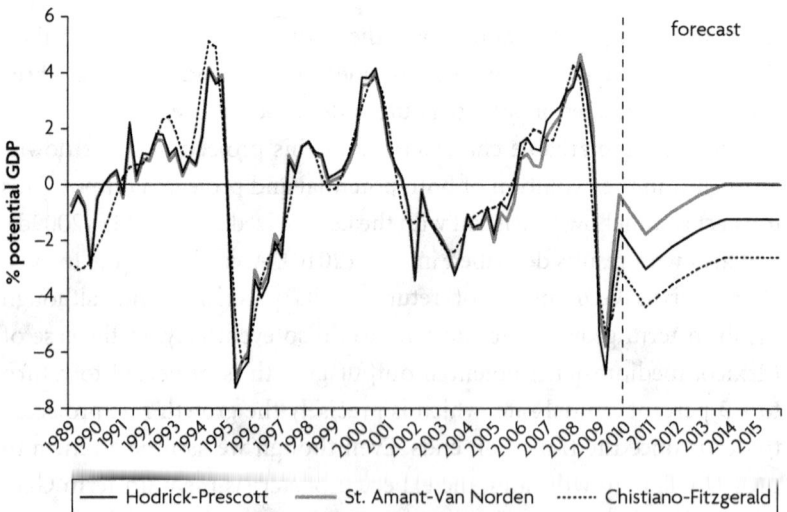

Source: Author's estimates.

resumption of strong and sustained economic growth. These obstacles are in the external, fiscal, and financial sectors.

External Sector. Mexico remains (and will probably continue to remain) strongly linked to the U.S. economy. The country's medium-term prospects thus depend heavily on the strength of the U.S. recovery. But given the significant loss of wealth suffered by an important segment of American consumers, and given the sizable U.S. external imbalances— which the national authorities will have to adjust sooner rather than later—the recovery of the U.S. economy is expected to be rather weak in the short and medium term (Blanchard 2009).

This scenario is obviously unfavorable for Mexico's economy since the U.S. market is by far the most important one for Mexican exports. In fact, since the passage of NAFTA, and despite having signed numerous free trade agreements with other countries and regions, Mexico has achieved little in terms of diversifying its export markets. This is partly because of its relatively poor infrastructure, but also because of its high logistical costs (e.g., transport, freight, and customs). Therefore, unless Mexico is able to gain access to other export markets, its medium-term growth prospects will be limited by the United States' ability to fully recover its growth capacity. Even if this happens, the United States' ability to pull the Mexican economy up could be diminished if the continuing large global trade and investment imbalances force a global realignment of exchange rates.

Fiscal Policy. The dramatic reduction in the price of Mexican oil (from US$140 a barrel in 2008 to an average of US$60 in late 2009) has definitely taken a toll on the country's public finances. Government expenditures, whose extraordinary increase in the early 2000s was fully financed with rising oil revenues, can no longer be sustained. This is because of the lower price of oil and the steady decline in Mexico's oil production since 2004—which, in turn, is at least partly the result of the lack of sufficient investment in the sector.

As a result, Mexico will inevitably need to go through a painful adjustment process that may take the form of either higher tax rates or lower government spending, or a combination of the two. It has become clear that current levels of government expenditures are incompatible with current tax revenues, which are among the lowest in the world (less than 9 percent of GDP).

Financial Sector. The financial (and especially the banking) sector may also be a drag on Mexico's medium-term economic prospects.[8] The banking sector's lending to the private sector, as a share of GDP, declined systematically from 1995 to 2004, and then expanded until 2007. Credit has begun to contract again since mid-2009, and it is expected to continue to do so at least throughout 2010.

The recent contraction seems to be, however, related more to specific domestic factors than to the international financial crunch.[9] This is because the credit expansion that started in 2002 concentrated on the most profitable of all credits, consumption credit, which increased five-fold between 2002 and 2008. But after years of focusing on this market and extracting huge rents,[10] the banking sector started to extend credit to riskier (or subprime) consumers, which, together with the weakening economic activity in the country, explains the substantial increases in defaults on this type of credit. This could explain why consumption credit in real terms began contracting in early 2008, well before commercial and total credit also began to decline.

The rapid increase in defaults on consumption and mortgage credits has had two different but related implications for the evolution of banking credit to the private sector. On the one hand, the rise in defaults by itself leads to more cautious behavior by banks at the moment of extending the credit, which in turns implies fewer loans to the private sector. On the other hand, since banks need to increase their reserves to prepare for defaults, they have substantially less in the way of resources available for loans. In this sense, the past practices of banking credit, together with the consequences of such behavior, will probably reduce the sector's ability to channel resources to foster economic activity for a couple of years. If we add to this the lack of international liquidity, we develop a very negative picture of the domestic financial sector, which explains the severity of the current credit crunch in the Mexican economy.

Perspectives on Poverty

The dismal performance of Mexico's economy in 2009 will surely lead to a sharp rise in poverty in the years to come. This rise in poverty comes on top of the increase that took place between 2006 and 2008, spurred by the rapid increase in food prices. That poverty uptick left almost half of Mexicans living in poverty conditions (assets-based poverty, as defined by the Mexican government) and almost one-fifth of the population living in an extreme poverty conditions (food-based poverty).

How much will poverty increase as a result of the global crisis and the output contraction in Mexico? We do not know for sure, but we can offer an educated guess based on previous experience and on the apparent relationship between per capita GDP growth and changes in poverty rates (that is, the unconditional output-poverty semi-elasticity). Figure 8.10 depicts the changes in the three official definitions of poverty rates and on per capita GDP growth in Mexico for the nine periods since 1992 for which we have data.[11]

Figure 8.10 also shows the fitted line for one of these poverty rates, as well as the estimated equation and its corresponding R-squared. The other two fitted lines are basically the same and are not shown for simplicity. The estimated equation suggests a negative relationship

Figure 8.10. Per Capita GDP Growth and Changes in Poverty Rates, 1992–2008

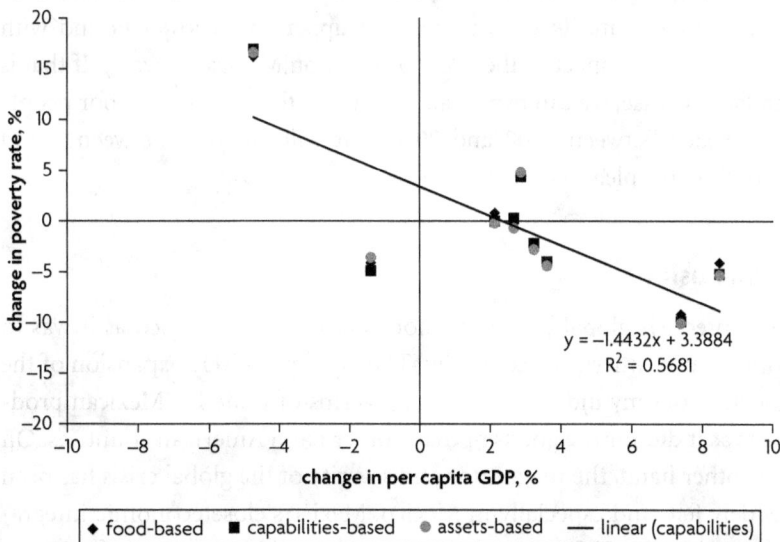

$$y = -1.4432x + 3.3884$$
$$R^2 = 0.5681$$

♦ food-based   ■ capabilities-based   ● assets-based   — linear (capabilities)

Source: INEGI; Consejo Nacional de Evaluación de la Política de Desarrollo Social (CONEVAL).

between these two variables (as expected), with a semi-elasticity greater than 1 in absolute terms. This estimate suggests that if Mexico's per capita GDP contracts by about 4 percent during 2008–10, poverty rates in Mexico could rise by almost 8 percentage points in the absence of policy responses.

Although such an increase in poverty seems too high, an impact of this magnitude cannot be completely ruled out since an even larger increase actually occurred during the crisis of 1994–95. Therefore, if this dismal scenario materializes, almost 60 percent of Mexico's population would be deemed to be poor, and almost one-fourth extremely poor. This scenario would thus be similar to the post-1994–95 period, and as was the case back then, it could take several years before poverty rates return to their precrisis levels. The pace of this recovery would critically depend on Mexico's economic growth rate.

Most probably, however, poverty in Mexico will not increase by as much as it did in 1994, since there are now mechanisms in place that could help mitigate the negative impact of the crisis on the poorest families and there has been a partial reversal of the sharp increase in food prices that occurred in 2008. In fact, some recent microsimulations by Habib and others (2010) suggest that poverty in Mexico may increase by only about 4 percentage points as a result of the crisis. In the end, these two estimates are likely to provide an upper and a lower bound with respect to the impact of the 2008–09 crisis on Mexican poverty. If that is in fact the case, we can expect an increase in the number of poor people in Mexico between 2008 and 2010 that will fluctuate between 4 and 8 million people.

Conclusions

The precrisis global boom was not as favorable to Mexico as it was to other Latin American economies. The rapid post-2002 expansion of the world economy did not improve the terms of trade for Mexican products as it did for the goods of many other Latin American countries. On the other hand, the magnitude and severity of the global crisis has been widely felt, and especially in Mexico. Mexico's close economic integration with the U.S. economy suggested a wide range of effects—or multiple channels of transmission—of the global crisis. Therefore, it is no surprise that Mexico was one of the countries in the world most affected by the crisis.

In addition, two other factors have hurt the Mexican economy during the crisis:

- Some of the government's fiscal and monetary policy responses were slow, timid, and clearly insufficient to cope with the magnitude of the external shock.
- The government's precrisis policy decisions barely helped improve Mexico's medium-term economic growth prospects, but they increased the economy's vulnerability to an external shock. This is because the government's policy decisions relied extensively on oil revenues to finance additional public sector spending and because Mexico has failed to diversify its export markets, which continued to be heavily concentrated on the United States.

As to growth prospects, we have cited three main obstacles that will limit the ability of Mexico's economy to grow over the medium term:

- The recovery of the U.S. economy, which could be relatively slow in the next few years
- A large fiscal imbalance that needs to be addressed relatively soon and that will imply either higher taxes or lower government expenditures
- A foreseeable contraction in banking credit to the private sector

These three factors may limit Mexico's ability to grow over the medium term and would be additional to the structural weaknesses that have already limited Mexico's economic growth during the past three decades.

Finally, we discussed the perspectives on poverty and growth in Mexico. Our conclusion is that poverty will probably soar as a result of the crisis and that it will take a relatively long time to return to the precrisis levels in terms of both poverty and income. We therefore see a need for the Mexican authorities to adopt measures to confront the short-run problems of poverty, unemployment, and low income levels, but, at the same time, to implement deeper reforms in a wide range of areas (education, building of a social safety net, infrastructure investments, and so on) in order to transform the Mexican economy and improve its medium- and long-term prospects.

Annex

Table 8A.1 Basic Macroeconomic Indicators

	1994	1995	1996	1997	1998	1999	2000	2001	2002	2003	2004	2005	2006	2007	2008
Gross domestic product															
GDP (current US$ bn)	421.7	286.7	332.9	401.5	421.2	481.2	581.4	622.1	649.1	700.3	759.4	847.0	948.9	1,022.8	1,086.0
GDP (constant US$ bn)	475.4	445.9	468.8	500.5	525.1	545.4	581.4	580.5	585.3	593.2	617.0	636.8	667.4	688.8	701.0
GDP (constant, LCU bn)	6,055.2	5,678.7	5,970.5	6,375.1	6,687.9	6,946.9	7,405.6	7,393.9	7,455.0	7,555.8	7,858.9	8,110.4	8,500.9	8,773.2	8,904.8
GDP per capita (current US$)	4,709.6	3,145.5	3,596.3	4,274.4	4,422.2	4,982.2	5,935.0	6,284.1	6,490.6	6,932.5	7,441.7	8,216.1	9,104.3	9,715.1	10,211.1
GDP per capita, PPP (current int'l $)	7,332.5	6,894.7	7,273.2	7,780.1	8,138.8	8,454.8	9,189.6	9,303.3	9,563.0	10,970.1	11,638.0	12,563.5	13,444.6	14,104.4	14,495.3
GDP per capita (constant US$)	5,309.1	4,891.6	5,063.8	5,328.9	5,512.6	5,647.1	5,935.0	5,864.1	5,853.0	5,872.3	6,046.3	6,176.9	6,404.0	6,542.6	6,591.5
GDP per capita, PPP (constant 2005 int'l $)	10,798.4	9,949.3	10,299.5	10,838.7	11,212.3	11,485.8	12,071.5	11,927.3	11,904.7	11,943.9	12,297.9	12,563.5	13,025.3	13,307.3	13,406.7
Population growth (% per year)	1.8	1.8	1.6	1.5	1.4	1.4	1.4	1.0	1.0	1.0	1.0	1.0	1.1	1.0	1.0

Growth

Total GDP growth (constant LCU)	4.5	-6.2	5.1	6.8	4.9	3.9	6.6	-0.2	0.8	1.4	4.0	3.2	4.8	3.2	1.5
GDP growth by sector (% per year)															
Agriculture	0.9	0.9	3.6	0.2	0.8	3.6	0.6	3.5	0.1	3.1	2.9	-0.7	3.9	2.1	3.1
Industry	4.8	-7.8	10.1	9.3	6.3	4.7	6.1	-3.5	-0.1	-0.2	3.7	2.6	5.3	1.9	0.5
Services	4.7	-6.2	3.3	6.4	4.7	3.6	7.4	1.0	1.3	1.8	4.2	3.8	4.6	3.9	2.3
GDP growth by demand component (% per year)															
Private consumption (% per year)	4.6	-9.5	2.2	6.5	21.2	4.4	7.4	1.9	1.4	2.1	5.6	4.8	5.6	4.2	1.9
Gross fixed capital formation (% per year)	8.4	-29.0	16.4	21.0	10.3	7.7	11.4	-5.6	-0.6	0.4	8.0	6.5	9.6	5.6	4.4
Share of GDP (%)															
Private consumption	71.4	66.9	65.1	64.2	67.4	67.0	67.0	69.6	69.0	66.7	66.4	66.9	65.2	65.4	65.5
Gross fixed capital formation	19.3	16.1	17.8	19.5	20.9	21.2	21.4	20.0	19.2	18.9	19.7	20.0	20.7	20.8	22.1
Gross domestic savings	17.1	22.6	25.3	25.9	22.2	22.0	21.9	18.6	18.8	21.4	22.9	22.3	24.3	24.4	24.2

(continued)

Table 8A.1 (continued)

	1994	1995	1996	1997	1998	1999	2000	2001	2002	2003	2004	2005	2006	2007	2008
External sector															
Trade balance (US$ bn)	-21.2	7.2	6.4	-0.8	-9.2	-8.4	-11.9	-14.1	-12.6	-11.3	-14.5	-12.9	-12.6	-16.5	-23.9
Current account balance (US$ bn)	-29.7	-1.6	-2.5	-7.7	-16.0	-14.0	-18.7	-17.7	-14.1	-7.2	-5.2	-4.4	-4.4	-8.2	-16.0
Foreign direct investment (US$ bn)	11.0	9.5	9.2	12.8	12.7	13.8	18.0	25.4	22.8	15.2	19.2	15.3	13.4	18.9	18.2
International reserves (US$ bn)	6.4	17.1	19.5	28.9	31.9	31.8	35.6	44.8	50.7	59.0	64.2	74.1	76.3	87.2	95.3
In months of imports	0.7	2.1	2.0	2.5	2.5	2.2	2.0	2.6	3.0	3.5	3.3	3.4	3.0	3.2	3.2
External debt (US$ bn)	138.6	165.4	156.3	147.7	159.2	166.7	150.9	163.9	164.5	170.9	171.2	167.9	162.5	192.3	204.0
External debt to exports (%)	194.6	185.2	146.4	121.5	123.2	112.6	83.9	95.6	94.7	96.3	84.7	72.9	61.0	66.4	65.8
Debt service (US$ bn)	20.1	26.1	40.4	41.8	29.2	35.3	58.5	47.4	43.8	42.2	50.5	45.1	56.1	39.9	41.3
Debt service of PPG-EL (US$ bn)	11.7	15.4	26.6	28.0	17.4	15.9	24.1	24.2	19.0	21.9	24.5	22.4	38.0	20.0	19.6

Debt service to exports (%)	28.2	29.2	37.9	34.3	22.6	23.9	32.5	27.6	25.2	23.8	25.0	19.6	21.1	13.8	13.3
Debt service of PPG-ED to exports (%)	16.4	17.2	25.0	23.1	13.5	10.7	13.4	14.1	10.9	12.4	12.1	9.7	14.3	6.9	6.3
Nominal exchange rate (average)	3.4	6.4	7.6	7.9	9.1	9.6	9.5	9.3	9.7	10.8	11.3	10.9	10.9	10.9	11.1
Nominal exchage rate (eop)	5.0	7.7	7.9	8.1	9.9	9.5	9.6	9.2	10.4	11.2	11.2	10.6	10.8	10.9	13.8
Real effective exch. rate (1990 = 100, eop)	87.8	119.4	96.2	81.4	88.0	73.7	65.1	59.8	64.9	77.2	78.4	69.1	73.1	76.8	87.7
Public sector (PS)															
PS primary balance (% GDP)	2.1	4.7	4.3	3.5	1.7	2.5	2.6	2.6	1.7	1.9	2.2	2.2	2.5	2.2	1.8
PS overall balance (% GDP)	-0.3	-0.2	-0.1	-0.6	-1.2	-1.1	-1.1	-0.7	-1.2	-0.6	-0.2	-0.1	0.1	0	-0.1
Net PS debt (% GDP)	21.1	30.3	26.8	20.8	21.4	20.7	18.9	19.4	20.7	19.0	18.7	17.0	15.9	15.9	14.9

(continued)

Table 8A.1. *(continued)*

	1994	1995	1996	1997	1998	1999	2000	2001	2002	2003	2004	2005	2006	2007	2008
Net augmented PS debt (% GDP)	—	—	—	—	—	—	—	—	—	—	36.8	35.2	32.4	31.4	35.8
Economic activity															
Unemployment (%)	4.2	6.9	5.2	4.1	3.6	2.5	2.6	2.5	2.9	3.0	3.7	3.5	3.2	3.4	—

Sources: World Bank; Banco de México.

Notes: bn = billions; eop = end of period; LCU = local currency units; PPP = purchasing power parity; PPG-ED = public and publicly guaranteed external debt; — = not available.

Table 8A.2. Decomposition of GDP Growth (Contribution to GDP Growth)

	1994	1995	1996	1997	1998	1999	2000	2001	2002	2003	2004	2005	2006	2007	2008
Total GDP growth rate (%)	4.46	−6.22	5.14	6.78	4.91	3.87	6.60	−0.16	0.83	1.35	4.01	3.20	4.81	3.20	1.50
Total GDP expenditures	100	100	100	100	100	100	100	100	100	100	100	100	100	100	100
Final consumption	**82.88**	**58.43**	**67.58**	**71.89**	**95.14**	**79.40**	**78.53**	**137.91**	**78.59**	**65.99**	**64.82**	**82.51**	**58.74**	**79.51**	**78.08**
Private consumption	67.57	51.76	60.08	60.97	82.39	65.24	66.69	115.38	61.80	55.59	62.15	71.02	51.06	72.15	66.77
Government consumption	15.31	6.67	7.50	10.92	12.75	14.16	11.83	22.53	16.79	10.40	2.67	11.49	7.68	7.35	11.31
Investment	**28.61**	**13.40**	**31.96**	**36.65**	**16.54**	**19.66**	**25.39**	**−31.83**	**18.15**	**33.74**	**37.91**	**12.20**	**40.82**	**30.36**	**30.99**
Gross fixed capital formation	24.93	5.24	22.39	25.94	27.58	22.57	22.35	−3.93	9.65	17.46	25.43	24.38	26.38	21.46	38.12
Increase in stocks	3.68	8.17	9.57	10.70	−11.03	−2.91	3.05	−27.90	8.49	16.28	12.48	−12.18	14.45	8.90	−7.13
Net exports	**−11.49**	**28.16**	**0.45**	**−8.54**	**−11.69**	**0.94**	**−3.92**	**−6.08**	**3.26**	**0.27**	**−4.06**	**2.63**	**0.08**	**−5.68**	**−9.07**
Export	28.37	76.69	36.65	23.22	32.73	30.96	31.97	−31.61	17.43	18.21	36.02	34.26	35.70	31.14	27.85
Import	39.86	48.52	36.20	31.76	44.41	30.02	35.89	−25.53	14.17	17.95	40.08	31.63	35.62	36.82	36.92

Source: INEGI; World Bank.

Table 8A.3. Growth Factor Decomposition
(annual average growth rates, %)

Period	Ouput per worker	Capital per worker	Total factor productivity
1950–81	3.11	5.17	1.36
1981–95	−2.24	−0.88	−1.95
1995–2007	1.80	1.73	1.21
1995–2002	1.67	1.81	1.05
2002–07	1.98	1.63	1.43

Source: World Bank; author's estimates.

Table 8A.4. Domestic and International Financial Intermediation

	1994	1995	1996	1997	1998	1999	2000	2001	2002	2003	2004	2005	2006	2007	2008
Money supply (LCUs, billions)	145.1	148.5	206.1	267.2	323.9	407.6	465.5	526.3	600.8	684.7	743.2	865.9	988.5	1,125.2	1,250.3
Annual growth M1 (%)	0.8	2.4	38.7	29.7	21.2	25.8	14.2	13.1	14.2	14.0	8.6	16.5	14.2	13.8	11.1
Interest rate (observed and target, 2008)	15.5	45.1	30.7	19.1	31.8	20.7	15.3	11.1	7.0	5.9	6.6	9.0	7.1	7.1	7.9
Credit market															
Net domestic credit growth (% per year)	35.0	30.8	3.6	78.4	15.1	14.2	4.2	5.2	10.3	3.8	2.4	3.9	15.4	11.1	4.1
Domestic credit by banking sector (% GDP)	49.0	49.6	37.4	42.1	39.0	36.3	34.1	33.1	36.5	33.2	31.8	32.1	34.8	37.7	37.5
Credit to the private sector (% GDP)	38.7	29.2	18.8	26.5	23.7	20.4	18.3	15.7	17.7	16.0	15.2	16.6	19.6	22.0	21.1
Headline lending interest rate	19.3	59.4	36.4	22.1	26.4	23.7	16.9	12.8	8.2	7.0	7.4	9.7	7.5	7.6	8.7
Capital markets															
Market capitalization (% GDP)	30.8	31.6	32.0	39.0	21.8	32.0	21.5	20.3	15.9	17.5	22.6	28.2	36.7	38.9	21.4
Inflation (% per year)	7.0	35.0	34.4	20.6	15.9	16.6	9.5	6.4	5.0	4.5	4.7	4.0	3.6	4.0	5.1
Consumer price index (2005 = 100)	24.3	32.8	44.1	53.1	61.6	71.8	78.6	83.7	87.9	91.9	96.2	100.0	103.6	107.7	113.3
Wholesale price index (2005 = 100)	23.7	32.9	44.1	51.8	60.1	68.6	74.0	77.7	81.7	87.8	96.0	100.0	106.6	110.5	117.7
Total capital inflows (net, % GDP)	4.6	−0.1	6.8	4.4	3.2	5.4	2.9	4.6	3.3	2.7	3.2	2.8	1.5	3.2	2.5
FDI (net, % GDP)	2.6	3.3	2.8	3.2	3.0	2.9	3.1	4.1	3.5	2.2	2.6	1.9	1.5	1.9	2.0
Portfolio (net, % GDP)	2.0	−3.4	4.0	1.2	0.2	2.5	−0.2	0.6	−0.2	0.5	0.7	0.9	0.0	1.3	0.4

Source: World Bank; IMF.

393

Table 8A.5. External Trade

	1994	1995	1996	1997	1998	1999	2000	2001	2002	2003	2004	2005	2006	2007	2008
Total exports of goods and services (% GDP)	16.79	30.36	32.08	30.27	30.69	30.74	30.94	27.56	26.82	25.35	26.62	27.16	28.08	28.31	28.27
Merchandise exports (current US$ bn)	60.88	79.54	96.00	110.43	117.46	136.39	166.37	158.55	160.68	165.40	187.98	214.21	249.96	271.82	291.81
Manufactured exports (current US$ bn)	47.11	61.64	74.97	89.14	100.00	116.10	138.80	134.95	135.00	134.67	150.14	165.02	189.15	194.95	215.90
Services exports (current US$ bn)	10.32	9.78	10.72	11.18	11.66	11.73	13.76	12.70	12.74	12.62	14.05	16.14	16.39	17.61	18.64
Total imports of goods and services (% GDP)	21.60	27.70	30.02	30.37	32.81	32.36	32.93	29.77	28.64	26.82	28.39	28.62	29.37	29.93	30.47
Merchandise imports (current US$ bn)	83.08	75.86	93.67	114.85	130.95	146.08	182.70	176.19	176.61	178.50	206.06	232.25	268.09	295.20	323.15
Manufactured imports (current US$ bn)	62.53	60.80	78.44	95.93	110.73	125.97	156.95	153.18	151.76	153.13	174.82	193.99	221.53	225.35	252.10
Services exports (current US$ bn)	13.04	9.72	10.82	12.61	13.01	14.47	17.36	17.19	17.66	18.14	19.78	21.44	22.83	24.06	25.32
Remittances (current US$ bn)	3.47	3.67	4.22	4.86	5.63	5.91	6.57	8.90	9.81	15.04	18.33	21.69	25.57	26.07	25.14
Terms of trade (index 2000 = 100)	95.92	92.45	96.12	97.06	94.00	95.00	100.00	97.43	97.88	98.91	101.61	103.60	104.04	104.59	105.95

Source: World Bank; Banco de México.

Table 8A.6. Summary Impact of the Crisis

	1997–2002	2003–07	Change from 1997–2002 to 2003–07	Highest 2-year average value before crisis	Expected potential value (prior to the crisis)	2008	2009	Total loss during 2008–09 compared to potential (% GDP)
GDP annual growth (%)	3.2	3.3	0.1	5.8 (1997–98)	3.0	1.5	-6.5	11
TFP annual growth (%)	0.6	1.4	0.8	2.5 (1999–00)	1.2	0	-6.2	8.8
Exports annual growth, US$ (%)	7.8	11.1	3.3	19.0 (1999–00)	10.0	7.4	-22.2	n.a.
Exports/GDP (%)	29.5	27.1	-2.4	30.8 (1999–00)	28.5	28.3	27.8	0.9
Investment (% GDP)	23.2	24.6	1.4	25.8 (2006–07)	25.0	26.4	22.3	1.3
Output gap 1 (%)	0.7	-0.1	-0.8	2.9 (2007–08)	0.4	3.1	-4.4	n.a.
Output gap 2 (%)	0.7	-0.4	-1.0	2.9 (2007–08)	0.2	3.5	-3.3	n.a.
Output gap 3 (%)	0.6	0.0	-0.6	2.2 (2007–08)	0.3	2.2	-4.3	n.a.
Capital inflows (% GDP)	4.0	2.7	-1.3	4.3 (1998–99)	3.3	2.5	2.2	1.9
Fiscal deficit (% GDP)	-1.0	-0.2	0.8	0 (2006–07)	0	-0.1	-2.3	n.a.

Source: Author's estimates.
Note: n.a. = not applicable.

Table 8A.7. Demand-Side Growth Projections
(annual average growth rates, %)

	2003–2007	2008	2009	2010f	2011f	2012f	2013f	2014f	2012–15f
GDP	3.3	1.5	-6.5	3.6	3.4	3.4	3.2	3.1	3.2
Gross fixed capital formation	6.0	4.4	-10.1	3.0	2.4	3.5	4.0	4.0	3.7
Private consumption	4.4	1.9	-6.1	3.8	3.6	3.5	3.0	2.9	3.2
Public consumption	0.6	0.9	2.3	1.7	1.5	1.8	1.4	1.4	1.6
Net exports (negative)	11.6	27.0	-45.4	36.2	18.7	13.1	8.2	8.6	9.7
Export growth	7.5	0.5	-14.8	9.6	3.7	8.9	6.9	4.5	6.6
Import growth	7.9	2.8	-18.2	11.6	5.1	9.3	7.0	4.9	6.8
Memo (as % GDP)									
Current acount balance	-0.7	-1.5	-0.6	-1.1	-1.2	-0.8	-0.8	-0.7	-0.7
Capital inflows	2.7	2.5	2.2	2.2	2.4	2.4	2.6	2.7	2.5
Change in reserve	0.9	0.8	0.6	0.8	0.7	1.0	1.1	1.2	1.1
Fiscal balance	-0.2	-0.1	-1.8	-1.0	-0.7	-0.4	0.0	0.0	-0.1
Augmented public debt	34.0	35.8	38.8	40.2	40.5	41.0	41.3	41.5	41.3

Source: Author's estimates.
Note: f = forecast.

Table 8A.8. Supply-Side Growth Projections
(annual average growth rates, %)

	2003–07	2008	2009	2010f	2011f	2012f	2013f	2014f	2012–15f
GDP	3.3	1.5	−6.5	2.5	2.8	3.0	3.0	3.0	3.0
GDP per worker	2.3	0.0	−8.0	1.3	1.6	1.8	1.9	2.0	1.9
Capital stock per worker	1.5	−0.2	−3.0	−1.0	0.3	1.0	1.1	1.3	1.1
Trend TFP growth	1.8	0.0	−6.2	1.6	1.4	1.5	1.5	1.5	1.5

Source: Author's estimates.
Note: f = forecast.

Notes

1. For a more thorough discussion of these issues, see Haber (2005) and Murillo (2005).
2. The opposite had been done through a unilateral decision of the Mexican government in the mid-1980s.
3. See Esquivel and Hernández Trillo (2009) on the first issue and Lehoucq and others (2005) on the second.
4. See Faal (2005) and García-Verdú (2007) and the references cited therein.
5. See, for example, the study summarized in IMF (2009a).
6. There are several alternative methods. See, for instance, Acevedo (2009) and Faal (2005) for other applications to the Mexican case. We also tried a production function approach, but our estimates were too sensitive to the specification.
7. Our data on TFP are based on the Penn World Tables 6.2 and have been updated to 2007 by staff at the World Bank's Latin America and the Caribbean Region Chief Economist's Office. We have completed these data until 2009 using domestic sources. Owing to data limitations, these estimates do not take into account either capacity utilization or human capital information.
8. At the end of 2008, the banking sector accounted for 60 percent of total domestic credit to the private sector and about 45 percent of total credit (internal and external). More importantly, the banking sector represented almost 75 percent of Mexico's total increase in credit between 2006 and 2008.
9. Of course, this does not mean that the international credit crunch is not playing a role in this trend. Since most of the banks operating in Mexico are now foreign owned, their decisions have a global dimension. Therefore, some banks could have received instructions from their owners to reduce their credit lines in order to boost their overall capital ratios.

10. The average annual real interest rate charged on credit cards, for example, exceeds 30 percent. According to a report by the central bank (Banco de México 2007), this particular segment of the credit market exhibits collusive behavior. For more details, see Esquivel and Hernández-Trillo (2009) and the references cited therein.
11. These periods are 1992–94, 1994–96, 1996–98, 1998–2000, 2000–02, 2002–04, 2004–05, 2005–06, and 2006–08.

References

Acevedo, Ernesto. 2009. "PIB Potencial y Productividad Total de los Factores. Recesiones y Expansiones en México." *Economía Mexicana* XVIII (2): 175–219.

Antón S., Arturo. 2010. "El Problema al Final de la Muestra en la Estimación de la Brecha del Producto." *Economía Mexicana* 19 (1): 5–30.

Banco de México. 2007. *Reporte sobre el Sistema Financiero 2006.* Mexico City.

Barro, R. J., and J. F. Ursúa. 2008. "Macroeconomic Crises since 1870." *Brookings Papers on Economic Activity* (Spring): 255–350.

Blanchard, Olivier J. 2009. "Sustaining a Global Recovery." *Finance and Development* (September): 8–12.

CEPAL (Comisión Económica para América Latina). 2009. *Estudio Económico de América Latina y el Caribe 2008–2009.* Santiago de Chile.

Christiano, Lawrence, and Terry J. Fitzgerald. 2003. "The Band Pass Filter." *International Economic Review* 44 (2): 435–65.

Esquivel, Gerardo, and Fausto Hernández-Trillo. 2009. "How Can Reforms Help Deliver Growth in Mexico?" In *Growing Pains in Latin America*, ed. Liliana Rojas-Suarez, 192–235. Washington, DC: Center for Global Development.

Faal, Ebrima. 2005. "GDP Growth, Potential Output, and Output Gaps in Mexico." Working Paper, International Monetary Fund, Washington, DC.

García-Verdú, Rodrigo. 2007. "Demographics, Human Capital and Economic Growth in Mexico: 1950–2005." Paper prepared for the Conference on Growth in Latin America, organized by the Economic Commission for Latin America and the Caribbean, Santiago, Chile, June.

Haber, Stephen. 2005. "Mexico's Experiments with Bank Privatization and Liberalization, 1991–2003." *Journal of Banking and Finance* 29: 2325–53.

Habib, B., A. Narayan, S. Olivieri, and C. Sánchez-Páramo. 2010. "The Impact of the Financial Crisis on Poverty and Income Distribution: Insights from Simulations in Selected Countries." http://www.voxeu.org/index.php?q=node/4905, accessed April 19, 2010.

Hodrick, Robert J., and Edward C. Prescott. 1997. "Post-war U.S. Business Cycles: An Empirical Investigation." *Journal of Money, Credit and Banking* 29 (1): 1–16.

IMF (International Monetary Fund). 2009a. "Mexico: Selected Issues." Country Report 10/70, International Monetary Fund, Washington, DC.

————. 2009b. "Mexico: Staff Report for the 2008 Article IV Consultation." International Monetary Fund, Washington, DC.

————. 2009c. "Mexico: Staff Report for the 2008 Article IV Consultation. Supplementary Information." International Monetary Fund, Washington, DC.

————. 2009d. "What's the Damage? Medium-Term Output Dynamics after Financial Crisis." In *World Economic Outlook: Sustaining the Recovery* Washington, DC: International Monetary Fund.

————. 2010. "Mexico: Selected Issues." Country Report 09/54, International Monetary Fund, Washington, DC.

Lehoucq, F., G. Negretto, F. Aparicio, B. Nacif, and A. Benton. 2005. "Political Institutions, Policymaking Processes, and Policy Outcomes in Mexico." Working Paper R-512, Inter-American Development Bank, Washington, DC.

Murillo, José Antonio. 2005. "La Banca Después de la Privatización. Auge, Crisis y Reordenamiento" in *Cuando el Estado se Hizo Banquero*, ed. G. del Angel-Mobarak, C. Bazdresch, and F. Suárez. Mexico City: Fondo de Cultura Económica.

OECD (Organisation for Economic Co-operation and Development). 2009. *Economic Outlook Interim Report*. OECD, Paris.

St. Amant, Pierre, and Simon Van Norden. 1997. "Measurement of the Output Gap: A Discussion of the Recent Research at the Bank of Canada." Technical Report 79, Bank of Canada, Ottawa.

Discussant Paper

Comment on "Mexico: Large, Immediate Negative Impact and Weak Medium-Term Growth Prospects"

Edgardo Favaro

The financial crisis originated in the United States in 2008 and was transmitted rapidly to the rest of the world, resulting in slower global economic growth. The crisis caused a sharp fall in the volume of world trade, 14.4 percent, and major disruption in the financial sectors of several high-income economies.

The impact of the crisis among low- and middle-income countries varied. It was less severe among exporters of minerals and agricultural products (e.g., most of Latin America) than among exporters of labor-intensive manufactured products (e.g., most of East Asia); it was more severe among countries with large current account deficits (e.g., most countries in Eastern Europe) than among countries with smaller deficits before 2008 (e.g., Latin America and East Asia). To its credit, Mexico was among the latter group as of 2008.

Edgardo Favaro is Lead Economist, Economic Policy and Debt Department, Poverty Reduction and Economic Management Network, World Bank.

Gerardo Esquivel's paper illustrates the usefulness of this country classification about the impact of the crisis, but also underscores the importance of a thorough grasp of country-specific factors in assessing what happened in Mexico and what is likely to happen in the next five years.

As noted above, Mexico did not have a large current account deficit on the eve of the crisis (the average deficit in 2003–07 was equal to 0.7 percent of GDP). The deficit widened as a result of the fall in oil prices after mid-2008, but not as much as in other Latin American countries; it also widened as a result of the fall in demand for exports from the United States, but the fall as a percentage of the total economy was lower than in most countries in East Asia (the share of exports in Mexican GDP remained fairly constant).

To understand the impact of the crisis on the Mexican economy, it is useful to look at the pattern of economic growth on the eve of the crisis. In 2001–03, per capita GDP fell at an annual rate of 0.3 percent; in 2004–07, it recovered to an annual average of 2.7 percent. What explains the difference between these two periods? A full discussion is beyond the scope of these comments, but the following ingredients must be part of the story: (a) an increase in the rate of growth of exports (from 0.1 percent in 2001–03 to 8.8 percent in 2004–07), (b) a steady increase in gross capital formation as a percentage of GDP, (c) a large increase in the saving rate (from 19.5 percent to 24.6 percent), and (d) a steady rise in the share of credit to the private sector as a percentage of GDP.

It would have been useful to better understand these changes. Which sectors explain the dynamics of 2004–07? What happened in the manufacturing industry? Where did the new investment go? Where did employment fall? Esquivel hints that there is more to the story of Mexico than the external crisis when he states that "the recent contraction seems to be ... related more to specific local factors than to the international financial crunch." However, he does not develop this important theme sufficiently in the analysis of the crisis and in the preparation of his medium-term forecasts.

This chapter tells us that the negative external shock spread by means of the decline in U.S. demand for Mexico's manufactured exports, the fall in remittances, and the fall in tourism. The author provides data on remittances but not on tourism and he does not offer details on Mexico's manufactured exports. For example, has the crisis impact been the consequence of a medium-term trend toward a loss of competitiveness of these activities relative to China and other Asian exporters, or is it more of a short-term effect? Is the pessimistic forecast associated with the prospects for the U.S. economy or is it related to the industries in which Mexico has invested?

The second part of the discussion features an analysis of the growth prospects for the Mexican economy. In this context, it is important to think carefully about what potential output means in the context of an economy that is severely distorted. Potential output provides a frontier, a technical maximum, given the available factors of production, technology, and so on. But productivity in the economy, and hence actual output, depends on policies and regulations that determine what level of activity is profitable at any given moment. Against this background, the author's estimate of potential output may underestimate Mexico's production and income opportunities provided it eliminates distortions that currently hamper total factor productivity.

Weak Investment Climate and Fiscal Deficit Constrain Growth Prospects

Eric Le Borgne and Sheryll Namingit

After two decades of stagnant growth—owing partly to political instability, fiscal crises, and natural disasters—the Philippine economy had begun gathering momentum prior to the global crisis. The growth momentum can be traced to both the broad-based reforms adopted in the early 1990s and the boom in the early 2000s.

While the 2008–09 global financial crisis and ensuing recession have had a relatively minor impact on the Philippines, the crisis has nonetheless underscored the need for fundamental reforms to tackle the country's long-standing growth bottlenecks, improve the investment climate and infrastructure, and renew fiscal consolidation efforts. Since the collapse

Eric Le Borgne is Senior Economist, and Sheryll Namingit is Analyst, East Asia and Pacific Poverty Reduction and Economic Management Department, World Bank. This chapter, drafted in July 2010, is part of background country studies that Development Economics (the research and development arm of the World Bank) commissioned to assess and explore the medium- and long-term implications of the crisis for growth, poverty reduction, and, more broadly, the development of low- and middle-income countries. The authors would like to thank Carlos Braga, Milan Brahmbhatt, Mustapha Nabli, Vikram Nehru, Manu Sharma, and the conference participants for excellent comments, and Marianne Juco for research assistance.

of Lehman Brothers, policy makers' focus has been on short-term issues, such as how to stop the financial chaos and economic collapse, initiate a recovery, and deal with the immediate economic and social disruptions created by the crisis. Understandably, less attention has been given to the medium- and long-term implications of the crisis for growth, poverty reduction, and, more broadly, the development prospects of low- and middle-income countries. This chapter aims to fill this gap for the Philippines.

The chapter begins with a review of the precrisis growth experience and its relationship to the global economy. It goes on to describe the immediate impact of the crisis and the policy response, and it concludes by exploring the medium-term prospects of the Philippines in light of the global recession.

Before the Global Crisis

In the early 1990s, a series of natural disasters and a power crisis that caused major outages (in 1991) caused the Philippines to suffer low growth. Large-scale reforms undertaken by the government of President Fidel Ramos in the early 1990s managed to address power constraints and liberalize key economic sectors. The reforms focused on promoting competition in the domestic market through privatization of government assets; deregulation of such critical sectors as banking, power, telecommunications, and transportation; and liberalization of selected sectors (e.g., trade and banking).[1] At the same time, emerging markets—particularly in East Asia—attracted massive foreign investment. As a result, economic growth resumed from 1995 onward (figures 9.1 and 9.2), notwithstanding the Asian financial crisis in 1998 and the bursting of the dot-com bubble in 2001.

Prior to the Asian crisis, growth was led by consumption and investment, which in turn were fueled by the large-scale reforms. Domestic demand played a key role in supporting growth in 1995–97. This was supported by ample global liquidity. Consumption, which had improved after the restoration of democracy in 1986, grew steadily during the period. The contribution of (mostly) private investment was also large, especially in 1996–97; it reached 26 percent of gross domestic product (GDP) in 1997, a 14-year high (figure 9.1).

Figure 9.1. GDP Growth and Investment, 1981–2009

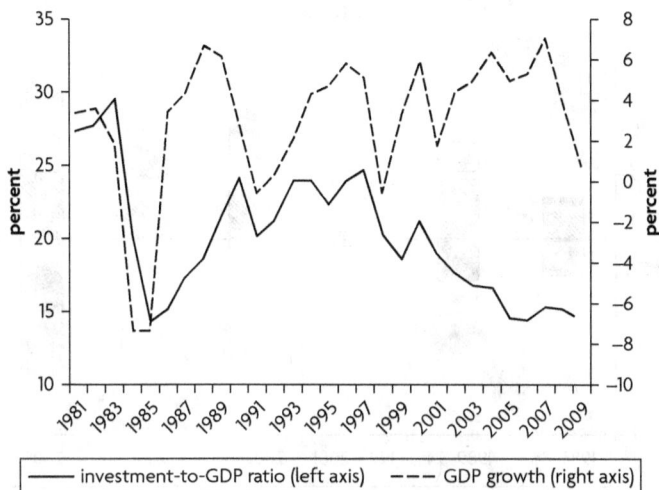

Source: National Statistical Coordination Board (NSCB).

On the supply side, the services sector, a beneficiary of deregulation, became a key contributor to growth before the Asian crisis (figure 9.2). All services subsectors, except government services, surged during the period. Industry also expanded, fueled by investments in construction and utilities (the heavy investment in utilities was the result of the power crisis of 1991). Manufacturing also contributed to overall growth, albeit to a lesser extent, as the share of electronics and semiconductor exports increased.[2] Owing to poor weather and weak technology, however, agricultural production was subdued over the period. The country's production structure thus shifted to one that was strong in industry and services and weak in agriculture.

A series of severe external shocks—the Asian crisis, a severe El Niño–related drought in 1998, and the 2001 dot-com bust—slowed the Philippines' growth momentum. In 1998, the Asian crisis and drought pushed the country into its second recession of the decade. It led to tumbling exports and capital outflows, which required a downward adjustment in domestic demand, as the country was a net capital importer. The construction boom ended abruptly. Meanwhile, the damage brought by the drought to agriculture was so bad that, in 1998, the sector contributed a greater decline to overall GDP growth than the

Figure 9.2. Contribution to GDP Growth

a. Demand side

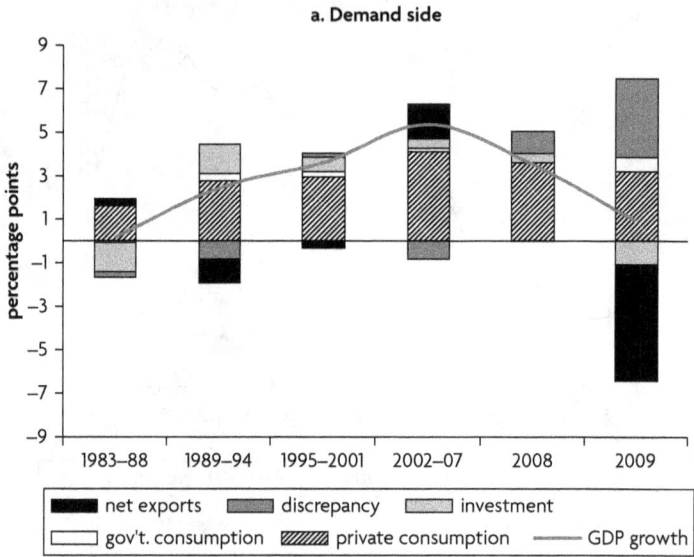

Legend: net exports · discrepancy · investment · gov't. consumption · private consumption · GDP growth

b. Supply side

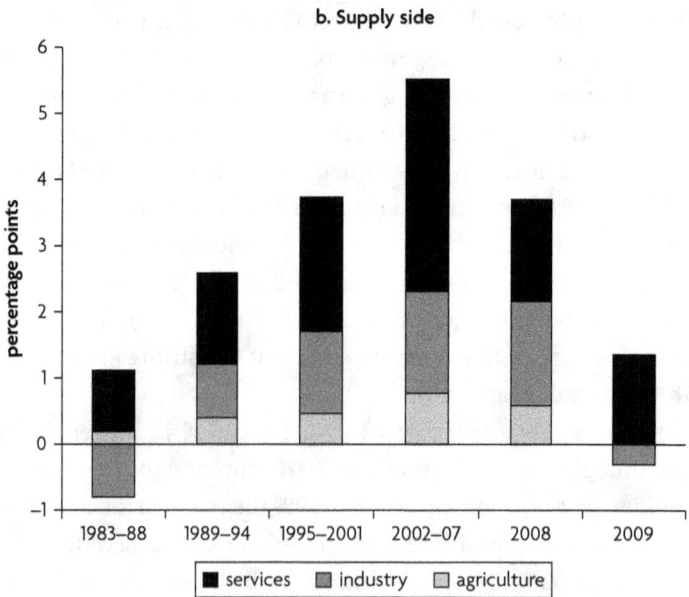

Legend: services · industry · agriculture

Source: NSCB.

crisis-hit industrial sector. The economy eventually recovered in 1999, but the global slump in 2001 led to a collapse of exports and investment, which once again dragged down the country's growth to just 1.8 percent.

Throughout the 1990s, the Philippines made headway in reducing poverty, although the gains were modest by regional standards (World Bank 2010d). Based on official estimates, the share of the population living below the national poverty line, which had reached about 45 percent in the mid-1980s, fell to some 30 percent by 2000. The World Bank's US$1.25-per-day income threshold measure of poverty provides a similar picture—the incidence of poverty fell from about 30 percent in the early 1980s to about 22 percent at the end of the 1990s. This decline was weak, however, relative to other countries in the region; indeed, poverty in the East Asia and Pacific region fell from nearly 80 percent in the early 1980s to about 50 percent in the late 1990s.

From 2003 to 2007, thanks to a favorable global environment and the postcrisis reforms, the Philippines enjoyed a prolonged period of economic growth (refer to figures 9.1 and 9.2). Heavy deployment of Filipino workers overseas generated huge remittance inflows (about 10 percent of GDP), which fed the robust domestic demand (and sustained domestic savings—figure 9.3). Coupled with strong global demand and trade, real annual GDP growth averaged 5.4 percent during 2003–06 and peaked at 7.1 percent in 2007—a growth performance not seen since the 1970s. On the production side, growth was led by the services sector, which benefited from the earlier liberalization of several services-sector industries. Subsectors that performed remark-ably well included transportation, communication, storage, private services (including the business process outsourcing [BPO] industry that emerged in the early 2000s), and financial services. The Philippine financial sector gradually regained its strength under regulatory reforms introduced after the Asian crisis. Growth in industry was driven by man-ufacturing, buoyed by electronics and semiconductor exports[3] and the utilities subsectors. Agriculture continued to be the least dynamic sector.

Investment, however, shrank steadily and markedly during the period. Public and private investment fell from a total of 26 percent of GDP in 1997 to less than 15 percent in 2005 (refer to figure 9.1). The decline in total capital formation was attributable mainly to a plunge in private investment and, to a lesser extent, lower public infrastructure investment.

Figure 9.3. Domestic and Foreign Savings

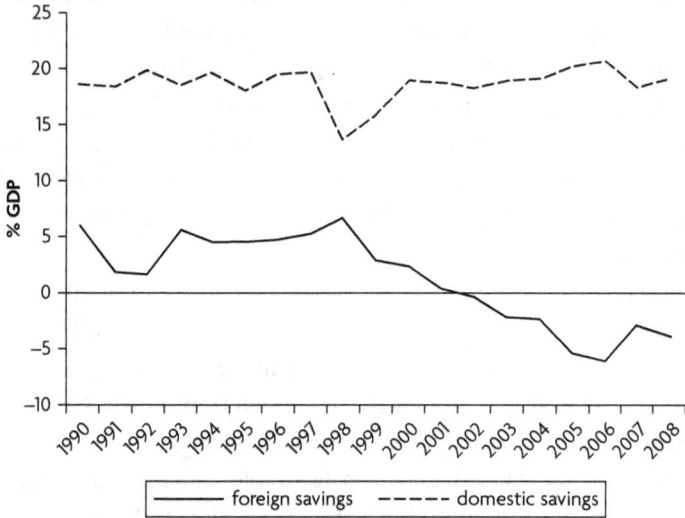

Source: NSCB; Bangko Sentral ng Pilipinas (BSP); Department of Finance (DOF).
Note: Foreign savings is the additive inverse of the current account surplus. Domestic savings is the difference of total investment and foreign savings.

In the power sector, persistent underinvestment raised concerns about supply shortages in the near term.[4] The reasons for the paradox of rising growth and declining investment can be traced to worsening public finances after the Asian crisis that limited the fiscal space for public investment; growth drivers that had low capacity intensity (such as the BPO sector); a capital-intensive private sector discouraged by insufficient public investment (especially in infrastructure); and the high cost of inputs stemming from elite capture in such industries as agriculture, maritime and air transport, electricity, and cement (Bocchi 2008). Key constraints to investment also included a poor investment climate, weak governance, and an unfavorable business environment (World Bank 2010c; refer to figure 9.4).[5] With the fiscal consolidation of 2005–06, however, government spending and private investment began to expand again, providing a modest boost to growth.

But the growth proved jobless, and the labor market stayed structurally weak. Despite the higher growth after the Asian crisis, unemployment did not fall. In fact, it climbed to an average 11.4 percent during 2000–04.[6] The composition of employment largely remained unchanged—50 percent of

Figure 9.4. Competitiveness Indicators

a. Governance-related competitiveness indicators

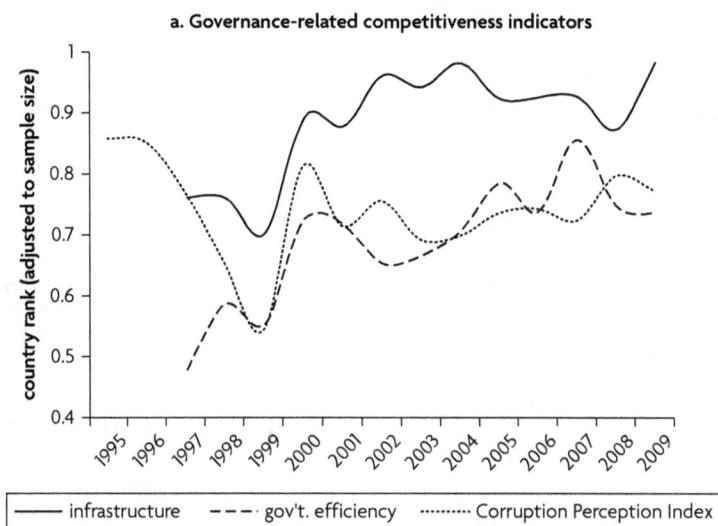

infrastructure   — — · gov't. efficiency   ········· Corruption Perception Index

Source: Infrastructure and government efficiency data are from IMD *World Competitiveness Yearbook;* Corruption Perception Index data are from Transparency International.
Note: On reading the ranking scale for both panels (a) and (b), a lower ranking (closer to zero) implies better performance.

b. Global Competitiveness Index

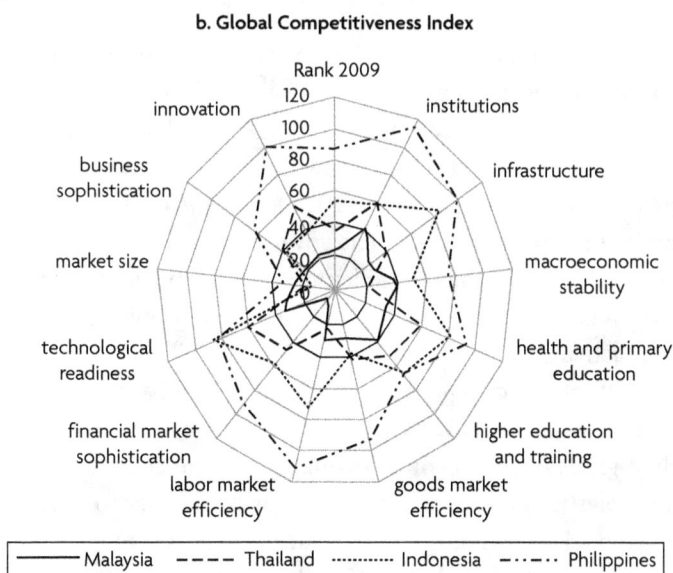

Malaysia   — — — Thailand   ············ Indonesia   —··—·· Philippines

Source: World Economic Forum Global Competitiveness Index, 2009.

Table 9.1. Labor and Employment Indicators, 2000–09

	2000	2001	2002	2003	2004	2005[a]	2006	2007	2008	2009
Employment Level (thousands)	28,285	29,157	30,062	30,628	31,248	32,189	32,635	33,560	34,090	35,060
percent change	−2.4	3.1	3.1	1.9	2.0	3.0	1.4	2.8	1.6	2.8
Employment by compensation type (% total employment)										
Wage and salaried	50.7	49.5	48.7	50.1	52.3	50.5	51.1	52.2	52.3	53.3
Own account	37.1	37.5	37.9	37.6	36.6	37.3	36.6	35.8	35.4	34.7
Unpaid family workers	12.2	13.0	13.3	12.3	11.2	12.2	12.3	12.1	12.3	12.0
Underemployment rate (%)	21.7	17.2	17.0	17.0	17.5	22.5	22.6	20.1	19.3	19.1
Unemployment rate (%)										
New definition[b]	—	—	—	—	—	7.9	8.0	7.3	7.4	7.5
Old definition	11.2	11.1	11.4	11.4	11.9	—	—	—	—	—
Poverty incidence	33.0	—	—	30.0	—	—	32.9	—	—	—

Source: NSCB; National Statistics Office (NSO).
Note: Figures from 2004 to 2008 are averages of quarterly surveys; estimates for these years are based on the 2000 census; the rest are based on previous censuses; — = not available.
a. April–October average.
b. A new unemployment definition was adopted in 2005 and includes all persons who are 15 years old and over as of their last birthday and are reported as (1) without work, (2) currently available for work, and (3) seeking work or not seeking work for valid reasons.

employed workers were either working on their own account (self-employed, largely earning meager incomes) or unpaid (table 9.1) (World Bank 2010d).

Growth did not bring greater progress in the reduction of poverty. The share of the population living below the national poverty line actually increased—from 30.0 percent in 2003 to 32.9 percent in 2006—and now stands at its late-1990s level. The government has made slow progress toward achieving some key Millennium Development Goal targets, such as universal access to primary education and improved maternal and reproductive health.

The lack of robust (on a per capita basis) and inclusive growth explain the failure in reducing poverty since 2000 (World Bank 2010d). The relatively high degree of income inequality has the effect of reducing the income elasticity of poverty, posing a further barrier to faster poverty reduction. These findings imply that the modest growth on a per capita basis that took place during 2003–06 must have had an anti-poor bias or been associated with a deteriorating distribution of income.

Several factors may have also contributed to such a bias and a worsening income distribution. Among these is an unequal sectoral distribution of growth—which could slow progress in poverty reduction if the poor are concentrated in the sectors that are stagnating or contracting—or an unequal spatial distribution of growth.

The Precrisis Boom and Policies

Ample global liquidity and the favorable global environment mitigated the pressure on the government to reduce fiscal spending. Still, in 2004 the government adopted a fiscal consolidation program.[7] As fiscal consolidation unfolded, ample liquidity and investor appetite for emerging-market debt narrowed spreads on sovereign debt. The peso appreciated. With stronger economic growth and a bullish market, the government engaged in an active privatization program and received Php 150.3 billion (2.3 percent of GDP) in proceeds between 2005 and 2008.[8] Public sector debt fell from 118 percent of GDP in 2003 to 64 percent in 2008 (figure 9.5). However, early and notable improvements in public finances eventually undermined the government's ability to sustain the early fiscal consolidation gains. Indeed, several crucial bills that were part of the 2004 fiscal program were never passed. As a result, the country's structural fiscal balance (i.e., excluding cyclical factors) stopped improving in 2006 (figure 9.6).

Government policies sought to boost investment in goods and services that enjoyed strong global demand. These are "priority sectors" in the Medium-Term Philippine Development Plan for 2004–10 and include information technology (IT) and IT-enabled services and electronics. The Investment Priorities Plan (IPP)[9] provides fiscal incentives to attract investors to these sectors.

As opportunities abroad increased, labor policies helped promote the employment of Filipino workers overseas. Indeed, the government's medium-term plan stipulates that it, in cooperation with the private sector, would pursue bilateral agreements to provide employment opportunities abroad. The Philippines has a long-standing tradition of sending workers overseas (dating back to the early 1970s), and the country is one of the most efficient in the world in helping its overseas workers. The deployment of these workers grew sharply and has contributed to strong remittance inflows since 2001 (figure 9.7). The Philippines ranks fourth in the world for remittance inflows (in absolute U.S. dollar terms).

Figure 9.5. Public Sector Debt and Sources of Debt Dynamics

a. Public sector debt

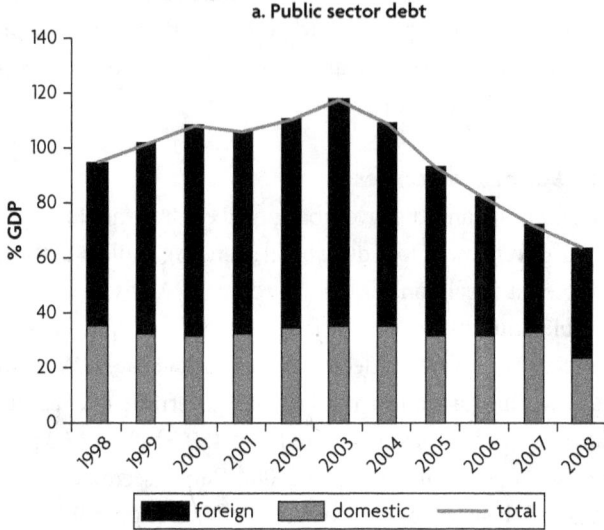

Source: NSCB; DOF.

b. Sources of debt dynamics

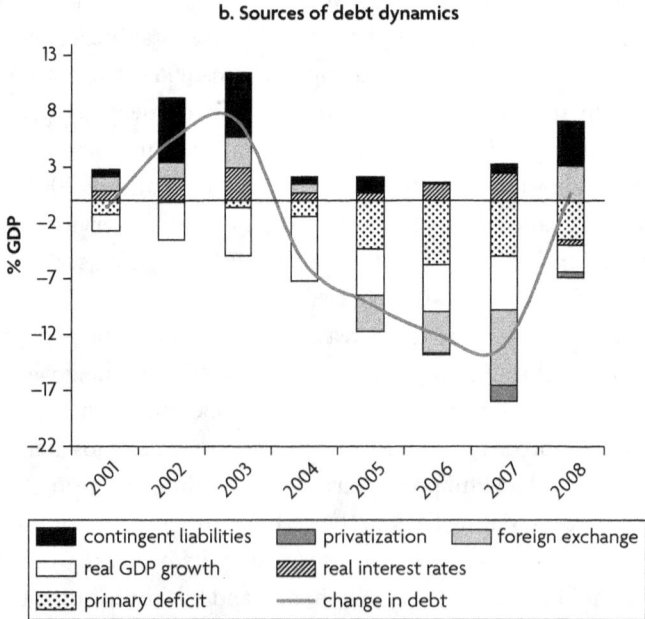

Source: World Bank staff calculations based on International Monetary Fund (IMF) staff Reports.

Figure 9.6. Fiscal Balance Decomposition and Structural Balance Components

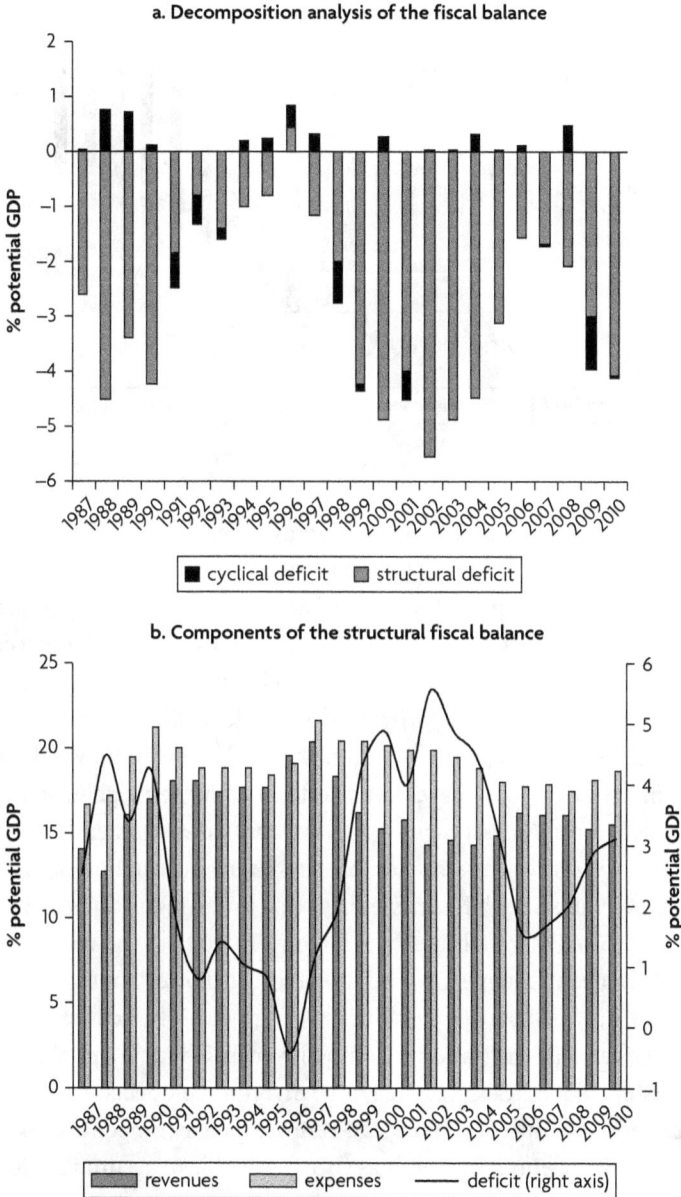

a. Decomposition analysis of the fiscal balance

cyclical deficit   structural deficit

b. Components of the structural fiscal balance

revenues   expenses   deficit (right axis)

Source: World Bank staff calculations based on the second method presented in Fedelino, Ivanova, and Horton (2009).

Note: The small share of cyclical factors in the overall fiscal balance is common in developing and emerging markets as automatic stabilizers are rather modest.

Figure 9.7. Deployment of Overseas Workers and Remittances

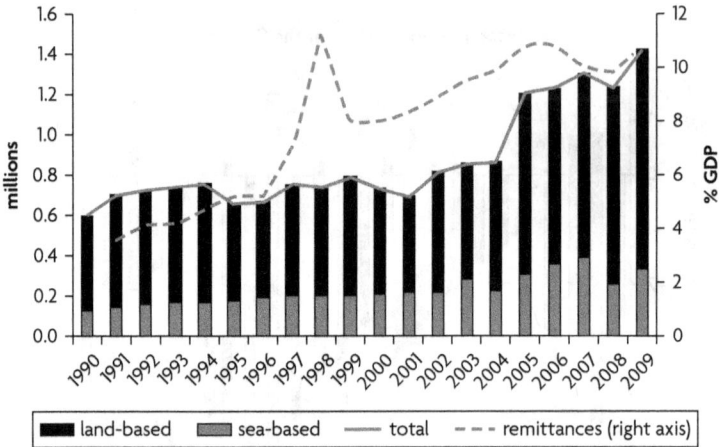

Source: CEIC Database; NSCB; BSP.

The government has passed laws to encourage foreign investment, but actual inflows were modest given the weak investment climate. One of the most important laws passed was the Minerals Act (2004), which eased the entry of foreign investors by allowing them to own up to 100 percent of mining corporations. The authorities also liberalized retail trade by reformulating the foreign equity participation rate, depending on the amount of paid-in capital for retail trade ventures. Overall, however, inflows of foreign direct investment (FDI) have been modest relative to neighboring countries, except for Indonesia (figure 9.8). Investors have consistently identified corruption as one of the strongest barriers to investment and doing business in the Philippines.[10] Businesses have also found regulations and procedures increasingly complicated and taxing. To address the country's low competitiveness, Congress passed the Electric Power Industry Reform Act of 2001, which sought to reduce the high cost of electricity; and the authorities created the National Competitiveness Council, a public-private partnership. Nonetheless, key markets remain to be opened up to greater competition to reduce input costs and enhance their competitiveness.

The Bangko Sentral ng Pilipinas (BSP) was able to accumulate foreign exchange reserves and increase external resiliency, thanks to the large supply of global liquidity. After the Philippines abandoned its currency peg (because of the Asian financial crisis), the government committed itself to

Figure 9.8. Entry of Foreign Direct Investment in Selected East Asia Countries

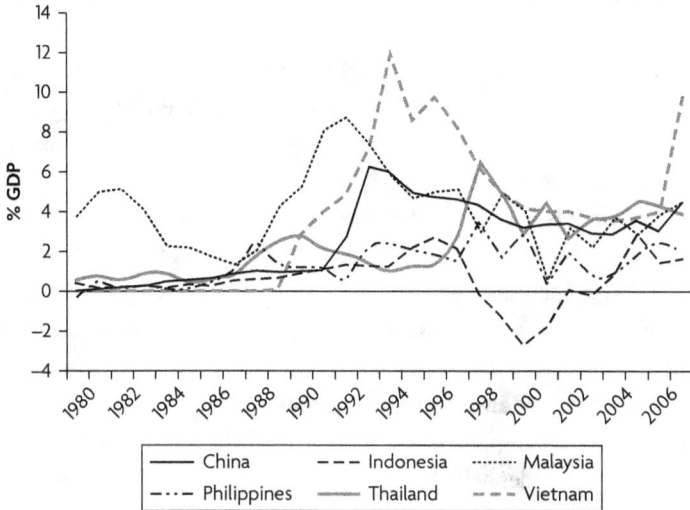

Source: World Bank, World Development Indicators Database.

boosting the country's external reserves. It has been largely successful; the balance of payments has posted increasing surpluses since 2004, and gross international reserves exceeded US$30 billion at the end of 2007.

After the Asian financial crisis, the government moved cautiously to liberalize the financial sector. Following up on the liberalization of foreign banks' entry in 1994, the government further encouraged the investment of foreign banks in the financial system—especially in troubled banks, where foreign banks could own up to 100 percent. Lessons learned after the Asian crisis also led to the strengthening of the regulatory and supervisory framework. Aside from the adoption of internationally accepted banking and supervisory practices for the BSP, the Securities and Exchange Commission, and the Insurance Commission (which are generally risk-based), the Securities Regulation Code was also passed into law in July 2000. The code strengthened the regulatory framework even as the government worked to develop the capital market. Progress on financial sector surveillance, however, was incomplete, as Congress resisted giving the BSP more power to supervise and close down ailing banks.

Globalization increased the impetus for greater openness to trade. Tariff reforms undertaken in 1991—partly in conjunction with negotiations in the Association of Southeast Asian Nations (ASEAN) Free Trade Agreement and the Uruguay Round of multilateral negotiations—continued. Nominal tariff and effective protection rates were reduced considerably with the implementation of the Tariff Reform Program (TRP) III in 1995 and TRP IV in 2001. The Philippines continued to liberalize trade with the ASEAN, while the ASEAN as a whole signed free trade agreements with China and the Republic of Korea. The country also signed and ratified the Japan-Philippines Economic Partnership Agreement. Nonetheless, several policies were reversed in the boom period (for example, Executive Orders 241 and 264, which favored such interest groups as agriculture), and the coefficient of variation of tariff rates increased (Aldaba 2005).

The Precrisis Boom and Potential Growth

The expansion during 2003–07 differed from the growth patterns of the preceding two decades, which were characterized by strong business cycles. While overall growth was closely tracking the potential growth path (zero output gap) from 2002, the election years (2004 and 2007) featured a strong cyclical component, owing to heavy election-related spending. During those years, the cyclical impact of net exports, investment, and consumption turned positive. The rise in investment was also driven by the surge in foreign equities late in the boom period—the same factor that led to the stock market boom. On the supply side, much of the cyclicality came from the services sector, especially trade, transportation, and communications.

During 2003–07, potential growth rose to an average 4.6 percent, compared to 3.8 percent in 1995–2002. The increase in potential growth was led by consumption and net exports, which, as noted earlier, were driven by earlier reforms and positive changes in the global environment (figure 9.9).

The global boom led to a surge in Filipinos deployed abroad and in associated remittances. From 2002, annual deployments of overseas workers increased substantially, reaching more than 1 million beginning in 2005 (figure 9.7). Remittances, a major source of household income, boosted private consumption, which has been the key contributor to growth. The remittance elasticity of private consumption in the past 10 years is estimated at 0.7; that is, a 1 percent increase in remittances raises private consumption by 0.7 percent. In addition, Granger causality tests reveal that remittance growth drives consumption at short horizons and that over longer time periods "hysteresis" effects play a role: higher

Figure 9.9. Growth Decomposition and Breakdown of Its Structural Components

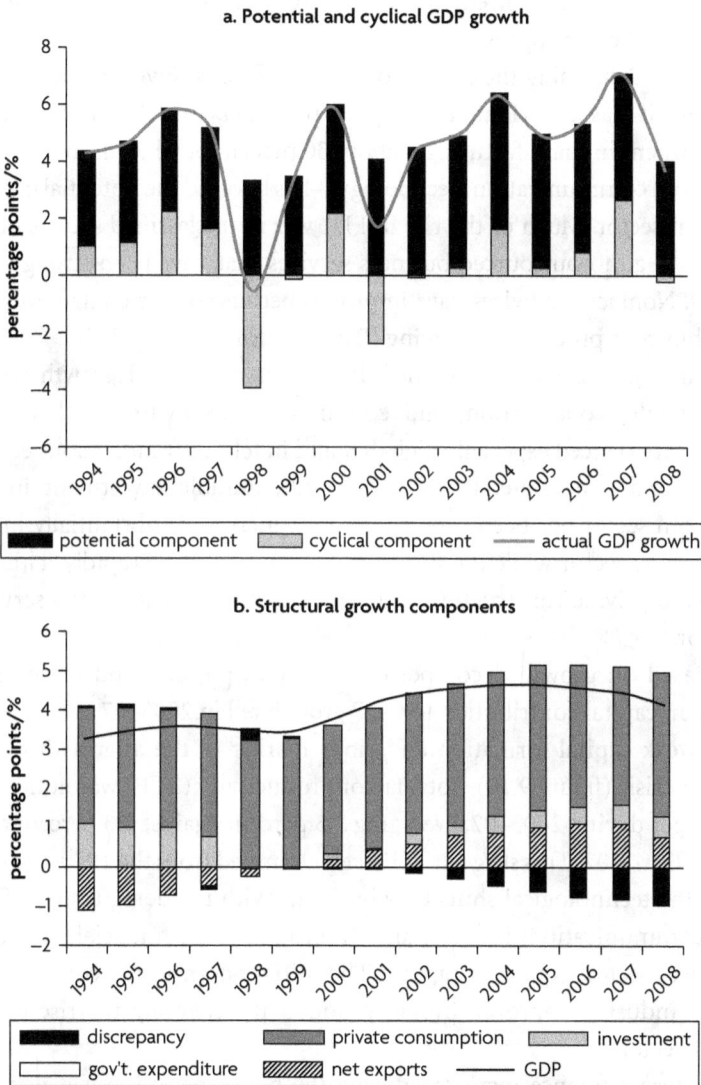

a. Potential and cyclical GDP growth

b. Structural growth components

Source: NSCB; BSP; CEIC Database; World Bank staff calculations.

consumption levels engendered by remittances later call for continued remittances, which strengthens the structural relationship of remittances and consumption.

Notwithstanding the overall low level of foreign investment, in some sectors it has contributed to higher potential growth. Most notably, investment in manufacturing—about 30 percent of which is in information and communications technology—has boosted the potential growth of that sector. Much of the rise in FDI was in unclassified sectors but is likely to go to outsourced business services that have been strong since 2000. Nonfactor services have improved because of the contribution of the business process outsourcing (BPO) sector.

The rapid expansion of the BPO industry spurred growth in the real estate, construction, and communications sectors. Call centers have experienced especially high demand in telecommunications equipment and real estate. Partly as a result, durable investment in the telecom sector has been robust, and FDI increased substantially in the real estate sector while the BPO sector was expanding rapidly. This has spurred private construction and expanded the capacity of the services sector.

Based on growth decomposition analysis, physical and (especially) human capital contribution to GDP growth fell in 2003–07 as a result of the weak capital formation and labor market in the aftermath of the Asian crisis (figure 9.10). Total factor productivity (TFP) was noticeably stronger during 2003–07, averaging 3.5 percent against 0.3 percent during 1994–2002. This surge in TFP likely stemmed from the 1990s reforms and the technological shifts they brought. With the deregulation of the telecommunications industry and the growth of the financial sector, the services sector expanded rapidly. The initial boom in the communications industry improved overall productivity, enabling the rise of the BPO sector.

External finance increased during the boom period, but it was not used to address binding constraints in infrastructure. Net external financing of the national government was higher in the boom period, especially in the pre–fiscal consolidation period (pre-2004). Public investment as a percentage of GDP, however, had been on a declining trend up to 2006 and has failed to address pressing infrastructure needs.

Figure 9.10. Growth Decomposition by Factors

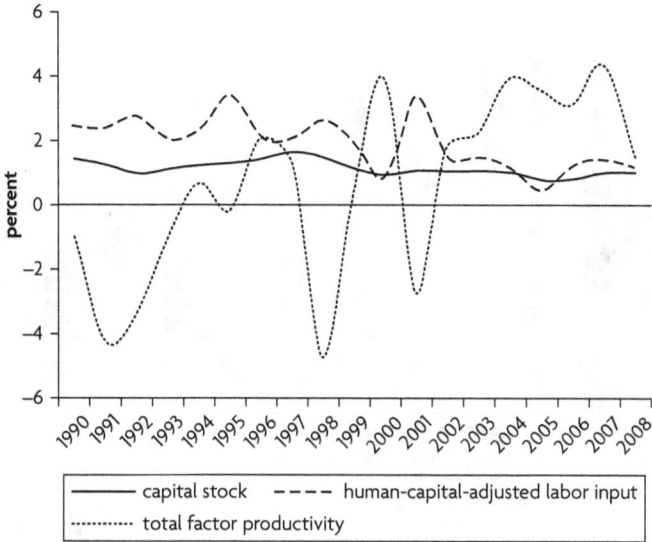

Source: World Bank staff estimates.

The Precrisis Boom and External Vulnerabilities

Thanks to lessons learned from the Asian financial crisis, the policies pursued in the precrisis period mitigated the vulnerability of the Philippine economy to external shocks. As the country was recovering from the Asian financial crisis—and banks and corporations were slowly rebuilding their balance sheets while public finances were being consolidated—the economy had no large imbalances at the onset of the global crisis. Monetary and financial market regulations put in place after the Asian financial crisis curbed the use of such risky instruments as structured products.[11] In contrast to the period before the Asian financial crisis, the BSP had accumulated large reserves during the high-growth period. Despite a large trade deficit, the current account has remained in surplus due to heavy net remittance inflows. The ratio of reserves to short-term external debt thus increased by a multiple of 5 in 2008 (figure 9.11), and both the government and corporate sectors sharply reduced their dependence on foreign financing. On the fiscal front, while the share of foreign-currency-denominated debt remained large, the debt is of long duration.

Figure 9.11. Total External Debt and Reserve Cover

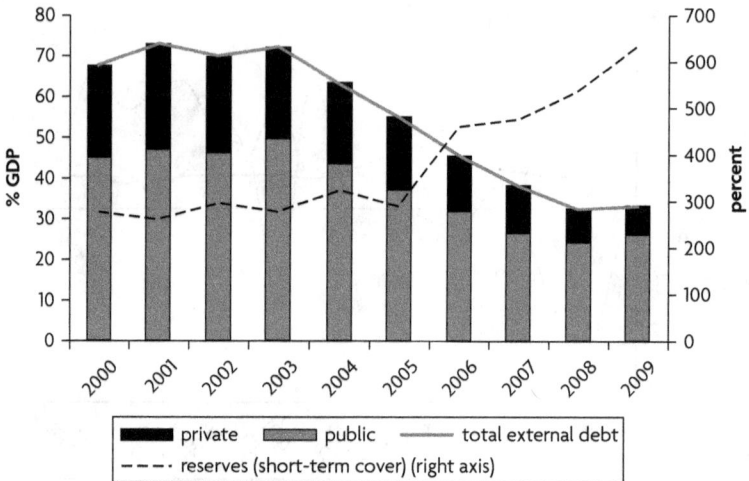

Banks assumed a cautious stance in lending to the private sector after the Asian crisis, when the nonperforming loan (NPL) ratio soared to more than 16 percent of total loans in 2001 (figure 9.12). Policies were put in place to gradually reduce banks' high NPLs.[12] In 2002, the Special Purpose Vehicle Act was approved and further extended up to 2008 to help banks dispose of their NPLs and other nonperforming assets. Moreover, banks also began strengthening their capital by raising tier-2 bonds to comply with the requirements of the Basel II.[13] The BSP has encouraged such capital raising by setting forth guidelines relating to the issuance of hybrid capital instruments. The stronger fundamentals of the banking sector thus helped banks withstand external pressure. However, their acquisition of substantial government debt securities heightened the banking sector's exposure to market and interest rate risk. (Such risk emerged during the global financial crisis, when yields on sovereign paper soared, albeit temporarily.)

As the Philippines was not, comparatively speaking, an attractive destination for foreign investors, it did not receive large capital inflows during the boom years. The relative lack of foreign investment (either FDI or portfolio flows) was due mostly to a weak investment climate, unfavorable laws

Figure 9.12. Total Loans and Nonperforming Loans

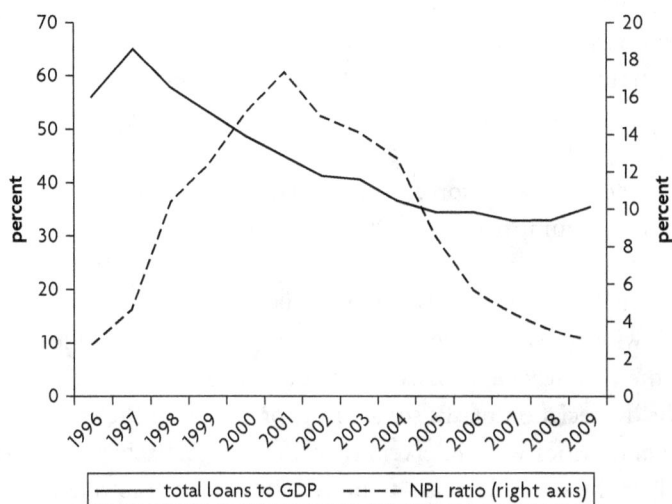

Source: BSP.

that work against foreign investors, and the perception of political instability and corruption. Since the country benefited less from these flows during the boom period, it also suffered less during the global downturn.

The Crisis

The key transmission channels through which the Philippines' economy has been affected by the global crisis are the following:

- Financial channel
- Noncommodity trade channel
- Commodity trade channel
- Remittance channel

All of these have led to a weaker real sector, although, as noted earlier, some sectors have benefited from the crisis.

Financial Contagion and the Banking System

Although banks had minimal direct exposure to distressed credit instruments, asset prices fell rapidly and sharply in 2008, only to recover in

2009. The impact of the global financial turmoil on the Philippines has been seen mainly in the (temporary) decline in stock market and asset prices; a large and rapid (again, temporary) rise in the spreads on its international bonds; and a modest and brief depreciation of the peso. Stock market prices declined by 49 percent in 2008, but fully recovered their losses following the collapse of Lehman Brothers in the third quarter of 2009. Borrowing spreads, which had fallen below 200 basis points (bps) in 2007, jumped to over 800 bps in October 2008; spreads returned to their precrisis levels a year later and were below their pre–Lehman Brothers collapse levels by December 2009.

Following the strong appreciation of the peso (relative to the dollar) in 2007, the currency depreciated by about 14 percent by the end of 2008. But the depreciation masks some of the pressures on the exchange rate, as the authorities were intervening in the foreign exchange markets— notably in the swap markets—to prevent unwanted peso volatility.

Banks' large concentrations of assets in government securities greatly affected profits in 2008. As banks took a cautious approach to lending to the corporate sector—especially to micro, small, and medium enterprises (MSMEs)—and to households, they expanded their trading and other sources of income to boost profitability. Given banks' large holdings of securities (especially government securities), mark-to-market losses contributed to a 41 percent fall in profits in 2008; the losses would have been larger had the central bank not allowed a change in accounting rules to enable banks to avoid further mark-to-market losses on their bond holdings.[14] Nevertheless, the overall banking system remained resilient, with banks' capital adequacy ratios still above the required level and with banks' profitability recovering in the first half of 2009.

The transmission of the international credit crunch to domestic banks in the Philippines in the wake of the Lehman Brothers collapse had a limited impact on domestic liquidity. This was because, in the period leading up to Lehman's collapse,

- foreign banks were not as active in lending to the Philippines as to other countries,[15] so that fund withdrawals owing to risk aversion or portfolio rebalancing were not highly disruptive;
- domestic banks were liquid, with relatively low loan-to-deposit ratios, owing to little dollar fund sourcing;

- the dollar liquidity of local banks was also ample, with foreign currency deposit unit (FCDU) assets tilted toward liquid security investments;
- money markets in the Philippines were underdeveloped, with a low degree of cross-border integration (Loretan and Wooldridge 2008);

While foreign banks operating in the Philippines were active in the foreign exchange market (and were occasionally net borrowers in the peso market), they constituted a small segment of the banking system (12 percent of total bank assets) and were on the periphery of the loan market, notably the credit card business (World Bank 2009a).

After some tumult in late 2008 and early 2009, asset prices and interest rates normalized in 2009. Following the strong appreciation of the peso in 2007 and in early 2008, the onset of the global financial crisis weakened the peso, causing it to finish out 2008 poorly—14.7 percent weaker against the U.S. dollar. Some of this depreciation was reversed in 2009 as the economy proved resilient; by the end of 2009, the peso had appreciated by 2.4 percent. Stock market assets lost 49 percent of their value in 2008, reflecting the massive (US$1 billion) sell-off of foreign equity holdings, but equity prices increased by 63 percent through the end of 2009. Borrowing spreads widened to more than 800 bps in October 2008 but fell to precrisis levels by the end of 2009 (200 bps in December 2009), notwithstanding the country's deteriorating structural fiscal balances. While the narrowing spreads were attributable partly to the ample global liquidity (owing to the central bank's large quantitative easing and easy monetary policies), they also reflected the region's stronger relative performance compared with other parts of the world, as well as the resulting strong demand for the region's global bonds.

Capital flows recovered, with a net portfolio investment inflow of US$1.4 billion in 2009, in contrast to a net outflow of US$3.8 billion the year before. Nonresident direct investment in the country, driven by equity placements, remained positive at the end of 2009 at US$1.9 billion, 39 percent higher than in 2008. Several large investments, such as Hanjin's second shipyard in Mindanao, encountered start-up delays linked to the global crisis and recession, but net inflows of portfolio and direct investment remained positive in 2009.

Gross international reserves continued to grow steadily throughout the global financial crisis, with only limited dips at the peak of the crisis.

Reserves reached a record high of US$44.2 billion at the end of 2009, versus US$38 billion in 2008 and US$33 billion at the end of 2007. Nonetheless, the relatively strong reserves position—equivalent to nine months' import cover and almost five times external liabilities by remaining maturity—remains vulnerable to shocks, especially peso weaknesses. To smooth excessive sudden exchange rate volatility, the BSP has intervened in the foreign exchange market using a mix of international reserves, swap markets, and nondomestic forward markets; in 2008, for example, the BSP's swap position fell by more than US$8 billion.

Financing the Corporate Sector and Trade

As corporations in the Philippines have difficulties accessing credit, they rely largely on retained earnings to finance themselves; indeed, nearly half of total financing of the corporate sector comes from retained earnings. Domestic loans are the second largest source of total financing, with foreign loans and bonds now accounting for only about 10 percent. Similarly, domestic bond financing remains marginal, as only top-tier corporations can tap the market. In early 2009, the San Miguel Corporation issued a record approximately Php 38 billion in retail bonds and paved the way for other large corporations to issue securities (table 9.2).

The crisis has left many exporters (particularly those in vulnerable industries and MSMEs) in a difficult financial position. Before the crisis, exporters—especially multinationals—maintained open accounts with

Table 9.2. Financing Sources
(share in total, %)

Year	Domestic bank loans	Domestic bonds	Foreign debt (loans + bonds)	Stockholders' equity
2002	38.2	0.1	22.1	39.7
2003	41.6	0.3	23.2	35.0
2004	38.1	0.8	21.2	40.0
2005	40.9	1.2	19.0	38.9
2006	39.9	2.1	14.4	43.5
2007	39.1	2.9	12.0	46.0
2008	38.0	3.3	10.4	48.3

Source: BSP; Asian Development Bank (ADB); Business World Top 1,000 Corporations data; World Bank.
Note: Stockholders' equity data are the total of the nonfinancial firms belonging to the top 1,000 corporations; actual data for 2008 are not yet available and the assumed growth rate is 14 percent, the same as in 2007.

their foreign counterparts, while others relied on letters of credit opened by their customers. But after the crisis, all banks became highly selective in extending credit to industries hurt badly by the crisis or whose long-term prospects were not particularly good. Examples of industries that faced reduced export credit availability included garments, furniture, small electronics firms, and automotive parts suppliers; also facing curtailed credit were exporters unable to provide collateral. On the other hand, food exporters were spared credit cuts, as they were not greatly affected by the crisis. In response to the credit squeeze facing exporters, the government sharply boosted official guarantees and credit insurance for the export sector (70.6 percent in the fourth quarter of 2008, relative to the year-earlier quarter).

Short-term foreign loan inflows, as noted earlier, account for 10 percent of corporate financing; these fell sharply in early 2009. Indeed, through May of that year, short-term credit inflows (mostly trade credits) totaled zero, owing to increased risk aversion and the global liquidity crunch. Until May 2009, no firm floated bonds denominated in foreign currency or received foreign equity capitalization, which underscores the high level of stress prevailing in the external financing market. During May–December, however, the market did show signs of stabilizing as some short-term loans, public bonds, and external equity (worth US\$1.1 billion) flowed in.

While the initial public offering (IPO) market in the Philippines Stock Exchange was robust in 2007, it effectively dried up in 2008. Several companies, such as Shell Philippines, Seaoil, and other oil refineries—which are mandated by the Oil Deregulation law to list at least 10 percent of their stocks with the Philippine Stock Exchange—have delayed their plans to tap the market as they wait for the market to normalize. The shallow capital market clearly limits the ability of the stock market to raise substantial equity.

Impact on Commodity and Noncommodity Trade

Although the Philippines has seen a collapse in its exports and imports, the impact on economic growth and employment has been moderate. In 2009, exports fell 22 percent and imports fell 24 percent with the collapse of global demand for electronics and semiconductors—which account for about 60 percent of the country's exports. All other major exports categories also suffered sharp drops. Exports rebounded toward the end of 2009 but, as of December, they remained at their 2005 levels. However, because a large share of Philippine exports has limited value added, owing to the large import component (as is the case in the electronics and semiconductor industry), the collapse in exports had a limited negative impact on GDP growth and on employment (as major exporters are relatively capital intensive). The impact of the global boom on trade in the Philippines was also modest relative to its peers. As a result, the damage inflicted by the contraction in global trade on overall GDP growth was modest relative to other countries in the region.

Impact on Remittances

Worker remittance inflows have slowed considerably in dollar terms but were strongly countercyclical in real peso terms—thanks to the country's strong deployment of overseas workers and their extensive diversification in terms of their skills, gender, education, and engagement in tradable versus nontradable sectors (World Bank 2010c). In 2009, remittance flows eased considerably, posting 5.6 percent growth in nominal dollar terms compared to 13.7 percent in 2008.[16] In real peso terms, however, remittances grew by 9.6 percent in 2009 relative to 0.3 percent in 2008, thanks to a combination of a weaker peso for much of the year and lower inflation. These helped drive a rebound in consumption in the last three quarters of 2009, following a contraction in the first quarter (quarter on quarter, seasonally adjusted; World Bank 2009b). Remittances have also boosted gross international reserves and bank deposits.

The economy contracted in the last quarter of 2008 and first quarter of 2009 owing to a sharp fall in industrial production and private consumption at the peak of the global crisis. A soft rebound in the remainder of 2009 pushed the economy out of negative territory, but just barely. GDP grew 1.1 percent in 2009, the slowest pace since the Asian crisis in 1998. On a per capita basis, GDP actually decreased by 0.9 percent, compared to an average growth rate of 3.2 percent in 2002–08.

The sharp falloff in growth was due to a major slowing of net exports and domestic demand. The decline in net exports—mainly of electronics and semiconductors, which constitute about 60 percent of Philippine exports and are tightly integrated into the global supply chain— contributed most to the growth slowdown. Private consumption, despite strong growth in real peso remittances, grew by 3.8 percent in 2009 (the slowest pace since the boom period) as consumer sentiment weakened and precautionary savings rose. Private investment dropped precipitously, and robust public spending was able to offset only some of the drop.

The crisis opened up an output gap in 2008 that widened further in 2009, even though the economy was operating at near potential level before the crisis. The fall in both domestic and external demand led to an increase in excess capacity in 2009 and a TFP decline of 1.9 percent.

Government Policy Responses

Overall, monetary and fiscal authorities have been prompt to react to the crisis and have introduced appropriate policies. The fiscal stimulus, however, has come at a heavy cost.

Monetary and Financial Regulation Policies

Monetary policy has been appropriately supportive of growth and financial system stability and liquidity during the crisis. As disinflation from the 2008 food and fuel price shock set in and the economy softened, the BSP cut policy rates substantially. Starting in December 2008, the central bank cut rates by 200 bps, bringing the key policy rate to a 17-year low of 4.0 percent (although banks were slow to follow the BSP cuts, trimming lending rates by just 146 bps in September 2009). The BSP has also taken preemptive measures to avoid a liquidity crunch, even though domestic liquidity remained adequate. The central bank lowered reserve requirement by 2 percentage points, doubling the peso rediscounting facility to Php 40 billion in November 2008 and further increasing it to Php 60 billion in February 2009. The BSP also increased the loan value of all eligible rediscounting paper from 80 percent to 90 percent of the outstanding balance of a borrowing bank's credit instrument.

The central bank has also relaxed accounting rules, enabling banks to avoid mark-to-market losses on their government bond holdings and to continue lending. In October 2008, the BSP authorized banks, through a one-time reclassification, to move some of their trading assets to hold-to-maturity (at a precrisis price). The BSP also eased its rules on the 100 percent asset cover of banks' foreign currency deposit units and opened an interbank dollar-denominated borrowing and lending facility to ease banks' liquidity constraints. Moreover, the BSP relaxed limits on related-party lending by excluding lending to affiliates and subsidiaries engaged in power projects certified as urgent under the Philippine medium-term investment plan.

In April 2009, the government also passed a law doubling the limit up to which bank account deposits are insured. Deposits are now guaranteed by the Philippines Deposit Insurance Corporation (PDIC) up to Php 500,000 (about six times annual GDP per capita), which covers about 97 percent of bank accounts in the Philippines (but only 31 percent of total deposits). The measure was deemed necessary to maintain public confidence in the financial system, especially as several regional banks from the Legacy Financial Group[17] were closed in December 2008. The law also reinforces PDIC's supervisory power by giving it the authority to determine insured deposits, conduct special bank examinations upon the impending closure of a bank, and examine deposit accounts in case unsafe or unsound banking practices are discovered. The examiners are now also immune from lawsuits.

Fiscal Policy: The Economic Resiliency Plan

To lessen the impact of the global recession, the government adopted a fiscal stimulus package in February 2009 whose magnitude was unprecedented in recent Philippines history. Also, a large part of the Economic Resiliency Plan (ERP)[18] was front-loaded. The fiscal easing from 2008 to 2009—equivalent to 2.6 percent of GDP—was the largest recorded since the 1986 People Power revolution (table 9.3). The government's ability to implement such a large countercyclical and timely fiscal stimulus contrasts with its previous fiscal record, which had been pro-cyclical (Zakharova 2006; Botman 2009). The government was able to launch the ERP because of the fiscal space created in previous years—and because of the strong balance of payments position resulting from large and sustained worker remittances. Overall, the ERP has buffered the deceleration in growth; government expenditure and investment contributed about 1.4 percentage points to overall growth in 2009, compared to 0.1 percentage point in 2008. The stimulus, however, has also led to a large fiscal deficit.

Moreover, a large component of the ERP consists of permanent measures, undermining fiscal consolidation efforts and reducing fiscal space for priority spending. The worsening in the fiscal balance from 2008 to

Table 9.3. National Government Cash Accounts, 2006–10
(% GDP, unless otherwise stated)

	2006	2007	2008	2009	2010 Revised budget	World Bank projections
Revenue and grant	16.1	15.7	15.8	14.6	14.8	14.6
Tax revenue	14.3	14.0	14.2	12.8	13.3	13.2
Nontax revenue[a]	1.9	1.7	1.7	1.8	1.5	1.4
Grant	0.0	0.0	0.0	0.0	0.0	0.0
Total expenditure[b]	17.5	17.4	17.3	18.7	18.6	18.7
Current expenditures	15.2	14.4	14.1	14.9	15.5	15.5
Personal services	5.4	5.3	5.1	5.4	6.0	6.0
MOOE	1.7	1.9	1.9	2.1	2.1	2.2
Allotment to LGUs	2.3	2.2	2.3	2.7	2.6	2.6
Subsidies	0.2	0.3	0.2	0.2	0.2	0.2
Tax expenditures	0.3	0.5	0.8	0.7	0.5	0.7
Interest payment	5.3	4.1	3.9	3.8	4.3	3.9
Capital outlays	2.3	2.9	3.0	3.6	2.9	3.1
Net lending	0.0	0.1	0.2	0.2	0.2	0.1
Balance (GFS definition)[c]	−1.4	−1.7	−1.5	−4.1	−3.8	−4.1
Balance (government definition)	−1.1	−0.2	−0.9	−3.9	−3.5	−3.8
Primary balance (GFS)[c]	4.0	2.5	2.3	−0.3	0.4	−0.2
Memorandum items						
Privatization receipts (Php billions)	5.8	90.6	36.0	1.4	12.5	12.5
CB-BOL interest payments (% GDP)	0.2	0.1	0.2	0.2	0.2	0.2
Nominal GDP (Php billions)[d]	6,031	6,647	7,409	7,679	8,405	8,405

Source: DOF; Bureau of Treasury (BTr); Department of Budget and Management (DBM).
a. Excludes privatization receipts (these are treated as financing items in Government Financial Statistics Manual)
b. Data from DBM; Allocation to LGUs excludes their capital transfer (it is included in capital outlays).
c. Based on IMF's Government Finance Statistics (GFS) concept.
d. Nominal GDP for 2010 is World Bank forecast.
Note: MOOE = maintenance and other operating expenses; LGU = local government unit; CB-BOL = Central Bank Board of Liquidators.

2009 was due mostly to a sharp deterioration in the structural fiscal balance, attributable mainly to large and permanent tax cuts. Hence, by early 2010, most of the gains from the 2005 revenue reforms were undone. The government has long pressed Congress to pass bills to rationalize the tax system and raise revenue (for example, by rationalizing fiscal incentives and increasing excise taxes on alcohol and tobacco), but so far with no success. Progress in tax administration reform has also been disappointing.

Medium-Term Prospects and Policies

The Philippines now finds itself at a crossroads, not only because of the post–global crisis environment, but also (and especially) because of the results of the general elections in May 2010, which offer unique prospects for reforms. The outcome of the presidential election has generated high hopes for reform, especially in the anticorruption and governance areas. Benigno Simeon "Noynoy" Aquino III of the Liberal Party won with a large majority. Mr. Aquino's core electoral platform rested on improving governance and reducing corruption so as to reduce poverty. These elections have generated widespread hope for reforms and the tackling of well-known structural bottlenecks, especially corruption. These elections also offer the possibility of renewed impetus on structural reforms as the need to fight sudden and large shocks abates.

Growth prospects for the Philippines are highly contingent on reform prospects, as a normalized post–global crisis environment would provide considerable rewards, especially in terms of business activity, reduced corruption, more infrastructure, and fiscal stabilization.

We envisage two outlook scenarios:

- *Baseline scenario:* Without reforms, medium-term economic growth would be lower than the average for the boom period (2003–07), given dimmer prospects for investment and net exports. Spare capacity would linger, while TFP growth would slow. Some sectors in which the country has comparative advantage would nonetheless benefit from global restructuring in the aftermath of the crisis.
- *Reform scenario:* Growth would accelerate as structural bottlenecks to inclusive growth are tackled and fiscal consolidation takes place.

Baseline Scenario

In the baseline scenario, growth is below precrisis levels, an annual average of 4.2 percent in 2012–15 versus 5.4 percent in 2003–08 (table 9.4). While the growth improvement in 2010 would be comparable to short-term

Table 9.4. Baseline Growth Projections, 2006–15
(percent)

	Actual			Avg.	Prel. Actual	Projection						Avg.
	2006	2007	2008	2003–08	2009	2010	2011	2012	2013	2014	2015	2012–2015
Private consumption	5.5	5.8	4.7	5.3	4.1	5.3	4.9	4.9	4.9	5.0	5.0	5.0
Government consumption	10.4	6.6	0.4	4.0	10.9	6.0	2.0	2.0	3.0	3.5	3.8	3.1
Capital formation	5.1	12.4	2.3	3.5	−5.7	9.4	4.5	4.0	4.0	3.9	3.7	3.9
Exports	13.4	5.5	−2.0	6.9	−13.4	9.6	5.5	5.8	6.4	6.4	6.5	6.3
Imports	1.8	−4.1	0.8	2.9	−1.9	12.0	7.0	7.0	7.1	7.2	7.3	7.1
Statistical discrepancy	−136.6	337.5	−16.2	55.8	−74.6	37.0	...	...	...	...	...	...
GDP	5.3	7.1	3.7	5.4	1.1	4.4	4.0	4.0	4.3	4.3	4.2	4.2

Source: NSCB; World Bank staff estimates.
Note: ... = zero growth.

recoveries in previous crises, the pace of medium-term recovery would be less robust (World Bank 2010a).

Unlike in previous recoveries when the global environment was strong, a soft recovery is now projected for the global economy. The pace of the global recovery and the new postrecession equilibrium will affect domestic growth via remittances, exports, capital inflows, and access to capital. Some of these effects will benefit the structure of the Philippine economy, such as the sea-based overseas workers (i.e., those working in ships and other sea vessels) and the BPO sectors. These sectors will benefit from the new wave of global restructuring induced by the crisis, as through the global effort to contain costs (Gereffi and Fernandez-Stark 2010). At the same time, structural impediments such as the weak investment climate and inadequate infrastructure will continue to be a major constraint on medium-term growth.

Private consumption would be hurt by the worsening fiscal stance, weak labor market, and investment climate; thus, more inclusive growth would remain a challenge. Private consumption would average about 0.3 point less during 2012–15 than in 2003–08. With growth projected to be moderate—and given the rapidly rising labor force—the labor market would likely remain weak, dampening private consumption despite favorable remittance prospects.

Although global remittance flows are projected to grow more slowly in the postcrisis environment (given the expectation that the global recovery will have limited job intensity and as immigration controls are tightened), remittances to the Philippines would grow by 9 percent annually during 2012–15. While this growth rate is 6 percentage points lower than the country's average remittance growth in the boom period, it compares favorably with global remittance growth prospects (figure 9.13). As noted earlier, this is largely explained by the wide geographic and skill distribution of overseas Filipinos and the rising number of deployed workers. Heavy deployment of workers overseas partly reflects recession-induced global staffing, restructuring, and the attractiveness of Filipino workers in the global labor market.[19]

Structural bottlenecks and weaknesses in the economy would likely result in a continued low investment-to-GDP ratio under the baseline scenario. In the absence of structural reforms to improve competitiveness, and with macroeconomic stability endangered by weakening public finances, private sector incentives to invest would be limited at the same time that public investment was constrained (figure 9.14). Total investment as a ratio of GDP is projected to decline from 15.6 percent in 2003–08 to 15.2 percent in 2015, continuing its slow trend from the

Figure 9.13. Remittances Are Projected to Do Well as Deployment Increases and the Peso Weakens

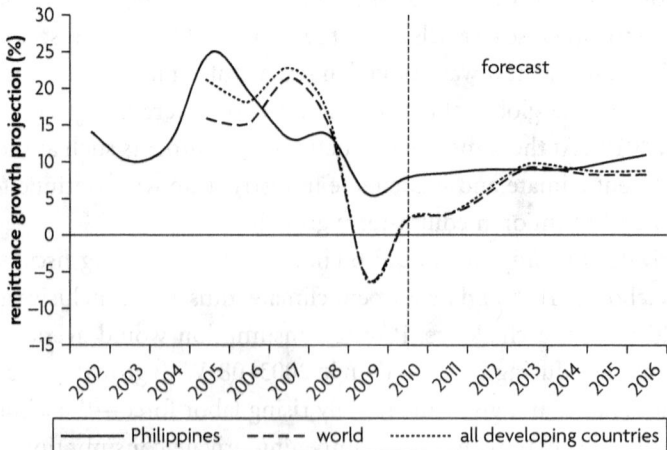

Source: BSP; World Bank.

Figure 9.14. Limited Fiscal Space would Constrain Public Investment

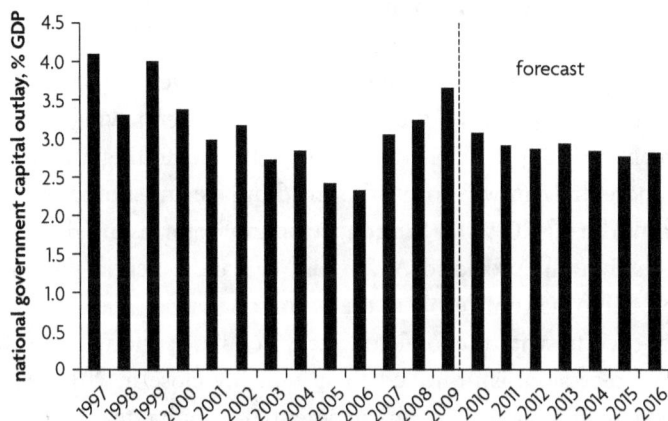

Source: DBM; World Bank.

boom period. Net FDI inflows would broadly track those of the pre-crisis period, although portfolio investment by foreigners would be lower than in the boom period. This is because global liquidity will be tighter when global fiscal and monetary stimuli are withdrawn. The electricity sector, which has suffered from insufficient investment, runs the risk of a supply shortage; this would hurt the economy from 2013 onward.

Net exports would not contribute much to GDP growth under the baseline scenario. Export growth would continue tracking developments in the market for electronics and semiconductors, which account for some 60 percent of the country's exports. While most of the Philippines' major exports are shipped to countries in the East Asian region, most ultimately go to high-income countries outside the region. With the recovery of high-income countries projected to be soft, the growth of exports of goods and services would average 6.3 percent, slightly below the boom period. Imports of goods and services would expand at a slightly higher rate than exports, as workers' remittance inflows continued to provide strong demand for consumer goods. The terms of trade would thus remain at the precrisis average level.[20]

Trade in services is expected to strengthen in the baseline scenario, partly because of the global recession. The BPO sector in the Philippines would continue to grow rapidly over the medium term as cost consolidation efforts accelerated globally. The country's competitive edge will continue to attract foreign investment in this sector. However, given its projected rapid growth, the industry may encounter growing problems in recruiting quality staff in sufficient numbers.

Potential growth in the baseline scenario is expected to remain below precrisis boom levels over the medium term, after having averaged 4.6 percent in 2002–08. Based on a growth accounting framework, annual potential growth over the medium term should slow to 4.2 percent during 2009–15. Without structural reforms, no new major growth catalysts are projected. As a result, TFP and potential growth are not expected to rise noticeably in the postcrisis period. The output gap, which opened up with the food and fuel price shock and widened with the global recession, is projected to sustainably close in 2013. This is partly due to the slow recovery in the potential growth rate (annual average of 4.2 percent), which reflects a slow increase in capital and a fall in productivity growth.

In a no-reform scenario, public finances would constitute an increasing source of risk to macroeconomic stability. With a weak structural tax effort and limited prospects for reducing primary spending, the overall fiscal balance would remain in deficit over the medium term. This, along with moderate growth and rising spreads, would keep public debt as a share of GDP rising over the forecast horizon (figure 9.15). Combined with the public sector's large gross financing requirements (currently about 19 percent of GDP), the potential for macroeconomic instability would increase.

Given moderate growth and labor market prospects, progress in fighting poverty would remain disappointing. The global recession would then (using micro-macro simulations) push 1 million more Filipinos into poverty in 2010 (Habib et al. 2010). Not surprisingly, the long-term effects of the crisis would mostly hurt the poor, as even a small reduction in their income can have lasting effects on their welfare (for example, by making households less likely to invest in education and health). Moreover, narrower fiscal space would also reduce government spending on the poor, although this could be cushioned by the large scale-up in the new Conditional Cash Transfers Program for poor households. The 2009 typhoons and the 2010 El Niño phenomenon are also expected to compound the duress of poor and near-poor households. The result could be large increases in hunger, as 74.8 percent of the poor

Figure 9.15. Debt Dynamics Worsen as a Result of High Deficit, Weak Growth, and Rising Spreads

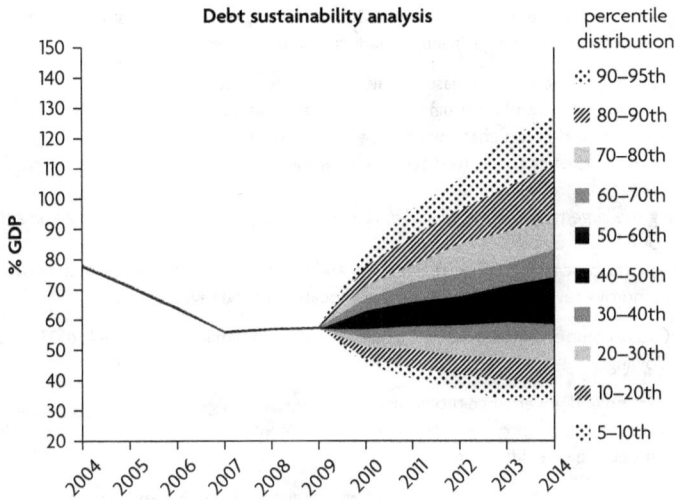

Source: BTr; World Bank staff calculations (for details, see World Bank 2009b).

reside in rural areas where self-subsistence farming is widespread (World Bank 2010d).

Reform Scenario

In the policy reform scenario, fiscal consolidation and reforms tackling growth bottlenecks would boost the economy's growth potential and result in inclusive growth (box 9.1). Fiscal reforms, particularly tax reforms, would raise the revenue necessary to finance badly needed social and infrastructure projects. Macroeconomic stability would also be preserved as the fiscal stance returns to a sustainable path. Also, robust and sustained reforms to boost the country's overall competitiveness would enable the Philippines to expand rapidly. Potential growth in this scenario would increase by an average of 6.1 percent during 2012–15, 1.9 percentage points higher than in the baseline scenario. The output gap would thus be closed by as early as 2010 (figure 9.16 and table 9.5).

The reform scenario would generate not only substantially higher growth, but also a rapid decrease in poverty over the medium term. Increased investment and exports, as the main beneficiaries of reform,

Box 9.1. Medium-Term Reform Agenda

The following specific fiscal reforms (World Bank 2010b) would promote the establishment of a sound tax policy framework and an efficient tax administration system:

- Raising and indexing excise taxes on gasoline, alcohol, and tobacco products
- Rationalizing tax incentives and reforming the corporate income tax system
- Implementing a moratorium on enacting revenue-eroding measures
- Appointing a commissioner for a fixed term, who would govern by an agreed-upon performance standard
- Strengthening the large taxpayer office and enforcement programs (for example, the Run After Tax Evaders, or RATE, program)
- Improving basic tax processes, such as registration, audits, and collection, and generating better fiscal data to improve revenue target setting and allocation to the revenue regions

Reforms to improve competitiveness and the overall investment climate (World Bank 2007, 2010d) include the following:

- Tackling corruption and governance problems
- Promptly addressing the country's weak business environment
- Enhancing competitive diversification by:

  - promoting the production and export of nontraditional manufacturing and services
  - increasing the efficiency of infrastructure and education spending
  - implementing gradual reforms to reduce elite capture in the agriculture, maritime, air transport, electricity, and cement industries to lower the cost of strategic inputs

- Improving MSMEs' and SMEs' access to finance to tap the potential growth contribution of lower-income segments of the population

would be the growth catalysts (figure 9.17). Investment growth would accelerate, and the reforms would enable the government to invest in infrastructure. This, in turn, would attract private investment, including large foreign direct and portfolio investment. Investments in the power sector would avert the potential power crisis seen in the baseline scenario, as reforms improve the business climate and institutional and regulatory framework. Private consumption, especially late in the forecast horizon, would also rise as fiscal consolidation and improved employment prospects boosted confidence. Government consumption would also improve toward the end of the forecast period, as revenue-driven fiscal consolidation created fiscal space for priority spending on health, education, and infrastructure. Finally, with more broadly shared growth, poverty would fall rapidly over the medium term.

Figure 9.16. Growth Path under Reform Scenario

Potential and actual growth path scenarios

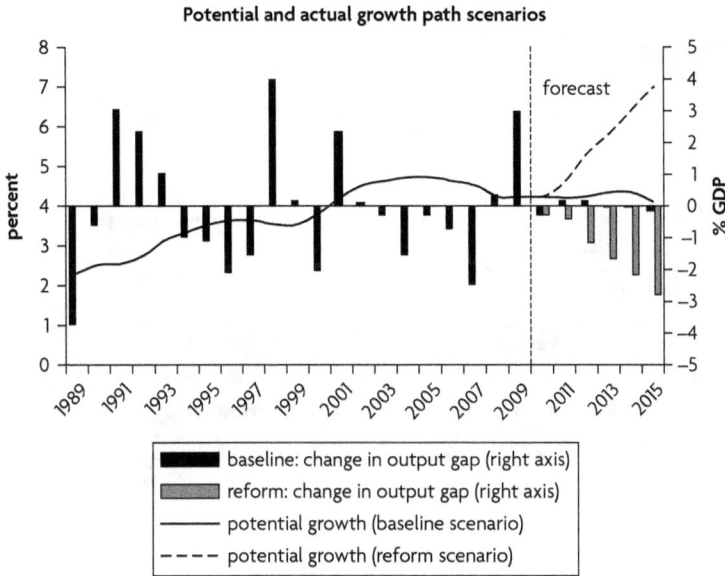

Legend:
- baseline: change in output gap (right axis)
- reform: change in output gap (right axis)
- potential growth (baseline scenario)
- - - - potential growth (reform scenario)

Source: NSCB; NSO; World Bank staff calculations.

Table 9.5. Growth Projections in the Reform Scenario, 2006–15
(percent)

	Actual			Avg.	Preliminary	Projection						Avg.
	2006	2007	2008	2003–08	2009	2010	2011	2012	2013	2014	2015	2012–15
Private consumption	5.5	5.8	4.7	5.3	4.1	5.3	4.9	4.9	4.9	4.8	4.8	4.9
Government consumption	10.4	6.6	0.4	4.0	10.9	6.0	2.6	3.0	3.5	4.0	4.0	3.6
Capital formation	5.1	12.4	2.3	3.5	−5.7	9.4	5.0	11.2	18.1	18.2	20.6	17.0
Exports	13.4	5.5	−2.0	6.9	−13.4	9.6	6.6	7.2	7.5	8.8	9.0	8.1
Imports	1.8	−4.1	0.8	2.9	−1.9	12.0	7.0	8.2	10.0	10.6	11.5	10.1
Statistical discrepancy	−136.6	337.5	−16.2	55.8	−74.6	37.0	...	...	...	...	...	...
GDP	5.3	7.1	3.7	5.4	1.1	4.4	4.6	5.4	6.0	6.5	6.8	6.2

Source: NSCB; World Bank staff calculations.
Note: ... = zero growth.

Figure 9.17. Reform Scenario Growth Path, Transition and Recovery

Growth scenarios: baseline vs reform path

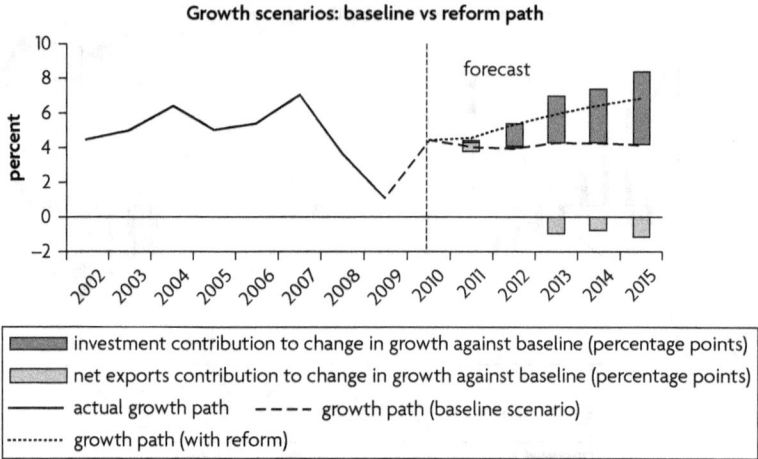

investment contribution to change in growth against baseline (percentage points)
net exports contribution to change in growth against baseline (percentage points)
——— actual growth path   – – – – growth path (baseline scenario)
.... growth path (with reform)

Source: NSCB; NSO; World Bank staff calculations.

Exports would also do well under the reform scenario, thanks to the rise in investment and a more enabling business environment. Real total export growth would rise, partly on the heels of a surge in commodity exports (agricultural, metals, and minerals); these commodities are currently badly undermined by an inadequate infrastructure, a high cost of doing business, and weak investment. Trade in services would expand substantially with increased competitiveness (tourism, for example, would benefit greatly from the structural reforms). Imports, however, would also accelerate as the investment surge would likely be more import-intensive. Overall, the trade deficit would widen in the medium term, but at a sustainable rate.

As the domestic economy strengthens, the growth of remittances can be expected to fall (as a percentage of GDP) as the upturn in the reform scenario encourages more Filipinos to stay in the country. This, together with a widening of the trade deficit, would drive the current account into a small deficit.

Notes

1. Key reforms include the amendment of the Foreign Investments Act of 1991 (which allowed up to 100 percent foreign ownership of a business enterprise

engaged in any activity not included in the foreign investment negative list) and the implementation of the build-operate-transfer projects (i.e., public-private partnerships, which also boosted private sector construction activity).

2. On the demand side, this development did not translate into notable increases in net exports because the country's exports have relatively low value added; a large share of the value chain comes from imports that are reprocessed for export.

3. Electronics and semiconductors accounted for more than 60 percent of total merchandise exports in 2002–08, versus 42 percent in 1995.

4. Major power outages already occurred in the first half of 2010 on the island of Mindanao, partly the result of low hydropower generation (because of El Niño). With no additional investment in the power sector, extensive power outages are also expected during 2012–14 on the island of Luzon, where most of the country's value added is created.

5. Surveys consistently cite poor infrastructure and governance as top constraints to competitiveness in the Philippines. For example, the country's ranking— based on the IMD *World Competitiveness Yearbook*—has been dragged down by an infrastructure sector that ranks among the worst in the sample countries and a deterioration in governance effectiveness in the boom period. Other surveys such as the one by Transparency International reveal an increased perception of corruption incidence, which has adversely affected the country's ability to efficiently deliver public goods and social services (see figure 9.4).

6. While unemployment is lower from 2005 onward than during the 2000–04 period, the two periods are not comparable as there has been a change in the unemployment definition since 2005 and no overlap year with the two definitions (refer to table 9.1).

7. The program centered on increasing revenue and reducing spending. During 2004–06, three tax laws were passed: an increase in excise tax for alcohol, cigarettes, and tobacco products; the Lateral Attrition Act; and the Reformed Value Added Tax Law.

8. Most of these proceeds were received in 2007 (Php 90.6 billion) and 2008 (Php 31.3 billion). The largest privatization operations were the sales of the Philippines National Oil Company–Energy Development Corporation in 2006 and 2007 (Php 66.8 billion), Petron Corporation in 2008 (Php 25.7 billion), and the Philippines Telecommunications Investment Corporation in 2007 (Php 25.2 billion).

9. The IPP is an annual listing of preferred sectors for investments eligible for greater tax and nontax incentives from the government.

10. For example, the World Bank and Asian Development Bank's *Investment Climate Survey 2004*, or the various annual business surveys conducted by the World Economic Forum and Makati Business Club.

11. The implementation of risk-based financial reporting also helped banks increase capital so that the capital adequacy ratio was well above the required level.

12. In contrast to many other Asian countries affected by the Asian financial crisis, the Philippines entered the crisis with a relatively high debt-to-GDP ratio, so it did not have the fiscal space to introduce a bailout for the banking industry. As a result, the writedowns of nonperforming assets and loans and the cleanup of bank balance sheets was protracted; NPLs returned to pre-Asian-crisis levels only by 2008 (figure 9.12).

13. The Basel II framework describes a more comprehensive measure and minimum standard for capital adequacy. It seeks to improve on existing rules by aligning regulatory banks' capital requirements more closely to underlying risks and also seeks to promote more forward-looking capital supervision.

14. About 26 out of 32 major banks took advantage of the accounting rule change to avert Php 30 billion in losses—equivalent to 48 percent of the total profits of the entire banking system in 2007 (World Bank 2009a).

15. Turner (2007) shows that while international bank lending to developing Asia doubled between 2000 and 2006, lending to the Philippines, comprising a mere 3 percent of the flows, grew by only 27 percent.

16. Remittance inflows, however, rose in the fourth quarter of 2009, as overseas Filipinos sent large amounts of money for the recovery and reconstruction needs of family members flooded by two severe typhoons that hit the country in September–October.

17. The Legacy Financial Group owner allegedly misused depositors' money, leading to the collapse of a number of rural banks.

18. The total ERP reached Php 330 billion (4.1 percent of GDP), of which 88 percent consisted of expenditure measures—Php 160 billion from increased national government spending, Php 100 billion to finance extrabudgetary infrastructure projects, and Php 30 billion for temporary additional benefits to social security members—with the remaining 12 percent consisting of general tax cuts for corporations and individuals.

19. For example, in the seafaring industry—which has been, and continues to be, sharply affected by the global recession and the collapse in global trade and cruise ship tourism—the pressure to drastically reduce costs has led some companies to accelerate their staff sourcing from countries such as the Philippines, which has a large pool of comparatively cheap English-speaking and well-qualified seafarers.

20. Developments in electronics and semiconductor prices have limited impact on the Philippines' terms of trade, as exports in that sector are part of a global supply chain where domestic value added is limited. The country's terms of trade are more sensitive to the prices of imported oil and consumer goods, especially rice. As international prices of these commodities are projected to be broadly stable, terms of trade over the medium term are projected to remain at the precrisis average level.

References

Aldaba, Rafaelita. 2005. "Policy Reversals, Lobby Groups and Economic Distortions." Discussion Paper 2005–04, Philippine Institute for Development Studies, Makati City.

Bocchi, Alessandro Magnoli. 2008. *Rising Growth, Declining Investment: The Paradox of the Philippines*. Washington, DC: World Bank.

Botman, Dennis. 2009. "Fiscal Policy during Downturns and the Pros and Cons of Alternative Fiscal Rules." Country Report 09/63, International Monetary Fund, Washington, DC.

Fedelino, Annalisa, Anna Ivanova, and Mark Horton 2009. "Computing Cyclically Adjusted Balances and Automatic Stabilizers. Fiscal Affairs Department Technical Notes and Manual, International Monetary Fund, Washington, DC.

Gereffi, Gary, and Karina Fernandez-Stark. 2010. "The Offshore Services Value Chain: Developing Countries and the Crisis." Policy Research Working Paper 5262, World Bank, Washington, DC.

Habib, Bilal, Ambar Narayan, Sergio Olivieri, and Carolina Sanchez-Paramo. 2010. "Assessing Ex Ante the Employment, Poverty and Distributional Impact of the Global Crisis in Philippines: A Micro-simulation Approach." Policy Research Working Paper 5286, World Bank, Washington, DC.

Loretan, Mico, and Philip Wooldridge. 2008. "The Development of Money Markets in Asia." *BIS Quarterly Review* (September).

National Economic and Development Authority. 2004. *Medium-Term Philippine Development Plan 2004–2010*. Manila: National Economic and Development Authority.

Turner, Philip. 2007. "Are Banking Systems in East Asia Stronger?" *Asian Economic Policy Review* 2: 75–95.

World Bank. 2007. "Invigorating Growth, Enhancing Its Impact, 2007." Philippines Development Report, World Bank, Manila.

———. 2009a. "Banking Sector Risks in the Philippines." Draft, World Bank, Manila.

———. 2009b. *Philippines Quarterly Update* (July). World Bank, Manila.

———. 2010a. *Philippines Quarterly Update* (February). World Bank, Manila.

———. 2010b. *Public Expenditure Review*. World Bank, Manila.

———. 2010c. "Managing the Global Recession, Preparing for the Recovery." *Philippines Development Report 2009*. World Bank, Manila.

———. 2010d. *Fostering Inclusive Growth* (June). World Bank, Manila.

Zakharova, Daria. 2006. "Cyclically-Adjusted Balances and Fiscal Sustainability in the Philippines." Country Report 06/181, International Monetary Fund, Washington, DC.

Comment on "Philippines: Weak Investment Climate and Fiscal Deficit Constrain Growth Prospects"

Milan Brahmbhatt and Manu Sharma

The paper by Eric Le Borgne and Sheryll Namingit provides a lot of interesting information about the precrisis period in the Philippines, what happened during the crisis, and the prospects for recovery and the medium-term future. Broadly speaking, we agree with the paper's expectation of only muted growth—a little above 4 percent—in the baseline scenario. The authors could, however, have dug more deeply into some aspects of the sources of growth before the crisis, which would help provide a better foundation for the baseline scenario. The authors may also be somewhat optimistic regarding the proposed reform scenario.

The chapter identifies three phases of precrisis growth:

1. The significant reforms under the Ramos administration of the early 1990s, followed by a significant but brief growth pickup in the

---

Milan Brahmbhatt is Senior Adviser, and Manu Sharma is Junior Professional Associate, Poverty Reduction and Economic Management Network, World Bank.

mid-1990s, accompanied by stronger investment and progress on poverty reduction.

2. The sharp deceleration in growth after the East Asian financial crisis, followed by the shock of the dot-com crash in 2001.

3. The substantial acceleration in growth during 2003–07, which, however, appears to have been quite different in important ways relative to the growth pickup of the 1990s.

This recent period of apparently robust growth is quite mysterious in at least a couple of respects. First, there is what one might call the mystery of capital. On a cross-country basis, substantial growth accelerations are typically accompanied by a boom in investment—as documented, for example, in the paper by Hausmann, Pritchett, and Rodrik (2005). In the Philippines in the early 2000s, however, it was accompanied by a major deceleration in capital accumulation and a sharp fall in the share of private investment in GDP. Employment growth also appears to have slowed.

Thus it would seem that most of the growth acceleration came from an improvement in total factor productivity (TFP) growth. That sounds good, but it does not dispose of the mystery entirely. It would be helpful to dig more deeply into the nature or decomposition of this boom period for TFP. Higher TFP growth should raise the marginal product of capital and, over time, also induce higher investment. Indeed, returns to assets rose from 5 percent in the mid-1990s to 9 percent in 2006; but this was apparently not enough to attract higher investment. Instead, a significant part of the rise in output and in TFP appears to have resulted from rising capacity utilization. Corporations also used rising profits to pay down debts and improve financial balance sheets, but not to invest. This raises the question of how sustainable TFP growth will be if it does not induce stronger investment over time. Some other things one might expect to accompany rising TFP—such as improved international competitiveness—also did not occur. Instead, the Philippines' share in world exports actually fell in the first part of the decade of the 2000s, and this was also true for such major export components as high tech and apparel.[1]

The analysis sometimes appears to be of two minds about the character of the precrisis boom. At one point, it attributes the boom in part to the reforms of the early 1990s, which seems like a long time to wait for reform payoffs. In other places, however, the paper points to continued problems of governance and corruption and, indeed, to policy reversals in various areas. In providing some explanations for the weakness of investment, the article cites such things as elite capture of key input-producing industries, a poor investment climate, and continued weak governance.

Here the discussion is on the right track, although it should address the point that many of these weaknesses are long-standing problems and would not by themselves explain the weakening of investment seen in the early 2000s. To strengthen its argument, the paper could present clearer evidence of deterioration in political and governance conditions in the period under review. The Transparency International index of corruption perceptions, for example, shows deterioration between the late 1990s and the late part of the following decade. The same is true of the International Country Risk Guide perceptions index for government stability (World Bank 2008). The chapter itself notes that businesses have found regulations and procedures not just complicated but "increasingly complicated" and that there were reversals on the trade policy front. In addition, progress on the fiscal front came to an end in 2006 with the failure of several proposed major fiscal bills. Also, as the paper notes, there is now some deterioration in the fiscal structural balance owing to the permanent character of many of the fiscal measures in the countercyclical fiscal stimulus program passed in 2009.

Summing up, we see a demand-led boom (fueled primarily by exceptionally strong remittances) accompanied by some deterioration in governance and general development policies. We see firms generally meeting rising demand through increased capacity utilization and some increase in the efficiency of use of the existing capital stock, but failing to make the substantial new investments needed to sustain long-run growth.

The second mystery that needs fuller explanation is the apparent failure of growth to have an impact on poverty. How do we explain this poverty-neutral or even anti-poor growth path? What happened to income distribution? It's possible, even likely, that it got more skewed, and one could link this to the supply-side decomposition of growth—that is, TFP-led growth that sharply boosted returns to capital but failed to raise returns to labor since weak investment was accompanied by weak employment growth.

Again, we have little argument with the modest medium-term baseline growth projections, although a few comments on the reform scenario may be in order.

First, it may be worth asking what it would take for a reform scenario to actually come about, in political-economy terms, and whether the political balance of forces in the wake of the recent presidential election gives room for hope. Second, we could question the economic realism of the reform scenario. Reforms of the type outlined might take years to design and implement in a country like the Philippines—and perhaps years more before they have an effect on growth and poverty. The projection of a near vertical acceleration in growth rates is perhaps meant to provide encouragement and incentives for reform, but it may not have this effect if it is seen as unrealistic. Arguably, growth acceleration could take place if the government sends strong, credible signals about its reformist intentions, even though the reforms themselves could take some time to implement. The paper could spell out more clearly the two or three highest-priority actions that the new government could take to send such credible signals.

Note

1. Information in this paragraph on capacity utilization, corporate profitability, and trade competitiveness draws on the Philippines Development Report (World Bank 2008).

References

Hausmann, Ricardo, Lant Pritchett, and Dani Rodrik. 2005. "Growth Accelerations," *Journal of Economic Growth* 10 (4): 303–29.

World Bank. 2008. "Accelerating Inclusive Growth and Deepening Fiscal Stability." Philippines Development Report, World Bank, Washington, DC.

From Crisis Resilience to Robust Growth

Kaspar Richter and Maciej Krzak

Poland's economic record after its transition to a market economy has been strong. In the two decades leading up to the global financial crisis, policy reforms and economic integration with Europe fueled a remarkable expansion. As the crisis broke out, this integration made Poland vulnerable to the collapse in international capital, trade, and labor flows. Yet Poland performed well during the crisis, reflecting a diversified and flexible economy, fairly strong macroeconomic balances going into the crisis, and sound policy responses during the crisis.

In this chapter, we examine Poland's growth prospects based on an investigation of its growth history. Drawing on an analysis of competitiveness, investment, and trade, we argue that growth drivers of the past might not sustain high growth in the future. To ensure prosperity in the future, Poland faces the need for reforms to shore up the productive capacity of its economy.

Kaspar Richter is Senior Economist, Europe and Central Asia Poverty Reduction and Economic Management Department, World Bank, and Maciej Krzak is Coordinator of the Macroeconomic Team, Center for Social and Economic Research (CASE), Poland. The authors are grateful to Ewa Kroczyc for outstanding research assistance.

Precrisis Years

Transition and European Union (EU) Accession

Poland's transition from a planned to a market economy was launched in 1989, when the economy was reeling under high inflation, large fiscal deficits, and large foreign debt. The first noncommunist government since World War II implemented a vigorous program of stabilization, liberalization, and privatization. In December 1989 the Parliament adopted a package of 11 acts prepared under the Balcerowicz Plan, covering state-owned companies, banking, credits, taxation, foreign investment, foreign currencies, customs, and employment. Rescheduling agreements with the Paris Club of sovereign creditors in 1991 and with the London Club of private credits in 1994 paved the way for access to international financial markets. Major banks were privatized, often with the help of foreign strategic investors. In 1999 Poland launched ambitious reforms of its public finances (including devolution of expenditure authority to local governments), health care (including reorganization into regional health care centers), pensions (introduction of a three-pillar system), and education (delaying the vocational training track in order to expand students' exposure to general secondary curricula). In 2004, after a political divide lasting over half a century, Poland, along with the other seven countries in Central and Eastern Europe, became a full EU member. Poland's overall economic integration into the EU was virtually complete by the date of accession. In preparation for accession, Poland undertook far-reaching structural reforms to enable it to integrate into the EU's system of political and economic governance. Negotiations covered 31 chapters, based on the key principle of no permanent derogation from EU rules, although transitional periods (ranging from 6 months to 12 years) were accorded. Entry into the EU signified a fully functioning open market economy and the adoption of the economic legislation included in the *acquis communautaire*. EU membership brought Poland access to the European single market, including rights to substantial freedom of movement of goods, people, services, and capital; it also enabled participation in the many institutions and financing mechanisms available to EU members. In addition, the legal and institutional stability and free trade flows within the EU brought foreign direct investment (FDI), especially from the

EU15. This helped Poland to overcome the lack of domestic savings and to increase investments. Polish growth accelerated as EU accession, supported by credit growth and a favorable external environment, bolstered business confidence, spurred investment, and boosted wages and employment.

Poland's average per capita growth after 1992 reached 4.6 percent, leading to an expansion of the economy by 120 percent (figure 10.1). This performance puts it on par with the Slovak Republic, and ahead of Hungary and the Czech Republic. Growth brought about rapid convergence to EU income levels, with especially sizable gains since 2005 (figure 10.2). Only two years after the launch of market reforms in late 1989, Poland emerged from a severe depression, ahead of other transition countries. Growth accelerated from –7 percent in 1991 to 6 percent in 1996 on the back of Poland's early stabilization program, the strength of market-oriented reforms, and an investment boom. The sharp expansion in trade and current account deficits in the second half of the 1990s made Poland vulnerable to financial market volatility. In response to the financial crises in the Russian Federation and East Asia, the National Bank of Poland (NBP) raised the policy rate from 13 percent in September 1999 to 19 percent by August 2000 to curtail domestic demand and inflation. Growth moderated to about 1 percent in 2001–02 as a

Figure 10.1 GDP per Capita Growth

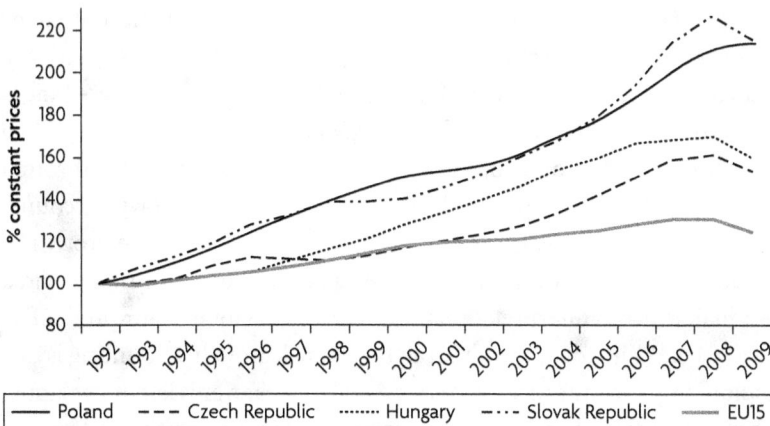

Source: EC Ameco Database.

Figure 10.2 GDP per Capita in Purchasing Power Standards

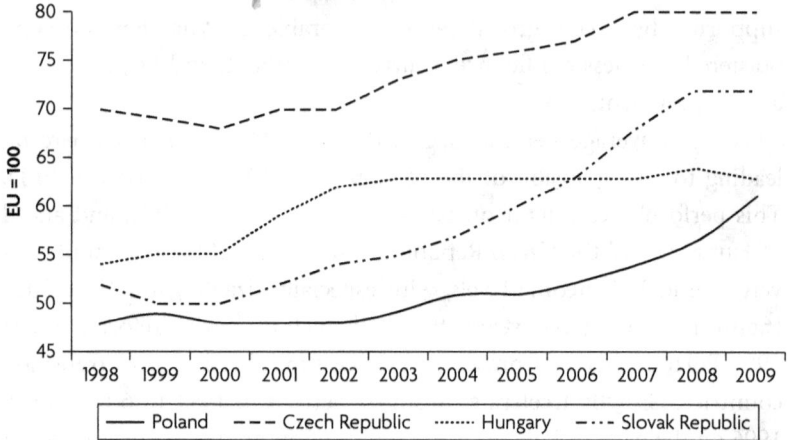

Source: EC Ameco Database.

result of the monetary tightening cycle, recessions in key Polish export markets, including Germany and Russia, and the loss of competitiveness owing to the rise in international oil prices. Growth resumed in the run-up to EU accession, supported by the upswing in the external economic environment and FDI flows.

Productivity Growth and Trade Integration

To what extent did Poland's growth rely on the accumulation of factor inputs rather than the more efficient usage of available factors? Extensive growth would support the notion that Poland's competitiveness hinges foremost on the availability of natural resources and labor force, while intensive growth would indicate that technological progress through innovation and competition plays an important role. Growth accounting sheds light on this issue. The main idea is to decompose growth in output into the contributions of higher quantities of factor inputs and a residual, which is interpreted as improvements in total factor productivity (TFP). While conceptually straightforward, growth accounting is difficult to implement. Since TFP is set equal to whatever is left unexplained by the identified factors, its measurement is highly sensitive to the precise method of constructing capital and labor inputs. In addition, lack of data typically restricts the analysis to a fairly aggregated level. Finally, the framework assumes that output is primarily supply constrained, which makes it difficult to accommodate episodes such as the global financial crisis or the subsequent recovery process where capacity utilization is increasing.

Growth accounting for Poland highlights two issues. First, economic growth is mostly due to TFP rather than to increases in capital and labor (World Bank 2008a; Burda and Severgnini 2009). From 1992 to 2009, TFP contributed 2.7 percentage points or 60 percent of the 4.5 percent average growth rate. This compares to 1.2 percentage points for capital, spurred by FDI and financial market integration in Europe, and 0.5 percentage points for labor and human capital. Second, similar to other EU10 countries, the drivers of TFP changed since early in the transition (World Bank 2008a). During the 1990s, the transition to a market economy involved a substantial reallocation of labor and capital from low- to high-productivity sectors. In addition, high TFP reflected heavy firm turnover, including the entry of new, more productive firms and the exit of obsolete firms. Furthermore, firms began using their excess labor and capital, which had become idle during the deep transitional recession; consequently, output increased, and this is captured in TFP estimates. By contrast, in the early 2000s, TFP reflected increasing productivity gains within firms. Furthermore, the EU accession boom from 2003 to 2008 relied more on larger contributions from labor, while the post-transition boom from 1996 to 2000 relied more on improvements in TFP (figure 10.3). The growth contributions from labor improved during the early 2000s for two reasons. The entry of baby boom cohorts from the early 1980s into the labor market expanded the labor force and led to higher growth. In addition, the education reforms launched in late 1990 improved the quality of human capital during the opening decade of the 2000s.

A key driver of TFP in the early 2000s was trade integration. While exports of goods and services remained at around 25 percent of GDP during the post-transition boom in the second half of the 1990s, the EU accession boom of the early 2000s was fueled by rising exports, which reached 40 percent of GDP in 2008. The increase in exports contributed to a decline in the trade deficit of about 1 percent of GDP, which in turn supported GDP growth during the EU accession boom even though

Figure 10.3 Growth Factor Decomposition by Growth Period

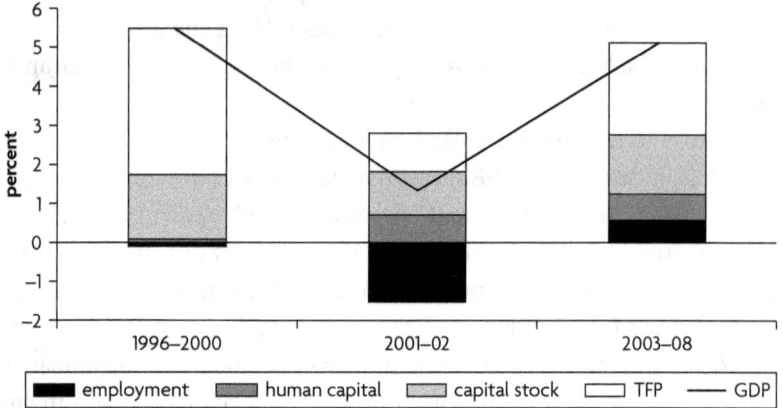

Source: The Conference Board Total Economy Database.

growth contributions from consumption and investment were lower than during the post-transition boom. Poland's trade links with other European countries increased strongly during the beginning years of the 2000s, as FDI brought knowledge spillovers, integration into vertical supply chains, and quality upgrading of products. Poland's export market share increased from 0.9 percent in 1999 to 1.9 percent in 2007 within the EU15, and from 2 percent to 3.7 percent within the EU10.[1] Trade integration was not limited to the EU. Trade with the rest of the world expanded rapidly, and Poland's global export market share rose from 0.5 percent in 1999 to 1.0 percent in 2007.

Before enlargement, Poland was expected to increase its specialization in labor-intensive export products during the 2000s to take advantage of low wages. Instead, FDI inflows attracted initially by large-scale privatization and later by a supportive investment climate, access to the EU market, and the growing role of cross-border production networks brought about an upgrading in the quality of the export basket. Many EU15 industries and companies took advantage of this by splitting their production chains and engaging in vertical specialization. Examples include the automotive industry, which expanded to Poland, as well as the Czech Republic, Hungary, Romania, and the Slovak Republic; the information and communication technology industries; and the financial sector, which opened up refinancing possibilities from abroad for foreign-owned banks, which contributed to substantial bank credit expansion. In Poland, the share of labor-intensive exports of total exports dropped from 34 percent in 1999 to 22 percent in 2006, while the share of research-intensive exports increased from 27 percent to 35 percent (figure 10.4). Similarly, in manufacturing exports, the share of low-technology exports declined over this period from 37 percent to 26 percent (figure 10.5). However, export classification of high-tech products is controversial and hard to interpret. The same high-tech exports gains can be the result of different production processes— improvements in product innovation and development, more sophisticated design and fabrication, or simply incorporating a relatively low-skill assembly process. The first process is the most, and the last process the least, integral to enhancing productivity. Even though Poland's export basket became technologically more sophisticated, Polish companies remain foremost "assemblers" rather than "designers" or even "innovators."

Trade integration and export expansion changed Poland's value added sectoral composition. Poland's gross value added growth rate of 4.4 percent over the period 1995–2008 is slower only than the Slovak Republic's (figure 10.6). As in the other Visegrad countries,[2] growth was

Figure 10.4 Composition of Exports by Factor Intensity

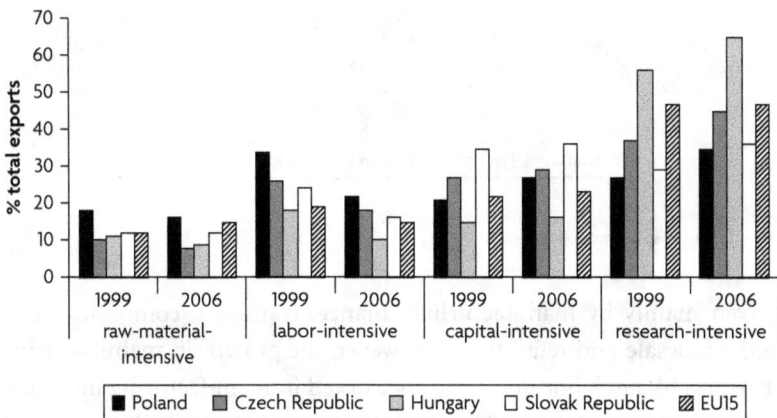

Source: UN Comtrade; EC 2009c.

Figure 10.5 Composition of Manufacturing Exports by Technology Intensity

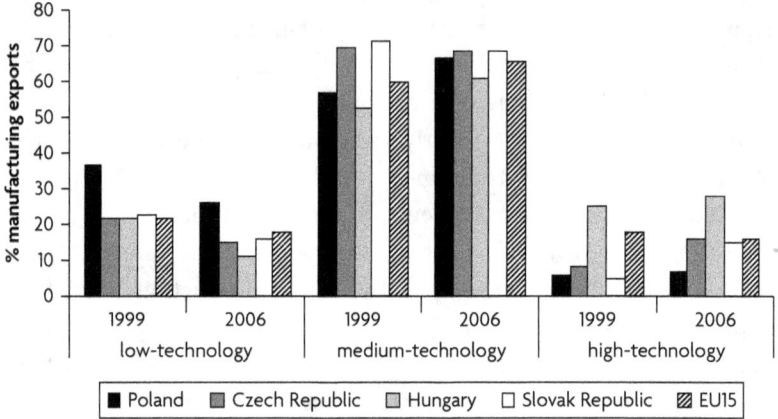

Source: UN Comtrade; EC 2009c.

Figure 10.6 Annual Sectoral Growth Rates of Gross Value Added (GVA), 1995–2008

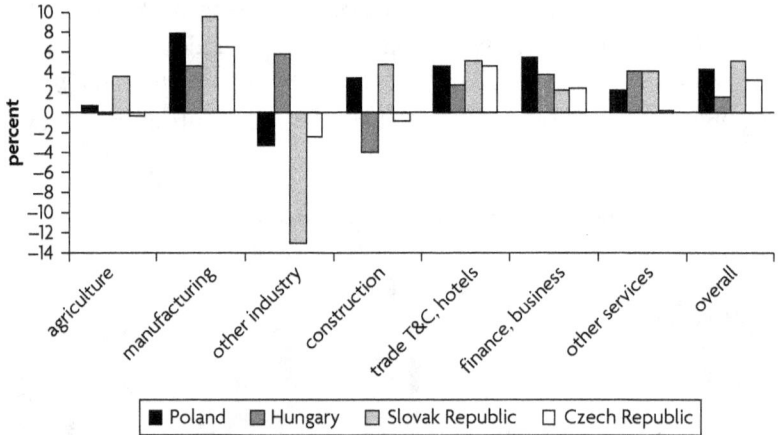

Source: Eurostat.
Note: T&C = transport and communication.

driven mainly by manufacturing, finance, transport, communication, and wholesale and retail trade. However, the growth in manufacturing relied on higher labor input. Hours worked in manufacturing increased in Poland from 1995 to 2008 by 45 percent, and remained constant or declined elsewhere (figure 10.7). As a result, gross value added (GVA)

Figure 10.7 Annual Growth Rates of GVA, Hours Worked, and GVA per Hour, 1995–2008

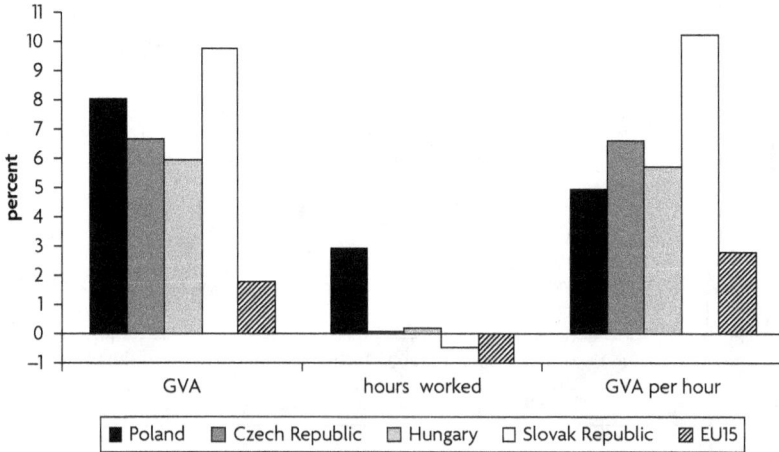

Source: Eurostat.

per hour increased in Poland just on par with the EU15, and far slower than in the Slovak Republic, the Czech Republic, and Hungary. In addition, Poland's manufacturing sector contributed in 2008 only 25 percent of gross value added, compared to 32 percent in the Czech Republic and 39 percent in the Slovak Republic.

Differences in productivity growth, nominal wage inflation, and exchange rate trends resulted in a 30 percent appreciation in Poland's real exchange rate since 2004 relative to the euro area. Real exchange rate appreciation—the ratio of nontradables to tradables prices—naturally accompanies economic convergence; for example, productivity growth in the tradables sector increases the relative prices of the nontradables sector via the Balassa-Samuelson effect (Mihaljek and Klau 2008). Indeed, Poland's real exchange rate appreciation was less than that in Hungary, and far less than that in the Slovak Republic and the Czech Republic, suggesting no major misalignment of the exchange rate (Darvas 2010). Real unit labor costs declined noticeably after 2001 (figure 10.8). Poland's labor costs per hour as a share of the EU15's remain moderate, even though they increased from 17 percent in 1997 to 26 percent in 2007.

Figure 10.8 Real Unit Labor Costs

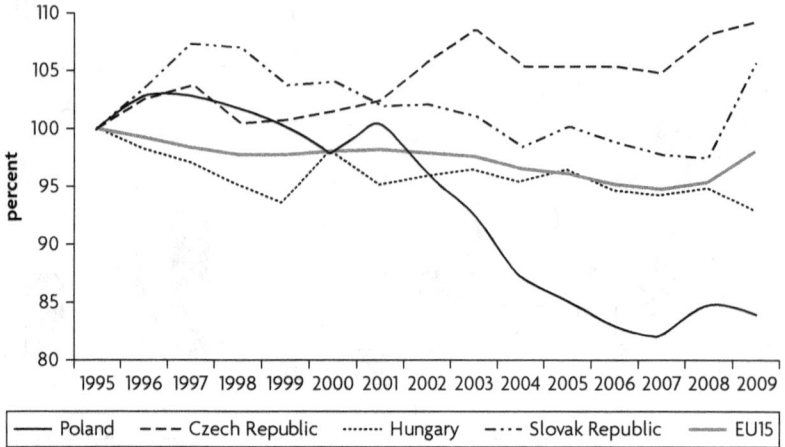

Source: EC Ameco Database.

Savings and Investment

A major economic difference between the EU15 countries and Poland, along with other EU10 countries, is the stock of productive capital. The estimated capital stock is about three times the size of GDP in the old member states, but only two times the size of GDP in Poland and other EU10 countries. This difference in capital endowment means that new member states are less productive than old member states. Hence, capital accumulation is crucial for raising productivity in Poland.

Tapping foreign savings can accelerate this process. International capital inflows and the accumulation of financial and equity claims by foreign investors on income generated domestically typically come along with current account deficits. Poland's net payments abroad turned negative from 2004 onward but remained fairly modest at 1.7 percent of GDP, compared to 4.1 percent to 7 percent of GDP in the Slovak Republic, the Czech Republic, and Hungary from 2004 to 2008. Likewise, Poland's current account deficits remained mostly below 3 percent of GDP, the lowest among the Visegrad countries and mostly financed by foreign direct investment, and reached 5 percent of GDP or more only in 1999–2000 and 2007–08. Nevertheless, a structural weakness of Poland's economy is low investment (figure 10.9). Its investment rate was about 7 percent of GDP lower than in the Slovak Republic and the Czech Republic, mainly because of lower private savings and lower private foreign investments. In particular, the private savings-investment gap from 1999 to 2008 was zero in Poland, but –2.8 to –3.7 percent of GDP in the Czech Republic, Hungary, and the Slovak Republic (figure 10.10). This translates to over 30 percent lower investment in machinery and equipment in Poland than in the Czech Republic and the Slovak Republic.

In contrast to the private savings-investment gap, Poland's public savings-investment gap was sizable. From 1995 to 2008, the overall fiscal deficit averaged 4.2 percent of GDP and the structural fiscal deficit 4.4 percent of GDP. Government expenditures exceeded revenues throughout this period, even at the peak of the economic cycle. In particular, from 2003 to 2008, fiscal policy was procyclical, with large increases in public spending masked by unsustainably high revenue growth. This allowed benign developments in headline fiscal deficits despite an unfinished agenda of public spending reforms.

Figure 10.9 Savings and Investment, 1999–2008

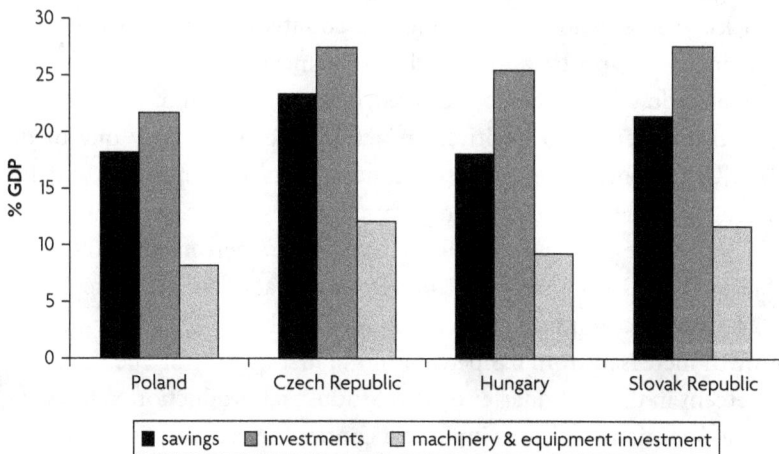

Source: EC Ameco Database.
Note: Machinery and equipment investment for Hungary is from 2000 to 2008.

Figure 10.10 Public and Private Savings and Investment Gaps, 1999–2008

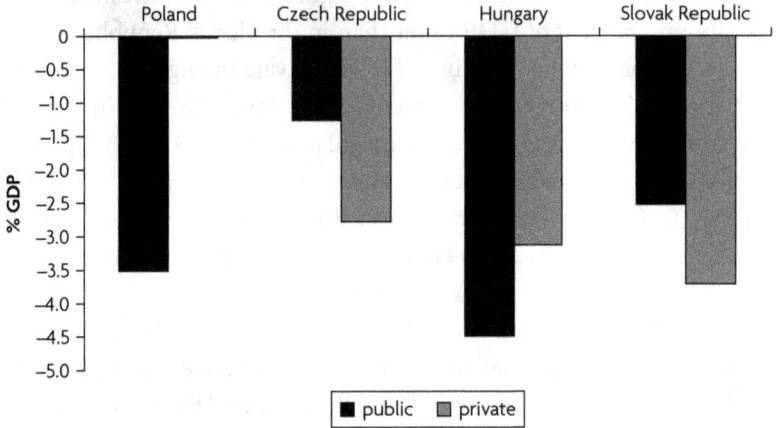

Source: EC Ameco Database.

Global Financial Crisis

Economic Impact

The global economic crisis ended Poland's speedy economic expansion, but in contrast to its neighbors Poland has avoided a decline in economic activity. Poland's growth started to slow in mid-2008 due to emerging capacity constraints. In late 2008, Poland was hit by two shocks: the recession in high-income countries, which hurt external demand for exports; and the global financial crisis, which reduced capital inflows and thereby lowered domestic demand. Nevertheless, growth has remained positive. In fact, Poland is the only one of the 27 EU member states whose economy has continued to expand throughout the crisis. According to preliminary European Commission (EC) estimates, Poland's economy grew by 1.7 percent in 2009, while that of the EU declined by 4.1 percent and that of the EU10 region by 4.2 percent. Economic activity rebounded further in 2010. Year-on-year growth increased from 0.8 percent in the first quarter of 2009 to about 3 percent in the first quarter of 2010. Industrial production, retail sales, and economic projections indicate a continuing recovery in the second quarter of 2010.

Poland's economic slowdown has been muted for a number of reasons (box 10.1). First, Poland entered the crisis with relatively moderate macroeconomic imbalances. This lessened the need for adjustment. While actual output exceeded potential output, as in Poland just prior to the crisis, the output gap in 2008 remained the smallest among the Visegrad countries according to EC estimates. Countries with the largest imbalances, as reflected in large bank-related capital inflows, high inflation, and large current account deficits, experienced the greatest downturns in economic activity in 2009 (figure 10.11).

- In Poland foreign-owned banks, representing about 70 percent of the banking sector's assets, fueled an expansion in credit that was more rapid than in other countries, and more focused on the household than the enterprise sector. Credit to the private sector remained below 50 percent of GDP in 2008, less than in the Baltic countries, Bulgaria, the Czech Republic, and Hungary. Moderate bank-related inflows also kept inflation at bay. Financial stability was strengthened by the adoption of banking supervision practices in line with the EU legal framework, the unification with the Polish Financial Supervision Authority (FSA) in January 2008, and the creation of a Financial

---

Box 10.1. Resilience of Poland's Economy in 2009: Indicative Quantification of Selected Factors

The following factors contributed to Poland's economic resilience in 2009:

- *Large domestic economy:* a 10-percentage-point increase in the export-to-GDP ratio lowered GDP growth in 2009 on average by about 0.5 percentage point. For example, the economies of the Czech Republic, the Slovak Republic, and Hungary, which all have export-to-GDP ratios of about 80 percent, declined by 4.2, 4.7, and 6.3 percent, respectively, in 2009, while Poland's economy expanded by 1.7 percent.
- *Exchange rate depreciation:* Poland's real effective exchange rate depreciated from July 2008 to March 2009 by about 30 percent. This may have boosted growth by 1.5–2.0 percentage points with a lag of about one year.
- *Countercyclical fiscal policy:* The large domestic market of the Polish economy and accommodative monetary policy stance are likely to have strengthened the impact of fiscal policy. The widening of Poland's fiscal deficit from 3.6 percent of GDP in 2008 to 7.2 percent could have added 1.5 percentage points to growth in 2009.

Source: European Commission 2009a; authors' calculations.

Figure 10.11 GDP Growth versus Bank-Related Inflows, Current Account Balance, and Inflation Rate

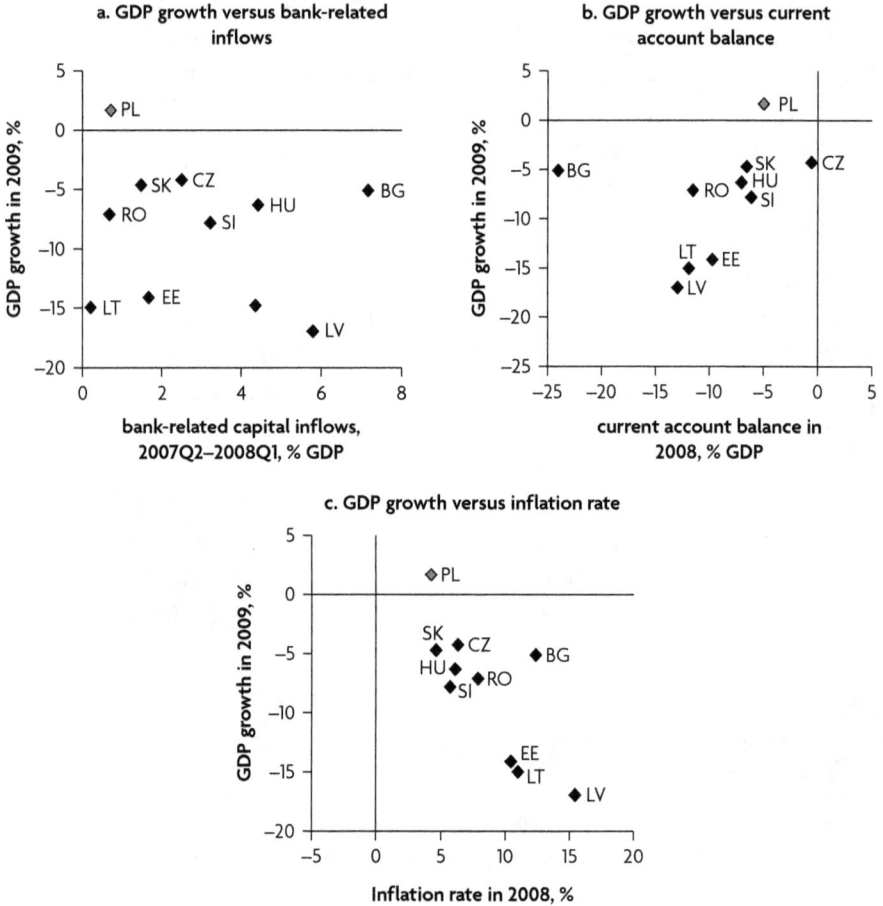

a. GDP growth versus bank-related
inflows

b. GDP growth versus current
account balance

c. GDP growth versus inflation rate

Source: Eurostat.

Stability Committee. The FSA also took measures to limit the expansion of foreign currency credit, which became more attractive with the rapid appreciation of the Polish zloty.

- The NBP's effective inflation targeting regime using a free-floating exchange rate helped anchor inflation expectations over the course of decade. With record-low unemployment pushing wage increases in excess of productivity gains and high international commodity prices, inflation peaked in July–August 2008 at 4.8 percent—above the upper end of the 1.5–3.5 percent tolerance range—but stabilized quickly thereafter. The central bank raised the policy rate by 200 basis points during 2007–08, ending the easing cycle only in November 2008 in response to the global financial crisis.

- Poland's current account deficit widened in 2007 and 2008 to around 5 percent of GDP, linked to rapid import growth and a rise in private investment, yet it remained fairly low compared to other EU10 countries.

Second, the country's relatively large domestic economy has limited its exposure to the decline in world trade. Exports of goods account for about 30 percent of GDP in Poland, only half of the share in other Visegrad countries. Moreover, the slump in global demand has been harsher for investment than for consumption goods. This has limited the impact on Polish exports, which are more oriented toward consumption goods. At the same time, the flexible exchange rate regime has facilitated the economy's adjustment to the external shock. While the zloty regained some value since March 2009 owing to strengthening investor confidence, the depreciation of the real exchange rate exceeds that of Poland's neighbors. This has supported the sharp turnaround in net exports. With the contraction in imports exceeding the contraction in exports, net exports turned positive and became the principal stabilizing force in 2009 (figure 10.12). The current account deficit narrowed to 1.6 percent of GDP in 2009 from 5.5 percent in 2008, reducing external vulnerabilities.

Third, as Poland entered the crisis with fairly moderate imbalances, the government was able to cushion the impact of the crisis. Fiscal policy has shored up growth through automatic stabilizers and discretionary measures, and it has also contained the rise in public debt through consolidation measures. The general government deficit doubled to 7.2 percent of GDP in 2009 from 3.6 percent in 2008. About two-thirds of the increase was due to lower revenues. Poland adopted fiscal recovery measures equal to about 2 percent of GDP in 2009, which was the largest stimulus among the EU10 countries. These included the reductions in personal income tax legislated in 2007 and entering into force in early 2009, and increases in social and infrastructure spending adopted as part of the July 2009 supplementary budget and supported through accelerated use of EU funds (figure 10.13). The supplementary budget also incorporated fiscal savings equal to about 1.4 percent of GDP through reductions in administrative spending

Figure 10.12 Contribution of Net Exports and Domestic Demand to GDP Growth

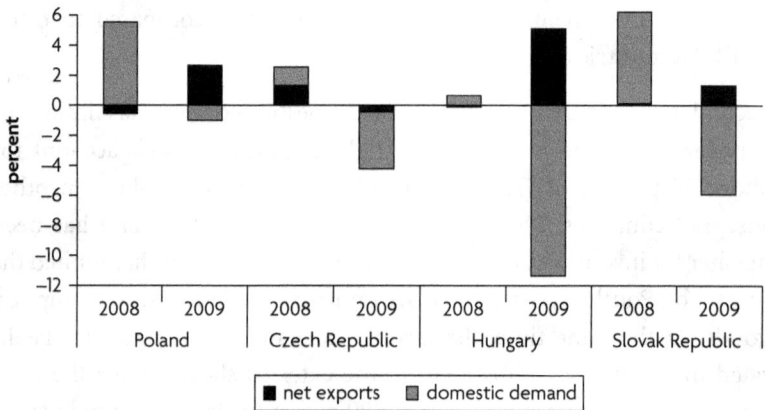

Figure 10.13 Growth Rates of Public, Private, and Total Investment

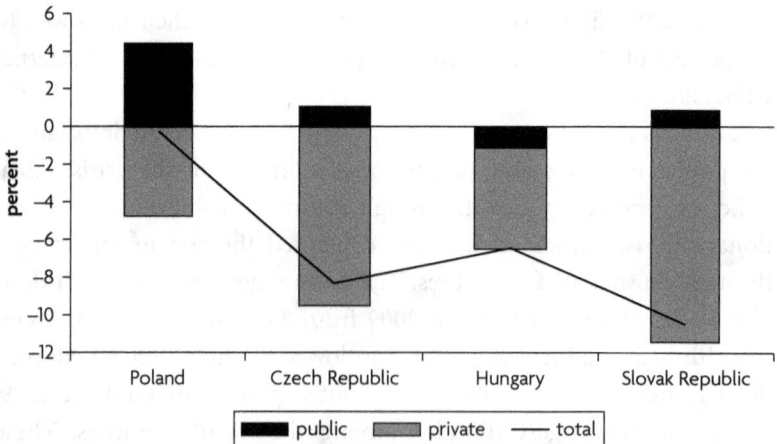

and increases in dividends from state-owned companies. Financial markets have responded well to the government's rising financing needs. Yields on government bonds have fallen since spring 2009, although they remain somewhat above precrisis levels. The government maintained access to international capital markets throughout the crisis.

Fourth, Poland's banking system has withstood the global financial crisis well. After the collapse of Lehman Brothers in September 2008, the Polish interbank market froze, the stock markets fell by nearly half, and the zloty depreciated by about a third. In response to the stabilization of global financial markets in the spring and the precautionary one-year US$20.5 billion facility under the International Monetary Fund (IMF) Flexible Credit Line from early May 2009, the appetite for risk returned to financial markets: the zloty appreciated, the stock market recovered, and yield spread declined. This has mitigated the strains on corporations and households carrying foreign currency debt and helped stabilize banks' profits in the third quarter of 2009. Subsidiaries of foreign banks, which hold about 70 percent of the banking sector's assets, have largely maintained their exposure, with private debt rollover rates of nearly 100 percent relative to late 2008 levels, and credit default swap spreads of parent banks have narrowed significantly. Most banks retained 2008 profits to strengthen their balance sheets, and the capital adequacy ratios remain safely above the minimum level of 8 percent specified in Basel II. Nonperforming loans have grown only moderately and remain modest as a percent of GDP. Credit growth to the private sector remains positive, and overall corporate profitability and corporate bank deposits remain high. The NBP has also reduced the policy rate from 6 percent in November 2008 to 3.5 percent in support of the recovery. While the interbank market is active only for short-term maturities, such liquidity preference of banks is also widespread in mature financial markets in the euro area.

The factors underlying Poland's resilience during the global financial crisis contribute also to its resilience against sovereign debt concerns in the euro area. While the risk appetite in financial markets in Poland moderated somewhat along with increases in default risk of major European banking groups during the second quarter of 2010 (figure 10.14), the risk of contagion to Poland is low as long as the crisis

Figure 10.14 Asset Class Performance in Poland

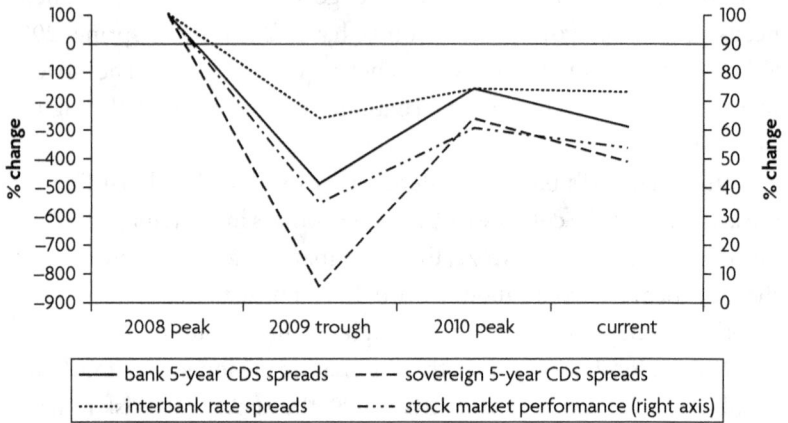

Source: Bloomberg; Reuters.
Note: CDS = credit default swap.

does not spread from the southern periphery to the major economies of the euro area (box 10.2).

Labor and Poverty Impact

The deterioration in labor market outcome was modest compared with that of other countries in the region. The steady growth in the economy contained the rise in unemployment, as have government schemes to strengthen the labor market. In addition, adequate funding of social and unemployment benefits protected household incomes. Unemployment increased, according to the Labor Force Survey, from 7.3 percent in April 2008 to 9.9 percent in April 2010. Job losses affected mostly young workers with basic education and limited work experience. The rise in unemployment by 2.5 percentage points was less than for the other Visegrad countries and the EU 10 region overall. The Labor Fund has sufficient resources to deal with increased spending on unemployment benefits and labor market program, thanks to the substantial surplus accumulated in the previous years when unemployment was falling. At the same time, Poland's unemployment benefit system is not overly generous and thus does not create significant labor supply disincentives (World Bank 2010b). The rise in unemployment was offset by an increase

Box 10.2. Contagion Risks from Sovereign Debt Concerns in the Euro Area

Financial Contagion
Downgrading of sovereign debt, rising nonperforming loans, and tightening of collateral requirements in the euro zone could reduce the exposure of parent banks to Poland. Subsidiaries and branches in Poland could come under additional pressure through a withdrawal of funds from depositors. This could derail the rebound in credit growth and hurt the recovery. However, Greek, Portuguese, and Spanish banks play only a minor role in Poland (figure B10.2.1). Their collective share in the assets of the Polish banking sector is no more than 7 percent. Furthermore, the condition of Poland's financial system remains strong, and market confidence in the country's central bank and the financial supervisor, Polish Financial Supervision Commission (KNF), is solid. The recovery in credit growth is well underway, as Poland continues to be a growth market for the main European banking groups. Furthermore, the newly established European financial stability mechanisms and the generally positive results of stress tests of European banking groups from July 2010 helped to improve the sentiment in European financial markets. Finally, Poland's external vulnerabilities have declined further with the reductions in current account deficits in 2009, and Poland's gross external debt remains low at around 55 percent of GDP.

Fiscal Contagion
Concerns over fiscal sustainability are at the core of the troubles in the euro zone. Markets could develop similar concerns for countries of Central and Eastern Europe. Poland has a public-debt-to-GDP ratio of about 50 percent, which is the second-highest among the EU10 countries after Hungary. Nevertheless, markets have so far shown little signs of concern over Polish public finances.

Figure B10.2.1. Claims of the Banking Sector in Poland by Country, December 2009 (percent)

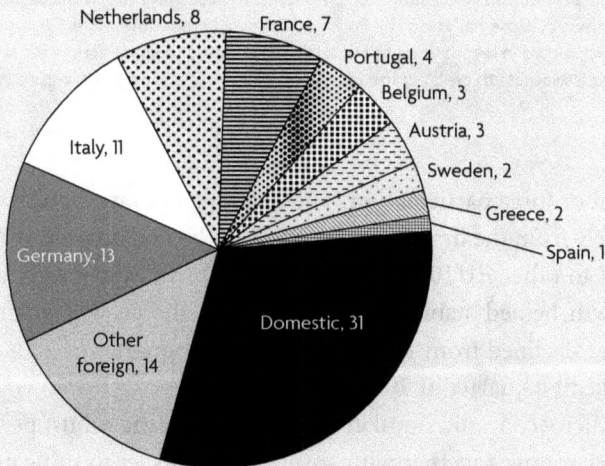

Source: Bank for International Settlements.

(continued)

a

Box 10.2 *(continued)*

A number of factors strengthen Poland's fiscal sustainability. First, Poland had already secured more than half its external budgetary financing needs by late April 2010. Second, aided by a better economic performance in Poland than in the euro zone, the fiscal position in Poland has deteriorated less than in the euro zone. For example, while the public debt increased from 66 percent of GDP in 2007 to 79 percent in 2009 in the euro zone, it increased only from 45 percent of GDP in 2007 to 51 percent in 2009 in Poland. Third, Poland's long-term fiscal sustainability is bolstered by favorable dynamics of age-related expenditures. According to EC projections, age-related spending is projected to increase from 2007 to 2060 by 2.7 percent of GDP in the EU, but to decline by 2.7 of GDP in Poland. Poland is the only EU country where age-related government spending is projected to decline. At the same time, unlike most other EU countries, Poland's general government fiscal deficit is inflated by about 3 percentage points of GDP, owing to public transfers to open pension funds. Fourth, Poland's fiscal rules underpin the fiscal adjustment. They include national public debt limits embedded in the public finance act and the constitution and commitments under the Stability and Growth Pact. Fifth, along with the other EU10 countries, external vulnerabilities in Poland have moderated with the sharp contractions in current account deficits in 2009. This has contributed to a notable increase in central bank reserves. Finally, Poland has the option to renew its Flexible Credit Line with the IMF.

Real Contagion

In view of Poland's deep market integration in the region, a recovery in the euro zone is needed to support exports, spur credit growth, and strengthen job prospects in the country. For example, about 55 percent of Polish exports go to the euro zone, but the euro zone's recovery from the global crisis could be sluggish or followed by a "double dip." This could undermine growth in Poland, which, according to latest forecasts, was expected to be approximately 2.5–3.0 percent in 2010. Mitigating factors include low inventory levels, low interest rates, and stepped-up utilization of EU funds. For example, Poland plans to increase spending of EU funds from 2.1 percent of GDP in 2009 to 3.7 percent in 2011. In addition, the depreciation of the zloty in the aftermath of the Lehman Brothers collapse has given the Polish economy a competitive edge. Finally, the authorities' solid track record in recent years has ensured good access to financial markets, which should provide adequate access to credit in the event of a further slowdown or downturn.

in labor force participation. The employment rate increased only moderately from the first quarter of 2008 to the first quarter of 2010, in contrast to other EU10 countries (figure 10.15). Moderation in real wages growth helped stabilize employment, as the growth in the labor cost index declined from 13 percent in the first quarter of 2008 to 2 percent in the first quarter of 2010.

Microeconomic simulations confirm that the robust performance of the economy, together with government policies to mitigate the impact of the slowdown on vulnerable households, has succeeded in limiting the increase in poverty and unemployment (box 10.3).

Figure 10.15 Employment Growth for 15- to 64-Year-Olds by Skill Level

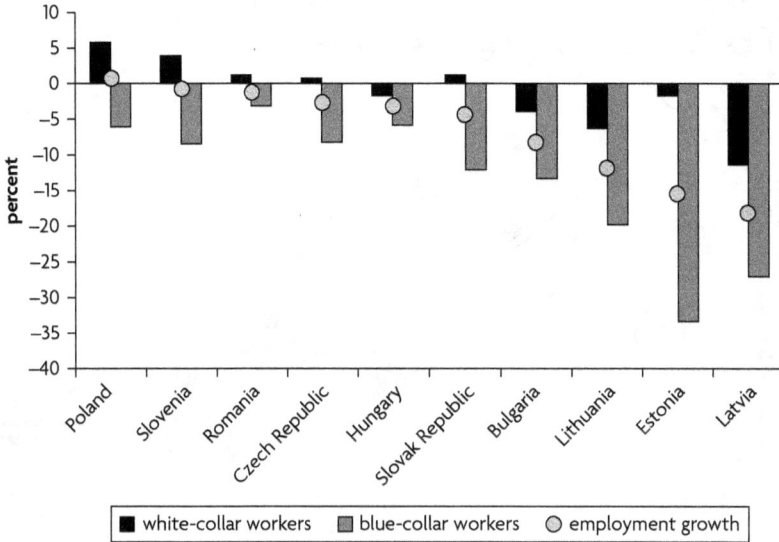

white-collar workers ■ blue-collar workers □ employment growth ○

Source: Eurostat.

Box 10.3. Simulating the Social Impact of the Slowdown

Simulation analysis suggests that the modest impact of the global financial crisis on Poland's economic performance, along with policies to strengthen social benefits, have mitigated the impact on household income and poverty. The results are derived through a simple economic model built on Polish household survey data from EU Statistics on Income and Living Conditions. The model generates microlevel outcomes such as income, poverty, and employment, drawing on two macroeconomic scenarios. The baseline scenario is hypothetical and captures the economic performance in the absence of a global financial crisis. The slowdown scenario presents the actual and projected economic performance reflecting the impact the global financial crisis and government responses. The macroeconomic assumptions are taken from the December 2008 convergence program for the baseline scenario, and from the January 2010 convergence program for the slowdown scenario.

The main results are as follows:

• The slowdown lowered the growth of household income by 1 percent in 2010 and 3 percent in 2011, but household income in 2011 is projected to remain 10 percent above the 2007 level.
• The slowdown increased the share of the population in poverty by 0.4 percentage point in 2010, and 0.7 percentage point in 2011 (figure B10.3.1). Accounting for increases in social benefits adopted in 2009, the increases were only 0.1 percentage point in 2010 and 0.5 percentage point in 2011. Overall, accounting for the decline in growth and increases in social benefits, the poverty head count in 2011 is projected to be 13.3 percent, versus 17.3 percent in 2007.

(continued)

Box 10.3 *(continued)*

Figure B10.3.1. Simulation Results: Poverty Head Count

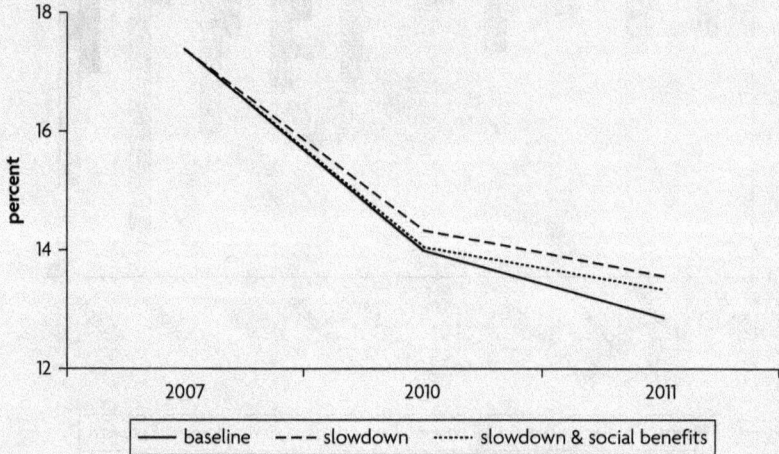

Source: Sanchez-Paramo 2010.

Postcrisis Recovery

Growth Outlook

This section develops an illustrative medium-term growth scenario. The objective is not to forecast growth in Poland, especially in light of the fact that the economic environment remains highly uncertain. Instead, the following discussion of the economic prospects serves to highlight salient growth drivers and emphasize areas of policy reform for strengthening growth. The growth scenario is built around four assumptions.

First, Poland performed well during transition, EU accession, and the global financial crisis, but the importance of growth drivers of the past is diminished in the postcrisis world. Growth was driven first by sectoral reallocation and firm turnover during the 1990s, and then by trade and financial integration (anchored in EU accession) and improved labor utilization during the 2000s. In addition, the rapid growth during 2003–08 was aided by a favorable external environment, marked by plentiful capital flows, rapidly rising global trade, and improving job markets.

The economic expansion in 2009 relied on a sharp decline in imports and a large increase in the fiscal deficit; on the other hand, trade balances are set to deteriorate with a rebound in imports, and the fiscal stimulus to decline with fiscal consolidation, in the next years. In a world of financial market fragilities, sovereign vulnerabilities, and global imbalances, economic growth is harder to come by across the region (Darvas 2010). According to EC estimates, all EU10 countries have seen a reduction in potential output growth from 2007 to 2011 due to factors including a drop in investment, the downsizing of sectors such as finance and real estate, and skill erosion among the unemployed (EC Ameco Database).

Second, Poland's growth is supported by sustainable macroeconomic balances. With actual output still below potential, inflation is projected to be moderate in 2010 and to remain subdued over the medium term. While the current account gap is set to widen in 2010 as imports pick up with stronger GDP growth, the recovery in exports and the adjustment in the zloty are expected to keep the current account balance at moderate levels. A competitive exchange rate, solid private sector flows, and continued favorable access to international capital markets all suggest that the balance of payments will remain robust. The sound initial condition of Poland's financial system, the central bank's credibility in conducting monetary policy, and the regular stress tests undertaken by the financial supervisor provide a strong base for financial markets. The government is committed to addressing the fiscal challenges, helped by the broad consensus for reducing the fiscal deficit. The consensus derives from the constitutional public debt limit of 60 percent of GDP and Poland's commitments under the EU Stability and Growth Pact (box 10.4).

Third, the rebound in the EU is central to Poland's growth prospects. The recovery in the EU will continue, supported by the return of confidence in financial markets, the turning of the inventory cycle, low interest rates, and positive feedback effects from the real and financial sectors. Similar to recent estimates of the World Bank (2010c), EC (2010a), and IMF (2010), growth in the EU is expected to improve from – 4 percent of GDP in 2009 to 2.3 percent in the coming years, just short of its 1994–2008 growth average of 2.4 percent. Poland's upturn will benefit from the EU15's rebound through trade, capital, and labor links:

- Poland's trade flows are mainly oriented toward the EU; for example, half of Polish exports go to the euro area.

Box 10.4. Poland's Fiscal Consolidation Strategy

Medium-term fiscal consolidation is crucial to the government's goal of early euro adoption, to stay clear of the 55 percent of GDP national public debt limit, and to protect priority spending for jobs and growth. In January 2010 the government presented its plan to reduce the fiscal deficit from 7.2 percent of GDP in 2009 to 2.9 percent of GDP in 2012. This target is consistent with the EC recommendations issued in July 2009 as part of the initiation of an excessive deficit procedure based on the 2008 fiscal deficit of 3.6 percent of GDP. The scale of the fiscal consolidation is set to increase over time, as selected expenditure savings are offset initially by higher capital investments, partly financed from EU structural funds. The rebalancing from public to private investment in 2012, together with faster growth of nominal GDP relative to index-based social expenditures, will support a major contraction of public expenditures as a share of GDP in 2012. In an alternative macroeconomic scenario that assumes a slower recovery in growth due to a weaker external environment, the government still anticipates bringing down the fiscal deficit to 3 percent of GDP by 2013.

The government is in the process of elaborating the details of the fiscal consolidation strategy. The main instruments identified to date for bringing about the reduction in the fiscal deficit are maintaining the public sector wage bill constant in real terms, limiting the growth in other discretionary budgetary spending to 1 percent in real terms against the backdrop of a robust economic recovery, rationalizing nondiscretionary spending, and broadening the tax base and strengthening tax administration. The government has prepared draft assumptions for four initiatives (law on the stability of public finance, integration of uniformed services into the main pension system, alignment of disability benefits with pension benefits, and removal of the floor on public defense spending). Preliminary estimates suggest that additional consolidation measures, including on the revenue side, will be needed to reach the fiscal deficit target of 3 percent of GDP by 2012, especially if growth in economic activity or revenue collection turns out to be lower than expected.

Beyond 2012, the government aims to achieve a structural fiscal deficit of 1 percent of GDP, in line with the medium-term objective of the EU Stability and Growth Pact. Such fiscal discipline is to be achieved with the help of a rule adopted as part of a new fiscal responsibility law that limits public expenditure increases during an economic upturn. Introducing multiyear binding expenditure ceilings and implementing a permanent fiscal rule would also contribute to keeping public expenditures below 40 percent of GDP over the long term compared to a rate around 45 percent of GDP in 2009.

- Poland's financial sector is well integrated into the EU economy, with about 70 percent of banking assets owned by European banking groups.
- EU accession in 2004 opened labor markets to Polish workers in EU countries. From May 2004 to June 2007, some 430,000 Polish nationals registered as workers in the United Kingdom. Even though such migration might have led to labor shortages in selected sectors at the time, it has provided important benefits in the form of knowledge transmission and remittances. For example, Polish workers' remittances reached 1 percent of GDP in 2008, compared to only 0.3 percent of GDP in the early 2000s.

Fourth, the forces of convergence to EU living standards will translate into higher growth in Poland than in the EU15, although the growth differential will be lower than prior to the crisis. From 1993 to 2008, Poland grew faster than the EU15 in every single year with the exception of 2001. And with exception of the Asian crisis in the early 2000s, Poland's growth differential with the EU15 was at least 1.5 percent of GDP (figure 10.16). For example, econometric estimates suggest that the economic integration in the EU provided a growth dividend to EU10 countries of around 1.7 percentage points, over and above the direct effects of higher capital and trade flows (EC 2009c). Going forward, higher growth in Poland than in the EU15 reflects capital inflows attracted by higher returns on investment compared with the EU15 due to capital scarcity and competitive labor costs, EU funds, and privatization; rising labor participation; the upgrading of skill levels; and rising TFP. While it is difficult to estimate the precise impact, reforms in these areas, anchored in the goal of euro adoption, will be crucial for shoring up long-term growth prospects and transforming the economy in line with the government's Vision 2030 (box 10.5). Most growth-oriented reforms are designed to foster the microeconomics of creation and destruction, aid structural change and innovation, and protect people who are adversely affected by these dynamics. Such structural reforms are also endorsed in the EU's Europe 2020 strategy. Based on the EC's macroeconomic model QUEST III, the main priority areas of this

Figure 10.16 Poland and EU15 Growth Differential

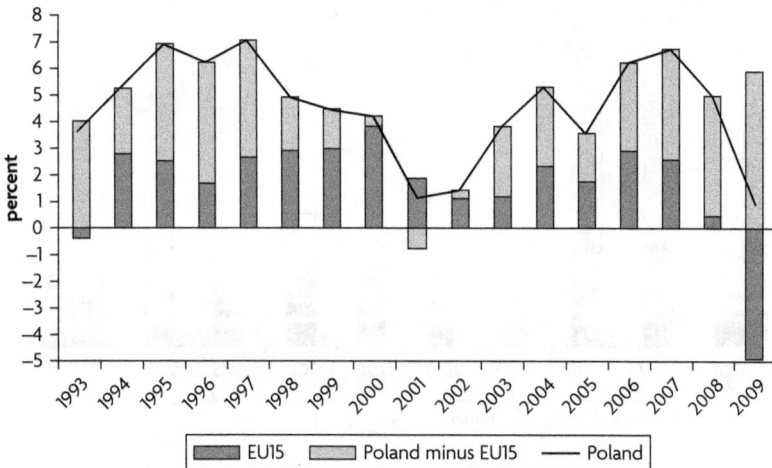

Source: Eurostat.

Box 10.5. The Government's Vision 2030

The government's strategy for 2030, announced in autumn 2009, argues for a fundamental trans-formation from a "welfare society to a workfare society." The need for this transformation arises from the challenges of globalization, energy deficiency, climate change, and population aging. The aim is to build a competitive, innovative, and energy-efficient economy supported by a perform-ing state for a socially and regionally cohesive society. Using the current economic crisis as a stepping stone for Poland's modernization, Vision 2030 provides a framework for long-term development anchored by specific targets to inform the process of designing, developing, and implementing public interventions.

strategy are estimated to boost growth in the EU by 2020 from 1.5 percent to 2.2 percent (Hobza and Mourre 2010).

What does Poland's illustrative growth path look like? The growth scenario draws on VisionMod, a dynamic stochastic general equilibrium model (box 10.6). Two features stand out. First, while growth will

Box 10.6. Assumptions for Macroeconomic Projections

The supply- and demand-side projections for 2010–15, along with historic (2003–08) and estimated (2009) data, presented in figure B10.6.1 and table B10.6.1 were derived as follows:

- The growth projections are based on VisionMod of the Institute for Structural Research (IBS) (Bukowski 2009). VisionMod is a large-scale dynamic stochastic general equilibrium model of the

Figure B10.6.1. GDP Growth Projections

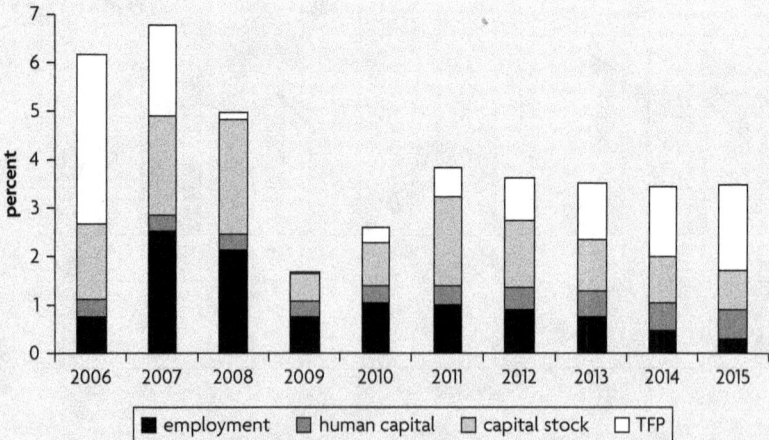

Source: IBS VisionMod; authors' calculations.

Polish economy. It is a multisectoral, open-economy, two-country model with sectoral production and labor markets. It was used to derive long-term macroeconomic projections for the government's strategy paper Vision 2030, fiscal simulations for the 2009 World Bank public expenditure review of social sectors and public wages, and low-carbon-growth simulations for the 2010 World Bank climate change report. The projections are based on Eurostat demographic projections up to 2030 and account for the impact of the global financial crisis of 2009. They also reflect the impact of announced government policies to spur growth and convergence to EU income levels through measures to bolster infrastructure via stepped-up utilization of EU finds, to raise employment rates, to increase the effective retirement age, to improve the productivity of the education system, and to boost spending on research and development.

- The supply-side trends from 2003 to 2008 are based on the Conference Board Total Economic Database. The supply-side projections for 2009–15 are constructed from the demand-side projections, along with the following assumptions: the labor share remains constant relative to 2008; labor grows in line with the IBS projections, including the impact of labor market reforms; the contribution of human capital doubles by 2015 relative to 2008 due to the impact of skill reforms; and TFP growth increases linearly to its projected value for 2015.

Table B10.6.1. GDP Growth Projections
(percent)

	2003	2004	2005	2006	2007	2008	2009	2010	2011	2012	2013	2014	2015
GDP (% per year)	3.9	5.3	3.6	6.2	6.8	5.0	1.7	2.6	3.9	3.6	3.5	3.5	3.5
Contributions													
Employment	−1.9	−0.2	0.1	0.8	2.5	2.2	0.8	1.1	1.0	0.9	0.8	0.5	0.3
Human capital	1.0	1.1	1.0	0.3	0.3	0.3	0.3	0.4	0.4	0.5	0.5	0.6	0.6
Capital stock	0.9	1.0	1.2	1.6	2.0	2.4	0.6	0.9	1.8	1.4	1.1	0.9	0.8
TFP growth	3.9	3.3	1.4	3.5	1.9	0.2	0.0	0.3	0.6	0.9	1.2	1.5	1.8

Source: IBS VisionMod; authors' calculations.

rebound, the growth rate will slow from 4.8 percent during 1993–08 to 3.5 percent during 2012–15. Second, growth is expected to accelerate steadily from 1.7 percent in 2009 to 2.6 percent in 2010 and to continue to accelerate in 2011 before converging to 3.5 percent during 2012–15. The following sections take a closer look at Poland's likely growth drivers based on the supply-side decomposition of growth projections.

EU Funds

VisionMod projects that the contribution of capital to growth will increase sharply until 2011 and then decline steadily until 2015. EU funds are the principal reason for these projected dynamics. Poland can draw on an increased supply of EU funds to overcome infrastructure and human capital bottlenecks at a time when the global financial crisis has reduced private capital inflows. Poland will receive about €9.6 billion (US$13.4 billion) annually from 2007 to 2013—more than any other EU country— compared to €2.8 billion (US$3.9 billion) from 2004 to 2006. Assuming that EU funds are available to 2015, two years after the end of the perspective (in line with the "n + 2" rule) EU funds will increase from 2.1 percent of GDP in 2009 to 3.7 percent in 2011, and to 3.5 percent in 2015 (OECD 2010). This, according to government plans, will help to boost public investment from 4.9 percent of GDP in 2009 to 7.5 percent in 2011. EU funds are likely to increase growth mainly through the demand side in the short term (increasing capacity utilization with multiplier effects) and mainly through the supply side in the long term (adding to physical and human capital).

Macroeconomic models used for ex ante evaluations of EU funds confirm a positive general impact, although the estimates vary (box 10.7).[3] This is consistent with the notion that the growth impact of EU funds hinges on macroeconomic and institutional factors. First, large increases in EU funds pose macroeconomic risks in the form of overheating that could hamper convergence. However, the decline in capital flows attributable to the global financial crisis and the spare capacity in the economy will mitigate this risk, at least in the short run. EU-funded investment is likely to have a greater growth impact during an economic downturn, when it is less likely to crowd out private and other public investment,

---

Box 10.7. Growth Impact of EU Funds

- Lolos (2001) finds, based on the HERMIN model, that EU funds of 1 percent of GDP increase GDP growth by 0.5 percent.
- Allard and others (2008) find, based on the IMF Global Integrated Monetary and Fund model, that the EU fund inflows invested in public infrastructure allow for a considerable acceleration in the catch-up process, by close to 5 percentage points of GDP in the early 2020s. Conversely, EU fund inflows supporting households' income would have virtually no impact on per capita GDP, because, as shown above, higher consumption is offset by a deterioration in corporate profitability, appreciation of the real exchange rate, and lost competitiveness.
- The European Commission (2009b) finds, based on QUEST III simulations, that EU funds from the 2007–13 perspective will lead to increases in productivity from more infrastructure spending, human capital investment, and research and development (R&D), resulting in a permanent increase of 4 percent of GDP even after the full absorption of these funds.
- The Organisation for Economic Co-operation and Development (2010) estimates, based on a literature review, that EU funds of 3.3 percent of GDP annually will increase Poland's growth rate by 0.5 percent to 1.5 percent per year from 2009 to 2015.

Box 10.8. Reform Issues in Poland's Land Transport Sector

The national roads sector achieved significant improvements and reforms, but the network is still in need of massive investment. The national road network condition has improved in recent years, as a result of a large increase in capital spending supported by EU structural grants and international financial institutions. Important institutional reforms were implemented, separating policy making from implementation, and an important effort was made to introduce use of modern planning tools for road asset management. About 40 percent of the network, however, is still in need of various types of repair and rehabilitation work, from strengthening to patching and surface repairs. There is still insufficient consistency in investment among the various levels of administration.

Despite the implementation of some EU-mandated reforms, the railway sector has lost market share. The railway has implemented important reforms, such as the separation of infrastructure from operations, to follow principles set by the EU railway directive for legal and institutional framework. These reforms, however, did not result in direct productivity and competitiveness improvements. Polish Railway has continuously lost freight market share to the roads sector, and the situation is similar for passenger services. The main obstacle faced by railway clients is low quality of infrastructure. Despite a considerable maintenance backlog since 1990, the executed annual track renewal works allotment is still only half the amount needed for rehabilitation and maintenance, and as a result the rail infrastructure continues to deteriorate.

Combined with pricing policies, this situation contributes to roads sector predominance for passenger and freight traffic, and to suboptimal use and higher cost of land transportation. The poor state of the rail asset requires more investment to achieve a certain performance standard than would be necessary if proper maintenance had been done. In combination with regulatory requirements, this results in higher operating costs for railway infrastructure, which is passed on to railway operators though track access charges. This, in turn, further reduces the competitiveness of railways with the roads sector, where user charges remain low. As road users are not charged for the full impact of road deterioration (which is especially true for trucks with the vignette system), the roads sector does not fully recover its costs, requiring higher government support effectively paid by nonroad users through taxation.

Source: World Bank 2010c.

generate inflation pressures, or trigger nominal appreciation—all of which would undermine the economic expansion. Second, both the overall spending mix and a favorable business environment help determine the impact of EU funds. Poland gives priority to investments in infrastructure and human capital (box 10.8), which are typically seen as being generally productive, and product and service markets have shown a remarkable flexibility during the global financial crisis.

Third, while EU funds could provide a timely stimulus to Poland's recovery, their effective absorption presents a major institutional challenge. Nevertheless, two factors suggest that the absorption of EU funds has improved relative to the past. Partly in response to the global financial crisis, the EC has improved the utilization of EU structural funds by increasing a country's flexibility in implementing the programs, extending the final date of eligibility for funding, and taking measures to reduce potential financing constraints for beneficiaries. Poland also gained valuable experience and built its capacity to absorb EU funds during 2004–06, after EU accession (Holda and Skrok 2010). Poland managed to use all the structural funds available from the 2004–06 perspective by the end of the period, and to advance the absorption of funds from the new perspective, 2007–13. By March 2010, Poland had contracted out nearly 60 percent of its total 2007–13 allocations of EU structural funds.

Foreign Direct Investment

The contribution of capital to growth in Poland will also be supported by FDI flows. FDI is likely to have both direct and indirect effects on growth. Direct effects include higher overall investment, production, and exports, which are crucial for a relatively capital-scarce economy such as Poland's. Indirect effects include higher productivity and competitiveness of domestic firms, thanks to spillovers and more intense competition. Knowledge spillovers from FDI could come from different sources, such as product or organizational limitations, rotation of employees, and backward or forward linkages. Foreign entrants also heighten the intensity of competition, especially in sectors otherwise isolated from global competition, thereby eliminating the most inefficient incumbents and forcing the survivors to reduce production costs and innovate. However, FDI benefits the economy only when inflows are matched by firms' capacity to absorb them, which is linked to such issues as labor quantity and quality, and innovation performance.

FDI inflows to Poland held up far better than those to other Visegrad countries. Poland has remained attractive for FDI during the global financial crisis because of its sound fundamentals, the growth and size of the domestic market, its access to regional markets, and the possibility it affords for integration with international production chains. Nevertheless, other Visegrad countries received substantially higher FDI inflows in the past and have thus built up large FDI stocks (table 10.1). As the case of the Slovak Republic suggests, dedicated reforms to strengthen the investment climate can be effective in attracting FDI (box 10.9).

In Poland, prospects for euro adoption can trigger increased FDI inflows by removing exchange rate risk. For example, the EC (2008)

Table 10.1. Selected Structural Growth Indicators

	Poland	Czech Republic	Hungary	Slovak Republic	EU/ OECD
FDI (% GDP)					
Flows, 1998–2008	3.9	7.0	4.7	7.6	—
Flows, 2009	2.7	1.4	1.1	−0.1	—
Stock, 2009	32.1	53.9	57.2	50.3	—
Employment					
Tax wedge (% total gross wage), 2006	42.5	40.1	43.3	35.6	41.1
Tax wedge (% total gross wage), 2009	33.4	40.1	46.7	36.0	40.8
Employment rate 55–64 (%), 2009	32.3	46.8	32.8	39.5	48.0
Female life expectancy at 65, 2008	19.1	18.8	18.1	17.8	20.6
Formal child care for children under 3 years of age (%), 2008	3.0	2.0	7.0	2.0	31.0
Nonnationals in labor force (%), 2008	0.2	1.2	0.8	0.2	6.5
Skills					
PISA test score reading, 2000	479	483	480	469	498
PISA test score reading, 2006	508	492	482	466	492
PISA test score mathematics, 2003	490	517	490	498	500
PISA test score mathematics, 2006	495	510	491	492	498
Four-year-olds in education (% 4-year-olds), 2007	44.4	87.8	92.4	74.1	88.6
Youth education (% 20–24-year-olds with upper secondary or more), 2008	91.3	91.6	83.6	90.2	75.8
Lifelong learning (% 25–64-year-olds), 2008	4.7	7.8	3.1	3.3	10.9
Productivity					
Labor productivity per hour worked (EU15 = 100), 2009	44.0	55.1	51.8	67.6	100.0
Average value of exports and imports, (% GDP) 2009	33	57	61	62	—
High-tech exports, (% total exports) 2006	3.1	12.7	20.3	5.8	16.6
Patent applications to European Patent Office per 1,000 inhabitants, 2007	3.8	15.8	17.2	7.8	116.5
Gross domestic expenditures on R&D (% GDP), 2008—business	0.19	0.77	0.48	0.16	1.09
Gross domestic expenditures on R&D (% GDP), 2008—nonbusiness	0.42	0.70	0.52	0.31	0.90

Source: Eurostat; EC Ameco Database.

Note: EU/OECD refers to OECD for test scores; it refers to EU27 female life expectancy at age 65, 4-year-olds in education, nonnationals in the labor force, patent applications, and high-tech exports; otherwise, it refers to EU15. PISA = Programme for International Student Assessment; R&D = research and development; — = not available.

Box 10.9. The Slovak Republic's Reforms of 2002

Eager to overcome the economic slowdown of the late 1990s, the Slovak Republic in 2002 adopted a strong reform program. It included the introduction of a flat income tax and a single-rate value added tax, and it linked social benefits to participation in labor market programs. Along with prudent macroeconomic policies and early privatization and enterprise restructuring, the reforms helped to turn the Slovak Republic into one of the most attractive places for doing business in Central and Eastern Europe. Large FDI inflows extended the Slovak Republic's productive capacity and contributed to strong, export-led economic growth.

finds that euro adoption will increase the growth of FDI inflows by 19 percent for Poland and 14 percent for the EU10 countries overall. In addition, the government's plan to reinforce the privatization agenda will also support a rebound in FDI flows. The Polish authorities foresee an acceleration of privatization in 2010–11 in line with the improvement of market conditions in sectors such as finance, power, oil refinery, chemicals, coal mining, copper, and defense. Receipts from privatization are expected to rise from 0.1 percent of GDP in 2008 to 0.5 percent in 2009 and to 1.8 percent of GDP in 2010.

Labor Participation

Poland's employment rate has improved sharply since the early 2000s. This reflects primarily the fall in unemployment owing to strong economic growth over much of the decade. In addition, labor migration to EU countries has reduced the labor supply and boosted the employment rate in Poland, and the baby boom of the early 1980s increased the number of core working-age people. Labor market reforms have also helped. From 2007 to 2009, disability contributions declined from 13 percent to 6 percent; the personal income tax was consolidated from a three- to a two-bracket system, and family allowances were introduced. This substantially reduced the tax burden for an employed person with low earnings, turning Poland into a low-tax-wedge economy within the EU and Central Europe (table 10.1). Finally, the government has phased out early retirement provisions, slashing the number of eligible workers from above 1 million to about 250,000, for an active labor force of about 17 million.

While these reforms will continue to yield dividends in the coming years, demographic trends will tend to lower the growth of the working-age population. According to Eurostat projections, the number of people ages 15–55 will shrink by 6 percent from 2009 to 2015. VisionMod projects that, even assuming policy reforms to increase labor participation (box 10.10), the contribution of labor to growth will peak in 2010 and then decline steadily until 2015, although remaining positive. Key structural changes needed to expand the labor supply include the following:

- *Raising the legal retirement age, especially for women.* While the main pension system will be fully actuarially fair from 2014 on, and there are no restrictions to continue working beyond retirement age, the statutory retirement age remains an important social norm that contributes to the employment rate of older workers, which is the main reason for Poland's low overall employment rate relative to the EU15 (Rutkowski 2010). The legal retirement age in Poland is 60 years for women and 65 years for men, which is below the corresponding ages (65 and 68 years) in many EU15 countries. Women's life expectancy after retirement is 23 years. This is one of the highest in the EU and is significantly higher than the 15 years for men. Together with the more interrupted nature of their working lives, this implies that pensions for women are only half those of men.
- *Advancing the reform of the social protection system.* Two key issues are the integration of the special pension schemes into the main system and the alignment of disability benefits with the core pension system.
- *Better integrating social assistance and labor market policies.* Poland has only recently started to implement activation policies, linking receipt of benefits to active job search and labor market attachment. Activation policies reintegrate social assistance recipients into the labor market by providing job search assistance, vocational counseling and

Box 10.10. Growth Impact of Labor Participation Measures

VisionMod projections incorporate measures to increase the contribution of labor to growth:

- Equalize the retirement age for men and women at age 65 and increase the effective retirement age by 3 years.
- Increase continuously the employment rate of 15- to 24-year-olds from 27.3 percent in 2008 to 41 percent in 2030, and the employment rate of 55- to 64-year-olds from 31.6 percent in 2008 to 47 percent in 2030.

(continued)

Box 10.10 *(continued)*

It is estimated that these measures will increase the employment rate of 15- to 64-year-olds by 6.5 percentage points by 2015 (figure B10.10). Projections indicate they will increase GDP growth from 3.2 percent to 3.4 percent in 2015. The growth impact is relatively modest for three reasons: the rise in total hours worked through the increased employment rate is offset partly by the reduction in the working-age population due to population aging, and partly by increases in leisure that accompany higher incomes; plus, the increased employment is concentrated among workers with low skills.

Figure B10.10.1. Selected Employment Indicators and Impact on Growth

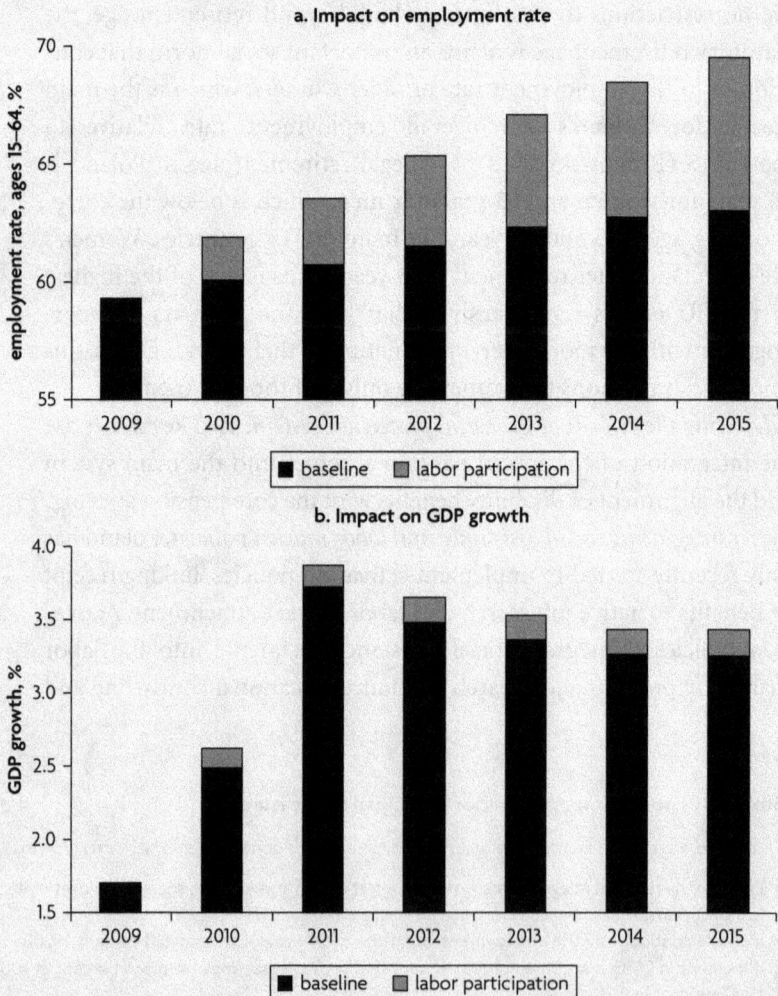

a. Impact on employment rate

b. Impact on GDP growth

Source: IBS VisionMod.

training, and work experience by means of enrollment in public works and workfare schemes.
- *Enabling women to find jobs* by providing nurseries and kindergartens for children, and nursing and retirement homes for the elderly.
- *Facilitating migration.* Only one in 500 workers was foreign in 2008. This share is among the lowest in the EU. Labor migration is one option to help fill the expected shortfalls in the workforce.

Skills

Low labor participation is also related to skills mismatch, along with low productivity. In the past, the workforce used an over-expansive system of primary vocational education that promoted the accumulation of specific, nonfungible skills that was badly adapted to a situation of intense restructuring. With transition and the integration into the global economy, firms have changed the skill composition of their workforce to raise productivity and improve competitiveness. As a result, labor demand has shifted away from low-skill occupations toward high-skilled ones. Workers without the skills to use the newly acquired technologies were often driven out of the labor market and, in many cases, became inactive. Returns to education have increased, and the wages of highly skilled professional workers have greatly improved, while those of less skilled workers have deteriorated. For example, from 1996 to 2006 wage growth among managers and officers increased relative to average wage growth by over 20 percent, while wage growth among machine operators and elementary occupations declined relative to average wage growth by 15 percent in Poland.

On the eve of the global financial crisis, firm managers in Poland and other transition countries reported in an enterprise survey that, among all the elements of their business environment, labor skills (along with infrastructure) were the most serious constraints on their ability to operate and expand their businesses. Complaints about the insufficiency of skilled labor had increased from previous survey rounds, suggesting that the demands for labor skills outpace their provision (Mitra, Selowsky, and Zalduendo 2009). During the crisis, employment growth among skilled workers remained positive, while employment growth turned negative among unskilled workers. Skills mismatch and skills shortages are related to two problems (World Bank forthcoming). While youth higher education attainment levels are high in Poland (around 90 percent in 2008), students graduate with diplomas, but not with skills, because the quality of the education for many students remains poor. In addition, there are few opportunities for adults to retrain, upgrade their skills, or acquire new skills.

Over the past decade, Poland has pursued education reforms to make workers more productive over time. It postponed by a year the time for graduates to move from lower secondary to vocational education, allowing students to avoid excessive early specialization and absorb more general knowledge. The reforms have led to some notable successes. In addition to Poland's high youth educational attainment levels, the performance of 15-year-olds in international proficiency tests for reading and mathematics improved over the decade (table 10.1). Remaining key skill challenges for Poland include shifting the focus of education to skills demanded in the labor market and promoting lifelong learning through formal, informal, and vocational training schemes. A number of reforms to address these issues are under way.

- Preschool education of 5-year-old children will become mandatory as of 2011–12, as will primary education of 6-year-old children as of 2012–13. This will ensure that education outcomes are more equitable, and it will mean that students enter the labor market a full year earlier than today.
- The government has begun rolling out a new syllabus with a greater emphasis on problem-solving skills. In the school year 2009–10, the reform covered kindergartens and the first grades of primary and middle schools. The syllabus reform will be completed in secondary and vocational schools by 2015, in secondary technical schools and artistic secondary schools by 2016, and in complementary secondary schools by 2017.
- The government has endorsed the higher-education reform plan to revamp the university system by classifying institutions into three groups: elite universities capable of competing with the European elite, well-performing universities at the national level, and local institutions. It will also limit tuition-free studies to one degree for most students and define a common list of free services in public and nonpublic

universities, including examinations, final examinations, and submitting and reviewing of theses. Additional reform areas include promoting a clearly distinct vocational education at the tertiary level and reinforcing the quality assessment of higher-education institutions.

- Under the "50-plus" program, several measures were introduced to help less qualified and older workers to upgrade their skills or change occupations.

The VisionMod projects incorporate a doubling of the contribution from human capital to growth from 0.3 percent in 2009 to 0.6 percent in 2015.

Productivity

Despite the rapid convergence to EU living standards over the past decade or so, Poland still faces a large productivity gap relative to advanced economies. Its hourly labor productivity is less than half that of the EU15, and considerably less than that of any of its Visegrad neighbors (table 10.1). The productivity gap is linked to a number of factors in addition to capital scarcity and skills mismatch.

First, as already discussed, Poland's transition and EU integration brought about an expansion of trade and sectoral transformation. The export composition shifted from traditional industries (textiles, basic metals, wood, and extraction activities) to more specialized sectors (vehicles, boilers and machinery, and electrical and electronic equipment), reflecting a move from low technology to medium-high technology. Despite Poland's technology upgrade, it lags its Visegrad neighbors in export specialization. Poland specializes in low- and medium-technology products, while the Czech Republic, Hungary, and the Slovak Republic specialize in high-technology products. Poland tends to import capital goods and export consumption goods. In addition, Poland is globalized mainly through its integration with the EU, while integration with countries of the Commonwealth of Independent States remains underdeveloped. This relates to the limited inflow of FDI into high-technology sectors, lower trade openness compared with the other Visegrad countries, and the small size of Polish firms—with limited capacity for absorption of new technologies and limited knowledge of the possibilities of cooperation with distant markets.

Second, Poland's markets are remarkably flexible, as shown during the global financial crisis. For example, Poland has a largely decentralized wage-bargaining system similar to that of the United Kingdom and the United States, with trade union density less than 25 percent and bargaining coverage between 30 percent and 40 percent. Nevertheless, some areas are still subject to stringent regulation, including network industries (where public ownership remains high), retail services, and professional services.

Third, Poland's technology structure, limited FDI, trade intensity, and low linkage between research centers and industry translate into low gross domestic expenditures on R&D, and even lower business expenditures on R&D (table 10.1).

Given that Poland's industries are well behind the global technological frontier (Veugelerspa 2010), the primary policy focus should be aiding the absorption of technology rather than innovation in technology. But also required are active efforts to learn about technologies and to absorb the technological advances of other firms. This implies that the government should put the emphasis on developing the prerequisites for knowledge-based growth. A key driver of economic growth is a country's absorptive capacity, or the ability to tap into the world technology pool (World Bank 2008b). Trade flows, FDI, and labor mobility and skills are important conduits for knowledge absorption. In addition to a favorable investment climate and a skilled workforce, knowledge absorption requires that Poland boost productivity in the medium to long run by emulating the best practices of management and using technologies available in advanced economies (Piatkowski 2010; World Bank forthcoming).

VisionMod projections suggest that productivity advances are crucial to improving Poland's medium-term growth prospects:

- The evolution of Poland's competitiveness will largely depend on its capacity to upgrade its export structure and continue to reorient it toward capital-intensive and high-technology industries.
- Further market reforms are needed to speed up technology diffusion, exploit economies of scale, and strengthen export performance. Privatization can bring about productivity gains, especially in network industries.
- Increased and better-targeted R&D spending can speed technology transfer and help Poland make the most of the foreign knowledge embedded in FDI.

Euro Adoption

The global financial crisis has derailed Poland's progress in meeting nominal convergence criteria central to euro adoption. According to the latest EC assessment, Poland does not meet the criteria on price stability, the government fiscal position, the exchange rate, and the interest rate (EC 2010b). In view of the uncertainty in Poland's progress in meeting the convergence criteria, the government has not announced a specific target date for the adoption of the euro.

Euro adoption will facilitate deeper market integration with countries of the euro zone, but premature euro adoption could derail Poland's competitiveness. The benefits of euro adoption are substantial, ranging from strong market integration of finance and trade to enhanced competition, reduction in exchange rate and country risks, enhanced macroeconomic stability, and reduction in transaction costs. These benefits will tend to strengthen growth. EU integration has also made euro adoption more attractive. Joining the euro area would further align Poland's economy to the euro area's volatility and business cycle. At the same time, euro adoption carries a heavy price: the loss of autonomous monetary policy making and exchange rate flexibility. The experiences of countries like Greece and Portugal point to the potential pitfalls of premature euro adoption. The convergence process to EU income levels implies that Poland's price level will rise to the higher levels of richer euro area countries. This could happen either through nominal exchange rate appreciation relative to the euro or through domestic inflation outpacing euro area inflation. At the same time, once Poland's exchange rate is fixed to the euro, the convergence of price levels has to operate through the inflation channel.[4] This could also lower real interest rates below levels consistent with keeping output at potential and stabilizing inflation at low levels. Given the scarcity of capital, Poland's marginal productivity of capital is higher than in the euro area, suggesting that the real interest in Poland should be higher than in the euro area. This exposes Poland's economy to the risk of overheating, especially if capital inflows translate mostly into higher investments in nontradable sectors, such as construction and real estate, and into a household consumption boom (Eichengreen and Steiner 2008). If wages and prices rise more than increases in productivity and more than those of trading partners, the competitiveness of the economy will be undermined and trade balances will deteriorate. The economies will then be exposed to the risk of slowdowns in capital inflows, implying the need to reduce current account deficits and regain competitiveness through a painful process of domestic price moderation.

Conclusions

Poland has done well during the two decades of transition. In spite of the transition shock of the late 1980s, the Asian crisis of the late 1990s, and the global financial crisis of 2007–08, Poland has maintained high growth and rapid convergence to EU living standards. Growth was driven by sectoral reallocation and firm turnover in the 1990s, and by trade and financial integration through EU accession and a favorable external environment in the early 2000s. Two years after the outbreak of the global financial crisis, Poland has managed to successfully shore up its economic expansion, strengthen financial markets, and maintain employment growth.

Now Poland faces the challenge of building on this record in the uncertain postcrisis world. Growth is set to decline with the slowdown in capital accumulation, the reduction in labor supply, and the moderation of productivity growth. Halting this trend will require Poland to address some of the long-standing weaknesses in its economy. Among the Visegrad countries, Poland's gaps with the EU in terms of living standards and labor productivity in manufacturing remain the largest, while its investment rate and export orientation gaps are the lowest. Our analysis suggests that Poland's economic prospects will depend on:

- The strength of the EU recovery and Poland's linkages to the EU economy
- The recovery of investment, supported by EU funds and FDI flows, from the slump during the global financial crisis
- Increased labor force participation to make up for the reduction in the working-age population and to boost private savings
- Improvement of workers' education and training to overcome skill shortages
- Market reforms to speed technology diffusion, exploit economies of scale, and strengthen export performance to make up for any shortfall in factor accumulation

This reform agenda, anchored in the government's Vision 2030 program and the goal of euro adoption, and aligned with the EU's Europe

2020 strategy, holds the promise of extending Poland's successful economic record into the next decade. Without such policy reforms, sluggish investment, a declining workforce, skill mismatches, low productivity growth, and a large public sector could become a drag on future growth.

Notes

1. The EU15 consists of Austria, Belgium, Denmark, Finland, France, Germany, Greece, Ireland, Italy, Luxembourg, the Netherlands, Portugal, Spain, Sweden, and the United Kingdom. The EU10 consists of countries from Central and Eastern Europe that joined the EU during the 2004 and 2007 enlargement. They include Bulgaria, the Czech Republic, Estonia, Hungary, Latvia, Lithuania, Poland, Romania, the Slovak Republic, and Slovenia.
2. The Visegrad countries include the Czech Republic, Hungary, Poland, and the Slovak Republic.
3. By contrast, the evidence from econometric models that measure the ex post macroeconomic impact of EU funds is mixed. This could reflect, among other issues, the inefficient use of EU funds or difficulties in disentangling the long-run effect of EU funds from the various factors that affect growth (EC 2009b).
4. However, a nominal appreciation does not have to undermine competitiveness, as long as it is in line with the appreciation of the real equilibrium exchange rate—for example, through the Balassa-Samuelson effect (Mihaljek and Klau 2008).

References

Allard, C., N. Choueri, S. Schadler, and R. van Elkan. 2008. "Macroeconomic Effects of EU Transfers in New Member States." Working Paper 223, International Monetary Fund, Washington, DC.

Bukowski, Maciej. 2009. *Poland 2030 VisionMod*. Warsaw: Institute for Structural Research.

Burda, Michael, and Battista Severgnini. 2009. "TFP Growth in Old and New Europe." Discussion Paper 2009-33, Humboldt Universitaet zu Berlin, Berlin.

Darvas, Zsolt. 2010. "Global Financial Crisis and Growth Prospects." Focus Note in World Bank EU10 Regular Economic Report July 2010. Warsaw: World Bank.

EC (European Commission). 2008. "Study on the Impact of the Euro on Trade and Foreign Direct Investment." Economic Paper 321, EC, Brussels.

———. 2009a. "Explaining Poland's Successful Performance during the Global Financial Crisis." EC, Brussels.

———. 2009b. "A Model-Based Assessment of the Macroeconomic Impact of EU Structural Funds on the New Member States." European Economic Paper 371, EC, Brussels.

———. 2009c. "Five Years of an Enlarged EU: Economic Achievements and Challenges." EC, Brussels.

———. 2010a. "European Economic Forecast—Spring 2010." European Economy 2/2010, EC, Brussels.

———. 2010b. "Convergence Report 2010." European Economy 3/2010, EC, Brussels.

Eichengreen, Barry, and Katharina Steiner. 2008. "Is Poland at Risk of a Boom-and-Bust Cycle in the Run-Up to the Euro Adoption?" NBER Working Paper 14438, National Bureau of Economic Research, Cambridge, MA.

Hobza, Alexandr, and Gilles Mourre. 2010. "Quantifying the Potential Macroeconomic Effects of the Europe 2020 Strategy: Stylised Scenarios." Economic Papers 424, EC, Brussels.

Holda, Paulina, and Emilia Skrok. 2010. "Absorption of EU Funds." Focus Note in World Bank EU 10 Regular Economic Report July 2010, World Bank, Warsaw.

IMF (International Monetary Fund). 2010. *World Economic Outlook, April 2010.* Washington, DC: IMF.

Lolos, Sarantis. 2001. "The Macroeconomic Effect of EU Structural Transfers on the Cohesian Countries and Lessons for the CEECs." Interim Report IR-01–044/October, International Institute for Applied Systems Analysis, Laxenburg.

Mihaljek, Dubravko, and Marc Klau. 2008. "Catching-Up and Inflation in Transition Economies: The Balassa-Samuelson Effect Revisited." Working Paper 270, Bank for International Settlements, Basel.

Mitra, Pradeep, Marcelo Selowsky, and Juan Zalduendo. 2009. *Turmoil at Twenty: Recession, Recovery, and Reform in Central and Eastern Europe and the Former Soviet Union.* Washington, DC: World Bank.

OECD (Organisation for Economic Co-operation and Development). 2010. *OECD Country Surveys: Poland 2010.* Paris: OECD.

Piatkowski, Marcin. 2010. *Poland—The Macroeconomic Setting.* Warsaw: World Bank.

Rutkowski, Jan. 2010. *Increasing Labor's Contribution to Growth.* Warsaw: World Bank.

Sanchez-Paramo, Carolina. 2010. "Distributional Impact of the Global Financial Crisis in Poland." World Bank, Washington, DC.

Veugelerspa, Reinhilde. 2010. "Assessing the Potential for Knowledge-Based Development in Transition Countries." Bruegel Working Paper, Brussels.

World Bank. 2008a. *Unleashing Prosperity: Productivity Growth in Eastern Europe and the Former Soviet Union.* Washington, DC: World Bank.

———. 2008b. "Globalization and Technology Absorption in Europe and Central Asia." Working Paper 150, World Bank, Washington, DC.

———. Forthcoming. *Fuelling Growth and Competitiveness in Poland.* Warsaw: World Bank.

———. Forthcoming. *Skills—Not Diplomas.* Washington, DC: World Bank.

———. 2010a. *Global Economic Prospects.* Washington, DC: World Bank.

———. 2010b. *Poland Public Expenditure Review: Analysis of Social Sectors and Public Wages.* Washington, DC: World Bank.

———. 2010c. *Poland Transport Policy Note: Toward a Sustainable Land Transport Sector.* Washington, DC: World Bank.

Discussant Paper

Comment on "Poland: From Crisis Resilience to Robust Growth"

Brian Pinto

The paper by Richter and Krzak takes a broad, chronological sweep through growth in Poland from 1996 to 2008, which it divides into two periods: (1) post-transition and (2) European Union (EU) accession, beginning in 2003. It then looks at the impact of the global crisis and presents medium-term growth projections.

It would be easier to grasp the points made in the paper if it had an explicit conceptual framework. Let's start with the conclusions. Essentially, these are that Poland is not in danger of a major collapse, that it has some fiscal room given its debt dynamics, and that its financial sector is resilient. Its growth prospects are tied to recovery in the EU15. And it has some scope to increase productivity, but how? The discussion does not shed light on this. Poland seems mired in the dreaded middle-income country trap: stability but no dramatic upside.

This is how I would formulate the policy challenge: "Is there anything the Polish government can do to engineer a positive productivity shock while keeping the public finances on a sustainable trajectory?"

Brian Pinto is Senior Adviser, Poverty Reduction and Economic Management Network, World Bank.

I believe this is the right question based on the evidence presented in the Richter-Krzak article. This is the sequence I see: a positive productivity shock leading to faster growth and, hence, a rise in national savings, leading to sustained faster growth. The focus on national savings makes sense given the external uncertainty and likely crowding out by the richer countries in the international capital markets. There are some key assumptions embedded in this proposition, and it points to the sort of growth analytics necessary to see if this sequence makes sense, and then to determine how to advise the government.[1]

Let's start with productivity. Figure 10.7 shows that Poland's productivity measured as output per worker hour was well behind that of Hungary, the Czech Republic, and especially the Slovak Republic in 2008–09. What have been the trends over time? Is Poland catching up to its accession neighbors and to the EU15? In a speech he made in June 2010 in Poland, Olivier Blanchard noted that output per capita there grew at 3.1 percent from 1989 to 2009, compared with 1.8 percent in Hungary and the Czech Republic (Blanchard 2010). But in 1989 Poland was much poorer: in terms of purchasing power parity (PPP), its per capita GDP was 54 percent that of the Czech Republic and 69 percent that of Hungary. I took a look at the latest PPP GDP numbers and found that Poland has indeed caught up. In 2009, its per capita GDP had risen to 78 percent of the Czech Republic's and to 99 percent of Hungary's.

This means that convergence is happening, but it raises some questions. First, is this an automatic process? Here's my interpretation of what Olivier Blanchard said in his Krakow speech: Poland had to develop the institutions, markets, and policies needed to spur convergence, and this was no mean accomplishment. But this prompts the question of whether the government needs to do anything beyond this or just sit back and let it happen.

Looking at Poland in a comparative context, did it do anything starkly different from what its neighbors did? And are there things it could do better? The Slovak Republic's experience may shed some light here. In the early 1990s, it was regarded as a "laggard" relative to the Czech Republic, and probably to Hungary as well. But it has done extremely well in the past 20 years.

The second broad area in which more systematic analysis is needed is public finances. We know that sustainability is not under threat because the dynamics, even if adverse, are likely to be under control; besides, Poland has a constitutionally mandated debt-to-GDP ceiling. It has a good track record and high credibility. They key issue is whether the management of the public finances can be tweaked to give growth a boost.

What do I mean by this? I would like to see a more systematic analysis of debt dynamics—what has happened to primary surpluses, real interest rates, growth rates, quasi-fiscal deficits. What are the trends in government savings and public expenditure composition? Are there good public investment projects, particularly those that might ease infrastructure bottlenecks and are "shovel-ready"? Poland stands to receive a substantial amount of EU funds from now to 2015—at least 3 percent of GDP a year. Assuming this is guaranteed given the fiscal woes in the EU15 and comes without restrictions, the question arises about the optimal use of this money. Should it be used to pay down public debt, augment spending on sound public investments, or reduce marginal tax rates?

The third broad area is how to increase the chances of a positive productivity shock. The most promising area probably is a campaign to woo foreign direct investment (FDI). Figure 10.17 shows that Poland has received about half of the FDI the Slovak Republic did during 1998–2008 as a share of GDP. The Slovak Republic had the highest output per worker among the Visegrad Group countries in 2009 as well as the highest share of FDI during 1998–2008. It's tempting to think there may be something more than just spurious correlation here. What does the Slovak Republic have that Poland doesn't? Poland has a much bigger domestic market, an equally favorable location, and an equally good reputation. Can it learn from the Slovak Republic? What should Poland do—improve its tax regime, cut red tape, privatize, strengthen infrastructure? In addition, what sorts of incentives can the government adopt to promote innovation, such as hardening budgets or further strengthening competition?

Fourth, I am not at all persuaded that the adoption of the euro is going to yield the benefits the authors suggest. For example, the authors argue that this would be the best way to boost FDI. But the Slovak Republic managed to get more FDI (as a percent of GDP) without being on the euro. And the disadvantages are severe, especially given the increased medium-run uncertainty that Poland faces. The ability to let the zloty depreciate quickly proved to be a valuable shock absorber by raising net exports, and such flexibility—plus the ability to use monetary policy that goes along with it—could prove valuable over the medium term.

To sum up: First, Richter and Krzak could do a more thorough job of assessing and analyzing productivity levels and growth rates, including at the sectoral level. Second, Poland's public finances need more careful analysis, incorporating the optimal use of EU funds. Third, examining how the government can engineer a positive productivity shock, if at all, is worth exploring. And fourth, a second look at the pace of euro adoption is important.

Let me end by referring to the five ingredients identified by the Growth Commission as necessary for rapid, sustained growth. Poland has done pretty well on all of them, but it could do better on importing knowledge via FDI in support of a positive productivity shock. And it would be useful to see how national savings and investment have evolved over the past two decades.[2]

Notes

1. One key assumption is that high growth leads to high saving and not the other way around, in keeping with the "habit formation" hypothesis of Carroll, Overland, and Weil (2000).
2. The five ingredients are openness, good governance and leadership, macro-stability, market-based resource allocation, and future orientation captured in high saving and investment rates Commission on Growth and Development (2008, 22).

References

Carroll, C. D., J. Overland, and D. N. Weil, 2000, "Saving and Growth with Habit Formation." *American Economic Review* 90 (3): 341–55.

Commission on Growth and Development. 2008. *The Growth Report: Strategies for Sustained Growth and Inclusive Development*. Washington, DC: World Bank.

Blanchard, Olivier. "Institutions, Markets, and Poland's Economic Performance." Speech on June 1, 2010, Krakow.

External Imbalances Amplify the Crisis, Domestic Strengths Limit the Damage

Cihan Yalçın and Mark Roland Thomas

Turkey was hit hard by the global crisis, suffering a dramatic fall in exports and industrial production, largely because demand in its export market, the European Union (EU), collapsed. Moreover, the industries in which Turkey had built up exports—such as consumer durables, automobiles, white goods, and machinery and equipment—have been sensitive to fluctuations in external demand. In addition to having trade and inventory effects, the crisis also hit through the financial channel. Domestic financial markets remain quite shallow, and amid concern about the availability of foreign finance, bank lending and other forms of finance collapsed. Despite some offsetting favorable factors, a severe domestic credit crunch, particularly for small and medium enterprises (SMEs), ensued.

Cihan Yalçın is Senior Economist, and Mark Roland Thomas is Lead Economist, Macroeconomics Unit, Europe and Central Asia Poverty Reduction and Economic Management Department, World Bank. The authors extend sincere thanks to Indermit S. Gill, Mustapha Kamel Nabli, and participants at several workshops at the World Bank. Discussions with Kamuran Malatyalı and Şeref Saygılı were very useful in building the medium-term growth scenario. The authors are also very grateful to Pınar Baydar and Muammer Kömürcüoğlu for their invaluable help formatting the text and updating data.

The impact on growth was severe. Year-on-year, gross domestic product (GDP) contracted by 7.0 percent in the last quarter of 2008, 14.5 percent in the first quarter of 2009, and 4.7 percent for the whole year. While government policies have helped mitigate the damage—especially quick central bank action to maintain liquidity of and confidence in banks, a moderate fiscal stimulus, and tax cuts—the crisis will have lasting effects on Turkey: the public debt ratio will take some time to return to precrisis levels, the fall in export demand will persist to some extent, and less foreign financing is likely to be available for investment. The potential growth rate over the medium term will therefore be lower than before the crisis.

In this chapter, we will consider the growth dynamics of the Turkish economy, emphasizing the 2002–06 boom period and the subsequent slowdown prior to the global crisis. We will then look at the impact of the crisis on the Turkish economy and the government's responses. We will then provide medium-term growth scenarios and assess the impact of the global crisis on potential growth.

Growth Dynamics Until 2008

Turkish economic growth has historically been volatile, as evidenced by a currency crisis in 1994, the contagion effects of the East Asian and Russian crises, the Marmara earthquake in 1999, and Turkey's own banking crisis in 2001. These contractions have all been followed by rapid expansions (figure 11.1, table 11.1). During the recoveries, the contribution of external demand (net exports) to growth was mostly negative, widening the current account deficit, which was financed in part through foreign-currency-denominated debt. And "sectoral transformation" (the shift to relatively capital-intensive technologies)—while fueling investment, total factor productivity (TFP) gains, and growth—appears to have limited employment gains associated with the upswing after the 2001 crisis, more specifically during the 2002–05 period.

After liberalizing its economy in the 1980s, Turkey experienced economic and political instability in the 1990s. Average GDP growth was volatile and below potential while inflation remained high (figure 11.1). High public sector borrowing requirements (nearly 10 percent of GDP) raised the cost of domestic funds in a shallow domestic financial market.

Figure 11.1. GDP Growth Rates

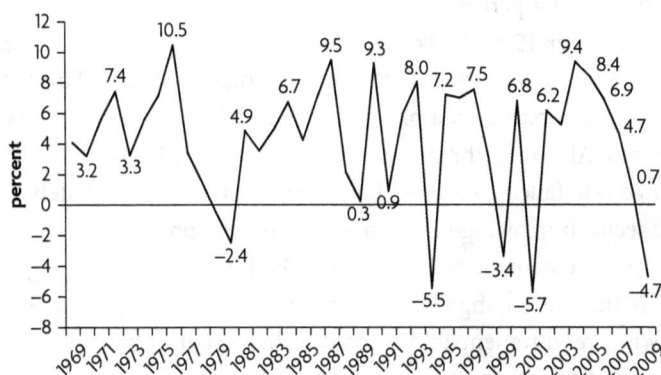

Source: TurkStat.
Note: Growth rates after 1998 are based on revised National Accounts series consistent with ESA95.

Table 11.1. Basic Macroeconomic Indicators and Their Volatility

	1988–2001	1995–2001	2002–07
GDP growth (%)			
Mean	3.1	3.4	6.8
Standard deviation	5.1	5.5	1.8
Fixed investment growth (%)			
Mean	2.8	3.2	15.5
Standard deviation	15.5	16.8	7.5
CPI inflation rate (%)			
Mean	73.2	73.9	17.6
Standard deviation	15.1	16.2	15.0

Source: TurkStat and authors' own calculations. GDP and investment growth rates after 1998 are based on new National Account series consistent with ESA95.

Public sector deficits were largely financed by banks, notably public banks through "duty losses." Bank lending to the public sector reached twice the level extended to the private sector, and empirical evidence suggests severe crowding-out effects in the second half of the 1990s (Kaplan, Özmen, and Yalçın 2006; Özatay 2008).

In 1994, an exchange rate crisis led to a 5.5 percent contraction in GDP. When growth resumed in 1995–97, it was accompanied by high inflation and current account deficits. Thus, when the Russian crisis broke out in 1998, it led to a further contraction of output in Turkey, reducing it by 3.4 percent in 1999.

In December 1999, Turkey launched an exchange-rate-based stabilization program supported by the International Monetary Fund (IMF). A crawling peg based on a preannounced exchange rate path served as the anchor. Although the program initially attracted capital inflows, the exchange rate failed to follow the peg and current account deficits and public sector borrowing requirements remained problematic.

Mismanagement of public finances had been a persistent problem and was the underlying cause of the 2001 crisis. A high public sector borrowing requirement and limited policy credibility raised the cost of domestic funds in the context of shallow financial markets. As is often the case in such environments, the corporate sector invested in interest-bearing assets (especially government securities) rather than fixed assets, to remain liquid in an uncertain macroeconomic environment. The net effect was that large firms tended to behave as financial intermediaries while small and medium firms faced severe financing constraints.

Despite strong export performance, driven by depreciation of the lira and strong external demand, in 2001 the economy contracted by 5.7 percent. Certain banks started to borrow short-term finance from abroad to on-lend to the public sector (Ertuğrul and Selçuk 2001), and the financial sector's resulting short net foreign exchange position and maturity mismatches created huge vulnerability. When market sentiment changed—the lira depreciated by 140 percent in 10 months and spreads on government securities shot up to 194 percent in March 2001 from 65 percent in January—the Turkish financial system was left insolvent.

The estimated fiscal cost of the subsequent financial restructuring was equivalent to some 15 percent of GDP. The public debt-to-GDP ratio, 51 percent at the end of 2000, reached 79 percent a year later. Credit to the private sector as a percentage of GDP fell below 10 percent, signaling a credit crunch. In short, poor public sector management, a weak balance of payments, political instability, a poorly regulated financial sector, rigid labor markets, the limited resources available for financially constrained households and firms, and overall macroeconomic instability all distorted resource allocation and led to extensive volatility in prices and economic activity.

Reforms in Response to the 2001 Banking Crisis

The economic program put into place after the 2001 crisis represented an unprecedented effort to address the fundamental weaknesses in economic management and financial oversight. Urgent measures were taken in the banking sector and macroeconomic policies focused on disinflation. Fiscal policy was tightened to stabilize the public debt stock and a new framework for monetary and exchange rate policy introduced inflation targeting and a flexible exchange rate regime.

The main innovation relative to earlier adjustment plans was improving overall expenditure efficiency and attaining relatively high primary surplus targets. The ratio of interest payments to GDP dropped sharply, from almost 18 percent of GDP in 2001 to 6 percent by 2007. Thanks to strong growth, revenue improved substantially and the public sector borrowing requirement (PSBR) fell dramatically. The debt-to-GDP ratio declined from 73 percent in 2002 to 43 percent in 2008 (table 11.2).

The banking sector's condition improved substantially, owing to a restructuring of assets, effective supervision and regulation, and strong economic growth. As a result, credit to the private sector as a percentage of GDP increased sharply. Foreign banks were brought in through mergers and acquisitions: the share of foreign commercial banks in total commercial bank assets reached 15.3 percent in 2008, versus 3.3 percent in 2002. The improvement in capital structure and the decline in the share of nonperforming loans (NPLs) increased the viability of the banking sector (table 11.3). As the public sector consumed a lower share of bank lending, the share of loans to the private sector recovered, to nearly

Table 11.2. Basic Indicators of Public Sector Balance
(% GDP)

	2001	2002	2003	2004	2005	2006	2007	2008
Gross public sector debt	78.9	73.3	65.4	59.5	54.1	48.2	42.2	42.9
Total PSBR	12.1	10.0	7.3	3.7	−0.3	−2.0	0.1	1.7
Interest payments	18.0	15.5	13.4	10.5	7.2	6.2	6.0	6.0
Public primary balance	4.1	3.2	4.8	5.5	5.0	4.6	3.1	1.7
Central gov't. tax revenues	18.2	17.2	18.1	17.9	18.4	18.1	18.1	17.7
GDP (TL billions)	**240.2**	**350.5**	**454.8**	**559.0**	**648.9**	**758.4**	**843.2**	**950.5**

Source: Treasury; Ministry of Finance.

Table 11.3. Selected Banking Sector Indicators
(percent)

	Net profits/assets	Loans/assets	Loans/deposits	Gross NPLs/loans	Capital adequacy ratio
2001	—	21.9	31.8	37.4	—
2002	1.1	26.5	39.6	18.5	24.2
2003	2.2	28.0	43.5	12.3	30.9
2004	2.1	33.7	52.3	6.2	28.8
2005	1.4	38.6	60.4	4.9	24.2
2006	2.3	45.0	69.7	3.8	22.0
2007	2.6	50.0	78.6	3.5	19.1
2008	1.8	52.0	80.9	3.6	18.1
2009[a]	2.7	48.4	75.0	5.3	20.0

Source: Banking Regulation and Supervision Agency (BSRA).
Note: NPL = nonperforming loan; — = not available.
a. By September.

Figure 11.2. Share of Consumer Credits in Total Credit

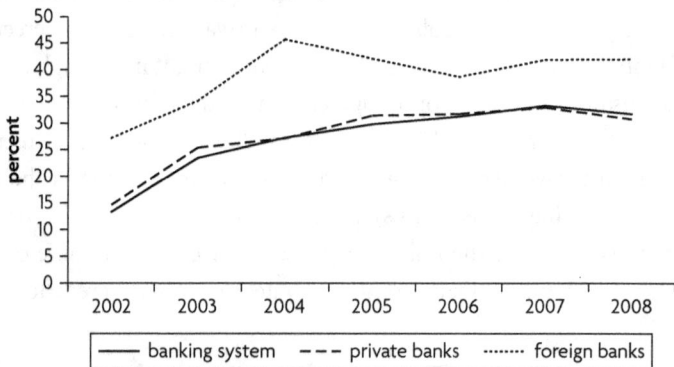

Source: Central Bank of the Republic of Turkey (CBRT).

30 percent of GDP in 2008 from 10 percent in 2002. The access to bank funds of financially constrained firms and consumers improved substantially. Even more striking was the rise in consumer loans, from 13 percent of total bank loans at the end of 2002 to 33 percent in December 2007 (figure 11.2). Despite the sharp rise in household loans, the share of household sector debt in GDP has remained below 15 percent.

Central bank independence was a crucial element. In the response to 2001, the Central Bank of the Republic of Turkey (CBRT) was granted full independence and authorized to design monetary strategy and select the policy instrument. This led to "implicit" inflation targeting and a flexible exchange rate as the framework for monetary policy. The consumer price index (CPI) inflation rate fell from over 50 percent in 2002 to single digits by 2006. In addition to tight monetary policy, capital inflows played a role in the 40+ percent real appreciation of the lira, which in turn supported disinflation (figure 11.3).

The flexible exchange rate regime not only supported disinflation but also discouraged dollarization. For example, corporate firms with limited foreign-currency-denominated revenues tended to avoid borrowing in foreign currency.

In addition to the macro-stabilization program introduced after 2001, a wide range of structural reforms also improved the outlook. Democratization, the abolition of regulatory obstacles to capital inflows, and other regulatory improvements linked to the EU accession process supported foreign direct investment (FDI), lengthened the maturity of foreign currency borrowing, and increased confidence over the period 2002–05. As a result, the volatility in prices and in economic activity declined substantially (table 11.1). Empirical evidence also supports the assertion that reforms in this period, as well as the monetary policy implemented by the Central Bank, reduced volatility and softened the impact of the recent global crisis on the Turkish economy.[1] More recently,

Figure 11.3. Inflation and Policy Rates, Real Effective Exchange Rate Index

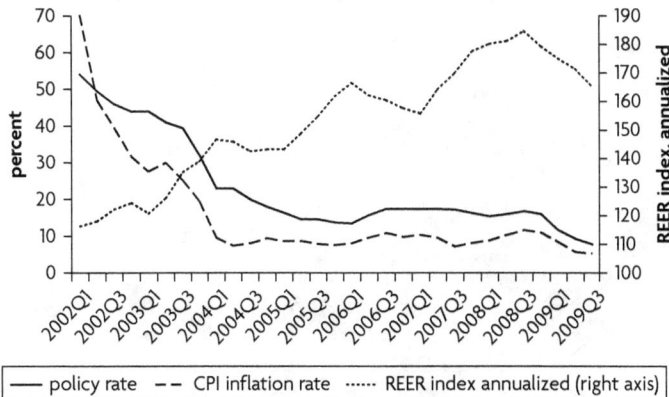

Source: TurkStat; CBRT.

however, the pace of reforms has slowed, partly due to unresolved issues in the EU accession process, partly as a result of the global crisis, and also partly as a reflection of internal political conditions.

Demand and Production Structure of Growth

Increased private sector productivity was the main engine of growth after the 2001 crisis. The Turkish economy grew 6.8 percent annually on average during 2002–07, versus 3.2 percent during 1995–2001. The rapid growth was facilitated by two developments.

First, the commitment to sound economic policy by a stable government reduced the country risk premium and boosted overall confidence (figure 11.4). Reforms that achieved macroeconomic stability, improved corporate governance, and higher labor productivity enhanced the contribution of TFP to growth.

Second, the extraordinarily benign global economic environment, in the form of high external demand and large capital inflows, supported exports and private investment.

The industrial and service sectors rapidly raised their productive capacity. These sectors—especially machinery equipment—played a leading role in GDP growth, whereas agriculture lagged. Services, led by transportation, trade, construction, and financial intermediation, contributed 4.3 percentage points to the average GDP growth of 6.8 percent in 2002–07. Manufacturing led industry and contributed nearly

Figure 11.4. The Emerging Markets Bond Index (EMBI) + Turkey Spreads

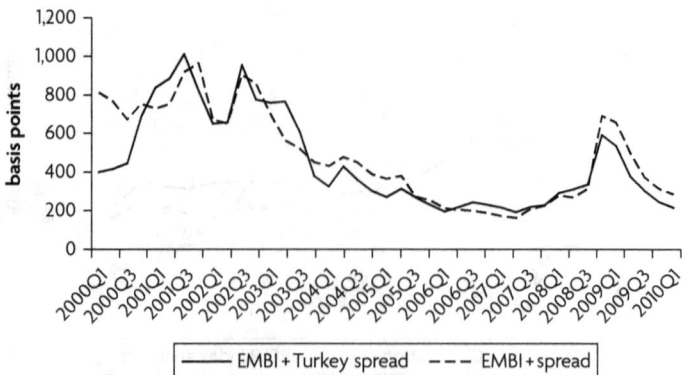

Source: JP Morgan.

2 percentage points while agriculture contributed only 0.2 percentage points.

The drivers of growth in 2002–07 were the activation of postponed private consumption, reduced private savings, capital inflows, and rising financial intermediation. Private consumption and investment contributed 5.4 and 3.0 percentage points, respectively, to the growth rate in the period. The contribution of public expenditures was modest, at 0.5 percentage points, owing to public sector reforms that moderated public spending. On the other hand, foreign trade was substantial; its share in GDP increased almost 10 percentage points during 2002–07, which made the economy more sensitive to external demand and financial conditions. But buoyant domestic demand, a somewhat appreciated currency, and the shift in industrial activity to sectors that used more imported inputs led to rapid growth of capital goods imports (30 percent annually during 2002–07). The average contribution of net exports to growth was negative as a result—on average –1.8 percentage points (figure 11.5).

Machinery-equipment investment played a large role in the boom period. Investment in capital goods imports supported the export activity of those sectors that invested heavily in capital-intensive technologies. The sectoral composition of exports changed dramatically, beginning in the mid-1990s. Labor-intensive exports lost pace, a trend that became

Figure 11.5. GDP Growth and Contribution by Expenditures

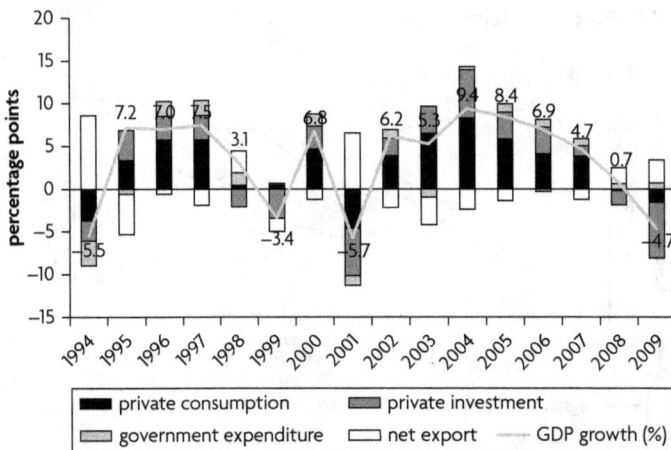

Source: TurkStat.

more marked as the currency appreciated. The decline in the share of exports of textiles and clothing and agricultural products was substantial, from 39 percent in 2002 to 20 percent in 2008. At the same time, motor vehicles, machinery, and basic metals expanded their shares sharply, from 25 percent to 39 percent. Thus the main driver of export growth was capital and intermediate goods, including motor vehicles, basic and fabricated metals, and machinery and equipment. Textiles and clothing in particular suffered beginning in the late 1990s from competition from China and India. Although export volumes were strong in 2002–07, imports grew faster (figure 11.6).

Strong demand from the EU and oil-exporting countries supported Turkey's solid export volume. Turkey realized more than half of its export trade with the EU during 2002–07. Although the share of exports to the EU declined after 2007, owing to a shift to neighboring countries and contraction in EU demand, it rose again in late 2009 but remained below the precrisis level. During the crisis, Turkey's exports to the Near and Middle East and North Africa partly offset the falling exports to the EU.

The content of imported intermediate inputs in production has increased substantially. Rapidly growing manufacturing sectors that adopted new technologies have fueled the import of intermediate capital goods (figure 11.7).[2]

Figure 11.6. Exports of Selected Sectors

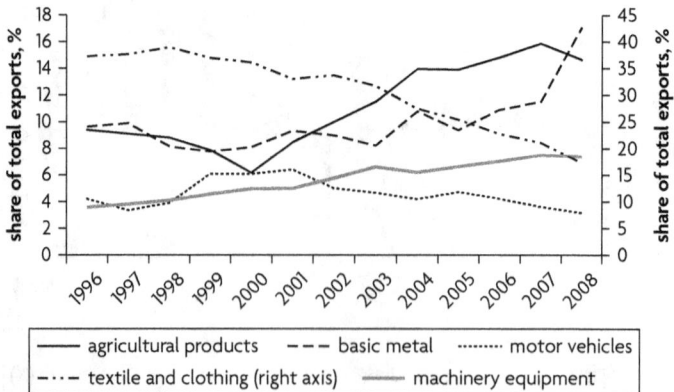

Source: TurkStat.

Figure 11.7. Decomposition of Intermediate Inputs in Production of Manufacturing Firms

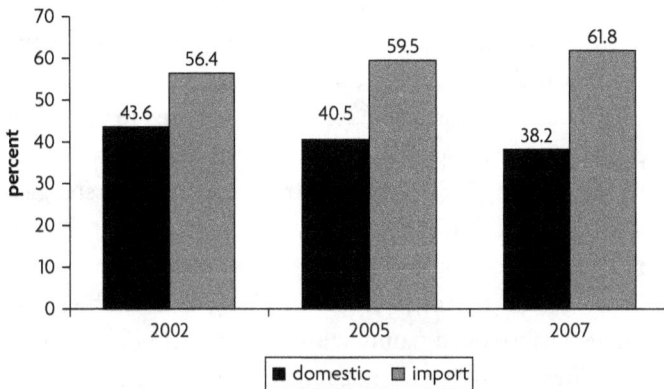

Source: Saygılı et al. 2010.

Exports were strong in 2002–07 despite real exchange rate appreciation of about 40 percent (based on monthly averages). This was partly
the result of a shift in the composition of exports to sectors that make
more intensive use of imported inputs. Exports of nontraditional industries, which have relatively high import content and are more sensitive to
external demand, exhibit less exchange rate sensitivity than traditional
ones. One side effect of the increase in imported inputs has been a
decline in the domestic content of value added created by exports as
international competition intensified and the relative cost of domestic
inputs rose. Sectors that made the most intensive use of domestic inputs
lost ground to East Asian countries. Yılmaz and Gönenç (2008) find that
sectors that used imported inputs most intensively enjoyed the strongest
productivity growth at moderate wage adjustments and, thus, enhanced
their competitiveness, while sectors engaged in lower-technology activities using lower-skilled labor saw less productivity growth. Because of
the latter sectors' high share in manufacturing employment, employment creation was limited, even during Turkey's high-growth period.

External Balance and Finance

Large current account gaps after 2002 were a source of vulnerability. Since
domestic savings have generally been insufficient to finance domestic

investment, particularly with rising commodity prices, Turkey has long
relied on foreign savings, which has been one of the most important
causes of volatility in its economic performance.

Alongside the strong domestic demand, the appreciating currency, and
the shift to imported inputs, a large portion of the post-2001 current account
deficit is attributable to worsening terms of trade linked to the sharp rise in
oil prices since 2002. The external deficit averaged 5.5 percent of GDP in
2005–08, more than half of which was attributable to higher energy costs.

The lack of domestic savings has been a binding constraint on growth for
much of Turkey's recent economic history. Boom-bust cycles have been
caused largely by short-term capital flows. The gains from the good times
have often been wiped out by contractions and crises, leading to lower trend
growth rates. Turkey's low saving rate translates into a higher average cost of
funds, relative to fast-growing emerging countries (table 11.4).

Table 11.4. Selected Indicators in High-Saving Countries and Turkey
(percent)

	Turkey	Korea, Rep.	China	Malaysia	Thailand	Iran, Islamic Rep.
				1980–89		
Dependency ratio	74.9	53.1	57.3	73.3	61.5	92.3
Labor force participation rate	60.0	60.4	84.1	62.0	85.2	52.6
Domestic saving rate	16.4	30.9	35.4	30.2	26.5	16.8
GDP growth rate	4.1	7.7	9.8	5.9	7.3	−0.3
Employment growth rate	1.5	2.8	2.9	3.8	3.4	—
				1990–99		
Dependency ratio	60.8	41.7	48.5	66.0	46.6	85.3
Labor force participation rate	57.6	63.9	84.2	64.3	79.9	52.6
Domestic saving rate	20.5	36.3	41.5	40.7	35.3	35.9
GDP growth rate	4.0	6.3	10.0	7.2	5.3	4.6
Employment growth rate	2.0	1.4	1.3	3.7	0.0	3.9
				2000–07		
Dependency ratio	52.4	39.0	43.1	56.7	42.3	54.5
Labor force participation rate	51.8	65.0	82.3	65.2	77.6	53.9
Domestic saving rate	17.5	32.1	45.1	43.0	31.6	39.3
GDP growth rate	5.2	5.2	10.1	5.6	5.0	5.9
Employment growth rate	0.6	1.5	1.0	3.0	1.7	3.6

Source: World Bank Development Data Platform (DDP) average employment growth figure of 1980–89 for Turkey from the
Organisation for Economic Co-operation and Development.
Note: — = not available.

Figure 11.8. Saving and Investment Rates and the Savings-Investment Gap

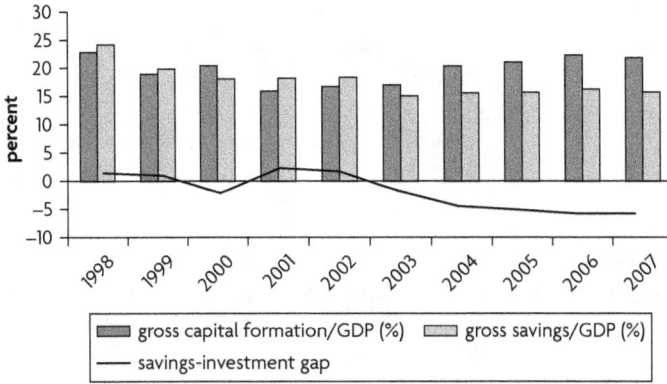

Source: World Bank, World Development Indicators Database.

The composition of domestic savings shifted to the public sector after 2001, and the overall savings rate remained about flat after 2003 (figure 11.8). The public sector savings rate increased with high public sector primary surpluses while the private savings rate declined as result of strong private consumption growth. Private consumption grew about 10 percent on average annually in the period 2003–05 as confidence and credit rebounded due to strong credit demand from constrained households. In essence, households borrowed from banks to finance a larger portion of their durable consumption while corporate firms financed their investments partly with foreign savings. The slowdown in capital inflows is therefore expected to be one of the factors hindering potential growth in the postcrisis global economy.

The quality of capital inflows, however, has improved substantially. The maturity of foreign debt owed by the private sector increased and the ratio of net FDI to total net capital inflows increased to 38 percent in 2007 (table 11.5). The increase in debt maturity and the decline in the liability dollarization reduced the vulnerability of the private sector, but a high net foreign exchange open position nonetheless is a concern. At the same time, average annual worker remittances fell sharply from nearly US$4 billion in 1995–2001 to about US$1 billion in 2002–07.

Table 11.5. Financing of Saving Investment Gap in Turkey
(% GDP)

	1998	1999	2000	2001	2002	2003	2004	2005	2006	2007	2008
Total capital inflows (net)	−0.3	3.2	3.9	−4.7	−0.1	2.2	5.3	8.6	9.7	8.1	5.1
FDI (net)	0.2	0.1	0.0	1.5	0.4	0.4	0.5	1.9	3.6	3.1	2.1
Portfolio (net)	−2.5	1.4	0.4	−2.3	−0.3	0.8	2.0	2.8	1.4	0.1	−0.7
Loans to private sector (net)	2.0	1.8	3.5	−3.9	−0.3	1.0	2.8	4.0	4.6	4.9	3.6
Banks	0.3	0.9	1.6	−4.1	−0.4	0.6	1.5	1.9	1.1	0.9	0.4
Short-term	0.0	0.8	1.8	−3.6	−0.3	0.7	0.9	0.6	−0.7	−0.3	0.3
Medium- to long-term	0.3	0.0	−0.1	−0.5	−0.1	0.0	0.6	1.4	1.8	1.1	0.1
Corporate	1.7	0.9	1.9	0.2	0.2	0.3	1.3	2.0	3.5	4.0	3.2
Short-term	0.2	0.0	0.0	0.1	−0.3	0.1	0.1	0.1	0.1	0.0	0.1
Medium- to long-term	1.5	0.9	1.8	0.1	0.5	0.2	1.2	2.0	3.5	4.0	3.1
GDP (US$ billions)	270.9	247.5	265.4	196.7	230.5	304.9	390.4	481.5	526.4	648.8	741.8

Source: CBRT.

Supply-Side Dynamics

During 1995–2001, capital accumulation was the driving force of economic growth in Turkey whereas the contributions of TFP and employment were limited. But during 2002–07, while capital accumulation remained strong, the contribution of TFP rose substantially, paced partly by improvements in human capital (via additional years of schooling). Adjusting the capital stock for cyclical variables reduces the contribution of TFP (the residual) to growth[3] (for a detailed analysis of growth accounting, see the annex).

Turkish companies, which invested heavily in financial assets before 2001, invested more in fixed assets and utilized capacity more effectively after the crisis. Intensifying external competition owing to import penetration and an appreciated currency pushed firms to adopt lower-cost production methods. A reallocation of resources to more labor-saving production processes raised productivity and improved the international competitiveness of industry. Capital inflows also relieved financing constraints and made room for small and medium firms to obtain bank financing.

The rise in labor productivity was supported by more rapid TFP growth in 2002–07. Labor productivity across all sectors was weak during the 1990s, with substantial improvement thereafter (figure 11.9). An analysis

Figure 11.9. Labor Productivity across Sectors

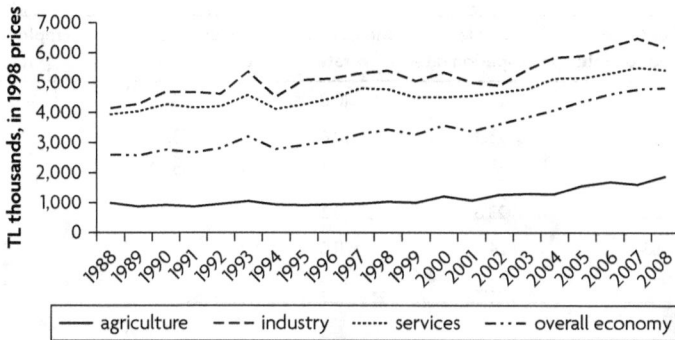

Source: TurkStat.

that controls for cyclical components, human capital, and the quality of
the existing capital stock (Altuğ, Filiztekin, and Pamuk 2007) nevertheless
shows that the contribution of TFP to growth has been limited in Turkey
relative to emerging East Asia. The reasons include inefficient institutions,
a low level of human capital, and macroeconomic instability. The acceleration of labor productivity growth occurred mainly in industry. The annual
average growth of labor productivity was 5.8 percent in 2002–07, versus
2.1 percent in 1995–2001. As a result, unit labor wages declined until 2007,
and there was only a slight rise in real wages.

Why has the contribution of labor to Turkish growth been so modest?
One might have expected a larger contribution from labor given favorable demographics. The working-age population has been growing by
1.7 percent a year on average in recent years, and more than half a million new workers enter the labor force every year. Indeed, the proportion
of the population under 35 years old was 61 percent in 2008.

The limited contribution of employment to growth can be attributed
to low labor force participation rates (below 50 percent) relative to
many emerging economies, a low female participation rate of less than
25 percent (table 11.6), and substantial changes in the composition
of production activity in favor of labor-saving technologies. Despite
strong economic growth, the Turkish unemployment rate hovered
around 10 percent during 2002–07.

The slower job creation in recent years can be explained by several
factors:[4]

Table 11.6. Selected Indicators in Labor Market
(percent)

	Labor force participation rate	Female participation rate	Unemployment rate	Nonagricultural unemployment rate	Employment rate
2004	46.3	23.3	10.8	14.2	41.3
2005	46.4	23.3	10.6	13.5	41.5
2006	46.3	23.6	10.2	12.7	41.5
2007	46.2	23.6	10.3	12.6	41.5
2008	46.9	24.5	11.0	13.6	41.7
2009	47.9	26.0	14.0	17.4	41.2

Source: TurkStat.

- The formal segment of the labor market (about half of total employment) is rigidly regulated.
- Public sector employment has declined substantially as state production has virtually disappeared in many sectors owing to privatization and a central government ceiling on new hiring.
- The share of labor-intensive activity (i.e., agriculture, textile, clothing) has declined and imported inputs have increased. (The share of agricultural employment in total employment declined from 35 percent in 2002 to 23.5 percent in 2007, while the share of agricultural value added in GDP declined to 7.6 percent in 2007 from 10 percent in 2002).[5]
- The movement of labor between sectors raises the issue of skills mismatches as labor released from rural activities lack the necessary skills to be channeled to non-agricultural activities in urban areas.

Although unemployment remained high, poverty and income distribution figures improved during 2002–07. This was partly due to the extension of social protections and a fall in the dependency ratio. Also, the incidence of absolute poverty has fallen considerably, although relative poverty has declined only modestly. Nonetheless, poverty should have increased during the global crisis.

In sum, Turkey's potential growth rate is estimated to have been just above 5 percent in 2002–07, driven by high investment, TFP gains, and the efficient utilization of factors. Clearly, structural reforms (which boosted efficiency and competition in goods and financial markets), favorable fiscal and monetary policies (which brought inflation and real interest rates down), and FDI expanded Turkey's productive capacity. But several risks pose problems for maintaining growth above 5 percent in the future. One risk is the ability of lower domestic and foreign savings to sustain a high investment rate. New investments are necessary for improving infrastructure and creating new jobs in areas of higher labor productivity. Nonetheless, Turkey has room for further TFP improvements; the question is how to unlock these in an environment of potentially lower investment.

The Transmission of the Global Crisis and the Policy Response

Private investment played a leading role both in the strong recovery during 2002–05 and in the subsequent slowdown from 2006. Following low gross fixed capital formation in the highly uncertain macroeconomic environment of 1998–2001, a strong recovery emerged after the 2001 crisis. But private investment had lost steam from the second half of 2006. By the time the global crisis hit in September 2008, the Turkish economy was already experiencing slower private investment growth (figure 11.10).

In a foreshadowing of the problems of 2008, Turkey experienced capital outflows after U.S. interest rate hikes in mid-2006. During May–June 2006, the lira depreciated by almost 20 percent, driven by portfolio outflows that reflected concerns about current account sustainability.

Figure 11.10. Private Investment, Public Expenditures, and GDP Growth Rates, Annualized

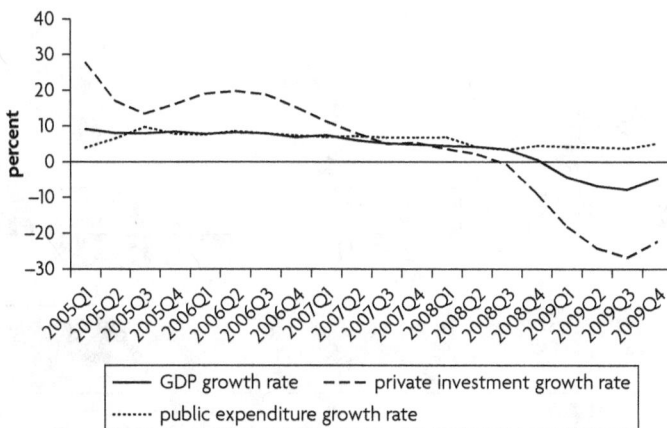

Source: TurkStat.

In an effort to contain inflation expectations, the CBRT raised interest rates by 425 basis points in June 2006. Confidence fell and private fixed investment subsequently slowed (figures 11.10 and 11.11). Moreover, capital inflows financed a growing import bill attributed to higher commodity prices and, to some degree, went into financial assets rather than new fixed assets.

The next two years—2007 and early 2008—were a period of political and economic uncertainty:

Figure 11.11. Confidence Indexes and Capital Account after 2006

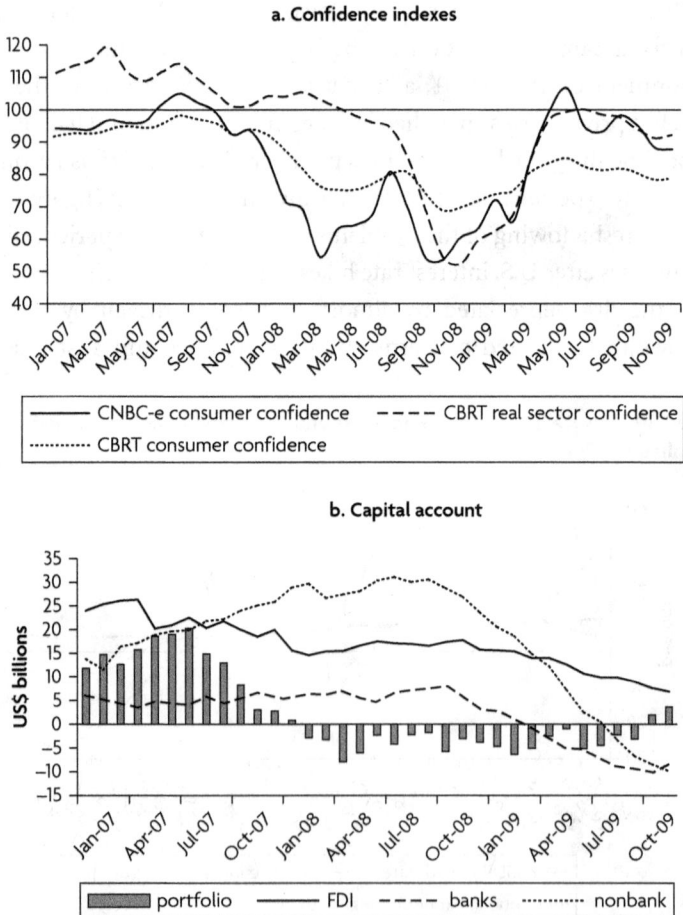

a. Confidence indexes

CNBC-e consumer confidence   — — — CBRT real sector confidence   ·········· CBRT consumer confidence

b. Capital account

US$ billions

portfolio   —— FDI   – – – banks   ·········· nonbank

Source: TurkStat.

- Monetary tightening was initiated in the second half of 2006 in response to inflation that exceeded official targets.
- Sharp rises in commodity prices affected financing needs and investor sentiment.
- Political tensions rose in light of a double election and an associated deterioration in the public sector balance.
- A drought hurt agricultural production.

Economic activity contracted sharply (by 7 percent) when the global crisis hit in the last quarter of 2008. The year-on-year contraction hit hardest in the first quarter of 2009, minus 14.5 percent, then eased in the second and third quarters. For 2009 as a whole, growth contracted by 4.7 percent (5.2 percent when adjusted for calendar effects).

Most destructive was the impact on unemployment, which jumped about 4 percentage points to 14 percent in the period 2007–09. The increase in nonagricultural unemployment was nearly 5 percentage points, to 17.4 percent relative to 2007 (figure 11.12a). A sharp rise in the labor participation rate—a response to the crisis—explains part of the jump in nonagricultural unemployment. In the first half of 2009, when the crisis hit the labor market, 2.2 million jobs were lost compared with a year earlier, most of them in manufacturing. At the end of 2009, industrial employment had declined 7 percent, while services and agricultural employment had increased by 4.7 percent and 1.3 percent, respectively. For the year as a whole, employment increased by just 0.4 percent. The rise in unemployment thus stemmed both from slower job creation and increased labor participation (figure 11.12b).

The sharp contraction in industrial output led to a fall in labor productivity in the early stages of the crisis due to a slower decline in employment relative to output even though labor productivity recovered toward the end of 2009. This drop in productivity was milder than that in real wages and resulted in a large decline in unit labor wages in industry in 2009 (figure 11.13a). Unlike industry, services have not posted job losses during the crisis (figure 11.13b). The net effect was a collapse of labor productivity and a rise in unit labor wages. Industry reacted aggressively by cutting jobs by 8.7 percent in the first nine months of 2009, which brought about a shift in labor productivity by the end of the year.

Figure 11.12. Labor Market Indicators during the Global Crisis

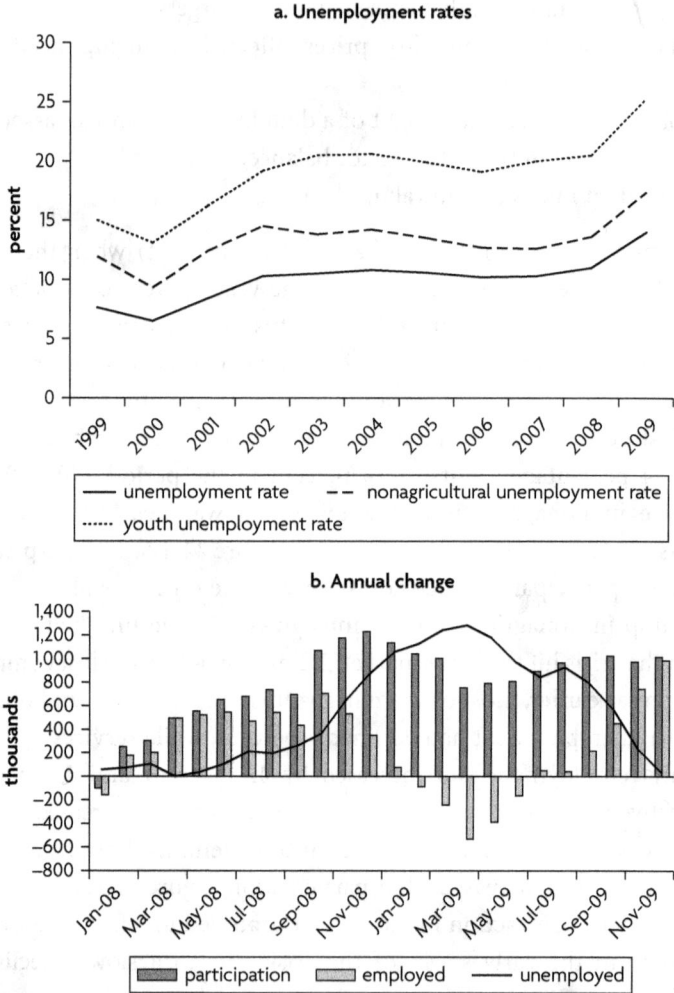

a. Unemployment rates

legend: —— unemployment rate   – – nonagricultural unemployment rate
········ youth unemployment rate

b. Annual change

legend: ▨ participation   ▨ employed   —— unemployed

Source: TurkStat.

Before the crisis, poverty had decreased sharply, to 17.1 percent in 2008 from 27.0 percent in 2002, but it worsened in the wake of the crisis. Simulations suggest a potential 5 percent rise in the poverty rate from 2008 to 2010, when it could be around 22 percent, which would mean more than 3 million people falling below the poverty line in 2009–10. These simulations also suggest that the most vulnerable groups are

Figure 11.13. Labor Productivity and Wages Indexes in Industry and Services Sectors

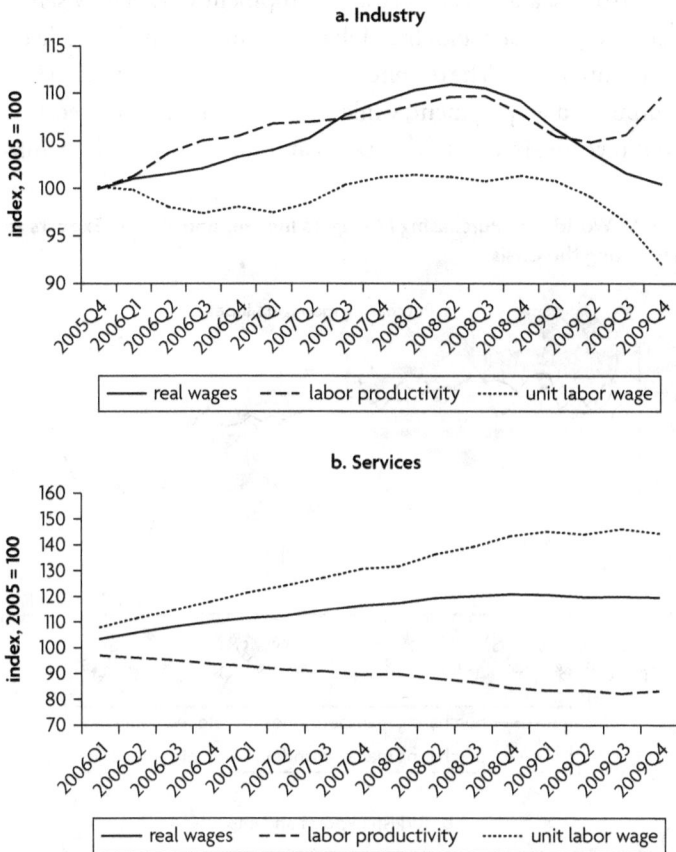

a. Industry

b. Services

Source: TurkStat.

informal nonagricultural workers (who account for nearly half the estimated increase in poverty), children, and young workers.

The impact of the crisis on the Turkish economy was transmitted through four channels: trade, inventory, financial flows, and confidence.

Exports Hit Hard

Exports were strong before the crisis: year-on-year export growth in 2008 was 23 percent, while import growth was 18 percent. Exports contracted by nearly 27 percent annually after the crisis hit, and imports dropped even faster (by nearly 35 percent), owing to declines in both prices and volumes. Since such export sectors as motor vehicles, basic metals, chemicals, electronics, and machinery and equipment were highly sensitive to cyclical changes in demand, the global crisis precipitated a trade crisis in Turkey (figure 11.14). The decline in exports fed the contraction in industrial output and employment, while the decline in imports reduced government revenue. In addition, exports and imports have close links with

Figure 11.14. Worldwide Purchasing Managers Indexes and Turkish Exports and Imports during the Crisis

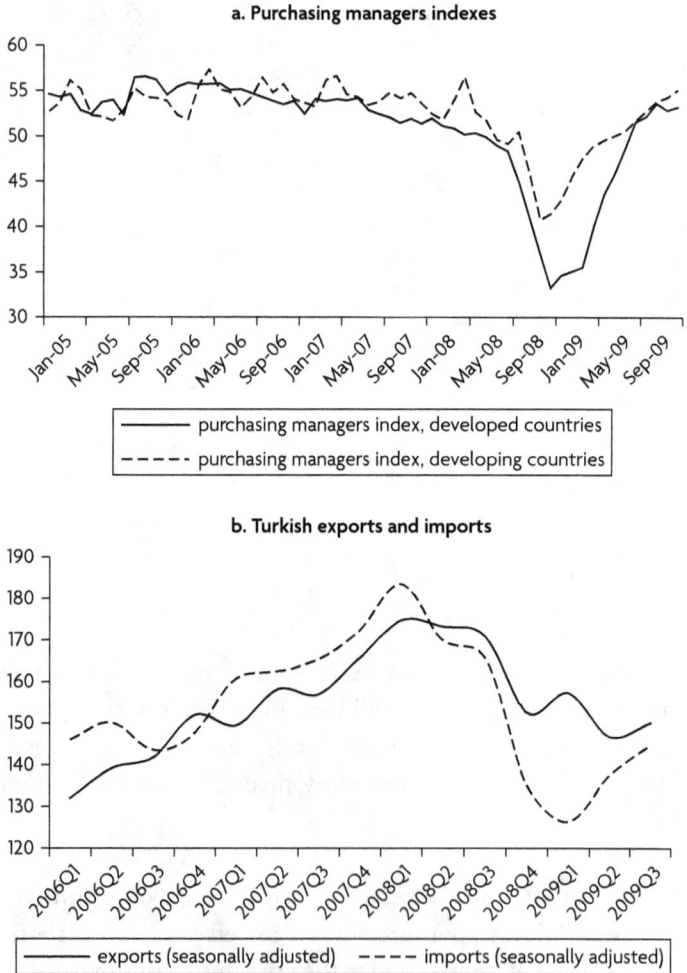

a. Purchasing managers indexes

— purchasing managers index, developed countries
---- purchasing managers index, developing countries

b. Turkish exports and imports

— exports (seasonally adjusted)   ---- imports (seasonally adjusted)

Source: Bloomberg; TurkStat.

services—including trade, transportation, tourism, and financial inter-mediation—and thus amplified the impact of the trade channel.

Declines in exports of motor vehicles, basic metal, machinery and equipment, and electronics were largely responsible for the 15 percent year-on-year fall in industrial production in the first nine months of 2009 (figure 11.15a). The production capacity of many SMEs (vital for employment) was hit especially hard. Survey data suggest that those firms with poorer governance, suboptimal size, engagement in informal activities, and limited equity bases have been exiting the

Figure 11.15. Industrial Production and Inventory Accumulation

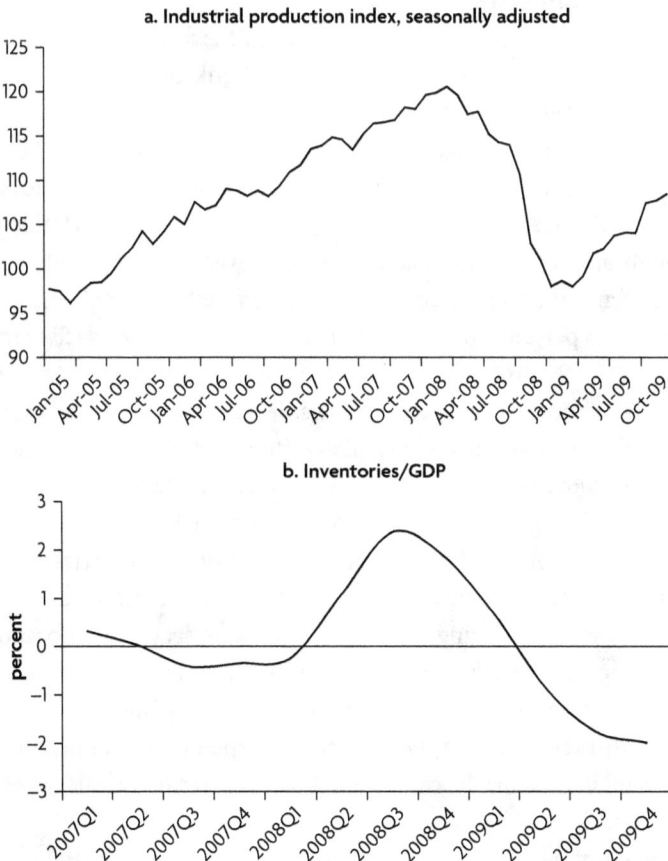

a. Industrial production index, seasonally adjusted

b. Inventories/GDP

Source: TurkStat.

market. Industrial production has, however, seen a gradual recovery since the last quarter of 2009.

Large Inventories Are Run Down
In addition to weak demand, the decline in industrial production was amplified by the high level of accumulated inventories prevailing at the start of the crisis. Inventory accumulation accounted for about 2 percent of GDP between the first quarter of 2007 and the third quarter of 2008. The running down of these high inventory levels may explain why export volumes declined more slowly than industrial output after September 2008 (figure 11.15b).

Financial Conditions Are Tightened
Turkey's financial system has been resilient in the face of the crisis. In past crises, banks had been the economy's weakest link, but thanks to the 2001 reforms, they have been the strongest component. Although the NPLs of SMEs have been growing, their strong capital structure and the rising profitability of the banking sector have been compensating factors; as a result, the capital adequacy ratio actually rose during the crisis (table 11.3). Although banks were liquid and solvent, the risks associated with global deleveraging led to tight credit conditions: interest rates on loans initially jumped to 25 percent from about 17 percent, followed by a decline toward the end of 2009. Although the spread of consumer loans over the deposit rate remains more than 5 percent, the spread of the corporate loans rate over the deposit rate eased substantially (to about 2 percent) in the third quarter of 2009. Loans to SMEs, however, contracted sharply and have recovered only slightly in recent months (figure 11.16a).

Turkey has not suffered as much as some other countries from the effects of financial balance sheet mismatches or remittances. First, in contrast to some emerging markets, the banking sector had no underlying currency mismatches when it entered the crisis. Second, as noted earlier, remittances are not an important item in the Turkish capital account. Turkey therefore did not need to spend any public resources on the banking sector; the capital adequacy ratio in early 2010 was above 20 percent.

Capital inflows, however, have fallen substantially, owing to both supply and demand influences. Large firms that had borrowed heavily from

Figure 11.16. Finance Channel

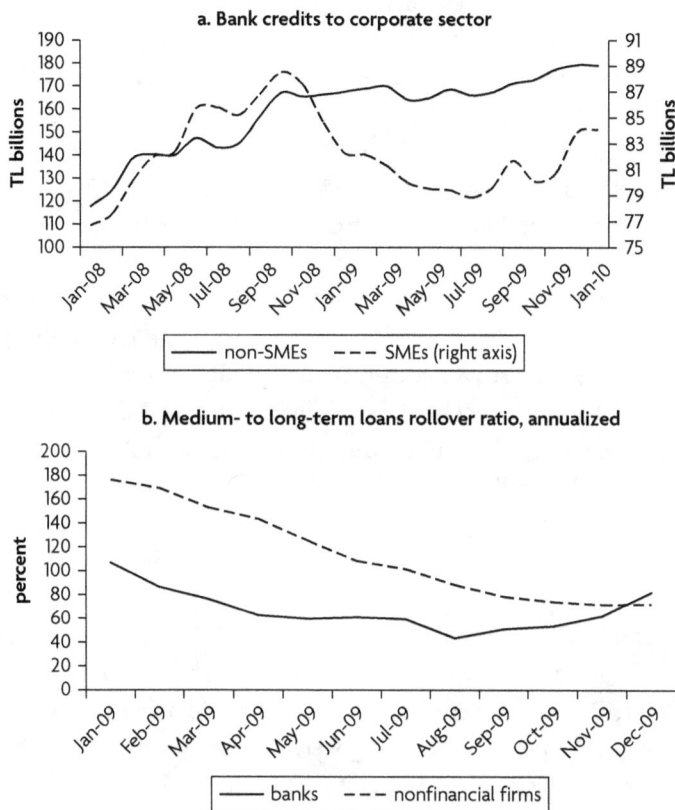

a. Bank credits to corporate sector

non-SMEs ---- SMEs (right axis)

b. Medium- to long-term loans rollover ratio, annualized

banks ---- nonfinancial firms

Source: BRSA; CBRT

abroad cut investments and, in 2009, rolled over only about 70 percent of their foreign currency liabilities (versus around 200 percent before the crisis). The banking sector's borrowing from abroad contracted less severely and recovered sooner; banks were rolling over more than 80 percent of their foreign currency liabilities by the end of 2009 (figure 11.16b). FDI, which had increased to 3.8 percent of GDP in 2006, fell to 2.5 percent in 2008 and to about 1 percent in 2009. In association with this, private investment contracted by 28 percent in the first three quarters of 2009. Partially offsetting this effect, net errors and omissions on the balance of payments showed inflows exceeding US$14 billion in the first half of 2009, reflecting repatriation of foreign currency assets.

In the wake of the global crisis, Turkey's sovereign spread (EMBI+) increased and then eased somewhat. Initially, spreads rose by about 280 basis points (bps) to 592 bps between the second quarter of 2008 and the first quarter of 2009. They then eased gradually to 215 bps in the first quarter of 2010. Overall, Turkey's sovereign spreads slightly outperformed the average for emerging market spreads (figure 11.4). A similar trend was seen in corporate spreads; they jumped nearly 300 bps between the final quarter of 2008 and the first quarter of 2009, then fell to pre-crisis levels—about 200 bps. Since the nonfinancial firms and banks that borrowed abroad were mostly large, blue-chip companies with strong balance sheets and export revenues, they managed to reduce their debt stocks during the crisis. Because the corporate sector managed risks well during the crisis, stock prices have nearly doubled since the onset of the crisis, reversing their 40 percent decline between August 2008 and February 2009. Finally, although portfolio inflows played a key role in the rise of stock prices in 2005–07, they had little impact on stock prices in 2009, during which time portfolio inflows were only US$198 million.

Impact on Public Finances

The crisis did, however, substantially worsen Turkey's public finances (figure 11.17). Real expenditures rose 10.9 percent in 2009, while real revenues fell 3.5 percent. General government expenditure as a share of GDP increased by nearly 6 points to 40.1 percent in 2009. The largest item was current transfers to the Social Security Institution (SSI), budgeted to rise by about 2 percent of GDP in 2009. As a result, the overall public sector deficit exceeded 5 percent of GDP in 2009. The primary balance is shifted to a deficit of 1.1 percent of GDP (the first primary deficit this decade), from a 1.7 percent surplus in 2008, owing mainly to the effect of automatic stabilizers. Public debt (EU definition) had risen to 45.4 percent of GDP at the end of 2009, from less than 40 percent a year earlier.

Confidence Is Hurt

Although the Turkish economy has witnessed a transformation in the past few decades, further reforms are needed to shore up its market economy and reduce volatility. Investors and consumers in Turkey remain sensitive not only to underlying vulnerabilities such as the reliance on

Figure 11.17. Central Government Balance

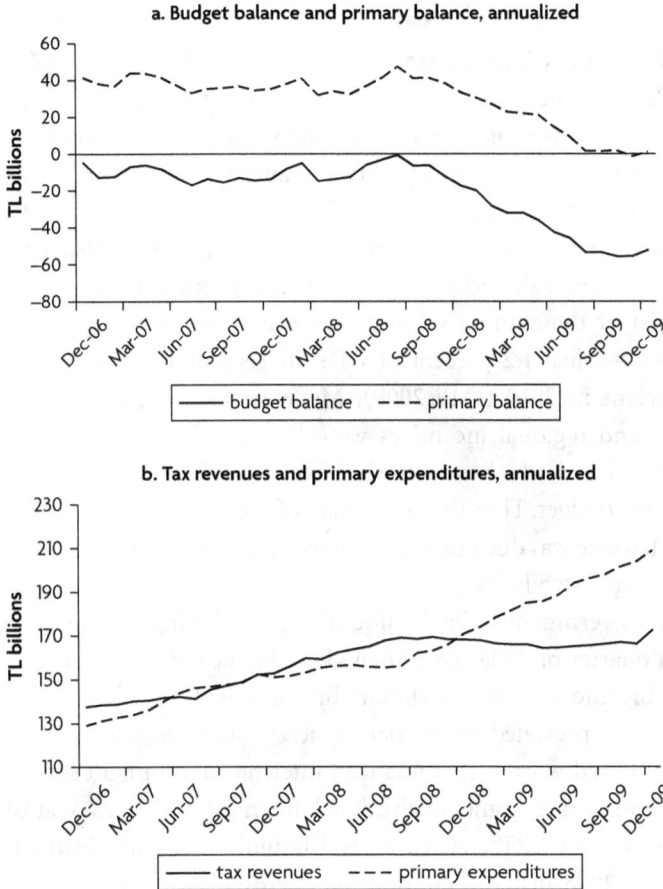

a. Budget balance and primary balance, annualized

b. Tax revenues and primary expenditures, annualized

Source: Ministry of Finance.

foreign finance, labor market problems, and public sector balances, but also to factors such as internal political tension and external developments in the wider region. In essence, investors had already adopted a cautious attitude toward Turkey before global imbalances transformed into a credit crisis. Although capital inflows were strong in 2007–08, investor and consumer confidence had shown a steady decline, mainly due to internal political tension and global imbalances. This was followed by a sharp decline in October 2008, in the wake of the global crisis. The real sector confidence index declined from 101 in May 2008 to 52 in December 2008 (figure 11.11).

The Government's Response

To offset the negative impact of the crisis, the Turkish authorities took steps to stimulate domestic demand. The measures took the form of monetary policy and liquidity enhancement, temporary tax cuts on durables consumption, regional incentives, financial incentives to promote employment, measures to encourage the repatriation of residents' capital abroad, and the extension of credit guarantee schemes. The cost of these anticrisis measures was moderate relative to richer economies—just 1.2 percent of GDP in 2009 and potentially another 0.5 percent in 2010 (IMF 2009). Measures associated with the labor market and regional incentives were financed by the Unemployment Insurance Fund, which reduced the direct burden of crisis-related spending on the budget. Thus the lion's share of the deterioration in the public sector balance was due not to these measures, but rather to the operation of automatic stabilizers.

The government's timely liquidity-provisioning measures in the fourth quarter of 2008 strengthened confidence in the financial sector. Following the failure of Lehman Brothers in September 2008, great uncertainty prevailed about banks' access to foreign exchange. This, in turn, raised worries that financial intermediation might stall, potentially threatening some institutions' financial viability. Against this backdrop, the CBRT enacted several liquidity measures in the fourth quarter of 2008, in addition to cutting interest rates by 1,025 bps between October 2008 and November 2009. The central bank preemptively addressed potential liquidity problems in currency markets by reintroducing its "blind broker" lending facility, restarting foreign exchange auctions, extending the terms of repo transactions, and reducing reserve requirements on foreign exchange deposits. The CBRT also increased the flexibility of the terms of its lender-of-last-resort facility, although this facility has in fact not been needed. The authorities also expanded credit for pre-exporting activities by increasing the EximBank credit line at the CBRT to US$2.5 billion from US$0.5 billion. The government also expanded the capacity of the existing Credit Guarantee Fund scheme in the last quarter of 2009. Finally, the Council of Ministers was given the authority to adjust the terms of the deposit guarantee scheme (although, again, no adjustments have actually been needed).[6]

A sharp decline in private investment demand and tightening credit conditions—particularly for riskier borrowers—led to an excess supply of loanable funds in the banking sector. The inflation-targeting regime allowed monetary policy to loosen in response to the slowdown. As noted earlier, between October 2008 and November 2009 the overnight interest rate was cut from 16.75 percent to 6.50 percent. This measure was timely but, given the supply conditions in credit markets, only partially transmitted to the credit market.

The easier monetary conditions allowed the government to use low-cost bank funds to finance a growing deficit in 2009. However, higher rates are likely soon as private demand rebounds. In a scenario of higher borrowing rates, the government will need to find additional spending cuts or revenue enhancements to stabilize the debt-to-GDP ratio.

Some measures have mitigated the credit effects on SMEs, which account for about three-quarters of employment in Turkey. With the decline in lending to SMEs, the government increased its contributions to Turkey's SME Development Organization to support existing credit subsidy and technical support programs. External lenders, including the World Bank, also increased intermediated lending to SMEs and exporters through public and private banks.

The government also introduced value added tax (VAT), or special consumption tax, exemptions for durable goods during March–September 2009. The affected sectors were new cars, white goods, and electronics. These measures were effective temporarily, leading to a run-down of inventories in these sectors and a rebound of consumption spending in the second and third quarters of 2009.

Finally, as the employment effects of the crisis became more apparent, the government took steps to strengthen labor markets and social safety nets. It introduced measures to encourage hiring, preserve existing jobs, and expand active labor market programs (including "short-time" compensation). The authorities also accelerated the scaling up of vocational training, public works programs, youth internships, business start-ups, and subsidies for women and youth hires. Although the total cost of these measures was small, they appear to have had an impact.

Results to Date

The Turkish economy has been recovering gradually since the second quarter of 2009, partly because of the measures taken by the government and partly because of the recovery of credit intermediation and returning confidence among consumers and firms. A fourth-quarter, year-over-year growth rate of 6 percent in 2009 signaled that the economy was returning to precrisis levels. Leading indicators—including confidence indexes, industrial production, and foreign-trade figures—in the first quarter of 2010 indicate a gradually strengthening recovery. Industrial production was up over 15 percent in the first two months of 2010. Imports grew by over 25 percent in the same period, implying a recovery in domestic demand, while exports also recovered somewhat in the first quarter of 2010. The unemployment rate declined from 14.9 percent in April 2009 to 12 percent in April 2010, and financial conditions are no longer constraining most parts of the credit market (although many SMEs still report a lack of access). Annual growth is expected to approach 6 percent in 2010. This growth rate will well exceed the projection of 3.5 percent originally included in the government's Medium-Term Program for 2010–12.

The crisis is expected to have lasting effects on the labor market and to increase the need for social safety nets. Unemployment has fallen somewhat from its peak of 16.1 percent in February 2009, but it is expected to remain in the range of 12 percent for the rest of the year. The elasticity of employment with respect to growth in Turkey has fallen and is low by international standards, making unemployment mainly a structural rather than a cyclical problem. Although the economy grew at an annual rate of 6.8 percent during 2002–07, unemployment stayed roughly constant (at about 10 percent), owing mainly to the shift to labor-saving, capital-intensive technologies described earlier and to labor exiting from agriculture. Higher growth rates together with labor market reforms will be needed to make further inroads into unemployment. Recent surveys also suggest that traditional safety net mechanisms (such as support from family, friends, and informal civil society) have been weakening recently, imposing increased demands on Turkey's social assistance programs. The crisis has highlighted the importance for Turkey of continuing labor market reforms, with a focus on flexibility and job creation, and of improving the social safety net for the most vulnerable.

Crowding out poses a potential risk to the recovery. Given global financial conditions, Turkey's access to foreign borrowing is likely to remain lower than before the crisis over the medium term. Although growth in 2010 is expected to exceed 5 percent, as private consumption and investment demand rebounds, heavy government financing needs could crowd out private borrowers from domestic credit markets and undermine the recovery. The risk of crowding out underlines the importance of fiscal consolidation. Any further increases in public sector deficits would also put pressure on the sustainability of public debt over the medium term and, thus, on the overall credibility of economic policy.[7]

The government's Medium-Term Program for 2010–12 uses realistic macroeconomic assumptions based on a gradual recovery. The program is aimed at reducing public sector deficits, adopting a fiscal rule to enhance the institutional base of fiscal sustainability, promoting private sector activity, and attaining sustainable growth. Despite forecasts of over 5 percent by market participants, the Medium-Term Program uses a growth assumption of just 3.5 percent in 2010, climbing to 4.0 percent in 2011 and to 5.0 percent in 2012.[8] Growth is expected to be led by the private sector, with an expected rise (over 8 percent) in private gross fixed capital formation. Although Turkey's pace of recovery is expected to be shaped mainly by global conditions—specifically external demand, financing opportunities, and foreign confidence in the Turkish economy—private consumption may continue to lead the recovery in GDP growth, once domestic banks ease credit conditions and the government's adjustment program reduces the need for banking resources.

The Medium-Term Program assumes only a gradual improvement in public sector balances. It projects a shift from a 2.1 percent primary deficit in 2009 (the realization likely having been better than this) to a 1.0 percent surplus in 2012. Half of the adjustment is expected to occur in 2010, with the deficit reduced to 0.3 percent of GDP. More ambitious fiscal adjustment may not be possible given the role of automatic stabilizers and fiscal pressure from social security and health expenditures.

Improvement in the primary balance in 2010 is the result of higher revenue; expenditure measures account for nearly all the planned adjustment in 2011–12. General government revenues should rise by 1.8 percent of GDP in 2010, and spending should remain roughly constant as a share of GDP. The government attributes about 0.8 percentage points of the rise in tax revenue to nominal GDP growth and the remaining 1 percentage point to tax policy changes. These developments include the adjustment of lump-sum taxes on petroleum and tobacco products; a VAT hike on luxury restaurants; new fees for imported mobile phones; increased fees for drivers licenses, identity cards, and passports; and increased highway tolls. During 2009–12, the Medium-Term Program calls for a total (cumulative) adjustment to central government primary spending equivalent to 1.3 percent of GDP. The main sources of this adjustment will be health expenditures, current transfers to the SSI, and public investments. Also, personal spending is assumed to fall slightly over the period. Key reforms to underpin this adjustment are global budgets for health spending and steps to increase the contribution of beneficiaries to health services.

Medium-Term Growth Prospects

The channels through which the global crisis has been transmitted will also shape the pattern of recovery in Turkey. A slow recovery is expected compared to the 2001 crisis. Following that crisis, exports increased, owing to a depreciated currency and buoyant external demand. This time, external demand is weak and will recover only gradually; foreign capital inflows will also be lower.

Demand-Side Dynamics
Nonetheless, Turkey could experience a faster recovery than the rest of the world if private demand rebounds relatively rapidly. Recent business confidence indexes and other leading indicators suggest such a rebound. The role of the public sector will be critical. First, a fiscal adjustment to reduce public sector demand for bank funds and increase the credibility of macroeconomic policies could boost confidence, supporting financial intermediation and private demand. Second, the inventory accumulation cycle, which is now starting from a low base, could also support a faster recovery. On the other hand, domestic resource mobilization will no longer guarantee average growth of more than 5 percent over the medium term. Also, exports are currently almost 25 percent below their precrisis level. Investment demand will thus be critical to stimulating overall growth. But even as overall demand recovers, it will take time to

offset the slower pace of capital accumulation since 2006. The potential medium-term growth rate will thus be lower than before the crisis.[9]

After contracting by 19.2 percent in 2009, investment is projected to grow by nearly 10 percent over the medium term (table 11.7). Owing to excess capacity, investment demand is expected to be relatively weak in the medium term compared with the precrisis period. Uncertainty still dominates, even though recent data indicate some recovery in confidence. But investment will be needed to support competitiveness in capital-intensive sectors, and privatizations in some sectors (particularly energy) may spur investment. A positive contribution from inventories is also expected in 2010–11.

We could thus see a steady rise in investment. Investment as a percentage of GDP has fallen to 14.9 percent in 2009 (from 21.8 percent in 2008), but it is expected to reach 19.0 percent in 2012 and 21 percent in 2015. The rise in investment is expected to be financed by rising domestic savings and by capital inflows.

Projections suggest that private consumption will grow by an average of 4 percent during 2012–15, significantly below the growth rate in

Table 11.7. Demand-Side Growth Projections

	2003–07	2008	2009	2010	2011	2012	2013	2014	2012–15
GDP (%/year)	6.9	0.7	−4.7	5.8	5.1	5.5	4.9	4.5	4.9
Gross fixed capital formation (%/year)	15.7	−8.2	−19.2	8.3	9.0	12.0	9.0	8.0	9.3
Private consumption (%/year)	7.7	0.5	−2.3	4.5	4.3	4.1	4.0	3.9	4.0
Public consumption (%/year)	4.2	1.7	7.8	5.2	4.3	4.5	5.2	4.5	4.3
Net exports (contribution percentage points)	−1.7	1.9	2.7	−1.5	−0.3	−0.4	−0.5	−0.3	−0.4
Export growth	8.0	2.7	−5.4	4.0	6.0	6.0	6.5	5.0	5.7
Import growth	14.8	−4.2	−14.4	10.0	7.0	7.0	7.7	6.4	6.8
Memo									
Current account balance (% GDP)	−4.6	−5.7	−2.3	−4.4	−4.6	−4.6	−4.4	−4.3	−4.3
Capital inflows (% GDP)	6.8	5.1	−1.2	4.4	4.6	4.6	4.4	4.3	4.3
Change in reserves (% GDP)	−1.5	0.1	0.0	0.0	0.0	0.0	0.0	0.0	0.0
Fiscal balance (% GDP)	−1.7	−1.6	−6.4	−4.2	−3.0	−2.1	−1.0	−0.5	−1.0
Public debt/GDP (% GDP)	52.9	39.5	45.4	50.0	49.1	47.9	47.0	45.5	46.0

Source: Author's projections based on Malatyalı (2010).

2003–07 (table 11.7). The projections assume that, unlike investment, private consumption was relatively strong in 2006–07 and that the contraction in 2009 was less than in 2001, which reduces the importance of the base effect. They also assume that the global crisis reduced household disposable income due to job losses and declines in real wages, but that low interest rates may provide room for some households to finance their consumption through bank loans, and that a large improvement in the fiscal balance could boost confidence and domestic credit. However, the risk of rising interest rates globally may hinder domestic consumption in the medium term.

The share of private consumption in GDP trended upward in the precrisis period, from 66.5 percent in 1998 to 71.0 percent in 2007. It reached a peak of 71.6 percent in 2009 because of the sharp contraction of investment and the effects of government stimulus packages. We project that the share of private consumption in GDP will decline to 70.7 percent in 2010 and ease to 70.2 percent in 2011. The share of private consumption is estimated at 68.8 percent for the end of 2015.

Projections suggest that government consumption will rise 4.5 percent during 2010–15, consistent with the government's fiscal targets (table 11.7). The recovery scenario envisaged is lightly stronger than that projected in the government's program, which creates room for slightly higher government consumption growth than government projections given in Medium Term Program due to stronger tax revenues. We project that government consumption as a percentage of GDP will decline only gradually over the medium term.

Exports and imports are expected to rebound relatively quickly. In addition to base effects, gradual recovery in overall demand and recent efforts to diversify trade with neighboring countries will support increased exports. On the other hand, we project that import growth will exceed export growth, given the sensitivity of imports to domestic demand—indeed, import growth is expected to top the import growth rates of Turkey's main trading partners. As a result, the contribution of net exports to GDP growth is estimated to be negative, nearly –0.6 percentage points on average during 2010–15. In addition to the faster relative growth of imports, Turkey's terms of trade are expected to deteriorate slightly in the face of rising commodity prices (mainly energy), which will widen the current account deficit over the medium term (table 11.7).

Potential Growth and Growth Accounting

The pace of capital accumulation and TFP growth is expected to be slower in the medium term than in the precrisis period, with obvious repercussions for potential growth. The slowdown in capital accumulation and TFP to date have led to lower potential growth and thus weakened job creation. Based on assumptions for investment, employment, and TFP, the potential growth rate is estimated to fall by nearly 1 percentage point—to 4.3 percent—over the medium term (table 11.8).

The output gap—the deviation of actual output from potential—is estimated to have fallen to about –6 percent in 2009, whereas its average value is estimated at about –0.1 percent during 1988–2008.[10] Actual growth rates are estimated to be above potential rates in the medium term, and the negative output gap is expected to disappear by 2012; this could then trigger inflationary pressures. The output gap is expected to be positive after 2012 mainly because of buoyant domestic demand and capital inflows, which will support the recovery of postponed consumption and investment.

The slowdown in capital accumulation is the leading cause of the lower potential growth rate for 2010–15; the recovery of capital accumulation will be gradual relative to 2002–06. One source of the weak investment is the sharp contraction in capacity utilization in manufacturing. It fell from 78 percent in 2007 to 65 percent in 2009 (table 11.9). A return to precrisis levels will therefore take time. In addition, TFP is estimated to have fallen by nearly 1 percent during the crisis, owing mainly to the smaller market size (TFP contraction in the recent crisis is less than the nearly 2 percent fall in 2001).

Table 11.8. Supply-Side Growth Projections

	2003–07	2008	2009	2010	2011	2012	2013	2014	2012–15
Potential GDP (%/year)	5.7	5.1	2.2	2.6	3.1	3.9	4.2	4.5	4.3
Employment (%/year)	1.1	2.2	0.1	0.9	1.0	1.2	1.3	1.3	1.3
Human capital (%/year)	1.8	2.5	1.0	1.5	1.8	2.0	2.1	2.1	2.1
Capital stock (%/year)	6.0	5.8	3.0	3.0	3.2	3.9	4.1	4.6	4.3
Actual TFP growth (%/year), including human capital	2.1	0.5	–0.8	0.0	0.8	1.2	1.3	1.4	1.4

Source: Author's projections based on Malatyalı (2010).
Note: Geometric means are used in calculating subperiod growth rates.

Table 11.9. Summary of the Impact of the Crisis

	Period 1997–2002	Period 2003–07	Change from 1997–2002 to 2003–07	Highest two-year average value before crisis	Expected potential value just prior to crisis	2008	2009	Total loss during 2008–09 compared to potential (% GDP)
GDP growth (%)	1.1	6.9	5.8	8.9	5.1	0.7	−4.7	14.2
TFP growth (%)	0.1	2.1	2.0	3.5	1.4	0.5	−0.8	3.1
Exports growth (%)	3.6	8.0	4.4	9.5	7.0	2.7	−5.3	16.6
Exports/GDP (%)	22.0	24.7	2.7	26.3	24.5	23.9	23.2	1.9
Investment (% GDP)	19.0	20.5	1.5	22.1	21.0	19.9	16.8	5.3
Capacity utilization rate (%)	76.3	80.6	4.3	81.4	79.0	75.1	65.0	17.9
Capital inflows (% GDP)	0.3	6.8	6.5	8.7	5.0	5.3	2.3	2.4
Fiscal deficit (% GDP)	9.2	1.8	−7.4	5.5	1.5	1.6	6.4	−5.0

Source: Author's projections based on Malatyalı (2010).
Note: Geometric means are used in calculating subperiod growth rates. Last column is calculated as the sum of deviations of figures in 2008 and 2009 from "expected potential value just prior to crisis." Minus in the last column shows a deterioration of budget compared to expected value just prior to crisis. TFP = total factor productivity.

Capital accumulation will continue to be the most important supply component of output growth in the medium term—as it was in the precrisis period. Almost 65 percent of potential growth was attributed to capital accumulation during 1988–2008. However, this figure is expected to decline to 55 percent in the medium term (table 11.10). In addition to a slowdown in investment, a higher pace of capital depreciation (attributable to the exit of firms during the crisis) is expected, modeled as lower capital accumulation.

Growth accounting also suggests a sizable, and steadily increasing, contribution from TFP in the medium term. We project that the contribution of TFP (including human capital) to output growth will exceed 30 percent in 2010–15, compared to less than 20 percent in 1988–2008. In this period, almost 11 percent of output growth and 63 percent of TFP growth were associated with human capital. In the medium term, the contribution of human capital to output growth will rise considerably. On the other hand, the contribution of labor to output growth has been relatively modest (only 17 percent in 1988–2008) and is expected to account for only 15 percent of potential output growth in 2010–15 (tables 11.10–11.13).

Table 11.10. Sources of Growth

Growth rates of potential GDP and factors of production (%)

	Potential GDP	Capital stock	Employment	TFP
1988–2008	3.8	4.6	1.3	0.7
2002–08	5.1	5.4	1.8	1.4
2010–15	3.3	3.4	1.0	1.0
2012–15	4.3	4.3	1.3	1.4

Contribution to potential growth (%)

		Capital stock	Employment	TFP
1988–2008	100.0	64.5	16.9	18.6
2002–08	100.0	56.2	18.4	25.4
2010–15	100.0	54.6	14.6	30.9
2012–15	100.0	53.1	14.2	32.6

Source: Author's projections based on Malatyalı (2010).
Note: Geometric means are used in calculating subperiod growth rates

Table 11.11. Contribution of Human Capital to TFP and GDP
(percentage points)

	TFP growth	Contribution of human capital	TFP growth (excluding human capital)	Contribution of human capital to GDP growth (%)	Contribution of human capital to TFP growth (%)
1988–2008	0.7	0.4	0.3	10.8	63.4
2002–08	1.4	0.5	0.9	9.6	35.1
2010–15	1.0	0.5	0.5	12.2	50.0
2012–15	1.4	0.6	0.9	14.0	42.9

Source: Author's projections based on Malatyalı (2010).
Note: Geometric means are used in calculating subperiod growth rates

Table 11.12. Growth Factor Decomposition
(percent)

	Output (Y)		TFP		Physical capital (K)		Labor (L)	
1994–2007	4.05		0.92	22.9	4.63	65.7	1.08	11.5
1994–96	4.47		0.21	4.7	5.26	67.3	2.93	27.9
1997–2002	2.79		0.83	29.9	3.29	67.9	0.14	2.2
2003–07	5.68		1.36	23.7	5.99	60.2	2.14	16.1
2008–09	2.33		0.61	25.7	2.97	72.9	0.07	1.4

Source: TurkStat; Malatyalı 2010.
Note: "Output" refers to geometric average potential GDP growth rates. Geometric average rates are shown in the first of the paired columns and percentage contributions to growth in the second. It is assumed that the contribution of human capital to growth is captured by TFP, whose decomposition is given in table 11.13.

Table 11.13. Decomposition of TFP Growth
(percent)

	TFP growth	Contribution of human capital	Contribution of human capital to output growth	TFP growth excluding human capital	Contribution of TFP (excluding human capital) to output growth
1994–2007	0.92	0.46	11.4	0.46	11.4
1994–96	0.21	0.42	9.4	−0.21	−4.7
1997–2002	0.83	0.45	16.1	0.38	13.6
2003–07	1.36	0.47	8.1	0.89	15.6
2008–09	0.61	0.26	11.1	0.34	14.6

Source: TurkStat; Malatyalı 2010.

Conclusion

After a decade of boom-bust cycles, Turkey experienced one of its largest economic contractions in 2001. The government responded with an economic reform program aimed at restoring macroeconomic stability and eliminating structural imbalances. Alongside these reforms, which were carried out in a relatively stable political environment, favorable external financial conditions supported a strong economic performance during 2002–07.

Tight fiscal and monetary policies combined with reforms in various areas, including the banking sector and capital market, have helped restore balance in the form of low inflation, low interest rates, and relative financial stability. In addition, the flexible exchange rate regime discouraged dollarization and encouraged agents to hedge themselves against unexpected external shocks. For example, firms with limited foreign-currency-denominated revenues tended to borrow less in foreign currency. Price and output volatility fell dramatically in this period compared to previous decades. Nevertheless, given structural problems associated with external sustainability, labor markets, competitiveness, and the investment climate, a return to economic volatility in the medium term remains a risk.

Strong economic performance in the 2002–07 period was driven largely by faster TFP growth and private fixed investment in relatively capital-intensive manufacturing sectors, as well as in such services sectors as telecommunications, financial intermediation, and transportation.

Although reforms have removed imbalances in the public and banking sectors and improved the investment climate, labor markets have improved only slightly, and external imbalances have continued. Persistent high unemployment rates and low job creation capacity are largely the result of the movement of labor from agricultural activity to urban areas and the shift to capital-intensive activity. At the same time, large current account deficits and accumulated foreign-currency debt have raised concerns about the sustainability of the growth model. Global imbalances have also made economic agents highly sensitive to global developments. The Turkish economy is more open now than ever. Reliance on foreign capital inflows to finance investments (capital goods and intermediate goods imports for domestic production) and a growing share of foreign trade in GDP have led the agents to consider underlying global risks.

Contrary to previous crises (and also somewhat to expectations), the Turkish lira's exchange rate played a limited role in transmitting the effects of the global crisis. The 37 percent depreciation of the currency (between late September 2008 and March 2009) had a limited impact on exports due to the sharp contraction in external demand. Its potentially stimulating effect on large exporting firms in growing sectors has also been limited.

On the other hand, high precrisis interest rates created room for the central bank to ease the monetary stance substantially, which reduced the pressure on financial markets. Alongside liquidity and monetary policy measures, the government also took steps to allay the impact of the crisis on labor markets—by adopting active labor market policies, including a short-term working allowance, the accelerated scale-up of vocational training, public works programs, youth internships, business start-ups, the extension of subsidies for women and youth hires, increased credit to SMEs (also financed by the World Bank), and the extension of existing credit guarantee schemes—and on domestic demand through temporary tax cuts. Despite the effectiveness of some of these measures, they could not prevent a large economic contraction in 2009.

The immediate effect of the global crisis on Turkey was magnified by the pattern of economic growth from about 2003 on. This growth had been capital intensive and was driven largely by fixed capital accumulation, which in turn had been partly financed by inflows—including external borrowing by corporations. By 2006, when the current account deficit exceeded 6 percent of GDP, investment and growth had already slowed. Turkish firms then entered the crisis with high fixed capital and high inventories. Compounding these problems, at the macroeconomic level, external debt accumulated during the growth period created high rollover needs in the private sector. This raised concerns in late 2008 and early 2009. In addition, Turkish banks, which had only started to lend significantly to the private sector after the financial restructuring sparked by the 2001 crisis, remained cautious and cut lending quickly. And finally, the effects of the crisis on world trade were particularly marked in sectors in which Turkey had rapidly increased its market share leading up to 2008, such as automobiles and white goods. Turkish exports in these sectors fell by more than half in the first six months of 2009. At its nadir in February 2009, Turkish monthly industrial production was down by nearly 24 percent from the previous year. GDP fell by 14.5 percent in the first quarter of the year. The government also retained a 2009 budget that had outdated forecasts and may have had the unintended consequence of amplifying the cautious stance adopted in the private sector—although it did afford government the fiscal space for discretionary measures.

The global crisis will have important and lasting effects on the economy. The unemployment rate has increased substantially and is likely to stay above 10 percent for quite some time, with important social implications. The potential growth rate has shifted down by an estimated 1 percentage point as a result of smaller export markets, lower availability of foreign savings, and slower sectoral transformation. Public debt dynamics have also deteriorated, a problem that will intensify as borrowing costs rise again. The decline in potential growth and the deterioration of public sector debt dynamics will entail further fiscal adjustment, which is also vital for avoiding a crowding out of a private sector–led recovery.

Over the medium term, Turkey's young labor force represents both an opportunity and a challenge. Reforms to education and labor markets are therefore central to Turkey's medium-term strategy. And in the long run, mobilizing domestic savings would create scope for higher growth rates and prevent the buildup of external imbalances—and the incidence of further boom-bust cycles.

The EU accession process appeared to provide a strong anchor for policy reforms, particularly in 2002–05, when a number of measures increased competitiveness, improved financial stability, and attracted non-debt-generating capital inflows. The EU process still has the potential to reinforce reform momentum, although uncertainty over the timetable and mixed signals from member states serve to attenuate this effect. At the same time, Turkey continues to invest in improving trade and financial relations with its non-EU neighbors, which should go some way to reduce volatility stemming from external demand.

Annex: Methodology for Potential Output and Growth Accounting

Potential output refers to the level of output an economy can produce with the efficient and full utilization of its resources. In this sense, potential output is the optimal production or supply capacity of an economy, given the supply of factors of production—namely, capital stock, labor, and the state of technology or knowledge. Consequently, a permanent rise in these production factors reflects an upward shift in potential output.

Potential output corresponds to the sustainable output level (aggregate supply) of an economy. The level of national income (GDP) is determined by aggregate demand in the short term, but is determined by aggregate supply (potential output) in the medium and long term. Therefore, depending particularly on developments in aggregate demand, the actual output level may deviate from the potential in the short run. This deviation is usually termed the "output gap." A positive output gap—where actual output temporarily exceeds potential—results from over-utilization of production factors. Conversely, the underutilization of factors of production yields a negative output gap. Actual output, therefore, involves both potential output and the effects of such short-run cyclical factors as the expansion or contraction of external or internal demand and seasonal factors.

Several methods are generally used to estimate the level or growth rate of potential output. One of the most widely used is the (aggregate) production function, in which the level of potential output is a function of capital stock, employment, and TFP. However, in contrast to the ordinary production function, the estimation of potential output requires accounting for the effects of cyclical variables and internal—or external—shocks on the level of output (and, hence, growth rate). In practice, this is usually addressed by including variables representing short-run fluctuations in demand (e.g., the capacity utilization rate for capital stock or average working hours for labor) in the production function.

The output (national income) of an economy can be described by using a Cobb-Douglas type of production function. The function is expressed in logarithmic form and has the property of constant returns to scale:

$$\ln Y_t = C_0 + \alpha_1 * \ln K_t + (1 - \alpha_1) * \ln L_t + \gamma T_t + e_t \qquad (11.1)$$

where Y, K, and L stand for output, capital stock, and employment, respectively, and T is the time variable. C_0 is the constant term, α is the output elasticity of capital stock, $(1 - \alpha)$ is the output elasticity of employment, γ represents the shift in the production function (the rate of technical change or TFP growth), e is the usual error term, and t is observations (years). Capital stock can be defined as the accumulated sum of previous investments after allowing for depreciation. Employment may be defined as depending on the labor supply (e.g., population growth or wage level), capital stock or investments, and the structure and functioning of the labor market. Technical change accounts for disembodied technical change and can be linked to such things as improvements in human capital, innovation, competitive pressures, sectoral reallocation of resources from less productive to more productive activities, or organizational changes in the firms.

As noted earlier, the output level in an economy is subject to cyclical changes in demand and external/internal shocks to the economy. These variables, in turn, lead to biased estimation results on the coefficients of the production function. One way to solve the problem is to include variables representing cyclical changes and external/internal shocks in the production function. Capacity utilization rates and average working hours are two widely used variables representing these factors. After taking into account these variables, equation 11.1 can be redefined as

$$\ln Y_t^p = C_0 + \alpha_1 * \ln(K_t * CU_t) + (1 - \alpha_1) * \ln(L_t * WH_t) + \gamma * T_t + \varepsilon_t \quad (11.2)$$

where CU is the capacity utilization rate and WH is working hours. In equation 2, $K * CU$ represents the effective capital stock and $L * WH$ is the effective labor (total number of hours worked) used to produce output or national income. Potential can be obtained by substituting average capacity utilization rate (CU_{avg}) and average number of hours (WH_{avg}) in the past observations instead of CU_t and WH_t in equation 11.2.[11] This definition of potential output is

$$\ln Y_t^p = C_0 + \alpha_1 * \ln(K_t * CU_{avg}) + (1 - \alpha_1) * \ln(L_t * WH_{avg}) \quad (11.3)$$
$$+ \gamma * T_t + \varepsilon_t$$

Note that equation 11.3 (potential output) and equation 11.2 (actual output) have the same parameters for the production function. This means that technology is the same in both equations.

Equation 11.2 is used to estimate the coefficients of capital and labor. In this context, the output elasticity of the capital stock and labor force are calculated as 0.57 and 0.43, respectively. TFP is a residual from this equation. Potential output is calculated after adjustment of production factors given in equation 11.3 (adjustment of employment by average working hours, of capital stock by average capacity utilization, and of TFP by Hodrick-Prescott filtering). The output gap is calculated as $(Y_t/Y_t^p - 1) * 100$.

TFP is decomposed into two components: gains from human capital, and everything else. In literature, several methods are used to estimate the contribution of human capital to growth or productivity. One of them introduces the human capital measure in the production function. However, as many empirical studies reveal, this method yields insignificant parameter estimates with a negative sign (Caselli, Esquivel, and Lefort 1996; Islam 1995). One other method uses the interaction term between labor and human capital, $(L * H)$, as an additional variable in the production function. We use the same methodology employed by World Bank (2006), where human capital (H) is calculated by using average years of schooling of the labor force (S) and a 7 percent return each year, $H = 1.07^S$. The following equation is estimated to decompose the sources of growth:

$$\ln(Y/L) = 0.33 * \ln(K/L) + 0.67 * \ln(H) - 0.07 * Dummy \quad (11.4)$$
$$ (3.65) (3.76) (-4.19)$$

This method requires an assumption on the return of human capital and explicitly assumes that human capital affects output by augmenting labor.

In this study, however, we assume that human capital affects output growth via productivity growth. In other words, we use regression results of Saygılı, Cihan, and Yavan (2006), where human capital (average schooling years of the labor force) is used to explain productivity growth, controlling for the relevant variables given in the following equation.[12]

$$ln(Y/L) = -0.088^* \ln(Y/L_{initial}) + 0.271^* (I/Y) + 0.470^* (FDI/Y)$$
$$\quad\quad\quad (-6.06) \quad\quad\quad\quad\quad (4.52) \quad\quad\quad (6.35)$$
$$+ 0.055^* (X/Y) - 0.057^* AGR + 0.063^* H$$
$$\quad (6.35) \quad\quad\quad (2.08) \quad\quad\quad (2.77)$$

$$(11.5)$$

where Y is GDP, I is investments excluding FDI, X is exports, AGR is the share of agricultural employment in total employment, and H is human capital, defined as average years of schooling of the labor force. Values in parentheses are t-statistics.

Notes

1. Model-based quantitative analysis by Alp and Elekdağ (2010) indicates that monetary reforms reduced the severity of the impact of the crisis on the real economy by over 50 percent.
2. Saygılı et al. (2010) provide detailed discussion on import penetration in Turkey based on firm-level surveys.
3. Saygılı and Cihan (2008) control for large investments in the forms of renewal and modernization and for strong cyclicality in capital and labor employments during 2002–07 by using such variables as renewal rate of capital (the ratio of investment to capital stock), capacity utilization rate, and hours worked, which are indirect contributions from capital and labor that "standard" growth accounting attributes to TFP (Solow residual).
4. Taymaz (2009) provides a detailed analysis of the relationships between growth, employment, skills, and the female labor force. It calculates a relatively low employment elasticity of output for manufacturing but a relatively high elasticity for services.
5. See also Türkan (2006) and Yükseler and Türkan (2008) for detailed discussions on imported inputs.
6. The CBRT announced an exit strategy in mid-April that allows gradual adjustment to a precrisis setup: it includes raising required reserve ratios, reducing the maturity of repo transactions, and giving up the blind broker function.
7. Growth figures for the first quarter of 2010 have already been released by TurkStat. Annual growth rate for the quarter is 11.7 percent. National account figures imply that the government has adopted a relatively tight fiscal policy in the first quarter of 2010, where government expenditures have declined sharply

and negatively contributed to growth (by 0.8 percentage points). It seems that the risk of crowding out is not very high in 2010.

8. The government's growth projections for 2010–12 are expected to be revised upward in the new Medium-Term Program.

9. Estimations are based on Malatyalı (2010).

10. Taking 2009 as a base, the cumulative potential growth during 2010–12 is nearly 9 percent, and 23 percent during 2010–15. If the output gap of the base year, about 6 percent, is added (i.e., actual growth rates may be higher than potential rates to close the gap), cumulative actual growth will reach 15 and 30 percent for the respective periods, yielding about 5 percent average annual growth. Thus, we can project an "optimistic" average growth rate of perhaps 4.8 percent during 2010–15.

11. It is also possible to use the maximum capacity utilization rate and maximum working hours instead of average values of these variables. In this case, potential output corresponds to the level of output that can be produced when the capital stock and labor are fully employed. This definition yields different values for the level of potential output, but similar potential growth rates.

12. Regarding the contribution of human capital to productivity growth, equations 11.4 and 11.5 give similar results.

References

Alp, H., and S. Elekdağ. 2010. "The Role of Monetary Policy during the Global Financial Crisis: The Turkish Experience." Unpublished manuscript.

Altuğ, S. G., A. Filiztekin, and Ş. Pamuk. 2007. "The Sources of Long-Term Economic Growth for Turkey 1880–2005." Koc University and CEPR Discussion Paper 6463, Center for Economic and Policy Research, Washington, DC.

Caselli, F., G. Esquivel, and F. Lefort. 1996. "Reopening the Convergence Debate: A New Look at Cross-Country Growth Empirics." *Journal of Economic Growth* 1 (3): 363–89.

Ertuğrul, A., and F. Selçuk. (2001). "A Brief Account of the Turkish Economy." *Russian and European Finance and Trade* 37 (3): 6–28.

IMF (International Monetary Fund). 2009. "State of Public Finances Cross-Country Fiscal Monitor." IMF Staff Position Note, IMF, Washington, DC.

Islam, N. 1995. "Growth Empirics: A Panel Data Approach." *Quarterly Journal of Economics* 110 (4): 1127–70.

Kaplan, C., E. Özmen, and C. Yalçın. 2006. "The Determinants and Implications of Financial Asset Holdings of Non-financial Firms in Turkey: An Empirical Investigation." Working Paper 06/06, Central Bank of the Republic of Turkey, Ankara.

Malatyalı, K. 2010. "Medium Term Growth Prospects for Turkey." Background paper prepared for this project.

————. Özatay, F. 2008. "Expansionary Fiscal Consolidations: New Evidence from Turkey." Working Paper 08-05, Department of Economics, TOBB University of Economics and Technology, Ankara.

Saygılı, Ş., and C. Cihan. 2008. "Growth Dynamics of Turkish Economy: Sources of Growth, Basic Issues and Potential Rate of Growth in 1997–2007" (in Turkish). TÜSİAD-CBT Joint Publication TÜSİAD-T/2008-06/462, TÜSİAD, Istanbul.

Saygılı, S., C. Cihan, C. Yalçın, and T. Hamsici. 2010. "The Import Structure of the Turkish Manufacturing Industry" (in Turkish). Working Paper 10/02, Central Bank of the Republic of Turkey, Ankara.

Saygılı, Ş., C. Cihan, and Z. Yavan. 2006. "Education and Sustainable Growth: Experience of Turkey, Risks and Opportunities" (in Turkish). Publication TÜSİAD-T/2006-06/420, TÜSİAD, Istanbul.

Taymaz, E. 2009. "Growth, Employment, Skills and Female Labor Force." SPO and World Bank Welfare and Social Policy Analytical Work Program Working Paper 6, World Bank, Washington, DC.

Türkan, E. 2006. "Import Dependency of Domestic Production and Export in Turkey." Working Paper, Central Bank of the Republic of Turkey, Ankara.

World Bank. 2006. "Promoting Sustained Growth and Convergence with the European Union." In Turkey Country Economic Memorandum, chapter 1. Washington, DC: World Bank.

Yılmaz, G., and R. Gönenç. 2008. "How Did the Turkish Industry Respond to Increased Competitive Pressures, 1998–2007?" Research and Monetary Policy Department Working Paper 08/04, Central Bank of the Republic of Turkey, Ankara.

Yükseler, Z., and E. Türkan. 2008. "Transformation in the Production and Trade Structure of Turkey: Global Trends and Reflections" (in Turkish). TÜSİAD-CBRT Joint Publication TÜSİAD-T/2008-02/453, TÜSİAD, Istanbul.

Discussant Paper

Comment on "Turkey: External Imbalances Amplify the Crisis, Domestic Strengths Limit the Damage"

Indermit Gill

The pace and pattern of Turkey's economic growth as recorded by the authors in this paper raise several questions. These should be part of the agenda of researchers interested in informing policy choices. The questions relate to the unusual volatility of Turkey's GDP growth since the 1970s, the abnormal relationship between growth and private savings since the 1990s, and the unexpectedly large impact of the global crisis in 2008 and 2009 on Turkey's enterprises.

Volatility of Growth

Perhaps the most striking feature of growth in Turkey is its variability, and reducing the volatility of growth should probably rank as high among policy objectives as increasing its average. Between 1969 and

Indermit Gill is Chief Economist, Europe and Central Asia Office of the Chief Economist, World Bank.

2009, there were 11 years with growth rates above 7 percent, and 11 years with growth rates below 2 percent. Annual growth exceeded 9 percent during four years, but was negative during five. This cannot be a healthy pattern for any country, and even less so for a country with unstable politics. Of course, political instability must be a part of the problem. But questions naturally arise: Has Turkey's policy mix exacerbated or dampened this volatility? Were the elements that generated the "excess volatility" purged during the reforms of the past decade, given that the volatility of GDP growth fell noticeably during the 2002–07 period?

The main candidates for examination in trying to answer these questions are the policies and institutions that influence (a) public sector finances and (b) private financial sector behavior.

The highly variable growth rate in Turkey is difficult to explain, but understanding it may well be the most important part of an inquiry into Turkey's growth performance and prospects. The explanation will help Turkey decide whether its economic structure is inherently more volatile, whether the government has been adding policy risk to economic risk through its fiscal and financial policies, and what changes are needed for the government to ameliorate these fluctuations and create the conditions for steadier growth.

Unusual Savings Patterns

The paper shows that Turkey's saving rates have been much lower than suitable comparator countries such as the Republic of Korea, Malaysia, and Thailand. During the 1980s, the domestic saving rate in Turkey was 16 percent (about half of the East Asian high growers), and GDP growth averaged 4 percent, compared with between 6 and 8 percent for the three East Asian countries. During the 1990s, the saving rate increased to 20 percent, but remained more than 15 percentage points of GDP below those of Korea, Malaysia, and Thailand. Turkey's annual GDP growth still averaged 4 percent, compared with 5 to 7 percent for the three East Asian economies. Between 2000 and 2007, the average saving-to-GDP ratio in Turkey inexplicably fell to 17.5 percent, even as the GDP growth rate increased to more than 5 percent, roughly the same as the growth rates in Korea, Malaysia, and Thailand.

Thus, since the 2001 crisis and until 2008, Turkey appeared to be doing better than its East Asian comparators in converting domestic savings to growth. But what matters more is the efficiency of investment, because the savings-investment gap was filled by foreign savings that flowed into Turkey. Investment-to-GDP ratios rose by more than 10 percent of GDP between 2001 and 2007, and the paper conjectures that future growth is likely to be driven by capital accumulation in the near future. But the questions remain: Why did savings fall? Which component of savings explains this anomalous relationship between faster growth and smaller saving in Turkey since 2001? Can changed policies help to increase savings, so that Turkey has less need to rely on foreigners to fuel growth?

The main candidates for explaining the behavior of savings are (a) the rapid fall of inflation resulting from tighter monetary policies and (b) accelerating demographic changes, if the trend is being driven by a fall in household saving.

Unexpectedly Severe Impact of the Global Crisis

Turkey was hit hard by the crisis in 2008 and 2009, much harder than Korea, Thailand, and Malaysia. The paper points to a sharp rise in unemployment and a sharp falloff in GDP growth (which had been slowing down since peaking at 9.4 percent in 2004).

It may be instructive to contrast the experience of Turkey during the crisis with that of Poland, the other large economy immediately to the east of developed Europe (see chapter 10 of this book). In 2008, Turkey's GDP was about US$795 billion; Poland's was about US$525 billion. Exports were about US$140 billion in 2008 (18 percent of GDP) in Turkey, and about US$190 billion (about 36 percent of GDP) in Poland, twice the ratio for Turkey. But while Turkey's GDP growth rates in 2008 and 2009 were 0.9 and –4.7 percent, respectively, Poland's GDP grew at 5.0 and 1.7 percent, respectively, during these two years. This raises a question: If Poland's economy is both smaller and more dependent on foreign demand, why did it weather the crisis so much better than Turkey's economy?

The obvious suspects are (a) Turkey's export destinations and structure and (b) Turkey's dependence on foreign capital inflows to fuel growth. Fragile investor confidence (reflected in "excess volatility" of growth) may also be a candidate.

Does Turkey's export destinations and structure make it more vulnerable to recessions abroad, essentially because it is more dependent on Western Europe? It is instructive to compare the destinations of Turkish and Polish exports. In 2007, a year before the crisis hit, the most important destinations of Turkey's exports were Germany (11 percent), the United Kingdom (8 percent), Italy (7 percent), France (6 percent), and the Russian Federation and Spain (4.5 percent each). For Poland, the major destinations were Germany (26 percent); Italy (7 percent); France, the United Kingdom, and the Czech Republic (about 6 percent each); and Russia (5 percent). If anything, the Polish economy seems more dependent on demand in Western Europe.

An alternative explanation is a difference in the structure of exports. It may be that Polish exports are more resource based or that Turkey competes with more efficient Asian economies in the markets for manufactured goods. Or the explanation may lie in Turkey's greater dependence on foreign savings as compared with Poland. In any case, the answer to this question will provide clues to understanding the high volatility of Turkey's growth rates.

The authors of this paper have made a good start in solving the puzzles related to the unusual volatility of Turkey's growth during the past 50 years, the odd behavior of savings during the past decade, and the unexpectedly severe impact of the crisis during the past two years. Identifying the reasons correctly will help policy makers increase Turkey's growth rate, make that rate steadier, and make the economy more resilient to external disturbances.

Surprising Resilience but Challenges Ahead

Nguyen Ngoc Anh, Nguyen Duc Nhat,
Nguyen Dinh Chuc, and Nguyen Thang

In the past 20 years, Vietnam has implemented comprehensive reforms. These reforms, together with an open-door policy to attract foreign direct investment (FDI) and trade liberalization (culminating in its World Trade Organization [WTO] accession in 2006), have created a growing and dynamic private sector. Since 2000, the government has pursued expansionary policies with extensive investment and has overseen a huge credit expansion, especially after the 1997–98 Asian financial crisis. These policies have helped Vietnam achieve high GDP growth rates since 1990.

But the situation has changed dramatically in recent years. In early 2008, concerns about an overheating economy forced the Vietnam government to shift priorities from high economic growth to stabilization,

Nguyen Ngoc Anh is Chief Economist, Nguyen Duc Nhat is Executive Director, and Nguyen Dinh Chuc is Senior Researcher, Development and Policies Research Center, Vietnam; Nguyen Thang is Director, Center for Analysis and Forecasting, Vietnamese Academy of Social Sciences, Vietnam. Helpful comments and suggestions from Thai-Van Can, John Gallup, Mustapha K. Nabli, Nguyen Tien Phong, Doan Hong Quang, and Martin Rama are gratefully acknowledged. This chapter also benefited from comments and suggestions by participants of the Vietnam Economists Annual Meeting 2009.

leading it to raise interest rates and cut government spending. By the end of 2008 and into 2009, Vietnam was faced with new problems and challenges caused by the global financial and economic crisis.

To date, the repercussions of the global financial and economic crisis have been felt all over the world. Economic growth has slowed in many developed countries, including the United States, countries of the European Union (EU), and Japan. In response, governments of developed countries have adopted economic stimulus packages to rescue their economies. These packages include such measures as writing off bad assets in the banking system, cutting taxes, investing in infrastructure, and paying out more social security benefits. Central banks in many countries have adopted a lax monetary policy, drastically cutting interest rates to levels not seen in many years and even using unconventional monetary tools to expand liquidity in the banking system. In developing countries—including Vietnam—the crisis has reduced investment inflows and lowered global commodity prices and trade. As a result, demand for Vietnamese exports and capital inflows have declined substantially. The government of Vietnam responded as many other countries did: by reversing its tight monetary policy stance and the fiscal austerity implemented in 2008. To stimulate the economy, the government also adopted a large fiscal stimulus package.

Although the global crisis originated in the developed world, it will have far-reaching consequences for the growth and development of developing countries for the foreseeable future. Since the recession hit Vietnam in December 2008, the government has focused on how to boost domestic demand in the short run and on how to deal with the immediate economic and social disruptions created by the crisis. Much less attention has been paid to the medium- and long-term implications of the crisis for growth, poverty reduction, and, more broadly, economic development.

In this chapter, we consider how the ongoing crisis, the policy responses to it, and the postcrisis global economy will shape the medium-term growth prospects of Vietnam. We first review the economic reforms and policies that Vietnam has pursued since mid-1990s and examine the economy's current economic performance. We examine how the global financial crisis has affected Vietnam, as well as the government's responses and their effectiveness. We assess the emerging patterns of the postcrisis world and their implications for Vietnam's development policy. We then provide medium-term projections for Vietnam's growth path until 2015 and discuss the crisis's implications for Vietnam in the postcrisis era.

Economic Reform and Development in Vietnam

The failure of the centrally planned model that Vietnam followed to develop its economy after national reunification in 1975 forced it to undertake comprehensive economic reforms. The first serious reform, in 1986, was known as the *Doimoi;* it was followed by more radical market-oriented reforms in 1989, which marked a turning point in the history of Vietnam's economic development. After some initial success, complacency built up and the reform process slowed during 1996–99, especially after the Asian crisis. But since 2000, the authorities have renewed their commitment to reform, and some progress has been achieved—especially with regard to the development of the private sector and trade liberalization.[1]

In the years immediately after the initiation of economic reform, the government focused on macroeconomic stabilization and price liberalization.[2] It introduced several measures to establish market institutions, including the recognition of a multisector economy in which the private sector exists alongside the state-owned sector, and protection of private property rights.

In agriculture, decollectivization took place and the farming household was recognized as a basic economic unit. Land was redistributed to households and output contracting arrangement whereby farmers were allowed to keep the surplus output beyond the contracted output was introduced. A particularly important reform was the new land law, introduced in 1987 and amended in 1993, which increased the security of land tenure and allowed the transfer of land use rights to others.

In the industry and services sectors, the government has been seeking measures to develop the private sector, while state-owned enterprises (SOEs) are either being equitized[3] or given more autonomy in business. The emergence of the private enterprise sector is an important development, and in 1991 the government introduced the company law and private enterprise law (later amended in 1994). These two laws, together with the adoption of the new land law in 1993 and a new labor code in 1994, have been important in stimulating the development of the private sector. However, the most significant reform in the development of private business came in 2000, with the new enterprises law. During 2000–04, about 90,000 private enterprises were registered under the new law (double the number of companies registered during the nine years under the two previous laws), with combined capital equivalent to about US$13 billion.[4] The private business sector, thanks to its increased freedom from the restrictions encumbering it under central planning, is making rapid gains in terms of its contribution to Vietnam's output growth. The one-tier banking system was replaced by a two-tier system that allows the State Bank of Vietnam to assume traditional central bank functions. Other major policy changes include the elimination of price controls, liberalization of foreign exchange, and the removal of barriers to the movement of labor and goods among regions in Vietnam.

Vietnam has substantially liberalized its trade and investment policies since the late 1980s. During the early years of economic reform, liberalization of the trade regime was achieved by the signing of trade agreements with about 60 countries. Vietnam has also implemented a preferential trade agreement with the EU since 1992 and it has actively sought membership in regional and global organizations.[5] Vietnam became a member of the Association of Southeast Asian Nations (ASEAN) in June 1995 and of the Asia Pacific Economic Cooperation in 1998. In 2000, Vietnam signed a historic comprehensive trade agreement with the United States to normalize trade relations between the two countries. And recently, by its membership within the ASEAN, Vietnam has joined regional integration clubs such as ASEAN—the China Free Trade Area and the ASEAN–Japan Comprehensive Economic Partnership. Most recently, in 2006, Vietnam became a member of the WTO.[6]

The Law on Foreign Direct Investment—first promulgated in 1987 and amended in 1990, 1992, 1996, and 2000—has helped Vietnam attract a large volume of foreign capital when domestic savings were insufficient to meet the country's investment needs.[7] Before 1987, there was virtually no private sector in Vietnam. By allowing FDI, Vietnam in effect imported/implanted a private sector of its own for the first time after its unification. Since then, FDI has become an integral part of the

Vietnamese economy and an important factor in the country's economic growth during the 1990s. In 2006, to create a more level playing field and ensure that its laws gave favorable treatment to FDI enterprises before Vietnam's accession to the WTO, Vietnam promulgated two important laws, the Investment Law and the new Enterprise Law,[8] which created a corporate-law regime for both foreign and domestic enterprises.

After 20 years of reform, Vietnam has put in place the fundamentals of a market economy and has opened up the economy to international flows of capital and trade in goods and services. The emergence of a market-based economy, with market-oriented institutions, a stable macroeconomic environment, and government support for business development, has allowed Vietnam to

- unlock the potential of its agriculture sector, turning Vietnam from a food-hungry country to the world's third-largest rice exporter;[9]
- encourage the development of a vibrant domestic private sector;
- attract substantial FDI; and
- realize its comparative advantages and gain more benefits from international trade.

These factors underlie the economic success that Vietnam has been experiencing since the early 1990s.

Economic Performance

Since the 1989 reforms, Vietnam has made remarkable achievements in terms of GDP growth, macroeconomic stabilization, export expansion, and poverty reduction. The country is now recognized as being among the most successful developing countries in terms of economic growth and poverty reduction. During 1990–2008, the annual GDP growth rate averaged more than 7 percent, and Vietnam's growth rates today remain among the highest in the region (second only to China's). The average annual GDP growth was about 5–6 percent during 1990–91 and climbed to and then stayed at about 8 percent during 1992–97 (figure 12.1). GDP growth, however, declined during 1998–99, partly because of the Asian crisis and the dissipation of the effects of reform.

Since 2000, the economy has regained its momentum. Its annual growth rate exceeded 7 percent—reaching 8.5 percent in 2007—then dropped back to an estimated 6.2 percent in 2008, owing to the effects of

Figure 12.1. Vietnam GDP Growth Rate, 1990–2009

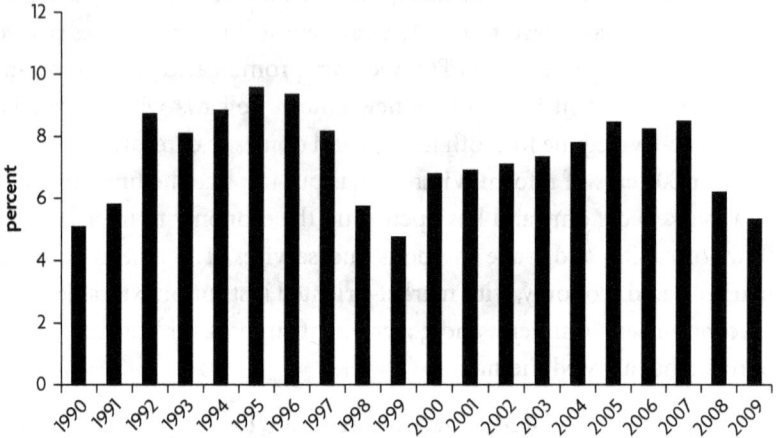

Source: Vietnam General Statistics Office (GSO) , http://www.gso.gov.vn.

the global recession. High and continuous GDP growth rates and successful economic development from 2000 to 2008 have resulted in significant improvements in the population's welfare and in substantial poverty reduction. According to the Vietnam Household Living Standard Survey, the total poverty incidence declined from 58 percent in 1993 to 37 percent in 1998, 29 percent in 2002, 19.5 percent in 2004, and 16 percent in 2006 (SRV 2003; Nguyen 2009). In addition, improvements have been made in other aspects of human welfare—such as the sharp rise in the percentage of literate adults (to over 90 percent), longer life expectancy (over 70 years), and a lower mortality rate for children less than five years old (40 per 1,000 live births in 2003).

During the course of transition to a market economy, Vietnam's economy experienced gradual changes in terms of sectoral and ownership structures. During this period, the focus of the economy shifted toward industrialization and modernization (table 12.1). The proportion of agriculture, forestry, and fisheries in GDP declined from more than 27.2 percent in 1995 to 22.1 percent in 2008. At the same time, the share of industry and construction in GDP rose from about 28 percent in 1995 to 40 percent in 2008. The share of the manufacturing subsector (within the industry and construction sector) increased from 15 percent

Table 12.1. GDP Structure by Sector and Ownership, 1995–2008
(% using current prices)

	1995	1996	1997	1998	1999	2000	2001	2002	2003	2004	2005	2006	2007	2008
GDP structure by economic sector														
GDP	100	100	100	100	100	100	100	100	100	100	100	100	100	100
Agriculture, forestry, and fisheries	27.18	27.76	25.77	25.78	25.43	24.53	23.24	23.03	22.54	21.81	20.97	20.4	20.34	22.10
Industry and construction	28.76	29.73	32.07	32.49	34.49	36.73	38.13	38.49	39.47	40.21	41.02	41.54	41.48	39.73
Manufacturing	14.99	15.18	16.48	17.15	17.69	18.56	19.78	20.58	20.45	20.34	20.63	21.25	21.26	21.10
Services	44.06	42.51	42.15	41.73	40.07	38.73	38.63	38.48	37.99	37.98	38.01	38.06	38.18	38.17
GDP share by ownership														
GDP	100	100	100	100	100	100	100	100	100	100	100	100	100	100
State sector	40.18	39.93	40.48	40.00	38.74	38.52	38.40	38.38	39.08	39.10	38.40	37.39	35.93	34.35
Nonstate sector	53.51	52.68	50.44	49.97	49.02	48.20	47.84	47.86	46.45	45.76	45.61	45.63	46.12	46.97
Collective sector	10.06	10.02	8.91	8.90	8.84	8.58	8.06	7.99	7.49	7.09	6.82	6.53	6.21	6.02
Private sector	7.44	7.40	7.21	7.24	7.25	7.31	7.95	8.30	8.23	8.49	8.89	9.41	10.19	10.81
Household sector	36.02	35.25	34.32	33.82	32.93	32.31	31.84	31.57	30.73	30.19	29.91	29.69	29.72	30.14
Foreign invested sector	6.30	7.39	9.07	10.03	12.24	13.27	13.76	13.76	14.47	15.13	15.99	16.98	17.96	18.68

Source: GSO, http://www.gso.gov.vn.

in 1995 to 21 percent in 2008, while the share of the services sector has remained at about 30–40 percent in recent years.

The second important structural shift has been the change in the ownership structure of the economy. This shift remains slow as reflected in the relatively stable and significant share of GDP owned by the state sector and partly explained by the slow progress of equitizing SOEs. The share of the state-owned sector has decreased from more than 40 percent in 1995 to 34 percent in 2008, whereas the FDI sector has steadily raised its share from 6.3 percent in 1995 to 18.7 percent in 2008 (table 12.1), demonstrating its increased role as an integral component of the economy. The private sector has also increased its role, accounting for more than 10 percent of the economy in 2008. Business households remain an important sector of the economy, accounting for 30 percent of GDP. However, in terms of growth, the domestic private sector and the FDI sector have the highest growth rates, typically over 10 percent per year.

Decomposition of GDP

Breaking down Vietnam's GDP to its demand components for the period 1996–2008 reveals the important and increasing role of domestic demand for growth (table 12.2). The most important component is domestic consumption. The second most important component is investment, which has grown consistently since 2000. More often than not, external demand contributed negatively to GDP growth during these years.[10]

After a dip in 1999 and 2000, domestic consumption has kept rising, serving as the single most important component of GDP growth. Total consumption in Vietnam has been growing at a considerably faster rate than GDP. Its contribution surged from 29.3 percent in 1999 to 89.6 percent in 2007 and to 106 percent in 2008. Private consumption growth clearly dominates total consumption growth, accounting for the lion's share of total consumption. Another interesting development in the last few years has been the rapid rise in stocks (inventory) from 8.32 percent in 2005 to 21.11 percent in 2007 when the economy overheated in 2005, 2006, and 2007 (table 12.2).

Vietnam has also seen a steady growth in its international trade over the period. The average annual growth rate of exports and imports was about 20 percent. The total value of international trade over GDP (trade-to-GDP ratio), an indicator of economic openness, soared to

Table 12.2. GDP Decomposition, 1996–2008
(% using current prices)

	1996	1997	1998	1999	2000	2001	2002	2003	2004	2005	2006	2007	2008
Expenditure on GDP	9.34	8.15	5.76	4.77	6.79	6.89	7.08	7.34	7.79	8.44	8.23	8.46	6.18
Share of GDP by component (%)													
Total	100	100	100	100	100	100	100	100	100	100	100	100	100
Gross capital formation	28.10	28.30	29.05	27.63	29.61	31.17	33.22	35.44	35.47	35.58	36.81	43.13	41.13
Gross fixed capital formation	26.32	26.70	27.02	25.70	27.65	29.15	31.14	33.35	33.26	32.87	33.35	38.27	36.00
Changes in stocks	1.78	1.60	2.03	1.93	1.96	2.02	2.08	2.09	2.21	2.71	3.46	4.86	5.13
Final consumption	82.79	79.90	78.51	75.43	72.87	71.19	71.33	72.58	71.47	69.68	69.38	70.81	73.42
State	8.35	8.13	7.62	6.79	6.42	6.33	6.23	6.32	6.39	6.15	6.03	6.05	6.15
Private	74.44	71.77	70.89	68.65	66.45	64.86	65.1	66.26	65.08	63.53	63.35	64.76	67.26
Trade balance (goods and services)	–10.97	–8.14	–7.30	–2.85	–2.46	–2.28	–5.17	–8.36	–7.55	–4.18	–4.56	–15.85	–16.54
Statistical discrepancy	0.08	–0.06	–0.26	–0.21	–0.02	–0.08	0.62	0.34	0.61	–1.08	–1.63	1.91	2.00
Contribution to GDP growth rate (%)													
Final consumption	77.63	56.82	59.62	29.35	36.29	49.62	75.24	77.87	66.52	62.65	72.39	89.63	106.17
Private consumption	71.13	52.88	55.30	38.35	31.29	43.23	70.19	71.46	60.00	56.30	65.66	82.76	98.18
Government consumption	6.50	3.94	4.31	–9.00	5.01	6.39	5.05	6.41	6.52	6.35	6.73	6.88	7.99
Investment	41.48	32.72	63.02	7.70	44.06	47.65	56.82	53.79	46.93	46.99	52.42	119.33	44.74
Gross fixed capital formation	38.12	33.05	58.12	9.48	41.71	44.62	54.02	50.81	43.79	38.67	40.76	98.23	24.46
Increase in stocks	3.36	–0.33	4.90	–1.78	2.34	3.03	2.81	2.97	3.15	8.32	11.66	21.11	20.28
Net exports	–12.62	13.95	–20.84	63.15	17.65	–3.23	–51.65	–43.73	5.06	18.58	–18.9	–156.37	–52.48
Export						71.61	90.74	113.61	152.25	69.4	112.73	91.88	57.72
Import						–4.85	–142.39	–57.34	–47.19	–0.82	–31.63	–248.24	–110.20
Errors	–6.49	–3.48	–1.81	–0.19	1.96	5.97	19.59	12.08	–18.52	–28.21	–5.93	47.36	1.49

Source: GSO, http://www.gso.gov.vn.
Note: Blank cells = not available.

150 percent in 2007 from 61 percent in 1994. Net exports accounted for only a small fraction of overall GDP growth.

The decomposition of GDP by demand factors using the traditional method is said to underestimate the contribution of exports to GDP growth. Therefore, we instead decompose the contribution of exports separately in order to determine the contribution of this component. The export component has been a significant contributor to GDP growth during the past 10 years, especially since 2000 (table 12.2). This reflects the trade liberalization and export-led growth policies pursued as part of the government's economic reforms. During the past 20 years, average annual export growth has stayed at about 20 percent.[11]

Investment and capital formation have played a key role in Vietnam's successful economic growth strategy. The investment-to-GDP ratio has increased considerably; during the 1990s, the ratio fluctuated around 28 percent before it started rising (beginning in 2000) and then peaked at 43 percent in 2007—after which it dropped moderately to 41 percent in 2008 (table 12.2). This is a high investment level, especially for a low-income country. According to the World Bank (2007), the large and increasing share of investment in GDP partly explains Vietnam's high and accelerating growth rate since 2000.[12]

Until 2006, the state sector was the most important source of investment in Vietnam. State investment is made either directly in public infrastructure or through loans to SOEs, or in the form of grants to municipalities and private enterprises. But the state's share in investment has declined from 60 percent in 2001 to 29 percent in 2008 as private domestic investment and FDI have increased. The recent decline in the state's share in GDP is due more to increased private investment than to new inflows of foreign investment. The nonstate domestic sector has increased steadily to become a key source of investment. Private sector investment increased from 27.6 percent in 1995 to 40 percent by 2008.[13] The increased saving and investment by Vietnam's private sector, along with the continued involvement of the state, have contributed to Vietnam's continuing high economic growth rates.

The share of the FDI sector in total investment during the 1990s and in early 2000 experienced a downturn. FDI accounted for 30 percent of investment in the mid-1990s, but fell to 20 percent in the wake of the Asia financial crisis. Since then, the share of FDI in total investment continued falling until 2006. In 2007–08, however, FDI inflows increased substantially, fueled partly by government reforms associated with WTO accession (figure 12.2), which created a buzz among international investors about Vietnam's prospects.[14] The reforms relaxed rules restricting FDI and made Vietnam a more attractive FDI destination. Indeed, in these two years, FDI became the country's most important source of investment. Notwithstanding Vietnam's success in attracting FDI, the actual benefits of FDI are subject to controversy. Previous studies have found little evidence of technical spillover from FDI enterprises to local counterparts (Nguyen et al. 2008). In addition, the country has become heavily dependent on FDI for sustaining its economic growth.

The high level of investment may also be partly attributable to the state and its expansionary policy adopted in response to the Asian crisis (table 12.3). The government maintained investment levels, and increased its share in GDP, to minimize the effects of the crisis and avoid recession. As a result, Vietnam continued to experience growth and was less affected by the crisis than most of its neighbors. In particular, during 2000–04, the authorities implemented a demand stimulus policy to revitalize the economy while upholding their commitment to reform. The demand stimulus included such measures as public investment in infrastructure projects, financial support to help SOEs deal with their

Figure 12.2. FDI in Vietnam, 1990–2008

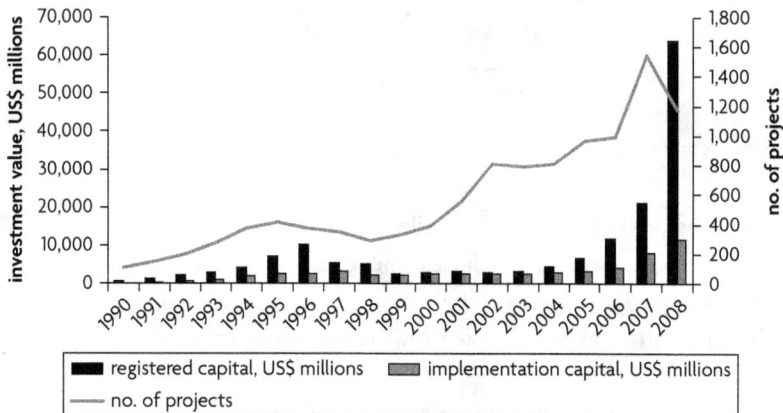

registered capital, US$ millions   implementation capital, US$ millions
— no. of projects

Source: GSO, http://www.gso.gov.vn.

Table 12.3. Structure of Investment by Ownership, 1995–2008
(% using current prices)

	1995	1996	1997	1998	1999	2000	2001	2002	2003	2004	2005	2006	2007	2008
Total	100	100	100	100	100	100	100	100	100	100	100	100	100	100
State sector	42.03	49.08	49.43	55.52	58.67	59.14	59.81	57.33	52.90	48.06	47.11	45.74	37.21	28.55
State budget	18.74	22.36	21.75	22.45	24.21	25.80	26.74	25.09	23.82	23.79	25.63	24.76	20.17	16.18
State credit	8.37	9.47	11.72	15.71	18.83	18.37	16.85	17.46	16.30	12.25	10.48	6.63	5.73	4.10
Owned equity of SOEs	14.92	17.24	15.96	17.36	15.63	14.97	16.22	14.78	12.78	12.03	11.00	14.35	11.31	8.28
Nonstate sector	27.61	24.94	22.61	23.73	24.05	22.88	22.59	25.29	31.09	37.73	38.00	38.05	38.47	39.96
Foreign invested sector	30.37	25.97	27.96	20.75	17.28	17.97	17.60	17.38	16.01	14.21	14.89	16.21	24.32	31.49

Source: GSO, http://www.gso.gov.vn, and authors' calculations.
Note: Data for 2006 adjusted by Vietnam Development Bank.

Figure 12.3. Vietnam Investment-Savings Gap, 1996–2008

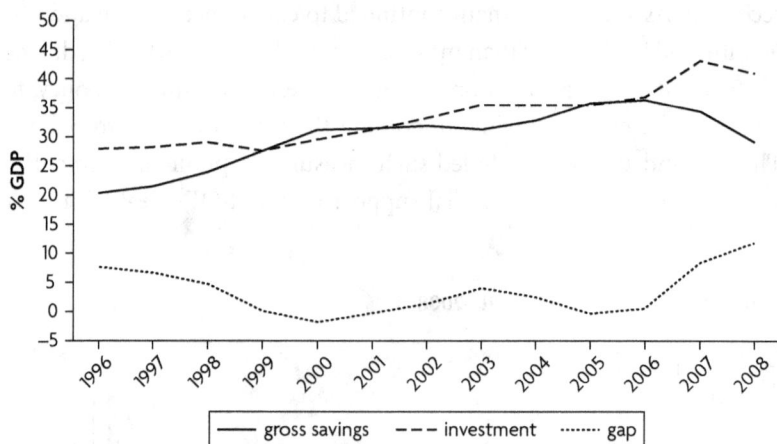

Source: World Bank Data Catalog.

mounting inventories, budget allocations for poverty reduction programs, raising wages and salaries, encouraging people to consume, and providing partial support to help enterprises expand their exports. This stimulus had a positive impact on the economy, minimizing deflation and economic stagnation.[15]

Vietnam's saving-investment gap has undergone considerable change (figure 12.3). In the mid-1990s, the gap was as large as 7.6 percent of

GDP. The gap then narrowed during the late 1990s and early 2000s but has widened since 2002, and in 2007–08 it became very large— 9.8 percent. To meet the county's investment needs and its growth target, the authorities would have had to mobilize foreign savings equal to about 10 percent of GDP if the domestic savings-to-GDP ratio did not improve. Relative to other countries—especially China, where the savings ratio reached 50 percent of GDP—Vietnam's saving ratio remains low. The ratio of saving to GDP tends to level off, thus widening the gap between domestic saving and investment.

Growth Accounting

Economic growth in the neoclassical framework derives from two sources: factor accumulation and productivity growth. Using a growth accounting framework, we break down GDP growth during 1986–2008 into three components: capital (K), labor (L), and total factor productivity (TFP) (A) (table 12.4).[16] The objective of this method is to determine how much economic growth is due to accumulation of inputs and how much to technical progress.

The data reveal an interesting TFP pattern for Vietnam. During the early economic reform period, TFP growth—and, hence, its contribution to GDP growth—was relatively high. However, in the years after the Asian crisis, the country's TFP almost ceased growing; it picked up after 2000 but then dropped again in 2008 during the global crisis, and posted negative growth in 2009. The growth accounting calculation also confirms the importance of investment to GDP growth in Vietnam. This

Table 12.4. Growth Accounting, 1986–2009

Year	GDP (constant 2000 US$ millions)	GDP growth (%)	Labor force, total	Labor growth (%)	Investment (constant 2000 US$ millions)	Gross capital stock (K/Y = 2)	Capital growth (%)	Growth rate of TFP (%)
1986–90	13,499	5	29,506,375	3	1,865	25,220	2	3
1991–96	19,809	8	33,840,536	2	4,279	29,811	6	5
1997–2002	30,595	7	38,071,353	2	9,167	54,555	11	2
2003–07	45,071	8	42,635,146	2	16,540	95,013	11	3
2008–09	57,279	6	22,803,368	2	25,233	138,709	13	0

Source: World Bank Data Catalog; GSO, http://www.gso.gov.vn; authors' calculations.

should be no surprise, as it is consistent with the decomposition previously discussed, where investment constitutes a large part of GDP for a sustained period.

The Run-Up to the Global Crisis

The years 2007–09 marked a memorable period for Vietnam. After a long-standing effort to achieve a high rate of economic growth for the first time in 2008, the government publicly conceded the trade-off between economic growth and macroeconomic stability. Vietnam had experienced a huge credit expansion in 2007, which, together with rising world energy and food prices, led to mounting inflationary pressures. In addition, in response to the heavy capital inflows (both FDI and portfolio investment), the government inappropriately attempted to absorb this inflow while maintaining a fixed exchange rate.

Given these problems, the Vietnamese government was forced, in 2008, to shift its priority from economic growth to stabilization; this meant a tight monetary policy and a cutback of public spending on large projects.[17] The policy worked and brought down inflation, but it also stalled the housing market and popped the financial bubble. While the macroeconomic situation improved by the end of 2008, the global crisis and recession took a heavy toll on the economy. As pointed out by the World Bank (2009), the policies implemented in 2008 were in a way good for Vietnam. But the economy was not well prepared for the crisis, given that it was suffering a self-induced recession in early 2008.[18] Thus, at the beginning of 2009, the global crisis compounded Vietnam's difficulties.

Box 12.1. Food-Fuel Crisis in Vietnam, 2007–08

The years 2007–08 saw unprecedented soars in world food and fuel prices, creating a global crisis and causing political and economical instability and social unrest in both poor and developed nations; Vietnam is not an exception.

In mid-2008, the food prices rose by about 60 percent and the fuel price index leaped 20 percent compared with the previous year. Rising prices of foods and fuels generated increases in the prices of most of other products and this, in turn, pushed the inflation up, even approaching the dangerous levels Vietnam's inflation rate topped to 21.4 percent in 2008. In order to stabilize prices, the State Bank of Vietnam tightened its monetary policy raising the prime interest rate to 14 percent in 2008, effectively raising the commercial lending rate to the prohibitive rate of 21 percent, resulting in nearly a liquidity crisis in 2008.

Source: Complied by the authors from various sources, primarily from http://www.vneconomy.vn.

Effects of the Global Crisis and Government Responses

As noted earlier, Vietnam's strong economic performance has been highly dependent on external demand, with the export-to-GDP ratio reaching 70 percent in 2007, and the FDI-to-GDP ratio reaching almost 10 percent. Although the country has witnessed strong domestic consumption growth in recent years, Vietnam's economy has continued to be driven by high external trade and increased FDI. The country's total trade is now equivalent to about 150 percent of GDP, which is the second highest in the region after Malaysia. Vietnam has also been one of the largest recipients of FDI in the world, relative to the size of its GDP. Therefore, the country was particularly vulnerable to the unexpected global economic slowdown and capital outflows.

The Effects of the Global Crisis

Up to the first half of 2008, Vietnam was relatively unaffected by the financial turmoil; but the financial and economic environment worsened in the final quarter of 2008 and first quarter of 2009 (table 12.5). The weak performance in the first quarter of 2009 confirmed fears that Vietnam was facing a full-blown recession for the year 2009.

The crisis has exposed Vietnam's vulnerability in its dependence on external stimulus. In the fourth quarter of 2008, Vietnam's exports fell substantially, due to the direct and immediate effects of the global crisis. According to official statistics from the country's General Statistics

Table 12.5. Basic Quarterly Macroeconomic Data during the Crisis

	2008Q3	2008Q4	2009Q1	2009Q2	2009Q3	2009Q4
GDP (% yoy)	6.5	5.7	3.1	4.5	5.8	7.7
Industrial production (% yoy)	15.8	14.1	2.9	6.8	10.7	14.0
CPI, end of quarter (% yoy)	27.9	19.9	11.3	3.9	2.4	6.9
Trade balance (% GDP)	−5.5	−5.9	8.5	−15.2	−19.7	−18.6
International reserves (US$ bn)	24.1	24.2	23.3	19.0	18.0	16.0
Policy rate, end of quarter (%)	14.0	8.5	7.0	7.0	7.0	8.0
5-year yield, end of quarter (%)	15.9	10.0	9.2	9.4	10.1	11.7
Dong/U.S. dollar, end of quarter	16,600	17,483	17,797	17,798	17,841	18,479
Dong/euro, end of quarter	23,572	24,301	23,492	24,917	26,048	26,425

Source: GSO, http://www.gso.gov.vn.

Office (GSO), over the first 10 months of 2009, Vietnamese exports fell 13.8 percent relative to 2008, with the full-year decline registering −8.9 percent. The export decline was the result of two developments:

- Decreased aggregate demand for its exports
- A substantial fall in the prices of its export commodities, especially crude oil and other primary commodities

Although some of Vietnam's major export products—such as coffee, rice, pepper, rubber, crude oil, and coal—showed volume increases in 2009, their lower prices raised concerns that Vietnam might even exceed the revised negative growth rate. For a country with annual growth in export values of about 20 percent, this is a serious setback. As the year 2009 closed, exports showed some signs of recovery, due to a global demand revival, but export values amounted to just US$56.6 billion—10 percent lower than in 2008.

A recent study by the Vietnam Academy of Social Sciences (VASS) finds that although several export manufacturing sectors—such as textiles, garments, leather, and seafood processing—were hit hard by the crisis, these industries are highly resilient and are capable of bouncing back once the world economy improves. This is because demand for the products of these industries is highly inelastic. On the other hand, several sectors or segments of the economy—such as furniture, electronics, and village crafts—are not resilient and may take longer to improve because world demand for these products is not inelastic.

In 2008, the heavy flows of registered FDI capital into Vietnam reached US$64 billion (triple the registered FDI capital in 2007), while flows of implementation capital totaled US$11.6 billion—versus US$8 billion in 2007.[19] In 2009, however, FDI inflows slowed because of capital constraints and the tightening of the world credit market. In the first eight months of 2009, Vietnam managed to attract about US$10.4 billion of registered capital, well below the figure for 2008. Actual disbursements for investment projects were about US$6.5 billion, also lower than in 2008. The slowdown of FDI inflows in 2009, with the expectation of continued lower levels in the years to come, will have serious consequences for Vietnam, especially in terms of its exports. According to official statistics, FDI has accounted for more than 50 percent of the country's exports over the past six years.

We might thus expect Vietnam's labor force to be highly vulnerable to the global financial crisis, given its heavy dependence on exports and relatively mobile international investment. Data on the impact of the crisis on the labor market and employment, however, are limited and not reliable, complicating the assessment of the social impact of the growth slowdown.[20] As the World Bank (2009) observes, current data show a mixed picture, and the effects are heterogeneous across enterprises and provinces. According to a survey conducted by VASS,[21] the effects have not been as bad as feared. Despite numerous job losses, frequent reductions in working hours and wages, reduced remittances, and increased reliance on informal sector jobs, major negative effects—such as rising poverty, food shortages, the need to pull children out of school or to sell land, or becoming homeless—have been relatively uncommon.

In addition to its impact on trade, FDI, industrial production, and the labor market, the global crisis has had implications for Vietnam's capital inflows, exchange rate, and stock market. Like other Asian countries, Vietnam suffered capital flight starting in the second quarter of 2008. Banks and financial institutions in the United States and the West reduced their international businesses and focused on their home markets. As a result, funds flowing into Vietnam fell sharply. In response to the booming stock and housing markets during 2006–07, short-term inflows had surged to high levels. The crisis then led to a reversal of these inflows. The reversal of portfolio capital flows significantly affected the stock market, with the VN-Index falling to a record low of about 300 points in 2009 from its high of over 1,000 points in early 2007.[22] Although the Vietnamese dong has long been pegged to the U.S. dollar, capital flows have had a major impact on the dong, with several small adjustments of the trading bands and devaluation. Generally, capital outflows depress the dong's value; indeed, since the beginning of 2009, the dong has lost up to a dozen percentage points in its value against the dollar.[23] Declines in exports, as well as in remittance and foreign capital inflows, have reduced the supply of foreign exchange, while expansionary monetary and fiscal policies have increased demand for it. Consequently, there has been a shortage of foreign exchange in the formal market, and the dong's exchange rate against the U.S. dollar has been transacted at the upper bound of its trading band.[24]

We now summarize the effects of the global crisis on Vietnam's economy (table 12.6). Before the crisis (2003–07), the economy was growing

Table 12.6. Summary of the Global Economic Crisis on Vietnam's Economy

	1997–2002	2003–07	Change from 1997–2002 to 2003–07	Highest 2-year average value before crisis	Expected potential value just prior to the crisis	2008	Forecast/ estimate 2009	Total loss during 2008–09 compared to potential
GDP growth (%)	6.58	8.05	1.48	8.45	7.5–8	6.18	5.32	–2.18
TFP growth (%)	1.66	2.99	1.33	3.21	2.75	0.20	–0.33	–3.08
Exports growth (%)	17.77	12.91	–4.86	27.74	0.25	5.05	–0.10	–0.26
Exports/ GDP (%)	50.73	68.98	18.25	75.25	0.65	78.21	0.62	–0.03
Investment (% GDP)	29.83	37.29	7.45	39.97	37.00	41.13	42.80	5.80
Capital inflows (% GDP)	0.054	0.048	–0.006	0.078	0.070	0.104	0.098	0.028
Fiscal deficit (% GDP)	—	0.051	—	0.055	0.050	0.041	0.070	0.020

Source: GSO, http://www.gso.gov.vn; World Bank Data Catalog; Ministry of Finance; authors' calculations.
Note: The potential GDP for Vietnam is expected to be in the range of 7.5–8 percent per year. In calculating the global crisis impact on Vietnam, we use the lower bound in order to be conservative. — = not available.

at an average annual rate of over 8 percent. We believe that this rate was the upper bound of the country's growth potential as signs of overheating emerged; specifically, the inflation rate was high by the end of 2007 and in early 2008, and investment in stock and inventory as a percentage of GDP was very high (more than 42 percent). We expect the potential growth rate for Vietnam to be between 7.5 percent and 8 percent. If we take the lower bound of 7.5 percent, the total loss during 2008–09, in terms of GDP growth, would be 2.18 percentage points. (In addition to the GDP loss, table 12.6 shows losses for TFP, exports, and other items.)

In addition to the direct effects of decreased exports and FDI inflows, the global crisis has reduced aggregate demand sharply, through the employment and income channels. The drop in domestic demand was the result of falling employment and delayed consumption and investment by domestic consumers and investors.

An indirect (but critical) effect of the global crisis on Vietnam has been the government's efforts to mitigate the impact on the domestic economy and stimulate short-term growth. These efforts may take the form of delaying or canceling some structural adjustment policies (reforms of SOEs and the banking sectors, as well as improvements in the business environment). These structural adjustments, however, are critical for sustainable growth. For example, to stimulate short-term economic growth, the Vietnamese government may resort to refinancing the inefficient banking sector, subsidizing loss-making state-owned conglomerates, and reviving real estate investment. Although these measures are useful and effective for stimulating short-term economic growth, they cannot ensure long-term sustainable growth and may in fact generate new risks. Therefore, the Vietnamese government should speed up structural adjustments to help to transform the country's growth model.

Remittances have long been seen as important sources of capital for Vietnam, and the crisis is expected to lower the inflow of this key source of capital. Other impacts include the decline in tourism and lower income for farmers, due to lower commodity prices.

Although the crisis has led to a steep fall in exports, it has also led to a more manageable trade deficit as of early 2009 (World Bank 2009). But the trade deficit is expected to grow significantly once the economy recovers. This is because of the import-export structure of Vietnam:

- Exports rely heavily on agriculture and raw commodities, and most manufacturing products still embody low value added.
- Imports of intermediate products and machinery for domestic production and export may rise more rapidly once the economy recovers.
- Overseas final-product imports, particularly luxury items, have high value, as they appeal to Vietnam's middle-income consumers.

Government Responses

The government of Vietnam quickly and decisively responded to counter the negative effects of the global crisis.[25] It reversed the course of the monetary tightening and fiscal austerity policy implemented in 2008 by announcing a US$6 billion stimulus package.[26]

As to monetary policy, the government aggressively loosened its stance by cutting the annual base rate from 14 percent to 7 percent within a few months. Ceiling lending interest rate (1.5 times base rate) offered by commercial banks was lowered accordingly, from 21 percent to 10.5 percent for productive activities. Lending interest rates for credit card and consumption are negotiable and fluctuating between 12 percent and 15 percent. The government also announced and implemented its plan to provide a 4 percent interest subsidy for working capital and short-term loans for enterprises; the subsidy cost totals US$1 billion.

Vietnam announced its fiscal stimulus in January 2009. The objective, of course, was to mitigate the impact of the global crisis on the economy and the population and prevent a general slowdown of economic activity. The initial US$6 billion figure was later revised to US$8 billion; this has raised some concerns about unsustainable spending.[27]

To put Vietnam's stimulus package into perspective, we compare it to the values of stimulus packages adopted by other ASEAN countries to fight the global recession (table 12.7). Based on a simple budget deficit metric, the budget plan of late 2008 put the Vietnamese stimulus package in the top tier within its region.

We also consider the fiscal stimulus package breakdown in terms of measures and in terms of how the fiscal stimulus package was financed (table 12.8).

The package includes a number of components, such as tax breaks and public investments in infrastructure, social transfers, and interest

Table 12.7. Proportion of Stimulus Package to GDP

Country	Stimulus package (US$ bn)	Proportion to GDP (%)
China	586.0	12.0
Indonesia	4.5	0.9
Malaysia	18.1	10.0
Philippines	6.1	4.0
Singapore	13.8	10.7
Thailand	8.3	3.3
Vietnam	8.0	10.0

Source: CIMB Research House; Ministry of Planning and Investment (MPI).

subsidies (table 12.8). For example, the stimulus package includes one-off support of Dong 200,000 (equivalent to US$12) per capita for the poor on the last New Year's holiday; a 30 percent reduction in corporate income taxes; an extension of nine months for the submission of 2009 tax payables; a temporary refund of 90 percent of value added tax for exported goods with "justifiable payment documents"; a personal income tax exemption for the first six months of 2009; and an extension of the 4 percent interest subsidy for long-term loans of up to two years for investment in agriculture and other productive activities.

Some researchers (Pincus 2009) have pointed out that the policy options available for Vietnam's government are much more limited than

Table 12.8. Vietnam's Fiscal Stimulus Package

Policy measure	Amount
Interest subsidy (for working capital loan)	D 17,000 billion
State development investment	D 90,800 billion
Tax holiday and exemption	D 28,000 billion
Other spending for social security and economic downturn prevention	D 9,800 billion
Total	D 145,600 billion (equivalent to US$8 billion)

Components and size (values in D trillions unless otherwise noted)	Amount
Revenue forgone	25.4
Corporate income tax	10.4
Personal income tax	6.5
Value added tax	7.4.0
Licenses and fees	1.1
Additional expenditures	117.6
Interest rate subsidy	17.0
Budget advanced from 2010	37.2
Government bond carried over from 2008	7.7
Investments funded by additional bond issuance	20.0
Expenditures carried over from 2008	22.5
Deferral of repayment of budget allowance for 2009	3.4
Social spending	9.8
Overall fiscal stimulus	143.0
% GDP	8.5

Source: Ministry of Finance; Ministry of Planning and Investment; World Bank; International Monetary Fund (IMF).

those for China or other neighboring countries. While China and other Asian neighbors have maintained current account surpluses and sound fiscal balances for several consecutive years, Vietnam has been plagued by twin deficits: a large current account gap of 12 percent of GDP in 2008 and double-digit fiscal deficits. The fall in world oil prices also constrained the Vietnamese government's fiscal policy, because 16 percent of government revenue comes from oil exports. A World Bank study (2009), however, suggests that there is still fiscal space for a stimulus policy in Vietnam and that the fiscal position of the country remains strong.

The Stimulus Package and Economic Recovery

According to the GSO (2009), signs of economic recovery in Vietnam emerged as early as August 2009. These signs were combined with the global recession bottoming out and recovery in other Asian countries. Domestic industrial production and GDP growth picked up in the third quarter of 2009; and in the fourth quarter, the year-on-year industrial production and GDP growth rates reached 14 percent and 7.7 percent, respectively (table 12.7). Some have attributed the economic recovery to the government's stimulus, but we see a number of factors at work here: the timely implementation of the stimulus, the intrinsic resilience of the economy, and—most important—the recovery of global demand for Vietnam's exports and the resumption of FDI inflows.[28]

Evaluating the effectiveness and efficiency of the government stimulus package is a daunting task in the absence of reliable data. We will therefore present only patchy evidence of the effectiveness of the stimulus package. The most obvious impact of the stimulus may be its having kept credit flowing to the economy and helping enterprises clean up their balance sheets. The government helped repair balance sheets by replacing the high-interest-bearing loans incurred during the turbulent year of 2008 (when the interest rate reached 21 percent) with interest rate–subsidized loans under an accommodative monetary policy. This reduced the financial burden of borrowing by easing costs during a period of economic pressure and enabled businesses to maintain production and jobs. According a government report, by September 2009, the government had spent Dong 17,000 billion (equivalent to US$1 billion) for interest rate subsidies, which led to Dong 405,000 billion (equivalent to

US$23.8 billion) worth of loans (for working capital); of this total, 16 percent went to SOEs and 84 percent to the nonstate-owned sector. Spurred by the introduction of government interest rate subsidies, the growth of credit and the money supply accelerated in the first half of 2009. The growth of total liquidity (M2) rose to 35.8 percent in the second quarter of 2009, up from 20.3 percent in the fourth quarter of 2008.

As noted earlier, the government also adopted an expansionary monetary stance to support economic activity. The growth of liquidity and credit, however, was relatively modest during the first quarter of 2009, owing to some lag. As time passed, economic activities increased; and, once the government's determination to boost growth rates became clear, bank lending picked up again. Any attempt to separate out the effects of monetary and fiscal policies on credit growth would be superficial, as monetary and fiscal policies in Vietnam are not independent of one another. The government thus adopted an unorthodox policy, using the fiscal budget to implement monetary policy (the interest rate subsidy). The interest rate subsidy under the stimulus package, together with the accommodative monetary policy, helped inject credit into the economy during this difficult time. Another effect of the package was to restore business confidence, as reflected in part by a rally in the stock market in mid-2009.[29]

The stimulus package has also helped mitigate the impact of the financial crisis on workers. In a recent study, Manning (2009) suggests that the impact on labor has been milder than might have been expected for a country so heavily exposed internationally. This can be partly attributed to the government's timely stimulus package.[30] In addition, the market for semiskilled and skilled workers recovered well after the Tet break (March 2009).[31] This is consistent with evidence from a rapid assessment survey conducted by VASS in May 2009, which found evidence of "green shoots," with enterprises receiving orders and recruiting more employees. The multiplier effect of the package may also help in the face of falling aggregate demand.

We now turn to the agricultural sector, which employs more than two-thirds of the country's population and accounts for most of Vietnam's exports. Needless to say, the sector has been hit hard by the global downturn, although the impact on rural areas has been limited.

In April 2009, the government introduced a series of stimulus measures targeting the rural economy. The new policies include interest-free loans for purchases of farm equipment and subsidized loans for fertilizer and other agricultural inputs. However, in the first stimulus package, farmers, who account for 70 percent of the population, were able to access only US$48 million of credit, too small a share of the total package of about US$22 billion disbursed.

In addition to the stimulus package, the resilience of the business sector appears to have been a major driver of the recent recovery. The stimulus has been seen as a "rescue remedy" to help enterprises access loans to get back on track, remain in production, and create jobs. It has been important in improving the liquidity of the banking system and maintaining debt payments. After all, it is the business sector that takes the risk in responding to the stimulus, and it is its investments that keep aggregate demand from falling too far. Another key factor in facilitating the recovery is the revival of world demand for Vietnam's exports and inflows of foreign investment.

Medium-Term Projections

The current global financial and economic crisis is the worst since the Great Depression, and Vietnam is being hit much harder than it was by the Asian financial crisis. But the crisis is also giving Vietnam an opportunity to review and redesign its economic development policy to sustain rapid growth, protect the country from future external shocks, and strengthen internal sources of growth.

The economic development policy that Vietnam pursued during the past 20 years has three important characteristics:

- Gradual domestic reforms: developing private businesses while maintaining a dominant role for the state sector
- Dependence on external stimulus: increasing export growth and attracting FDI
- Overreliance on investment as a source of economic growth

Over these years, the government tried to increase employment and eradicate poverty with a strategy of export-led, investment-based growth—with state intervention. The state developed five-year plans and an industrial policy based largely on the above features. This approach, however, must be reevaluated. Alternative strategies are needed to prepare for what could be a prolonged period of lower demand for Vietnam's exports, lower inward FDI, and shifting patterns of global economic growth. Adopting an updated and effective strategy to drive economic growth will be difficult, however, because it requires that some of the assumptions that have traditionally driven policy making be reexamined or replaced.

The global financial crisis and resulting recession will have profound long-term implications for many developing countries, including Vietnam. How will the Vietnamese economy fare in the medium term? What course of economic development will it follow?

One of our main tasks in this chapter is to apply the lessons of past experience to the new and changed postcrisis world so as to analyze the likely course of the Vietnamese economy. Much of what has happened in the past, however, will only have limited value for predicting the future. This is particularly true if we think of the recent crisis as causing a structural break that heightens the risks associated with projections using past trend data. Therefore, although we use contextual information and concentrate on the issues, factors, and trends that have some forward-looking elements, our projections may suffer from subjective bias and judgment. We next provide our projections for Vietnam's economic growth from both the demand and supply sides, using our forecasts for global external factors as well as key domestic factors.

Projections of Global Exogenous Factors

We now turn to assessing medium-term prospects for the Vietnamese economy, based on the performance of its export sector and capital inflows.

Demand for Exports. As discussed earlier, Vietnam is highly dependent on exports for growth. In 2009, although some of Vietnam's major export products (such as coffee, rice, pepper, rubber, crude oil, and coal) showed increases in volume, depressed world prices led to marked decreases in export values. In the first quarter of 2010, exports registered a positive growth rate of 3.8 percent.[32] Although this is modest relative to the yearly average growth rate of about 20 percent during the past decade, we expect that Vietnam's export performance will soon recover and may return to precrisis growth levels after 2012. There are a number of reasons for this belief.

First, as pointed out by the World Bank (2010), China's stimulus package has helped trade in Asia recover faster than elsewhere. According to recent official statistics (figure 12.4), China is the third-largest importer of Vietnam's products (after the United States and Japan) and we thus expect that Vietnamese exports to China will increase. And once economic recovery takes hold in the United States and Japan, exports from Vietnam to these large markets will also improve.

Second, higher export prices in 2010 (relative to 2009) will lead to higher export values.

Third, Vietnam's export sector also shows potential for dynamism. During the crisis year of 2009, Vietnam still managed to diversify away from its traditional export markets, and it is these markets that sustained Vietnam's export growth in 2009 (figure 12.5). If Vietnam manages to maintain and expand its newfound nontraditional markets while benefiting from recovery in its traditional markets, its export performance will strengthen in the next few years.

Based on these considerations, we expect Vietnam's export performance to be stronger than the average growth rates for Asia and the Pacific estimated by the World Bank (2010). In particular, we expect that Vietnam's export growth will return to its precrisis growth rate of 20 percent earlier than 2015. According to the latest statistics issued by the GSO, the export growth rate of Vietnam in the first half of 2010 was over 15.7 percent. We believe that this would be the growth rate in 2010,

Figure 12.4. Main Export Markets, 2008

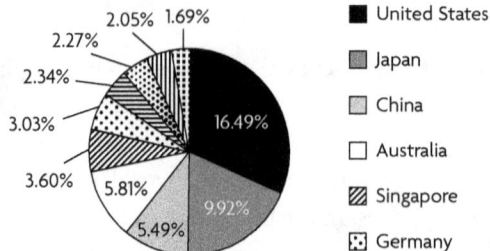

Legend:
- United States
- Japan
- China
- Australia
- Singapore
- Germany

Values: 16.49%, 9.92%, 5.49%, 5.81%, 3.60%, 3.03%, 2.34%, 2.27%, 2.05%, 1.69%

Source: GSO, http://www.gso.gov.vn.

Figure 12.5. Diversification of Export Markets

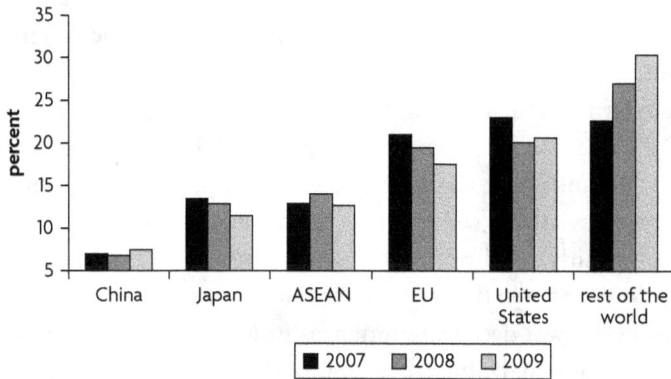

Source: GSO, http://www.gso.gov.vn.

which is then expected to increase gradually to 16 percent in 2011, 17 percent in 2012, and 18 percent in 2013, and we expect it to return to the long-term rate of about 20 percent by 2014.[33]

Capital Flows and Access to International Finance. In 2007–08, Vietnam experienced new and large FDI inflows—partly because of reforms committed to as part of WTO accession, which relaxed rules restricting FDI and made Vietnam a more attractive FDI destination. Indeed, in those two years, FDI became the most important source of investment in Vietnam.[34] But in 2009, FDI inflows slowed due to the constraints of available capitals and the tightening of the world credit markets. In the first eight months of 2009, Vietnam attracted about US$10.4 billion of registered capital, much lower than in 2008. Also, although actual disbursements under investment projects exceeded US$6.5 billion, this figure was also lower than that for 2008.

The World Bank (2010) expects external financial inflows to developing countries to decline over the medium term, depending on the type of capital flow. The study suggests that the decline in FDI inflows into developing countries will be less than for other types of finance. FDI as a percentage of GDP is thus expected to decline from 3.9 percent to about 3 percent, a decrease of 30 percent. Traditionally, Vietnam has been able to attract more FDI than its proportionate share. During 2003–07, for example, Vietnam attracted a large inflow of FDI equivalent to 7.3 percent of GDP. Although we expect FDI flows into Vietnam to be higher than the world average over the medium term, the country will also suffer from the general global decline. We project that, over the medium term, Vietnam will attract FDI inflows equivalent to 5.1 percent of GDP (a decline of 30 percent). With regard to portfolio investment, the World Bank study (2010) expects it to be severely constrained. To be safe and relatively conservative, and since portfolio investment in Vietnam is fairly small relative to FDI, we project that portfolio investment into Vietnam in the medium term will be negligible.

During the past decade, remittances from overseas Vietnamese have played an increasingly important role, both in terms of macroeconomic stability as well as constituting a cheap source of financing. During the crisis, although remittances fell from a high of US$7.2 billion to US$6.8 billion, the decline was not as bad as many expected. To make some projections about future remittances (table 12.9), we rely on the scenario developed by the World Bank, in which the growth rates for remittances are given.

Medium-Term Projections for Key Domestic Variables

During the early 2000s, Vietnamese inflation rates were relatively low (under 10 percent). But because of sustained debt-financed investment by the government combined with accommodative monetary policy, inflation accelerated in 2007 and peaked at over 23 percent in 2008. In switching from a high-growth strategy to one of stabilization, the government tightened monetary policy in 2008 (in combination with nontraditional and administrative methods) to curb the accelerating inflation rate. As a result, inflation in 2009 fell back to less than 10 percent. The government's ability to control inflation in 2009 was made easier by the lower commodity prices (especially oil) associated with the crisis.

To counter the effects of the global crisis, however, the government reversed the course of monetary tightening. Money supply and credit expansion, together with the large stimulus package, have put renewed pressure on inflation. As the economic recovery began toward the end of 2009, there were worrying signs of accelerating inflation.[35] The government has openly set the inflation target at about 8 percent for 2010. Thus, on the one hand, we expect that for now the lessons of high inflation in

Table 12.9. Projections of Key External Variables
(current US$ millions)

	Actual				Projected					
	2003	2007	2008	2009	2010	2011	2012	2013	2014	2015
Vietnamese exports	23,045.9	52,769.2	70,891.2	63,802.1	73,372.4	85,112.0	99,581.0	117,505.6	141,006.8	169,208.1
Exports growth (%)	20.0	11.3	5.1	-10.0	15.0	16.0	17.0	18.0	20.0	20.0
Foreign direct investment	1,450.0	6,516.0	9,279.0	9,514.7	9,999.9	10,509.9	11,045.9	11,609.2	12,201.2	12,823.5
Portfolio investment	0	6,243	-578	—	—	—	—	—	—	—
Total capital flow	1,450.0	12,759.0	8,701.0	9,514.7	9,999.9	10,509.9	11,045.9	11,609.2	12,201.2	12,823.5
Remittances	2.6	5.5	7.2	6.8	7.0	7.1	7.3	7.5	7.7	7.8

Source: World Bank Data Catalog; GSO, http://www.gso.gov.vn; authors' calculation.

Note: — = not available.

2007 will be a good reminder of the costs and difficulties associated with controlling high inflation. On the other hand, the government is under great pressure to boost economic growth in the absence of an independent central bank. On balance, we see a low likelihood of double-digit inflation in the next few years, as the government tries to check inflation pressures. But we see much uncertainty in achieving the government's inflation target of 8 percent for 2010. We project that inflation will be about 10–12 percent in the next few years, before the government is able to reduce it to 7–8 percent (figure 12.6).

Although the decisive implementation of Vietnam's economic stimulus package is encouraging, the government's aggressive approach has also raised concerns about its impact on public finances. Since 2000, the government's operating expenditures have risen more sharply than its tax revenues (figure 12.7). Vietnam has a narrow tax base, and most of the working population are low wage earners; thus, only a small segment

Figure 12.6. Inflation and Cost of Capital, Actual and Projected to 2015

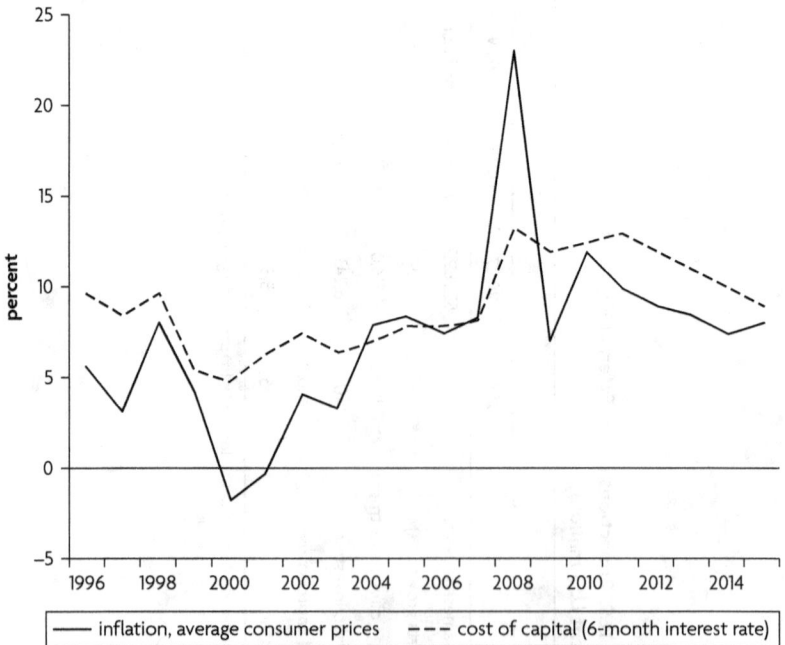

Source: World Bank Data Catalog; Asian Development Bank (ADB) Key Indicators; authors' calculations.

Figure 12.7. Budget Collections and Expenditures

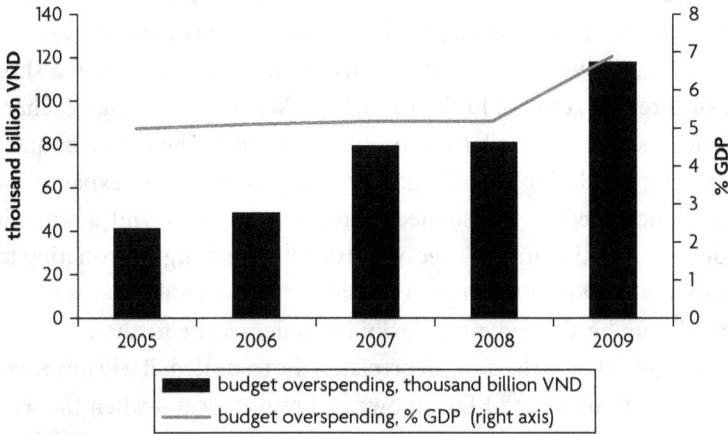

Source: Ministry of Finance.

of the Vietnamese working population pay income tax. Owing to the fiscal stimulus package, the deficit in 2009 is much higher than in previous years; the deficit in 2010 is expected to be 6 percent of GDP and, according to a recent report by the Ministry of Planning and Investment, could reach 6.5 percent.[36] The implication is that with a large budget deficit, there is less fiscal space for the government to make direct investments in the economy—and this raises the cost of funding. At present, the government has to deal with a difficult balancing task: controlling inflation while also stimulating economic growth. With the expanding budget deficit and public debt, it will be hard for the government to obtain funding at low interest rates. Therefore, we expect interest rates to be somewhat higher than in the precrisis period, peaking by 2011 at about 13 percent before falling to 9 percent in 2015 (figure 12.6).

Along with the fiscal deficit, Vietnam faces a chronic current account shortfall, which has led to episodes of near crisis in the balance of payments in recent years. The trade and current account deficits have reached levels that are much higher than the level of 5 percent of GDP that is commonly believed sustainable. The continuing current account deficit has been mainly driven by the growing domestic credit associated with financing the fiscal deficit, the increase in private consumption by households, and an overvalued currency (partly because of a rigid exchange rate policy) and loss of competitiveness. As noted earlier, in 2009 declines in exports, remittances, and foreign capital inflows reduced the supply of foreign exchange, while expansionary monetary and fiscal policies increased demand for it. Consequently, there has been a shortage of foreign exchange in the formal market, and the dong's exchange rate against the U.S. dollar has been transacted at the upper bound of its trading band. Rapid credit growth—together with an expansionary fiscal policy—led to a sustained increase in imports and a widening trade deficit in the first quarter of 2010, with the dong depreciating to a record low of Dong 19,000 per U.S. dollar. The general belief is that the dong should be allowed more flexibility to depreciate further.

We expect that as the dong depreciates, the trade deficit will improve—together with increased FDI inflows and remittances—when the world economy recovers, lessening pressure on the dong. However, it will take some time for the government to wind down its expansionary program (the government has a growth-driven target in mind). We expect the dong to depreciate by a few more percentage points in the next few years before it stabilizes. As the dong depreciates, it will reduce the current account deficit—but we do not expect the deficit to shift into surplus in the medium term. Rather, we expect that in 2010–11, Vietnam will still have a large current account gap (equal to about 5 percent of GDP), but the situation should improve by 2015.

Table 12.10. Inflation, Interest Rate, Current Account, and Exchange Rates, Actual and Projected to 2015

	Actual				Projected					
	2003	2007	2008	2009	2010	2011	2012	2013	2014	2015
Inflation, average consumer prices (%)	3.2	8.3	23.1	7.0	12.0	10.0	9.0	8.5	7.5	8.0
Cost of capital (6-month interest rate, %)	6.5	8.2	13.3	12.0	12.5	13.0	12.0	11.0	10.0	9.0
Current account balance (US$ bn)	–1.9	–7.0	–10.7	–8.9	–9.8	–9.3	–8.8	–7.9	–7.1	–6.4
Exchange rate (Dong per US$)	15,509	16,105	16,302	19,000	19,570	20,549	21,576	22,223	22,668	22,894

Source: World Bank Data Catalog; authors' calculations.

Figure 12.8. GDP Growth and Investment

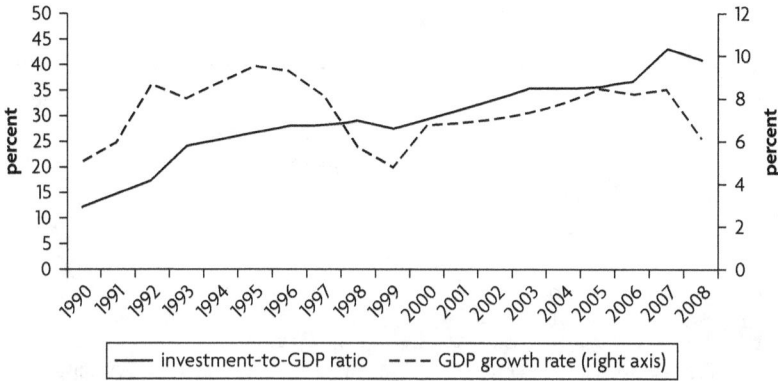

Source: World Bank Data Catalog; authors' calculations.

Projections for Investment. The investment ratio and GDP growth in Vietnam go hand in hand for the period under study (figure 12.8). This suggests that investment is critical for any medium-term GDP growth projection. Actually, according to the World Bank (2007), the large and increasing share of investment in GDP partly explains the growth rate acceleration since 2000.

Vietnam's economic growth strategy, which relied on extensive investment, was made possible by increasing government debt and heavy inflows of foreign savings (FDI and official development assistance [ODA]). FDI inflows have been an important source of funds for investment in Vietnam, accounting for over 30 percent of total investment.[37] Since the early days of economic reforms in the 1990s, Vietnam has enjoyed considerable transfers of resources in the form of ODA, most of which was in the form of nonrefundable grants or loans on highly favorable terms (with a large grant component). ODA has facilitated the construction of important infrastructure projects, rural development, education, training, and administrative reform. In the foreseeable future, given the commitments of donors, ODA will remain available, but the terms of ODA loans are bound to become less advantageous as Vietnam grows.

Unlike the situation in other countries, the private sector in Vietnam plays an important—but not a dominant—role in investment; instead,

Figure 12.9. Investment Structure by Ownership

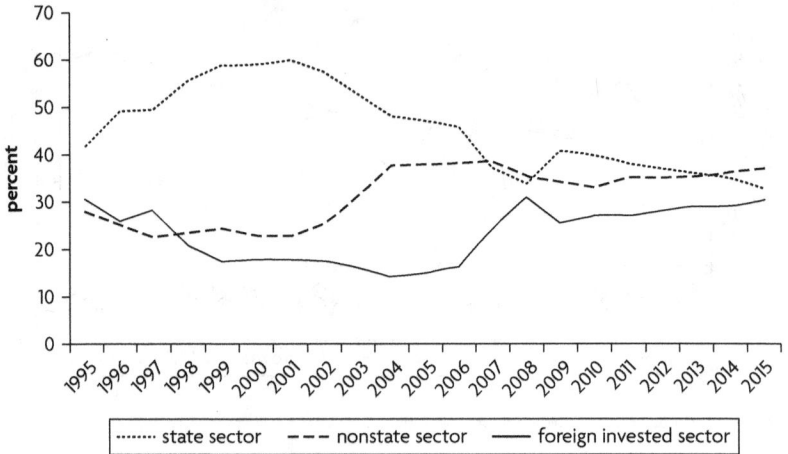

Source: GSO, http://www.gso.gov.vn; authors' calculations.

the state sector has played the most significant role of the three sectors (figure 12.9). Until 2006, the state sector was the most important source of investment, but its share in investment has declined from 60 percent in 2001 to 33.9 percent in 2008, before rising again to more than 40 percent because of the fiscal stimulus package.[38] By the end of the past decade, the three sectors—state-owned, domestic nonstate-owned, and FDI—were more or less equal in terms of investment shares in the economy.

The general declining trend of the state sector is irreversible and contrasts with the increasing roles of the private domestic and FDI sectors. During the crisis, the investment share of the state sector recovered, but we do not expect the state's role to rise over the long term. Our projections for the three economic sectors are for the general declining trend of the state sector to continue and for the shares of FDI and domestic private sectors to increase—with the domestic private sector becoming the most prominent.

The question Vietnam faces now is whether it can still rely on the old strategy of investment-based development. The answer depends in part on its ability to sustain the inflows of foreign savings and on how the country uses such inflows. In the face of the government's growing need to secure additional funding, ODA takes on greater importance. This is especially true when FDI inflows and export earnings are falling. On this front, the Japanese government has resumed its ODA for Vietnam; the Asian Development Bank granted Vietnam budget support of US$500 million; and, most recently, the government has secured an unprecedented level of ODA—US$8 billion—from international donors. While we expect that such cheap ODA funding will still be available in the medium term, ODA funds will become more expensive over the long term, and Vietnam may have more difficulty competing for them as its economy develops.

Given the worsened fiscal balance, owing to the fiscal stimulus and reduced future revenues caused by weaker economic activity, Vietnam will find it more difficult to sustain high economic growth with expansionary policies. But relative to the level of public debt among other ASEAN countries (ranging from 30 percent for Indonesia, over 42 percent for Thailand and Malaysia, 56 percent for the Philippines, and 113 percent for Singapore), Vietnam's public debt, at (44.4 percent of GDP), is moderate and expected to be sustainable. The debt level is similar to those of other ASEAN countries. Therefore, we expect that a moderate fiscal stimulus package would not cause serious fiscal impairment. Furthermore, joint IMF–World Bank analysis (2009) suggests that there is scope for further fiscal policy maneuvering in Vietnam, as the fiscal position remains strong.[39] We therefore project that in the medium term, the government may continue its investment-based growth strategy of incurring more debt and that the public-debt-to-GDP ratio will keep increasing.

As noted earlier, we expect that FDI inflows, although possibly lower than in precrisis years, will still be higher than the world average. Domestic interest rates may be a bit higher than in other countries, given the potential high return to investment in Vietnam. But we do not expect a sharp decrease in domestic private investment. Overall, we expect that in the next few years, the growth of investment in Vietnam will be slower than in 2009. According to the latest statistics from GSO, the investment growth rate in the first half of 2010 was 13.4 percent, lower than the 15 percent growth rate in 2009. We suspect that the growth rate will slow down gradually toward the 11 percent level during 2012–15.[40]

Medium-Term Growth Projection and Recovery Path

To assess Vietnam's recovery path after the global crisis, we use projections for various factors to derive the GDP growth path to 2015. On the demand side, what would be the growth trajectory for Vietnam in the next few years to 2015? To answer this question, we look at the trends of the main components of aggregate demand—consumption, investment, and net exports. We do not expect consumption to change abruptly or significantly. However, the consumption level in Vietnam is already relatively high, particularly for the last few years, a condition we consider to be unsustainable. We thus expect that although consumption will keep growing, or even accelerating its medium-term growth rate will be around 7 percent by 2015, returning to the precrisis (2004–05) levels. However, in the meantime, the actual consumption growth rate would deviate from 7 percent. According to the latest statistics released by the GSO, the retail sales and private consumption increased by 16.4 percent in the first six months of 2010. This figure is used in our projection for private consumption growth in 2010. We expect that this figure would decline toward 7 percent by 2015.

Based on our projections about investment growth above, we are also able to project the investment trajectory for Vietnam to 2015. The last and most uncertain component is net exports. Vietnam has more than a decade-long trade deficit, which has worsened recently—due mainly to budget deficits and the overvalued exchange rate. As the share of investment by the state sector is expected to decline over the medium term, together with the expected depreciation of the Vietnam dong, in theory we would expect the trade balance to improve. But the trade balance may get worse before improving. As discussed above, the global crisis may help improve the trade deficit but the shortfall may worsen once the economy recovers. Since the beginning of the year, the economy is doing quite well and a number of international organizations have revised their estimate of Vietnam's GDP growth rate upward. Goldman Sachs revised up Vietnam's GDP growth rate to 8.2 percent in 2010 from its earlier estimate of 6.7 percent.[41] Similarly, in June 2010 the IMF revised its estimate to 6.5 percent from its earlier 6 percent in 2010, arguing that such projection is supported by a continued recovery in private investment, consumption, and nonoil export growth.[42] The government, however, has been even more ambitious, sketching a plan to achieve a GDP growth rate in the range of 7.5–8.5 percent from 2011 to 2015 while the growth rate for 2010 is targeted to be 6.5 percent.[43] The discussion above suggests that Vietnam may soon enjoy solid growth rates in

Table 12.11. Medium-Term Growth Demand-Side GDP Projection
(percent)

	Actual							Projected					
	2003	2004	2005	2006	2007	2008	2009	2010	2011	2012	2013	2014	2015
Private consumption growth	8.0	7.1	7.3	8.3	10.8	9.2	8.4	16.0	11.0	10.0	9.0	8.0	7.0
Government consumption growth	7.2	7.8	8.2	8.5	8.9	7.5	9.0	7.0	7.0	6.0	5.0	5.0	5.0
Investment growth	11.9	10.5	11.2	11.8	26.8	6.3	15.0	13.4	12.0	11.0	11.0	11.0	11.0
GDP growth	7.3	7.8	8.4	8.2	8.5	6.2	5.3	7.5	8.0	8.2	8.3	8.5	8.5

Source: ADB Key Indicators; World Bank Data Catalog; GSO; authors' calculations.

the years to come provided the trends stay favorable (see table 12.11 for our medium-term projections).[44]

On the supply side, using the growth accounting framework, we also derive the potential GDP growth path for Vietnam up to 2015. In estimating potential output, we assume that the TFP growth rate will stay at about its annual average precrisis rate of 2.85 percent. Similarly, we assume employment growth of 2.28 percent per year, equivalent to the average of the last five years. Vietnam's potential output will then be about 8 percent per year (table 12.12). According to our projection, the economy of Vietnam will need another two years before it fully recovers from the crisis.

Policy Implication and Conclusion

Thanks to Vietnam's rapid economic growth over the past 20 years, it is expected to join the middle-income country group in the next year. The country's past success has been fueled partly by a series of gradual reforms and expansionary investment. But it must now decide how to sustain economic growth and avoid the "middle-income trap" in which many countries in the regions are stuck. The experience of China and other East Asian countries suggests that high growth rates can be sustained for more than 20 years, but other South-East Asian countries have shown that high economic growth cannot be sustained for so long.

In 2008, as the global financial crisis unfolded, its severe effects were felt on all continents, including in Vietnam. The crisis, together with the

Table 12.12. Medium-Term Potential Output Projection

Year	GDP growth (%)	Labor growth (%)	Investment (constant 2000 US$ millions)	Gross capital stock (K/Y = 2)	Capital growth (%)	Growth rate of TFP (%)
Actual						
2003	7.34	2.32	12,892	76,500	10.67	2.24
2004	7.79	1.82	14,251	84,802	10.85	2.96
2005	8.44	2.16	15,840	93,965	10.81	3.40
2006	8.23	2.38	17,715	104,167	10.86	3.02
2007	8.46	2.20	22,000	115,632	11.01	3.32
2008	6.18	2.45	23,872	130,694	13.03	0.20
2009	5.32	2.34	26,594	146,724	12.27	−0.33
Projected						
2010	8.20	2.18	28,987	164,515	12.12	2.90
2011	8.07	2.28	31,596	183,631	11.62	2.85
2012	8.08	2.28	35,160	204,209	11.21	2.85
2013	8.09	2.28	39,126	227,116	11.22	2.85
2014	8.10	2.28	43,539	252,615	11.23	2.85
2015	8.10	2.28	48,451	280,998	11.24	2.85

Source: World Bank Data Catalog and authors' calculations.

recent turbulence of macroeconomic development in the past two years, has revealed several economic weaknesses in Vietnam and raised the question of whether the country can continue on its current course of economic development in a changing world.

Rebalancing

With the current global imbalances, characterized by a huge deficit in the United States and surpluses in many Asian countries (especially China), the issue of rebalancing must be addressed. Although global rebalancing implies strengthening domestic demand in Asian countries, the optimal policy mix for rebalancing will necessarily differ across countries. As in other Asian countries, the issue of rebalancing growth has been hotly debated in Vietnam; the debate centers on whether the country should shift its focus to raising domestic demand instead of external demand. The following arguments have been put forward in favor of shifting toward domestic demand:

- For an export-oriented economy, a decrease in external demand would be more deflationary to the domestic economy than a similar decrease in domestic consumption.
- Given the United States' huge current account deficit, the export-led countries—such as China and Japan—should be less willing to finance U.S. imports.
- Vietnam is potentially a huge market for its own production given its large population (approaching 86 million), its high economic growth rate, and its becoming a middle-income country (Ohno 2009).

Admittedly, in view of the current global crisis, Vietnam inevitably will have to readjust its short-term growth strategy and shift away from its emphasis on export-oriented growth, especially if the crisis is prolonged. But Vietnam cannot rely on domestic consumption for long-term economic growth in the face of its already high level of consumption. Although domestic demand is currently substantial and keeps growing, household income is still low. Furthermore, unlike such large countries as the United States, China, and India, where domestic markets are large enough to sustain economic growth and absorb excessive production capacity, Vietnam has a domestic market that is much smaller. On the other hand, compared to China, Japan, and other large exporters, Vietnam is a small, open country and has the scope to increase its exports without worsening global imbalances. Moreover, in recent years, Vietnam has accumulated a large current account deficit.[45] Therefore, if Vietnam decides to sustain high economic growth in the medium term, it should continue with its export-oriented development strategy.

The above argument does not mean, however, that Vietnam's domestic market will play a less important role in the long run. Indeed, the government should emphasize some elements of domestic consumption—for example, it should provide more public goods, particularly those affecting the well-being of individuals—and address such economic bottlenecks as a lack of skilled workers and inadequate health care system. Global growth rebalancing will also affect Vietnam's macroeconomic variables; the country could see an increase in its saving rate as well as decreases in domestic consumption and investment.

Shifting Consumption Patterns

One of the often-cited structural causes of the global crisis is the unsustainable global imbalance between overconsumption in the United States (as reflected in its large current account deficit) and over-saving in China and other emerging East Asian countries (with large current account surpluses). Such unsustainable global imbalances will necessarily be rebalanced, either with a gradual adjustment or a sudden sharp adjustment caused by, for example, a global crisis. As a result, either the world consumption map may evolve into a multipolar one (featuring the United States, the European Union, Japan, and emerging consumer nations in Asia), which is the more likely scenario, or it may evolve into an Asia-centered, unipolar map.

In either case, the emergence of a consumption center in Asia (China, India, and other current account surplus countries) may have important implications for Vietnam's export strategy. With already high consumption and a low saving rate, Vietnam may not be able to become part of the consumption center. Instead, it may need to foster more domestic saving and rein in domestic consumption. In this case, resources would be shifted from manufacturing industries that are concentrated on exports to developed countries to industries and services that serve markets in China, India, and other emerging Asian countries.[46]

Another important consequence of China's rising wage is that the lower-end manufacturing is beginning to shift into other countries that are lower on the development ladder such as Bangladesh, Cambodia, Vietnam. The lower-end products include cheaper, labor-intensive goods like garments, toys and simple electronics that do not necessarily require skilled workers and can tolerate unreliable transportation systems and electrical grids.[47] This would surely create an opportunity for Vietnam to fill the vacuum left by China. However, this may not come automatically and may require active policy from the government (See also Nguyen and Nguyen 2010).

Economic Reform: Unfinished Agenda?

Vietnam's recent economic growth has its roots in policies of economic openness, with trade liberalization at center stage in recent decades. Since its joining the WTO in 2006, the country has experienced tremendous economic changes and fluctuations. Although it has received a large amount of FDI and (presumably) technology transfer, as a result of its cheap labor cost and abundant natural resources, Vietnamese products and services are still less internationally competitive than regional competitors (See Nguyen and Nguyen 2010), due to high transaction costs.

Vietnam's WTO accession and membership is neither the beginning nor the end of the country's international integration. But the question is: Will traditional trade liberalization and openness policies still drive—and ensure—Vietnamese growth in the future? For many researchers and policy makers in Vietnam, economic reform based on traditional trade liberalization theory seems to have lost its momentum, as most of the country's tariff and nontariff barriers have already been removed. Finding a new engine for growth is a high priority. This is even more important in a time of crisis when the economy's competitiveness and advantages, relative to its trading partners and competitors, are most openly visible.

The following challenges, old and new, thus face Vietnam in the postcrisis era:

- *Infrastructure limitations:* The absence of good infrastructure could potentially obstruct the country's economic growth. One of the most pressing risks is a potentially serious power shortage, in which the national electricity system is unable to cope with the increased power consumption in the near future.
- *The need for a more skilled workforce:* A slow pace of human capital development can put an end to fast economic growth. The domestic supply of skilled labor remains a constant challenge and is mainly the result of a weak education system whose outdated curricula do not meet current work requirements.
- *The need to reform the state-owned enterprise sector:* The reforms of the SOEs have not seen much progress and recently slowed down significantly due to the global crisis. To improve the efficiency of the sector as a whole, particular attention should be paid to the contingency liabilities risk of SOEs. It is undeniable that guaranteeing these enterprises' borrowing is a good and efficient way of supporting them because it is less costly than a direct subsidy. However, by doing this, governments have to suffer potential risks such as having to pay the outstanding loans when borrowers default. The most recent case of near-collapse of a giant shipbuilder Vinashin testifies this risk (see Nguyen and Nguyen 2010).

Macroeconomic Stability and Crisis

Crises are very costly to long-term growth and development. Our previous calculations show that the current crisis is imposing heavy economic costs on Vietnam and that it will take until 2011 for the country to fully recover. Macroeconomic stability is very important in preventing potential crises, and Vietnam macroeconomic indicators are not good at present:

- Although inflation remains stable, it can get out of control once the world economy recovers.
- Trade deficits have recently been a recurrent problem for Vietnam and have reached unsustainable levels. Although most of the widening of the trade deficit is due to purchases of intermediate goods and capital equipment, many imported items have been semi-finished products and luxury consumption goods.
- The government has continued to run a budget deficit for many years. In 2009, the deficit is estimated to have increased because of the stimulus package. But even more worrying is the substantial off-budget spending in Vietnam.
- The volatile inflow of hot money into real estate and stock markets is cause for concern.
- Vietnam is hindered by the weakness of risk management and financial capacity supervision in many companies and financial institutions.
- Finally, Vietnam's inadequate system of gathering and analyzing information on financial market fluctuations and the lack of a reasonable roadmap for capital account liberalization remain challenges for its policy makers.

Notes

1. During 1980–88, some spontaneous microeconomic reforms such as the "output-based illicit contracting" in agriculture and "fence breaking" in the manufacturing sector were introduced (as early as 1981). These microreforms revitalized the economy and helped raise the production during 1982–85. However, such reforms were not sufficient to sustain economic growth, owing to the fundamental problems of resource misallocation and macroeconomic imbalances. In the mid-1980s, the inflation rate accelerated to several hundred percent, forcing the government to change the denomination of its currency. The privatization

process was accelerated in 2006 when the government allowed some large monopoly firms in the banking, insurance, petroleum, and telecommunication sectors to be privatized.

2. As other economies in transition, Vietnam has had to deal with three key sets of reforms: liberalization and stabilization; institutional changes that support market exchange and encourage private ownership; and the establishment of social programs to ease the pain of transition (World Bank 1996). The implementation has been successful, resulting in price stabilization and reduction of the fiscal burden. In 1989, inflation was under control and has remained low, except for 2004 and 2008.

3. The word "privatization" is often avoided in the context of Vietnam SOE reform. Instead, the conversion of state-owned enterprises into public limited liability companies is referred to as equitization.

4. Some evidence suggests that the private sector may not be quite as healthy and robust as the numbers imply. See the paper by the International Finance Corporation (IFC), "Beyond the Headline Numbers: Business Registration and Startup in Vietnam," http://www.ifc.org/ifcext/mekongpsdf.nsf/Attachments-ByTitle/PSDP-20/$FILE/PSDP-No-20-EN.pdf.

5. International integration efforts picked up beginning in the early 1990s, after the collapse of the Berlin wall and several years after Vietnam lost its traditional markets in Eastern Europe and the Russian Federation. The U.S. trade embargo against Vietnam was lifted only in 1994, and the relationship with the United States was normalized in 1995. Also, since 1993 Vietnam has began receiving official development assistance (ODA), which has contributed to the substantial increase in financial resources for investment in Vietnam's development.

6. In a recent paper, Abbott, Bentzen, and Tarp (2009) observe that each time Vietnam reached a significant bilateral agreement, trade flows with that partner surged.

7. Apart from FDI, Vietnam also started receiving ODA from international donors, and the amount committed and disbursed has been increasing since then. These capital sources have helped advance infrastructural construction in such areas as transportation and communication, information, agricultural and rural development, public health, education and training, administrative reform, legislation, and structural reform.

8. Specifically, on November 29, 2005, the National Assembly of Vietnam adopted the Law on Investment No. 59/2005/QH11 ("New LOI") and Law on Enterprises No. 60/2005/QH11 ("New LOE"), which apply to all enterprises established by domestic foreign investors.

9. Che, Kompas, and Vousden (2003) report that market reform leads to increases in rice productivity, pointing to the importance of market competition, secured property rights, and efficient use of resources. See http://www.crawford.anu.edu.au/degrees/idec/working_papers/IDEC03-7.pdf.

10. There are some limitations to this decomposition method as pointed out by Kranendonk and Verbruggen (2008). This method underestimates the importance of exports to the growth in GDP and overestimates the importance of domestic expenditure categories. The authors suggest an alternative method called "import-adjustment." However, owing to time limitations, we use the traditional method and estimate the contribution of exports and imports to GDP separately instead of using net exports.

11. The structure of imports and exports has been substantially changed over the course of development. Vietnam has exported oil and various manufacturing and agriculture processing products, and imported not only consumption goods, but also (and mainly) raw materials for domestic production, and initially progressive techniques and technology to promote the growth and efficiency of the economy. The composition of Vietnamese exports has gradually reflected the success of the industrialization process. The share of manufactured products—particularly labor-intensive products like textile and garments, footwear, and seafood—has been increasing and these now have replaced traditional agricultural products. In 2005, the share of manufactured handicraft products alone accounted for more than 40 percent of total export values (CIEM 2005).

12. The efficiency of the high level of investment has been questioned by various researchers owing to the high integrated capital-output ratio relative to other economies, such as Taiwan, China, or the Republic of Korea, when these economies were at the same stage of economic development. See also Rebalancing Growth in Asia by Prasad (2009).

13. Jensen and Tarp (2006) point out that private savings to fund private investment come as much from retained earnings of firms as from savings by households. Reinvestment of corporate profits appears to be an important means of maintaining high rates of investment and growth.

14. Vietnam requires registration of intended FDI, and not all such registrations are implemented.

15. In the debate about the current economic stimulus package, there has been little reference to the previous prolonged demand stimulus implemented in 2000–04.

16. A Cobb-Douglas function, $Y = AK^a L^{1-a}$, is assumed. L = employment or labor force (depending on whether or not employment data are available) and K = capital stock, computed using a perpetual inventory method. As there are no data on capital stock for Vietnam and these are needed to estimate TFP, we need to build a time series on capital stock for Vietnam using available information and some common assumptions. In Vietnam, although there are no capital stock data, investment data are available. We construct a capital stock series based on the following assumptions:

   (i) The capital stock in the initial year is proportional to output (GDP) in that year, that is, $K_0 = \lambda Y_0$. The parameter λ is referred to as the capital-output ratio. This assumption follows from the Harrod-Domar model, which argues that there is a stable relationship between output and capital stock depending on the structure of the currently used technology.

(ii) The capital stock can be estimated using the perpetual inventory method, that is, $K_t = K_{t-1} - \delta K_{t-1} + I_{t-1}$, where δ is the depreciation rate and I is the gross investment during period $t - 1$. Usually, the depreciation rate is assumed to be about 6 percent a year. In our estimation, the initial year is 1986, and we assume that the capital output ratio is 2. We acknowledge that different capital output ratio would lead to different results.

17. For further details, see World Bank (2008).

18. Some would go further to say that without the global crisis, Vietnam would still have fallen into a recession on its own.

19. When investing in Vietnam, foreign investors are required to register their planned total investment capital (often referred to as registered investment capital), which in practice may differ substantially from the actual amount invested (implementation capital).

20. See also a study by UNDP (2009). Other effects include lower demand for Vietnamese workers in other countries, such as Malaysia; Taiwan, China; and Middle East countries.

21. Since early 2009, VASS conducted repeated Rapid Assessment Surveys to assess the impact of the global crisis on Vietnam. The first survey, in early 2009, found that job losses were widespread in industrial zones (both in the North and the South), but few took the form of open layoffs. Nonrenewals of contracts and incentives for voluntary departures were more common. Job losses were frequent among seasonal workers and those on short-term contracts. Some enterprises attempted labor-hoarding measures to retain their skilled employees. Unemployed immigrants were highly vulnerable, owing to the lack of social security and nonreversibility of immigration (the immigrant workers largely come from areas where arable land is scarce and other opportunities are few). Another survey of the impact of the global financial crisis on labor in industrial parks was conducted by the Central Institute for Economic Management (CIEM). Evidence from this survey suggests that job losses were widespread in industrial parks in late 2008 and early 2009. Remittances to families staying in rural areas suffered as a result.

22. The Vietnamese banking system has suffered only indirectly from the crisis. This is because the financial and banking sector was not fully integrated with the global network. Furthermore, the absence of such regulation as mark-to-market has helped the banking system in a time of crisis.

23. This decline in the dong's value is due mainly to the declining demand in exports and to portfolio outflows. The depreciation of the dong may help to improve Vietnam's export performance, limiting the negative impact from the global recession. However, a study by Jongwanich (2010) of a group of nine Asian countries finds a very weak link between the real exchange rate and export performance in these countries. On the contrary, world demand and production capacity play a more important role in determining exports of these groups of Asian economies.

24. The dong has been devalued by 2 percent by the widening of the trading band, to ±5 percent from ±3 percent around the central bank reference rate. Rapid credit growth, together with an expansionary fiscal policy, have led to a sustained increase in imports and a widening trade deficit. A larger demand for foreign exchange by importers, combined with market expectations that the dong would be devalued, led to a shortage of foreign exchange that was particularly severe in May–July 2009, and again in November 2009, imposing significant costs on enterprises. On the one hand, the shortage of foreign exchange in the formal market has helped narrow the trade deficit, but it has also created difficulties for businesses at a time when the government would most like to stimulate business activities.

25. The effectiveness of the fiscal stimulus packages that countries, developed and developing alike, are implementing is questioned by Foster (2009), http://www.heritage.org/Research/Economy/bg2302.cfm.

26. In some respects, the large state-owned sector has made the task of stimulating the economy much easier.

27. Since the first announcement of the stimulus package, several additional stimulus polices were adopted or announced, creating some confusion and prompting understandable concern about potentially unsustainable government spending.

28. See www.vneconomy.vn/20090828091054122P0C10/kinh-te-8-thang-buc-tranh-dang-sang.htm. In order to assist the economy further, the government is considering the second stimulus package; see http://vneconomy.vn/20090901102716178P0C5/he-mo-kha-nang-tao-buoc-dem-cho-nen-kinh-te.htm.

29. While most have agreed that the prompt introduction of the stimulus package provided quick protection for the economy, some debate continues about whether or not the package was able to target the most effective businesses and sectors. An overall and full assessment of the stimulus package may be necessary, but this falls outside the scope of this discussion. But another important impact, not often mentioned, of the strong response by the government was to restore the confidence of the business sector.

30. Other factors include the tight labor market before the crisis, the competitive nature of Vietnam's key exports, and the private sector's capacity to compete globally, despite cutbacks in demand for key export commodities (Manning 2009).

31. Tet break is Vietnam's traditional New Year holiday.

32. Positive growth of 3.8 percent is attributable to price increases and (re)export of gold. If gold (re)export is excluded, Vietnam would register negative export growth of 1.6 percent.

33. Our scenario proposed here resembles the last episode that Vietnam suffered in 2000.

34. Although Vietnam has been successful in attracting FDI in recent years, the real benefits from FDI still appear to be controversial. Previous studies have found little evidence of technical spillover from FDI enterprises to local counterparts (Nguyen et al. 2008). In addition, the country has become heavily dependent on

FDI capital as an important way to sustain economic growth. In 2008, FDI into Vietnam reached US$64 billion of registered capital (triple the registered FDI capital for 2007) and US$11.6 billion of implementation capital (versus US$8 billion in 2007).

35. Vietnam's economy depends heavily on imports (especially intermediate goods); therefore, once the world economy recovers, higher prices for Vietnam's key imports should lead to higher pass-through of import inflation. On top of that, the depreciation of the dong would lead to further pressure on inflation.

36. In Vietnam, increasing government spending at a time of recession with contracting revenues poses complicated questions. The national budget, which was already in deficit, was put under further strain by a marked reduction in revenue (lower revenue from lower economic activities attributable to the global crisis, and lower crude oil royalties owing to falling prices). When the crisis hit in 2008, the national budget was already under strain by a marked reduction in revenue. In the recent past, crude oil royalties have been an important source of revenue (and export earnings) for the government—with 16 percent of government revenue coming from oil export—but with global oil prices falling sharply from the highs reached in 2008, the government's revenue position is weak, leaving less scope for generous spending plans. In 2009, the government actually used up Dong 37.2 trillion (US$2.2 billion) from the budget for 2010 (budget advancement). This is not a healthy fiscal practice, and some expect it to lead to under-reporting of the budget deficit.

37. The current financial crisis has put Vietnam in a delicate position. On the one hand, it now would like to be more selective in attracting FDI; but on the other hand, it still needs to compete against other countries for the smaller pool of capital. The comparative advantages offered by Vietnam's abundant, cheap, skillful, and compliant labor force has largely disappeared and will become less important. Vietnam cannot rely on an unskilled-labor advantage to compete for FDI as it could in the past 20 years. Therefore, rather than seeking greater investment for its own sake, policy makers should concentrate on building a climate conducive to efficient investment. Vietnam still lags far behind other countries in the region in this respect. The supporting domestic manufacturing sector has not emerged.

38. State investment is made either directly into public infrastructure or through loans to SOEs, or in the form of grants to municipalities and private enterprises.

39. The baseline scenario of the most recent debt sustainability analysis (DSA) by the World Bank and the International Monetary Fund (IMF) estimates public and publicly guaranteed debt to increase from 44 percent of GDP in 2007 to around 51 percent by 2016, and decline slightly thereafter. There are two important aspects of Vietnam's debt. First, the government has a long history of prudent external debt, and a large component of its external debt is highly concessional—with long repayment periods and low interest rates. Therefore, although this increase is large, it is still considered manageable. External debt,

both public and private, is projected to decline somewhat—from a little over 30 percent of GDP to just under 26 percent in 2017. The ratio of external-debt-service payments to exports is estimated to remain about 4 percent during 2007–17. The DSA concludes that Vietnam should thus remain at low risk of external debt distress. Further details of the DSA can be found at http://imf.org/external/pubs/ft/dsa/pdf/dsacr09110.pdf.

40. Except for 2007, when the investment growth rate was 26 percent, owing to large FDI inflows.

41. See http://74.53.24.87/news/articles/economy/111283045.shtml.

42. http://www.imf.org/external/np/dm/2010/060910.htm.

43. http://vneconomy.vn/20100517094952600P0C9920/tang-truong-5-nam-toi-muc-tieu-85-la-chap-nhan-duoc.htm and http://www.maivoo.com/2009/10/20/Dong-thuan-muc-tieu-GDP-nam-2010-tang-6-5-n79242.html.

44. It should be noted that due to large statistical errors in the national account, using projection methods based on components of GDP is difficult. We instead use these trends in informing our subjective judgment.

45. Unlike many export-oriented Asian economies, Vietnam has been running a trade deficit.

46. Global saving glut in the words of Ben Bernanke, the chairman of U.S. Federal Reserve in 2005. See www.brookings.edu/opinions/2009/0802_china_spending_prasad.aspx and http://blogs.harvardbusiness.org/hbr/hbr-now/2009/08/trend-to-watch-shifting-consum.html.

47. See http://www.theepochtimes.com/n2/content/view/39318/.

References

Abbott, Philip, Jeanet Bentzen, and Finn Tarp. 2008. "Trade and Development: Lessons from Vietnam's Past Trade Agreements." *World Development* 37 (2): 341–353.

Che Tuong Nhu, Tom Kompas, and Neil Vousden. 2003. "Market Reform, Incentives and Economic Development in Vietnamese Rice Production." Asia Pacific School of Economics and Government, The Australian National University. http://www.crawford.anu.edu.au/degrees/idec/working_papers/IDEC03-7.pdf.

CIEM (Central Institute of Economic Management). 2005. "Vietnam' s Economy 2005." CIEM, Political Theories Publisher, Hanoi.

Foster, J. D. 2009. "Keynesian Fiscal Stimulus Policies Stimulate Debt—Not the Economy." Backgrounder 2302, The Heritage Foundation, Washington, DC.

GSO (General Statistics Office). 2009. "Annual Socio-Economic Report for 2009." http://www.gso.gov.vn/default.aspx?tabid=507&ItemID=9449.

IFC (International Finance Corporation). 2005. "Beyond the Headline Numbers: Business Registration and Startup in Vietnam." http://www.ifc.org/ifcext/mekongpsdf.nsf/AttachmentsByTitle/PSDP-20/$FILE/PSDP-No-20-EN.pdf.

IMF (International Monetary Fund)-World Bank. 2009. Joint IMF/World Bank Debt Sustainability Analysis 2008. http://www.imf.org/external/pubs/ft/dsa/pdf/dsacr09110.pdf.

Jensen, H. T., and Tarp, F. 2006. "A Vietnam Social Accounting Matrix SAM for the Year 2003." Discussion Paper PRG1.06.02, Central Institute of Economic Management (CIEM), Hanoi.

Jongwanich, Juthathip. 2010. "Determinants of Export Performance in East and Southeast Asia." *The World Economy* 33 (1): 20–41.

Kranendonk, Henk, and Johan Verbruggen. 2008. "Decomposition of GDP Growth in European Countries." CPB Netherlands Bureau for Economic Policy Analysis, The Hague.

Manning, Chris. 2009. "Globalisation and Labour Markets in Boom and Crisis: The Case of Vietnam." Working Paper 2009–17, Australian National University, Canberra. http://rspas.anu.edu.au/economics/publish/papers/wp2009/wp_econ_2009_17.pdf.

Menon, Jayant. 2009. "Managing Success in Vietnam: Macroeconomic Consequences of Large Capital Inflows with Limited Instruments." *ASEAN Economic Bulletin* 26 (1): 77–95.

Nguyen, N. A., and D. N. Nguyen 2010. "Vietnam's Industrial Policies and Large Economic Groups: A Discussion." Report prepared for the World Bank and the Vietnam Academy of Social Sciences.

Nguyen, N. A., T. Nguyen, D. T. Le, Q. N. Pham, D. C. Nguyen, and D. N. Nguyen. 2008. "Foreign Direct Investment in Vietnam: Is There Any Evidence of Technological Spillover Effects?" DEPOCEN Working Paper, Development and Policies Research Center, Hanoi.

Nguyen, Viet Cuong. 2009. "Can Vietnam Achieve Millennium Development Goal on Poverty Reduction in High Inflation and Economic Stagnation?" DEPOCEN Working Paper, Development and Policies Research Center, Hanoi.

Ohno, Kenichi. 2009. "Avoiding the Middle-Income Trap: Renovating Industrial Policy Formulation in Vietnam." *ASEAN Economic Bulletin* 26 (1): 25–43.

Pincus, Jonathan. 2009. "Vietnam: Sustaining Growth in Difficult Times." *ASEAN Economic Bulletin* 26 (1): 11–24.

Prasad, Eswar. 2009. "Rebalancing Growth in Asia." Discussion Paper 4298, Institute for the Study of Labor, Bonn. http://ftp.iza.org/dp4298.pdf.

SRV (Socialist Republic of Vietnam). 2003. "The Comprehensive Poverty Reduction and Growth Strategy." Official Document, Government Office, Hanoi, November.

UNDP (United Nations Development Programme). 2009. "The Impact of the Global Economic Downturn on Employment Levels in Viet Nam: An Elasticity Approach." Vietnam Technical Note, UNDP, New York. http://www.undp.org.vn/digitalAssets/12/12563_undp_viet_nam_technical_note_employment_elasticities.pdf.

World Bank. 1996. *World Development Report, From Plan to Market.* Washington, DC: World Bank.

———. 2007. "Taking Stock: An Update on Vietnam's Recent Economic." For Report prepared for the Mid-year Consultative Group Meeting for Vietnam, Ha Long City, June 1–2.

———. 2008. "Taking Stock: An Update on Vietnam's Recent Economic Developments." Report prepared for the Annual Consultative Group Meeting for Vietnam, Hanoi, December 4–5.

———. 2009. "Taking Stock: An Update on Vietnam's Recent Economic Developments." Report prepared for the Mid-year Consultative Group Meeting for Vietnam, Buon Ma Thuot, June 8–9.

———. 2010. *Global Economic Prospects: Crisis, Finance, and Growth.* Washington, DC: World Bank.

Discussant Paper

Comment on "Vietnam: Surprising Resilience but Challenges Ahead"

Sudarshan Gooptu

The authors have carefully reviewed the structural transformation that took place in Vietnam over the past two decades until the global crisis in 2008. They appropriately discussed how the Vietnamese economy was affected by the crisis in spite of the government's sustained and comprehensive policy reforms. These reforms included an "open-door policy to attract foreign direct investment (FDI) and trade liberalization," which was instrumental in creating a "growing and dynamic private sector." The country achieved remarkable poverty alleviation, with the total poverty incidence falling from 58 percent in 1993 to 16 percent by 2006. Literacy and life expectancy were rising and the under-five mortality rate was declining. A stable macroeconomic environment and high GDP growth seemed likely to continue—until 2008. This backward-looking part of the article is highly informative and contains a rich analysis of key economic variables and a lucid, though brief, discussion of the immediate impact of the fiscal stimulus implemented post-2008.

Sudarshan Gooptu is Sector Manager, Economic Policy and Debt Department, Poverty Reduction and Economic Management Network, World Bank.

595

Among the country case studies in this book, Vietnam's experience stands out in that even before the September 2008 global financial crisis hit, the Vietnamese authorities were implementing stringent fiscal consolidation measures to cope with the effects of the global food and fuel price hikes it faced at the end of 2007. Concerns of overheating had also emerged in early 2008, owing partly to the rapid increase in the role of domestic demand in GDP growth between 2005 and 2007. (Table 12.2 is telling in this regard; it shows the importance of domestic spending on the build-up of gross domestic capital formation, inventories, and a rapid increase in imports in Vietnam's GDP growth decomposition.) Vietnam's fiscal consolidation, together with its reserve build-up (a result of continued high export revenues and FDI inflows) helped the country to cope with the global downturn of late 2008, relative to other developing countries, as it had adequate room to undertake a rapid countercyclical fiscal expansion.

The question remains: how important have total factor productivity (TFP) increases been (especially in agriculture) to Vietnam's growth path? In the section on growth accounting, the choice of the Cobb-Douglas production function assumes that the relationship between output and the capital stock is stable for the period 1986–2008. Does this mean that the structure of the technology in production in Vietnam did not change during this period? Also, it would be useful to compare the growth trends of TFP between Vietnam and its main trading partners and developing countries with similar production structures. This would shed more light on the importance of TFP to Vietnam's growth process relative to, for example, China's.

Where the paper needs a bit more attention is in the forward-looking part, that is, in the discussion of the country's medium-term outlook. Here, the focus should be on the need for better risk management going forward—whether it is the fiscal risks attributable to contingent liabilities of state-owned enterprises or large business houses that dominate Vietnam's economy today, the risk of increasing job losses, or the risk of a drop in foreign demand and/or remittances. Managing these risks will not be easy, especially in a volatile global environment where the shape and speed of recovery in the advanced countries (many of which are Vietnam's trading partners) are being hotly debated today. In forming an opinion about Vietnam's export price outlook, one may need to look a bit deeper at the composition and destination of exports. What are the "newfound nontraditional markets" the authors refer to? Similarly, where is Vietnam's FDI coming from and to what sectors is it going? Answers to these questions will provide a better foundation for projecting Vietnam's medium-term growth prospects. The paper notes that Vietnam's comparative advantage of having an "abundant, cheap, skillful, and compliant labor force has largely disappeared and will become less important." Where will Vietnam's future GDP growth come from? This uncertainty poses risks to Vietnam's medium-term outlook as well. Undertaking more detailed growth diagnostics may be in order, but that may be beyond the scope of the analysis.

The authors rightly point out Vietnam's infrastructure limitations, but how infrastructure is financed will be important as well. The government's capacity to measure, evaluate, and manage the risks (fiscal, financial, and operational) associated with these financing structures will be all the more important going forward. While the paper cites the "volatile inflow of hot money into real estate and stock markets" as cause for concern, and weaknesses in financial capacity for financial sector risk management and supervision, the transmission mechanism by which the above-mentioned problems could pose fiscal risks to the government should be highlighted.

Index

Boxes, figures, notes, and tables are indicated by *b, f, n,* and *t,* respectively.

www.ingramcontent.com/pod-product-compliance
Lightning Source LLC
Chambersburg PA
CBHW070238290326
41929CB00046B/1752